NEWS DICTIONARY 1972

NEWS DICTIONARY

an encyclopedic summary of contemporary history

Editor-in-Chief, Books: LESTER A. SOBEL

Editor: SUSAN ANDERSON

Staff: Foreign Affairs—HAL KOSUT, JOHN MINER, MYRNA LEBOV, CHRISTOPHER HUNT

National Affairs—JOSEPH FICKES, BARRY YOUNGERMAN, MARY ELIZABETH CLIFFORD, SETH ABRAHAM, SUSAN J. SCHOCH, DAVID SEISMAN

Associate Editors—DOROTHY KATTLEMAN, SUSAN GINZBURG, MARJORIE B. BANK

Facts on File, Inc.

119 West 57th Street, New York, N.Y. 10019

NEWS DICTIONARY 1972

Using the News Dictionary

You will find the 1972 NEWS DICTIONARY as easy to use as the WEBSTER'S that stands beside it on the shelf. The editors of FACTS ON FILE—who themselves spend much of their time buried in reference books—designed the NEWS DICTIONARY to overcome the shortcomings of the typical yearbook: a complicated index, nine-month coverage, and an eclectic choice of material. Here you will find a self-index, complete ·coverage from January 1 through December 31, and the details of *every* significant news development of 1972.

The principle of the NEWS DICTIONARY is the alphabet. To find the story and facts of an event, the researcher simply looks up—as he would in a dictionary—the subject, the country concerned, or the name of a key person or organization involved in the event; if the story is not found in the first place he looks, an explicit cross-reference will direct him to the proper location without further effort or guesswork. Thus, the record of the kidnaping and murder of Israeli athletes during the summer Olympics and the events following the murder is found under OLYMPIC TERRORISM; but the researcher would also be referred to the proper location from cross-references under MIDDLE EAST; OLYMPICS; TERRORISM; and other headings.

A useful feature of the NEWS DICTIONARY is the system of numbered paragraphs to make the work of the researcher less time-consuming. Whenever there are more than a few paragraphs under any heading, numerals in the margin number the paragraphs consecutively. The cross-references refer the researcher—by number—to the specific paragraph(s) in which the desired information is recorded. For example, a researcher seeking material involving the Supreme Court's decision curbing capital punishment will find after Capital Punishment the reference "See CRIME [10-11]; ELECTIONS [44]"; this refers him to paragraphs 10 through 11 of the CRIME entry and paragraph 44 of the ELECTIONS entry.

ABDUCTION—*See* ARGENTINA [10-11]; BRAZIL; COLOMBIA; GREECE [12]; HIJACKING [1-13]; MEXICO; OLYMPIC TERRORISM; SECURITY, U.S.; TURKEY; UNION OF SOVIET SOCIALIST REPUBLICS [10]; URUGUAY [7]; VENEZUELA

ABORIGINES—*See* AUSTRALIA [1]

ABORTION—Vermont throws out law. The Vermont Supreme Court Jan. 14 ruled unanimously that the state's 125-year-old abortion statute, which permitted an abortion only if the mother's life was in danger, was unconstitutional. The court upset a lower court decision which dismissed a request by a welfare recipient for a declaratory judgment to block prosecution if she obtained an abortion.

ABA convention approves abortion 'on demand.' In a surprise move, the American Bar Association's 307-member House of Delegates Feb. 7 approved a uniform statute to permit women to obtain abortions "on demand" during the first 20 weeks of pregnancy. The House of Delegates, traditionally a conservative body on social issues, approved the model plan with only 30 dissenting votes. Under the proposal (drafted by the National Conference of Commissioners on Uniform State Laws, a legal group seeking to reduce disparities in state laws), abortions would be permitted beyond the 20th week of pregnancy only to preserve the expectant mother's mental or physical health, or if the fetus was gravely deformed, or if the pregnancy was the result of incest or rape. The proposal was more liberal than abortion laws in any state except New York and Hawaii.

New Jersey law voided. By a 2-1 decision Feb. 29, a federal court in Trenton, N.J. struck down the state's 122-year-old abortion law, which prohibited abortions performed "without lawful justification." The court held that the statute was unconstitutional on the grounds that it was vague and was an invasion of privacy. The decision said that the wording of the law "provides not one glimmer of notice" as to what one could or could not do and that the application of the law had not been clear. In a key passage of the decision, the court said that the 9th and 14th Amendments' constitutional right of privacy extended to a woman's decision to "terminate a pregnancy in its early stages." The court also held that the New Jersey statute "chills" doctors' exercise of their constitutionally guaranteed free speech rights and violated their 14th Amendment rights to "freely practice" the profession of their choice.

1

Liberalized laws urged, rejected. The Commission on Population Growth and the American Future, appointed by President Nixon, March 16 formally recommended that all states greatly liberalize their abortion laws and permit women to obtain abortions on request. Nixon, however, formally rejected the recommendation May 5. In its report, the commission called for government to fund abortion services and urged that health insurance plans be tailored to cover the cost of abortions. The panel had been set up to study population growth, but had based its report solely on another ground—that "all Americans, regardless of age, marital status or income should be entitled to avoid unwanted births." The commission, using New York City and its liberalized abortion law as a guidepoint *(see below)*, linked a reduction in the number of illegal abortions to a decrease in maternal mortality and a decline in illegitimacy. In his rejection of the recommendation May 5, President Nixon said that he regarded abortion as "an unacceptable means of population control" and that he did not support "unrestricted abortion policies."

The commission's report had roused strong opposition. Calling abortion an "unspeakable" crime, 240 U.S. Roman Catholic bishops April 13 had condemned the commission's recommendation. The commission itself revealed May 10 that mail it was receiving was running 5-1 against the recommendation. According to report, some of the opposition to the panel's proposal appeared to be organized. Some of the critical mail was on form letters, and other mail was composed of antiabortion letters allegedly distributed in churches.

Worldwide use widespread. The United Nations' Population Division March 19 made public a 162-page report indicating that abortion "may be the single most widely used method of birth control in the world today." The report noted that abortion seems "to be common in many countries, whether legalized or not," and that "the death rates among women undergoing legal abortions have been very low."

Connecticut laws upset. In a 2-1 decision, a panel of federal judges in Hartford, Conn. April 18 struck down the state's 112-year-old abortion statutes which had allowed abortions only to protect the life of the mother. The judges, in ruling the laws unconstitutional, said that "what was considered to be due process with respect to permissible abortions in 1860 is not due process in 1972." Connecticut officials, however, arguing that the ruling had left the state without any valid laws concerning abortion and had caused confusion among physicians and legal authorities, May 9 were granted a temporary stay of the ruling. The decision of the 2nd U.S. Circuit Court of Appeals made it unnecessary for the Connecticut legislature to convene in special session to pass an abortion law that might satisfy the federal courts. Despite the stay, Connecticut legislators during May enacted a new abortion law, stronger than the old one, allowing abortions only when the "physical" life of the mother was threatened (eliminating the possibility of performing an abortion to preserve a mother's mental health). The same federal panel in Hartford ruled 2-1 Sept. 20 that the new law also was unconstitutional. Connecticut appealed to Supreme Court Justice Thurgood Marshall to grant a stay of the new court order, and succeeded in having the full Supreme Court consider the question after Marshall Oct. 3 refused to grant the stay. The full court Oct. 16 granted the stay by an 8-1 ruling (Marshall dissenting), thus keeping the law in force until the Supreme Court could decide on its constitutionality.

Rockefeller vetoes N.Y. repeal. New York Gov. Nelson Rockefeller May 13 vetoed a bill that would have repealed the state's liberalized abortion law. The repeal bill would have struck down the two-year-old law which allowed abortion on demand up to the 24th week of pregnancy and would have restored New York's old abortion law under which a woman could obtain an abortion only if her life were in jeopardy. Rockefeller had been under heavy pressure from the Catholic Church and state groups organized under the "right-to-life" banner to sign the repeal bill. The pressure had been increased May 6 when the Archdiocese of New York released a letter from President Nixon to Archbishop

Terence Cardinal Cooke expressing the President's support for the repeal movement. The letter, which the White House said was private correspondence and not meant to be publicized, called the drive of the antiabortion forces "truly a noble endeavor." Rockefeller took note in his veto message that the state legislature was under election-year pressure to repeal the liberal law. He said that the "personal vilification and political coercion" surrounding the issue "raised doubts" that the legislature's votes "represented the will of the majority of the people of New York State." (Rockefeller had stated April 25 that he would approve a "desirable" modification in the liberal law reducing the 24-week period for abortions to a 16-week limit.) The liberal bill was upheld July 7 by New York's Court of Appeals.

  California law ruled too vague. The California Supreme Court ruled Nov. 22, by a 4-3 vote, that certain requirements in the state's abortion law were too vague to enforce. The decision meant that a woman in the first 20 weeks of her pregnancy could obtain a legal abortion if it were performed by a licensed doctor in an accredited hospital—with the decision to abort resting solely on the woman and her doctor. Among the provisions ruled unconstitutionally vague were the medical criteria for an abortion and a requirement that abortions be approved by local hospital committees. (In a related development, Pennsylvania Gov. Milton J. Shapp Nov. 30 vetoed a tough anti-abortion bill that would have allowed an abortion to be performed only when a panel of three hospital-based physicians decided that the continued pregnancy could endanger the life of the mother. In vetoing the bill, Shapp termed it "so restrictive that it is unenforceable.")

  See also ELECTIONS [16]; WOMEN'S RIGHTS

ABRAMS, CREIGHTON—*See* MILITARY [3, 6-8]
ABU DHABI—*See* OIL & NATURAL GAS
ACADEMY AWARDS—*See* MOTION PICTURES

AFGHANISTAN—Famine. Two rainless years followed by a severe winter caused a major grain shortage in the country during 1972, resulting in the reported deaths of tens of thousands of persons from hunger during the first six months of the year. During the worst of the famine, in April, an estimated 100,000 to 1,000,000 persons suffered from hunger. (In the fall of 1971, the U.S., the Soviet Union and several other European countries had responded to Afghanistan's plea for emergency aid by providing wheat and advice.)

  See also DRUG USE & ADDICTION [18]

AFRICA—West African economic group. Seven French-speaking African states June 3 signed a treaty setting up the West African Economic Community (CEAO). Plans for the organization, which was designed to promote regional trade among its members, had been announced at an April 25-26 summit meeting of the Common Organization of Africa, Malagasy and Mauritius (OCAM). Those signing the treaty were Ivory Coast, Dahomey, Upper Volta, Mali, Mauritania, Niger and Senegal. (Zaire had withdrawn from the group April 19, explaining that its membership in the exclusively French-speaking group would jeopardize its "policy of friendly relations with all the African states.")

  See also BRAZIL; CHURCHES; ENVIRONMENT; FOREIGN POLICY; HIJACKING [2]; INTERNATIONAL MONETARY DEVELOPMENTS [5]; NEGROES; OLYMPICS [3]; POLITICS [8]; SPACE [23]; ZAIRE

AFRICAN NATIONAL COUNCIL—*See* RHODESIA
AGING—*See* AUSTRALIA [6]; ELECTIONS [22, 24, 33]; NIXON, RICHARD MILHOUS; STATE & LOCAL GOVERMENTS
AGNEW, SPIRO THEODORE—*See* CRIME [2]; ELECTIONS [14, 22, 24, 26, 37]; JAPAN [4]; PENTAGON PAPERS

AGRICULTURE—1971 subsidies. The Agriculture Department announced March 7 that more than $3.1 billion in federal farm subsidy payments was paid out to 2,396,094 farmers in 1971. The reduction from 1970, when more than $3.6 billion went to 2,424,687 farms, was attributed more to reduced benefits for some crops than to a $55,000 per crop limitation for payments to individual farmers enacted under the 1970 Agricultural Act. Because of exemptions under the law for sugar payments and farms operated by states or other government bodies or on Indian reservations, and because of payments incorporating payments for several crops, 1,192 payments in 1971 exceeded $55,000. In the $50,000-$55,000 range, there were 1,105 payments in 1971 compared with only 452 in 1970.

Price supports disputed. According to a report Sept. 20, a Department of Agriculture study recommended that federal price supports and subsidies be abandoned in favor of funding used to create alternative job opportunities for farmers displaced from the land. According to the report, the study said that the U.S. listed 2.9 million farmers in 1970, but less than 1.5 million of that number had sales of $5,000 or more. The inclusion of small farmers, according to the report, "tends to exaggerate the low-income position of commercial farmers relative to the rest of the economy, and, hence, adds pressure" to raise farm commodity prices although the net effect could be economically inefficient. The study, commissioned by former Secretary of Agriculture Clifford Hardin, was disavowed by the present secretary, Earl L. Butz. A disclaimer reportedly was attached to the study saying that its views "aren't representative of the policy of the department."

    See also BUDGET; ELECTIONS [33]; EUROPEAN ECONOMIC COMMUNITY [1-2]; LABOR; SOVIET-U.S. RELATIONS [1, 7-10]

AIR FORCE, U.S.—*See* DEFENSE: DRUG USE & ADDICTION [2]; MILITARY [5, 7-8]; SPACE [3, 21]
AIR POLLUTION—*See* AUTOMOBILES; POLLUTION [1-8]
ALASKA PIPELINE—*See* ENVIRONMENT
AL FATAH—*See* HIJACKING [9]; JORDAN; MIDDLE EAST [7, 10, 17]; OLYMPIC TERRORISM

ALGERIA—Land redistribution. The government June 17 gave some 740 acres of land to 200 sharecroppers at Khemisklkhethna, 15 miles east of Algiers, as part of Algeria's program of land redistribution.

    See also CUBA; HIJACKING [4-5]; INDOCHINA WAR [25]; MIDDLE EAST [26]; YEMEN

ALI BHUTTO, ZULFIKAR—*See* BANGLA DESH [3]; PAKISTAN [5-12, 15, 17]
ALIOTO, JOSEPH L.—*See* CRIME [3]
ALLENDE GOSSENS, SALVADOR—*See* CHILE [1-5, 7, 9-12, 14, 16-22]
ALLIANCE FOR LABOR ACTION—*See* LABOR
ALL-STAR GAMES—*See* BASEBALL; BASKETBALL [7]; FOOTBALL; HOCKEY
AMERICA FIRST PARTY—*See* ELECTIONS [37]
AMERICAN BAR ASSOCIATION (ABA)—*See* ABORTION; JUDICIARY; POLICE
AMERICAN BASKETBALL ASSOCIATION (ABA)—*See* BASKETBALL [5, 7, 9, 12-14]
AMERICAN CIVIL LIBERTIES UNION (ACLU)—*See* CRIME [5]; SECURITY, U.S.
AMERICAN FEDERATION OF LABOR-CONGRESS OF INDUSTRIAL ORGANIZATIONS (AFL-CIO)—*See* ECONOMY [8, 10]; EDUCATION [9]; ELECTIONS [28]; LABOR; RAILROADS; SHIPS & SHIPPING
AMERICAN FEDERATION OF TEACHERS (AFT)—*See* EDUCATION [9]
AMERICAN INDIAN MOVEMENT (AIM)—*See* INDIANS, AMERICAN
AMERICAN LEAGUE (AL)—*See* BASEBALL
AMERICAN MEDICAL ASSOCIATION (AMA)—*See* MEDICINE
AMERICAN PARTY—*See* ELECTIONS [21, 37]

ANGOLA—New fighting reported. The Popular Movement for the Liberation of Angola (MPLA), a black nationalist group based in Brazzaville, Congo, announced Feb. 10 that the Cunene District of Angola, near the Ovamboland area of Namibia (Southwest Africa), had been in "armed revolt" against the government of the Portuguese colony since Jan. 12. The MPLA communique said that Camilo A. Rebocho Vaz, Angola's governor general, had visited the area Jan. 31 to study the situation. A report Feb. 12 confirmed Rebocho Vaz's visit and said that Portuguese and South African forces were conducting joint patrols in the region with the aim of preventing unidentified "outsiders" from spreading unrest.

    Nationalists unite. The Western-oriented Angolan National Liberation Front (FLNA) and the pro-Communist MPLA—Angola's two principal black liberation movements—Dec. 13 signed an agreement to form a united Supreme Council. Each side was to appoint 14 members to the council and seven members to the United Military Command and the Angolan Political Command. MPLA was to name the military leader of the union, and FLNA would choose the political chief. A committee composed of representatives from Zaire, Congo, Tanzania and Zambia was to supervise application of the agreement.

    See also BRAZIL; CHURCHES; HEALTH; PORTUGAL

ARAB REPUBLIC OF EGYPT—New Cabinet formed. President Anwar Sadat Jan. 16 named Aziz Sidky to succeed Mahmoud Fawzi as premier. After the Central Committee of the Arab Socialist Union (ASU), Egypt's only political party, approved Sidky's appointment as premier, Sadat issued a decree naming Fawzi second vice president, a post that had been vacant since the arrest and ouster of Aly Sabry in 1971. (The other vice president was Hussein el-Shafei.)

    Sidky Jan. 17 named a new Cabinet, which was to follow guidelines that called for more production, less consumption and restrictions on middle-class privileges in order to prepare the country for war with Israel *(see* MIDDLE EAST). The Cabinet had five deputy premiers: Gen. Mohammed Sadek, minister of war and production; Mohammed Abdullah Marzeban, minister of economy; Mamdouh Salem, interior minister; Mohammed Abdul Salam el-Zayyat, first secretary of the ASU (replaced in the ASU post by former Deputy Premier Sayed Marei); and Abdel Kader Hatem, minister of information and culture. Mohammed H. el-Zayyat, chief delegate to the United Nations, was recalled to become a minister of state for information. He was also appointed Sept. 8 to replace Foreign Minister Murad Ghaleb, who was dismissed Sept. 8 without explanation.

Military shakeup. Two top military commanders reportedly opposed to President Sadat's efforts to improve strained relations with the Soviet Union *(see* MIDDLE EAST [32]) resigned Oct. 26 and Oct. 28. Gen. Sadek resigned Oct. 26, reportedly under pressure from charges of insubordination, and was replaced as war minister and commander in chief by Maj. Gen. Ahmed Ismail, who was promoted to the rank of general. President Sadat announced Oct. 28 that he had replaced Rear Adm. Mahmoud Abdel Rahman Fahmy, a close friend of Sadek, as navy commander with Vice Adm. Fuad Zikry. (Sadat reportedly had discovered at an Oct. 24 meeting of the Armed Forces Supreme Council that "some directives to Gen. Sadek had not reached the various commands, while others had not been implemented." Some Egyptian sources said that Sadek had failed to pass on to senior officers under him the results of an Oct. 16-18 Moscow visit by Premier Sidky.)

Anti-Sadat plot reported crushed. A series of press reports indicated that a right-wing military coup aimed at overthrowing President Sadat was crushed Nov. 11, but Cairo officially denied the reports Nov. 19. According to the press accounts, the conspirators—led mostly by anti-Soviet colonels—had planned to oust Sadat Nov. 15 and form a military junta with Gen. Sadek as figurehead. (Sadek was said to have no knowledge of the plot.) The planned uprising allegedly was thwarted with the arrest of 25-30 officers, including Gen. Mustafa Mehrez, chief of military intelligence. The coup reportedly had been set to start before the ouster of Soviet military experts in July *(see* MIDDLE EAST [32]), then was delayed and revived about the time of Premier Sidky's Moscow visit. Arab diplomatic sources in Lebanon reported Nov. 19 that 35-40 Egyptian military officers had been seized in connection with the alleged conspiracy.

See also EUROPEAN ECONOMIC COMMUNITY [9]; HIJACKING [9]; IRAQ; MIDDLE EAST [1, 15-17, 26, 29-37]; OLYMPIC TERRORISM; PHILIPPINES [3]; SYRIA; YEMEN

ARAB WORLD—See ARAB REPUBLIC OF EGYPT; HIJACKING [15]; JORDAN; MALTA; MIDDLE EAST; OLYMPIC TERRORISM; PAKISTAN [1]; SYRIA; YEMEN

ARAFAT, YASIR—See JORDAN; MIDDLE EAST [6]

ARCHEOLOGY & ANTHROPOLOGY—B.C. calendar found in Mexico. A fragment of a pre-Christ calendar chiseled in stone was found in Mexico, according to a report Feb. 16. The stone fragment, together with a companion slab found in 1939, proved that an extinct people—the Olmecs—and not the later Mayas invented the calendar in the Western Hemisphere. The date on the stone—equal to the Christian year 31 B.C.—was represented by a column of bars and dots.

Philippine cave dwellers found. Manuel Elizalde Jr., president of Panamin (the Philippine presidential agency in charge of national minorities), announced March 26 that the Tasadays, a Stone Age tribe discovered in the southern Philippine rain forest in June 1971, were cave dwellers. They were the first primitive people to be discovered in modern times who still lived in caves as permanent homes.

2.6-million-year-old skull found. Richard Leakey, director of the National Museum of Kenya, reported Nov. 9 the discovery of an approximately 2.6-million-year-old skull of early man that he said challenged the current theories of human evolution. (The definitive age of the skull had not yet been determined by radioisotopic tests, but radioactive dating methods had established that the volcanic ash in which the skull was found and two thigh bones found in the same area were 2.6 million years old.) Leakey said that the skull and the thigh bones presented "clear evidence" that a large-brained "truly upright and bipedal form" of man had lived in East Africa contemporaneously with a more primitive African near-man known as Australopithecus. Leakey postulated that modern man evolved from the line represented by the newly found skull, rather than from Australopithecus. He said that, "while the skull is different from our own species, Homo sapiens, it is also different from all known forms of early man." Leakey said that the cranial cavity indicated a capacity of more than 800 cubic centimeters, as compared to almost 500 cubic centimeters for Australopithecus, and that "the whole shape of the brain case is remarkably reminiscent of modern man." He said further that the two intact thigh bones were "practically indistinguishable from the same bones of modern man," indicating that the 2.6-million-year-old man was able to walk upright.

ARGENTINA—During 1972, Argentina was plagued with an economic crisis brought on by the highest inflation in the world and an almost total loss of foreign reserves. The crisis resulted in the March resignation of the Cabinet, the president of the Central Bank and the governors of Argentina's provinces *(see* [2]) and in the July resignation of the new Central Bank president *(see* [4]) because of his opposition to inflation-breeding government spending *(see* [5]). The economic situation was aggravated by widespread and violent strike actions *(see* [13-18]) which caused the government to grant large wage increases *(see* [15]). The government of Argentina was also preparing, throughout the year, for planned 1973 elections and a return of the country to institutional rule *(see* [6]). Election developments were marked by the return to Argentina of former-dictator Juan Domingo Peron after 17 years in exile and by Peron's subsequent departure *(see* [7]). In other actions, acts of terrorism continued through the year *(see* [9-12]) and evoked strong reaction from the government *(see* [8]), including what was widely considered to be the retaliatory murder of 16 persons involved at a hijacking near Trelew *(see* [12]).

[2] Cabinet resigns. All 12 Cabinet ministers, the president of the Central Bank and the governors of Argentina's 21 provinces resigned March 3, leaving President Alejandro Lanusse free to form a new administration. Lanusse, who had announced plans for a major reorganization of the government Feb. 24, was reportedly seeking a Cabinet able to control the country's economic crisis and to prepare for the elections scheduled for March 1973. According to a report March 8, Lanusse rejected the resignations of all but four of the Cabinet members. Lanusse March 10 swore in Daniel Garcia to replace Alfredo Girelli as commerce minister, Enrique Juan Parellada to replace Carlos Casale as industry and mining minister, and Ernesto Jorge Lanusse (a first cousin of the president) to replace Antonio Americo Di Rocco as agriculture and livestock minister. The president accepted the resignation of Defense Minister Jose Rafael Caceres Monie, but did not replace him until May 9, when Eduardo E. Aguirre Obarrio was appointed defense minister. In other Cabinet changes: Foreign Minister Luis Maria de Pablo Pardo resigned June 19, reportedly at President Lanusse's insistence, and was replaced June 22 by retired Brig. Gen. Eduardo McLoughlin; Justice Minister Ismael Bruno Quijano resigned July 4, claiming he did so to protect himself from a charge that he had sought to influence an appeals court in the 1971 bankruptcy case of Swift de la Plata, and was replaced July 11 by Gervasio Colombres; Social Welfare Minister Francisco Manrique resigned Aug. 9, facilitating his presidential candidacy (announced Aug. 31) in the 1973 elections, and was replaced Aug. 13 by Oscar R. Puiggros. (Officials wishing to run in the 1973 elections were required to leave their posts by Aug. 25.) Finance Minister Cayetano Licciardo resigned Oct. 8 and was replaced Oct. 11 by Jorge Wehbe.

[3] Chile pact voided. Argentina announced March 12 that it would withdraw from a 1902 treaty with Chile under which the two countries agreed to settle by British Crown arbitration a long-standing dispute over the Beagle

Channel and three small islands at the southern tip of South America. Argentina's announcement meant that it would invoke an article in the treaty which allowed either nation to withdraw on six-months' notice at the end of each 10-year period. Argentina said that ways of resolving international disputes had evolved so much since 1902 that it was necessary to bring the treaty up to date. The foreign ministers of the two countries April 5 signed a 10-year arbitration agreement replacing the 1902 treaty. Under the new agreement, the two countries would take unresolvable differences to the International Court of Justice at The Hague. However, the new pact did not affect arbitration under the 1902 treaty of disputes over the three contested islands.

[4] Brignone resigns in economic crisis. The government announced July 25 that Central Bank President Carlos Brignone, a strong opponent of inflation-breeding government deficit spending, had resigned and been replaced by Jorge Bermudez, head of the state-owned National Bank. Brignone had been severely criticized for his inability to pull Argentina out of a severe economic crisis. Critics alleged that his tight money policy, often eroded by government spending, had caused a severe shortage of liquidity in the economy and had not prevented inflation from reaching a record 37% in the first half of 1972. (Argentine inflation for the year ending May 31 was 56.5%, the highest in the world.) Brignone had also been criticized for his inability to obtain significant foreign loans required to meet debt payments of $600 million due by July 1973. (Argentina's foreign reserves were only about $150 million, down from $800 million in October 1970. The reserves had been virtually wiped out by trade deficits and the flight of capital.) Brignone had embarked on a Jan. 30-Feb. 26 U.S. and European tour to try to find $1 billion in foreign credits to restore confidence in the Argentine economy. However, hopes of achieving the $1 billion goal were dashed May 14 when the International Monetary Fund (IMF) removed from its agenda an Argentine loan request for $119 million. The IMF had negotiated an economic stabilization agreement with Brignone as a basis for the loan and considered the agreement violated by an Argentine wage hike announced in April *(see* [15]) and by cancellation of an electricity rate increase *(see* [14]). Many potential creditors were unwilling to lend to Argentina unless the IMF also contributed.

[5] *Economic decisions announced.* The government July 25 also announced a series of economic measures which had been opposed by Brignone. One of the measures provided that the minimum wage—about $40 a month—would be increased by about 25% within a few weeks. Another provided for the speeding of pension and welfare checks. (Some payments had been in arrears since November 1971 because of the shortage of funds.) A third measure promised that, despite the government's record internal deficit and the low point of foreign exchange reserves, there would be no increases in utility rates, subway and commuter fares or costs for other public services. (Despite its pledge, the government Oct. 24 increased the minimum bus fare in Buenos Aires from 3¢ to 4¢. In protest over the increase, 17 buses were burned in different parts of the city that day.)

[6] Constitutional amendments. President Lanusse Aug. 24 decreed a series of constitutional amendments designed "solely to guarantee the stability of authorities elected by the people" in the projected 1973 elections. The measures, altering the constitution of 1853, would remain in effect until May 24, 1977 and for four years after that if a special constitutional convention was unable either to incorporate them into the constitution or overturn them. The measures provided for: direct election of the president and vice president rather than the old system of election by electoral colleges; reduction of the presidential term of office from six to four years, with a limit of two terms to any president; establishment of four-year terms of office for governors, national and provincial legislators and municipal intendents and councilmen; allocation of three Senate seats, instead of two, to each province and the federal capital, with one of the three senators from each area representing the minority of voters; and extension of the normal congressional session from four to seven months, with provisions to facilitate quorums and allow the government budget to encompass projects lasting more than a year.

[7] **Peron returns, leaves.** Ex-President Peron returned to Argentina Nov. 17, ending 17 years of exile which had begun in 1955 when his government was overthrown. His arrival followed months of negotiations with the military government, which reportedly believed that an arrangement with Peron's Justicialista party was necessary to insure the success of the 1973 elections and a return to institutional rule. The ex-dictator returned under heavy security precautions. The airport where Peron arrived was cordoned off by tanks, cannon and 30,000 troops; police and army patrols were increased in Buenos Aires and other cities to prevent large demonstrations and quell raucous celebrations; a paid holiday was declared to prevent factory workers from massing to march on the airport and to defuse a general strike called by the Peronist-dominated General Confederation of Labor (CGT). Peron was rushed upon arrival to the heavily guarded airport hotel, where he canceled a scheduled press conference and message to the country as a protest over the strict security measures. Peron's return to Argentina had been cleared by court decisions March 24 and April 7, clearing him of charges of fraud and treason, respectively. The Justicialistas had proclaimed him their presidential candidate June 25. Peron was also nominated Dec. 5 by the Justicialista Liberation Front, a coalition formed by the Justicialistas and some 14 minor parties and political groups. However, Peron left Argentina Dec. 14, after 28 days of political consultations, and announced that he would not accept the presidential nomination. (Peron legally was unable to run for the presidency under residency requirements imposed by the government.) During the 28 days of consultations, Peron attempted to build a broad-based civilian coalition for the 1973 elections, but the coalition's progress was hampered by Peron's insistence on being the coalition's candidate. The Justicialistas Dec. 15 again renominated Peron for the presidency, but Peron refused the further nomination.

Guerrilla Developments

[8] **Report accuses police of torture.** Lawyers and relatives of 30 persons held in Argentine jails Jan. 14 released a report accusing police of torturing prisoners. The report contained statements from the alleged victims, most of whom were linked by police to various guerrilla organizations. The reports of torture grew later in the year, with a report May 26 that more than 50 persons had been tortured at prisons and military installations during the previous year. The army May 25 issued instructions intended to prevent the mistreatment and torture of political prisoners, but government sources admitted that authorities were virtually powerless to stop torture, since the names of torturers were not on staff lists of any of the police security forces. In a related development, some 25,000 lawyers June 23 staged a nationwide day of protest against repressive laws and the alleged torture of political prisoners. In Buenos Aires, police armed with tear gas and fire hoses broke up the lawyers' demonstration.

[9] **Bank robbery.** Fifteen members of the People's Revolutionary Army (ERP), a Trotskyite guerrilla group, Jan. 30 took as much as $800,000 from the state-owned National Development Bank in Buenos Aires. It was the biggest bank robbery in Argentine history. Notices distributed later in Buenos Aires said the money was "expropriated for the people's cause, and will be used to continue the revolutionary war."

[10] **March-April wave of attacks.** A wave of political assassinations and kidnapings swept Argentina during March and April, threatening President Lanusse's plans to hold elections in 1973. Participating in the terrorist campaign were Peronist urban commandos, who had defied a plea from Peron to his followers for a halt to violence. Among the incidents of violence: a policeman was killed and the owner of a refrigerator firm was seriously

wounded March 13 in Buenos Aires when about 10 terrorists fired on them; members of the Armed Forces of Liberation March 17 kidnaped an executive of a leading wine company, but released him after payment of $37,000 in ransom; unidentified assailants March 17 shot to death a former police chief of the province of Tucuman; members of the Peronist Montonero guerrilla organization March 18 set fire to an office of the New Force party in Buenos Aires and killed a leader of the New Force; at least 10 members of the Armed Forces of Liberation were reported March 19 to have blown up the clubhouse of the exclusive Buenos Aires San Jorge Polo Club with three bombs; members of the ERP March 21 kidnaped Oberdan Sallustro, president of Argentina's Italian-owned Fiat automotive industries, and April 10 killed him during a shootout with police at the guerrilla's hideout outside Buenos Aires; the ERP and the Revolutionary Armed Forces (FAR) April 10 machine-gunned to death Gen. Carlos Sanchez, commander of the Army's 2nd Corps, allegedly in reprisal for his antiguerrilla campaign.

[11] *Other kidnapings.* Ernanno Barca, president of the Buenos Aires branch of the Italian-owned Banco di Napoli, was kidnaped by four armed men June 30 and released a few hours later, after the bank had paid a $200,000 ransom. Two Argentine businessmen—Adolfo Kaplun and Eduardo Falugue—were abducted Sept. 4 and released unharmed Sept. 6 after their families reportedly ransomed them for $150,000 and $250,000. Jan J. Van de Panne, a Dutch citizen who headed the Philips Argentina electronics firm, was kidnaped Sept. 5 by alleged Montonero guerrillas and released Sept. 6 after his company paid them $500,000. Aldo Benito Roggio, an engineer in the industrial city of Cordoba, was kidnaped Sept. 21 and released Sept. 22 after his family paid a reported ransom of $130,000-$170,000. Enrico Barrella, an Italian industrialist, was kidnaped in Buenos Aires Nov. 7 and released unharmed Nov. 10 after his family reportedly paid a $500,000 ransom. Falix Azpiazu, a Spanish industrialist, was abducted Dec. 6 by unknown persons demanding $180,000 ransom. He was released Dec. 8 after his firm paid a reported $100,000 ransom. Ronald Grove, managing director of Great Britain's Vestey industrial group in South America, was kidnaped Dec. 10 and released Dec. 19 after Vestey paid a reported $1 million ransom. Vicente Russo, an executive for a subsidiary of the International Telephone and Telegraph Corp., was kidnaped Dec. 27 and released Dec. 29 after reported payment of $500,000-$1 million.

[12] **16 killed after prison break, hijacking.** A group of political prisoners reportedly escaped from the maximum-security prison at Rawson Aug. 15. Some of the prisoners allegedly were members of a group of 10 guerrillas who Aug. 15 hijacked an Austral Airlines jet at Trelew Airport and forced the pilot to fly them and 96 passengers to Chile, where the guerrillas surrendered to police and requested political asylum. (The 10 hijackers were sent to Cuba by the Chilean government Aug. 25 to avoid extradition requested by Argentina.) Following the hijacking, 19 guerrillas who had assisted in the hijacking surrendered to police at the Trelew Airport and were imprisoned. Sixteen of the 19 were shot to death Aug. 22 while allegedly trying to escape from prison. The three others of the group were reportedly wounded. The killings were widely assumed to be a retaliatory execution ordered by the government and provoked widespread protests in Cordoba, Buenos Aires, La Plata, Rosario, Santa Fe, Tucuman, Corrientes and Bahia Blanca. The government gave two conflicting versions of the Trelew killings, one "off the record" and one an official version. In the informal version, the prisoners reportedly escaped from their cells early Aug. 22 and, after seizing the second-in-command of the base, Capt. Luis Sosa, were proceeding toward the armory when they were engaged in fierce combat by guards. The official version held that Sosa had ordered the prisoners out of their cells and was inspecting them in a narrow passage when he was siezed by a guerrilla, who took his submachine gun and began shooting at the guards. (There was some question why the guerrilla had missed his targets and why

Sosa alone had escaped unharmed from a fusillade that cut down the guerrillas.) The three survivors of the killings gave a different version. According to their story, the 19 guerrillas had been lined up outside their cells by guards and officers, who then shot them down with automatic rifle fire.

Labor Developments & Civil Disorder

[13] **General strike cripples nation.** Approximately five million workers from 110 unions remained away from their jobs Feb. 29 and March 1, closing down an estimated 85% of Argentina's industry, commerce and transportation. The general strike had been called by the powerful CGT Feb. 12 to protest the government's economic policies and the government's refusal to grant a CGT request for a 10% wage increase. The shutdown, which had been declared illegal by President Lanusse, affected factories, shops, banks, subways and trains. Government sources estimated it would cost the nation $104 million in lost production and wages. Government troops guarded important installations throughout the country, and extra police details patrolled the heart of Buenos Aires. Although there was little violence, arsonists in Buenos Aires reportedly set fire to more than a dozen buses and railway coaches.

[14] **Violence in Mendoza.** The western city of Mendoza was placed under a curfew April 4 after a two-hour general strike that paralyzed the province of Mendoza and after violent clashes between police and demonstrators protesting a 110% increase in electricity rates. The government in Buenos Aires declared a state of emergency and sent in army troops, which were able to restore order only after five hours of street battles. By April 7, the disorders, said to be the worst since President Lanusse seized power in 1971, had resulted in three deaths. More than 100 persons were wounded in the fighting and about 500 were jailed. The protests, which ended after Lanusse announced April 7 the suspension of electricity payments for January-April and the creation of a special commission to overhaul the rate structure, were accompanied by daily general strikes called by the CGT to protest the electricity increases. (The government April 5 blocked CGT funds in an attempt to break the union's strikes.) The general strike April 7 left Mendoza with low food and medical supplies. Sympathy strikes the same day halted virtually all activity in Cordoba and in the western province of San Juan. Mendoza was calm April 8 as most citizens ignored a CGT call for another strike. Troops continued to patrol the streets April 9, but the curfew was lifted and air and train service to the city (suspended April 7) was resumed.

[15] **Wage increases.** Although President Lanusse had said Feb. 3 that he would not change his policy on wages (which guaranteed a 15% wage increase in January and a further 10% increase in July), he ordered April 26 that the July increase be moved up to May 1 and be increased to 15%. (Lanusse reportedly made the decision over the objections of Finance Minister Licciardo and Central Bank President Brignone.) The CGT bitterly attacked the wage increase May 16, charging it already had been swallowed up by price increases. Following a series of strikes in August and September, Lanusse Sept. 20 decreed further across-the-board wage increases of 12%.

[16] **June disorders.** One person was killed and more than 500 arrested June 22-30 as protests against the government erupted in several major cities. The disturbances began June 22 in Tucuman with a strike for higher wages by teachers and civil servants. The strike led to riots in which more than 100 persons were arrested. The rioting in Tucuman continued June 24-26, and the army occupied the city June 27 in the midst of a general strike called by the CGT to protest government economic policies and repression. As the violence diminished in Tucuman, disturbances spread June 27 to Cordoba, Santa Fe, Salta and La Plata. Students and police clashed in Cordoba and Salta, while about 1,500 students and workers in Santa Fe demonstrated before provincial government buildings. Troops and police massed in the streets of Buenos Aires and other main cities June 28 to prevent anti-government demonstrations on

the anniversary of the 1966 coup which brought the military to power. Further violence was reported from Tucuman, and Cordoba was the scene of another general strike. Students occupied university buildings in Buenos Aires June 30, demanding the release of other students detained by the police. Violence continued the same day in Tucuman and Cordoba, where at least 40 persons reportedly were arrested, and in Santa Fe, where troops and police clashed with striking workers.

[17] Disturbances in Malargue. The closing of the Santa Cruz manganese mine, which left 200 families in the Andean mining town of Malargue without work, set off protests July 2 which led to army occupation of the town July 3. Residents of the town began their protest against the area's high rate of unemployment July 2 by taking control of Malargue, blocking access from the north and appointing five citizens to assume the functions of the municipal government. Municipal Intendent Jose Ranco resigned in sympathy with the protest, and police refused to take action against the insurgents. The same day, about 100 residents of Malargue arrived in the provincial capital of Mendoza after a 250-mile "hunger march" made to dramatize their region's economic situation. Most commercial activity stopped in Malargue July 3 as residents began a general strike to protest the army occupation. Shopowners reportedly refused to sell food to security officers, forcing the government to send in supplies from Mendoza, but no serious incidents were reported. The National Development Bank July 14 agreed to furnish the credit necessary to reopen the Santa Cruz mine.

[18] Emergency in General Roca. In a development similar to that in Malargue, troops July 4 occupied the town of General Roca in Rio Negro province after residents occupied the municipal government building and began to form a "provisional committee of government." The protest reportedly grew out of a decision by the provincial governor to establish a court in a neighboring town, allegedly discriminating against General Roca. Emergency measures were imposed in General Roca July 10-18 to quell continuing civil disturbances. President Lanusse July 10 declared the town an emergency zone and named Lt. Gen. Guillermo Anibal With as the military commander and supreme authority in the region. Assuming command of General Roca July 11, Gen. With issued a series of decrees barring strikes, ordering prison sentences for persons disobeying military or security forces and imposing press censorship. Most businesses resumed operations the same day, but the town newspaper struck to protest the censorship decree. After a week of relative calm, the emergency measures were lifted July 18. Troops were withdrawn and a new municipal intendent, Col. Enrique Pellicetti, was installed. However, demonstrations resumed that night, with townspeople building bonfires and racing cars through the streets. Thirty-two persons were arrested during protests July 19 and released the next day. About 2,500 persons demonstrated in front of the municipal building July 20, but no police action was reported.

See also BOLIVIA; CONSERVATION; DRUG USE & ADDICTION [16]; INTERNATIONAL MONETARY DEVELOPMENTS [9]; LATIN AMERICA; URUGUAY [7, 13]

ARMAMENTS, INTERNATIONAL—Latin America. U.S. Defense Secretary Melvin R. Laird Feb. 15 warned in a defense policy statement that the U.S. would limit arms sales to Latin America where an arms race could develop. However, less than four months later, June 7, Laird urged a Senate Appropriations subcommittee to abrogate the $100 million ceiling on military aid to the area. Laird's February statement was reportedly aimed at Venezuela and Colombia—both of which had increased weapons purchases since a border dispute developed over the Gulf of Venezuela, which was believed to cover a wealth of petroleum. Laird's statement declined to bow to Congressional pressure to end military assistance to Latin America. The defense secretary pledged to continue such assistance to protect the interests of "the U.S. as well as the hemisphere." Venezuelan President Rafael Caldera Feb. 16 responded to

Laird's statement by pointing out that arms were readily available from Europe. Laird acknowledged the European supplies in his June statement, conceding that the U.S. had "forced [its] neighbors to look toward other governments...to buy more expensive and less satisfactory equipment. As a result, he said, several Latin American countries had run into difficulties in locating replacement parts and munitions, and had spent more for military supplies than Congress had estimated when it approved the $100 million ceiling.

In a related development, it was reported July 28 that Venezuela had ordered $60 million worth of arms from France—the largest single Latin American purchase of ground weapons since World War II. The order, which reportedly would give Venezuela the most advanced tank force in Latin America except for Cuba, allegedly included 142 French AMX-30 medium-size tanks for delivery in 1972-73, plus more than 20 self-propelled 155-mm. howitzers. Venezuelan Foreign Minister Aristides Calvani said July 28 that Venezuela's recent purchases did not mean that the country was in an arms race. He said the transactions were "simply for re-equipment." (The International Institute for Pacifist Research in Stockholm reported June 15 that Latin American countries had engaged in a massive purchase of jet fighter planes and other war materiel since 1968. The purchases included 478 military aircraft—from propeller-driven transport carriers to French Mirage and Soviet MiG-21 jet fighters.)

See also ATOMIC ENERGY [2, 7-8, 13]; BAHRAIN; CYPRUS; DISARMAMENT; ENVIRONMENT; FOREIGN POLICY; GREECE [1, 6]; IRELAND; JAPAN [4]; LATIN AMERICA; MIDDLE EAST [26-27, 34]; NIXON, RICHARD MILHOUS; POLAND; SOVIET-U.S. RELATIONS [5]; SWITZERLAND

ARMY CORPS OF ENGINEERS—See FLOODS; POLLUTION [14]
ARMY, U.S.—See DEFENSE; DISARMAMENT; DRUG USE & ADDICTION [2]; ESPIONAGE; GERMANY, WEST [3]; MILITARY [1,4-6,9];WAR CRIMES
ART—See ITALY [9]
ASHBROOK, JOHN M.—See ELECTIONS [3-6, 8]

ATOMIC ENERGY—Suit against AEC's conflicting functions. Six environmental groups Jan. 6 filed suit to force the Atomic Energy Commission (AEC) to divest itself of one of two competing functions—the promotion or the regulation of the nuclear power industry. The plaintiffs also asked for a temporary injunction barring the AEC from issuing permits for the construction or operation of any new nuclear plants. The suit, filed in the U.S. District Court for the District of Columbia, charged that the law granting the commission the conflicting powers violated constitutional due process rights, since "there is no unbiased legal forum before which a citizen or group can secure a fair hearing in matters relating to atomic energy." As a result of AEC bias, the groups said, the public was deprived of a voice in protecting its health and safety and in the matters of plant financing and eventual consumer power rates.

[2] **U.S. to build breeder reactor.** AEC Chairman James R. Schlesinger announced Jan. 14 that the Tennessee Valley Authority (TVA) and the Commonwealth Edison Co. of Chicago would construct a breeder nuclear power plant in Tennessee, the first of a type that was expected to become the mainstay of future power needs. The facility, which would begin construction in about two years, would provide 350,000-500,000 kilowatts to the TVA when completed in 1980. It would cost $500 million, with the federal government and the TVA each supplying $100 million and public and private utilities and other corporations supplying the rest. Schlesinger said that breeder reactors would reduce thermal pollution of the environment and would present a solution to the problem of rapidly dwindling sources of power. (The breeder reactor created more fuel than it consumed, converting uranium to plutonium.) Despite the advantages named by Schlesinger, however, environmentalists urged reconsideration of the disadvantages of the breeder reactor program. The

Scientists' Institute for Public Information brought a suit in federal district court in Washington to force the AEC to issue a general environmental impact statement on the program, but Judge George L. Hart Jr. dismissed the suit March 24. The institute had charged that breeder reactors would entail greater risk of explosion, thermal pollution and plutonium emission and produce more radioactive wastes, than other types of reactors. The institute also charged that the AEC plan to give the breeder reactor top priority and annual federal expenditures of $100 million together constituted a major federal act and a legislative proposal, thereby invoking the impact statement requirement. Hart ruled that the breeder program would have no tangible impact for some time and that "there is no certainty any kind of system will ever be economically feasible." The AEC defended the reactor April 14 in a specific environmental impact statement for the Tennessee plant, but a group of 31 scientists and other experts April 25 asked Congress to deny an Administration request for development funds for the reactor. The group based its statement on safety and environmental hazards, warning that the heat generated in a breeder reactor could lead, in cases of human or mechanical error, to a substantial atomic explosion. Problems of plutonium transport and disposal also were raised, as well as the danger of black-market plutonium diversion for weapons manufacture.

[3] **AEC asks interim licenses.** The AEC, backed by top Administration environment officials, asked Congress March 16 for an amendment to the National Environmental Policy Act to permit the AEC to grant interim emergency operating licenses to new nuclear power plants before filing complete environmental impact statements. AEC Commissioner Schlesinger said that, without emergency licenses, five completed nuclear plants would be unable to meet possible 1972 and 1973 power shortages in New York City, Illinois, Iowa, Michigan and Wisconsin. Under the proposed amendment, the AEC would have the power through June 1973 to issue licenses without public hearings and without submitting statements to the Council on Environmental Quality. After July 1, 1973, no new interim licenses would be issued, but any license could be continued if the AEC declared the emergency still in effect. Congress May 19 passed an amendment to the Atomic Energy Act allowing temporary emergency permits until October 1973; but the amendment to the National Environmental Policy Act was tabled by the Senate Interior Committee July 19, killing chances for 1972 passage.

[4] **Safety left to federal government.** In a 7-2 ruling April 3, the Supreme Court ruled that the AEC alone had the authority to regulate radiation control standards for nuclear power plants. The decision dealt a serious setback to efforts by local governments to seek tighter safety controls. The ruling came in a case involving the state of Minnesota and a nuclear power plant built by the Northern States Power Co. 30 miles north of Minneapolis. The company had received an AEC license allowing it to discharge more radioactive debris than permitted by Minnesota's State Pollution Agency.

[5] **Surface waste storage planned.** In the face of opposition to its plans to bury radioactive wastes underground, the AEC announced May 19 that it would build a huge steel and concrete waste-storage facility above ground or just below the surface. The facility would be ready by 1979 or 1980, at an estimated cost of $100 million. In the meantime, the AEC said, it would continue research on burying the waste products of power plant fission reactions in abandoned salt mines or other underground formations. (A 1966 report by the National Academy of Sciences had advised the underground alternative. About $8 million already had been spent to prepare a salt mine near Lyons, Kans. to receive the wastes, before opposition from the state of Kansas and the Sierra Club blocked the project in 1971.)

International Developments

[6] **Australia, Japan sign accord.** Australia and Japan Feb. 21 signed an agreement on the peaceful uses of atomic energy. The accord would facilitate commercial agreements for the sale of Australian uranium to Japan and would provide for future collaboration between the two nations in research and commercial ventures. The two countries July 28 exchanged notes formally notifying each other of the completion of the procedures required for implementation of the agreement. At the same time, the two nations and the International Atomic Energy Agency (IAEA) signed a safeguards agreement covering the export of uranium from Australia to Japan. (In a related development, the Board of Governors of the IAEA March 1 approved previously negotiated accords with 12 nations providing for the application of IAEA safeguards to the nations' nuclear material to insure its peaceful use. The nations were Czechoslovakia, Denmark, East Germany, Greece, Iraq, Ireland, Malaysia, New Zealand, Norway, Rumania, Yugoslavia and Zaire. Similar accords with Mauritius, Morocco and the Netherlands were approved by the IAEA Oct. 3. *See also* [8].)

[7] **Taiwan reactor to use natural uranium.** According to a report July 19, Taiwan's (Nationalist China) Institute for Nuclear Energy Research, in collaboration with Canada, was constructing a $35 million atomic research reactor that could produce 22 pounds of plutonium annually, 8.8 pounds more than enough for the fabrication of an atomic bomb. The reactor, expected to go into operation in 1973, would be fueled by natural uranium, which could be purchased on the open market without any safeguards, in contrast to the restricted purchase of enriched uranium. The use of natural uranium fuel aroused fears among arms control experts that Taiwan might divert the plutonium to the construction of nuclear weapons. The reactor would be Taiwan's fifth, but its first fueled by natural uranium.

[8] **IAEA approves Euratom accord.** The board of governors of the IAEA Sept. 22 approved a cooperation agreement with the five non-nuclear members of the European Atomic Energy Community (Euratom). The accord would cover the current members of Euratom, except France, and two of the future members, Denmark and Ireland *(see* EUROPEAN ECONOMIC COMMUNITY [10]). France and Britain were not included in the accord because they already possessed nuclear weapons. The agreement provided for the coordination of IAEA and Euratom safeguards systems to verify that atomic material was used for peaceful purposes. Under the accord, Euratom would conduct the basic inspection, but would adapt some of its procedures to conform with IAEA requirements.

[9] **U.S., U.S.S.R. set joint effort.** The AEC announced Sept. 29 that the U.S. and the Soviet Union had signed an agreement to expand their cooperative efforts in the peaceful uses of atomic energy to cover controlled thermonuclear fusion reactions and fast breeder reactions. Other exchanges covered by the joint memorandum—the fifth since 1959—included atom-smasher machine studies, radiation chemistry, energy conversion and disposal of radioactive wastes.

Testing

[10] **Chinese tests.** China conducted nuclear tests in the atmosphere Jan. 7 and March 18. The tests—the 13th and 14th since China's first nuclear explosion in 1964—were at the Lop Nor nuclear test site in northern China. The Jan. 7 test had the force of less than 20 kilotons (equivalent to the explosive force of less than 20,000 tons of TNT). The March 18 test had the force of 20-200 kilotons.

[11] **Soviet tests.** Seismic signals from what were presumed to be underground Soviet nuclear tests were reported March 28, June 6, Aug. 16, 19, 26 and 28, Sept. 21, Oct. 1 and 3,Nov. 1 and Dec. 10. The March 28, June 26, Aug. 16, 19 and 26, Sept. 21 and Oct. 1 and 3 tests, all recorded at the

Semipalatinsk nuclear testing ground in eastern Siberia, reportedly each had a force of 20-200 kilotons. The Nov. 1 test had a force of 200-1,000 kilotons. The Aug. 28 test, at the Novaya Zemlya test area of the Soviet Arctic, was in the one-megaton range (equivalent to one million tons of TNT). The Dec. 10 blast registered 7 on the Richter scale, indicating one of the strongest explosions in recent years.

[12] **U.S. tests.** The AEC conducted underground nuclear tests in the low-yield range (less than 20 kilotons) at its Nevada test site April 19, May 17 and 19, July 20 and Sept. 26. Tests in the low-intermediate-yield range (20-200 kilotons) were held at the site Sept. 21 and Dec. 21.

[13] **French tests.** Despite sharp protests from many countries, France reportedly began a controversial series of atmospheric atomic tests at the Mururoa Atoll in the South Pacific June 25. A second test was said to have taken place June 30, and the third and last test allegedly occurred July 29. (There was some doubt as to the accuracy of the test dates because the French Defense Ministry refused to officially confirm or deny the reports.) The French government had defended the planned series of tests on the grounds that they were of low yield and removed from population centers. The purpose of the series was to test the igniting device of the French hydrogen bomb. Among the incidents of international protest over the tests: Australian longshoremen boycotted French shipping and cargo June 1-Aug. 3; Peru threatened in early June to break relations with France if the tests were carried out; the foreign ministers of Bolivia, Chile, Colombia, Ecuador and Peru June 19 condemned the blasts and demanded an immediate halt to preparations for the series; Australia, New Zealand and Peru had formally protested the tests to the Geneva Disarmament Conference June 20; and Japan and Canada had urged cancellation of the tests at the Geneva conference June 22. The foreign ministers of New Zealand and Australia, joined by U.S. Secretary of State William P. Rogers, June 29 issued a statement indirectly condemning the French tests and affirming their hope that all nations would adhere to the treaty banning atmospheric nuclear tests. (France had not signed the treaty.)

See also CANADA [3]; DISARMAMENT; ENVIRONMENT; EUROPEAN ECONOMIC COMMUNITY [12]; HIJACKING [6]; JAPAN [4]; MEDICINE; NIXON, RICHARD MILHOUS; POLLUTION [3, 13]; SECURITY, U.S.; SPACE [6]

ATOMIC ENERGY COMMISSION (AEC)—See ATOMIC ENERGY [1-5, 9, 12]; HIJACKING [6]

ATTICA PRISON—See ELECTIONS [25]; PRISONS

AUSTRALIA—**Aborigines given limited land rights.** Prime Minister William McMahon Jan. 25 announced a new policy enabling aborigines to lease government-owned tribal areas provided they "have the intention and ability to make reasonable social and economic use of the land." The policy, which was called inadequate by leaders in national movements promoting aboriginal rights, in effect reaffirmed a 1971 Supreme Court decision denying aboriginal claims to ownership of tribal areas. Under the policy, the government would set up an initial fund of $5.95 million and allot an additional $2.8 million annually for the purchase of privately owned land on aboriginal reserves to lease to the aborigines. The policy would also grant licenses for mineral exploration to qualified aborigines on a preferred basis in areas where they had a "special interest" and would require mining companies to hire more aborigines. McMahon's statement followed the formation in Brisbane Jan. 18 of Australia's first Black Panther party by militant aborigines under the leadership of Dennis Walker. Walker, who assumed the post of party defense minister, said the movement would be modeled after the U.S. Black Panthers and would engage in militant action. Militant aborigines Jan. 26 set up an encampment in front of Parliament in Canberra to protest the government's refusal to grant aborigines legal freehold land titles. The tent encampment was forcibly broken up by police July 20.

[2] **Government changes.** Minister for the Army Andrew Peacock was sworn in Feb. 23 as external territories minister, replacing Charles Barnes, who retired. Robert C. Katter was installed as minister for the army.

[3] **Oil strike.** Australia was plagued during June-August by an off-again, on-again strike of oil refineries which crippled fuel supplies and disrupted industry and transportation. The strike, by metal tradesmen responsible for maintenance and other work at the refineries, was over demands by workers for a 35-hour workweek and a weekly pay increase of $A26 ($31.95). The strike was temporarily ended June 26, when strikers agreed to defer for nine months their workweek demand. However, the workers' insistence on the wage demands resulted in a quick resumption of the strike. Most of the strikers agreed July 17 to end the strike, but July 19 the workers rejected an interim pay award of $A3.60 and $A4.80 weekly pay increases granted by the Federal Arbitration Court in Sydney. The workers immediately walked off their jobs again in the states of Victoria, New South Wales, Queensland and South Australia. The workers Aug. 3 accepted the recommendation of the Australian Council of Trade Unions (ACTU) to end the strike and accepted an offer from the arbitration court to reconsider their wage claims if they returned to work. The workers Aug. 28 accepted a wage and benefits offer from the oil companies which provided for an immediate $A7 increase in pay with another $A4 in June 1973. The unions agreed to postpone negotiation of their workweek claim for another nine months.

[4] **Closer New Zealand defense link agreed.** The formation of a joint Australian-New Zealand Consultative Committee on Defense Cooperation, to develop closer defense links between the two nations, was announced July 27 by Defense Minister David Fairbairn and New Zealand Defense Minister Allan McCready. The committee would be headed by the permanent heads of each Defense Department and their service chiefs of staff. The permanent heads of the respective Foreign Affairs Departments would participate in issues involving basic strategy and policy.

[5] **Independence moves for Papua-New Guinea.** Minister for External Territories Peacock and Michael Somare, chief minister of Papua and New Guinea, Aug. 8 issued a joint communique announcing agreement on the transfer of constitutional powers over wages and industrial relations, migration and land policies from Australia to the Papua and New Guinea government. The agreement was conditional on the approval of the National Assembly. (The Papua-New Guinea House of Assembly Sept. 20 approved a timetable for implementation of the agreement.) During talks between the two ministers July 27-Aug. 8, agreement was also reached on creation of defense and police ministerial posts in the Papua and New Guinea government. Somare would act as spokesman in those areas until the posts were set up. Peacock also agreed to seek an amendment to the Papua and New Guinea Act to give Somare authority to enlarge the territory's ministry. In later developments in the territory: the Administrator's Executive Council of Papua and New Guinea Aug. 31 approved in principle authorization for foreign countries to establish consulates in the territory as a prelude to the region's independence; a decision to establish a national airline in Papua and New Guinea, to be controlled eventually by the territory's government, was announced Sept. 5.

[6] **1973 deficit budget presented.** Treasurer Billy M. Snedden Aug. 15 presented to Parliament a deficit budget for fiscal 1973 designed to stimulate the nation's flagging economy. Total government expenditures were estimated at $A10.078 billion, resulting in a budget deficit of $A630 million. The budget reduced personal income tax rates by an average 10% and raised the minimum taxable income from $A417 to $A1,041. It also increased old age pensions to $A20 a week for single persons and $A34.50 for couples. The qualifying test for old age pensions, known as the means test, would be abolished within three years. Defense expenditures were increased by $A106 million to $A1.32 billion. The budget also provided for $A220 million in economic aid to developing

nations, with $A145 million earmarked for Papua and New Guinea. Nearly $A14 million was allotted for defense aid to certain Southeast Asian nations. Other budget measures included small estate and gift duty concessions and increases in shipping fees and air navigation charges at airports.

[7] Norfolk Island demands self-rule. Hundreds of the more than 1,000 residents of Australian-administered Norfolk Island, according to a report Sept. 14, demanded self-government in the wake of a proposal by Canberra to abolish the island's tax-exempt status and establish an animal quarantine station there. The residents had reportedly petitioned Queen Elizabeth II of Great Britain the previous week, condemning Australian rule and maintaining that their land was a separate territory under the British crown—assigned to Australian jurisdiction in 1955 more for protection than administration.

[8] Clunies-Ross yields Cocos Islands rule. John Clunies-Ross Sept. 15 relinquished his family's authority over the Cocos Islands—which had been permanently granted to the family by Queen Victoria in the nineteenth century—to the Australian government. Clunies-Ross announced he had dropped an earlier demand for more home rule—a demand he had made to counter the government's hints that it would curb his power on the islands. The home-rule demand had won unexpected support from a number of press members, who wrote glowing accounts of Clunies-Ross's paternalistic rule of the islands. Clunies-Ross provided the islands' Malay natives, employed by his huge coconut plantation, with free housing, free medical care and retirement pensions, as well as with stable prices.

[9] Foreign takeovers bill approved. Following Senate approval Oct. 31, the government Nov. 9 enacted an interim foreign takeovers bill empowering the responsible minister to prohibit implementation of a foreign takeover proposal that he deemed contrary to the national interest. The legislation also authorized the minister to limit the beneficial interests a particular foreign interest or associated interests could have in a company. The breach of an order prohibiting a foreign takeover would carry a fine of $A50,000 or six months in jail. The bill also set a fine of $A200 a day for anyone holding a greater interest in an Australian company than permitted by the government. The bill would be replaced before 1974 by other legislation establishing an independent authority to investigate and report on takeover proposals.

[10] Labor party wins elections. The Australian Labor party returned to power in parliamentary elections held Dec. 2, ousting the Liberal-Country party coalition that had ruled since 1949. The results represented a stunning victory for Labor leader Gough Whitlam, who formally took over as prime minister Dec. 5 after McMahon resigned the post. The voting results indicated a 3%-4% nationwide swing to Labor. Labor won 50% of the national vote for 62 seats in the House of Representatives (an increase of three seats); the Liberal-Country parties won 41.3% of the vote for 50 seats (a loss of 26); the Democratic Labor party won 5.1%; and the Australia party won 2.3% (see [12]). Most news reports attributed Labor's victory to a general desire for change after 23 years of the Liberal-Country coalition.

[11] _Whitlam outlines plans._ Following the Dec. 5 installation of Whitlam as prime minister and Lance Barnard as deputy prime minister, and the temporary assumption by the two of responsibility for all other ministerial offices pending final election results (see [12]), Whitlam outlined some of the policies his administration would pursue. Whitlam immediately announced an end to the military draft and the start of talks on establishing diplomatic relations with the People's Republic of China. (Diplomatic relations were established Dec. 22.) He also announced the release from jail of all draft offenders and abandonment of pending prosecutions of offenders. He said his administration would not raise the issue of U.S. military installations in Australia, a favorite target of Australia's leftists and nationalists. He backed self-government for Papua and New Guinea by December 1973 and said he expected complete independence of the territory within two years. Announcing a change in Australia's recent votes in the United Nations, Whitlam said his government would oppose independence for Rhodesia before it instituted majority rule. (Whitlam Dec. 14 announced a ban on the export of wheat to Rhodesia.) He also called for sanctions against South Africa and Portugal and said he would review foreign policy to develop "more constructive, flexible and progressive approaches" for Australia. In later actions, Whitlam Dec. 7 abolished the federal government's nominations for British knighthoods and other royal honors and made the following announcements: that equal pay for women (unconditionally approved Dec. 15 by the Federal Arbitration Commission, an independent body that determined the nation's basic wage rates) would be enforced; that the government was canceling the Australian passport of Vice Marshal Harold Hawkins, a long-time resident of Rhodesia and a Rhodesian diplomat; that the New South Wales state government was being asked to close a Rhodesian information center in Sydney; and that the government was restoring the Australian passport of Wilfred Burchett, an expatriate left-wing journalist living abroad.

[12] *Cabinet sworn in.* Final election results, announced Dec. 17, gave Labor 67 seats in the House of Representatives, the Liberals 38 seats and the Country party 20 seats. Following the announcement of the results, a new 27-member Cabinet was sworn in Dec. 19. The departments of interior, environment, aborigines and the arts, education and science, trade and industry, and national development and social sciences were abolished; and 16 new departments were created. The new Cabinet: prime minister and foreign—Whitlam; deputy prime minister and defense—Barnard; overseas trade—James F. Cairns; social security—William G. Hayden; treasurer—Frank Crean; attorney general, customs and excise—Lionel K. Murphy; special minister of state—Donald R. Willesee; media—Douglas McClelland; northern development—Rex Patterson; repatriation and assistant defense—Reginald Bishop; property and services—Frederick M. Daly; labor—Clyde R. Cameron; urban and regional development—Thomas Uren; transport, civil aviation—Charles K. Jones; education—Kim E. Beazley; tourism and recreation—Francis E. Stewart; works—James L. Cavanagh; primary industry—Kenneth S. Wriedt; aboriginal affairs—Gordan M. Bryant; minerals and energy—Reginald F. X. Connor; immigration—Albert J. Grassby; housing—Leslie R. Johnson; Capital Territory and Northern Territory—Keppel E. Enderby; postmaster general—Lionel F. Bowen; health—Douglas N. Everingham; environment—Moss H. Cass; science, external territories—William L. Morrison.

See also ATOMIC ENERGY [6, 13]; AVIATION; CONSERVATION; HEALTH; HIJACKING [15]; INDOCHINA WAR [38]; INTERNATIONAL MONETARY DEVELOPMENTS [8]; MINES; PAKISTAN [7]; SINO-U.S. RELATIONS [8]; SPACE [23]; TERRITORIAL WATERS

AUSTRIA—Nazi trials. In the first trial in Austria for crimes committed in Auschwitz, the World War II Nazi extermination camp for Jews, a Vienna court March 10 acquitted two admitted officers in the Nazi SS (Elite Guard) of murder and other criminal charges for designing and constructing the gas chambers in the Polish camp. The jury unanimously acquitted Walter Dejaco and a former aide, Fritz Karl Ertl, of directly aiding and abetting the murders. It ruled, by a 5-3 vote, that Ertl, but not Dejaco, had "remote responsibility" for the deaths but not enough to justify a conviction because he was acting under the "duress of orders." The two defendants had contended that they were acting under military orders and were unaware of the purpose of the ovens. The state prosecutor announced that he would ask for a retrial on the basis of newly revealed charges that Dejaco had helped select prisoners to be gassed.

In other trials of former Nazis for World War II crimes: Franz Novak, a former SS captain who had been Adolph Eichmann's chief transport official, was sentenced by a Viennese court April 13 to seven years imprisonment for organizing the transport of Jews to Auschwitz; a Vienna court May 4 acquitted Johann Gogel, a former SS officer, of charges that he murdered and tortured prisoners at Mauthausen, a Nazi concentration camp in Austria; the trial of Ernst Lerch and Helmut Pohl, both charged in connection with their alleged roles in the selection and murder of an estimated two million Eastern European Jews in 1942, was suspended indefinitely in Klagenfurt May 17 because the prosecution was unable to produce key witnesses from outside Austria; Otto Graf and Franz Wunsch, both former SS officers, June 27 were acquitted by a Vienna court of charges that they murdered and tortured Jewish prisoners in Auschwitz.

Czech ties curbed. A border incident May 2 resulted in the announcement May 9 by Foreign Minister Rudolph Kirchschlaeger that Austria would "limit its relations with Czechoslovakia to the absolute minimum necessary" pending resolution of the incident. According to Czech officials, Jaromir Masarik, a Czech emigre residing in South Africa, had gone to the Czech border to talk with his mother and had stepped into Czech territory. When border guards demanded his papers, he reportedly ran back into Austria and was shot and dragged into Czech territory. Czechoslovakia said May 10 that Masarik had been shot on Czech territory and had dragged a frontier guard into Austrian territory. Masarik reportedly was then "overpowered" and pulled back into Czechoslovakia. The Austrian government protested the incident and demanded Masarik's return, but the Czech government refused on the grounds that Masarik was still a Czech citizen and had left the country illegally in 1969 with false documents.

Protest over Slovene language rights. Some 15,000 persons demonstrated in southern Carinthia province Oct. 15 to protest a government decision approved in July to provide dual-language road signs for the Slovene minority in accord with the 1955 quadripartite treaty granting Austria independence. The demonstration followed several nights of rampaging and property destruction and about two weeks in which the signs had been ripped down nightly.

See also DRUG USE & ADDICTION [18]; EUROPEAN ECONOMIC COMMUNITY [8]; INTERNATIONAL MONETARY DEVELOPMENTS [2, 9]; OLYMPICS [2]; SOVIET-U.S. RELATIONS [2]

AUTOMOBILES—Air bag delay granted. The Department of Transportation (DOT) Feb. 24 published new regulations granting auto manufacturers a two-year delay in mandatory installation in all cars of automatically inflatable air bags—a passive restraint system designed to cushion passengers during head-on crashes of up to 60 m.p.h. impact. The regulations were published after the U.S. Court of Appeals in Washington dismissed a suit brought by consumer activist Ralph Nader to enforce DOT's original 1974 deadline. (After the industry claimed it could not meet the 1974 deadline, DOT in September 1971 granted a delay until the 1976 model year, provided that 1974 and 1975 model cars would be equipped with systems preventing start-ups until front-seat passengers fastened their seat belts.) General Motors Corp. (GM) Feb. 25 and Ford Motor Co. March 9 announced plans for large-scale testing of the air bag system under normal driving conditions, but said that the tests could not be made early enough to enable a decision on mass production by July, when tooling orders would have to be made in order to meet the 1976 model year deadline. (A federal court of appeals in Cincinnati ruled Dec. 5 that the government must further postpone the deadline.

GM, Ford sued on fleet prices. GM and Ford were indicted by a federal grand jury in Detroit May 1 on charges of violating the Sherman Antitrust Act by conspiring to keep prices of fleet cars at an artificially inflated level. The indictment charged that the companies—supported by the National Automobile Dealers Association and Peterson, Howell & Heather, Inc. (the nation's largest auto leasing company) as co-conspirators—conspired during 1969 and 1970 through public statements and talks to third parties in the industry to end the practice of discount pricing on fleet cars. The Chrysler Corp. had originated the practice of discount pricing on fleet cars in 1962 and had only partially curtailed it when GM and Ford moved out of the discount market. (Chrysler was currently being sued by retail dealers contending that the two-price system itself violated antitrust laws.) The indictment against GM and Ford carried criminal penalties of up to $50,000 for each of two counts for each company. A conviction would open the companies to customer damage suits.

Hawaii limits autos. Hawaii Gov. John A. Burns (D) May 25 signed a bill setting up a Transportation Control Commission that would make annual recommendations to the legislature on the maximum number of automobiles and other transportation vehicles to be permitted on each island. No other state currently had such a law on its books.

Federal insurance plan shelved. The Senate voted 49-46 Aug. 8 to send a no-fault auto insurance bill back to the Judiciary Committee for further study, effectively shelving the proposal for the 1972 session of Congress. (The Judiciary Committee had approved the bill May 24 by a vote of 15-4.) The bill, sponsored by Sens. Philip A. Hart (D, Mich.) and Warren G. Magnuson (D, Wash.), was opposed by the Nixon Administration, the American Trial Lawyers Association and by many insurance companies. It would have established minimum standards for the enactment by state legislatures of no-fault auto insurance plans. If the states failed to adopt laws measuring up to the federal guidelines, the federal standards would take effect automatically. The bill would have provided minimum payments of $25,000 in medical expenses, $25,000 in rehabilitation costs and $75,000 in economic loss. Lawsuits for recovery of tangible damages would be permitted when costs exceeded the minimum federal standards. General damage payments for "pain and suffering" would be prohibited except in specific cases of severe disfigurement, loss of body function or prolonged disability. In the case of death, the victim's family might sue for tangible loss. The Nixon Administration had favored voluntary state action on no-fault auto insurance. However, only four states (Massachusetts, Florida, Connecticut and New Jersey) had passed no-fault plans and none would have met the federal guidelines. No-fault plans had been rejected in Maryland, Colorado, Virginia and New York. Illinois's plan was ruled unconstitutional March 24.

Safety test cover-up charged. Ralph Nader's Center for Auto Study Aug. 22 charged that the National Highway Traffic Safety Administration (NHTSA) had suppressed test results of crash helmets in which only eight of 75 types complied with minimum safety standards. The center said that an estimated 3,000 motorcyclists would die in accidents during 1972. According to the center, 44 states and the District of Columbia required that crash helmets be worn by cyclists.

GM to offer Wankel. GM announced Aug. 28 that it would offer the rotary-powered Wankel engine as optional equipment in its Chevrolet Vega model in "about two years." GM expected approximately 20,000 rotary engines would be produced by 1974. The engine (named after its inventor, Feliz Wankel), a radical departure from the conventional piston/cylinder machine, was lighter and quieter than ordinary engines, used fewer moving parts and was smoother running than present engines. It was powered by triangular rotors revolving in an elliptical chamber. Its size (⅓ smaller than ordinary types) would permit easy installation of bulky pollution control devices required in cars by federal law. GM was reportedly paying $50 million over five years for production rights to the Wankel. (Curtiss-Wright Corp. of New Jersey held North American rights to the engine.) GM had been experimenting on the Wankel for 2½ years. Ford and Chrysler were also working on the engine, but were not expected to produce rotary-powered cars until after the GM cars were introduced.

See also CONSUMER AFFAIRS [5, 16]; ECONOMY [4]; LABOR; POLLUTION [2, 4-8]

AUTO RACING—Indy 500. Mark Donahue steered his Penske McLaren Offenhauser racer through the pack and into the lead just 13 laps from the finish on his way to winning the Indianapolis 500 May 27 at the Motor Speedway in Indianapolis. He collected $218,768 in prize money. Donahue covered the 200-lap run in 3 hours, 3 minutes, 31.55 seconds for an average speed of 163.465 m.p.h. That eclipsed the old mark of 157.73 set by Al Unser in 1971. (In qualifying runs, Bobby Unser set a spectacular qualifying record May 14, covering the required 10 miles at an average speed of 195.94 m.p.h. The old mark of 178.69 was set in 1971 by Peter Revson.) Jerry Grant finished 47.1 seconds behind Donahue, but was dropped to 12th place May 28 when a post race contest confirmed an illegal refueling. Second prize money went to Al Unser.

AVALANCHES—*See* FLOODS

AVIATION—Concorde purchases. The state-owned British Overseas Airways Corp. (BOAC) announced May 25 that it would buy five Concorde supersonic jet aircraft for an estimated $299 million—nearly twice the price estimated for such a purchase in December 1971. (BOAC signed a contract for the jets July 28, at the same time that Air France signed a contract for four of the jets.) The British order was the first firm sale for the controversial Anglo-French plane. BOAC planned to put the jets into service in 1975 and to charge fares "a notch or two" above present first-class rates in subsonic planes. The initial guaranteed payload for New York-London flights would be 20,000 pounds, a lower figure than previously estimated. The planes would be fitted to carry 100-104 passengers. BOAC planned to operate two daily round-trip flights from London to New York, three weekly round-trip flights from London to South Africa and Australia and two weekly flights to Tokyo. The announcement of the BOAC order came as Britain planned to send its 002 prototype on a 10-nation sales tour to Greece, the Middle East and the Far East. The tour, which lasted from June 2 to July 1, resulted in a firm order for three planes for Air Iran. In other purchase developments: Canada, one of the 16 nations which had originally taken options to buy the Concorde, July 5 formally renounced its options on four of the jets; Communist China July 24 signed a preliminary agreement to buy two Concordes and Aug. 28 signed a preliminary agreement for a third; the West German airline Lufthansa Aug. 8 decided not to exercise its options to buy three Concordes; United Airlines Oct. 26 cancelled its options to buy six of the jets. (The development cost of the Concorde, according to a report May 4, had risen $221 million to $2.5 billion.)

Extortion actions. An anonymous phone call March 7 led officials of Trans World Airlines (TWA) to a locker in the TWA terminal at New York's Kennedy airport, where the officials found a note warning that four TWA planes would be blown up at six-hour intervals if the airline did not pay a $2 million ransom. The note prompted TWA to recall to Kennedy a jetliner that had just taken off. After clearing the plane, police, using specially trained dogs, found six pounds of plastic explosive in a case by the plane's cockpit. The bomb was defused by police. The following morning, a TWA jetliner parked on an apron at the Las Vegas, Nev. airport was severely damaged by a bomb that exploded in the cockpit area. The bombing was believed to be part of the extortion plot, but TWA refused to pay the ransom on the advice of federal officials, who believed that to do so would only encourage more blackmail. Later March 8, a caller warned United Air Lines of a bomb in a plane that had arrived in Seattle from San Francisco. A search led to the discovery of several sticks of dynamite in two aerosol cans in a piece of unclaimed luggage. The device was described as inoperable as constructed. An attempt was made by United to pay the extortionists March 10, but the contact was broken off and no money was paid.

In response to the extortion threats, President Nixon March 9 ordered the nation's airlines to immediately adopt tighter air and ground security measures. The new regulations were published in the Federal Register March 7. Under normal circumstances, they would not have been implemented for 90 days; but Nixon used his executive authority to put them into effect at once. Among the tighter security measures were more electronic surveillance, tighter checks of baggage and closer inspection of boarding passengers to deter "carriage of weapons or explosives" aboard the aircraft. The new regulations would cover all U.S.-flag aircraft, including those that fly domestic routes.

CAB bars discount fares. The Civil Aeronautics Board (CAB) Dec. 9 announced that it would eliminate discounted youth fares, family fares and Discover America fares on domestic airline tickets because the promotional fares were discriminatory and were expensive operations which had not significantly increased passenger travel. The discount rates, which the CAB estimated had lowered total airline revenue per passenger mile by 7.8% in 1971, would not be canceled until after hearings could be held to consider a simultaneous reduction in regular fares. (In a compromise action, the CAB voted Dec. 14 to retain the international youth fare, but to increase rates by 21%.)

Air travel impasse. Negotiations by the International Air Transport Association (IATA) to settle North Atlantic air fares collapsed Dec. 13 in Geneva; and industry officials, representing 40 airlines, declared that scheduled carriers were free to set their own price levels on all routes, beginning Feb. 1, 1973. According to a report Dec. 13, European and American disagreement was evident in two areas: a U.S. proposal for higher fares was opposed by European airlines, which sought lower rates to meet competition from chartered flights; and a European proposal, which would have cut fares for Europeans visiting the U.S. but increased fares for Americans flying to Europe on American carriers, was rejected by the U.S.

Air disasters. The National Transportation Safety Board, according to a report Jan. 2, disclosed that deaths involving regularly scheduled U.S. airlines jumped sharply in 1971 to 203 recorded over 6.5 million flying hours. In 1970, when the carriers had their best safety record in history, the total was 146 recorded over 6% more flying hours.

In major 1972 crashes: An Iberia Airlines Caravelle jet on a scheduled flight from Valencia, Spain to the Mediterranean island of Iviza, 90 miles southeast, crashed into a mountainside Jan. 7 as it was approaching the Iviza airport. All 104 persons aboard were killed. Fifty-five persons died Jan. 21 in two separate incidents involving Colombian airlines planes. A Satena Airlines DC-3 with 35 people aboard including the Roman Catholic bishop of Buenaventura, the Rev. Gerardo Valencia Cano, crashed and burned in the Andes Mountains in Northern Colombia. Shortly afterwards a Uraca Airlines turboprop crashed on takeoff in Bogota during a rainstorm. A Danish Sterling Airways charter plane carrying 112 persons from a holiday in Ceylon "smashed to pieces" March 14 near Kalba, 60 miles east of Dubai in the Union of Arab Emirates. The manager of the airline said there was no hope of survivors. Overshooting a runway, an East Africa Airways VC-10 with 107 people aboard struck a farmhouse April 18 in Addis Ababa, Ethiopia. The death toll reached 41 April 20, including many British schoolchildren returning from a vacation. Trevor Hill, director of operations of the airline, said April 21 that the accident "had nothing to do with the plane or the pilot," and that the cause was a mystery. An Alitalia DC-8 jetliner with 115 aboard struck a mountainside near the Palermo Airport in bad weather May 6 and burst into flames. There were no survivors. An airline spokesman said the disaster was the worst in Alitalia history. A Soviet plane crashed near the Ukrainian city of Kharkov May 18, killing 158 persons. A Japan Air Lines DC-8 caught fire in midair and crashed in flames as it attempted a landing June 14 in New Delhi, India. At least two persons on the ground and all but six of the 89 people on board were killed. All 81 persons aboard a Cathay Pacific jetliner were killed June 15 in a crash over the Central Highlands in South Vietnam. A British European Airways Trident Airliner crashed minutes after takeoff from London's Heathrow Airport June 18, killing all 118 aboard. It was Britain's worst air disaster.

An Ilyushin-62 chartered by Interflug, the East German state airline, crashed after takeoff Aug. 14 from East Berlin's Schonefeld Airport. All 156 aboard were killed. A Korean War-vintage F-86 Supersabre jet skidded on takeoff from the Executive Airport in Sacramento, Calif. Sept. 24 and plowed into an ice cream parlor filled with some 100 birthday party celebrants, killing 22. A Canadian government official said Oct. 14 that the jet had been stripped down and sold to a Canadian firm to be used as a monument. In accordance with government regulations, the vital center section supporting the wings had been removed and the plane was unflyable. A Soviet Ilyushin-18 passenger plane crashed Oct. 4 near the Black Sea resort of Sochi, killing all 100 persons aboard. A Soviet Ilyushin-62 airliner, attempting to land in a heavy rain, reportedly crashed Oct. 14 three miles from the Sheremetevo Airport in Moscow. All 176 persons aboard (including 55 foreign tourists) perished. According to the reports, the airport's instrument landing system was inoperative and the plane made three passes before crashing on the fourth attempt. The crash was the worst air disaster in history.

A Uruguayan air force plane with 47 persons aboard disappeared Oct. 13 on a flight over the Andes Mountains to Chile from Argentina. All aboard were assumed dead, but 16 of the passengers were rescued Dec. 22-23 after having survived for 69 days in sub-freezing weather. The survivors subsisted on melted snow, food from the plane and the remains of their dead companions. A twin-engine aircraft carrying House Democratic Leader Hale Boggs (La.) and Representative-at-Large Nich Begich (D, Alaska) apparently crashed Oct. 16 on a flight between Anchorage and Juneau, Alaska. Also aboard were Begich's aide, Russell Brown, and the pilot, Don E. Jonz. The biggest air search in Alaskan history was carried out Oct. 16-Nov. 24 for the missing plane. Judge Dorothy Tyner Dec. 29 in Juneau signed jury findings of presumptive death for Begich, Brown and Jonz. (A petition for presumptive death hearings for Boggs was not filed at the request of Boggs's family.) A French domestic airliner with 68 persons aboard slammed into a hill 38 miles from Clermont-Ferrand Oct. 28 after a flight from Lyons. Rescue workers said there were about 20 survivors. A Japan Air Lines DC-8, en route to Tokyo from Copenhagen via Siberia, crashed minutes after takeoff from a Moscow airport Nov. 28. At least 42 of the 76 passengers and crew members were killed. A chartered Spanish airliner carrying 155 people exploded and burst into flames shortly after takeoff Dec. 3 from an airport in the Canary Islands. All aboard were killed. A United Air Lines Boeing 737 jet carrying 61 persons from Washington, D.C. to Omaha, Neb. with a stopover in Chicago, Dec. 8 crashed into a row of houses on Chicago's residential southwest side prior to a scheduled landing at Midway Airport. Forty-five persons were killed. At least 98 of 177 persons aboard an Eastern Airliners L-1011 Tristar jetliner were killed Dec. 29 when the plane crashed into the Florida Everglades 17 miles west of Miami International Airport, where it was making an approach for landing. It was the first fatal accident involving a jumbo jet.

See also BUSINESS; CANADA [8]; CHILE [21]; DEFENSE; HIJACKING; MIDDLE EAST [1, 22-24]; SWITZERLAND

AWARDS—*See* MOTION PICTURES; NOBEL PRIZES; PULITZER PRIZES; RECORD INDUSTRY; TELEVISION & RADIO [8]; THEATER

BACON, LESLIE—*See* CIVIL DISORDERS

BAHAMAS—Elections. Prime Minister Lynden O. Pindling led his Progressive Liberal party (PLP) to an overwhelming victory in general elections Sept. 19. The PLP, in power since 1967, won 30 of the 38 seats in the islands' House of Assembly, an increase of eight seats. The opposition Free National Movement (FNM), which had held 15 seats, won only eight. (The race for one seat had ended in a tie. A runoff election Oct. 6 resulted in another victory for the PLP.) The month-long campaign had centered around the issue of independence from Great Britain, which controlled the islands' foreign affairs and defense. Pindling had promised independence in less than a year. The FNM had charged that independence would lead to poverty and hunger and would leave the islands vulnerable to attacks from Cuba or the Soviet Union. Pindling had countered with pledges to remain in the British Commonwealth, seek membership in the Organization of American States and maintain conditions favorable to foreign investment in the islands. Pindling announced his new Cabinet Oct. 5.

Independence approved. Great Britain agreed Dec. 20 to end nearly 200 years of rule in the Bahamas and to grant the islands independence July 10, 1973. Britain rejected all objections to granting independence, basing its rejection on the ground that the PLP election victory demanded it. A joint communique issued by British officials and representatives of Bahamian political parties said agreement had been reached on "the substance of the provisions" of a new Bahamian constitution.

BAHRAIN—U.S. sets up base. The U.S. State Department Jan. 5 disclosed that an agreement to establish an American naval base at Bahrain had been signed Dec. 23, 1971. The leasing of the former British naval facilities in the Persian Gulf state was arranged in the form of a Presidential executive agreement that did not have to be submitted to the U.S. Senate for ratification. A State Department official said that the U.S. needed the base to continue the Middle East naval force as a "flag-showing operation to manifest the United States interest in the area" following the 1971 end of Britain's protectorate role in Bahrain. State Department officials said that the agreement was not announced at the time of its signing at the request of the Bahrain government.

See also EUROPEAN ECONOMIC COMMUNITY [7]; HEALTH; INTERNATIONAL MONETARY DEVELOPMENTS [10]

BALANCE OF PAYMENTS—See ECONOMY [2]

BANGLA DESH—The new country of Bangla Desh celebrated its first year of existence in 1972, as the government tried to heal the war scars left from the December 1971 civil war in which the former East Pakistan broke away from West Pakistan with the help of India *(see also* PAKISTAN). Sheik Mujibur Rahman, the Bangla Desh leader who had been imprisoned in Pakistan during the war, was released in January and returned to Bangla Desh to set up a new government *(see* [3-5]). The nearly 10 million refugees who had fled to India during the December fighting also returned to their country during the early part of the year *(see* [2]). The Indian troops who had aided Bangla Desh during its struggle against Pakistan withdrew from Bangla Desh during March, but returned the same month to assist Bangla Desh in fighting rebel tribesmen *(see* [9]). The new country strengthened its ties with the Soviet Union and India *(see* [10-11]) and was formally recognized by the United States *(see* [13]). Internally, the government began a sweeping program of nationalization *(see* [12]). Although Mujibur issued an order calling for Bangla Desh guerrillas to surrender their arms *(see* [6]), there were still heavy clashes during the early part of the year between guerrillas and Pakistan-sympathizers *(see* [7-8]).

[2] **Refugees return.** The mass return of refugees from India to Bangla Desh formally began Jan. 1, although figures released by Indian officials revealed that more than one million refugees had unofficially returned since the end of the Indian-Pakistani war Dec. 16, 1971. The last refugee camp in India for Bangla Desh refugees closed March 25, after the repatriation of virtually all the 10 million Bengalis who had fled to India during the 1971 fighting. (About 600,000 remained in India with friends and relatives.)

[3] **Mujibur freed.** Sheik Mujibur was freed from detention in West Pakistan Jan. 8 and returned to Dacca Jan. 10, via London and New Delhi, to take over leadership of the government. Pakistan President Zulfikar Ali Bhutto saw off Mujibur and Kamal Hossain (Mujibur's Bengali advisor, who also had been imprisoned) at the Rawalpindi airport. Pakistani officials indicated that Mujibur wished to go to London before flying to Dacca, but Mujibur said Jan. 8 in London that the decision had been a Pakistani one. Mujibur said he had been condemned in "a mock trial" for treason by the regime of former Pakistan President Agha Mohammad Yahya Khan and placed in solitary confinement prior to his planned execution by hanging. The sheik said that Bhutto called off the execution after his assumption to office and released Mujibur from prison (placing him under house detention) Dec. 22, 1971. Bhutto reportedly suggested that both men negotiate new ties between the east and west wings of Pakistan, but Mujibur refused to make any commitments.

[4] Mujibur left London Jan. 9 and arrived the following morning in New Delhi, where he was welcomed by Indian Prime Minister Indira Gandhi, President V.V. Giri and representatives and ambassadors of 20 countries. (U.S. Ambassador Kenneth B. Keating was absent.) Mujibur said he had made the flight to New Delhi "to pay special tribute to the best friend of my people, to the people of India and its government under the leadership of your magnificent prime minister, Mrs. Indira Gandhi." Mujibur flew on to Dacca later Jan. 10 and received a tumultuous welcome. A crowd of 10,000 lined the mile-and-a-half route from the airport to the center of the city. Another 500,000 turned out to hear him address a mass rally at the Dacca Race Course. He appealed to the rally audience not to seek revenge for the three million Bengalis he claimed had been slain by the Pakistani army during the nine-month drive to suppress the Bengali secession movement. "Forgive them," he said. "There should not be any more killings."

[5] In his first official act, Mujibur expanded his powers Jan. 12 by declaring a temporary constitution in effect and appointing Sabusadat Sayem as new chief justice of the High Court. (The Bangla Desh National Assembly Nov. 4 approved a permanent constitution. The charter was signed by the Constituent Assembly Dec. 14 and became effective Dec. 16.) Mujibur then resigned as

president and Sayem swore in Abu Sayeed Choudhury as the new president. Choudhury in turn swore in Mujibur as prime minister. Mujibur immediately appointed a new Cabinet, that included only one member—Hossain—not previously associated with the provisional government. Hossain was assigned to head the Ministry of Law and Parliamentary Affairs. Mujibur Jan. 13 assumed the additional posts of defense, home affairs, information and Cabinet affairs. Abdus Samad Azad continued as foreign minister. Former Prime Minister Tajuddin Ahmed was appointed finance and planning minister. Syed Nazrul Islam, who had served as acting president until Mujibur's return, was named minister of industry, trade and commerce. Former Home Affairs Minister A. H. M. Kamaruzzaman was appointed relief and rehabilitation minister. Yusuf Ali became educational and cultural affairs minister.

[6] Guerrilla arms surrender ordered. Mujibur Jan. 17 issued an order calling on an estimated 100,000 Bengali rebels to turn in their arms and ammunition within 10 days. (A similar order had been issued Dec. 27, 1971.) The prime minister warned that possession of weapons after the 10-day period "will be construed as unauthorized and illegal." The order was aimed at curbing the irregular armed bands of former guerrillas, who had fought the Pakistanis and who were now engaged in robbery and other acts of lawlessness. In some areas, particularly in districts north of Dacca, the former guerrilla groups had established de facto governing authority. Mujibur announced Jan. 24 that he had extended the deadline for turning over the arms to Jan. 31 because of a Moslem holiday.

[7] Bengali-Bihari clashes. Heavy casualties were reported Jan. 28-Feb. 4 in clashes between Bangla Desh soldiers and armed Bihari civilians in the Dacca suburbs of Mirpur and Mohammedpur. By Feb. 4, the death toll was reported at 350—about 250 civilians and 100 Bangla Desh security forces. Former Bengali guerrillas and civilian-garbed Pakistani soldiers reportedly also were involved in the fighting. (Some Pakistani soldiers were known to have gone into hiding among the Biharis, who had collaborated with the Pakistanis during the 1971 war, rather than surrender to Indian troops at the end of the war.) The clashes were said to have started after the Biharis accused Bengalis of looting. An army cordon was placed around two Bihari enclaves and a curfew was imposed to stop the violence. Bengali-Bihari clashes were also reported in Rangpur, 160 miles northwest of Dacca, the last week of January. It was said that at least 200 Biharis had been killed by former guerrillas in the area after Indian troops had withdrawn. Following the violence, Indian troops moved back into the town to protect the Biharis. Heavy casualties were reported in further clashes between Biharis and Bengalis in Khulna March 10-12. Indian troops on their way back to India were the first forces to enter the area and brought the situation under control. There were conflicting reports of how the violence erupted. One report said the Biharis were angered over the loss of their jobs to Bengalis in a Khulna jute mill. When the body of a Bengali was found in the Bihari section of the city, Bengalis poured into the area, attacking residents. Bangla Desh officials said no more than 60 persons were killed or wounded, but press sources said that between 300 and 1,000 persons had been killed and hundreds injured. The press sources said that most of the victims were Biharis.

[8] *Biharis removed from Mirpur.* Bangla Desh troops and police began Feb. 4 to shift Biharis from Mirpur to a camp 12 miles from Dacca. The removal was said to be only temporary, to permit security forces to search the Bihari sections in Mirpur for arms without resistance. By Feb. 7, about 4,000-5,000 Biharis had been removed from Mirpur to the camp. Bangla Desh authorities were also reported Feb. 7 to have arrested about 1,500 Biharis as suspected collaborators with Pakistan. The Biharis were jailed following the arms search in their enclave in Mirpur. A government spokesman said the Biharis would be brought to trial. Pakistan protested the encampment and the Bengali-Bihari clashes Feb. 5, appealing to the foreign ministers of 13 Western nations to prevent what it called "atrocities" against the Biharis. Students in Karachi, Pakistan Feb. 7 organized a general strike to protest the plight of the Biharis. The strike disrupted business life in the city and forced the closing of all schools and colleges. The demonstrations were climaxed by street rioting. Prime Minister Mujibur proposed Feb. 15 that the Biharis in Bangla Desh be exchanged for Bengalis living in Pakistan. He suggested that the United Nations administer the transfer.

[9] **Indian troop withdrawal.** India and Bangla Desh issued a joint communique Feb. 7 announcing that India had agreed to complete withdrawal of its troops from Bangla Desh by March 25. The last contingent of the Indian troops allegedly left Bangla Desh March 12, 13 days ahead of schedule. However, it was reported March 20 and confirmed by Indian sources in Dacca March 22 that Indian troops were assisting Bangla Desh forces in fighting Mizo tribal rebels in the southeastern section of the country. According to Western sources, the Indian troops had returned to Bangla Desh March 16; but other reports indicated that the small Indian support units involved in the Mizo fighting had never left Bangla Desh. (The Indians had been combatting the Mizos for six years in Assam State, which bordered on Bangla Desh and Burma. The Mizos had fled to Bangla Desh and joined the Pakistani army in its unsuccessful drive in 1971 against Bengali independence forces and Indian troops. Bangla Desh was said to have called on India to help it oust the Mizos.)

[10] **Moscow ties strengthened.** Bangla Desh and the Soviet Union signed two agreements strengthening economic ties March 2 during a March 1-5 visit to Moscow by Mujibur. Under one of the accords, Mujibur's government was to receive $45 million originally pledged to Pakistan for projects in its east wing, which was now Bangla Desh. The funds were to be used for construction of an electrical engineering plant, oil and gas exploration and the purchase of radio equipment. The other agreement provided for "immediate assistance in the reconstruction of vital branches" of Bangla Desh's war-torn economy. A joint declaration signed by Mujibur and Soviet Premier Aleksei N. Kosygin March 3 paved the way for regular political consultations between the two countries and set up a broad program of exchanges and contacts on all levels.

[11] **India ties strengthened.** Bangla Desh and India acted to strengthen their defense and economic ties in March and June, respectively. Mujibur and Indian Prime Minister Gandhi signed a 25-year mutual defense treaty March 19, pledging that, "in case either party is attacked or threatened with attack, the high contracting parties shall immediately enter into mutual consultations in order to take effective measures to eliminate the threat." The two leaders the same day also signed three other joint declarations. In the first agreement, India agreed to cooperate with Bangla Desh in trying persons responsible for the slaughter of thousands of Bengalis during the 1971 conflict. In the second declaration, the two leaders "took note of the forces threatening the security, stability and territorial integrity of countries of the region." The third agreement called for a renewal of trade between India and Bangla Desh and joint action on flood control and hydroelectric power. Indian and Bangla Desh officials met June 8-10 in New Delhi and agreed on a plan to integrate the economic development programs of both countries. The two nations were to cooperate within the context of India's five-year plan, while programs in Dacca were to be drawn up at a later date. The two countries agreed to hold periodic discussions on expanding bilateral trade. (The Dacca government had also announced the first week in June an agreement by which India would train and equip Bangla Desh's armed forces.)

[12] **Nationalization program.** The government March 26 announced a sweeping nationalization of the country's major industries. Under the program, the government would take control of all jute, textile and sugar mills, domestic banks, domestic insurance countries and a "major portion" of inland and coastal shipping. Foreign banks and insurance companies were not affected.

The majority of the domestic firms to be taken over had belonged to Pakistani businessmen, who were either in West Pakistan or in Indian prison camps.

[13] U.S. recognition. The U.S. April 4 formally extended diplomatic recognition to Bangla Desh. Asked by reporters why the U.S. had delayed recognition while 60 other nations already had established ties with Bangla Desh, State Department spokesman Robert J. McCloskey replied "we had other considerations." He explained that the U.S. was awaiting the withdrawal of Indian troops and was concerned about the "general stability" of the region. (In another action marking Bangla Desh's new participation in the community of nations, it joined the British-led Commonwealth of Nations April 18.)

[14] Mujibur scored at rallies. Prime Minister Mujibur came under severe public criticism for the first time at anti-government rallies in Dacca Sept. 3 and 17. In the first demonstration, 20,000 Bengali workers protesting against rising prices and government corruption demanded Mujibur's resignation and the establishment of a coalition government of all political parties. Charges that Mujibur was not coping with the problem of starvation were raised at the second protest meeting. (Several volunteer agencies had reported cases of starvation in the previous few months, but attributed them to failures in the distribution of food.) Addressing the rally of 50,000 persons, left-wing student leader Abdur Rab said that members of the Constituent Assembly were growing rich while Mujibur had reneged on his pledge that "no one would be allowed to die of starvation after independence."

See also EUROPEAN ECONOMIC COMMUNITY [7]; FOREIGN AID; HEALTH; INDIA [8]; PAKISTAN [1, 7-9, 16-17]; PULITZER PRIZES; TARIFFS & WORLD TRADE; UGANDA [1, 7, 9]; UNITED NATIONS

BANKRUPTCY—See RAILROADS

BANKS—FRB changes. The Federal Reserve Board (FRB) June 21 adopted two major changes in bank reserve requirements and check collection procedures, effective in fall, 1972. Under the reserve change, banks of the same size would have the same reserve requirements, no matter where they were located, and reserve requirements would be reduced, with the largest reductions going to the smallest banks. Under the check change, same-day payment would be required for all checks cleared through the FRB system, even if the checks were from non-FRB members. The check-collecting change was expected to eliminate the $2 billion "floating" of uncollected checks.

The changes were altered slightly from the form in which they were proposed March 27, in order to lessen transition difficulties in implementing the new rules. Penalties would be waived temporarily for banks showing reserve deficiencies resulting from the new requirements, and an additional reduction in reserve requirements would be provided for banks with deposits of $10 million to $100 million. The changes, aimed at an overall release of reserve funds, would make smaller FRB member banks more competitive within the system and would reduce the reserve "inequity" arising from bank classification by location rather than size.

Brazilian merger. It was reported March 13 that the Brazilian government had created the largest private bank in Latin America by approving the merger of the Banco Brasileiro de Descontos and the Uniao de Bancos Brasileiros. The new bank, to be known as the Uniao de Bancos Bradesco, would have resources of $1.6 billion, deposits of about $800 million and control of about one-fourth of Brazil's mutual funds.

See also ARGENTINA [9]; BRAZIL; CHURCHES; CIVIL DISORDERS; HIJACKING [2]; INTERNATIONAL BANK FOR RECONSTRUCTION & DEVELOPMENT; LATIN AMERICA; MINES; SOVIET-U.S. RELATIONS [12]

BARBADOS—See INTERNATIONAL MONETARY DEVELOPMENTS [8]

BASEBALL—A's win World Series. The Oakland Athletics, who originated in Philadelphia and were transplanted to the West Coast by way of Kansas City, won baseball's 69th World Series Oct. 22 as they beat the Cincinnati Reds in the seventh and deciding game. The A's went into the series as underdogs because two of their top players—slugger Reggie Jackson and relief pitcher Darrell Knowles—were out with injuries. The A's overcame the odds with timely, if erratic, hitting and solid relief pitching. The game-by-game scores were: Oct. 14 in Cincinnati—Oakland 3, Cincinnati 2; Oct. 15 in Cincinnati—Oakland 2, Cincinnati 1; Oct. 18 in Oakland—Cincinnati 1, Oakland 0; Oct. 19 in Oakland—Oakland 3, Cincinnati 2; Oct. 20 in Oakland—Cincinnati 5, Oakland 4; Oct. 21 in Cincinnati—Cincinnati 8, Oakland 1; and Oct. 22 in Cincinnati—Oakland 3, Cincinnati 2. Dick Williams managed the A's. Sparky Anderson managed the Reds. The series hero and outstanding player was A's catcher Gene Tenace, who tied a series mark by hitting four home runs.

The A's and the Reds captured their leagues' pennants by each winning the fifth and deciding game of the American League (AL) and National League (NL) playoffs. It was the first time since the leagues were divided in 1969 that the pennant winners were decided in the final game of the best-of-five playoffs. In the AL, Western winner Oakland beat the Eastern champions, the Detroit Tigers, 3-2, 5-0 in the first two games. Detroit rallied to win games three and four, 3-0, 4-3; but the A's won the deciding game Oct. 12, 2-1. Cincinnati, the NL's Western champion, twice overcame a deficit against the Pittsburgh Pirates to win the pennant Oct. 11, 4-3. The Reds dropped the opener, 5-1, won game two, 5-3, and lost game three, 3-2. Cincinnati won the fourth game, 7-1.

Nationals win All-Star game. Joe Morgan of the Cincinnati Reds singled home the winning run in the 10th inning July 25 in Atlanta to give the NL a 4-3 triumph over the AL in baseball's 43rd All-Star Game. A crowd of 53,107, the largest baseball crowd in Atlanta's history, attended as the NL increased its lead in All-Star competition to 24 wins against 18 defeats and a tie. They had won nine of the last 10 games and all seven extra-inning All-Star contests. Danny Murtaugh, the former manager of the world champion Pittsburgh Pirates, came out of retirement for a day to manage the NL. Earl Weaver of the Baltimore Orioles managed the AL.

Strike delays opener. A strike by the Major League Baseball Players Association forced the cancellation of the first 86 games of the season and postponed the opening of the season from April 5 to April 15. The players, through their representatives, had voted 47-0 March 31 to strike. The strike ended April 13. The original issue which led to the strike was the players' pension fund. The players' association wanted increased contributions by the owners for health care benefits and a 17% increase (from about $5 million to about $6.2 million) for the pension plan to "make up for the loss occurred due to cost-of-living increases since the last owner-player pension agreement. (The owners had offered an additional contribution of $400,000 to the plan's health care benefits.) Settlement of the pension dispute came when the owners agreed to add an additional $500,000 to the fund, but a new problem arose during negotiations to settle the pension dispute. While most of the AL club owners favored resuming the schedule without making up for lost time, most of the NL owners stood firm for a full 162-game season. Marvin Miller, executive director of the players' association, said the players would play a full season if they were paid the full worth of their contracts, but would not play a full season if their pay was reduced by the number of days missed due to the strike. After several days of discussions, the NL owners dropped their demand for a full schedule and an agreement was reached among the owners to have a shortened schedule. The settlement meant that the 600 major leaguers would lose nine days' pay.

Indians' sale approved. The AL owners March 22 unanimously approved the sale of the Cleveland Indian franchise to a group of businessmen headed by Nick Mileti, a sports magnate who also owned the Cleveland Cavaliers of the National Basketball Association. Mileti pledged to keep the team in Cleveland.

His group had purchased the Indians for a reported $9 million from Vernon Stouffer, a Cleveland restaurant and food products entrepreneur.

Yankees to stay in New York. The AL New York Yankees agreed to continue playing ball in New York City for 30 years after the city's Board of Estimate March 23 approved a plan to buy and renovate the club's home park, Yankee Stadium in the Bronx. Under the agreement, the city would buy the stadium from Rice University in Houston and the land on which it stands from the Knights of Columbus. Renovation would begin in 1974 and be completed in time for the 1976 baseball season. During the renovation, the Yankees would play home games in Shea Stadium, the home of the NL's New York Mets. The stadium and its renovation would cost an estimated $24 million.

Supreme Court upholds status. The Supreme Court, in a 5-3 ruling June 19, refused to lift the immunity from federal antitrust laws given to major league baseball by Congress in 1922 and subsequently upheld by the court in two prior rulings. At the same time, however, the court acknowledged that the status of baseball, which alone enjoyed immunity from federal antitrust laws, was an "aberration" and an "anomaly" and that Congress should settle the matter. The ruling came in the case of Curt Flood, a former star outfielder, who was traded to Philadelphia from St. Louis after the 1969 season. Flood sued baseball, challenging the sport's reserve clause, which bound a player to one team indefinitely and would not allow him to voluntarily change teams if he were dissatisfied with the team he played on. Flood had quit baseball to press his suit, which called for $3 million in damages. The court bypassed the merits of Flood's argument against the reserve clause and instead stressed its unwillingness to overturn two earlier rulings in 1922 and 1953 which upheld baseball's exempt status.

BASKETBALL—College. Kentucky State wins NAIA. Kentucky State showed itself to be the cream of the small-college crop March 18 as it rallied behind All-American Travis Grant to defeat Eau Claire State, 71-62, in Kansas City, Mo. in the final of the National Association of Intercollegiate Athletics (NAIA) tournament. Grant finished the game with 39 points to give him a tournament total of 213, one better than the old mark set in 1957.

[2] Maryland wins NIT. Maryland's tall front line was too big and strong for Niagara March 25 as the Terrapins overwhelmed the Eagles, 100-69, in the final of the National Invitation Tournament (NIT) in New York's Madison Square Garden. The NIT triumph gave Maryland a 27-5 mark, the best in the school's history. Maryland, coached by Lefty Driesell, was also the first team in the NIT's 35-year history to score 100 points in the final game of the tournament. Niagara, coached by Frank Layden, finished the season with a 21-9 record.

[3] UCLA wins NCAA. The University of California, Los Angeles (UCLA) March 25 defeated Florida State University (FSU), 81-76, in Los Angeles to win its sixth consecutive National Collegiate Athletic Association (NCAA) basketball championship. It was UCLA's and coach John Wooden's eighth NCAA title in nine years. The victory also gave the Bruins a 30-0 season and a 45-game winning streak. (FSU's presence evoked critical remarks from some coaches, who said the team did not belong in the finals after having been put on probation by the NCAA three years before for infractions of player recruiting regulations.)

[4] NCAA removes freshman ban. The NCAA, in a surprise move Jan. 8 at its convention in Hollywood, Fla., voted to give major colleges permission to let freshmen play varsity basketball, effective Aug. 1. The new freshman eligibility rule was permissive and not mandatory. It did not affect NCAA members with small-school status since they were already allowed to use freshmen in their basketball programs.

[5] NCAA files suits. The NCAA Feb. 23 filed a $216,663 suit against Howard Porter, a former Villanova All-American, and the American Basketball Association (ABA). The NCAA April 5 filed an almost identical suit for $285,763 against Jim McDaniels, the ABA, the Carolina Cougars and others. Both suits, the first ever to be inaugurated by the NCAA, were filed for alleged illegal action by the players for playing collegiate ball after they signed professional contracts. The suits sought to enjoin the ABA from concealing further signings of collegiate players with remaining eligibility. Porter had led Villanova to a second-place finish in the 1971 NCAA basketball championships. Villanova's runner-up position was forfeited, however, and its share of the tournament receipts was revoked when it was learned that Porter had signed a professional contract in 1970. McDaniels, another former All-American, had played in the 1971 NCAA championships with Western Kentucky after he had signed a professional contract in 1970 with the Cougars. (Western Kentucky March 6 forfeited its third-place finish in the NCAA championship and returned its share of tournament receipts.)

[6] *Foul shooting rule changed.* The National Basketball Committee of the United States and Canada March 28 adopted a proposal to change foul shooting rules for college and high school competition by dropping most one-shot fouls. Under the revised setup, teams would no longer take one foul shot after each of the first six common fouls charged to an opponent during a half. Instead, the team that was fouled would put the ball in play "from the point out of bounds nearest to the point of the foul" after the early fouls. The change would not affect the one-and-one situation, in which a team was given a bonus free throw—if the first was made—once their opponents fouled seven or more times in a half.

[7] **Professional.** *All-star games.* The Western Division all-stars of the National Basketball Association (NBA) rallied behind the fourth-quarter shooting of Jerry West Jan. 18 to nip the East all-stars, 112-110 in the NBA's 22nd all-star game in Inglewood, Calif. West scored the winning basket with 12 seconds remaining to give the Western Division its eighth all-star triumph. Tom Heinsohn of the Boston Celtics coached the East. Bill Sharman of the Los Angeles Lakers coached the West. McDaniels of the Cougars and Dan Issel of the Kentucky Colonels paced the ABA's East all-stars to a 142-115 pasting of the West all-stars in the ABA's fifth annual all-star game in Louisville Jan. 29. Utah's Ladell Anderson coached the West, and Kentucky's Joe Mullaney coached the East. Bob Lanier of the Detroit Pistons rallied his NBA teammates from a 19-point deficit to a 106-104 victory over a team of ABA all-stars May 25 in Uniondale, N.Y. Nine NBA players who participated in the game were fined $3,000 each June 16 for playing without the permission of their clubs. Those fined were Lanier, Wilt Chamberlain and Gail Goodrich of Los Angeles, Archie Clark of Baltimore, Oscar Robertson of Milwaukee, Bob Love of Chicago, John Havlicek of Boston, Nate Archibald of Kansas City-Omaha and Dave DeBusschere of New York. The ABA club owners had sanctioned their players' participation in the game.

[8] *NBA title.* The Los Angeles Lakers, coached by Sharman, turned key steals into fast break baskets May 7 to break open a close game and defeat the New York Knicks, 114-100, in Inglewood, and to give the Lakers their first NBA title since they moved to the coast from Minneapolis (where they had won five league crowns). The Lakers took the best-of-seven series 4 games to 1. The Lakers came into the finals as champions of the West by ousting the defending NBA champions, the Milwaukee Bucks, 4 games to 2. The Knicks, coached by Red Holzman, made it into the final round by defeating the Boston Celtics, 4 games to 1.

[9] *ABA title.* The Indiana Pacers regained the ABA crown they had given up in 1971 by trouncing the New York Nets, 108-105, in Uniondale, N.Y. May 20 to win the league championship 4 games to 2. Indiana, coached by Bob Leonard, had entered the final round as the Western Division champion by eliminating the Denver Rockets and the Utah Stars in a seven-game playoff series. The Nets came into the finals as the Eastern champions by beating the Colonels and the Virginia Squires. Lou Carnesecca coached New York.

[10] *NBA revises divisions.* The NBA's board of governors announced Feb. 15 that the Western Conference's Pacific and Midwest Divisions would be realigned for the 1972-73 season. Under the shift, the Phoenix Suns would move from the Midwest to the Pacific Division, joining Los Angeles, Seattle, Golden State and Portland. Completing the realignment, Houston would move from the Pacific to the Midwest Division, pairing the team with Chicago, Milwaukee and Detroit. The board also made a change in the league's playoff system. For 1973, the four division leaders would automatically qualify for the playoffs, but the other two playoff berths in each conference would go to the teams that had the best won-lost percentage in the conference. Under the former setup, the other playoff spots went to the division runners-up.

[11] *Royals moving.* The NBA Cincinnati Royals announced March 14 that they were shifting the franchise to Kansas City, Mo. at the end of the 1971-72 season. In Cincinnati, the Royals were beset with poor attendance, averaging about 3,500 fans a game in the 11,650-seat Cincinnati Gardens. The Royals' front office said the club hoped to play at least 21 games in Kansas City and approximately 10 each in Omaha, Neb. and St. Louis.

[12] *ABA files antitrust suit.* The ABA March 22 filed a $300 million antitrust suit against the NBA in the U.S. District Court in San Francisco, charging the older league with conspiring to "monopolize and eliminate competition" in professional basketball. In its suit, the ABA cited the recent number of defections of players who quit ABA clubs to sign with NBA teams. The suit asked the court to grant damages and to issue an injunction prohibiting NBA teams from contacting ABA players or in any way inducing them to jump leagues. (In a related development, the 4th U.S. Circuit Court of Appeals in Richmond, Va. ruled April 6 that Billy Cunningham, a perennial NBA all-star, must play for the ABA Cougars if he was to play professional basketball for the next two seasons. Cunningham, a Philadelphia 76er forward, signed a contract with Carolina in August 1969. The case went to court after Cunningham, claiming a breach of contract, disregarded the Carolina contract and signed a new four-year pact with the 76ers.)

[13] *San Diego joins ABA.* The ABA awarded San Diego a league franchise July 28, bringing the number of clubs in the ABA to 10. (The league's Floridians and Pittsburgh Condors had folded June 13 because of precarious financial situations. Players from the two clubs were dispersed to other ABA clubs in a common draft June 13.) The San Diego team, owned by Leonard Bloom and coached by former Celtic star K. C. Jones, was to be known as the Conquistadors. The new ABA alignment: Eastern Division—Cougars, Colonels, Nets, Squires and Memphis Tams; Western Division—Stars, Conquistadors, Rockets, Pacers and Dallas Chaparrals.

[14] *Merger bill dies.* The Senate Judiciary Committee Sept. 16 approved a bill to permit the NBA and the ABA to merge into a single league, but the legislation died when the Senate and House failed to act. The bill would have waived antitrust laws to permit the merger if the leagues abandoned the reserve clause, which bound a player to the team that held the rights to his contract. Opponents of the proposed NBA-ABA merger had contended that formation of a single professional league would deprive players of the possibility of negotiating with two potential employers.

See also OLYMPICS [11]

BASQUES—*See* SPAIN
BAYH, BIRCH—*See* CRIME [9]; POLITICS [5]
BEAGLE CHANNEL—*See* ARGENTINA [3]
BEARD, DITA—*See* POLITICS [4, 6]
BEGICH, NICK—*See* AVIATION

BELGIUM—New Cabinet. Gaston Eyskens, premier of the government which had resigned following general elections in November 1971, ended a 10-week government crisis by forming a new Christian Social-Socialist coalition Jan. 20. The crisis had stemmed from party differences on a wide range of issues, particularly rivalry between the French-speaking and Flemish-speaking communities. Edmond Leburton, co-president of the Socialist party, had attempted a mediation effort between the two parties, but had abandoned his effort Jan. 4. Following the failure of the Leburton mediation, the two parties resumed talks and announced Jan. 14 agreement on the formation of a new Cabinet and approval of a new program.

The government was sworn in by King Baudouin Jan. 21 and won, by a 124-73 vote (four abstentions), a vote of confidence in the Chamber of Deputies Jan. 28.

The new Cabinet (CS=Christian Socialist; S=Socialist): premier—Eyskens (CS); deputy premier—Andre Cools (S); defense—Paul Vanden Boeynants (CS); foreign affairs—Pierre Harmel (CS); post and telegraphs—Edouard Anseele (S); health—Leon Servais (CS); home affairs—Renaat van Elslande (CS); justice—Alfons Vranckx (S); public works—Joseph de Saeger (CS); labor—Louis Major (S); culture (French)—Charles Hanin (CS); social affairs—Louis Nameche (S); agriculture and middle class affairs—Leo Tindemans (CS); culture (Flemish)—Frans van Mechelen (CS); finance—Andre Vlerick (CS); traffic—Fernand Delmotte (S); education (Flemish)—Willy Claes (S); education (French)—Leon Hurez (S); and economics—Henri Simonet (S). Ten junior ministerial posts were divided evenly between the two parties.

Retailers strike. Some 700,000 small businessmen struck Oct. 23 to protest government red tape, taxes and alleged bias toward large department stores and supermarkets. The strike closed groceries, laundries, cafes, most restaurants, other small enterprises and the stock exchange. Strikers also forced the large department stores and supermarkets to close. Doctors and druggists joined the protests. Gasoline stations remained closed at the end of the strike to press the owners' demand for higher prices to cover the cost of recently increased gasoline taxes.

Cabinet again resigns. The coalition government resigned Nov. 22 over the continuing dispute between the French-speaking and Flemish-speaking communities. The government collapsed over the rejection Nov. 22 by parliamentary members of Premier Eyskens' Flemish CS wing of a compromise government plan aimed at resolving the language dispute. The plan proposed to transfer control of the Fourons (a group of six small villages in eastern Belgium which had both Flemish- and French-speaking inhabitants) from Flemish administration to the central government—a solution aimed at giving the French-speaking community more rights. The Flemish CS members had insisted that such a move be matched by similar autonomy for a Dutch-speaking community near the town of Mons in French-speaking Wallonia. The Flemish CS members had also insisted on the strict enforcement of the current geographical boundaries of predominantly French-speaking Brussels to prevent the expansion of the capital's political and economic power to the surrounding Flemish-speaking suburbs. King Baudouin accepted the Cabinet's resignation Nov. 23, and Nov. 25 named outgoing Public Works Minister de Saeger (Flemish CS) to sound out other political leaders on the formation of a new Cabinet. Edmund Leburton, French-speaking president of the Socialists, Dec. 14 accepted a mandate from Baudouin to form a new government.

See also CONSERVATION; EUROPEAN ECONOMIC COMMUNITY [1]; INTERNATIONAL MONETARY DEVELOPMENTS [2, 6, 9]; POLLUTION [13]; TERRITORIAL WATERS

BELIZE—*See* LATIN AMERICA
BERLIN—*See* GERMAN CONSULTATIONS; GERMANY, WEST [8]; SOVIET-U.S. RELATIONS [6]
BERRIGAN, PHILIP F.—*See* SECURITY, U.S.

BHUTAN—King dies. King Jigme Dorji Wangchuk, 45, of Bhutan died July 22 in Nairobi, Kenya, of a heart ailment. He had arrived in Nairobi the previous week for medical treatment. Dorji's son, Crown Prince Jigme Singye Wangchuk, 16, was enthroned as the new king July 24.

See also EUROPEAN ECONOMIC COMMUNITY [7]

BICYCLES—*See* CYCLING
BIOLOGICAL WARFARE—*See* CHEMICAL & BIOLOGICAL WARFARE

BIRTH CONTROL—Massachusetts law upset. The Supreme Court, in a 4-3 vote March 22, struck down as unconstitutional a 93-year-old Massachusetts statute under which persons who sold or gave birth control devices to unmarried persons were subject to prison terms. Under the law, the same devices were legally available to married persons. The court's majority opinion rejected Massachusetts's argument that the law was a proper exercise of the state's power to discourage fornication and protect people from harmful products. The opinion held that this could not have been the state's real purpose, since the statute applied only to unmarried persons.

The court's ruling came in a case involving birth control advocate William R. Baird, who had been convicted in April 1967 of distributing birth control devices to a coed at Boston University and sentenced to three months in jail. State courts had sustained the conviction, but the 1st U.S. Circuit Court of Appeals voided the law under which Baird was convicted. (In a separate vote, the Supreme Court voted 6-1 March 22 to overturn Baird's conviction.)

See also ABORTION; IRELAND; POPULATION; WOMEN'S RIGHTS

BLACK CAUCUS—*See* CONGRESS
BLACK LUNG—*See* MINES

BLACK MILITANTS—Louisiana unrest. A street corner rally by black militants in Baton Rouge Jan. 10 turned into a wild gunfight that left two white deputy sheriffs and two young black men dead and 31 other persons reported injured. The violence erupted when police moved to break up the rally. According to the police, they opened fire when a black man was spotted pulling a pistol from his jacket. Other witnesses, however, said that the militants were unarmed. Mayor W. W. Dumas of Baton Rouge ordered a tight 10 p.m.-to-6 a.m. curfew in the wake of the violence. The curfew was enforced by about 600 National Guardsmen who had been called to duty Jan. 10 by Louisiana Gov. John J. McKeithen.

Brown resentenced. Black militant leader H. Rap Brown was resentenced in New Orleans June 2 by District Court Judge Lansing L. Mitchell to five years in prison and a $2,000 fine for a 1968 conviction on a federal weapons charge. Mitchell had given Brown the same sentence in absentia in 1970 for carrying a rifle in Baton Rouge, La. while he was under indictment elsewhere. Brown had been flown to New Orleans for the resentencing, despite objections by his attorneys that the flight was at risk to his health. He had been in custody in New York since his capture by New York police in October 1971. (Mitchell ordered that Brown's five-year sentence would not start pending the outcome of other criminal charges Brown faced in New York.)

Angela Davis acquitted. An all-white jury in San Jose, Calif. deliberated 13 hours before returning a verdict June 4 acquitting Angela Y. Davis, a black militant and avowed Communist, of all charges of murder, kidnap and conspiracy in connection with an August 1970 Marin County courtroom escape and kidnap attempt. Miss Davis had allegedly supplied weapons which were smuggled into the Marin County courtroom by Jonathan Jackson, a companion and bodyguard of Miss Davis'. Inside the courtroom, Jackson was joined by three San Quentin inmates—James McClain, then on trial for stabbing a guard, and Arthur Christmas and Ruchel Magee, witnesses at McClain's trial. Jackson, McClain and Christmas were killed in the escape attempt, along with Judge Harold J. Haley, who had been seized as a hostage. (Three jurors and Gary Thomas, assistant district attorney of Marin County, had also been taken as hostages.) Although Miss Davis had not been present at the courtroom, under California law her alleged involvement in supplying the weapons used and in helping to plan the escape and kidnap made her equally responsible with those who had committed the actions.

The Davis trial had begun March 27. During the seven-week prosecution presentation which ended May 15, the state tried to establish a link between Miss Davis and the Marin County shootout with testimony that the weapons used belonged to her, that the hostages taken were intended to be exchanged for the three imprisoned Soledad Brothers *(see* PRISONS*)* and that Miss Davis was motivated in her alleged conspiracy by passionate love for George Jackson, one of the Soledad defendants and brother of Jonathan Jackson. Several of the first prosecution witnesses testified that they heard the escapees demand that the Soledad Brothers be freed in exchange for the hostages, although one of the hostages, Mrs. Maria Elena Graham, admitted March 30 under cross-examination that she may have been influenced by chief prosecutor Albert Harris Jr. to recall the Soledad demand, after she neglected to mention it at an earlier police interview. The three other surviving hostages testified March 30 and April 5 that they had heard no mention of Soledad, but a newspaper photographer and three law officers claimed April 3 that they heard a demand that the Soledad Brothers be freed the day of the crime. Assistant District Attorney Thomas testified April 5 that the shot killing Judge Haley had come from a shotgun held by Magee in the escape vehicle. A witness testified April 17 that the shotgun had been purchased by Miss Davis two days before the crime. In order to demonstrate Miss Davis's love for George Jackson, the prosecution read to the jury three letters written by Miss Davis to Jackson in June and July 1970. The defense had objected to the reading on grounds that the letters, which expressed Miss Davis' love for Jackson, had been illegally seized, were irrelevant and would prejudice the jury. Presiding Judge Richard E. Arnason refused, however, to allow the prosecution to introduce into the record an 18-page document, written by Miss Davis after her arrest in October 1970 and found among Jackson's possessions after he was killed in an alleged August 1971 San Quentin escape attempt. The prosecution later read excerpts from the document which expressed Miss Davis's love for Jackson and referred to him as her husband. In the last weeks of prosecution testimony, several witnesses reported that they had seen Miss Davis with Jonathan Jackson in the days before the kidnap attempt; but some of the witnesses, under cross-examination, admitted uncertainty about their identification of Miss Davis as the woman with Jackson.

The defense rested its case May 24 after only three days of testimony, mostly by Miss Davis's friends or associates, who testified that they were with her at the times she was said by the prosecution to have been with Jonathan Jackson. One witness said that the guns registered in Miss Davis's name and used by Jackson had been borrowed from the witness without Miss Davis's knowledge. Fleeta Drumgo, one of the Soledad Brothers, testified that he had heard nothing about the alleged plot while he was at San Quentin.

(Miss Davis had been freed on $102,500 bail Feb. 23, 16 months after her arrest. In granting bail, Judge Arnason ruled that the state law denying bail to defendants in "capital cases" was nullified by the California Supreme Court ruling abolishing the death penalty. *See* CRIME [11].)

Hanrahan acquitted. Cook County Criminal Court Judge Philip J. Romiti Oct. 25 acquitted State's Attorney Edward V. Hanrahan and 13 co-defendants on charges of conspiring to obstruct justice in the shootout slaying of Black Panthers Fred Hampton and Mark Clark during a December 1969 gun raid on the Panthers' apartment. The 14 defendants, including eight policemen who conducted the raid, were specifically accused of conspiring to withhold and falsify evidence to prevent prosecution of the policemen and to obstruct the defense of seven Panthers indicted for attempted murder on charges brought by Hanrahan after the raid. (Hanrahan had later dropped the charges for lack of evidence.) All of the defendants had waived jury trial. Romiti ruled in his acquittal that no defense witnesses need be called because "evidence is simply not sufficient to establish or prove any conspiracy against any defendant." Romiti said the evidence presented by special county prosecutor Barnabas Sears amounted to "not much more than conjecture and speculation." (The prosecution's case had been damaged by the discovery during the trial of written statements made to their lawyers by four Panthers who had survived the 1969 raid. The statements contradicted their testimony before a grand jury that they had not fired shots at the police.)

See also AUSTRALIA [1]; HIJACKING [5]; NEWSPAPERS; POLITICS [8]; PRISONS

BLACK PANTHERS—*See* AUSTRALIA [1]; BLACK MILITANTS; HIJACKING [5]; NEWSPAPERS
BLACK POLITICAL CONVENTION—*See* POLITICS [1, 8]
BLACK SEPTEMBER ORGANIZATION—*See* HIJACKING [9]; MIDDLE EAST [7, 29]; OLYMPIC TERRORISM
BLINDNESS—*See* CONSUMER AFFAIRS [8, 11]
BLOOD BANKS—*See* CONSUMER AFFAIRS [13]
BOGGS, HALE—*See* AVIATION

BOLIVIA—Cabinet changes. As the result of a shuffle within the Cabinet, it was announced Jan. 6 that Interior Minister Col. Andres Selich, a strongly anti-Communist member of the regime and one of the leading figures in the overthrow of President Juan Jose Torres in August 1971, would resign his post to become ambassador to Paraguay. (Selich May 14 was relieved as ambassador and retired from the armed forces on the orders of President Hugo Banzer Suarez.) Information Minister Hugo Gonzalez Rioja said that Selich's dismissal from the Cabinet and the replacement of three other Cabinet officers (announced Dec. 28, 1971) had "no political significance." However, Selich attributed his resignation to disagreements between the two political parties supporting the government—the Nationalist Revolutionary Movement (MNR) and the Bolivian Socialist Falange (FSB). The new Cabinet members were: interior—Col. Mario Adett Zamora; education and culture—Mario Mendez Elias; mines and petroleum—Edmundo Nogales Ortiz; and urban planning—Julio Prado Salmon. Agriculture Minister Col. Jose Gil Reyes resigned June 23, reportedly due to differences with the government over the price of sugar, which had been increased during 1972.

In a later Cabinet change, President Banzer Aug. 24 appointed new ministers of mines (Raul Lema Patino), finance (Luis Bedregal Rodo) and information (Guillermo Fortun Suarez) in an attempt to ease tensions within the ruling military-civilian coalition. All three appointees, like their predecessors, were members of the MNR. Former Finance Minister Edwin Rodriguez had resigned Aug. 23, but the two other replaced ministers learned that they were being replaced only minutes before the new appointments were announced. According to a report Sept. 1, the chief conflicts within the government involved: the status of the MNR's ex-vice president, Guillermo Bedregal, at that time in temporary exile (permanently exiled to Brazil Sept. 30); military feeling against MNR president Victor Paz Estenssoro; and attacks from the FSB on Paz Estenssoro and his colleague, Walter Guevara Arce, presently ambassador to the United Nations. The three new ministers reportedly were selected because they were young technocrats not directly associated with the government's internal political conflicts. In a similar move, Banzer Sept. 4 removed Education Minister Mendez and Urban Planning Minister Prado (both FSB members) and replaced them with Jaime Tapia Alipaz and Mario Rivera (both MNR members).

'Death Squad' appears. A communique issued in Santa Cruz March 23 announced that a Brazilian-style, right-wing political "death squad" had been formed to eliminate subversives and that, "for every nationalist killed, 20 traitors will die." Interior Minister Adett Zamora April 20 declared the death squad "outside the law." (The death squad had claimed five victims by April 20.)

Soviet diplomats expelled. Foreign Minister Mario Gutierrez announced March 29 that the government had ordered 119 staff members of the Soviet embassy in La Paz to leave Bolivia within a week. Gutierrez called the expulsions "a question of sovereignty" and said that several sectors of the nation—including the armed forces—had been concerned over the large number of officials at the embassy. Gutierrez pointed out that there were only three officials in the Bolivian embassy in Moscow. The foreign minister also said documents that had fallen into his hands had outlined a plan for "foreign intervention in Bolivia" and had given instructions for the "landing of men" in various parts of the country April 4. Gutierrez emphasized that the expulsion did not mean an end to Soviet-Bolivian relations. The Soviet ambassador to Bolivia, Alexei F. Shcherbachevich, March 30 denied any misconduct on the part of his embassy, adding that it had only 40 attaches in Bolivia. Shcherbachevich said the list of officials to be expelled was headed by the name of a four-year-old daughter of an embassy official, and included the names of diplomatic couriers, members of trade missions and journalists who had visited La Paz at one time or another. The government announced April 19 that 62 Soviet diplomats and dependents had left the country, reducing the Soviet embassy staff to 13.

Peso devaluation, strikes. President Banzer Oct. 27 decreed a 66.7% devaluation of the peso and a price freeze on essential goods and services, including rents. The measures were accompanied by compensatory raises for workers and employees and by a two-day suspension of private and public activities. The actions roused immediate protest. The Bolivian Manufacturing Workers Confederation, one of the strongest unions in La Paz, and the Bolivian University Students Confederation condemned the measures Oct. 27. Other unions added their protests Oct. 28 as official prices on basic goods rose by about 40% and widespread speculation and hoarding of goods were reported. Only the Peasants Confederation and members of the governing coalition came to the defense of the new economic measures. The Peasants Confederation urged its rank and file to support the government by "increasing production and selling all products directly to the consumer." In order to deal with increasing protests, the army Oct. 29 decided to take "direct control of the situation." Armored cars moved into the center of La Paz Oct. 30 and used tear gas to disperse demonstrators. One person was killed and at least 40 injured in the clashes in the capital. The influential Federation of Private Businessmen came out against the government decrees Oct. 31, leaving Banzer with little support for his economic policies.

Siege declared in protest strike. The government Nov. 23 imposed a nationwide state of siege (a form of martial law suspending some constitutional rights and forbidding rallies and demonstrations) at the beginning of a protest strike by thousands of factory, commercial and bank workers. The state of siege was ordered after textile workers in La Paz declared a 24-hour work stoppage to protest the October austerity measures and charges made Nov. 22 by Interior Minister Adett Zamora that unions were being infiltrated by extreme leftist elements. (Workers' rights to free association, suspended since the August 1971 military coup, had been recognized by the government, effective Nov. 10.) Tanks, troops and police surrounded the textile factory district in La Paz Nov. 23 as workers barricaded themselves inside factories. Army assault cars were positioned in working-class neighborhoods; and numerous persons were arrested, including workers, union leaders and the news director of a radio station. Thousands of bank and commercial employees joined the strike later in the day, after the arrest of members of the National Confederation of Bank Employees. Tanks and troops were withdrawn from the factory district Nov. 24 as some workers returned to work, but bank employees continued to strike. Interior Minister Adett Zamora claimed authorities had discovered a plot by extremists to take advantage of the strike to overthrow the government. The strike was suspended Nov. 25 after the government agreed to release the arrested strikers and to negotiate wage increases, but the siege regulations remained in effect.

Guerrilla 'plot' reported. Adett Zamora Dec. 20 claimed to have uncovered a plot by exiled Bolivian guerrillas to assassinate President Banzer and "Vietnamize" Bolivia. He said that more than 30 persons had been arrested in connection with the plot, which allegedly had Cuban financial backing and support from guerrilla movements in Chile, Argentina and Uruguay. According to Adett Zamora, exiles under the leadership of Ruben Sanchez (a former army major living in Chile) had planned to invade Bolivia from Chile, Argentina and Brazil to sabotage mining centers and to organize peasants against the government. The plotters allegedly had planned to assassinate Banzer Dec. 20. According to Adett Zamora, four would-be assassins—all members of the left-wing National Liberation Army (ELN)—had been arrested Dec. 20 after killing a soldier. Observers maintained that the real motive for Adett Zamora's charges was a new round of plotting among high military officers.

See also ATOMIC ENERGY [13]; DRUG USE & ADDICTION [16]; FOREIGN POLICY; LATIN AMERICA

BOMBS—*See* ARGENTINA [10]; AVIATION; CANADA [2]; CIVIL DISORDERS; DRAFT & WAR PROTEST;GERMANY, WEST [3]; GREECE [12]; HIJACKING [2, 18]; IRELAND; MEXICO; MIDDLE EAST [1, 24-26]; NORTHERN IRELAND [3-5, 12-14]; PHILIPPINES [1, 5]; SECURITY, U.S.; SHIPS & SHIPPING; SPAIN; STUDENT UNREST; SWITZERLAND; TURKEY; UNION OF SOVIET SOCIALIST REPUBLICS [9]

BOOKS—Hughes hoax. Writer Clifford Irving and his wife, Edith, March 13 pleaded guilty to federal conspiracy charges in their scheme to swindle $750,000 from McGraw-Hill Publishing Co. with a fake autobiography of billionaire recluse Howard R. Hughes. Irving had claimed that he authored the book after extensive face-to-face meetings with Hughes and had signed contracts with McGraw-Hill and Life magazine for publication of the book. A voice which seven reporters accepted as that of Hughes Jan. 9 said in a telephone conversation between Los Angeles and the Bahamas (where Hughes was believed to be living) that he had never met with Irving and that the autobiography was "totally fantastic fiction." Irving disclosed Jan. 28 that a $650,000 check, drawn on McGraw-Hill and intended for Hughes, was cashed by Edith Irving in one Swiss bank and deposited in another under the name of "Helga R. Hughes."

McGraw-Hill and Life concluded Feb. 11 that the Irving book was a fraud and canceled plans for publication. McGraw-Hill said much of the material in the book could have been drawn from a manuscript about Hughes written by Noah Dietrich, a former Hughes aide, and John Phelan, an investigative reporter.

Irving, his wife and Richard Suskind, a researcher for Irving, had been indicted on the conspiracy charges March 9. The same day a New York County grand jury indicted the three on charges of grand larceny, conspiracy and possession of forged instruments. The county and federal governments dropped some charges when the Irvings pleaded guilty. Irving was sentenced to 2½ years in prison on federal fraud and conspiracy charges. He entered prison Aug. 28. The Swiss government had issued warrants for the arrest of the Irvings Jan. 31 on charges of fraud in connection with Mrs. Irving's bank manipulations. Swiss authorities Feb. 22 ruled out any deals concerning Mrs. Irving, a Swiss national. Mrs. Irving returned to Switzerland Sept. 4 and was immediately jailed.

See also NOBEL PRIZES; PULITZER PRIZES

BORDABERRY, JUAN MARIA—*See* URUGUAY [2-4, 6, 8, 11-12, 14-15]
BOTSWANA—*See* INTERNATIONAL MONETARY DEVELOPMENTS [8]

BOWLING—Johnson wins U.S. Open. Don Johnson Jan. 9 bowled six straight strikes to defeat George Pappas, 233-224, in the finals of the $100,000 Bowling Proprietors Association of America U.S. Open in New York's Madison Square Garden. Johnson won $10,000; Pappas earned $6,000.

BOYLE, W.A. (TONY)—*See* MINES
BRANDT, WILLY—*See* EUROPEAN ECONOMIC COMMUNITY [17]; GERMANY, WEST [2, 5, 12-13]

BRAZIL—Mass arrests. Members of the army, navy and air force joined police in rounding up over 200 "suspected subversives" in Rio de Janeiro, Sao Paulo, Porto Alegre and Recife during the week ending Feb. 5. The arrests were the largest since the November 1970 "Operation Birdcage" which put an estimated 2,000 persons in jail or under house arrest pending the outcome of parliamentary elections. Most of those jailed in the February roundup were students, many of whom were said to belong to the Communist Workers party and the terrorist National Liberation Alliance. Authorities released 50 students Feb. 5 after lecturing them on the dangers of Communism. In other actions against terrorism: nine persons, six of them still at large, were sentenced to life imprisonment by a military court in Rio de Janeiro April 16 for the 1970 kidnaping of West German Ambassador Ehrenfried von Holleben; a military court Aug. 24 sentenced two men and a woman to life imprisonment for the 1970 kidnaping of Swiss Ambassador Giovanni Enrico Bucher.

Portugal relations. A convention conferring mutual rights of citizenship on Portuguese and Brazilian citizens, approved by the government in 1971, went into effect April 22. Portuguese President Americo Tomaz arrived in Brazil the same day to return the remains of Pedro I, the Braganza monarch who declared Brazil independent in the 19th century. According to a report July 7, Brazil and Portugal had also strengthened their economic ties. One measure signed by the two countries established custom-free zones for each other's exports. (The zones were in the Brazilian ports of Sao Paulo and Rio de Janeiro, in Lisbon and in the Portuguese colonies of Angola and Mozambique. Other measures signed by the two countries provided for: an easier flow of capital between the two, particularly to Portugal's colonies; direct participation of Portuguese capital in Brazilian development; investment by Brazil's state oil company in exploration in Africa; increased shipping services; and the establishment of a multinational investment bank that would operate in Portuguese colonies, Rhodesia and South Africa. (Brazil reportedly had difficulty penetrating European markets and was also interested in trade with Africa.)

Indian policy criticized. According to a report May 24, Antonio Cotrim, one of Brazil's top Indian specialists, had resigned from the National Indian Foundation because, he said, he was tired of being a gravedigger for Indians dying as a result of government policies. Cotrim charged that the rights of Indians in Brazilian forests were being violated by land development companies; and that the National Indian Foundation, which was supposed to protect the Indians, did nothing more than manipulate public opinion. In later developments, it was reported Aug. 5 that a virtual state of war existed between Xavante Indians and Caucasian settlers in the western state of Mato Grosso. The Indians claimed that their land was being invaded and fenced off by the settlers. According to a report Aug. 18, 100 Xavantes had died in Mato Grosso during July in an outbreak of flu and measles. The deaths were attributed to increased contact between Indians and non-Indian highway workers and to failure by authorities to provide adequate medical care for the victims. According to a report Sept. 26, the government later ordered the creation of special areas for the Xavantes to live in "free from interference from outsiders."

Church renews torture charges. The National Conference of Bishops (Roman Catholic Church) charged June 10 that, despite government denials, torture and illegal arrests had continued in Brazil during the previous two years. (The group had asked authorities to investigate reports of official torture in May 1970, but the government had denied the reports were true.) The bishops condemned the use of physical, psychic and moral torture during interrogation of suspected criminals and deplored the "atmosphere of insecurity" allegedly created among citizens by the authorities. The group alleged that many arrests by security forces had all the characteristics of abductions, with families unable for months to obtain news of detained relatives. The bishops also expressed support for demands by lawyers' organizations for immediate restoration of the right of habeas corpus. The bishops' statement followed similar charges by the Inter-American Commission on Human Rights of the Organization of American States, reported June 4, and charges leveled in two letters allegedly sent by Brazilian political prisoners, published April 14. The two letters, addressed to judges of Brazilian military courts, had charged that political prisoners in Sao Paulo's Tiradentes jail were jammed into cells designed to hold one-fourth their number, denied adequate medical care and physical exercise and tortured or threatened with torture. One of the letters also charged that unnatural sex acts were forced on prisoners for the amusement of prison guards. Amnesty International, an independent organization working for the release of political prisoners, issued a report Sept. 26 naming 1,000 Brazilians it said were tortured and asserting it had the names of 472 Brazilian torturers. (The report said the names of the torturers would be made available only to the Brazilian government and to a limited number of international organizations.) The report charged that physical and mental torture was practiced by the police and military in virtually all Brazilian prisons.

Agrarian reform initiated. Agriculture Minister Luis Cirne Lima announced Aug. 5 that the government's promised land reform would begin in the northeastern states of Paraiba, Pernambuco and Ceara, all highly agrarian areas where the predominant social problems stemmed from unequal land distribution and where unemployment or underemployment affected nearly 30% of the rural population. Under the plan—which was immediately met with strong opposition by landowners and members of the ruling National Alliance for Renewal (ARENA)—owners of more than 2,470 acres would have to cede 20% of their land for redistribution among peasants. Owners of more than 7,410 acres would lose 30%, and those with over 13,350 would have to give up 50% of their holdings. The owners would lose the land within six months, but would be compensated immediately in cash, at a rate still to be fixed. According to Lima, the confiscated land would comprise 30% of Paraiba, 14% of Pernambuco and 40% of Ceara. However, the redistribution would benefit only about 15,000 families.

New censorship measures. The military government Sept. 15 imposed severe curbs on political and economic debate by the press, radio and television. The action followed growing criticism of the regime in conservative newspapers and speculation on who would succeed President Emilio G. Medici in 1974. The Justice Ministry communique prohibited publication or broadcast of "news, commentaries, interviews or opinions of any nature concerning political openings, democratization or issues related to amnesty for those who have lost their political rights, or partial revision of procedures taken against them; criticism, commentaries or editorials of an unfavorable nature on the economic and financial situation; and [news of] the problems of presidential succession and their implications." The document also forbade any reference to "the events which led to approval of Institutional Act No. 5," which gave the government virtually dictatorial powers. There reportedly had been increasing public pressure for repeal of the act, imposed in 1968 following a year of civil disturbances.

See also BANKS; BOLIVIA; DRUG USE & ADDICTION [20]; INTERNATIONAL MONETARY DEVELOPMENTS [9]; LATIN AMERICA; TARIFFS & WORLD TRADE; TERRITORIAL WATERS; URUGUAY [7]

BREMER, ARTHUR—*See* CRIME [7-8]; ELECTIONS [10]
BREZHNEV, LEONID I.—*See* DISARMAMENT; SOVIET-U.S. RELATIONS [1, 3, 6]
BRINEGAR CLAUDE S.—*See* NIXON, RICHARD MILHOUS
BRITISH COMMONWEALTH—*See* BAHAMAS; BANGLA DESH [13]; CEYLON;
JAMICA; PAKISTAN [7]
BRITISH HONDURAS—*See* LATIN AMERICA
BROWN, H. RAP—*See* BLACK MILITANTS

BUDGET—President Nixon Jan. 24 presented to Congress a $246.3 billion
budget for fiscal 1973 (July 1, 1972 through June 30, 1973). Predicated on a
"full employment" concept (spending and revenue calculated on the basis of an
economy operating at 3.8% unemployment rather than actual expected levels of
unemployment), the budget estimated receipts at $220.8 billion and a deficit of
$25.5 billion—the largest peacetime deficit in U.S. history. (The fiscal 1972
deficit, forecast in January at $38.8 billion was reported July 24 to actually be
$23 billion.) The central purpose of the budget, President Nixon said, was "a
new prosperity for all Americans without the stimulus of war and without the
drain of inflation." The budget contained no new major tax increase proposals.

The large deficit and a request to increase the authority for military
programs by $6.3 billion, the largest new initiative of the budget, were major
features of the new budget. The President justified both as necessary—deficit
spending to increase jobs and spur the economy and a rise in defense fund
obligations to modernize the U.S. arsenal. Nixon pointed out that the increase
in federal spending was only 4.1% from the previous year, that 71% of federal
spending was "uncontrollable," or built into the budget from ongoing programs
enacted by Congress, and that tax revenues were $22 billion less because of
reductions for individuals since he assumed office. In the area of defense, Nixon
said, "A demagogue may find it easy to advocate that we simply allocate
necessary defense dollars to social programs, but a responsible Congress and a
responsible president cannot afford such easy answers." Despite this view, and
largely because of built-in budget programs, outlays for domestic "human
resource" programs exceeded those for defense. For the first time, the budget
for the Department of Health, Education and Welfare ($79 billion) exceeded
that for the Defense Department ($76.5 billion). (See chart, p. 43.)

Spending ceiling recommended. In a separate message Jan. 24, the
President requested Congress to enact "an absolute limit on spending" for the
new budget at the $246.3 billion level, beyond which the Congress or the
Executive branch could not go. It was vital, he said, that both branches "act
together to stop raids on the treasury which would trigger another inflationary
spiral." (In a later development, the President Aug. 16 vetoed a $30.5 billion
appropriations bill for fiscal 1973 for the Departments of Labor and Health,
Education and Welfare because the bill would have provided $1.76 billion more
than requested in the budget. Nixon had threatened July 6 to veto any bill
which exceeded his budget requests. The House Aug. 16 voted 203-171 to
override the veto, but fell short of the necessary two-thirds margin.)

Spending curb actions. The House Oct. 10 voted 221-163 to approve a
$250 billion spending limit for fiscal 1973. The measure, which gave the
President unrestricted power to cut back federal programs of his own choosing,
was passed as an amendment to an extension of the debt ceiling *(see below)*. The
House version of the spending curb was reported to the Senate Oct. 12 after the
Senate Finance Committee deadlocked 8-8 on its own version of the bill. The
Senate Oct. 13 passed the House version of the debt ceiling, but substituted for
the House spending curb a spending ceiling amendment prohibiting cutbacks
on an explicit list of government programs—military pay, interest on the public
debt, veterans' benefits and services, Social Security payments including
Medicare, Medicaid, public assistance, social service grants, the food stamp
program and judicial salaries. The amendment also required proportional
reductions on the remaining federal programs and permitted a maximum cut of
only 10% (totalling $7.5 billion) in the allowable areas. The amendment was

aimed at preserving the authority over power of the purse granted Congress by the Constitution. The House-Senate conference committee reconciling the House and Senate versions of the bill produced a compromise version that retained restrictions on appropriation reductions for certain programs—such as military pay, Social Security payments, public assistance and judicial salaries. However, the compromise permitted presidential cuts of up to 20% in 50 broad functional categories, such as national defense, agriculture and pollution control. No restrictions were put on spending cuts made within individual programs in these categories. The Senate Oct. 17 voted 39-27 to reject the spending ceiling compromise and to detach it from the debt ceiling bill. The House Oct. 18 followed the Senate lead and approved the debt ceiling bill without any provision for a spending curb. President Nixon Oct. 19 reacted to the defeat of the spending curb legislation by revealing that he intended to impound funds already appropriated by Congress in order to remain under a spending limit of $250 billion for fiscal 1973.

Debt ceiling actions. A temporary $20 billion increase in the national debt ceiling was approved March 15, by a 237-150 House vote and by a 55-33 Senate

Budget Receipts

(In billions of dollars for the fiscal year)

	1971 actual	1972 estimate	1973 estimate
Individual income taxes	86.23	86.5	93.9
Corporation income taxes	26.785	30.1	35.7
Social insurance taxes and contributions:			
Employment taxes and contributions	41.699	46.367	55.113
Unemployment insurance	3.674	4.364	5.016
Contributions for other insurance and retirement	3.205	3.361	3.554
Excise taxes	16.615	15.2	16.3
Estate and gift taxes	3.735	5.2	4.3
Customs duties	2.591	3.21	2.85
Miscellaneous receipts	3.858	3.525	4.052
Total receipts	**188.392**	**197.827**	**220.785**

Budget Outlays

(In billions of dollars for the fiscal year)

	1971 actual	1972 estimate	1973 estimate
National defense*	77.661	78.03	78.31
International affairs and finance	3.095	3.96	3.844
Space research and technology	3.381	3.18	3.191
Agriculture and rural development	5.096	7.345	6.891
Natural resources and environment	2.716	4.376	2.45
Commerce and transportation	11.31	11.872	11.55
Community development and housing	3.357	4.039	4.844
Education and manpower	8.654	10.14	11.281
Health	14.463	17.024	18.117
Income security	55.712	65.225	69.658
Veterans benefits and services	9.776	11.127	11.745
Interest	19.609	20.067	21.161
General government	3.970	5.302	5.531
General revenue sharing	——	2.25	5.0
Allowances for:			
Pay raises (excluding Department of Defense)	——	.25	.775
Contingencies	——	.3	.5
Undistributed intrabudgetary transactions:			
Employer share, employe retirement	−2.611	−2.687	−2.893
Interest received by trust funds	−4.765	−5.19	−5.697
Total outlays	**211.425**	**236.61**	**246.257**
Budget deficit	**23.033**	**38.783**	**25.472**

*Includes allowances for military retirement systems reform and civilian and military pay raises for Department of Defense.

vote. The bill raised the level of the federal debt to $450 billion through June 30. (President Nixon had requested a $50 billion rise to cover expected borrowing until 1973.) Congress June 30 then acted to approve a bill extending the $450 billion debt ceiling until Oct. 31. The last-minute congressional action averted a temporary fiscal paralysis of government, since government spending was well in excess of the $400 billion limit to which the ceiling would have reverted without legislation. (The Administration had requested an extension of the debt ceiling to $465 billion to cover borrowing until February 1973.) Congress Oct. 18 passed (by voice vote in both chambers) a bill authorizing an extension of the debt ceiling until June 30, 1973 and raising the ceiling from $450 billion to $465 billion. President Nixon signed the measure Oct. 28. (The measure also provided for the establishment of a permanent Joint Budget Committee, empowered to set spending guidelines at the beginning of each congressional session and to oversee appropriations requested in order to head off fiscal confrontations between the Congress and the President.)

See also BUSINESS; DEFENSE; ELECTIONS [9, 23]; FOREIGN AID; HEALTH; NIXON, RICHARD MILHOUS; POLLUTION [15-16]; SOCIAL SECURITY

BULGARIA—1971 economic report. Results of the 1971 economic development plan were disclosed Feb. 1. Measured against the results for 1970, the following major increases were reported: real income 5%; industrial production 9.5%; oil output 29.2%; ferrous ore production 24.6%; chemical and rubber industries 11.4%; chemical fiber and silk 22.5%; foreign trade 11.6%.

See also CUBA; DRUG USE & ADDICTION [18]; ENVIRONMENT; ESPIONAGE; HIJACKING [11]

BUREAU OF CUSTOMS—See DRUG USE & ADDICTION [17]
BUREAU OF INDIAN AFFAIRS (BIA)—See INDIANS, AMERICAN
BUREAU OF MINES—See FLOODS; MINES
BUREAU OF NARCOTICS & DANGEROUS DRUGS—See DRUG USE & ADDICTION [3-4, 10-11, 16-17, 19]
BURGER, WARREN E.—See CRIME [10]; ESPIONAGE; JUDICIARY; VOTING RIGHTS

BURMA—Civilian government formed. The government announced April 20 that Gen. Ne Win, the country's ruler, had resigned from the army and his post as army chief of staff to become premier of the nation's first civilian government in 10 years. Ne Win kept his positions as chairman of the ruling Revolutionary Council and of the Burma Socialist Program, the country's only political party. Most of the Cabinet's army members also resigned from the armed forces, and most of the Cabinet members retained their posts. Brig. Gen. San Yu, the deputy premier, was appointed chief of staff and given the rank of general. Col. Tin U was appointed deputy minister of defense and was promoted to the rank of brigadier.

The government changeover paved the way for the announcement April 22 of a new constitution which provided for the establishment of a Socialist Republic of Burma and retained the one-party system with an elected unicameral 600-member People's Congress.

See also DRUG USE & ADDICTION [12, 18]

BURUNDI—Coup sentences. A military tribunal Jan. 24 sentenced nine persons to death for plotting to overthrow the government. Seven other defendants were given life sentences and six were acquitted. President Michel Micombero Feb. 4 pardoned the nine sentenced to death. Those affected by the move included two former ministers—Libere Ndabakwaje, who was set free, and Marc Manirakiza, whose sentence was commuted to life at hard labor.

Former king seized, killed. Charles Ndizeye, the exiled King Mioame Ntare V of Burundi, was arrested March 30 in Bujumbura after being taken to the capital by Ugandan authorities upon a written promise by President

Micombero that Ndizeye would not be harmed. (Ndizeye had been deposed in 1966 by Micombero, who had warned that he would be treated "like a criminal" if he ever returned to Burundi.) Burundi announced March 31 that the former ruler had been arrested while trying to invade the country with the help of foreign mercenaries, but Uganda denied having returned Ndizeye either to have him "answer for any alleged crimes" or "to invade Burundi with the assistance of mercenaries." Ndizeye was killed April 29 while he was under house arrest at Gitenga, some 60 miles east of Bujumbura. According to an official government report, Ndizeye was killed in fighting when dissident forces attempted to free him from house arrest *(see below)*. In response to Ndizeye's death and to rebel uprisings in the southern province of Bururi, Micombero dismissed his entire Cabinet April 29 and appointed military governors for each of Burundi's eight provinces April 30.

Thousands killed in fighting. The death of Ndizeye was the apparent start of fighting which resulted in the death of undetermined thousands in Burundi. Accounts failed to give a clear picture of the fighting, but it appeared to be caused by efforts to settle tribal grievances and to overthrow the government. According to eyewitness accounts, the fighting began April 29 when Bahutu tribesmen and Simba tribesmen who were followers of the late Congolese rebel Pierre Mulele (in some accounts, supported by Watusi monarchists) attacked Burundi from Tanzania and Zaire. After killing some 20,000 persons, most of them Tutsis, the invaders, reportedly under the influence of drugs, were opposed by a joint force of Watusi and Bahutu. The government of Zaire announced May 3 that it was sending troops to help Burundi "overcome agents of imperialism." News sources gave no clear indication of the role taken by Zaire troops, but they reportedly were sent to oppose the Simba. The fighting in Burundi was largely indiscriminate. There were reports that the Bahutu (who were sometimes identified as supporters of Micombero) were carrying out massacres of the Watusi minority (considered to be monarchists opposed to Micombero) in southern Burundi. (The Watusi, who composed 14% of the population, had long subjugated the Bahutu, who composed 85%.) Order was reportedly restored May 6 by forces loyal to Micombero. Reprisals carried out beginning May 10 by Watusi organizations—including the army, the police, the ruling UPRONA party and the youth movement—reportedly resulted in the death of a further 100,000 Bahutu *(see below)*.

Government version of fighting. Nsanze Terence, Burundi's delegate to the United Nations, gave a different version of events June 3. Terence declared that the invading forces had been "largely destroyed" after the death of "some 50,000" persons. He said that in the April attack, a main force of Mulele followers had been joined in Burundi by a smaller group, which "composed their fifth column." Terence did not specify the tribal origin of the Burundi rebels, but he claimed there was no ethnic warfare in the country. He said that, "in everyday life, Hutu and Tutsi live side by side in harmony and peace in one neighborhood, cultivate their land and raise cattle together." The government June 7, however, released a white paper at the U.N. contradicting Terence's version. The white paper said members of the Bahutu had tried to "systematically exterminate" the Watusi, performing such "barbarous acts" as "crucifixions, mutilation and impalement." According to the report, Ndizeye had been killed by Hutu, who had attacked April 29 at five places in Burundi. President Micombero June 11 confirmed that the fighting had been caused mainly by Bahutu. Micombero said the plotters had attempted to use the prestige of Ndizeye, whom Micombero revealed had been tried and executed by the government April 29. Micombero said that the invaders had killed all Watusi and those local Bahutu who would not help them.

Reprisals. The government May 10 began to carry out a program of political executions of members of the Bahutu. Four Hutu members of the government, according to a report June 11, were arrested. A report June 21 said: "Many Hutus are being buried while still alive. Leadership elements have been slaughtered. The rest are docile and obedient. They are digging graves for themselves and are thrown in afterwards." The office of Sen. Edward M. Kennedy (D, Mass.), chairman of the Senate Judiciary subcommittee on refugees and escapees confirmed that some 25,000 Hutu refugees had fled to Tanzania, Zaire, Rwanda and the Central African Republic. According to Kennedy's office, relief organizations were at work, but the government's relief program was "not uniformly administered." Male refugees reportedly were being "summarily" slaughtered despite government assurances to them of safe conduct back to their villages. Kennedy said July 28 that the reprisals were still continuing, with "hundreds of people" being killed each day.

U.N. mission. U.N. Secretary General Kurt Waldheim announced June 16 that the U.N. would send a three-man mission to Burundi, having obtained permission from Burundi officials. The team arrived June 22 and issued a report July 28 that "the proportions of the human tragedy which the people of Burundi are experiencing is staggering." The report said the mission had been informed by the Burundi government "that 500,000 persons, including 50,000 widows and tens of thousands of orphans, are experiencing great suffering and are in need of humanitarian assistance." A second U.N. technical mission was reported Aug. 3 in Burundi to study emergency aid requirements. However, the International Committee of the Red Cross announced Aug. 3 that it was withdrawing a relief team from the country because government authorities had refused to allow Red Cross representatives to supervise distribution of relief supplies.

New Cabinet formed. President Micombero July 15 appointed a new prime minister and a 13-member Cabinet to replace the one dismissed April 29. The new Prime Minister Albin Nyamoya, formerly the agriculture minister, was also given the post of interior minister. (Micombero had no prime minister in his previous government.) Micombero remained head of state and minister of defense. Five ministers were retained from the previous government. The Cabinet included members of both the Hutu and the Tutsi, but no proportional breakdown was given.

BUSH, GEORGE H.—*See* POLITICS [15]

BUSINESS—FTC charges cereal companies. The Federal Trade Commission (FTC) Jan. 24 voted 3-2 to file a proposed complaint against the nation's four largest breakfast cereal companies (Kellogg Co., General Mills Inc., General Foods Corp. and the Quaker Oats Co.) for illegally monopolizing the market, preventing "meaningful price competition" and forcing consumers to pay "artificially inflated" prices estimated as 20%-25% higher than they would be in a competitive market. The FTC attached a consent order which would require divestiture of some or all of the firms' manufacturing assets to permit new competitors to enter the industry. The complaint did not charge the firms—which comprised 91% of the ready-to-eat cereals market—with conspiracy, but accused them of individually violating Section 5 of the FTC Act which prohibited restraint of competition. They were charged with "proliferation of brands and trademark promotion; artificial differentiation of products; unfair methods of competition in advertising and product promotion; restrictive retail shelf space control programs and acquisitions of competitors."

FCC resumes AT&T probe. The Federal Communications Commission (FCC) Jan. 28 voted unanimously to resume an investigation of costs and investments of the American Telephone & Telegraph Co. (AT&T), reversing its Dec. 23, 1971 vote to drop the probe. The investigation—part of a two-part probe authorized in 1965—was to examine AT&T cost estimates, on which the FCC was to base future rulings on interstate rates, and was to include management practices, investments, allocation of costs to different services and the prices and profits of Western Electric (AT&T's manufacturing subsidiary). The FCC, which had come under severe public pressure after its 1971 decision, said President Nixon's proposed fiscal 1973 budget (*see* BUDGET) provided for additional funds for the Common Carrier Bureau, which oversees AT&T,

enabling the probe to resume. Pressure on the FCC had included: a threat by Sen. Fred Harris (D, Okla.) to institute court action to force the FCC investigation; the scheduling of Senate Appropriations subcommittee hearings on the matter by Sen. John O. Pastore (D, R.I.); and petitions by the Defense Department and the governments of Chicago and Pennsylvania to resume the hearings. (The FCC Nov. 22 approved an estimated 2% rate increase for AT&T which would insure the company a revenue return of 8.5%-9% or $145 million a year in pretax profits. The increase was lower than AT&T's request, but higher than recommended by the FCC's staff report and its hearing examiner.)

U.S. sues aircraft makers. The Justice Department March 29 filed a civil suit in federal district court in New York charging the 20 major aircraft manufacturing companies and their trade association with suppressing competition in research and development. The suit charged that the companies, since 1928, had agreed to mutual licensing of patents, but had refused to buy patent rights from non-members of the Manufacturers Aircraft Association, Inc. The Department asked the court to dissolve the association and to prohibit the companies from entering into any patent agreement that would reduce competition in research. The companies named were manufacturers of airplane bodies and non-engine parts; engine manufacturers were not involved.

Xerox charged with monopoly. The FTC Dec. 12 accused the Xerox Corp. of illegally monopolizing the $1.7 billion office copier machine market by engaging in unfair marketing and patent practices and by preventing competition in the U.S. from foreign affiliates. Among the illegalities alleged by the FTC were Xerox's "lease only" policy which did not permit sale of office copier machines; its policy requiring exclusive maintenance and repair contracts; and its price discrimination among customers. In a proposed consent agreement, the FTC asked changes in 10 illegal patent practices and eight illegal sales practices. The company, which controlled 86% of the office copier machine market, would be required to: provide royalty-free licensing for all existing and pending patents and those obtained within the next 20 years; disclose to licensees all technology related to those patents; divest itself of a British subsidiary, Rank Xerox Ltd., and end the alleged practice of "false disparagement of competition"; and refrain from entering into new joint ventures with any manufacturer of office supplies or copiers.

See also CHILE [1, 7-9, 11-13]; CONSUMER AFFAIRS [5-6, 15]; ECONOMY [1, 3-6, 9-11]; ELECTIONS [33]; POLITICS [1-7]; RAILROADS; SOVIET-U.S. RELATIONS [1, 7-10, 12]

BUSING—*See* CIVIL RIGHTS [1-5, 7, 9, 12]; EDUCATION [2]; ELECTIONS [6, 16, 21, 23, 35, 44]; POLITICS [8]

BUTZ, EARL L.—*See* AGRICULTURE; NIXON, RICHARD MILHOUS; SOVIET-U.S. RELATIONS [8-9]; WELFARE

CABINET COMMITTEE ON INTERNATIONAL NARCOTICS CONTROL—*See* DRUG USE & ADDICTION [17-19]
CABLE TELEVISION (CATV)—*See* TELEVISION & RADIO [3]

CAMBODIA—Lon Nol assumes total power. The Cambodian government March 10 underwent a major revision as Lon Nol assumed supreme power as head of state, nullified the nearly completed republican constitution, dissolved the National Assembly and ousted his entire Cabinet—including Gen. Sisowath Sirik Matak, who had been serving as deputy premier since Lon Nol suffered a stroke in April 1971. Lon Nol's assumption of power had been preceded March 10 by the resignation of Cheng Heng as chief of state in the Sirik Matak government. In a broadcast to the nation the same day, Lon Nol explained that his actions against the proposed constitution and the Assembly had been taken because the special convention of former deputies drawing up the new charter had made alterations in the document since it had been approved by the Cabinet.

Lon Nol swore himself in as president March 14 and named Son Ngoc Thanh, a long-time nationalist leader, as premier March 18. At least five political leaders were said to have rejected offers to become premier before Thanh accepted Lon Nol's bid. A new 17-member Cabinet, reportedly provisional and subject to further change, was announced March 21. Eight ministers had been in the previous Cabinet and most of the others were well-known government officials. Thanh held the post of foreign minister. Two of Lon Nol's supporters—Maj. Gen. Sak Suthsakham and Maj. Gen. Thapana Nginn—held the key posts of defense and interior. The only member of the new government who had been associated with the opposition was Yem Sambaur, who was appointed chief justice. Sirik Matak, whose ouster from government had been demanded by protesting students for two weeks, was not appointed to the new regime. Despite his exclusion and announced retirement from public life, students of Pnompenh University and of the city's high schools, who accused Sirik Matak of corruption and of denying them free speech during his term in office, continued their protests and boycotted all classes.

Lon Nol elected. Lon Nol was elected June 4 to a full five-year term as president and swore himself into office July 3. Running against candidates In Tam, former chairman of the National Assembly, Keo An and Hou Mong, Lon Nol received slightly less than 55% of the vote. Lon Nol further consolidated his rule June 21 by announcing the formation of a new political organization—

48

the Nationalist Union Movement—with himself as its head. Political circles in Pnompenh expressed shock at the news and at the similarity of the new movement with the Sangkum—the political organization with which exiled former Chief of State Prince Norodom Sihanouk had effectively controlled political life from 1955 until his overthrow in 1970.

Thanh assassination attempt. Premier Thanh Aug. 21 escaped an assassination attempt which wounded three of his bodyguards. Thanh was riding to the Foreign Ministry in Pnompenh when an abandoned car at a roadside blew up. Two of three suspected assailants were captured by Thanh's security staff.

Food riots. Riots and looting of food stores broke out in Pnompenh Sept. 7-8 as the result of an acute shortage of rice. The shortage was officially attributed to the Communists' closure of all but one of the key roads leading into the capital *(see* INDOCHINA WAR [7]), but many city residents charged that it was the result of speculation by merchants, who were primarily Chinese. Following clashes between civilians and police-army forces Sept. 7, troops raided more than 100 stores and forced the owners to sell rice at new, lower prices announced earlier by the Commerce Ministry. (The ministry had said it was requisitioning all low-grade rice in the city and putting it on sale at less than half the current market price.) Troops joined civilians in rioting and looting Sept. 8. Gunfire was heard throughout the city, and a Chinese merchant was shot to death. Police did not interfere in any of the incidents.

Elections. The pro-government Social Republican party won all 32 seats in the upper house of the National Assembly in elections held Sept. 17. The Social Republicans reportedly won 96.19% of the vote, with the remainder going to the Popular Assembly party. Following the elections, Premier Thanh's Cabinet resigned Oct. 14. A new Cabinet, under the premiership of Social Republican Secretary-General Hang Thun Hak, was presented to the National Assembly Oct. 17. Several members of the outgoing Cabinet retained their posts. Among the changes in the new Cabinet were the appointment of Lon Nol's younger son, Col. Lon Non, as pacification minister, the appointment of Interior Minister Thappana Ngin as defense minister and the appointment of San Hor as interior minister.

Army scandal. The government said Dec. 27 that it had "at times" paid salaries to as many as 100,000 nonexistent soldiers because of corruption by military commanders and other "irregularities." It was estimated that the false pay rolls submitted by unit commanders had resulted in a loss of $2 million a month—virtually all of which came from U.S. aid.

See also DRAFT & WAR PROTEST; ELECTIONS [34]; FOREIGN AID; INDOCHINA WAR [1-7, 17, 44, 49]; SINO-U.S. RELATIONS [8]

CAMEROON—Unitary Cabinet established. President Ahmadou Ahidjo July 3 issued a decree establishing the first Cabinet of the United Republic of Cameroon. (A plebiscite in East and West Cameroon had resulted in the decision to establish a unitary state.) Vincent Efon was named foreign minister. Of the 19 other ministers and four vice ministers, eight were from the English-speaking former state of East Cameroon.

CAMPAIGN GM—*See* CONSUMER AFFAIRS [5]

CANADA—Cabinet shuffle. Prime Minister Trudeau Jan. 28 announced a major Cabinet shuffle in an apparent attempt to bolster the image of his Liberal party. Justice Minister John Turner was named finance minister to replace Edgar J. Benson, who would succeed Donald MacDonald as defense minister. MacDonald would replace J. J. Greene, who was retiring as energy minister for health reasons. Labor Minister Bryce Mackasey was appointed minister for manpower and immigration, replacing Otto Lang, who was appointed justice minister. Patrick Mahoney, the one new appointee to the Cabinet, was named minister of state without portfolio to replace Martin O'Connell, who became labor minister. Ronald Basford, consumer and corporate affairs minister, exchanged posts with Robert Andras, urban affairs minister. Public Works Minister Arthur Laing switched posts with Veterans Affairs Minister Jean-Eudes Dube. (The moves involving Benson, Basford and Mackasey—all three involved in controversial economic and labor policies—were seen as attempts to reduce friction between the government and the business community.)

[2] **Cuban office bombed.** Two plastic bombs exploded April 4 at the Cuban Trade Commission offices in Montreal, killing a Cuban security guard and badly damaging the building. Authorities arrested seven Cuban officials and charged six of them with interfering with a police investigation, but the charges were later dropped. Cuban Premier Fidel Castro alleged April 5 that Montreal police had used "brutal and fascist methods" in their handling of the incident and that the blast had been a "sad event" engineered by the U.S. Central Intelligence Agency (CIA). Acting Canadian External Affairs Minister C. M. Drury April 6 apologized to Cuba for the police intrusion into the commission's offices, which "enjoyed diplomatic immunity." An anonymous caller April 5 had said that the bombings had been carried out by a group called the Young Cubans "in the name of Alejandro Del Valle, who died in the [1961] Bay of Pigs invasion" of Cuba.

[3] **Nixon visit.** President Nixon concluded a two-day visit to Canada April 15 with the signing of an agreement pledging the two nations to joint efforts to combat pollution in the Great Lakes. The pact, known as the Great Lakes Water Quality Agreement, pledged that, by 1976, the amount of phosphorus dumped into the lakes would be reduced by about 50%. The U.S. was to spend approximately $3 billion on the project, and the Nixon Administration was to attempt to persuade industry to give up to about $1 billion of that sum. The remaining $2 billion, to be provided half by the federal government and half by state and local governments, was to come from funds already authorized. Canada's share of the cost would be nearly $500 million, all of it from government funds not yet appropriated. The agreement also specified the construction of municipal and industrial waste treatment facilities and the establishment of controls on thermal pollution, radioactive wastes, pesticide residues and storm-water discharges. The U.S.-Canadian International Joint Commission was to set up a Great Lakes Water Quality Board to insure compliance with the pact. (During his visit to Canada, Nixon April 14 also addressed the Canadian Parliament and held talks on Canadian-U.S. trade with Prime Minister Trudeau.)

[4] **Deficit budget presented.** Finance Minister John N. Turner May 8 presented to the House of Commons a budget for fiscal 1972-73 totaling $16.1 billion, an increase of $1.4 billion over the figure for the previous year. A $450 million deficit was expected. Turner said that the government's "first priority" was jobs in order to decrease unemployment. To stimulate growth of the economy, the budget reduced the general corporate tax rate for manufacturers and processors from an average 50% to 50%, effective Jan. 1, 1973. Firms would be allowed to write off the cost of machinery in two years. (The previous system had allowed companies to write off 20% of the costs of machinery each year on a diminishing basis.) Small businesses would be taxed at the rate of 20% of income instead of 25%. Foreign-owned small businesses would continue to be taxed at the rate applying to large corporations. The budget included increases in old age and veteran allowances. Persons over 65 could claim tax exemptions of $1,000 instead of $650. Exemptions of $50 a month could be claimed by students taking post-high school training courses.

[5] **Ontario sets Cabinet rules.** Ontario Premier William Davis Sept. 14 announced a code of rules limiting the financial holdings of members of his Progressive Conservative government. The action followed public debate over the financial interests of two Ontario ministers. (Attorney General Dalton Bales had offered to resign Aug. 9 after public disclosure that he and two partners had purchased land in the Markham Township which the government

would expropriate for development of a new city near the proposed site of an international airport. Davis had refused to accept the resignation, saying that the decision about the airport was made two years after Bales purchased the land. Financial and Intergovernmental Affairs Minister Darcy McKeough resigned Aug. 31 after it was revealed that he had approved the subdivision of land owned by a development company in which he had a business interest. His resignation was accepted by Davis "with great regret" Sept. 6.) The new code of rules would: require all ministers to publish a list of their land holdings and those of their immediate families; ban ministers from acquiring interest in a land development company or from conducting any business activity "on a day-to-day basis"; and oblige Cabinet officials either to sell their shares in public corporations or to put such shares in a "blind trust" for the duration of their term in office. In cases where a minister could benefit personally from a decision falling within the competence of his department, another minister would be appointed to handle the matter.

[6] Liberals lose majority. In the closest federal election in Canadian history, the Liberal government Oct. 30 emerged with 108 seats in the 264-seat House of Commons—one less than the opposition Progressive Conservatives. A Nov. 2 recount added one seat to the Liberal tally, and Prime Minister Trudeau that day announced his intention of remaining in power. Further recounts Nov. 6, 11 and 16 resulted in the net loss of two seats to the Conservatives. The amended totals: Liberals—109; Progressive Conservatives—107; New Democrats—31; Social Credit—15; Independents—2. When the Parliament was dissolved for the elections in September, Liberals held 147 seats and Conservatives 73. The New Democrats had held 25 seats, the Social Credit 13 and Independents 2. There had been four vacancies. Trudeau said Nov. 2 that he would "ask the governor general to call Parliament as soon as possible after the final results are in. The existence of my government will depend on Parliament." (Trudeau announced Nov. 16 that the House of Commons would be called into session Jan. 4, 1973.) Trudeau remarked that no single issue was responsible for his government's near-defeat and that it would be unfair to blame it on Liberal sponsorship of the Official Languages Act, which had ensured that French Canadians could use their language in conducting government and legal business and had required English-speaking Canadian civil servants to learn French as a condition of promotion. Opposition to the act was believed to have cost the Liberals votes in the western provinces. (The government announced Dec. 14 that it was delaying by three years its target dates for the achievement of bilingualism in the civil service.) Trudeau also announced that his government's new legislative proposals would include tax cuts, anti-inflation measures, a tightening of immigration laws and a revamping of unemployment insurance programs, which had cost considerably more than government estimates. The Oct. 30 elections were the first in Canada since June 1968. Trudeau had announced the elections Sept. 1, shortly after Parliament passed measures ending a dock strike (see [13]).

[7] New Trudeau Cabinet. Prime Minister Trudeau Nov. 27 revealed the composition of his new Cabinet. Of the 30 ministers (including Trudeau), eight were new appointees, 10 members changed portfolios and 12 remained in their old positions. The new ministers: Warren Allmand became solicitor general, replacing Jean-Pierre Goyer; Goyer was named minister of supply and services; Hugh Faulkner was appointed secretary of state, replacing Gerard Pelletier; Pelletier became minister for communications; Stanley Haidasz became minister of state without portfolio; Marc Lalonde a former private secretary and close friend of Trudeau, was appointed minister of health and welfare, succeeding John Munro, who took over the labor portfolio after the defeat of Labor Minister O'Connell in the election; Daniel MacDonald was named veterans affairs minister and Andre Ouellet became postmaster general, both filling posts vacated by men who had resigned earlier; Jeanne Sauve, the only woman in the Cabinet and the first in a Trudeau government, took over the science and technology portfolio from Alastair Gillespie; Gillespie was given the post of minister of industry, trade and commerce; Eugene Whelan replaced Horace Olson as agriculture minister; Consumer and Corporate Affairs Minister Andras replaced Manpower and Immigration Minister Mackasey, who was resigning; Andras was replaced as consumer and corporate affairs minister by Revenue Minister Herbert Gray; Gray's post was taken over by Robert Stanbury, who vacated the communications portfolio. James Richardson became minister for defense, replacing Benson, who had resigned earlier; Donald Jamieson moved from the Transport Ministry to the Department of Regional Economic Expansion, changing jobs with Jean Marchand.

Labor Developments

[8] Air controllers strike. Some 1,450 traffic controllers thoughout Canada went on strike Jan. 17-28, closing the country's airports, forcing the rerouting of hundreds of international flights that normally used Canadian airspace and resulting in airline losses of more than $1.5 million a day. Only 136 controllers remained on the job to handle emergency flights. The walkout began following the failure of the Canadian Air Traffic Control Association, representing the controllers, and government negotiators to reach agreement on a new wage contract. The controllers had originally asked for a 50% increase in a two-year contract. The unions and the government Jan. 22 reached a tentative settlement providing for a 17% pay increase and a reducton of the work week from 36 to 34.5 hours, but union members rejected the agreement Jan. 24. The strikers began returning to work Jan. 28-29 after leaders of the union and government negotiators agreed Jan. 27 to submit their contract differences to binding arbitration.

[9] Ontario services strikes. A coalition of the Confederation of National Trade Unions (CNTU), the Quebec Federation of Labor and the Quebec Teachers Corp., asking for a 8.3% increase in salaries for Quebec public service employees over a three-year period, carried out strikes in the province throughout the second quarter of 1972. A one-day strike March 28 closed some 5,000 schools and forced hospitals and government officials to operate at minimum efficiency. The strike followed rejection by Marcel Pepin, president of the CNTU, of a government offer of a 4.8% salary increase over three years. Members of the coalition April 11 began a general strike of unlimited duration after Quebec Civil Service Minister Jean-Paul L'Allier refused their demand that he negotiate for the government in wage talks with union leaders. The strike, involving some 200,000 teachers and civil servants and nearly 1.5 million schoolchildren, ended April 22 after the Quebec National Assembly April 20 approved emergency legislation ordering the strikers back to work. The legislation provided heavy fines for individuals who stayed away from work and for unions which did not get their men to return; it also ordered negotiations to continue until June 1 and public hearings to be held. If negotiations did not produce results, the government would impose a two-year contract, to take effect June 30, with an average pay increase of 5.3% and a 6% increase for those in the lowest-paid categories. The law also revoked the right of civil servants to strike.

[10] Public services strikes began again May 8 when Superior Court Justice Pierre Cote sentenced Pepin, Louis Laberge of the Quebec Federation of Labor and Yvon Charbonneau of the Quebec Teachers Corp. to a year in prison for contempt of court. (The three had urged workers to defy injunctions ordering the maintenance of essential services during the April strike.) The Canadian Labor Congress May 15 passed a resolution presented by Fernand Daoust, secretary general of the Quebec Federation of Labor, pledging that strikes and walkouts would continue in Quebec until the three union leaders were given an amnesty and the legislation ending the April strike was revoked. (Five judges of the Quebec Appeal Court Nov. 13 upheld the prison terms for the three labor leaders.) Workers in Montreal disrupted traffic May 11 by sprinkling nails on one of the bridges leading into the city. Canadian Broadcasting Company journalists in Quebec city held a one-day walkout May 12, and Montreal's six daily newspapers were shut down the same day. About 30,000 construction workers and 8,000 city blue-collar workers in Montreal stayed off the job May 15. Workers in Sept Iles May 10 blocked roads, jammed telephone lines and took over the local radio station. (Police regained control of the city May 11.) The series of strikes ended May 19 in what labor leaders called a show of "good faith." Talks between the government and the unions resumed June 6, with newly appointed Quebec Civil Service Minister Jean Cournoyer (who replaced L'Allier May 12) taking part in the talks. Cournoyer announced June 15 that he had obtained Cabinet authorization to postpone by four or five weeks the June 30 deadline by which the government would impose a contract. The Quebec National Assembly June 30 extended the deadline to Sept. 15 and limited until 1975 the suspension of the right to strike.

[11] Parliament ends Quebec port strike. In emergency legislation passed July 7 (after postponement of its summer recess), Parliament ordered an end to the seven-week strike by longshoremen at the St. Lawrence River ports of Montreal, Quebec City and Trois Rivieres. Dock workers, who reportedly were striking to protest their assignment to other than longshoreman duties, began returning to their jobs July 10; but industry spokesmen said the ports would not recover fully from effects of the walkout for at least six weeks. The legislation barred strikes, slowdowns or lockouts at the three ports until the end of 1974, during the life of a three-year collective agreement signed in March. The bill also provided for appointment of an arbitrator to modify terms of a job-security program in the March contract and empowered the labor minister to appoint arbitrators in contract disputes between longshoremen and their employers. The strike was estimated to cost the ports a total of $125 million in lost business as ships were diverted to other ports.

[12] *British Columbia dock strike ended.* The federal legislature Sept. 1 adopted emergency laws requiring 3,200 longshoremen in British Columbia to resume cargo-handling operations after their strike had curtailed foreign shipment of iron ore, forest products and wheat. The legislation demanded an immediate return to work and a continuation of the old contract, which had expired July 31, until Dec. 31 or until a new contract could be worked out. The bill banned lockouts during negotiations and provided that all benefits in a new contract would be retroactive. The strike had begun Aug. 7 when 1,800 dockworkers in Vancouver had walked off the job over a hiring issue apparently unrelated to negotiation of their contract. The men were joined Aug. 23 by another 1,400 workers at Victoria, New Westminster, Nanaimo, Prince Rupert and Port Alberni. They reportedly had been asking for an increase of 50¢ an hour on rates ranging from $5.05 to $5.30, as well as for an increase in fringe benefits.

[13] New job training program. Federal Manpower Minister Mackasey Sept. 27 announced that the government would implement a $40 million job training program Dec. 1. Mackasey said the government would pay 75% of direct wages during the first half of training and 50% during the second half. Mackasey also said that there would be closer ties between his department and the Unemployment Insurance Commission, with creation of a job information center where unemployed persons could obtain information from computerized job banks.

See also ATOMIC ENERGY [7, 13]; AVIATION; BASKETBALL [6]; CONSERVATION; CRIME [8]; DRUG USE & ADDICTION [1, 6, 18]; ENVIRONMENT; EUROPEAN SECURITY; HEALTH; HIJACKING [17]; HOCKEY; INDOCHINA WAR [52]; INTERNATIONAL MONETARY DEVELOPMENTS [2, 9]; LATIN AMERICA; SPACE [23]; STUDENT UNREST; TARIFFS & WORLD TRADE; TURKEY; VIETNAM, NORTH

CANAL ZONE—*See* DRUG USE & ADDICTION [11]
CANCER—*See* CONSUMER AFFAIRS [2, 4, 8]; DRUG USE & ADDICTION [8]; MEDICINE; PESTICIDES; SOVIET-U.S. RELATIONS [4]
CAPITAL PUNISHMENT—*See* CRIME [10-11]; ELECTIONS [44]
CARIBBEAN COUNTRIES—*See* JAMAICA; POLITICS [8]; TERRITORIAL WATERS
CASTRO, FIDEL—*See* CANADA [2]; CHILE [4]; CUBA; ELECTIONS [20]; POLITICS [9]
CATHOLIC CHURCH—*See* ROMAN CATHOLIC CHURCH
CENSORSHIP—*See* ARGENTINA [18]; BRAZIL; KOREA, SOUTH; PERU; PHILIPPINES [5-6, 9]; PORTUGAL; URUGUAY [4-6]
CENSUS, U.S.—*See* ECONOMY [2]; NEGROES; POPULATION

CENTRAL AFRICAN REPUBLIC—Bokassa named president for life. Gen. Jean-Bedel Bokassa was named President for Life Feb. 22 by a meeting of the country's only political party, the Movement for Social Evolution in Black Africa (MESAN).

Campaign against theft. The government July 29 published a decree prescribing that a thief's ear be cut off after a first offense, his other ear after a second, his right hand after a third and that he be publicly executed after a fourth. In reaction to the apparent ineffectiveness of the decree, President Bokassa led soldiers July 31 into the prison at Bangui (the capital) and supervised the beating of 46 inmates. Four of the men later died, and the surviving 42 were placed on public display Aug. 1. Bokassa said July 31 that such beatings would continue every Saturday until there was "no more theft" in the country.

See also BURUNDI

CENTRAL INTELLIGENCE AGENCY (CIA)—*See* CANADA [2]; CHILE [11]; DRUG USE & ADDICTION [13, 17]; INDIA [8]; INDOCHINA WAR [23]; OLYMPIC TERRORISM; POLITICS [9]; VIETNAM, SOUTH
CERRO CORP.—*See* CHILE [1, 9]

CEYLON—Republic proclaimed. Ceylon became the independent Socialist republic of Sri Lanka (great and beautiful island) May 22 under a new constitution adopted by a 120-6 vote of the constituent assembly. Ceremonies breaking the island's 157-year link with the British crown and renaming the country were held in Colombo. The first premier of Sri Lanka, Mrs. Sirimavo Bandaranaike (the last premier of Ceylon), took the oath of office and nominated William Gopallawa (the last governor-general, the local representative of the British queen) as the first president. The new republic was to remain a member of the British Commonwealth.

The charter establishing Sri Lanka had been approved after 22 months of deliberation. The opposition right-wing United National party, led by J. R. Jayewardene and former Prime Minister Dudley Senanayake, cast the only votes against the constitution. Senanayake said his party adopted the principle of adopting a resolution to establish a republic but contended that the charter had been formulated in haste. The Tamil Federal party, representing the largest minority in Ceylon, had boycotted the constituent assembly meeting to protest the charter's failure to recognize Tamil as an official language in addition to Sinhalese. (Residents of the Tamil-speaking Northern and Eastern Provinces staged a one-day strike Oct. 8 to protest the charter.)

Land reform. The National Assembly, according to a report Aug. 19, approved a land reform program limiting individual land holdings to 50 acres. The measure, which exempted foreign-owned tea and rubber plantations, would put nearly 400,000 acres under government control.

See also INTERNATIONAL MONETARY DEVELOPMENTS [8]; MIDDLE EAST [18]

CHAFEE, JOHN H.—*See* MILITARY [2]

CHEMICAL & BIOLOGICAL WARFARE—Germ treaty signed. More than 70 nations April 10 signed a treaty prohibiting the development, production, stockpiling or other acquisition or retention of biological weapons and pledging the nations "to destroy or divert to peaceful purposes" such weapons "as soon as possible but not later than nine months" after the treaty came into force. The treaty, which had been worked out in 1971 by the United Nations Conference of the Committee on Disarmament and approved by the General Assembly, was signed in ceremonies in Washington, London and Moscow. The treaty was to go into effect when it had been signed by 22 nations, including the three host nations—the U.S., the Soviet Union and Great Britain. The treaty included a pledge that signatory nations would negotiate for a ban on chemical weapons.

See also DISARMAMENT; POLLUTION [13]; SOVIET-U.S. RELATIONS [6]

CHEMISTRY—*See* NOBEL PRIZES

CHESS—Fischer wins world championship. Bobby Fischer of the United States became the world chess champion Sept. 1 when defending champion Boris Spassky of the Soviet Union conceded defeat in the 21st game of their scheduled 24-game match in Reykjavik, Iceland. Spassky delivered his resignation by telephone to referee Lothar Schmid. His resignation gave Fischer the 12½ points he needed to become the first American to win the title, which had been in the hands of Soviet grandmasters without interruption since 1948. Fischer fashioned his victory with seven wins (one point each) and 11 draws (½ point each). Spassky finished with 8½ points. For his victory, Fischer picked up $156,000 of the $250,000 purse.

The play, game-by-game: **game 1** (July 11) to Spassky after Fischer conceded on the 56th move and after a 35-minute walkout by Fischer to protest the presence of cameras; **game 2** (July 13) to Spassky by forfeit after Fischer failed to appear in continued protest over the presence of film and television equipment; **game 3** (July 17) to Fischer on the 41st move; **game 4** (July 18), a draw after five hours of play and 45 moves; **game 5** (July 20) to Fischer after a blunder by Spassky forced him to concede after only 27 moves; **game 6** (July 23) to Fischer on the 41st move; **game 7** (July 26), a draw after 49 moves; **game 8** (July 27) to Fischer after the 37th move; **game 9** (Aug. 1), a draw after 27 moves; **game 10** (Aug. 4), to Fischer on the 56th move; **game 11** (Aug. 6), to Spassky on the 31st move, after Spassky trapped Fischer's queen on the 24th move; **game 12** (Aug. 9), a draw after 55 moves; **game 13** (Aug. 11), to Fischer after 74 moves; **game 14** (Aug. 15), a draw after a blunder by Spassky lost him the lead in a game which most experts had conceded to him; **game 15** (Aug. 18), a draw after 43 moves; **game 16** (Aug. 21), a draw after 60 moves; **game 17** (Aug. 23), a draw on Fischer's request under a rule specifying that a game was drawn "at the request of one of the players when the same position appears three times, and each time the same player has had the move"; **game 18** (Aug. 25), a draw after 47 moves; **game 19** (Aug. 27), a draw after 40 moves; **game 20** (Aug. 30), a draw after 54 moves; **game 21** (Sept. 1) to Fischer after Spassky resigned without resuming play in a game adjourned Aug. 31 after 40 moves.

The match almost failed to begin because of Fischer's pre-game maneuvering. Spassky had arrived in Reykjavik at the end of June to prepare for the opening game scheduled to begin July 2. However, Fischer remained in New York until July 3, arguing over the size of the purse involved. After seeking and obtaining a two-day postponement of the opening game, Fischer flew to Reykjavik following an offer of $125,000 by London investment banker James D. Slater to double the size of the purse. It was Spassky's turn to protest July 3 when Fischer sent a second to represent him at a meeting to draw lots for the right to the white pieces and the first move in the first game. Spassky charged that Fischer had personally insulted him and the Soviet Chess Federation. He demanded a written apology from Fischer and insisted that Fischer be "punished." Fischer submitted the apology July 5. Dr. Max Euwe, president of the International Chess Federation, consented to another Soviet demand and admitted that he had erred in granting Fischer the two-day postponement.

Even after the tournament began, it was plagued by complaints by the players. Fischer repeatedly protested the presence of cameras during the opening games and succeeded in having them removed. During the final games, Fischer protested the noise being made by observers and said Aug. 16 that he would "demand" that the match be moved to a private room unless playing conditions were improved. Spassky's second, Efrim Geller, charged Aug. 22 that the Americans might be using "electronic devices and chemical substances" to weaken Spassky's playing ability. A thorough examination of the playing area revealed nothing unusual.

Soviets retain title. The Soviet Union won its 11th consecutive world Chess Olympics championship Oct. 13 in Skoplje, Yugoslavia, scoring a 1½-point victory over Hungary. The Soviet winning streak had begun in 1952 and had continued every two years to the 1972 competition. The Soviets finished with 42 points. Hungary was second with 40½, Yugoslavia third with 38 and Czechoslovakia fourth with 35½. The U.S., playing without Fischer and other top players, finished in a tie with the Netherlands for eight place.

CHIANG KAI-SHEK—*See* CHINA, NATIONALIST; SINO-U.S. RELATIONS [5]; UNITED NATIONS
CHICAGO PLAN—*See* CIVIL RIGHTS [19]
CHICAGO 7—*See* CIVIL DISORDERS

CHILE—The Chilean government was plagued during 1972 by serious economic difficulties, a nationwide strike in October (*see* [19-22]) and opposition political strength within the Congress and on the universities (*see* [14]). Economic troubles caused the government in February to end its subsidy of basic foodstuffs and thus raise prices drastically (*see* [6]). There were widespread protests against food shortages within the country (*see* [18]). Chile's economic problems were also international in scope, necessitating an agreement, signed in April, to refinance part of the country's foreign debt (*see* [13]). Opposition to the Socialist government of President Salvador Allende Gossens within the Congress resulted in the impeachment of two government ministers (*see* [2, 4]) and in the passage of amendments restricting Allende's efforts to give Chile a Socialist economy (*see* [10]). However, the restrictive amendments were vetoed by Allende. The government's difficulties resulted in three resignations by the Cabinet and the formation of new Cabinets (*see* [2-3, 5]). In other developments, the government reached agreement with the Cerro Corp. for compensation on the nationalization of its copper interests in Chile (*see* [9]), but failed to reach similar agreements with Kennecott Copper Corp. or the Anaconda Co. (*see* [7-8]). Relations between Chile and the United States were adversely affected during March by the revelation that International Telephone & Telegraph Corp. had exerted pressure on the U.S. government to subvert the Allende government.

[2] Cabinet changes. The entire Chilean Cabinet resigned three times in 1972 to give President Allende a chance to form a new government. The first mass resignation came Jan. 20 after the defeat of candidates of the government's Popular Unity coalition (UP) in two by-elections. A new Cabinet was formed Jan. 28 in changes which affected six of the 15 posts. Jose Toha Gonzalez, who had been suspended as interior minister Jan. 6, was named defense minister. (Toha had been impeached by the Senate Jan. 22 for failure to oppose left-wing extremist groups and for violating the right of Chileans to protest peacefully.) The new interior minister was Hernan del Canto, secretary general of the Central Labor Union. Orlando Cantuarias moved from the Ministry of Mining to the Ministry of Housing. Alejandro Rios Valdivia, a former defense minister until his appointment Jan. 7 to replace Toha as interior minister, became minister of education. Manuel Sanhueza became justice minister (replaced April 7 by Jorge Tapia), and Mauricio Yungk Stahl became minister of mining (replaced April 7 by Gen. Pedro Palacios Cameron). In another Cabinet change,

Labor Minister Jose Oyarce resigned May 9 to take up "important duties" in the central committee of the Chilean Communist party.

[3] *2nd resignation.* The entire Cabinet resigned again June 12 to facilitate a change in the government's economic policies. President Allende formed a new government June 17, replacing six Cabinet officials. Controversial Economy Minister Pedro Vuskovic, a member of Allende's Socialist party, was replaced by Carlos Matus Romo, also a Socialist but reportedly more pragmatic and less of a Marxist ideologue than Vuskovic. (Vuskovic remained in the government as director of the Executive Economic Committee—a new presidential unit to coordinate economic programs—and as vice president of the State Development Corp.) In other changes June 12: Labor Minister Oyarce was replaced by Mireya Baltra; Finance Minister Americo Zorrilla was replaced by Orlando Millas; Education Minister Valdivia was replaced by Anibal Palma; Housing Minister Cantuarias was replaced by Luis Matte; and Mining Minister Palacios was replaced by Jorge Arrate.

[4] *Del Canto suspended, impeached.* Interior Minister del Canto was suspended by the opposition-controlled Chamber of Deputies July 5 and censured and dismissed by the Senate July 27. Del Canto was charged with refusal to order the arrest and prosecution of leftist agitators who had seized private farms and factories to force an acceleration of President Allende's Socialist program and with allowing the entry of 18 mysterious packages from Cuba without proper customs checks. (The opposition had charged that the packages, which were taken from a Cuban plane to a secret destination by plainclothes policemen, might contain illegal arms. The government maintained that they contained only gifts for Allende from Cuban Premier Fidel Castro. The Santiago customs administrator ruled Sept. 1 that del Canto was not guilty of smuggling in regard to the Cuban packages.) Foreign Minister Clodomiro Almeyda assumed del Canto's duties until Aug. 2, when Jaime Suarez Bastidas was named to replace del Canto. Del Canto assumed Suarez's post as secretary general of the Cabinet.

[5] *3rd resignation.* The Cabinet resigned again Oct. 31 to give President Allende a freer hand in resolving a strike crisis *(see* [18-21]). The resignations followed a move Oct. 31 by the five opposition parties to impeach Interior Minister Suarez, Economy Minister Matus, Agriculture Minister Jacques Chonchol and Education Minister Palma for "repeated violations of the constitution and the law." (The opposition parties Nov. 8 dropped their charges against the ministers.) Allende named a new Cabinet Nov. 2. The new Cabinet: foreign affairs—Almeyda; interior—Gen. Carlos Prats Gonzalez; economy—Fernando Flores Labra (switched to finance minister Dec. 29); finance—Millas (switched to economy minister Dec. 29 after being censured and suspended as finance minister by the Chamber of Deputies); education—Tapia; justice—Sergio Izunza Barrios; public works and transportation—Rear Adm. Ismael Huerta Diaz; agriculture—Pedro Calderon Aranguiz; land and colonization—Humberto Martones; labor—Luis Figueroa; public health (temporary)—Juan Carlos Concha Gutierrez; mining—Gen. Claudio Sepulveda Donoso; housing (temporary)—Matte; defense—Toha; Cabinet secretary general (temporary)—del Canto. The new Cabinet retained a left-wing orientation, with a majority of ministers from the Communist, Socialist and Radical parties. The appointment of military officers was seen as a way of placating anti-Marxists, at least until March 1973 congressional elections.

[6] **Price increases.** In a sharp reversal of economic policy, the government decided Feb. 1 to end its subsidy of basic foodstuffs and to raise prices. Affected were costs of such items as bread, milk, sugar, oil and tea—which rose by an average of 25%-30%—and public transportation—which rose by 60%. To offset the price increases, the government announced plans to order employers to pay a differential of about $4.10 a month to each family, varying with the number of children. (Many Chileans felt the bonus would barely cover the increase in bus fare for a family of four.) The government Aug. 18

announced another increase in food prices. Apart from chick peas, which rose by only 3.87%, food prices rose by 36%-117%. The government simultaneously announced that wages and salaries would increase by 100% from the beginning of October and that everyone would receive an unprecedented $23.90 bonus for Sept. 18 independence celebrations.

[7] Kennecott sues Chile. The Kennecott Copper Corp. announced Feb. 4 that it had brought two suits against Chile on 111 notes held by the corporation on the El Teniente Mine, expropriated by Chile in 1971. The suits, which sought payment of a $5.7 million first installment on the notes, was filed by the Braden Copper Co., a Kennecott subsidiary, in the U.S. District Court for the Southern District of New York. The payment of the first installment had been suspended by President Allende Dec. 30, 1971, two days before it was due. In response to the suits, the court Feb. 18 blocked the U.S. bank accounts of nine Chilean agencies. Faced with the blocking of the accounts, Allende announced Feb. 25 that Chile would pay $84,618,000 to Braden. (Allende said $8,125,000 of the debt had been deducted because that much of the original sum had not been "usefully" invested.) Braden received the first installment March 31, and a U.S. federal judge vacated attachments on the Chilean accounts in the U.S. In a related development, a special Chilean copper tribunal ruled Aug. 11 that the Chilean government could bill Kennecott and the Anaconda Co. (whose major Chilean copper properties had also been assumed by the government—*see below* **[8]**) for repayment of $774 million in "excess profits" from mining operations since 1955. The tribunal ruled 4-1 against appeals by the two companies that Chilean law at the time of the operations did not set a ceiling on profits. The decision set a legal precedent for denying the companies further compensation for the takeover of their Chilean copper properties. The tribunal refused to review its ruling; and, in response, Kennecott announced Sept. 7 that it was withdrawing from further legal proceedings in Chile and would "pursue in other nations its remedies for the confiscated assets." Kennecott refused to specify the "remedies" it planned to pursue in other nations. (Kennecott Oct. 4 succeeded in having a French civil court suspend $1.3 million in payments for a 1,250-ton shipment of copper from Chile. The freeze was granted on Kennecott's charges that it had not been compensated for the nationalization of its properties. In response to the ruling, the shipment, on its way to France, was rerouted to avoid confiscation by Kennecott, but finally was unloaded in Le Havre Oct. 23 and turned over to its French purchasers. A Paris civil court Nov. 28 released the payment, but ordered Chile to deposit an equal amount in escrow pending settlement of its dispute with Kennecott.).

[8] *Anaconda developments.* The New York State Supreme Court Feb. 29 blocked the New York bank accounts of the Chilean State Copper Corp. (CODELCO) and the State Development Corp. (CORFO) in response to a suit against the agencies by Anaconda. Anaconda was demanding $11.8 million in unpaid interest on promissory notes issued by Chile in 1969 as security for the purchase of 51% of Anaconda's Chilean copper properties. In response to the court action, Chile March 1 suspended a shipment of copper consigned to Anaconda and announced that it would not honor the $203 million in notes held by the company. The government retaliated further March 9 by blocking the remaining Chilean real estate and bank accounts of both Anaconda and Kennecott. The copper tribunal July 7 reportedly approved a government request to suspend payment on the notes on grounds that Anaconda had made "excess profits" in the country *(see also* **[7]**).

[9] *Cerro compensation set.* Chile's special copper tribunal Dec. 1 set compensation to the U.S.-based Cerro Corp., for nationalization of its copper properties, at $34,544,000. The amount, to be owed by Chile as of Dec. 31, included $13,254,000 for Cerro's 70% equity in the Andean Mining Co., plus $24,300,000 in notes and interest. Cerro was exempted from any charges for excess profits because its Rio Blanco mine was a new property that had not begun operations when Allende took office. The mine project had been carried out with government cooperation since its inception under a previous government, and Chile's relations with Cerro had remained friendly. Cerro had continued to aid Chile in operating the Rio Blanco mine after its nationalization.

[10] Anti-Socialist bill. Congress Feb. 19 passed a series of amendments which would restrict the efforts of President Allende to give Chile a Socialist economy. The measures, passed by a vote of 100-33, prohibited the government from fully or partially expropriating any enterprise without specific authorization by Congress, retroactive to Oct. 14, 1971. Allende March 21 suspended sessions of the Senate and the Chamber of Deputies for a week to gain time for negotiations with the opposition Christian-Democratic party (DC) on a compromise on the anti-expropriation legislation. The move effectively postponed the March 22 deadline by which Allende would have been forced to submit planned vetoes of the measures. The negotiations failed to reach a compromise, however; and Allende vetoed the measures April 6. (In a protest against certain ideas expressed in the veto, the moderate Radical Left party withdrew from the UP April 6. The move was a blow to the government, since the PIR was important among Chile's influential middle classes, which Allende sought to attract to his program.)

[11] ITT and U.S. policy. Syndicated columnist Jack Anderson March 20-21 revealed material purporting an effort by International Telephone & Telegraph Corp. (ITT) to influence U.S. policy in Chile, where the conglomerate had six affiliates, and to have the U.S. take a stronger stance, protective to U.S. corporate interests, in Latin America in general. Anderson March 22 released to the news media the allegedly private ITT documents which comprised the basis for his disclosures. According to Anderson, the documents revealed ITT efforts and "fervent hopes for a military coup" in Chile and the "generally polite but cool reception" it got from the White House and the State Department. A "more friendly" reception was attributed to the Central Intelligence Agency's (CIA) William V. Broe, who was reported to have visited ITT Vice President E. J. Gerrity Jr. to "urge ITT to join in a scheme to plunge the Chilean economy into chaos and thus bring about a military uprising that would keep Allende out of power." The Anderson documents also revealed that ITT had received a report from its representatives in Santiago that the State Department had given a "green light" to U.S. Ambassador to Chile Edward M. Korry "for maximum authority to do all possible, short of a Dominican Republic-type action" (a reference to U.S. military intervention), to "keep Allende from taking power." In a later development, a letter and "action" memorandum from ITT to the White House, submitted Oct. 1, 1971 (two days after Chile placed the ITT-controlled Chilean Telephone Co. under provisional state supervision), was revealed July 3. The documents contained an 18-point plan to assure that the Allende government would not "get through the crucial next six months." In the documents, ITT called for extensive economic warfare against Chile to be directed by a special White House task force, assisted by the CIA. ITT further recommended subversion of the Chilean armed forces, consultations with foreign governments on ways to put pressure on Allende, and diplomatic sabotage. ITT proposed putting an "economic squeeze" on Chile through denial of international credit, a ban on imports of Chilean products and a similar ban on vital exports to Chile. The company suggested that the CIA would help in the squeeze and urged a deliberate interruption of fuel supplies to the Chilean air force and navy. The measures, ITT held, should cause sufficient "economic chaos" to convince the armed forces to "step in and restore order."

[12] *ITT seizure bill submitted.* President Allende May 12 sent to Congress a bill that would nationalize the Chilean Telephone Co. The bill, approved by the Chilean Senate July 7, did not provide for expropriation of ITT's other properties in Chile. ITT properties had been the subject of purchase talks between Chile and ITT that had begun in 1971. The talks had been stalemated April 10 when ITT rejected a series of Chilean proposals.)

[13] **Credit pact signed.** Chile and 11 creditor nations, including the U.S., reached an agreement in Paris April 20 for the refinancing of an estimated $600 million of Chile's $3.7 billion foreign debt. The agreement obligated Chile to remit by 1975 only 30% of the debt and interest payments falling due from November 1971 through December 1973. After that, Chile would have six years to repay those debts in full. The creditors also agreed to study "with good-will" the refinancing of all Chilean debts due in 1973. The Chilean government had asked for a three-year moratorium on all payments and had insisted that the subject of compensation for nationalized U.S. copper intersts *(see* [7-9]) not be a factor in the negotiations. However, at the insistence of the U.S., Chile accepted "the principles of payment of a just compensation for all nationalizations in conformity with Chilean law and international law." The clause would presumably protect U.S. copper interests and ITT. Chile also reached agreement with a group of U.S. banks Feb. 9 for refinancing $300 million of its foreign debt. Agreement was reached between Chile and a group of 28 U.S. banks June 12 on refinancing $160 million in foreign debts.

[14] **Opposition wins university vote.** The ruling UP suffered a setback April 27 as opposition candidates won control of the University of Chile. In balloting for rector, CD candidate Edgardo Boeninger, who had resigned as rector in January in a dispute between Marxist and anti-Marxist forces over control of the university, won with 51.8% of the vote. UP candidate Felipe Herrara, a close associate of President Allende, received 43.8% of the vote; Revolutionary Left Movement (MIR) candidate Andres Pascal Allende, a nephew of the president, received 3.4%; and Revolutionary Communist party (PCR) candidate Luis Vitale received less than 1%. Anti-Marxist candidates also won a slim majority in the 100-member university council, which had been controlled by UP sympathizers. Chile was so bitterly divided between supporters and opponents of the government that the university vote had taken on the importance of a national plebiscite. (Balloting had been weighted so that faculty votes counted 65% of the total, student votes 25% and employee ballots 10%.) Opposition candidates also won elections of state university branches in Concepcion, Chillan and Los Angeles.

[15] **Copper strikes.** A 48-hour strike by 8,000 workers at the Chuquicamata copper mine, Chile's largest, ended May 6 after the government made concessions on bonuses, work regulations and promotions. The strike had been voted by a workers' assembly May 3 in support of five worker representatives on an 11-member management council which ran the mine, mill and smelter operations. The representatives had protested that, because they were outnumbered on the committee, they were given too little say in running the mine. The strike cost $1.5 million in lost production, apart from the additional costs involved in the concessions to worker demands. In a related development, more than 3,000 workers May 18 staged a work stoppage at the El Teniente copper mine to protest allegedly poor transportation between the mine and nearby housing projects.

[16] **Economic plan set.** President Allende July 24 announced a new government plan to combat inflation and accelerate national development. Under the program, the government would invest more than $760 million in industrial and farm production over the following two years. (Most of the money would come from Communist countries which already had pledged, according to Allende, $400 million in credits.) The plan also provided tax increases for the wealthy and the middle classes, compulsory insurance on virtually everything from life to private automobiles and further price controls to force the nationalization of 91 large industries left in private hands. Allende said the controls would permit government-administered industries to become self-financing, give small and medium private enterprises a "reasonable" profit and give big industries "strictly enough to operate."

[17] Top police officials dismissed. President Allende Aug. 6 dismissed civil police chief Eduardo Paredes and subchief Carlos Toro in response to protests from most political sectors over a bloody police raid on a Santiago shantytown Aug. 5. The raid had been conducted by more than 100 policemen searching for members of the extremist July 16th National Liberation Movement. Residents of an encampment known as Assault on Moncada Barracks, which reportedly had been organized by the MIR, attempted to prevent a house-to-house search; and a battle ensued in which one person was killed, 60 injured and 160 arrested. The incident reportedly caused a political crisis, stirred initially by angry editorials in opposition newspapers and aggravated by hostile communications from the MIR. The MIR claimed that the government's "reformist sectors" (implicitly the Communist party) were responsible for the violence.

[18] Food shortage protests. President Allende Aug. 21 declared a state of emergency in Santiago province after violent protests against Chile's acute food shortage erupted out of a one-day strike that day by most of the capital's shopkeepers. The shopkeepers were complaining that inflation, the scarcity of goods, price controls and other official restrictions were squeezing retailers out of business. The government had declared the strike illegal. Santiago housewives staged a pot-banging demonstration Aug. 21, while police riot squads clashed with anti-Marxist demonstrators. About 160 young demonstrators were arrested after police used tear gas and clubs to break up groups shouting slogans against the Allende administration. Clashes spread to residential areas by nightfall, with demonstrations outside the homes of four government officials. Santiago was reported calm Aug. 22—as most shops reopened and government troops and police returned to their barracks—but street fighting again broke out Aug. 29-Sept. 1 in Santiago and Concepcion. The state of emergency in Santiago, lifted Aug. 28, was not reimposed; but Concepcion was placed under army control Aug. 31. Thousands of pro-Marxist youths battled government opponents in Concepcion Aug. 30 after each group held illegal demonstrations. Police using water hoses and tear gas broke up the fighting, but one policeman was killed and two policemen and seven civilians injured in the action. In Santiago, high school students from the Marxist-controlled Chilean Students Federation and the anti-government Federation of Secondary Students battled each other and police Aug. 29-Sept. 1. The opposition students claimed Education Minister Palma was not working to solve student problems, and protested the appointment of a government supporter as principal of a Santiago girls' high school. Roving gangs of students fought in the streets of Santiago the night of Sept. 1, often eluding riot police. Anti-Marxist students set bonfires, blocking intersections; and housewives, angered by food shortages, shouted encouragement from apartment houses. Police reportedly re-established order after arresting 154 persons. (Defense Minister Toha Dec. 12 announced a series of government measures to combat the scarcity of essential goods. The measures included proposed legislation providing severe punishment for black marketeers and monopolists, and establishment of a special commission to improve systems of distribution and commerce.)

[19] Nationwide strikes bring crisis. One of the worst series of strikes in Chilean history began Oct. 10 when the Confederation of Truck Owners called a nationwide strike to demand higher rates and to protest the establishment of a state trucking agency in the southern province of Aysen. The government immediately termed the strike "seditious" and arrested 159 persons, including four national leaders of the confederation. The strike spread Oct. 11, and a state of emergency was declared that day in the central agrarian provinces of Curico and Talca. Eleven more of Chile's 25 provinces, including Santiago, were placed under military control Oct. 12 as filling stations began to run out of gasoline and bakeries closed for lack of flour. The government requisitioned all trucks belonging to striking enterprises and assumed control of distribution of fuel in Santiago. Most of Chile's shopkeepers and small businessmen joined the strike Oct. 13. Organizations of taxi drivers, construction workers and independent farmers also called on their members to join the protest. The government took control of all radio stations "until further notice," stifling most opposition opinion about measures being taken against the strike. About 1,000 striking truck drivers were reported arrested Oct. 13. In an effort to end the strike Oct. 14, President Allende offered truck owners and drivers a number of concessions, including release of all imprisoned strikers; but strike leaders reportedly refused to end their walkout until plans for the Aysen trucking agency were dropped. Four more provinces were placed under a state of emergency, but many private radio stations were returned to their owners. Many Santiago shops were reported open, and a government directive authorized official takeover of any that remained closed. The anti-Marxist opposition parties expressed support for the strikes Oct. 15 after the government threatened to requisition all stores that refused to open for business.

[20]   Violence erupted Oct. 16 as the government resorted to force against striking shopkeepers. Riot police, using tear gas and a water cannon, broke up anti-Marxist demonstrations and broke locks on stores in downtown Santiago, forcing them open. Pro- and anti-government youths clashed in rock-throwing street battles in the center of the city, and the government again took control of all radio stations as 7,000 engineers announced their support for the strikers. (Chile's controller general Oct. 21 declared the government takeover of the stations illegal, and the government Oct. 27 relinquished control of all private stations.) Physicians, merchant marine captains, private school students and many bank employees joined the walkouts Oct. 17. Riot police attempted that day to force open more stores in Santiago, but reportedly were beaten back by rock-throwing demonstrators. The main rail line between Santiago and the port of Valparaiso was bombed, and at least two trucks carrying supplies to the capital were fired upon. President Allende Oct. 17 prevented widening of the strike by reaching an agreement with bus owners who had threatened to join the action. (Allende pledged to keep transportation in the private sector.) Two more provinces were placed under military control Oct. 18. In a further move against the strike, the government Oct. 18 requisitioned the last large wholesale distribution company in private hands.

[21]   The crisis worsened Oct. 20 when bus service was cut off after union members voted a 24-hour strike despite Allende's concessions to the bus owners. The 180 pilots of the government airline LAN also joined the strike. Two more provinces were placed under military control Oct. 20. Army commanders Oct. 21 banned the sale of gasoline to private consumers for two days as a result of delays in deliveries. Striking bank employees announced Oct. 22 that they would return to work, but warned that they would resume their stoppage if any reprisals were taken against them. The striking LAN pilots returned to work the same day, following a military takeover of the airline. Opposition leaders called for a "day of silence" protest Oct. 24, but the protest was only partially successful. President Allende and the striking truck owners reportedly reached agreement Oct. 25 on settling the truck strike; but Allende Oct. 28 broke off negotiations with the owners and dissolved the truckers' union, charging the strike leaders had made "unacceptable" political demands which would mean "the limitation of presidential powers."

[22]   *Strikes end.* The strikes ended Nov. 5 after Allende revised his Cabinet (see [5]), and new Interior Minister Prats negotiated a settlement with strike leaders. Prats, former commander in chief of the army, reached the agreement after threatening strike leaders with "severe action." The government acceded to a number of the strikers' "strictly labor" demands, but ignored others which it termed "political," including a reported demand for a plebiscite on Allende's economic policies. The government also agreed to continue negotiations with labor leaders on a series of specific grievances. Terms of the settlement included: immediate abandonment by the government of all legal actions and

sanctions against striking unions; no reprisals by the government against strikers or strike leaders; no reprisals by striking employers against employees who worked or attempted to work during the strikes; full pay for those laid off by the strikes; removal of a wholesale distributing firm, owned by small businessmen and industrialists, from the list of firms to be nationalized; a new pledge not to nationalize trucking; return of private businesses and property taken over or requisitioned by the government during the strikes; and enactment of legislation to protect small businessmen, artisans and industrialists. In announcing the settlement, Prats also announced the return to civilian officials of the 21 provinces placed under a state of emergency. The strike had cost the country an estimated $200 million.

See also ARGENTINA [3, 12]; ATOMIC ENERGY [13]; BOLIVIA; CONSERVATION; DRUG USE & ADDICTION [16]; FOREIGN POLICY; LATIN AMERICA; MEXICO; TERRITORIAL WATERS

CHINA, COMMUNIST (PEOPLE'S REPUBLIC OF CHINA)—1971 economic gains. An increase of "about 10%" in China's industrial and agricultural output was announced Jan. 1. Measured against 1970 figures, the following major gains were reported: steel production 18%; grain output 2.5%; pig iron 23%; crude oil 27.2%; coal "over 8%."

Government changes. Chi Peng-fei, acting foreign minister since early 1971, was appointed foreign minister following the death of Foreign Minister Chen Yi Jan. 6. (The Foreign Ministry was expanded May 15 in order to cope with China's expanded international affairs. Five new deputy foreign ministers and two assistant foreign ministers were appointed.) In another government change, it was announced Feb. 24 that Tung Pi-wu had been named acting chief of state, filling the vacancy created by the ouster of Liu Shao-chi. Tung had served as one of the two deputy chiefs of state and was a member of the Communist party's Central Committee. The appointment of Li Chen as minister of public security, Chang Wen-pi as minister of water conservation and power and Yu Chieu-li as director of the state planning commission (ministerial rank) was disclosed Oct. 21. All three ministers had military backgrounds, increasing the ratio of military men to civilians in the government. Key vacancies in the State Council (cabinet) existing since the Cultural Revolution purge included defense, finance, commerce and public health.

Territory claimed. China officially claimed the British Crown colony of Hong Kong and the Portuguese colony of Macao in a letter filed with the United Nations Committee on Decolonization, which was made public March 10. Huang Hua, China's chief delegate to the U.N., who had submitted the letter, said that the U.N. had no right to discuss the question of Hong Kong and Macao, which he called "part of the Chinese territory, occupied by the British and Portuguese authorities." He said that the two islands "belong to the category of questions resulting from...unequal treaties...which the imperialists imposed on China." At a meeting March 3 of the U.N. General Assembly's Committee on Peaceful Uses of the Seabed, China also reportedly "laid claim to certain territories" known to the Philippine government as the Spratly Islands. At a meeting of the committee March 10, China reiterated its right (reportedly first claimed Jan. 1) to the Senkaku Islands, which were claimed by the Japanese as part of its Ryukyu Islands and which were believed to contain substantial seabed deposits of oil.

Militia rearmed. According to a report July 1, China's militia was being rearmed and new emphasis was being placed on training of the regular army. The new program represented a shift from the previous stress on political indoctrination of the armed forces as advocated by former Defense Minister Lin Piao (see below) to a policy of professionalism in the country's armed forces. The reorganization of the general staff of the armed forces was indicated by the appointment of Hsiang Chung-hua, a former political commissar of the armored corps, as a new deputy chief of the general staff. The trend toward military professionalism was borne out by an editorial in the official newspaper of the armed forces, Chiehfang Chun Pao, which had stated: "In order to win victory in a future war against aggression, we must exert great efforts to master highly developed modern military technique."

Lin plot detailed. A U.S. newspaper July 22 quoted from a Chinese Communist party document, dated Jan. 13 and classified "absolutely secret," detailing the smashing of a "counter-revolutionary plot" in which former Defense Minister Lin planned to oust Chairman Mao Tsetung in 1971. The document was said to have been obtained by the Nationalist Chinese intelligence service from agents in China. According to the document, the plot, which was said to have taken shape after Lin and Mao became engaged in a sharp policy dispute following the second plenary session of the ninth Central Committee of the party Aug. 23-Sept. 6, 1970, was to result in Mao's capture and in his forced acceptance of the plotters' terms. The plotters, who were said to have planned on getting Soviet military aid and diplomatic support for their coup, said Mao had "abused the confidence and status given him by the Chinese people" and had moved China toward a "peaceful transition" in domestic and international affairs. Among the other plotters identified in the account were: Huang Yung-sheng, former chief of the general staff of the armed forces; Wu Fa-hsien, air force commander; Li Tso-peng, deputy chief of staff and political commissar of the navy; Chiu Hui-tso, deputy chief of the army and head of the logistics department; Yeh Chun, Lin's wife, a member of the Politburo and director of the administrative office of the party's military affairs committee; and Lin's son, Lin Li-kuo, deputy director of the air force operations department. The document gave no indication of the ultimate fate of any of the plotters.

Lin's death confirmed. Wang Hai-jung, a Chinese assistant foreign minister, July 18 confirmed that Lin had been killed Sept. 12, 1971 in a plane crash as he attempted to flee China after his plans to seize power had failed. Wang's statement confirmed a statement issued earlier July 28 by the Chinese embassy in Algiers and a report July 27 that Chairman Mao had given a similar account of Lin's death to Prime Minister Sirimavo Bandaranaike of Sri Lanka (formerly Ceylon) and French Foreign Minister Maurice Schumann during their recent visits to China. A Chinese official, according to a report Aug. 12, said that Lin had been on the way to the Soviet Union when his plane crashed.

See also ATOMIC ENERGY [10]; AUSTRALIA [11]; AVIATION; CHINA, NATIONALIST; CYPRUS; DISARMAMENT; ENVIRONMENT; FOREIGN POLICY; INDOCHINA WAR [20, 22]; JAPAN [7]; KOREA, SOUTH; SINO-SOVIET RELATIONS; SINO-U.S. RELATIONS; SPACE [21]; UNITED NATIONS

CHINA, NATIONALIST (REPUBLIC OF CHINA or TAIWAN)—U.S. to reduce air strength.

U.S. officials said March 17 that a substantial part of the U.S. Air Force on Taiwan would be withdrawn from the island gradually over the next year or two. The withdrawals reportedly would affect four squadrons of C-130 transports which had been supporting American operations in Indochina from their Taiwan base. The number of men connected with the mission accounted for about half of the 8,600 U.S. personnel stationed on Taiwan. The decision to reduce U.S. air strength came after President Nixon's return from Communist China Feb. 28 *(see* SINO-U.S. RELATIONS [3-6]), but reportedly was connected with American disengagement in Vietnam *(see* INDOCHINA WAR [35-36]) more than with the new policy of better relations with Peking.

Chiang re-elected. Generalissimo Chiang Kai-shek March 21 was re-elected to his fifth six-year term as president. He was sworn in May 20. Chiang had run unopposed and had received 99.9% of the votes cast by the National Assembly. (Eight of the 1,316 ballots were blank.) Chiang had told the Assembly Feb. 26 that he would not run for re-election and had urged it to "choose a new person to succeed me." He reversed his decsion March 4 following a nationwide movement to draft him. He was nominated for the presidency by the ruling Kuomintang party March 10.

Chiang's son elected premier. The Yuan (parliament) May 26 elected Deputy Premier Chiang Ching-kuo, son of President Chiang, as premier by a 381-13 vote with 13 abstentions. The standing committee of the Kuomintang had recommended the younger Chiang's promotion May 18. The outgoing premier, C.K. Yen, had resigned May 11 with the rest of the Cabinet to allow the president to create a new government following his re-election. In other appointments, President Chiang May 29 moved to broaden support for the government and to unify the population by appointing three Taiwanese to high-level administrative positions which had been held by natives of mainland China. The appointees were: Interior Minister Hsu Ching-ching, named deputy premier; Taipei Mayor Henry Kao, appointed communications minister; and Provincial Assembly Speaker Hsieh Tung-ming, promoted to governor of Taiwan Province, a position usually held by a military man.

Mixed results in elections. The Kuomintang won nearly all contested seats in national and local elections Dec. 23. Several anti-government independents, however, defeated Kuomintang candidates in balloting conducted to fill 51 additional seats in the Yuan, 53 additional seats in the National Assembly (which convened every six years to elect the president and revise the constitution), all 73 seats in the provincial assembly, mayoralty posts in four large cities and the magistrate's office in 16 counties. Elections to the Yuan, the first such elections since the Nationalists had moved to Taiwan in the 1940s, were to elect new legislators with fixed terms. Incumbent legislators, who had been chosen when the Nationalists still controlled most of the China mainland, were to retain their seats until a "return to the mainland."

See also ATOMIC ENERGY [7]; CHINA, COMMUNIST; FOREIGN POLICY; JAPAN [7]; SINO-U.S. RELATIONS [1, 5-8]; UNITED NATIONS

CHISHOLM, SHIRLEY—*See* ELECTIONS [3-4, 6-8, 15, 17, 19]
CHOLERA—*See* HEALTH; STORMS
CHOU EN-LAI—*See* JAPAN [7]; SINO-U.S. RELATIONS [1, 3-5, 9]

CHURCHES—South Carolina Methodist merger. The white and black Methodist conferences in South Carolina, segregated since the Civil War period, voted separately in Columbia Jan. 27 to accept a plan of union. The white conference voted 573-247 in favor of the merger and the black conference voted 135-44 in favor. Under the plan, the present church structure of 11 geographical districts of the white conference and four districts of the black conference would be reorganized into 12 districts with nine white and three black district superintendents. A system calling for racial quotas for chairmen of committees, boards and commissions—included in a 1971 merger plan rejected by the white conference—was not included in the approved plan. (In a related development, the United Methodist Church's all-white North Mississippi Conference Nov. 27 overwhelmingly approved a merger with the all-black Upper Mississippi Conference, which earlier had supported the move.)

Lutheran issues orthodox guidelines. The Rev. Dr. Jacob A. O. Preus, president of the Lutheran Church-Missouri Synod, issued guidelines on his own authority to bar the historical-literary-critical method of scriptural interpretation at his church's main seminary. The special statement to the church's 2.8 million members, according to a report March 11, grew out of a three-year struggle between Preus and the moderate leadership of Concordia Seminary in St. Louis over Preus's insistence on a fundamentalist interpretation of the Bible.

Explo '72. More than 75,000 young people met in Dallas June 12-17 for Explo '72, an evangelical conference which utilized training seminars, prayer meetings and a music festival toward reaching its goal of a "spiritual explosion." Organizers of the meeting said its aim was to "evangelize the whole world by 1980." The meeting, variously termed a "religious Woodstock" and the "largest camp meeting in the U.S.," featured addresses by the Rev. Billy

Graham (honorary chairman of Explo '72), folksinger Johnny Cash and Dallas Cowboys quarterback Roger Staubach. Participants at the conference were each expected to recruit five more persons into the movement.

Orthodox Church names Dimitrios I. The Holy Synod of the Eastern Orthodox Church July 16 selected Metropolitan Dimitrios as patriarch of the faith, succeeding Athenagoras I, who died July 6. Dimitrios I was formerly a theologian and archbishop for two Turkish islands in the Dardanelles. The Turkish government, representing a primarily Moslem population, had barred the candidacy to the patriarchate of Metropolitan Meliton, a progressive archbishop and dean of the Holy Synod. (The Turks had won control of the church hierarchy in the 15th century by their defeat of the Byzantine Empire.) However, Dimitrios was supported by the Meliton faction in balloting and was expected to maintain close ties with Meliton. The Turkish government had also exerted its influence over the church July 9 by barring Archbishop Iakovos, primate for the Greek Orthodox Church of North and South America, from attending Athenagoras's funeral and from participating in the election of the new patriarch. Officials charged Iakovos with "anti-Turkish activities," but a report July 10 attributed the Turkish action to its policy of harassment aimed at forcing the church to abandon Istanbul as the seat of the patriarchate. An ecumenical delegation of four U.S. prelates canceled plans to travel to Istanbul as a gesture of support for Iakovos.

World Council, Vatican study on ecumenism. The World Council of Churches' central committee, meeting Aug. 17, discussed a joint study undertaken by the council and the Vatican on council membership by the Roman Catholic Church. According to a report Aug. 17, the Vatican had delayed the release of the study because it was embarrassed by the findings, which concluded that the initiative for membership and ecumenical action remained with the Vatican. The joint study group which authored the report had been established in 1965, during the reign of Pope John XXIII, but the study was not begun until after the 1969 visit by Pope Paul VI to the council's Geneva headquarters.

Council drops stocks to combat racism. The council's central committee also voted Aug. 22 to liquidate its $3.5 million holdings in all corporations doing business with Rhodesia, Angola, Mozambique, South Africa and Portuguese Guinea—all white-ruled countries of Africa. The action, which was meant to symbolize the group's "commitment to combat racism" and which would affect 22 corporations, was followed by an announcement that no council funds would be deposited in banks that "maintained direct banking operations" in the proscribed African countries. The council took the action despite the opposition of the central committee's financing unit, which questioned the effectiveness of the strategy. The finance committee had suggested that the council instead take action as stockholders to bring pressure on corporations.

See also CYPRUS; EDUCATION [2, 4, 7]; MALAWI; NORTHERN IRELAND; ROMAN CATHOLIC CHURCH

CIGARETTES—*See* HEALTH
CITIZENS' COMMITTEE TO INVESTIGATE THE FBI—*See* FEDERAL BUREAU OF INVESTIGATION
CIVIL AERONAUTICS BOARD (CAB)—*See* AVIATION

CIVIL DISORDERS—Bombs found in 8 banks. Ronald Kaufman, a 33-year-old psychologist and AWOL army private, was indicted Jan. 13-19 in San Francisco, Chicago and New York on charges of placing time bombs in safe deposit boxes in eight bank branches in those cities. (Kaufman was still at large.) The bombs, which were attached to nine-month timing devices, had been defused by police Jan. 7 after identical unsigned letters were received by several newspapers listing the bombs' locations and warning that the "Movement in Amerika" could "kidnap property" by planting powerful bombs in office buildings or highways under construction and could reveal their location in return for the release of imprisoned radicals. The Federal Bureau of

Investigation (FBI) said it had identified Kaufman's fingerprints on applications for the safe deposit boxes. A ninth bomb mentioned in the letters had exploded prematurely Sept. 7, 1971 at a San Francisco Bank of America branch.

Leslie Bacon indicted, charge dropped. Antiwar activist Leslie Bacon was indicted March 24 in Seattle on charges of perjuring herself while testifying in May 1971 as a material witness before a grand jury investigating a bomb blast at the Capitol building in Washington, D.C. However, the Justice Department announced Aug. 4 that it had secured the dismissal of the indictment "because the decision was made not to answer defendant's motions of disclosure of electronic surveillance" regarding the case. The perjury charge had contended that Miss Bacon had been "at the U.S. Capitol building and the U.S. House of Representatives office building" on or about Feb. 28, 1971, which she had specifically denied. (The Justice Department announced Nov. 1 that it also was dropping a bomb conspiracy charge against Miss Bacon rather than reveal contents of surveillance material.)

Bomb damages Pentagon. An explosive device was detonated in a section of the Pentagon building early May 19, causing damage estimated at $75,000 but no injuries. Just before the explosion occurred, two newspapers received telephone calls announcing the bombing. One call, from someone identifying himself as "a Weatherman," announced the explosion. The second call said the explosion was in honor of the birthday of the late North Vietnamese leader Ho Chi Minh and directed the newspaper to a phone booth where a six-page statement criticizing President Nixon's war policies was found. Another statement was received May 19, signed by "Weather Underground No. 12," and bearing insignia identical to markings on 1971 Weather Underground letters claiming credit for the bombing of the Capitol building.

Six antiwar vets indicted. Six members of the Vietnam Veterans Against the War (VVAW) were indicted July 14 in Tallahassee, Fla. on charges of conspiring to disrupt the Republican National Convention in Miami Beach *(see* ELECTIONS [22-26]) with bombings and shootings. The six were charged under provisions in the 1968 civil rights bill against crossing state lines to stir disorder. According to the indictment, at least four meetings were held April 1-June 24 to plan the disorders, and a variety of weapons was assembled. The six charged were John W. Kniffen, William J. Patterson, Peter P. Mahoney, Alton C. Foss, Donald P. Perdue and Scott Camil. Camil was also indicted for manufacture and possession of a firebomb and with instructing others in the use of explosives. VVAW leaders charged July 15 that the indictments were based on false evidence given by William Lemmer, a former VVAW official who had been an informer for the FBI and provocateur. The group claimed to have tape recordings in which Lemmer admitted the charges. The Justice Department announced Oct. 18 that a federal grand jury had expanded the indictment by two additional conspiracy counts and by the addition of John King Briggs and VVAW member Stanley K. Michelson as defendants. Briggs was brought under the original conspiracy charge, and Michelson was charged with concealing an unlawful act and with being an accessory after the fact. The seven VVAW members and Briggs pleaded innocent Nov. 6 on all five counts of the indictment.

Chicago case overturned. The U.S. Court of Appeals for the 7th Circuit Nov. 21 overturned the convictions of five defendants (David T. Dellinger, Rennard C. Davis, Thomas E. Hayden, Jerry C. Rubin and Abbie Hoffman) in the "Chicago 7" trial because of improper rulings and conduct by District Court Judge Julius J. Hoffman during the 1969 trial for crossing state lines with the intent to start a riot at the 1968 Democratic National Convention in Chicago. (Two other defendants—Lee Weiner and John R. Froines—had been acquitted during the trial. An eighth defendant—Black Panther leader Bobby Seales—had charges against him dropped. Charges against Seales for contempt of court during the trial had been dropped by the government Sept. 27 rather than disclose electronically overheard conversations that had been introduced in

Judge Hoffman's chambers during the trial.) The appeals court rebuked Judge Hoffman in unusually emphatic terms for his "deprecatory and often antagonistic attitude toward the defense" from "the very beginning of the trial," both "in the presence and absence of the jury." Judge Hoffman's statements and a series of incidents and rulings, according to the appeals court, "must have telegraphed to the jury the judge's contempt for the defense." The appeals court said that Hoffman's attitude alone would have justified reversal of the decision. However, in addition, Hoffman had not adequately questioned potential jurors about their attitudes toward the defendants and about the effect of pre-trial publicity, had improperly sent notes to the jury during deliberation without telling the defense, had rejected defense evidence relating to the defendants' intentions and had excluded expert witnesses who would have testified on police tactics. The court also said that the prosecution, led by U.S. Attorney Thomas A. Foran, had frequently made remarks before the jury, "not called for by their duties," which "fell below the standards applicable to a representative of the United States." The appeals court refused, by a 2-1 vote, to find unconstitutional the interstate riot act under which the five Chicago defendants had been tried. The court found that there was enough evidence legally to justify another trial, but said the Justice Department then would have to disclose electronically overheard conversations made under national security wiretaps, since found unconstitutional by the Supreme Court (see SECURITY, U.S.). (The court May 11 also had ordered retrials for the Chicago 7 on contempt of court charges. The court cited a 1971 Supreme Court ruling that a judge might impose contempt sentences only at the time of the contempt. If action were deferred until the end of the trial—as was the case with the Chicago 7—the sentencing must be left to another judge. The appeals court had ruled in addition that no contempt sentences longer than six months could be imposed without a jury trial.)

See also AUSTRIA; BLACK MILITANTS; DRAFT & WAR PROTEST; ELECTIONS [20, 25-26]; INDIA [4, 8, 10]; IRELAND; NIXON, RICHARD MILHOUS; NORTHERN IRELAND; SECURITY, U.S.; STUDENT UNREST; SWITZERLAND

CIVIL RIGHTS.—President Richard M. Nixon during March proposed legislation denying courts the power to order busing of elementary schoolchildren to achieve racial integration (see [2-3]). While the House of Representatives passed a bill retaining the major provisions of the President's proposals, the legislation died when the Senate failed to end a filibuster against it (see [4]). However, the Congress did pass three moderate antibusing proposals as amendments to a higher education-integration aid bill (see [5]). In other school action, a district judge ordered the Department of Health, Education and Welfare (HEW) to cut off funds to school districts which were violating the 1964 Civil Rights Act (see [6]). (For state-by-state developments in school desegregation, see [7-13].) In the field of equal employment, Congress passed a bill giving the Equal Employment Opportunity Commission (EEOC) increased power and jurisdiction (see [14]). The Federal Power Commission (FPC) ruled that it did not have the power to enforce equal job opportunities for minorities within utilities companies (see [16]). President Nixon banned minority employment hiring quotas in the federal government, throwing into doubt government minority hiring plans (see [17]).

School Desegregation

[2] **Nixon busing message.** President Nixon March 17 sent a message to Congress proposing legislation to deny courts the power to order busing of elementary schoolchildren to achieve racial integration. He asked Congress for a moratorium on all new busing orders, a clear Congressional mandate on acceptable desegregation methods and a program to concentrate federal aid to education more effectively in poor districts, in order to substitute "equality of educational opportunity" for racial balance as the primary national education

goal. The President's legislative program consisted of two separate bills. The first, on which he requested immediate action, was the Student Transportation Moratorium Act. The act would prohibit all new court busing orders immediately on passage until July 1, 1973 or until Congress passed appropriate legislation. It "would not put a stop to desegregation cases," however. Where "lower courts have gone beyond the Supreme Court" in ordering massive busing, Nixon promised "intervention by the Justice Department in selected cases." Nixon said that passage of the act would "relieve the pressure on the Congress to act on the long-range legislation without full and adequate consideration."

[3]   The second Nixon bill, the Equal Educational Opportunities Act, would define the responsibilities of school districts concerning integration and minority opportunities, specify remedies for violations and stimulate improvements in poorer schools. Deliberate segregation would be prohibited, and previously dual school systems would "have an affirmative duty to remove the vestiges" of segregation. No student could be assigned to a school other than the one nearest his home, or allowed to transfer to another school, if greater racial segregation would result. Voluntary transfers to promote integration would be encouraged. However, "racial balance" would not be required, and "the assignment of students to their neighborhood schools would not be considered a denial of equal educational opportunity" unless the schools had been located for purposes of segregation. Faculty and staff employment and assignment bias would be banned. If a court found violations of the law, it could impose remedies only "to correct the particular violations" and could not change or ignore district lines unless thay had been drawn up deliberately to prevent integration. All desegregation orders would expire after 10 years, or five years if busing were involved; and subsequent orders could be imposed only if new violations were found. Courts would have to choose from a list of preferred remedies, using the least severe that would correct the situation. The remedies would be: (1) assigning students to the school nearest their homes, taking "natural physical barriers" into account; (2) assigning students to the nearest school regardless of physical barriers; (3) permitting voluntary transfers to promote integration; (4) revising attendance zones or grade structures without new busing; (5) building new schools and closing inferior schools; (6) establishing "magnet schools" or educational parks; and (7) any other feasible plan, excluding any new busing of sixth grade or younger students, and allowing busing of older children on a temporary basis only, and only where no health or educational risk were involved, and provided the order was stayed until approved by an appeals court. The fiscal basis for the Equal Educational Opportunities Act would be the Title I program of aid to poor districts under the 1965 Elementary and Secondary Education Act, and the Emergency School Aid Act requested by the President in 1970 to aid districts undergoing desegregation. (The emergency bill had been passed in different versions by the House and Senate. *See* [5].)

[4]   *Congressional action.* The House Aug. 18 passed, by a 282-102 vote, legislation barring court-ordered busing across school district boundaries for the purpose of school integration. The bill retained the major provisions of the President's antibusing proposals. However, the President's program was killed for the Congressional session Oct. 12 when the Senate failed for the third time to end a filibuster by Northern liberals against the House bill. The bill passed by the House would have preserved the sanctity of existing school district boundaries unless the districts were "drawn for the purpose and had the effect" of segregation. It would have permitted the continued pairing of schools, an action in which selected grades of predominantly white schools were combined with grades in nearby black schools. It included amendments by Rep. Edith Green (D, Ore.) permitting the reopening of court-settled desegregation suits to determine whether the court rulings conformed with the new legislation and barring the busing of any student, regardless of grade-level. The House bill

arrived in the Senate Oct. 6 after Sen. James B. Allen (D, Ala.) had succeeded through parliamentary maneuvers in getting the bill directly on the floor without committee approval. Opponents to the bill, charging that it would have unconstitutionally interfered with court powers and that it would have undone progress in desegregation, immediately began a filibuster to block passage during the last scheduled week of the 92nd Congress. Cloture motions, requiring a two-thirds majority, were defeated Oct. 10, 11 and 12. The Senate then agreed by a 50-26 vote to go on to other legislation.

[5] **Congress clears busing curbs.** The House June 8 approved (by a 218-180 vote) and sent to the President a combined higher education-integration aid bill with three moderate antibusing provisions *(see* EDUCATION [8] for education provisions). The bill, a compromise resulting from a House-Senate conference, had been approved by the Senate in a 63-15 vote May 24. (The conference bill was a compromise on bills passed by the Senate March 1 and by the House Nov. 5, 1971.) President Nixon signed the bill into law June 23, while criticizing its antibusing provisions as an "inadequate, misleading and entirely unsatisfactory" response to "one of the most burning social issues of the past decade." The bill delayed all new court busing orders until appeals had been exhausted or until Jan. 1, 1974. Federal funds could not be used to finance busing for desegregation unless requested by local authorities; nor could federal officials order or encourage districts to spend state or local funds for busing, in cases where busing endangered pupils' health or education, "unless constitutionally required." The bill also authorized $2 billion over two years to school districts in the process of desegregation. Of these funds, 4% were earmarked for bilingual programs, 3% for educational television and 5% for metropolitan-area education plans, which would be implemented only if two-thirds of the districts in an area approved them. The approval of the bill in the House June 8 came despite House votes March 8 and May 11 instructing House conferees not to water down tougher provisions approved by the House. (The House provisions had set no deadline for an end to the delay in court busing orders and had totally prohibited federal funds or encouragement for busing.)

[6] **Court orders fund cuts.** U.S. District Court Judge John H. Pratt ruled Nov. 16 that HEW had unlawfully refrained from cutting off federal funds to school districts officially found to be not in compliance with the 1964 Civil Rights Act. Since 1970, the Administration had almost entirely avoided using the cutoff provisions of the law, preferring to seek voluntary compliance— which Pratt said had been "unsuccessful in the case of many state and local agencies." An attorney for the NAACP (National Association for the Advancement of Colored People) Legal Defense and Educational Fund (which had brought the suit in which the decision was handed down) said "the court has held that cutting off funds is not discretionary."

[7] **State-by-state desegregation developments.** *Georgia.* Supreme Court Justice Lewis F. Powell Sept. 1 refused to stay a busing plan for Augusta. The stay had been requested under the provisions of the higher education-integration aid bill *(see* [5]), but Powell held that the bill applied only to orders issued for achieving racial balance and that the Augusta plan was instead ordered to correct illegal segregation. (Powell had also refused to grant a stay of the plan Feb. 11.) In the Atlanta school district, the 5th U.S. Circuit Court of Appeals Oct. 7 ruled that the district school system was "virtually totally segregated" and ordered the Atlanta school board to implement an integration plan within seven weeks. The court ordered the school board to devise a plan that would, "at a minimum," use "pairing or grouping of contiguous segregated schools," paying "special attention" to 20 schools "which have never been desegregated." (The Nov. 27 deadline for the plan was delayed Nov. 24 when a three-judge panel of the 5th Circuit Court of Appeals remanded the case to a lower court.)

[8] *Massachusetts.* A Massachusetts Superior Court judge Sept. 27 ordered the state to grant $52 million in withheld school aid to Boston, but ordered the

city to devise a school integration plan. The state had found Boston in violation of a Massachusetts law which barred any school from having more than 50% minority students, and had cut off the funds in September when the Boston School Committee revoked a plan to integrate one school after both white and black parents protested. The judge ordered the School Committee to draw up a temporary integration plan by mid-November and to make "maximum progress" toward racial balance by June 1973. (The Boston school system was also under a federal investigation, announced June 2, to determine if the School Committee maintained a racially segregated system.) The School Committee drafted a plan, but it was rejected by the court Nov. 6.

[9] *Michigan.* The Ferndale school district April 19 became the first in the North to be cut off from federal aid because of violation of desegregation laws, but HEW Secretary Elliot Richardson June 2 granted a deferral of the cutoff. U.S. District Court Judge Stephen J. Roth June 14 ordered a massive busing effort to integrate Detroit city and suburban schools. The plan, based largely on a proposal of the NAACP, was the most extensive desegregation order issued by a federal court. Under it, 310,000 of 780,000 pupils in Detroit and 53 suburban school districts would be bused across Detroit city lines. City high school districts would be paired or clustered with suburban districts, and teachers would be reassigned so that each school had at least 10% black faculty and staff. Roth set up a nine-member panel to fill in the details and establish a schedule within 45 days, with full implementation set for the fall 1973 term. The panel July 5 recommended that Michigan be ordered to pay $3 million for 295 available school buses to begin busing 50,000-80,000 children in the fall of 1972. Roth issued the order July 10. However, the 6th U.S. Circuit Court of Appeals July 21 issued a stay on the July 10 order. (The Justice Department had joined Michigan's appeal of the order July 17, relying in part on the higher education-integration aid bill provisions. *See* [5].) The court Aug. 24 extended the stay indefinitely, but ruled Dec. 8 that a city-suburb integration plan was necessary to assure equal rights for black schoolchildren in Detroit.

[10] *Tennessee.* The 6th U.S. Circuit Court of Appeals June 5 granted a stay to the Memphis Board of Education, which had been under a lower court order to begin a busing program in the fall. The Board of Education had claimed that, without a stay, it would have to commit itself to buy or lease buses before it knew the final disposition of the case. The appeals court Aug. 29, however, ordered the plan into effect.

[11] *Texas.* The 5th U.S. Circuit Court of Appeals, sitting en banc rather than in the usual three-judge panel, Aug. 2 reversed lower court school integration rulings for Austin and Corpus Christi and rejected the use of large-scale busing until all neighborhood-oriented remedies had been tried. In the Austin case, the court ordered a U.S. district court judge to request new plans for further desegregation plans from all parties, with a final plan required in time for the fall 1972 term. The district court judge had rejected plans for crosstown busing and ordered instead that special learning centers be set up for visits from neighborhood schools. The appeals court ruled that the judge could not "totally reject the use of busing as a permissible tool." In Corpus Christi, the appeals court reversed a U.S. district court ruling that called for extensive crosstown busing and ordered instead that the district judge adopt a new pupil reassignment plan. The appeals court also ordered the use of pairing and clustering of schools and relocation of portable classrooms, but barred the pairing of noncontiguous school districts "until the court had exhausted every other possible remedy which would not involve increased student transportation." A minority of the appeals court dissented in both cases, claiming that all remedies short of large-scale busing had already been unsuccessfully tried.

[12] *Virginia.* District Court Judge Robert R. Merhige Jr. Jan. 10 issued a landmark desegregation decision, ordering the merger of Richmond's predominantly black public schools with those of suburban Henrico and

Chesterfield Counties (who both had almost all-white enrollments) into a new metropolitan school district. In his opinion, Merhige held that busing schoolchildren within a predominantly black school system like Richmond had not increased integration. His decision, in effect, held that the constitutional requirement that blacks and whites have an opportunity to attend an equal, unitary school district loomed as more important than the right of local governments to set educational boundaries. Merhige followed his decision with an order Jan. 11 setting down specific guidelines for the consolidation of the three districts. He gave the governmental units involved 30 days to "take all steps necessary" to merge the school systems by September. The state board of education was given 30 days to name an administrative staff for the new metropolitan district and 90 days to submit a plan for the financial operation of the new district. The 4th U.S. Circuit Court of Appeals Feb. 8 granted a stay on Merhige's order and June 6 overturned the order on an appeal by the Justice Department and Henrico and Chesterfield Counties. The appeals court ruled that Merhige, in handing down the order, had exceeded "his power of intervention."

[13] In its first nonunanimous decision on a modern desegregation case, the Supreme Court ruled 5-4 June 22 that the town of Emporia could not constitutionally remove its schools from the Greenville County school system, which had a higher percentage of blacks. All four Nixon appointees to the court dissented. Emporia had decided to operate its own school system in 1969, when the county was under a court order to pair its largely segregated schools to increase integration. An appeals court had found that the purpose of the Emporia withdrawal from the county system was educational quality and local control. The Supreme Court decision overturned the lower court's finding and added that "inquiry into the 'dominant motivation' of school authorities is as irrelevant as it is fruitless."

Equal Employment Developments

[14] **Rights bill passed.** The Senate March 6, by a 62-10 vote, and the House March 8, by a 303-110 vote, approved a bill giving the EEOC power to seek court enforcement of its findings of job discrimination and expanding EEOC jurisdiction. The bill, signed by President Nixon March 24, was the result of a House-Senate conference compromise between a bill passed by the Senate Feb. 22 and one passed by the House Sept. 16, 1971. It followed the more liberal Senate version in extending EEOC coverage to 10.1 million state and local government workers, all employees of public and private educational institutions and all companies and unions with at least 15 workers (instead of the previous minimum of 25). Two House provisions that would have curbed class action suits and made the EEOC the only federal agency with job bias authority were dropped in the conference. The conferees gave the EEOC, rather than the Justice Department, power to bring suits against a "pattern or practice" of union or employer bias. An independent EEOC general counsel was provided for—appointed by the President and subject to Senate confirmation, but acting only under orders from the EEOC.

[15] **U.S. efforts scored.** Federal programs to assure equal job rights at government agencies and among government contractors were criticized as ineffective by George Holland, outgoing head of the Office of Federal Contract Compliance (OFCC), and by the Public Interest Research Group, a Ralph Nader research organization. Holland, director of the OFCC since February, submitted his resignation June 1, effective July 1, charging that a recent reorganization of the agency had diminished its effectiveness in enforcing equal job opportunities in firms doing business with the federal government. Holland charged that the reorganization, which decentralized the agency and merged its field offices with other Labor Department units, "diminishes program impact, diffuses program authority and denies program uniformity." The Public Interest Research Group issued a report June 24

charging the Civil Service Commission with inadequate and unsympathetic supervision of job rights complaint procedures in government agencies and with failing to require agencies to provide training and promotion programs to compensate for past discrimination against blacks and women. The report charged that half of all complaints closed in the 1970 fiscal year and reviewed by the commission had taken over six months to process, despite regulations requiring action within two months. Of those cases reviewed by the commission, a finding of discrimination was made in only 7.4% of the cases in fiscal 1970 and in 4.8% of the cases in the first half of fiscal 1971. In 1970, supervisors were disciplined in only 1.8% of the cases, and only through reprimands or training classes. The Civil Service Board of Appeals and Review had rejected complaints in over 98% of the cases it reviewed.

[16] **FPC bars bias role.** The FPC July 11 issued a ruling that it did not have power under federal law or the "public interest" concept to enforce fair employment practices by utilities. The ruling came after 12 civil rights groups petitioned the FPC June 23 to take such action, charging "rampant discrimination against blacks, women and Spanish-surnamed Americans" by gas and electric utilities. The groups cited a September 1971 letter to the FPC from David L. Norman, assistant attorney general for the Justice Department's Civil Rights Division, which said the FPC could exercise such powers. However, the commission said that Congress had relegated fair employment powers to the EEOC and that its "public interest" regulatory functions no more covered employment practices than they covered securities, taxes, wages or advertising, all of which were regulated by other agencies.

[17] **Nixon bans quotas.** President Nixon Aug. 24 banned minority employment hiring quotas in the federal government. The order was in response to a letter sent Aug. 4 by the American Jewish Committee (AJC) to President Nixon and Democratic presidential nominee George McGovern expressing concern over the use of job quotas. As a result of the President's order, Labor Secretary James D. Hodgson revealed June 3 that the Philadelphia Plan (designed to increase minority employees on federal construction projects) was "being reviewed." Hodgson Sept 15 also released a memo to "all heads of agencies" in the federal government, stating that the OFCC did not require "quotas or proportional representation" of minorities, although "the goals required of government contractors" may have been "misinterpreted or misapplied" as requiring such quotas. Hodgson said the goals were merely "targets," and that failure to reach them "is not to be regarded as, per se, a violation." Responding to the memo, civil rights groups charged that it had nullified minority hiring plans.

[18] **HEW sets guidelines.** At the request of educators faced with a loss of federal contracts for inadequate affirmative action plans, HEW Oct. 4 issued a set of minority employment guidelines for about 2,500 colleges and universities holding federal contracts. The guidelines ruled out quotas for women or minority groups, but said that numerical "goals and timetables" would be required. The goals would be determined by "an analysis by the contractor of its deficiencies and of what it can reasonably do to remedy them, given the availability of qualified minorities and women and the expected turnover of its work force." If "changed employment conditions" or other factors prevented the school from reaching the goal despite "good-faith effort," as determined by an investigative team, the school would be considered to have "complied with the letter and the spirit" of an executive order requiring affirmative action by federal contractors.

[19] **New Chicago job plan.** The Labor Department announced Oct. 18 that nine Chicago building contractor associations and 15 building trades unions had signed a voluntary agreement to employ 9,820 additional minority workers by 1976, with specific yearly hiring goals for each trade. No minority representatives signed the agreement. However, the Chicago Urban League, under the agreement, would run a $1.7 million recruitment and training

program with funds supplied by the Labor Department's Manpower Administration. An earlier Chicago plan had begun in 1970 but had placed only 150 minority workers by May 1971, when it was disbanded after the disappearance of its director, Chicago Alderman Fred Hubbard. (Hubbard was arrested in Los Angeles in September and charged with embezzling $100,000 from the plan's funds.)

Miscellaneous Developments

[20] **Segregated clubs to be taxed.** A three-judge federal court in Washington Jan. 11 struck down the special tax status and concomitant tax benefits granted to fraternal organizations that excluded non-whites from membership. The ruling, handed down as an opinion of law, would bar federal income tax exemptions to fraternal orders investing portions of their funds for charitable and other purposes, and would deny individuals the right to claim tax deductions for their charitable contributions to the lodges. The decision said that the ruling would help "quarantine racism" by eliminating the involvement of the government. The court decided, however, that private nonprofit clubs that discriminated against minorities would not lose their tax exemptions, since the money generated by club members' dues "has simply been shifted from one pocket to another, both within the same pair of pants." The court ruling came in a suit against Treasury Secretary John B. Connally Jr. and other government officials by Clifford V. McGlotten, a black who had been denied membership in the Benevolent and Protective Order of Elks in Portland, Ore., allegedly because of his race.

See also CONSUMER AFFAIRS [5]; CRIME [12]; EDUCATION [2, 8]; ELECTIONS [6, 16, 21, 23, 35, 44]; NIXON, RICHARD MILHOUS; POLITICS [8]; VOTING RIGHTS; WOMEN'S RIGHTS

COLOMBIA—Guerrilla raids. Some 200 guerrillas, identified as members of the leftist National Liberation Army (ELN), seized the mountain town of San Pablo for several hours Jan. 7, killing two policemen, wounding four others, allegedly stealing $400,000 from public offices, and fleeing in stolen trucks with four hostages. Three persons were killed and eight wounded Jan. 16 in simultaneous ELN raids on the northeastern towns of Remedios, Santa Isabel, El Tigre and Yali. The guerrillas reportedly opened the Remedios jail, robbed banks and set several fires. As they had in many of their raids, the guerrillas assembled townspeople to lecture them on their plans to seize political power in Colombia. Army regiments moved into the area after the guerrillas Jan. 17. About 100 ELN guerrillas occupied the town of Vengache in the northwest state of Antioquia May 6. Two persons, including a Catholic priest, were killed May 7 when a group of ELN commandos attacked a government building in San Jeronimo in Antioquia. An ELN ambush of a military patrol in Antioquia April 20 resulted in the death of seven soldiers and two civilians. During November and December, the ELN raised large sums of money from ransom payments in a number of kidnapings of wealthy landowners.

Teachers strike. Teachers in technical and intermediate schools throughout the nation went on strike Feb. 21, beginning a series of walkouts which virtually paralyzed the educational system. The National Association of Secondary School Teachers announced March 6 that its affiliates would join the walkout, bringing the number of striking teachers to 40,000 in more than 600 schools. The union said that high school teachers would not go back to work until the government increased wages by 40% and revoked the decree establishing the "Teaching Statute," which regulated teacher salaries and promotion. The Colombian Federation of Educators (FECODE), representing 70,000 primary school teachers, voted March 14 to join the strike March 20. The strike widened as university students boycotted classes April 5 in solidarity with the striking teachers. Students at Bogota's National University voted a strike April 5 and were joined by 4,000 students at the city's Pedagogic University. The country's private universities began 48- and 72-hour strikes April 5. A student strike at the University of Antioquia also began the same day, after striking students and teachers at the university clashed violently with the police April. 4. Police also clashed with the strikers at other universities.

The government initially refused to negotiate with the strikers because, since they were public employees, their walkout was illegal. The government had attempted to halt the spread of the strike March 18 by creating a commission of 10 public officials and seven teacher representatives to review the "Teaching Statute," but the FECODE refused to participate because the 10-7 ratio insured its "interests will not be sufficiently guaranteed." Teachers voted April 4 to extend the strike indefinitely, charging that the government was not interested in a solution to the walkout. The strike was finally settled April 17 when the government agreed to raise the teachers' salaries and repeal the Teaching Statute. In the aftermath of the strike, the rector of the National University, Jorge Arias de Greiff, resigned April 25 as a result of a police raid on the University's women's dormitories April 7 during the strike. Following the raid, in which an arsenal of weapons allegedly was found, Gen. Luis Camacho, a senior army officer, asked Arias to control the activities of his students. Arias complained to Colombian President Misael Pastrana Borrero that the request was a threat to the University's autonomy. When Pastrana refused to support him, Arias resigned in protest.

Liberals win elections. The traditional Liberal and Conservative parties remained the dominant political forces in Colombia April 16 as the Liberals won municipal and provincial elections, taking about 47% of the vote. Results April 19 gave Liberals 876,451 votes, Conservatives 632,661 votes and ex-dictator Gustavo Rojas Pinilla's National Popular Alliance (ANAPO) 339,410 votes. Approximately 8,800 posts were at stake in 906 municipal councils and 22 provincial assemblies. Only 2 million of the 8.3 million registered voters went to the polls. Many voters reportedly were confused by the large numbers of candidates presented by the parties—particularly ANAPO—and splinter groups. In some municipalities, there reportedly were as many as 400 candidates for 10 offices. Many of the candidates were unknown to the vast majority of the voters. The voting took place amid relative calm as troops patrolled the major cities. The government earlier had put into effect new and drastic measures to maintain public order during the campaigns and elections. However, violence related to the elections claimed five lives during the campaigns.

Cabinet changes. President Pastrana May 4 appointed two Liberal party members to the Cabinet and confirmed 10 other ministers, resolving a Cabinet crisis that had arisen in the wake of the elections when 12 of the Cabinet's 13 ministers resigned May 2. (The Liberals and Pastrana's Conservatives had exchanged attacks during the April elections.) Hernando Agudelo Villa, an economist and senator, replaced Jorge Valencia Jaramillo as minister of economic development. Juan Jacobo Munoz, a physician, took over the Education Ministry from Luis Carlos Galan. The appointments raised to six the number of Liberals in the Cabinet. The other ministers included six Conservatives and Defense Minister Gen. Hernando Correa Cubides, who had not resigned because he was "apolitical."

Record budget proposed. The government July 28 proposed a 1973 budget of $2.3 billion, the highest in Colombia's history. According to Finance Minister Rodrigo Llorente, the new budget would emphasize education, payment of the public debt and national defense, in that order. Llorente said it would also focus on public investment, practically freezing bureaucratic expenditures. The budget was immediately attacked by members of the opposition, who charged that government economic policies had set off an inflationary cycle. The inflationary situation, according to a report Aug. 4, had virtually paralyzed investment in Colombia.

Student unrest. Fifteen policemen were reported injured Oct. 5 during clashes with students at the National University and the Free University in Bogota. Activities at the National University were halted Oct. 11 after the school's governing council suspended some 4,500 students (nearly one-third the student body) and expelled about 50 others in response to student strikes. The strikers had demanded greater internal democratization and student participation and an end to the tight military surveillance of the school, imposed Sept. 22 after a violent disturbance. The student protests continued through October and early November. Several departments of the National University's Manizales campus and the Universidad del Atlantico in Barranquilla announced Nov. 3 that they would close for the second semester in response to student strikes and demonstrations for academic reforms. The University of Antioquia closed for the second semester Nov. 6. University students clashed with police in Bogota, Medellin and Barranquilla Nov. 9.

See also ARMAMENTS, INTERNATIONAL; ATOMIC ENERGE [13]; DRUG USE & ADDICTION [20]; TARIFFS & WORLD TRADE

COMMISSION ON POPULATION GROWTH & THE AMERICAN FUTURE—*See* ABORTION; POPULATION

COMMITTEE OF 20—*See* INTERNATIONAL MONETARY DEVELOPMENTS [9]

COMMITTEE ON MOTOR VEHICLE EMISSIONS—*See* POLLUTION [4]

COMMITTEE ON POLITICAL EDUCATION (COPE)—*See* ELECTIONS [28]

COMMITTEE TO RE-ELECT THE PRESIDENT—*See* ELECTIONS [47]; POLITICS [9-10]

COMMON CAUSE—*See* ELECTIONS [47]; VOTING RIGHTS

COMMON MARKET—*See* EUROPEAN ECONOMIC COMMUNITY

COMMON ORGANIZATION OF AFRICA, MALAGASY & MAURITANIA (OCAM)—*See* AFRICA

COMMONWEALTH OF NATIONS—*See* BAHAMAS; BANGLA DESH [13]; CEYLON; JAMAICA; PAKISTAN [7]

COMMUNICATIONS SATELLITE CORP. (COMSAT)—*See* SPACE [23]

COMMUNISM, INTERNATIONAL—*See* CZECHOSLOVAKIA; ELECTIONS [23]; EUROPEAN SECURITY; POLAND; RUMANIA

COMMUNIST PARTY OF THE U.S.—*See* ELECTIONS [37]

COMPUTER TRAINING—*See* EDUCATION [6]

CONFERENCE ON THE HUMAN ENVIRONMENT—*See* CONSERVATION

CONGO, REPUBLIC OF (BRAZZAVILLE)—Coup defeated. Maj. Joachim Yhombi-Opango, army chief of staff, Feb. 22 led forces loyal to the government of President Marien Ngouabi in defeating an attempted coup d'etat which occurred while Ngouabi was visiting the coastal town of Pointe Noire, 240 miles southwest of the capital. Following his return, Ngouabi said the revolt had been led by Lt. Ange Diawara, who had temporarily taken over the Brazzaville radio station with the aid of an infantry battalion. It was reported March 9 that Diawara had escaped but 1,006 other persons were arrested, including Maj. Alfred Raoul (a former vice president), Ambroise Noumazalaye (a former premier), Bernard Kombo-Matsiona (former president of the Socialist Youth Union) and members of the ruling Congolese Labor party.

A court martial trying more than 170 persons accused of participating in the coup March 7 returned its verdicts. Nine of the defendants, including Diawara, were sentenced to death in absentia; 13 others, including Noumazalaye and Kombo-Matsiona, were sentenced to death; 30 were given life sentences; and the remainder received sentences ranging from two to 20 years. Ngouabi March 17 commuted all the death sentences to life imprisonment. He reduced 20 army officers, including Raoul and Diawara, to the ranks March 22.

See also ANGOLA; GABON; ZAIRE

CONGRESS—92nd Congress reconvenes. The 92nd Congress reconvened Jan. 18 to begin its second session. On hand were 336 House members and 56 senators. The political lineup in the Senate was 55 Democrats and 45 Republicans. The House of Representatives lineup was 254 Democrats and 178 Republicans (three vacancies).

Mundt loses committee posts. Sen. Karl E. Mundt (R, S.D.), who had not appeared on the Senate floor or in committee meetings since suffering a stroke in November 1969, was removed from his Senate committee posts (Appropriations, Foreign Relations, Government Operations) Feb. 3. His seniority standing on the committees—ranking Republican on one and second-ranking on the other two—had been removed in 1971. Mundt's removal from the committee posts was taken by the Senate Republican Conference at the instigation of Sen. William B. Saxbe (Ohio) as a spokesman for some of the younger GOP senators.

Stokes new Black Caucus head. Rep. Louis Stokes (D, Ohio) Feb. 8 was elected chairman of the Congressional Black Caucus, replacing Charles C. Diggs Jr. (D, Mich.) who resigned. Diggs had served as leader of the blacks in Congress since 1969 when there were six black congressmen. When the caucus (presently made up of the 13 black members of the House—all Democrats) was formally organized in 1971, Diggs continued as its chairman. In selecting Stokes, the caucus denied reports that it was dissatisfied with Diggs's leadership. There had been some reports that several caucus members considered Diggs too conservative and that his private and House business affairs interfered with his caucus duties.

House probes Dowdy status. The House Ethics Committee voted unanimously March 2 to examine the appropriateness of a continued voting role in Congress for Rep. John Dowdy (D, Tex.). Dowdy, who had been convicted in 1971 of bribery and perjury and sentenced Feb. 23 to 18 months in prison and a $25,000 fine, had announced Jan. 18 that he would retire from Congress at the end of his present term. (Dowdy had been found guilty of receiving a $25,000 bribe to thwart a federal probe of a home improvement firm.) It was the first time in the four-year history of the Ethics Committee that the panel had agreed to consider disciplinary action against a member of Congress.

Guam, Virgin Islands delegates. The Senate March 28 cleared a bill passed by the House Jan. 18 authorizing non-voting delegates in the House for the territories of Guam and the Virgin Islands. The bill was signed by President Nixon April 10. The new delegates, to be elected for the 93rd Congress, would join two other non-voting members of the House from Puerto Rico and Washington, D.C.

2 senators get seniority edge. Two newly elected senators—Sam Nunn Jr. (D, Ga.) and J. Bennett Johnston (D, La.)—gained important seniority edges when they were sworn in Nov. 7 and 14, respectively, to fill unexpired terms. Nunn was sworn in to fill the late Sen. Richard Russell's remaining two months in office. Nunn, who had been elected to a full term and to Russell's remaining term in elections Nov. 7, replaced Sen. David H. Gambrell (D, Ga.), who had been appointed in 1971 to fill Russell's seat but had failed to gain renomination in the Georgia primary. Johnston was appointed by Louisiana Gov. Edwin W. Edwards (D) to serve the remainder of the term of Sen. Elaine Edwards, the governor's wife. Mrs. Edwards, who had been appointed July 27 to the seat vacated by the death of Sen. Allen J. Ellender *(see* OBITUARIES [Allen J. Ellender]), resigned early.

See also ARMAMENTS, INTERNATIONAL; ATOMIC ENERGY [2-3]; AUTOMOBILES; AVIATION; BASEBALL; BASKETBALL [14]; BUDGET; BURUNDI; CIVIL RIGHTS [1-5, 14, 16]; CONSUMER AFFAIRS [3, 9, 15-16];

CRIME [9-10, 12]; DEFENSE; DISARMAMENT; DRAFT & WAR PROTEST;
DRUG USE & ADDICTION [5, 11]; ECONOMY [8-10]; EDUCATION [4, 8];
ELECTIONS [1, 3, 18, 28, 34, 36, 38-41, 46]; ENVIRONMENT; FLOODS;
FOREIGN AID; FOREIGN POLICY; GREECE [5-6]; HEALTH; HEALTH
CARE; HORSE RACING; HOUSING; INDIANS, AMERICAN;
INTERNATIONAL MONETARY DEVELOPMENTS [3]; JUDICIARY; LABOR;
LATIN AMERICA; MILITARY [5-9]; MINES; NEWSPAPERS; NIXON,
RICHARD MILHOUS; OLYMPIC TERRORISM; PAKISTAN [3]; PENTAGON
PAPERS; PESTICIDES; POLITICS [3-7]; POLLUTION [10, 13, 15];
POPULATION; POVERTY; RAILROADS; RHODESIA; SELECTIVE
SERVICE SYSTEM; SHIPS & SHIPPING; SINO-U.S. RELATIONS [9];
SOCIAL SECURITY; SOVIET-U.S. RELATIONS [2, 8, 12]; SPACE [18]; STATE
& LOCAL GOVERNMENTS; STOCK MARKET; STORMS; TARIFFS &
WORLD TRADE; TAXES; TELEVISION & RADIO [4, 10]; TERRITORIAL
WATERS; TRANSPORTATION; UNEMPLOYMENT; UNION OF SOVIET
SOCIALIST REPUBLICS [8, 11]; UNITED NATIONS; VOTING RIGHTS;
WELFARE; WOMEN'S RIGHTS

CONNALLY JR., JOHN B.—*See* CIVIL RIGHTS [20]; ECONOMY [5];
ELECTIONS [13-14]; NIXON, RICHARD MILHOUS

CONSERVATION—Fishing bans. Japan, the U.S., Canada, Costa Rica,
Mexico and Panama—all members of the Inter-American Tropical Tuna
Commission—agreed Jan. 14 to reduce their 1972 overall catch quota of yellow-
fin tuna in the eastern Pacific by 20,000 short tons to 120,000 short tons. The
nations agreed to the reduction because of a shrinking supply in the fishing
ground. In other action, Denmark and the U.S. tentatively agreed Feb. 24 to a
ban of high seas salmon fishing in the Atlantic Ocean off Greenland, effective
in 1976. The agreement, approved by the Danish Folketing (parliament) Dec.
15, was to be presented for final approval at the next annual meeting of the
International Commission for the Northwest Atlantic Fisheries. It was aimed
primarily at barring Danish fishermen from the Greenland waters and
provided for the gradual reduction of Denmark's permissible salmon catch
prior to 1976. (American fishing interests had claimed that increased catches
off Greenland in recent years had reduced salmon stocks in U.S. rivers.)
Canada May 29 also charged that Denmark's failure to impose curbs on its
salmon fishing would cause the species to wither away and would end the
annual spawning runs up Canadian rivers. In an attempt to conserve the
salmon, Canada May 1 banned all commercial salmon fishing in New
Brunswick and Newfoundland and May 29 banned such fishing off the tip of
the Gaspe peninsula.

Predator poisons suspended. The Environmental Protection Agency
(EPA) March 10 ordered a halt to shipments and sales of 19 commercial poisons
registered for predator control and began procedures to ban them
permanently. The poisons posed a danger to innocent species as well as
predators. In a related development, the federal government Feb. 8 prohibited
the poisoning of predators on U.S. lands or in federal programs, except in
emergencies.

Big cats on danger list. Eight species of big cats were put on the
endangered foreign wildlife list April 1 by Interior Secretary Rogers C.B.
Morton. Importation of cheetahs, leopards, tigers, snow leopards, jaguars,
ocelots, margays and tiger cats was banned, as was importation of their furs or
derivative products. The only exception to the ban was for use of the cats, their
furs or derivative products in zoos or for research or educational purposes.

Seal protection. A new convention prohibiting the hunting of certain
species of Antarctic seals and curbing the hunting of other species was signed in
London June 9 by Argentina, Belgium, Norway, South Africa, New Zealand
and the United Kingdom. Signatures were also expected from the United
States, Japan, France, Chile and Australia. (Restrictions on sealing elsewhere

had caused Norway, the Soviet Union and Japan to form plans to begin Antarctic harvesting of seals.)

Whale hunting curbed. The International Whaling Commission, meeting in London June 28-30, approved a series of curbs on commercial whale hunting, but defeated a U.S. proposal for a 10-year moratorium on all whale hunting. (The U.S. had banned all commercial whale hunting in 1971 and had barred imports of whale products in 1970.) The U.S. had proposed a moratorium resolution passed overwhelmingly June 9 by the United Nations Conference on the Human Environment (see ENVIRONMENT); but the Soviet Union and Japan, who together harvest 80%-85% of the world's annual whale catch, rallied Iceland, Norway, Panama and South Africa to defeat the proposal. The U.S. position was backed by Britain, Argentina and Mexico. France, Canada, Denmark and Australia abstained. The commission, which included representatives of government and private whaling interests, agreed, however, to reduce quotas for 1973 catches of fin, sei and sperm whales in the North Pacific and Antarctic Oceans. A quota was set for the first time on the smaller Minke whales, to which whalers had turned as the larger varieties diminished. Total catches for the two oceans would decline in 1973 to 34,000 whales, from about 40,000 in 1972, with further reductions promised the following year. Quotas were also established for the North Atlantic. The Soviet Union and Japan, for the first time, agreed to allow observers on board their whaling ships to assure compliance with the agreement. In other steps, the conference continued the ban on hunting humpback and blue whales and put the bowhead, right and gray whales on the proscribed list.

See also ENVIRONMENT; PUBLIC LAND

CONSPIRACY—*See* SECURITY, U.S.

CONSUMER AFFAIRS—FDA to review nonprescription drugs. The Food and Drug Administration (FDA) Jan. 4 unveiled plans for a long-range plan to review the safety and efficacy of all nonprescription drugs on the markets. The three-year review, the first of its kind, was being undertaken to assure the consumer that medications sold over the counter did what the label promised. Presently, consumers relied on previous experience and the manufacturer's word in selecting from more than half a million drugs available without a prescription. The FDA had tested for safety most of the drugs to be reviewed, but such testing had rarely included examination for efficacy. As part of the review program, the FDA June 21 requested drug manufacturers to submit data within 90 days to help the agency extend safe packaging rules to nonprescription drugs. The FDA also published July 7 a report by the National Academy of Sciences-National Research Council that found most claims on cold remedy labels to be unsubstantiated. (Twenty-seven representative cold remedies were reviewed in the study. Of 45 claims, the NAS-NRC said manufacturers had substantial evidence for only four, while 14 were found "probably effective," five "effective, but," 14 "possibly effective" and eight "ineffective as a fixed combination.") In a related development, the FDA Aug. 16 published proposed rules to begin regulating the diagnostic product, or test kit, industry. Some 4,000 diagnostic products—used for a variety of self-tests, including tests for diabetes, vaginal cancer, pregnancy or drunkenness—would be subject to new labeling requirements, including performance characteristics, directions and warnings. The FDA Oct. 8 also released a survey on the use of patent medicines and nonprescription drugs, concluding that "it is probable that there is an enormous waste of money, not to mention adverse health effects, from misguided consumer experimentation with health products." The survey was particularly critical of the labeling and advertising of nonprescription drugs and urged that regulation of their advertising be switched to the FDA from the Federal Trade Commission (FTC).

[2] **DES curbs.** The federal government took several actions in 1972 to curb the use of diethylstilbesterol (DES), a growth hormone used for food animals. Large doses of DES had been found to induce cancer in test animals. The

Agriculture Department Jan. 4 announced new regulations, effective Jan. 8, by which DES could not be fed to cattle or sheep within seven days of slaughter and by which animals brought to slaughter would have to be certified in compliance. The FDA March 10 banned the use of liquid DES in cattle and sheep feed after tests uncovered residues in nearly 1% of sample animals, despite the Agriculture Department's rules. Further tests showed that liquid DES had adhered to feed processing equipment, contaminating later batches of feed supposedly free of the chemical. The FDA acted further Aug. 2, banning all further production of DES but allowing cattlemen to continue using DES in feed until Jan. 1, 1973. The order permitted continued implanting of DES pellets in cattle and sheep. The pellets, which contained one-thirtieth the amount of DES in direct food supplements, had not been known to leave detectible residues. In a related development, the FDA March 17 issued proposals banning the use of the PCB group of chemicals (polychlororinated Biphenyls) in plants processing food or animal feed and in food packaging or recycled paper. The chemicals, which do not occur in nature and which tend to persist in the environment, had been linked to skin irritations, liver damage and birth defects.

[3] **Lead paint curbs.** In separate actions, the FDA, the Department of Housing and Urban Development (HUD) and the Senate acted to curb the use of lead in paints. Poisoning from lead paints resulted in 200 deaths annually. From 50,000-100,000 children a year reportedly required treatment for lead paint poisoning. HUD Jan. 1 banned all paints containing over 1% lead by weight from all uses in all properties owned or insured by the department. The FDA March 10 ordered lead content in all household paints limited to no more than .5% after Dec. 31 and to no more than .06% after Dec. 31, 1973. The Senate June 14 passed a bill authorizing $100 million a year to combat lead poisoning of slum children. The bill adopted the FDA limits on lead content in paint and further banned the use of lead-based paints on toys, furniture and utensils.

[4] **Saccharine curbed.** The FDA Jan. 28 removed saccharine from its list of food additives "generally recognized as safe" after studies showed that mice fed large doses of the artificial sweetener developed bladder tumors. If further research showed the tumors to be cancerous, the FDA said, it would outlaw the product. The removal of saccharine from the safe list would require food processors to list saccharine content on package labels. The FDA recommended a maximum daily adult use of one gram, the equivalent of seven 12-ounce bottles of diet beverage or 60 small tablets.

[5] **Corporate reform expanded.** The Project on Corporate Responsibility, which sponsored Campaign GM, Feb. 3 announced expansion of its reform program, originally aimed at General Motors Corp., to nine additional companies (Chrysler Corp., Ford Motor Co., American Telephone and Telegraph Co., American Cyanamid Co., Bristol-Myers Co., Eli Lilly & Co., Merck & Co. Inc., Smith Kline & French Laboratories and Warner-Lambert Co. The last six companies named were drug manufacturers.). GM, AT&T and Warner-Lambert would be the project's principal targets in 1972—GM because it was the largest corporation; AT&T because of alleged job bias against women; and Warner-Lambert because of different labeling practices in the U.S. and abroad of the drug Chloromycetin. (When the drug was distributed in the U.S., it carried a warning that it could cause "serious and fatal blood diseases." Labeling on the drug abroad carried no such warning.)

[6] **FTC power broadened.** The Supreme Court ruled unanimously March 2 that the authority of the FTC to protect consumers from immoral or unfair trade practices went beyond its power to enforce the letter or even the spirit of the nation's antitrust laws. FTC officials had sought the broadened powers to help them fight unfair schemes against consumers. With the court's decision, the FTC apparently would have the authority to investigate such practices as the mailing of unsolicited credit cards and the high-pressure tactics of some door-to-door salesmen. In the past, these practices did not clearly fall within the

FTC's jurisdiction. (In a related development, U.S. District Court Judge Aubrey E. Robinson Jr. ruled April 4 in Washington that the FTC lacked the legal authority to issue broad regulations on unfair trade practices. The decision marked the first time the federal courts had challenged the FTC's power to issue trade rules.)

[7] FDA to open files. The FDA May 4 proposed new rules to open as much of 90% of its correspondence to public scrutiny. Under former rules, which remained in effect for 60 days, about 90% of the FDA's documents had confidential status. Under the new rules, the public would have access to most information on the safety and effectiveness of thousands of drugs and food additives. Letters and any recorded summaries of phone calls to the agency from businessmen and congressmen would also be available, as well as internal operating manuals, informal enforcement actions, reports of factory investigations and the results of the FDA's own research. Trade secrets, such as manufacturing processes and commercial and financial information, would be kept secret, as would information on new drugs being tested and files of active law enforcement probes.

[8] NTA curbed. The Department of Health, Education and Welfare (HEW) May 5 released a study which found that the possibility of harm to humans from NTA (nitrilotriacetic acid) in laundry products had not been conclusively disproved. There had been reports that the Administration was pressuring HEW to approve the renewed use of NTA, suspended in 1970 after laboratory tests had disclosed cancer and birth defects in rats fed large amounts of the chemical. Soap and chemical manufacturers had reported losses of over $20 million since suspension of the chemical, but agreed to abide by the HEW opinion—although they reiterated their belief that the product was safe. (In a related development, undisclosed HEW tests, reported April 9, had allegedly concluded that detergents containing caustics threatened irreversible blindness, even if rinsed away minutes after contact. The caustics had been introduced to detergents as a substitute for water-polluting phosphates.)

[9] FDA plans more food inspection. FDA Commissioner Charles Edwards May 17 announced a stepped-up program of food plant inspections, after the General Accounting Office (GAO) reported "deteriorating" sanitary conditions in the food processing industry. The GAO report, presented to Congress April 18, found that 40% of a sample of 97 food plants operated under unsanitary conditions, 24% with "serious" sanitation problems. Among the violations found were rodent excreta and insects in raw or finished products, use of pesticides near processing areas, use of unsanitary equipment and "dirty and poorly maintained areas over and around food processing locations." The GAO claimed that the FDA had been unable to "provide the assurance of consumer protection required by the law," partly because of staff shortages and obsolete record-keeping. Congress was advised to give the FDA fine-levying power as a middle course between warning letters and time-consuming court action.

[10] Mattress fires curbed. The Commerce Department June 1 adopted a new mattress flammability standard that would require all mattresses produced after May 31, 1973 to be 99% resistant to cigarettes. The department said that current mattresses ignited 50% of the time when exposed to burning cigarettes.

[11] FDA curbs cosmetic mercury. The FDA June 30 proposed a ban on the use of mercury in cosmetics, with the exception of those used near the eye. Mercury was used in concentrations of up to 3% in skin-lightening creams, and at lower levels as a preservative in other types of cosmetics. The element was known to cause neurological damage. Eye-area cosmetics would be permitted to contain low levels of mercury, which was also an effective preventative against a harmful bacteria that could cause blindness.

[12] Vaccine review set. The FDA announced Aug. 17 that it was beginning a complete review of the safety, effectiveness and labeling of over 1,000 vaccines and other biological products. (HEW Secretary Elliot Richardson had announced May 2 that the FDA would be responsible for the regulation of vaccines and other biological drugs. In the past, that regulatory power had been in the hands of the National Institute of Health's Division of Biologic Standards, and the products had been reviewed only for safety.) The products covered by the FDA review, manufactured from live ingredients, included antitoxins, blood and blood derivatives, and allergenic extracts.

[13] **Blood bank licenses seen.** The FDA Aug. 26 published proposed procedures to begin licensing the nation's 5,000 blood banks and 200 processing centers to establish a "uniform, nationwide system" to reduce the risk of "unsafe blood" and "exploitation" by some concerns. Commissioner Edwards said that 1,500-3,000 hepatitis deaths were caused annually by contaminated blood. The new rules would require that donors be tested for the disease. The federal government already regulated 530 blood banks shipping across state boundaries, which collected over 75% of the eight million pints collected annually. Edwards said that the 200 plasma distributing centers were included in the new order because of "increasing demand for a variety of blood products useful across a broad spectrum of medical practice from the treatment of shock to hemophilia."

[14] **Hexachlorophene curbed.** The FDA Sept. 22 issued an order curbing the use of the germicide hexachlorophene. The FDA, which had originally proposed curbs on the product Jan. 5, issued the more stringent rules after 39 babies died in France in August after being treated with talcum powder containing an accidentally high 6% level of hexachlorophene. The new order would ban all production or shipment of 400 categories of over-the-counter products containing less than .75% of the chemical, a dose widely considered ineffective as a germicide. The ban would not apply to products already on retail shelves, or those containing minute amounts of hexachlorophene as a preservative. Medical products containing over .75% hexachlorophene, used mostly to treat skin outbreaks and dandruff, would continue to be sold, but only by prescription. However, all baby powders containing hexachlorophene would be recalled "because they are not rinsed off, are applied repeatedly and are covered by diapers." The January proposal would have permitted the sale of over-the-counter hexachlorophene products with a cautionary label. The September action was taken, according to the FDA, because, at high concentrations, the chemical acts as "a very, very potent neurotoxin." The order would serve to ban unnecessary exposure "to assure continued safe use of this effective germ fighter" in special cases.

[15] **Filibuster kills consumer agency.** A bill to set up an agency to defend consumer interests before other federal agencies, which had provoked a heated lobbying battle between consumer and business groups, died in Congress after supporters failed Oct. 5 for the third time to limit debate. The cloture vote was 52-30, three short of the required two-thirds. The House had passed the bill in a different version in 1971. The bill would have established a Consumer Protection Agency with a right to intervene before federal agencies as a full participant—with witness and subpoena rights—in all regulatory hearings and investigations, formal or informal. The agency, headed by a three-member presidentially appointed board, would have had power to ask court reviews of regulatory decisions, to engage in consumer research and education and to compile records of consumer complaints. The bill had been opposed by a coalition of some 150 major companies and business groups, who favored the House-passed version, which would have denied the agency power to intervene as a party in penalty proceedings and informal investigations. The Nixon Administration, which had supported the weaker House bill, was reported to have covertly encouraged the Senate filibuster.

[16] **Safety commission OKd.** A House-Senate conference committee reached agreement Oct. 11 on a bill to create an independent consumer product safety commission, and President Nixon signed the legislation into law Oct. 28. The conference agreement on the bill came after Senate conferees abandoned a

provision in the Senate bill that would have transferred the functions of the FDA to the new commission. The new commission, with five members named by the President and confirmed by the Senate, would set and enforce safety standards for thousands of household, school and recreation products, including some formerly regulated by other agencies. (Included in coverage by standards of the new agency were toys, flammable fabrics, poisons and hazardous substances; excluded were tobacco, automobiles, pesticides, weapons, food, drugs and cosmetics.) The commission would have the power to ban the sale, order the recall or seek court seizures of unsafe products, and could inspect factories, conduct tests and subpoena records. It would regulate safety aspects of performance, composition, design and packaging of products. Violators of the standards would face criminal or civil penalties, and some private suits requiring the commission to enforce standards or seek damages from manufacturers would be allowed. Individuals could sue the commission to begin developing standards on a product, but no such suits would be permitted in the first three years of the commission's operations. (The Nixon Administration originally had opposed the bill, favoring instead an expansion of FDA authority. However, the Administration decided against introducing its proposal to expand the FDA on the House floor, fearing that an overwhelming defeat for the amendment—predicted by House observers—might threaten the continued existence of the FDA when the conference committee met.)

[17] **Vitamin doses curbed.** The FDA Dec. 13 announced a proposal, effective in 60 days, to sharply restrict the amounts of vitamin A and D that could be sold in over-the-counter products. The agency said the substances were "known to be toxic" and were "heavily promoted in high doses to the consumer." Overdoses of either vitamin could retard physical growth in children. Too much vitamin A also could cause bone lesions, irritability, or enlargement of the liver or spleen. An excess of vitamin D could cause nausea, listlessness or a rise in calcium deposits leading to hypertension and kidney failure. Currently marketed multivitamin products contained as much as 10 times the new permissible limit of vitamin A and 60 times the limit of vitamin D.

See also ATOMIC ENERGY [1]; AUTOMOBILES; BUSINESS; EDUCATION [6]; NIXON, RICHARD MILHOUS; POVERTY

CORPORATION FOR PUBLIC BROADCASTING—*See* TELEVISION & RADIO [10]

COSTA RICA—**Rail takeover.** According to a Jan. 7 report, President Jose Figueres Ferrer had ordered the temporary takeover of the administration of the British-owned Northern Railroad after railroad officials said they could not meet salary demands by 2,000 striking employees. The strikers reportedly returned to their jobs after the government promised to meet their demands. Officials said the government would eventually buy out British interests in the railroad and remain as the official owner.

See also CONSERVATION

COST OF LIVING COUNCIL (CLC)—*See* ECONOMY [4, 6, 8]; NIXON, RICHARD MILHOUS

COUNCIL OF ECONOMIC ADVISERS (CEA)—*See* ECONOMY [9]; UNEMPLOYMENT

COUNCIL ON ENVIRONMENTAL QUALITY—*See* ATOMIC ENERGY [3]; POLLUTION [3]

COUNCIL ON INTERNATIONAL ECONOMIC POLICY—*See* TARIFFS & WORLD TRADE

CRIME—**Rise slowed in 1971.** The Federal Bureau of Investigation (FBI) announced in its annual crime survey, released Aug. 28, that the rate of serious crime reported to police rose more slowly in 1971 than in any previous year since 1965. The FBI report showed that the slowdown had resulted from a slower rise in the rate of crimes against property, and not from the rate of crimes of violence. A total of 5,185,200 crimes against property were reported in 1971 (a rise of 7%), and 810,000 crimes of violence were reported in the same time (a rise of 11%). In a further breakdown, the report gave the following increases in crime categories: murder 11%; forcible rape 11%; forcible robbery 11%; aggravated assaults 10%; burglary 9%; and larceny 7%. (The FBI announced July 12 that its statistics showed that the rate of serious crime had increased only 1% in the first quarter of 1972 over the same period in 1971. It was the lowest percentage increase for the quarter in 11 years.)

[2] **8 cities to get funds.** The Nixon Administration announced Jan. 13 that Atlanta, Baltimore, Cleveland, Dallas, Denver, Newark, Portland and St. Louis would each receive about $20 million over the next three years to help their police departments fight street crime. Vice President Spiro Agnew said that the Administration hoped "to reduce street crimes and burglaries by 5% in two years and as much as 20% in five years in each of the cities." Under the program, known as the High Impact Anti-Crime Program, each city would receive $5 million in 1972, $10 million in 1973 and $5 million in 1974 for new and improved crime-fighting efforts. The funds were to come from the Justice Department's Law Enforcement Assistance Administration (LEAA). Most of the funds were to help cities improve new crime-fighting controls involving better radio-dispatch systems, increased use of helicopters, expanded public education campaigns and better training techniques for policemen.

[3] **Alioto, 2 others cleared.** San Francisco Mayor Joseph L. Alioto, former Washington state Attorney General John J. O'Connell and former Washington state Assistant Attorney General George K. Faler were cleared March 26 by a county jury in Vancouver, Wash. of civil charges stemming from their alleged splitting of $2.3 million in legal fees. (Washington state and 12 publicly owned utilities had sought to recover the legal fees paid to Alioto for antitrust work he did for them while he was a practicing attorney. The suit had charged that Alioto had improperly split the fees with O'Connell and Faler.) A. U.S. judge in Tacoma, Wash. announced June 19 a directed order of acquittal for the three on federal charges of bribery, conspiracy and mail fraud in connection with the same alleged incident. The judge's order meant that the trial would not go to jury and the government would not appeal the case.

[4] **New York Mafia war.** A reputed struggle for power within the Mafia was signaled March 31 when Conrad Greaves, the owner of a New York nightclub, was lured into a darkened street and riddled with bullets. Greaves had been cooperating with city officials investigating organized crime. In the early morning of April 7, Joseph ("Crazy Joey") Gallo, a reputed Mafia kingpin long suspected of having engineered the unsuccessful attempted assassination of Mafia leader Joseph Colombo in June 1971, was shot and killed in front of his wife and daughter as they were celebrating his 43rd birthday in a New York City restaurant. The shooting prompted speculation that Colombo's men had disregarded their superiors' orders not to avenge Colombo (critically wounded in the assassination attempt) and had acted on their own. By May 2, the alleged Mafia war had claimed 10 victims, all slain gangland style. Joseph Luparelli, an associate of the Colombo Mafia family, surrendered to the FBI in California because he feared he was marked for assassination and was reported May 3 to have told federal and New York City lawmen that he and four other men allied with the Colombo family had carried out the Gallo killing. Luparelli said that he had remained at the wheel of one of two getaway cars while Philip Gambino, Carmine Di Biase and two other unidentified men entered the restaurant where Gallo was eating. Gambino was arrested in New York May 4 for violating parole by associating with known criminals. In a later development, Thomas Eboli, a reputed East Coast Mafia leader, was shot and killed on a New York street July 16 by a gunman who pumped five bullets into him at point-blank range. Police said July 18 that they were not near an arrest in the case. (*Time* magazine reported July 31 that the gang war was an outgrowth of an effort by Carlo Gambino, a New York Mafia boss, to seize control of all New York Mafia families.)

[5] D.C. bars homosexual prosecution. The District of Columbia city government and the American Civil Liberties Union (ACLU) filed an agreement May 31 in U.S. District Court in Washington under which private, consenting homosexual acts among persons 16 years old and over would not be subject to criminal prosecution. The agreement resulted from a lawsuit against D.C. police by four homosexuals charging harassment.

[6] Wiretap law held unconstitutional. For the first time in a U.S. Court, judge ruled June 1 that the 1968 federal law authorizing law enforcement agencies to wiretap phones under certain circumstances was unconstitutional. In more than a dozen other cases, federal judges had upheld the law. However, Judge Joseph S. Lord 3rd in Philadelphia June 1 found the law "unconstitutional on its face" because it violated the Fourth Amendment protection of citizens against "unreasonable searches and seizures." At issue in the case was a motion sought by seven defendants in a gambling case to suppress evidence gathered by electronic surveillance. Attorney General Richard G. Kleindienst said June 9 that wiretapping "is a legitimate, constitutional means to root out organized crime," and asserted that the Administration would continue to use it. *(See also* SECURITY, U.S.)

[7] Bremer guilty in Wallace shooting. Arthur H. Bremer, an itinerant jobholder from Milwaukee, was found guilty Aug. 4 of shooting Gov. George C. Wallace of Alabama and three other persons at a political rally in Laurel, Md. *(see* ELECTIONS [10]). The main issue before the Upper Marlboro, Md. jury was whether Bremer was sane when he fired the shots or whether, as the defense had tried to establish, he was insane and unable to distinguish between right and wrong. Bremer was found guilty on all nine counts submitted to the jury. (Fifteen other charges had been dropped by the prosecution before the trial opened. Federal charges against Bremer were still pending.) After the jury's verdict was read, Judge Ralph W. Powers sentenced Bremer to 63 years in prison—15 years for assault of Wallace with intent to murder, 15 years for use of a handgun in a crime of violence against Wallace, three years for illegally carrying a handgun, 10 years for assault of Secret Service agent Nicholas Zarvos with intent to murder, 10 years for assault of Wallace campaign worker Mrs. Dora Thompson with intent to murder, 10 years for assault of Alabama State Police Capt. Eldred C. Dothard with intent to murder, and 30 years (to run concurrently with the three 10-year assault sentences) on gun charges. (A Maryland appeals court panel Sept. 28 dropped 10 years from the sentence.)

[8] The most dramatic moment of the Bremer trial came Aug. 3, when Bremer's defense attorney, Benjamin Lipsitz, read to the court excerpts from Bremer's diary. In the diary, Bremer described in detail a trip he took to Ottawa, Canada, where he had gone to assassinate President Nixon, who was in Ottawa on a state visit April 14-15. Lipsitz read to the court Bremer's narrative of how he was frustrated several times from using his .38-caliber revolver when the Nixon motorcade passed him in Ottawa. Bremer said he never got close enough to pull the gun from his pocket because the security was too tight or because the President's car sped by too fast. Bremer attributed the tight security to the presence of anti-Nixon demonstrators, whom he called "radical Commies." He closed that portion of his diary with an explanation: "Can't kill Nixie boy if you can't get close to him." Earlier in the trial, psychiatrists were examined and cross-examined by prosecution and defense lawyers who were at odds over Bremer's sanity at the time of the shooting. Most of the psychiatrists agreed that Bremer had the capacity to determine the culpability of his deed. Bremer was taken Aug. 5 to an isolated hospital cell at the Maryland Penitentiary in Baltimore, where a guard was posted for 24-hour duty. A prison spokesman said Bremer was being "handled as if he had suicidal tendencies."

[9] *Senate passes handgun curb.* The Senate voted 68-25 Aug. 9 to ban the manufacture and sale of snub-nosed handguns, low-cost firearms that were the most commonly used pistols in violent crimes. Under the bill, sponsored by Sen. Birch Bayh (D, Ind.), the manufacture and sale of most short-barreled guns would be outlawed. Guns of that type were used in the Wallace shooting and in the assassination of Robert F. Kennedy in 1968. The primary target of the bill was the low-cost, easily obtainable revolver commonly known as the "Saturday Night Special." The bill would limit the sales of such guns to law enforcement agencies and the military unless the pistols were found suitable for "lawful sporting purposes" under standards established by the secretary of the Treasury. The bill would not ban possession of short-barrel pistols already in the hands of Americans, but, according to Bayh, would ban the sale of 1 million of the 2.6 million handguns sold annually in the U.S. Among the criteria determining if a weapon was covered by the bill were overall size, safety features, weight and frame construction. The Senate approval of the bill followed the rejection Aug. 9 of proposals by Sens. Roman L. Hruska (R, Neb.) and Ted Stevens (R, Alaska) that would have watered down the bill and the rejection Aug. 7 of efforts by Sens. Edward M. Kennedy (D, Mass.) and Philip A. Hart (D, Mich.) that would have broadened the bill to ban possession of all handguns. The Kennedy-Hart amendment also would have required registration of all guns and licensing of all gun owners. The Hruska proposal would have permitted licensed gun dealers to continue the sale of existing stocks of snub-nosed handguns and the sale of second-hand guns of the type and would have outlawed the manufacture of new handguns only if they failed to win the approval of the secretary of the Treasury after adequate tests. The Stevens proposal would have changed the standards under which the secretary of the Treasury could determine what handguns were unsuitable for sporting purposes. The approved bill did include an amendment repealing controls over the sale of .22-caliber rimfire ammunition which could be used in both sporting rifles and low-cost handguns.

[10] **Supreme Court curbs capital punishment.** The Supreme Court ruled 5-4 June 29 that the death penalty as usually enforced in the U.S. was a violation of the Eighth Amendment prohibition against cruel and unusual punishment. However, the five justices in the majority (Justices Potter Stewart, Byron R. White, William O. Douglas, Thurgood Marshall and William J. Brennan Jr.) wrote separate opinions giving three different arguments against the death sentence, and the four dissenters (Chief Justice Warren E. Burger and Justices Lewis F. Powell Jr., Harry A. Blackmun and William H. Rehnquist) suggested that Congress and the state legislatures might comply with the court's ruling by "more narrowly defining the crimes for which the penalty is to be imposed" and by setting precise standards for judges and juries to follow in enforcing the laws. Stewart and White based their decisions on the arbitrary manner in which the death penalty was imposed. Douglas wrote that the disproportionate number of minority group or lower class individuals sentenced to death were victims of unconstitutional discrimination. Marshall and Brennan ruled that any form of capital punishment must be considered cruel and unusual punishment under current moral standards. The court's ruling set aside the sentences of two Georgia men—Henry Furman, convicted of murder, and Lucious Jackson, convicted of rape—and a Texas man—Elmer Branch, convicted of rape. Death sentences were also set aside for 128 other convicts who had petitioned the court for review. (It was estimated that 600 men and women were awaiting execution at the time of the ruling. That number included 329 blacks, 14 Mexicans, Puerto Ricans or American Indians, and 257 whites.) The defendants had been represented by the NAACP Legal Defense and Educational Fund, which had led a national drive against the death penalty that had successfully blocked all executions since June 2, 1967.

[11] *State actions.* The New Jersey Supreme Court ruled Jan. 17 that the state's death penalty was unconstitutional because it violated Fifth Amendment guarantees against self-incrimination. The justices held, in a 6-1 vote, that the death penalty coerced defendants into pleading no defense as a means of

avoiding a trial by jury of first-degree murder charges that could lead to the electric chair. The court noted that a plea of no defense was tantamount to a plea of guilty. Because of the ruling, the sentences of 20 condemned men on death row at the state prison in Trenton would be reduced to life imprisonment. The California Supreme Court ruled 6-1 Feb. 18 that the death penalty was cruel and unusual punishment and was in violation of the state's constitution. In its decision, the court said that the death penalty "degrades and dehumanizes all who participate in its processes. It is unnecessary to any legitimate goal of the state and is incompatible with the dignity of man and the judicial process." California Attorney General Evelle Younger March 3 filed a formal petition asking the court to reconsider its decision. California also appealed the state decision to the U.S. Supreme Court, which refused May 30 to hear the appeal. One hundred and seven condemned convicts were spared by the ruling. In another action, the Texas Court of Criminal Appeals March 15 upheld the constitutionality of the death penalty in Texas.

[12] **Supreme Court procedural decisions.** During 1972, the Supreme Court reached the following decisions pertaining to procedural matters (date of decision and the court vote are given in parentheses); that a prosecutor only had to show that contested confessions of criminal defendants were voluntary "by a preponderance of the evidence" to have them admitted as evidence (Jan. 11, 4-3); that trial judges cannot increase a defendant's punishment on the basis of earlier convictions obtained when the defendant was not represented by counsel (Jan. 11, 5-2); that juries need not return unanimous verdicts to convict defendants in state criminal court cases (May 22, 5-4), but must return unanimous verdicts to convict defendants in federal criminal court cases (May 22, 5-4); that prosecutors could use the threat of imprisonment to induce recalcitrant witnesses to testify without violating the Fifth Amendment, so long as the compelled testimony or any leads developed from it were not used against the witnesses (May 22, 5-2); that the court's 1967 ruling allowing criminal suspects to have counsel present at police lineup identifications applied only when the suspects had been indicted or otherwise formally charged (June 7, 5-4); that the court's 1963 *Gideon v. Wainwright* decision entitling poor defendants to free lawyers in felony trials applied to cases involving misdemeanors as well (June 12, 9-0); that a white defendant had as much right as a black to challenge a conviction on the ground that blacks were systematically excluded from the grand jury that indicted him (June 22, 6-3); and that a defendant who had not been brought to trial for murder for more than five years after his arrest was not denied a speedy trial, because he did not seek one and was not disadvantaged by the delay (June 22, 9-0). The court Nov. 20 also issued the first nationally uniform evidence standards in history. The rules of evidence, to be used by federal courts in both civil and criminal cases, were to be effective July 1, 1973, unless vetoed by Congress. They would permit the use of more kinds of evidence and do away with many old restrictions on admissibility. Cross-examination would be wide open and no longer limited to the scope of a witness's direct examination. The rules also eliminated some of the present restrictions on the opinion testimony of witnesses claiming to be experts on the matters at issue.

See also AVIATION; BLACK MILITANTS; BOOKS; CIVIL DISORDERS; CIVIL RIGHTS [19]; CONGRESS; DRUG USE & ADDICTION; ELECTIONS [6, 10, 17, 21, 44]; FEDERAL BUREAU OF INVESTIGATION; HIJACKING; HORSE RACING; HOUSING; INDIANS, AMERICAN; ISRAEL; JUDICIARY; MEDICINE; MILITARY [3]; MINES; NIXON, RICHARD MILHOUS; PENTAGON PAPERS; PESTICIDES; POLICE; POLITICS [9-12]; PRISONS; RHODESIA; SECURITY, U.S.; STUDENT UNREST

CROATIA—*See* HIJACKING [13]; YUGOSLAVIA

CUBA—U.S. orders warships to resist seizures. In a change of policy, reported April 13, the U.S. ordered its military command in the Caribbean to protect merchant ships from harassment by the Cuban navy. The new instructions—which reversed previous nonintervention directives that had been in effect during the December 1971 Cuban seizure of two Panamanian-registered ships—reportedly authorized military commanders in the area to "interpose" U.S. warships between Cuban attackers and endangered merchant ships to block the Cuban line of fire and thwart any boarding attempts. The "interposition" could be ordered without instructions from Washington or even a request from the country whose ship seemed threatened. The only requisites for ordering such action were: that the merchant ship facing seizure be sailing in international waters at least three miles from the Cuban shore; the commander giving the order must have "no knowledge" that the threatened ship had been engaging in illegal activities against Cuba; and the U.S. commander must have reason to believe some U.S. citizens were aboard the threatened ship. The report on the new directives noted that the commander need not make certain either that the ship was not engaged in illegal activities or that U.S. lives were in danger. (The orders stated that, "in the absence of other certification" that a U.S. citizen was aboard the ship, the U.S. commander could "take the word" of the ship's captain.)

Castro tour. During an unprecedented two-month absence from Cuba, Premier Fidel Castro visited 10 nations in Africa and Eastern Europe May 3-July 6, capping his tour with a 10-day visit to the Soviet Union, where he received assurances of continued economic assistance and support for Cuba's foreign policy. Castro's itinerary: Guinea May 3-8; Sierra Leone May 8; Algeria May 8-17; Bulgaria May 17-26; Rumania May 26-30; Hungary May 30-June 6; Poland June 6-13; East Germany June 13-21; Czechoslovakia June 21-26; and the Soviet Union June 26-July 6. Castro held long talks with leaders of each country he visited except in Sierra Leone, where he remained only a few hours. He spoke in public frequently, asserting Cuba's support for socialist and revolutionary governments and making constant references to the Indochina war. According to a press report June 23, the trip gave Cuba a forum in which to express solidarity with revolutionary regimes, such as those in Algeria and Guinea, and gave Communist bloc countries the opportunity to showcase Castro, whose vitality and unconventionality caused a sensation among Eastern Europeans. The Cuban press repeatedly stressed the length of the journey, saying it showed the strength and unity of Cuban leadership and disproved the frequent charge that the government could not make day-to-day decisions without Castro.

Anti-Castro plot uncovered. Justice Department officials in New Orleans July 2 announced the arrest of nine men (including two Mexicans and a former U.S. immigration official) and seizure of seven tons of contraband ammunition allegedly to be used to overthrow Premier Castro. The arms were reportedly taken at an airport near Shreveport, La., and the suspects were arrested in Louisiana and Texas. According to one official, the ammunition was to have been shipped clandestinely to Veracruz, Mexico, from which point it would have gone to Cuba to be used by Anti-Castro insurgents.

Sugar harvest ends. The 1972 sugar harvest ended July 18. President Osvaldo Dorticos was quoted July 19 as saying the harvest had been "bad," but "the workers of this nation have made an effort that saves our honor and prestige and meets the vital needs of our economy." According to estimates July 28, the harvest had been 4.1 million tons—lower than recent harvests, but higher than the most pessimistic forecasts. Cuba reportedly would still earn as much as $560 million from sugar exports in 1972, since a scarcity of sugar had pushed the world market price up to nearly 10¢ per pound.

Government reorganized. Cuba's governmental structure was reorganized Nov. 25 following a "reorientation" of the Communist party. Under the change, seven Cabinet ministers were promoted to vice premier. Each of the seven new deputies would supervise several ministries and previously independent state agencies, with direct responsibility to Premier Castro. With Castro, Dorticos and First Vice Premier Raul Castro, they would form a new executive committee of the Council of Ministers, whose decision would have to be followed to the letter by local officials. Six of the new ministers—Majs. Ramiro Valdes (construction and related agencies), Guillermo Garcia Frias (communications, transport, merchant marine and ports), Pedro Miret Prieto (basic industries, mines and metallurgy), Flavio Bravo Pardo (light industry, food and internal commerce), Belarmino Catillo Mas (education, culture and science) and Diocles Torralba Gonzalez (sugar)—were army officers, continuing a trend toward military influence in the government. The lone civilian promoted was Carlos Rafael Rodriguez, an old-line Communist party leader who, as minister without portfolio, had been Premier Castro's chief foreign policy operative. Rodriguez would be in charge of the Foreign Ministry and the economic, scientific and technical collaboration commission. President Dorticos was assigned control of the Central Bank; the Foreign Trade, Labor and Justice Ministries; the Central Planning Commission; and the National Fishing Institute. Raul Castro was given no new duties, but remained head of the armed forces.

See also ARGENTINA [12]; ARMAMENTS, INTERNATIONAL; BAHAMAS; BOLIVIA; CANADA [2]; CHILE [4]; EUROPEAN ECONOMIC COMMUNITY [7]; HIJACKING [1-3, 6, 19]; KOREA, SOUTH; LATIN AMERICA; POLITICS [9]; SINO-U.S. RELATIONS [2]; SOVIET-U.S. RELATIONS [11]; STORMS

CULEBRA ISLAND—*See* PUERTO RICO

CYCLING—Merckx wins Tour de France. Eddie Merckx of Belgium, one of the greatest cyclists in the history of the sport, won his fourth consecutive Tour de France race July 23, crossing the finish line in Paris more than 10 minutes ahead of his closest challenger, Felice Gimondi of Italy. Merckx's time for the 3,840-kilometer race was 108 hours 27 minutes 59 seconds. Only France's Jacques Anquetil, with five wins (1957, 1961-64), had won the Tour de France more times than Merckx.

CYPRUS—Greek demands to Makarios. Greek Foreign Affairs Undersecretary Constantine Panayotakos Feb. 11 delivered a strongly worded note to Archbishop Makarios, president of Cyprus, urging the Cypriot government to take a series of actions to avoid open conflict between opposing elements of the Greek-Cypriot population. The note asked Makarios to surrender to the United Nations Force in Cyprus (UNFICYP, a peacekeeping force) a $2.5 million shipment of arms allegedly imported secretly from Czechoslovakia in January. Panayotakos warned Feb. 12 that bloodshed would result if Makarios enlarged his police force and distributed arms to "irresponsible elements," a reference to Makarios's reported plans to combat what the Cypriot government described as an anti-government conspiracy spearheaded by Gen. George Grivas, the leading advocate of enosis (union of Cyprus with Greece). The note to Makarios also called for the formation of a new anti-Communist Cypriot government of national unity and for Cyprus's acknowledgement of "Athens as the center of Hellenism, of which Cyprus is only a part." Turkey Feb. 15 expressed support for the Greek demands.

Makarios formally replied to the Greek demands March 14. The text of the reply was not made public, but an unidentified Greek official said "at first sight, it looks satisfactory." The reply reportedly informed the Greek government of an agreement made with the UNFICYP March 10 by which the UNFICYP would verify and inspect the Czechoslovakian arms. Makarios also took action in May and June to reform his government. Foreign Minister Spyros Kyprianou resigned May 5, apparently yielding to pressure from the Greek government. Makarios June 16 appointed seven new members to his 10-man Cabinet to replace Kyprianou and six other ministers. The new ministers: foreign affairs—Ioannis Christofides; education—Andreas Kouros; justice—

Christos Vakis; agriculture and natural resources—Odyssefs Ioannides; labor and social insurance—Markos Spanos; communications and works—Yiangos Zamparloukos; and commerce and industry—Michael Colocassides. Those retaining their posts were Interior Minister Georghios Ioannides, Finance Minister Andreas Patsalides and Health Minister Michael Glykys.

Bishops ask Makarios to resign. The Holy Synod of the Cypriot Orthodox Church—composed of Bishops Anthimos of Kitium, Gennadios of Paphos and Kyprianos of Kyrenia—March 2 called on Makarios to resign as president of Cyprus. The bishops based their demand on a canonical law prohibition in the Orthodox Church against an archbishop holding temporal power. Makarios March 19 refused to quit the presidency, but said that he might be obliged to resign if the bishops insisted. He warned that such a move could lead to a "national disaster" and charged that the bishops' request bore "evident signs of nonecclesiatical inspiration," an apparent reference to the Greek government's pressure on Makarios to accede to its demands. The bishops March 27 reiterated their demand and accused Makarios of abandoning the ideal of enosis, of tolerating the growth of Communism in government and public life and of permitting the rise of anti-Greek attitudes as well as the rise of atheism and nihilism. The bishops June 2 again reiterated their demand for Makarios's resignation, this time warning that they would expel the archbishop from the church if he failed to comply. Makarios June 10 rejected the renewed demand.

Intercommunal talks resumed. Under pressure from United Nations Secretary General Kurt Waldheim, a new round of the deadlocked talks between the Greek and Turkish Cypriot communities resumed June 8 in Nicosia, Cyprus. Attending the meeting were Glafkos Clerides and Rauf Denktash, the Greek and Cypriot negotiators respectively, as well as the U.N. special representative on Cyprus, Bibiano F. Osorio-Tafall, and advisers from Greece and Turkey. The presence of the U.N. representative and the Greek and Turkish advisers was part of a formula for broadened intercommunal talks agreed upon in 1971. The first working phase of the talks was held in Nicosia July 3-21.

UNFICYP extended. The U.N. Security Council June 15 voted 14-0 to extend the UNFICYP to Dec. 15. (China abstained.) In a sharply pessimistic report to the council prior to the vote, Waldheim warned that the situation in Cyprus was "anything but encouraging." He said the mutual suspicion between the Greek and Turkish communities in Cyprus had led to "a political instability and an atmosphere of tension and recrimination, which is extremely dangerous, especially in view of the relatively large number of persons bearing arms."

See also EUROPEAN SECURITY; GREECE [10]; INTERNATIONAL MONETARY DEVELOPMENTS [8]

CZECHOSLOVAKIA—1971 economic results. Results of the 1971 economic development plan were announced Jan. 27. Increases over 1970 figures were reported on the following major items: industrial production 6.9%; foreign trade 9.4% (with imports up 8.7% and exports increasing 10%); agricultural production 2.8%; building work 9.7%; personal incomes 5.5%; and personal consumption 5%.

Subversion trials. In nine trials July 19-Aug. 10 the government convicted 46 supporters of former Communist party First Secretary Alexander Dubcek on charges of subversion and of distributing anti-state leaflets prior to 1971 general elections. Some of the accused, several of whom had been members of the party Central Committee about the time when the Soviet Union invaded the country in 1968 to reverse the liberalization which had taken place under Dubcek, were charged with forming illegal organizations and maintaining contact with Czechoslovak emigres.

Those found guilty (jail sentences in parentheses): former Czechoslovak radio employee Premysl Vondra (28 months) and former Communist party college professor Ota Krizanovsky (18 months), sentenced July 19 on charges of subversion; historian Josef Belda (12 months, suspended), sentenced July 19 on charges of incitement; former Prague Central Committee Secretary Jiri Littera (2.5 years), Josef Stehlik (2 years) and Milan Rocek (1 year, suspended), sentenced July 20 on charges of distributing anti-government . pamphlets between 1970 and 1972; historian Jan Tesar (6 years), former student leader Jiri Mueller (5.5 years), sociologist Rudolf Battek (3.5 years), former Czechoslovak Student Union Secretary Jaroslav Jira (2.5 years), former army officer Stanislav Furek (2 years, suspended) and computer engineer Pavel Maries (1 year, suspended), sentenced July 21 on charges of having "duplicated various leaflets of an antistate character, which they disseminated together with inciting literature published in unfriendly foreign countries" and on various individual charges; the Rev. Jaromir Dus (15 months), sentenced July 25 on charges of subversion; historian Vladislav Hejdanek (9 months), his wife Hedvika (suspended) and lawyer Jiri Jirasek (suspended), sentenced July 25 on charges of incitement for distributing pamphlets in 1971 reminding voters of their right to cross out names on the election ballot; six persons, none of the well known, sentenced to 2-5 years July 26 for allegedly having formed an "illegal group" between 1970 and January 1972 which "carried out concrete hostile activities" with the aim of overthrowing "the Socialist state system"; Jan Sabata (2.5 years), Vaclav Sabata (2 years), Zuzana Richterovl (suspended) and Ales Krehulka (suspended), sentenced July 26 on charges of subversion; Marek Golias (suspended) and Tomas Bochorak (suspended), sentenced July 26 on charges of aiding a felony by allegedly passing out antistate leaflets and attempting to get others to help them; former Communist party political college head Milan Huebl (6.5 years) and former radio commentator Kael Kyncl (20 months), sentenced Aug. 1 on charges of subversion for allegedly distributing "illegal leaflets" and for allegedly compiling an underground chronicle of events following the 1968 invasion; historian Karel Bartosek (suspended), sentenced Aug. 1 for aiding a felony; former Central Committee member and Communist party secretary in Brno, Moravia Joroslav Sabata (father of Jan Sabata) (6.5 years), former Central Committee member Alfred Cerny (3 years) and five other persons (ranging up to 5 years) sentenced Aug. 8 on charges of plotting to overthrow the Socialist system; Vlastmila Tesarova (4 years), Anna Sabatova (Joroslav Sabata's daughter) (3.5 years) and six others, sentenced Aug. 10 for subversion.

Although foreign reaction tended to see the defendants as having been tried for their political opinions, the Communist party newspaper Rude Pravo argued Aug. 2 that they had been prosecuted only for breaking the law. The paper said those being sentenced had "spread doubts and hostility against the leading representatives of our Socialist state, tried to undermine the process of political consolidation and our relationship with the U.S.S.R." They had "maintained contact with some emigres who are carrying on hostile activities against our state, incited them to these activities and gave them for this purpose various pamphlets which grossly slandered our state.... They spread lack of confidence. They began activities aimed at creating organized groups of citizens of the same political opinions in order to misuse them for subversive activities." Rude Pravo added that "Nobody in Czechoslovakia denies them their personal opinions, whatever kind they are. But they cannot with impunity change their hostile and subversive opinions into acts and concrete deeds by which they break the law and threaten the calm and security of the state and its citizens."

See also ATOMIC ENERGY [6]; AUSTRIA; CHESS; CUBA; CYPRUS; ENVIRONMENT; ESPIONAGE; HIJACKING [10, 15]; HOCKEY; POLAND; SPACE [22]

DAHOMEY—Assassination attempt foiled. President Hubert Maga Feb. 23 announced that eight soldiers, four of them officers, had been arrested after trying to assassinate Col. Paul-Emile de Souza, the army chief of staff. De Souza was wounded during the attempt. A military tribunal May 16 sentenced six soldiers, including Col. Maurice Kouandete (assistant secretary general for defense), to death for their part in the assassination attempt. Eleven soldiers were given sentences ranging from five years to life. A civilian and five other soldiers were acquitted.

Powers transferred. President Maga May 7 transferred his powers to Justin Ahomadegbe under an arrangement by which the leadership of the country changed hands each two years among members of a presidential triumvirate. Each president assumed the portfolios of defense and interior and nominated four of the 12 Cabinet ministers.

Coup ousts Ahomadegbe. Elements of the army Oct. 26 seized power in Cotonou, ousting President Ahomadegbe and other members of the ruling triumvirate and replacing them with an 11-man military government. (It was the 11th coup since Dahomey became independent from France in 1960.) Troops reportedly surrounded the presidential palace while the Cabinet was in session and entered the building, "shooting as they went." Maj. Mathieu Kerekou, deputy chief of staff of the armed forces and leader of the attack, was named president and defense minister Oct. 27. Maj. Michael Alabaye became foreign minister, and Maj. Thomas Lahami was named minister of finance. The new government announced Oct. 28 that it was holding an unspecified number of national leaders under arrest. The dispatch did not mention Ahomadegbe or Maga, but called upon Sourou Migan Apithy, the third member of the Presidential Council, to return from France or be considered an exile.

See also AFRICA

DEFENSE—STRAF units found ill-prepared. The General Accounting Office (GAO) May 17 released a 1970-71 study of the Strategic Armed Forces (STRAF) in the U.S. that concluded that many STRAF units "are not combat ready." The GAO, the auditing authority of Congress, said it had based its report on a review of selected units of three out of the four and one-third divisions that made up the STRAF in 1970-71. (Since the time of the study, the Army had increased STRAF to six full divisions.) According to the GAO, STRAF units based in the U.S. were supposed to be "constantly available on short notice for deployment in an emergency," but in the units reviewed "more than one-third of the essential combat and combat support equipment was unable to perform its primary mission." The GAO report concluded that "so many tanks, radars and rifles are defective that these three divisions are not considered ready for combat." (The fourth STRAF division at the time of the report, the 82nd Airborne at Fort Bragg, N.C., was not reviewed by the study, but was considered then and presently to be the most combat-ready Army division in the U.S.)

New fighter unveiled. The Air Force June 26 put on display for the first time its new F-15 fighter, the plane designed to maintain U.S. air superiority into the 1980s. Grant L. Hansen, assistant secretary of the Air Force, said that the twin-tail F-15 (manufactured by McDonnell-Douglas) "will outclimb, outmaneuver and outaccelerate any fighter threat in existence or seen on the horizon." The plane had a planned top speed of Mach 2.5 (2.5 times the speed of sound). The 20 F-15s and equipment to be used in development and testing would cost nearly $1.2 billion. The Air Force planned to have a fleet of 749 F-15s.

Helicopter program dropped. The Army announced Aug. 9 that it had dropped its Cheyenne helicopter program, which was started in 1965 and had cost a reported $401 million, but which had failed to progress beyond the development of 10 test models. The Cheyenne helicopter, contracted to the Lockheed Aircraft Corp., was to have been a high-speed, heavily armed antitank craft. The Army also planned to use it to provide close air support for ground troops. However, troubles at Lockheed over rising costs and technical difficulties *(see below)* prevented the firm from meeting its contractual schedule to deliver the first Cheyennes by September 1969. The entire Cheyenne fleet of 375 aircraft was to have been ready by 1973. (The Senate Armed Forces Committee April 26 had virtually doomed the Cheyenne program by rejecting an Army request for $58.6 million for further production of the helicopter. The committee move came in consideration of a Defense Department procurement authorization bill. *See below.*)

Defense Spending Developments

GAO assails extra buying. Rep. Les Alpin (D, Wis.) Feb. 21 released a report by the GAO charging that the Air Force had wasted millions of dollars on spare parts for new planes. The GAO indicated that its indictment was directed at Air Force policy as it applied to all new aircraft, but the report singled out the accident-plagued F-111 fighter-bomber. According to the report, it cost the Air Force $56 million in markup to buy F-111 spare parts through the General Dynamics Corp., the plane's principal contractor. If the parts had been purchased from subcontractors making the parts, the GAO charged, a "significant" portion of that amount could have been saved. The GAO report also said that almost $116 million was spent for F-111 spare parts before they were needed and that $9.6 million worth of that purchase already had been "declared excess." In addition, the report charged that many spare parts common to more than one of the F-111 models were bought more than once, even when experience with the original part "indicated little or no usage." In related developments, General Dynamics and four present or former company officials were indicted by a federal grand jury in Dallas May 30 on charges of conspiring to defraud the Air Force by making it pay $300,000 for defective F-111 parts made by a subcontractor, the Selb Manufacturing Co. of

Walnut Ridge, Ark. (The defective parts reportedly were never turned over to the Air Force or used in construction of the planes.) The Air Force June 20 suspended flight operations of virtually all its F-111 fleet following two unexplained crashes of the aircraft June 15 and June 18. The suspension of operations was lifted June 26 after an investigation revealed no common cause to link the two crashes. (It had been the seventh time the Air Force had grounded the F-111.)

C-5A inquiry sought. Sen. William Proxmire (D, Wis.) March 27 asked the Justice Department to open a criminal investigation into a report that the government had made a $400 million overpayment to Lockheed Aircraft for development of the Air Force's C-5A cargo plane, the largest aircraft in the world. Proxmire acted on the basis of a GAO report which he had commissioned in 1971 to investigate accusations made by a former Lockheed employee that the C-5A development had been marked by "waste and mismanagement." The GAO report, according to Proxmire, "found that the Air Force paid $400 million in excess payments to Lockheed because the company understated the value of the work completed and overstated the value of the work in progress." At the same time, Proxmire made available a report by the Pentagon's Defense Contract Audit Agency which said that the $400 million overpayment exceeded the entire net worth of Lockheed. (The GAO also submitted an unpublicized study, according to a report April 6, which detailed known C-5A problems—including difficulties with the plane's wings, landing gear and engine mounts—and questioned the plane's ability to perform certain tactical combat missions. The study also questioned maintenance difficulties with the plane.)

F-14 contract unchanged. The Senate Armed Services Committee July 17 refused to rewrite a government contract with the Grumman Corp. to give the firm more money for construction of the Navy's swing-wing F-14 fighter plane, which was to be the backbone of the Navy's air arm in the mid-1970s. The committee's decision was made despite a claim April 17 by E. Clinton Towl, Grumman's chairman, that its subsidiary building the F-14, Grumman Aerospace Corp., would be "financially unable" to build 48 more of the fighters if it failed to get more money for work on the plane. (Grumman had announced Jan. 20 that the subsidiary expected to lose about $65 million on the contract.) The committee's decision was written into the military procurement authorization bill. (Sen. Proxmire April 16 had released a GAO report which contended that the F-14 would be inferior in some ways to the F-4, a plane that cost only one-fourth as much.) The Navy announced Dec. 11 that it would exercise its option to purchase the 48 additional planes. Grumman announced the same day that it would not honor the existing contract and would not build the aircraft under the old terms.

Spending defended. The Pentagon, in a sweeping defense of its economic policies, struck back at critics Aug. 10 in a report it said was designed to "debunk the view" that defense spending excessively strained the nation's budget. The report, titled "The Economics of Defense Spending—A Look at the Realities," was compiled by Robert C. Moot, comptroller of the Defense Department. The study made the following statements: that, once the effects of inflation were calculated, defense spending was at its lowest point in 21 years; that defense presently accounted for 20% of all government spending—federal, state and local—and about 30% of all federal spending; that defense now accounted for a smaller portion of the nation's manpower than at any other time since 1953; and that, in terms of current dollars, weapons procurement now was $300 million more than eight years before, prior to the Vietnam war. The report also disclosed that the extra cost of the Vietnam war resulting from the increased actions of U.S. forces in response to the North Vietnamese spring offensive *(see* INDOCHINA WAR [15]) would be $1.1 billion.

See also BUDGET; DISARMAMENT; ELECTIONS [5, 8-9, 16, 23, 34-35]; ESPIONAGE; EUROPEAN SECURITY; GREECE [5]; MILITARY; NIXON,

RICHARD MILHOUS; SELECTIVE SERVICE SYSTEM; SOVIET-U.S. RELATIONS [2]; SPACE [21]

DEMOCRATIC PARTY—*See* CIVIL DISORDERS; CONGRESS; ELECTIONS [1-10, 12-13, 15-20, 22-23, 27-34, 36, 38-42]; POLITICS [1, 8-14]

DENMARK—King dies, first reigning queen proclaimed. King Frederick IX, 72, died Jan. 14 in Copenhagen following more than two weeks of illness caused by pneumonia and a heart attack. He had reigned for 25 years. Princess Margrethe, the king's eldest daughter, Jan. 15 was proclaimed Queen Margrethe II, Denmark's first reigning queen, by Premier Jens Otto Krag. (Denmark's constitution had been amended in 1953 to enable Princess Margrethe to succeed her father because he had no male heir. Margrethe I had ruled the country in the 14th and 15th centuries, but was never crowned because there was no female right of succession.)

1973 budget approved. The Folketing (parliament) April 6 unanimously approved the Danish budget for fiscal year 1973 (April 1, 1972-March 31, 1973). Expenditures were estimated at 45 billion krone ($6.4 billion), an increase of 5 billion krone over the previous year.

Krag resigns. In an unexpected move, Premier Krag Oct. 3 announced his resignation to the opening session of the Folketing. Krag later cited personal reasons for his resignation, such as his desire to write and paint. Krag had been a central figure in Danish politics for 25 years. He had served as premier from 1962-68 and returned to office in 1971.. His Social Democratic party immediately named as his successor Anker Jorgensen, leader of the General Workers Union and a parliamentary deputy since 1964. Jorgensen had never held a government post. Pending Jorgensen's formal installation as premier, Foreign Minister Knud Boerge Andersen was designated interim premier. Jorgensen was formally invested by Queen Margrethe Oct. 5.

See also ATOMIC ENERGY [6, 8]; CONSERVATION; ESPIONAGE; EUROPEAN ECONOMIC COMMUNITY [1, 10-12, 18]; INTERNATIONAL MONETARY DEVELOPMENTS [6]; POLLUTION [13]; TERRITORIAL WATERS

DENT, FREDERICK BAILY—*See* NIXON, RICHARD MILHOUS
DES—*See* CONSUMER AFFAIRS [2]
DE VALERA, EAMON—*See* IRELAND
DEVALUATION—*See* BOLIVIA; INTERNATIONAL MONETARY DEVELOPMENTS [3, 5-6]
DEVELOPING NATIONS—*See* EUROPEAN ECONOMIC COMMUNITY [7, 10]; TARIFFS & WORLD TRADE
DEVLIN, BERNADETTE—*See* NORTHERN IRELAND [3]
DIMITRIOS I—*See* CHURCHES

DISARMAMENT—Senate ratifies seabed treaty. The Senate, by an 83-0 vote Feb. 15, ratified a treaty barring deployment of nuclear weapons on the ocean floor beyond the 12-mile territorial limit recognized by most nations. The treaty had been signed by the U.S. and 85 other nations in 1971. France and China, both nuclear powers, had not signed. The treaty came into force May 18 after it had been ratified by 28 nations.

Geneva conference. The United Nations Conference of the Committee on Disarmament, meeting in Geneva, began its 1972 session Feb. 29. Opening discussions centered on the need for an underground nuclear test ban and on the need for encouraging the participation of China and France in the conference. (France, one of the original 26 members of the conference, had never participated.) U.N. Secretary General Kurt Waldheim told the delegates that there was "an increasing conviction among nations of the world that an underground test ban is the single most important measure, and perhaps the only one in the near future, to halt the nuclear arms race, at least with regard to its qualitative aspects." The Canadian representative to the talks, George Ignatieff, asserted March 2 that the U.S.-Soviet failure to achieve an underground test ban was responsible for the "evident lack of interest" on the part of China and France in nuclear talks. The Mexican delegate, Alfonso Garcia Robles, Feb. 29 suggested that France and China might be induced to join the conference if the U.S. and the Soviet Union relinquished their co-chairmanship of the body and allowed the chairmanship to be rotated on a monthly or yearly basis.

Work on chemical ban. Much of the work done throughout 1972 by the Geneva conference centered on achieving a ban on chemical weapons. However, the conference adjourned for the year Sept. 7 with no apparent progress in resolving a U.S.-Soviet deadlock on a means of verifying such a ban. (The U.S. insisted on on-site inspection to verify compliance, while the U.S.S.R. opposed on-site inspection.) The Soviet Union March 28 had presented a draft treaty banning chemical weapons. The text of the treaty, similar to the treaty banning biological weapons accepted by the U.N. General Assembly in 1971 (see CHEMICAL & BIOLOGICAL WARFARE), asked all nations to agree "never in any circumstances to develop, produce, stockpile or otherwise acquire or retain" the means of chemical warfare. Those means were defined as "chemical agents of types and in quantities that have not justification for peaceful purposes" and "weapons, equipment, or means of delivery designed to use such agents for hostile purposes or in armed conflict." The U.S. had argued that it was too early to start work on a draft treaty and that the conference should first explore a U.S. "working paper" presented March 21 which had reviewed means of defining the chemical substances to be controlled and had put forth tentative suggestions on ways of assuring compliance with such a ban. Joseph B. Godber, British minister of state for foreign and commonwealth affairs, Aug. 8 put forward to the conference a proposal to end the deadlock over means of verification on a chemical weapons ban, but the Soviet Union rejected the proposal Sept. 5. The plan would have provided a two-stage process in which "one stage would be the elimination of stockpiles (with a freeze on production) and the other would be the elimination of productive capacity." Godber said it made no difference which step was taken first, provided there was a commitment to take the second step.

Arms limitation agreements signed. U.S. President Richard Nixon and Soviet General Secretary Leonid I. Brezhnev May 26 signed two agreements in Moscow limiting offensive and defensive strategic weapons. One of the agreements limited antiballistic missile (ABM) systems, and the other limited offensive missile launchers. Both accords had been worked out in months of Strategic Arms Limitation Talks (SALT) between U.S. and Soviet officials. The ABM accord allowed each nation two antiballistic missile systems—one "centered on the party's national capital" and the other located elsewhere to guard a portion of the nation's offensive missile force. No site could employ more than 100 ABM interceptor missiles and the same number of launchers. Radar complexes at each site were to be limited. The "modernization and replacement of ABM systems and their components" were to be permitted. Violations were to be monitored by spy satellites, referred to in the treaty as "national technical means of verification," and each side agreed not to interfere with the other's satellites or to "use deliberate concealment measures which impede verification." A "standing consultative commission" was to be established to deal with such questions as "unintended interference" with satellites, "possible changes in the strategic situation which have a bearing on this treaty" and "procedures and dates for destruction and dismantling of ABM systems" in excess of what the treaty allowed. The treaty was to be of "unlimited duration."

The agreement on offensive weapons was classified as an interim agreement. In it, the parties agreed "not to start construction of additional land-based intercontinental ballistic missile (ICBM) launchers after July 1, 1972." Submarine-launched ballistic missile (SLB) launchers and "modern ballistic missile submarines" were to be limited "to the numbers operational and under construction on the date of signature" of the agreement. Modernization and replacement of existing missiles and launchers could be undertaken. The accord was to last five years. It also provided that there was to be no interference with satellites and contained an agreement "to continue active negotiations for limitations on strategic offensive weapons." The agreement was accompanied by a protocol limiting the U.S. to no more than 710 SLBMs and no more than 44 missile-launching submarines, and limiting the Soviet Union to 950 SLBMs and 62 modern submarines. Some replacements were to be allowed for "launchers of older types deployed prior to 1964."

 Pacts submitted to Congress. The pacts required approval by the U.S. Senate, although both Nixon and Brezhnev promised May 26 to abide by them immediately. (Defense Secretary Melvin Laird May 27 ordered the U.S. Army to halt construction work on a Safeguard ABM base at Malmstrom Air Force Base in Montana and to drop construction plans for projected ABM sites not already under way. The order did not affect the nearly completed Safeguard site at the Grand Forks Air Force Base in North Dakota.) The interim agreement, signed as an executive agreement, required approval by both the Senate and the House. President Nixon submitted the pacts to Congress June 13 along with the texts of 18 understandings reached with the Soviet Union on "agreed interpretations," including "unilateral statements" specifying areas of disagreement. The areas of disagreement included: a Soviet refusal to agree to a ban on mobile land-based offensive weapons that could be mounted on railroad cars and trucks; the Soviet refusal to subscribe to the U.S. interpretation of a "heavy" missile as any ICBM having a "significantly greater" volume than the largest "light" ICBM (barred by the treaty from being converted into a "heavy" ICBM); and the U.S. refusal to accept a Soviet position that the U.S.S.R. would limit its submarine force to 62 in exchange for a limitation to 50 such vessels for the Atlantic alliance, which included Britain and France. (The U.S. refused to encompass other countries in the bilateral agreement.)

 Approval in Congress. The ABM pact was approved by an 88-2 vote in the Senate Aug. 2. Quick ratification of the offensive weapons pact was expected, but approval was delayed when Sens. Henry Jackson (D, Wash.), Hugh Scott (R, Pa.) and Gordon Allott (R, Colo.) Aug. 3 offered a substitute resolution asking that any future treaty on arms following the five-year interim pact be based on numerical equality. The Jackson resolution also contained a Congressional warning that, if the Soviet Union took any steps—even those permitted under the agreement—that threatened America's land-based strategic forces, that would be grounds for abrogation of the interim agreement and for U.S. countermoves. The White House Aug. 7 gave its support to an abridged version of Jackson's proposal, but withdrew the approval Aug. 9, resuming its no-compromise position on the interim agreement. The Senate Foreign Relations Committee Aug. 10 cleared the way for a floor vote on the interim agreement by defeating Jackson's substitute resolution and other proposals offered as amendments to the accord. The House backed the interim agreement Aug. 18 by a 329-7 vote, and the Senate cleared the measure Sept. 14 by an 88-2 vote. The Senate approval included a Jackson amendment calling upon the President in any future treaty on offensive nuclear weapons not to limit the U.S. "to levels of intercontinental strategic forces inferior to the limits provided for the Soviet Union." The House Sept. 25 voted 306-4 to accept the Senate version, obviating a conference on the Senate and House bills. President Nixon signed the bill Sept. 30, after the Presidium of the Supreme Soviet ratified both arms pacts Sept. 29. Following two days of talks in Washington, Nixon and Soviet Foreign Minister Andrei A. Gromyko Oct. 3 signed documents putting both agreements into effect.

 See also ATOMIC ENERGY [13]; CHEMICAL & BIOLOGICAL WARFARE; ENVIRONMENT; EUROPEAN SECURITY; FOREIGN POLICY; POLAND; SOVIET-U.S. RELATIONS [1, 4-6]

DISASTERS—*See* AVIATION; EARTHQUAKES; FLOODS; INDIA [6]; MINES; RAILROADS; SHIPS & SHIPPING; STORMS; TELEVISION & RADIO [5]

DISTRICT OF COLUMBIA—*See* CONGRESS; POLITICS [8]
DIVORCE—*See* HAITI; IRELAND; ITALY [6]
DOCK STRIKES—*See* CANADA [11-12]; ECONOMY [10]; GREAT BRITAIN [1,
12-14]; INTERNATIONAL MONETARY DEVELOPMENTS [6]; LABOR
DOLE, ROBERT J.—*See* POLITICS [15]
DOLLAR—*See* ECONOMY [2]; INTERNATIONAL MONETARY
DEVELOPMENTS [2-3, 5-6, 8, 11]
DOMESTIC INTERNATIONAL SALES CORPORATIONS (DISCS)—*See* SOVIET-
U.S. RELATIONS [10]

DOMINICAN REPUBLIC—12 die as police battle guerrillas. A day-long battle
Jan. 12 between police forces, using bazookas and mortars, and a band of leftist
guerrillas, wanted in a $50,000 robbery of the Royal Bank of Canada in
November 1971, was reported to have resulted in the deaths of eight policemen
and four guerrillas. The battle, which began at a guerrilla hideout 14 miles east
of the capital, touched off riots in Santo Domingo as students supporting the
terrorists took to the streets, throwing rocks and smashing windows. Gen. Neit
Nivar Seijas, national chief of police, ordered schools closed and imposed strong
security measures to head off further incidents.

University occupied. Ten persons were wounded and more than 150 were
arrested April 4 as police and soldiers searching for Tacito Perdomo Robles,
leader of the extremist Dominican Popular Movement (MPD), occupied the
Autonomous University of Santo Domingo (UASD) and fired on students and
teachers. Police invaded the campus after demanding that UASD rector Jotin
Cury produce Perdomo, who reportedly was hiding at the university. Cury
refused to allow the police to enter the university. (He and vice rector Tirso
Mejia later were detained by the police.) Political, labor, student and
professional organizations scored the government for the shooting. Students
from the Catholic University in the northern city of Santiago assembled on a
highway April 5 to protest the UASD occupation, but dispersed after police
briefly surrounded their university. Public schools in Santo Domingo and a few
other Dominican cities closed indefinitely April 5 in another protest against the
university's invasion. In a later development, several policemen were arrested
and charged with stealing university property during the UASD occupation,
according to a report April 11.

Land reforms passed. It was reported April 19 that the Dominican
Congress had passed a series of administration agrarian reforms which, if
enforced, would reduce the holdings of some of the landed rich and the military.
The most controversial of the reforms, and one which was likely to affect large
landowners, was the so-called ricelands law which required all publicly irrigated
land parcels of 80 acres or more used to cultivate rice to be turned over to the
government's Agrarian Institute, presumably for sale to poor farmers. A
second measure, which would take more than 200,000 acres of land already
technically in the hands of the Agrarian Institute and divide it among farmers,
reportedly affected many ranking army officers who had built homes on the
land after it was taken from the family of dictator Rafael Leonidas Trujillo
after he was murdered in 1961. According to report, President Joaquin
Balaguer also planned government purchase of uncultivated and vacant land
for distribution among the peasantry. In a move to accelerate agrarian reform,
the government Nov. 20 also decreed expropriation of more than 9,000 acres
acquired by large landowners in allegedly "irregular" transactions.

Subversive plot charged. Manuel Jimenez Rodriguez, mayor of Santo
Domingo and a member of President Balaguer's Reformist party, was
dismissed by Congress April 27 and ordered to stand trial for subversion.
Balaguer charged that Jimenez Rodriguez and unidentified "radical" groups
had plotted to overthrow the government. Jimenez Rodriguez took refuge in
the Mexican embassy April 27 and was reportedly allowed to leave the country
a few days later. From his sanctuary in the Mexican embassy, he denied
Balaguer's charges, claiming the accusations were the work of Gen. Nivar

Seijas, whose enmity he had incurred. (Nivar Seijas, considered one of the nation's most powerful men, was himself dismissed as national police chief Dec. 27.) Juan Estrella Rojas, also a Reformist, was inaugurated as mayor of Santo Domingo April 28.

 Teachers' strike. At least 10,000 public school teachers went on strike Nov. 13 for higher salaries, a teacher promotion law and higher budget allocations for university education. The strike began in Santiago and spread within 10 days to Santo Domingo and 25 other localities. Public schools in the capital were virtually paralyzed Nov. 23 following two days of violent student demonstrations which ended with military occupation of a high school. Students again clashed with police Dec. 5. (The students were supporting the teachers' strike and protesting a ruling by the administration of the UASD which decreed the expulsion for at least two semesters of students in the preparatory course with averages below 60 points and of students in the university with scores below 70. Students claimed the ruling would hurt the university in its campaign to persuade the government to double the university budget in 1973.) The teachers' strike ended Dec. 9 after President Balaguer threatened severe measures against the strikers.

DRAFT & WAR PROTEST—Protests renew over bombing escalation. The escalation of bombing in Indochina (see INDOCHINA WAR [15]) provoked a new wave of protests during April and early May—the first major antiwar protests of 1972. Most of the demonstrations centered on college campuses and near military or military-industrial installations. Demonstrations against the war and the Reserve Officers Training Corps (ROTC) began at the University of Maryland April 17—culminating in two days of pitched fighting between state police and up to 2,000 students, the arrest of several hundred students and an order by Gov. Marvin Mandel sending 800 National Guardsmen onto the campus and imposing a curfew. Some 250 students at Columbia University in New York—protesting the university's summoning of police to the campus to enforce a court injunction barring coercive picketing of buildings—broke up a meeting of the University Senate April 20, prompting university President William J. McGill to suspend all classes. Police were called into Columbia April 25 to clear one of several buildings occupied by protesters, and at least five students were arrested and several injured in the ensuing melee. Other campus violence was reported at: the University of Wisconsin at Madison and Stanford University in California April 17; Harvard University April 18-26; Rutgers University in Newark (N.J.), the University of Oregon in Eugene and Madison April 19; Boston University and the University of Massachusetts in Amherst April 20; Boston University, the University of Michigan at Ann Arbor, the University of Texas in Austin, Stanford, Syracuse University, Boise State College (Ida.), Yale University, Fordham University in New York and the University of California in Berkeley April 21; Princeton University April 22; Boston University April 24; Reed College in Portland (Ore.) April 25; Cornell University April 26; and the University of Pennsylvania April 27-May 1. A survey by the American Council on Education reported May 5 that war protests took place on 27% of a representative sample of college campuses in April, compared with 16% reported after the 1970 invasion of Cambodia. National Student Association (NSA) President Margery Tabankin issued a call April 17 for a national one-day student strike in protest over the bombing of Indochina, but the strike failed to materialize.

 Military installation demonstrations. Some 41 demonstrators were arrested April 17 at the Alameda Naval Air Station in California, and 16 protesters were arrested the same day while occupying an Air Force recruiting station in San Francisco. Police April 17 arrested 60 persons standing in the entrance of a United Aircraft plant in Stratford, Conn., protesting production of assault helicopters used in Vietnam. In Dayton, Ohio April 20, 160 persons, most of them Antioch College students, were arrested while trying to block the gates of Wright Patterson Air Force Base. About 95 protesters were arrested

April 21 and another 35 April 24 for trying to block the gates of the Westover Air Force Base in Chicopee, Mass. Some 21 protesters were arrested April 23 for attempting to interfere with loading operations of a Navy munitions ship near Middletown, Mass. An attempt to blockade the Groton, Conn. submarine base ended in 42 arrests April 26.

Other demonstrations. The protest over the increased bombing also took other forms. More than 200 persons were arrested April 15 for demonstrating without a permit in Lafayette Park, across from the White House. About 200 law school students protested at the Supreme Court building April 21 against the court's refusal to review the constitutionality of the war. In Boston the same day, police arrested 15 demonstrators for blocking a federal building. In antiwar rallies April 22, a crowd of 30,000-60,000 marched in New York, while 30,000-40,000 protesters marched in San Francisco and 10,000-12,000 marched in Los Angeles. Smaller marches were held in Chicago and other cities April 22, and a few thousand marched in Salt Lake City April 24. Police in Boston April 27 arrested 44 demonstrators at a television studio when they demanded time to reply to a speech by President Nixon on the bombing. Twelve nuns lay down in the aisles of St. Patrick's Cathedral in New York April 30 to symbolize the Indochina war dead, while 60 other nuns (mostly from the Order of Sisters of Charity) simultaneously conducted an anti-war vigil outside the cathedral. Police arrested seven of the 12 nuns, but the archdiocese announced later that it would not press charges. At least 29 congressmen and 80 congressional staff members supported an anti-war vigil on the steps of the Capitol in Washington May 3-4. The presidents of 60 Midwestern private colleges May 6 issued a statement calling for a total immediate withdrawal of U.S. forces from Indochina. (The presidents of the eight Ivy League Colleges and the Massachusetts Institute of Technology had issued a statement April 19 condemning the renewed bombing raids on North Vietnam and supporting peaceful anti-war demonstrations.)

May protests. President Nixon's May 8 announcement that he had ordered the mining of North Vietnamese harbors and the interdiction of land and sea routes to North Vietnam *(see* INDOCHINA WAR [20]) touched off an intense wave of antiwar protests on college campuses and in major cities May 8-11; and widespread use of civil disobedience tactics led to violent clashes with police, scores of injuries and a reported total of 1,800 arrests in several cities. The protests continued through mid-May, but their scale and extent seemed to decline from the first week. Serious incidents were reported: in Berkeley May 8-11 as police fired wooden and putty bullets and used tear gas to disperse as many as 1,000 rioters; in San Jose, Calif., where suspected arson at a Naval Reserve armory and an Army veterinary center caused over $200,000 damage May 9; in Boulder, Colo., where at least 70 persons were arrested while 1,000 protesters blocked intersections with burning automobiles and cars May 9; In Gainesville, Fla., as 1,000 students from the University of Florida fought police May 9-10, resulting in 395 arrests; in the Chicago area, as more than 22 persons were arrested for blocking expressways May 9-11; in Albuquerque, N.M., where at least nine persons were injured, one seriously, by police fire during disorders involving University of New Mexico students May 10-11; in Madison, Wis., where three policemen were shot May 11 while pursuing bomb suspects after three nights of clashes in which over 50 demonstrators had been arrested; and in Minneapolis, where Minnesota Gov. Wendell Anderson May 11 activated 715 National Guardsmen after an outbreak of violence May 10 between city police and as many as 2,000-5,000 students which resulted in injury to at least 25 students and three policemen. Sporadic demonstrations, violence or arrests occurred at varying locations in New York, Boston, Washington, San Francisco and Philadelphia, among other cities, while demonstrations or rallies were reported in dozens of areas. More than 400 protesters were arrested in Washington, D.C. May 21-22 during battles between police and war protesters, while up to 15,000 demonstrators attended a peaceful antiwar rally on the Capitol grounds May 22.

Ban on Capitol protests lifted. Without hearing arguments, the Supreme Court Nov. 6 unanimously affirmed a lower court ruling that held an 1882 law banning all unauthorized demonstrations on the U.S. capitol ground to be unconstitutional. The law had often been used by the District of Columbia prosecutors as a basis for federal "unlawful entry" charges against antiwar and other protesters demonstrating on the Capitol grounds. The decision upheld a May ruling by a three-judge federal panel in Washington that the law was an improper restriction of the public's First Amendment rights of free speech and free assembly. The case grew out of an attempt by a now-defunct peace group, the Jeanette Rankin Brigade, to stage a protest against the Vietnam war in January 1968 on the Capitol grounds.

See also CIVIL DISORDERS; FEDERAL BUREAU OF INVESTIGATION; GERMANY, WEST [3]; HIJACKING [7]; INDOCHINA WAR [39, 41]; SECURITY, U.S.; SELECTIVE SERVICE SYSTEM; UNITED NATIONS

DROUGHT—*See* INDIA [6]

DRUG USE & ADDICTION—The fight to control the flow of narcotics into and throughout the United States continued with increased efforts in 1972. While the use of drugs within the military reportedly was decreasing *(see* [2]), the international flow of heroin and related drugs was continuing unchecked *(see* [17-18]). In action to crack down on drug peddling in the U.S. and to stop the illicit traffic from abroad, President Nixon created a new drug abuse program *(see* [3]) and strengthened and coordinated existing programs *(see* [7]). The government also established a heroin "hot line," by which anyone in the U.S. could report information on drug trafficking *(see* [9]), and set up guidelines on the use of methadone, used in the rehabilitation of heroin addicts *(see* [8]). The U.S. acted to control amphetamines crossing the border from Mexico *(see* [10]), but reports were made implicating government officials in Panama and Paraguay in drug trafficking *(see* [11, 13]). The U.S. also gave its ambassadors more authority in combatting the narcotics flow into the U.S. from abroad *(see* [19]) and signed a pact with six Latin American countries to check the production, sale and consumption of narcotics *(see* [20]). Recommendations came from several sources to ease marijuana laws *(see* [4]). Those recommendations included proposals by the National Commission on Marijuana and Drug Abuse to drop all criminal penalties for the private use and possession of marijuana *(see* [5]). In Canada, the LeDain Commission recommended the abolition of all penalties for marijuana possession *(see* [6]).

[2] U.S. military addiction trend reversed. Dr. Richard S. Wilbur, assistant secretary of defense for health, said Jan. 8 that the Army had reversed what had been a rising rate of heroin use among servicemen. Wilbur said that the number of servicemen who were hard-core drug addicts had fallen from a peak of 600 in June and July of 1971 to slightly more than 200 in October of 1971 and that the downward trend was continuing. He also said that 2.5% of the GIs who returned to the U.S. from South Vietnam in December 1971 were using drugs, compared to 4.2% of those tested in August 1971 (shortly after the Army instituted urinalysis testing to determine drug usage). Wilbur attributed the downward trend to the military's mandatory drug tests, the success of rehabilitation plans for drug users and the education program alerting soldiers about the dangers of hard drugs. (In a related development, the Pentagon Jan. 16 released the results of its latest tests for drug use by servicemen. The new figures showed the following incidence of drug users according to the branch of service: Army 2.8%; Air Force .5%; Navy .3%; and Marine Corps .2%. The figures also showed that 4.1% of the soldiers in Vietnam, 1.6% of those in other Pacific area countries, .9% of those in Europe and 1.3% of those in other areas overseas were on drugs.)

[3] Nixon sets drive by new agency. President Nixon Jan. 18 announced a sweeping program intended to crack down on narcotics peddling in the U.S. and on illicit drug traffic from abroad. To press the drive, Nixon created a new office of Drug Abuse Law Enforcement, to be headed by Commissioner of Customs Myles J. Ambrose, in the Justice Department. Ambrose was to be a special assistant attorney general, with broad powers to use the pool of enforcement personnel in the Justice and Treasury Departments to carry out Nixon's orders. Nixon also designated Ambrose to be a special consultant to the President on drug abuse law enforcement. The new drug abuse office was to oversee the creation of a nationwide network of prosecutors and investigators and the summoning of special grand juries to help state and local authorities in detecting, arresting and convicting persons dealing in drugs. (The new office would assume many of the investigative duties previously assigned to the Justice Department's Bureau of Narcotics and Dangerous Drugs.) The new office's legal staff had the authority to convene grand juries and to grant immunity to witnesses to obtain information or the arrest and conviction of suspected narcotics dealers.

[4] **Marijuana law easing recommended.** Criticism of laws against the use of marijuana and recommendations that the laws be eased came from several sources during 1972. John H. Finlator, who had resigned as deputy director of the Bureau of Narcotics and Dangerous Drugs Jan. 1, urged Feb. 9 that laws against the use of marijuana be repealed. Finlator stopped short of recommending that marijuana be sold legally, but he said that both tobacco and alcohol had proved to be more dangerous than marijuana. (Finlator said he had been "told to be quiet" about his views on marijuana while he worked with the federal bureau.) Dr. Bertram S. Brown, director of the National Institute of Mental Health (NIMH), Feb. 11 released an NIMH report on marijuana which urged that penalties for its use be lessened. The report pointed out that use of marijuana adversely affected responses while driving an automobile, that marijuana could lead to psychotic breakdowns in people who were already unstable and that it could retard the emotional development of the very young; but said that moderate use of marijuana for stable persons posed no major problem. The report also said that there was "little evidence" tying marijuana use to birth defects or to a progression to hard drugs and that acute reactions to the use of marijuana were rare.

[5] The National Commission on Marijuana and Drug Abuse (consisting of nine members appointed by President Nixon, two members of the House of Representatives and two senators) March 22 submitted to the President and Congress a report recommending that all criminal penalties for the private use and possession of marijuana be abolished. The commission took note that the question of marijuana was a political issue and called for an end to further debate on such grounds. A major portion of the report dealt with the impact of marijuana on the user's health. The panel said "there is little proven danger of physical or psychological harm from the experimental or intermittent use" of marijuana. Instead, the commission said, the risk lay in heavy, long-term use. The panel said that, from what is known about marijuana's effects, its use did not present "a major threat to public health." Although the panel recommended the repeal of federal and state laws making it a crime to possess marijuana for private use or to distribute it in small quantities without remuneration, it also recommended that the cultivation, sale or distribution for profit, and possession with intent to sell marijuana should remain felonies, with states imposing uniform penalties. The commission also said that state laws should make the public use of marijuana and the public possession of more than one ounce of marijuana criminal offenses punishable by a $100 fine. (The panel recommended that federal law merely provide for the seizure of marijuana used publicly.) In addition, the panel recommended that state laws should make disorderly conduct associated with the public use of marijuana a misdemeanor punishable by up to 60 days in jail, a fine of $100 or both.

[6] *Canadian recommendation.* In Canada, the LeDain drug inquiry commission May 17 released a report recommending abolition of penalties for possessing marijuana. The commission, which had taken three years to assemble

its findings, recommended repeal of the prohibition against possession of marijuana and substantial reduction of the penalties for its sale. Cultivation for sale would be regarded as trafficking, but cultivation for personal use would carry no penalty, nor would giving a small quantity to someone else. However, the report also recommended that police should have the power to seize marijuana wherever it was found, regardless of the circumstances, in order to discourage use.

[7] **Jaffe given wide powers.** President Nixon March 21 signed into law legislation that would empower Dr. Jerome H. Jaffe, director of the Special Action Office for Drug Abuse Prevention, to act as steward of federal funds being used in the Administration's war against narcotics. The law gave Jaffe the final word on the budgets of the 13 agencies in the drug abuse program insofar as they were concerned with the narcotics effort. The total program was to have a $1 billion budget, with about $200 million going to the Special Action Office and $800 million to be spent by the Department of Health, Education and Welfare under Jaffe's guidance.

[8] **Methadone rules set.** The Food and Drug Administration (FDA) April 3 lifted the investigational status label for methadone, the drug most commonly used to help rehabilitate heroin addicts, and pledged that it would be available through approved treatment programs to all addicts who consented to use it. (The move was part of a government drive to eliminate the siphoning of methadone from approved treatment programs to illegal street sales. While methadone did not produce in users the euphoric effects of heroin, it was an addictive narcotic and was increasingly making its way into the sales of underworld drug peddlers.) Under the new rules (approved Dec. 15), methadone would be removed from all drugstores where it was available as an ordinary prescription drug and would be dispensed only through government-approved programs for addicts or through hospital pharmacies for use as a pain killer for certain groups of patients, such as those with terminal cases of cancer.

[9] **Heroin 'hot line' set up.** The White House April 7 announced the opening of a 24-hour telephone "hot line" to give the public a chance to help fight drug traffic by passing on to law enforcement authorities any information about heroin dealers. The telephone line would enable any person in the continental U.S. to call a toll-free number to give information to a central information collecting point in Washington. The identity of those calling with information would be protected so that they need not fear reprisals, and callers would not have to identify themselves.

International Traffic

[10] **Amphetamines control.** The Bureau of Narcotics and Dangerous Drugs Jan. 18 began legal action to cut off the illegal return flow of amphetamines exported to Mexico by an American firm back across the border into the U.S. The bureau ordered the Pennwalt Corp., described as the largest exporter of amphetamines, and its Strasenburgh Prescription Products Division to show why its export license for amphetamines should not be revoked. The bureau action followed a 10-month investigation which purportedly showed that much of Strasenburgh's exported amphetamine was returning illegally across the border. Pennwalt said Jan. 27 that it had decided not to seek renewal of its export license in response to a new Mexican law banning the production and sale of amphetamines in Mexico by July 12. (The U.S. bureau Feb. 9 also issued an order reducing the 1972 federal production quotas of amphetamines and methamphetamines by almost 82% of the 1971 total.)

[11] **Panama officials implicated in heroin trade.** U.S. Rep. John M. Murphy (D, N.Y.) March 15 charged that an investigation of heroin smuggling into the U.S. by the Bureau of Narcotics and Dangerous Drugs had touched "the highest levels" of the Panamanian government. Murphy said that information given him by the bureau indicated that Panamanian Foreign Minister Juan Antonio Tack and Ambassador to Spain Moises Torrijos

(brother of Panama's ruler) were involved in the narcotics trade. Columnist Jack Anderson March 14 had revealed a report by Murphy's House subcommittee on the Panama Canal which accused the U.S. State Department of following "an historic policy of ignoring or denying the involvement in the narcotics traffic into the United States of high-ranking officials of friendly foreign governments." Disclosure of the report led to the expulsion from Panama of two narcotics bureau agents March 14 and another March 15, leaving no bureau agents in the country. Anderson charged Aug. 3 that angry protests from the Panama government over the March story had led the State Department to ask federal narcotics agents to "tread softly" in Panama and even in the U.S.-controlled Canal Zone.

[12] **36 nations sign drug pact.** Thirty-six countries March 25 signed a series of U.S.-sponsored amendments to a 1961 narcotics convention. When the amendments (agreed upon at a United Nations-sponsored conference) were signed and ratified by 40 countries, they would become a protocol to the 1961 convention. The amendments would: give the U.N.'s International Narcotics Control Board wider powers to fight narcotics traffic; increase the board's membership from 10 to 13 and lengthen the terms of members from three to five years; and pledge recognition by all parties to the 1961 convention that trafficking, production and cultivation of narcotics were extraditable offenses. A number of countries which produce opium, from which heroin is derived, did not sign the accord. Among them were India, Burma and the Soviet Union. Among opium-producing countries that did sign were Turkey, Iran and Yugoslavia.

[13] **Stroessner linked to smuggling.** Jack Anderson charged April 22 that a Central Intelligence Agency (CIA) report in his possession indicated that Paraguayan President Alfredo Stroessner was "up to his epaulettes in international smuggling" of heroin. Anderson said that Stroessner "parcels out smuggling franchises to his generals to keep them from overturning his...regime." Anderson also said that, while Stroessner stopped short of personal involvement in the drug traffic, his generals and civilian aides conspired with "world dope gangsters to make Paraguay the 'heroin crossroads' of South America." According to Anderson's account of the CIA report, heroin originating in Turkey and refined in France was sent to the Western Hemisphere "inside dead bodies being returned to South America for burial and other methods equally bizarre. The largest part of this traffic passes through Paraguay with bulk shipments of as much as 100 kilograms (220 pounds)." Anderson wrote May 24 that, at the request of Stroessner, he had given Ambassador Roque Avila the names of top officials who were allegedly deeply involved in the international drug trade. The officials named included the chief of investigative police, the commander of 3,000 U.S.-equipped troops based near Ascuncion, a light infantry commander, an artillery commander who controlled contraband, the chief of the Paraguayan gunboat navy, an air force chief, Interior Minister Sabino Augusto Montanaro, National Police Chief Gen. Francisco Britez, Defense Minister Gen. Leodegar Cabello and Secretary of State Raul Sapena Pastor. The U.S. State Department May 26 claimed that it had no "definitive evidence" that the Paraguayan government was involved in drug smuggling.

[14] *Ricord extradited, convicted.* Paraguay Sept. 2 extradited Auguste-Joseph Ricord, an alleged heroin-smuggling kingpin sought by U.S. authorities for the previous 17 months. Ricord, a former French citizen, had been jailed in Paraguay. U.S. officials estimated that he was responsible for smuggling more than $2.5 billion worth of heroin into the U.S. over the previous five years. A Paraguayan judge Jan. 5 had rejected a U.S. request for Ricord's extradition on grounds that the 1913 extradition treaty between the two countries made no provision for such an extradition. However, a Paraguayan appeals court Aug. 13 agreed to extradite Ricord. Two appeals by Ricord's lawyers—that the appeals court ruling was unconstitutional and that Ricord should first be tried

for possible violations of Paraguayan law—had been rejected. Following Ricord's extradition, his lawyer Sept. 28 filed a motion in federal court in New York challenging Ricord's extradition. Ricord was convicted Dec. 15 on one count of conspiring to smuggle narcotics. His sentencing was set for Jan. 29, 1973.

[15] **U.S.-Turkey opium accord signed.** Turkey and the U.S. May 7 signed an agreement providing for $18.4 million in U.S. aid to help compensate Turkey opium farmers for a ban on opium poppy cultivation imposed by Turkey in 1971. The grant was part of a $35 million U.S. commitment to Turkey revealed by Turkish Premier Nihat Erim Feb. 27. (The U.S. had also agreed to provide an additional $700,000 in technical aid to offset the problems incurred by the ban.)

[16] **Chilean drugs increase in U.S.** According to a report Aug. 7, Chile had become the major source of cocaine smuggled into the U.S. and was gaining in importance as a supplier of heroin. The Bureau of Narcotics and Dangerous Drugs, agents and unidentified Chilean officials said that Chilean cocaine shipments intercepted in Central America, Mexico and the Caribbean averaged 80-100 pounds—indicating well-organized smuggling operations—and contained increasing amounts of heroin. Most of the cocaine reportedly was produced in Peru, Bolivia and Ecuador and sent to Chile for refinement in clandestine laboratories and for shipment to the U.S. and other countries. Heroin entered Chile for refinement from Argentina, Paraguay and Uruguay—all of which obtained it from southern Europe and the Middle East. The traffic allegedly had been facilitated by difficulties with the Chilean currency. Ordinary goods were being smuggled out of the country at an unprecedented rate, giving drug merchants a useful cover. In addition, the value of the U.S. dollar in Chile was such that the cocaine price there was far lower than in other countries.

[17] **U.S. concedes heroin flow unchecked.** A report on the world heroin trade, nine months in preparation, was released by the U.S. government Aug. 16. The report was prepared by the Cabinet Committee on International Narcotics Control from information gathered and collated by the State Department, the CIA, the Bureau of Narcotics and Dangerous Drugs, the Customs Bureau and the Treasury Department. The report said that heroin dealers and traffickers were continuing to ply their world trade with relative ease despite increased efforts by the U.S. and other countries to disrupt the smugglers' pipelines. It said that the increased level of heroin seizures during recent years "still represents only a small fraction of the illicit flow" and that "the international heroin market almost certainly continues to have adequate supplies to meet the demand in consuming countries." According to the report, most of the heroin traffic appeared to be financed by international criminal "cartels," who reaped "high rates of return on their investment." (According to the report, such returns could be $1 million for a $120,000-$300,000 investment in unadulterated heroin by an international trafficker, with a domestic dealer realizing a $21 million profit on his $1 million purchase from the trafficker.) The authors of the report used caustic language to speak of the cooperation of some nations in joining the drug fight. Efforts to bring about a coordinated world-wide drive against heroin had been hampered, the report said, "largely because of widely varying national attitudes toward the drug problem." These differences, the report added, "are regularly and skillfully exploited by the illicit international trafficker."

[18] *Routes traced.* The report divided the illegal traffic of opium, from which heroin is made, into three complexes. The primary complex, which contained most illegal traffic, consisted of Turkey as a supplier, countries in Western Europe and the Western Hemisphere as shippers and refiners and the U.S. as a final deposit point. The second complex was the Southeast Asia market, with most of the opium coming from Burma, Thailand and Laos. A third complex was found in the Eurasia area of India, Pakistan, Iran and

Afghanistan. The report said that the second and third complexes could take on increasing importance in coming years "because of their potential for becoming international suppliers of opium for the international heroin market, particularly if the primary complex falters." The report also detailed the routes used by traffickers in the primary complex. According to the report, virtually all the opium from Turkey passed overland among consignments of legitimate cargo (sealed with a customs band) through Bulgaria or Greece to Yugoslavia. From there, the pipeline channeled the opium to Austria, West Germany or to France through northern Italy. Smuggling by sea was losing its popularity and smuggling by air was "the least favored smuggling method." According to the report, the morphine base derived from the opium was refined into heroin, once in France, in small clandestine laboratories—most of them in the Marseilles area. The French dealers, most of them French Corsicans, then smuggled the drugs across the Atlantic directly to the U.S. (usually to New York, described in the report as the main distribution center in the U.S. for heroin smuggled from Europe). Some smugglers, however, sent the heroin through third countries, such as Canada, Mexico or other nations in Latin America.

[19] *Ambassadors given new authority.* The Cabinet Committee on International Narcotics Control announced Aug. 17 that U.S. ambassadors in a foreign country henceforth would have undisputed authority to deal with U.S. narcotics matters overseas. Previously, the Bureau of Narcotics and Dangerous Drugs had held that responsibility. The move was seen as an effort to strengthen the State Department's hand in fighting the international narcotics trade and to prevent jurisdictional disputes. Under the new setup, all government agencies doing narcotics work abroad would be represented equally on committees in each country headed by coordinators named by the ambassadors. The coordinators were to meet in Washington with top narcotics officials to discuss the new arrangement.

[20] **6 nations, U.S. set campaign.** The U.S. and six Latin American countries (Brazil, Venezuela, Peru, Ecuador, Panama and Colombia) agreed Nov. 18 on a program to combat the production, sale and consumption of narcotics. The campaign, to be coordinated by the Latin American division of Interpol, was organized at a narcotics conference in Bogota. The campaign would include the burning of drug-yielding crops, the confiscation of fields in which such crops were cultivated, creation of an international agency to store information on persons implicated in narcotics traffic, control of laboratories primarily using narcotics, easing of border controls for narcotics agents, extradition of drug offenders and uniform punishment for those convicted of drug dealing.

See also CONSUMER AFFAIRS [1, 5, 7, 12, 16]; ELECTIONS [21, 44]; HORSE RACING; MEDICINE; MEXICO; NEWSPAPERS; NIXON, RICHARD MILHOUS; OLYMPICS [10]; POLITICS [8]; STATE & LOCAL GOVERNMENTS

EAGLETON, THOMAS F.—*See* ELECTIONS [2, 19, 29-31]; NIXON, RICHARD MILHOUS

EARTHQUAKES—Peru. A violent earthquake shook the sparsely populated northern states of San Martin and Amazonas March 20, reportedly destroying half of the town of Juanjui, 340 miles from Lima, and completely destroying the neighboring towns of Mercedes, Huacho and Churuspa. Unofficial estimates of the deaths caused by the quake ranged from 6 to 30. Poor communications hampered efforts to determine the extent of the damage caused by the earthquake.

Iran. An earthquake struck about 600 miles south of Teheran April 10, sending tremors over a 250-mile radius, leveling nearly 45 villages and killing some 5,000 people. The center of the quake included the villages of Ghir and Karzin—both totally devastated. (New tremors rocked Ghir April 13, causing landslides.)

Thousands killed in Managua. A series of increasingly strong earthquakes, lasting 2.5 hours, destroyed much of Managua, Nicaragua early Dec. 23, killing an estimated 7,000 persons and injuring about 10,000-15,000. The tremors were among the worst in Nicaraguan history, with the strongest registering 6.25 on the Richter scale. The quakes leveled 60%-75% of the city, touching off explosions and fires and reportedly leaving at least 200,000 of Managua's 325,000 residents homeless. A large portion of the city was engulfed in flames as long as 15 hours after the quakes first struck, and fires continued to smolder for several days. Most of the survivors of the tremors fled Managua Dec. 23-24, settling in outlying towns and refugee stations. Ex-President Anastasio Somoza Debayle, who effectively ruled Nicaragua as commander of the National Guard, ordered the city evacuated Dec. 24, fearing that decaying bodies buried under the rubble might cause an epidemic. However, some residents remained to search for belongings and to loot stores. The government Dec. 25 ordered emergency stations in Managua to stop serving food in a further move to clear out the city, but looting continued despite an official order for soldiers to shoot looters on sight. Order reportedly was restored in the city Dec. 27. A major portion of the city was declared "contaminated" Dec. 26, and a fire department official said it would be leveled and covered with lime as a mass grave for those who had died in the quakes. Demolition experts said Dec. 29 that it would take eight months to a year to clear away the wreckage.

Gen. Somoza Dec. 28 asked the U.S. for aid, which President Nixon quickly granted. The U.S. provided more than $3 million in relief supplies and other aid over the next few days, including medicine, food, tents, water purification plants and manpower teams. Seventy-four doctors, nurses and other health workers flew from New York to Managua Dec. 27 with a 100-bed portable hospital and other equipment and supplies. Aid and volunteer workers also were sent by other countries and international relief agencies.

See also ENVIRONMENT; FOREIGN POLICY

EAST CAMEROON—*See* CAMEROON
EASTERN ORTHODOX CHURCH—*See* CHURCHES
EAST PAKISTAN—*See* BANGLA DESH
EAST-WEST RELATIONS—*See* DISARMAMENT; ESPIONAGE; EUROPEAN ECONOMIC COMMUNITY [17]; EUROPEAN SECURITY; FOREIGN POLICY; GERMAN CONSULTATIONS; GERMANY, WEST [5-8]; GREECE [5-6]; NORTH ATLANTIC TREATY ORGANIZATION; SINO-U.S. RELATIONS; SOVIET-U.S. RELATIONS; SPACE [7]; TELEVISION & RADIO [4]
ECOLOGY—*See* ENVIRONMENT
ECONOMICS—*See* NOBEL PRIZES

ECONOMY—Economic controls, originally imposed by President Nixon on Aug. 15, 1971, continued through 1972. The functioning of the controls did not proceed without criticism, however. Four of the five labor members of the Pay Board resigned from the board during March to protest the Nixon Administration's economic policies and alleged favoritism to big business *(see* [10]). The resignations forced President Nixon to restructure the board *(see* [11]).

[2] 1971 figures. The U.S. gross national product (GNP)—the nation's total output of goods and services—grew by 2.7% in 1971 as measured by constant (1958) dollars. The rise was far below the level economists considered necessary to reduce the unemployment rate. In terms of current dollars and reflecting persistent inflation, the total GNP for 1971 rose 7.5% ($73 billion) to a record $1,046.8 billion. The increase incorporated a 4.6% rise in prices—an improvement over 1970's 5.5% increase, which had been the steepest annual rise since a 6% jump in 1951. According to Census Bureau figures announced July 17, the median income of U.S. families rose by $418 to $10,285 in 1971— exceeding $10,000 for the first time. However, the figures showed that the increase was erased by inflation. In constant dollars, the median family income actually decreased by $4 from 1970 to 1971. The Census Bureau also reported that the number of persons classified as poor (with incomes below $4,000 for an urban family of four) remained at 25.6 million (about 13% of all U.S. families)—the same figure as in 1970. The Commerce Department Feb. 15 issued preliminary figures showing that the U.S. had suffered its worst payments imbalance in its history in 1971. The official reserve transactions (official settlements) measure—one of the department's four balance of payments measurements and the measure which reflected losses of U.S. monetary reserves, accumulations of dollars by foreign central banks and immediate foreign exchange market pressures on the dollar—showed a deficit of $29.63 billion in 1971, on a seasonally adjusted basis. The deficit was nearly triple 1970's deficit of $9.82 billion.

[3] Price Commission actions. The Price Commission Jan. 6 detailed a new procedure for price increase approvals for tier one companies—those with sales of $100 million or more a year. The firms had been required to seek advance approval for price rises, but the new rule would permit them to raise prices by 2% or less over a year period, with quarterly reports submitted to the commission for application of guidelines. However, the commission March 15 announced that the 2% price rise allowed for tier one companies would be reduced to 1.8%. The commission July 24 also issued an amendment to its regulations, effective July 20, to require that the quarterly corporate profit statements submitted to it be corroborated by semiannual statements from certified accountants. The accountants would be obligated to make eight statistical comparisons, checks and inquiries developed by the commission. The commission March 19 issued new regulations to help low-profit companies improve their economic picture by raising prices at a controlled level. Under the regulations, companies with sales of $1 million or more annually (14,000-15,000 companies in the country) could raise their prices to achieve a profit of between .2% and 3% of sales, depending on each firm's capital turnover. Companies with sales of under $1 million could increase prices to realize a margin of profit of up to 3%, regardless of their capital turnover. However, the commission said that a company could not raise the price of any individual product or service by more than 8%—even if the company was suffering a loss or had low profits.

[4] *Auto prices.* The Price Commission Jan. 12 approved a second round of price increases on 1972 automobiles to cover costs of new safety devices and antipollution equipment. (The first price rise had been approved in November 1971.) The price increase grants included .9% to General Motors Corp. (GM), 1.07% to Ford Motor Co. and .83% to American Motors Corp. Chrysler Corp., which previously had been permitted a 4.5% price increase but imposed only 3%, was to raise prices within the remaining 1.5% for new equipment. The Commission Aug. 24 approved selective price adjustments to cover the cost of optional equipment which would be standard in 1973 model cars, and suspended pending price increases until the commission could hold public hearings on the issue. (Ralph Nader and Consumers Union July 26 had brought suit in federal district court to require the commission to hold public hearings before approving car price increases. The case was dismissed Aug. 11 when Price Commission Chairman C. Jackson Grayson announced that hearings would be held.) The increases requested by the car companies were: $110 for Chrysler, $78 for American Motors, $90 for GM and $92 for Ford. Following talks with Donald Rumsfeld, director of the Cost of Living Council (CLC), GM Aug. 17 and Ford Aug. 19 announced reductions in their requested price increases—to $59 for both companies. Chrysler and American refused to reduce their requests. The Price Commission Aug. 29 refused the price increases for Ford and GM because the increases could push the companies' profit margins above the government-imposed ceiling. (Under the profit margin test, companies could pass on cost increases to customers only if the price rises did not result in higher profit margins than those of the base period, which was the average of any two of a company's last three fiscal years ending before Aug. 15, 1971.) Following public hearings Sept. 12-15, the commission Oct. 17 approved a 1.92% increase for Chrysler and a 5.3% increase for American Motors. The price rise, applicable only to cars which left the factory after Oct. 16, would average $60.10 a unit on Chrysler cars and $144.28 on American Motors cars. (Chrysler said its actual price rise would average $20 a unit; American Motors said its actual price rise would average $38 a unit.) The commission acted to allow the car manufacturers to cover the costs of federally required safety and antipollution features; American was also allowed an increase to cover ordinary manufacturing costs. GM reapplied to the Price Commission Nov. 2 and Ford reapplied Nov. 6. The commission Dec. 1 approved an average $54 price increase for GM and an estimated $63 price boost for Ford, effective Dec. 2, to cover increased costs necessitated by federal standards requiring installation of new pollution control and safety devices.

[5] *Food prices action.* In order to ease the high demand for meat, which was in short supply and which was an important factor in the rising retail cost of food during 1972, President Nixon March 9 signed a proclamation that, in effect, raised by 7% the U.S. meat import quota for 1972. Under the proclamation, meat imports would increase by 80 million pounds to 1.24 billion pounds. The Administration June 26 announced that all meat import quota restrictions would be lifted, effective immediately for the remainder of 1972. (Nixon Dec. 21 extended the suspension for all of 1973.) Rising meat prices were also the focus of a meeting in Washington March 29 between Treasury

Secretary John B. Connally Jr. and the heads of 12 major supermarket chains. The retailers were asked at the meeting to monitor their profit margins and to submit a weekly report on meat prices to the CLC. The Price Commission May 3 announced that it was forming a "food watch" unit to monitor supply and demand in the food industry and to analyze inflationary trends. In related action, CLC Director Rumsfeld June 29 announced President Nixon's decision, effective July 16, to impose price controls on unprocessed agricultural products and seafood at the wholesale and retail levels. Prices for fresh fruit, vegetables, eggs, and raw seafood were stabilized by the action; but prices for grains, soybeans and livestock continued to be exempt from controls until food processing or slaughtering began. Prices at the farm production level remained exempt from stabilization. (The Agriculture Department Sept. 28 issued a report indicating that middlemen were not passing along to consumers the increasingly cheaper farm prices for beef. According to the report, cattlemen lowered beef prices 8.4% during August, while retail prices dropped only 1.5¢ a pound. Packers and retail stores reportedly widened their margins 12.6%.)

[6] *Some rental, retail controls lifted.* The CLC Jan. 19 exempted from price controls about 40% of the country's rental units and 75% of the retail firms (those with under $100,000 in annual sales). The retail order, which did not apply to service establishments, involved companies which accounted for only 15% of the country's retail sales. The rent decontrol also applied to small units: luxury apartments renting for $500 or more a month; apartment buildings with four or fewer units that were owner-occupied and rented under leases running longer than from month-to-month; and single-family homes renting for longer than month-to-month where the landlord owned four or fewer units. The Price Commission May 18 issued further regulations on rent increases for tenants with leases for more than a year's period signed before Dec. 29, 1971. The regulations required landlords to offer tenants an option of a new lease of one year with an increase of up to 8% or a lease of at least the previous length with the up-to-8% increase. The 8% ceiling could be exceeded only to pass on increases in property taxes and municipal service costs.

[7] **Pay Board actions.** The Pay Board Jan. 13 approved retroactive payment of wage increases frozen during the 90-day wage-price freeze that ended Nov. 14, 1971. Payment of increases of up to 7% would be permitted in general, and the full increase was authorized if prices or taxes had been raised to cover the wage boosts. The board Feb. 9 announced that pay increases due in the second or later years of multiple-year labor contracts affecting 1,000 or more workers would be subject to advance notification to the board if the increases exceeded 7%. The notification would have to be accompanied by justification for the excess. The board Feb. 8 and Nov. 9 revised its policy on merit wage increases. The Feb. 8 revision applied the policy to union as well as nonunion wages. The Nov. 9 change limited merit increases to the 5.5% annual wage increase standard. (Workers previously had been allowed an additional 1.5% merit wage boost over the 5.5% limit.) The board Feb. 23 announced that it would allow annual increases in fringe benefits equal to .7% of total compensation in excess of the 5.5% wage guideline. In cases where fringe benefits had been raised less than 1.5% during the previous three years, the board would permit catch-up increases totaling up to 1.5% beyond the guidelines. In cases where employer expenditures for fringe benefits amounted to less than 10% of total compensation costs, additional fringe increments would be allowed up to the 10% ceiling, up to a maximum increment of 5%. The board also permitted exemptions from its guidelines for many employee-incentive plans. The board May 1 exempted from the guidelines employees working in firms that employed 60 or fewer persons. However, the board announced Sept. 21 that all employees of local governments would be subject to the guidelines, regardless of size.

[8] *Minimum wage exemptions.* The CLC Jan. 29 exempted from wage controls workers earning $1.90 an hour or less. (The figure earlier had been rejected by the Pay Board as too low.) The CLC arrived at the figure starting with a Bureau of Labor Statistics standard of an adequate annual budget in 1970—$6,690—for an urban family of four with the wage earner between 35 and 54 years, then applying adjustments for cost of living, an average of 1.7 workers per family, an average family size of 3.6, and other factors. A federal district court in Washington, D.C. July 14 ruled that the CLC acted "in excess of agency authority" and in violation of the intent of Congress by exempting only wages below $1.90 an hour from Pay Board controls. The decision, which barred enforcement of the CLC's ruling, came in a suit brought by the AFL-CIO and its affiliate, the International Union of Electrical, Radio and Machine Workers. Following the court ruling, the CLC July 25 announced that controls would be lifted for workers earning less than $2.75 an hour.

[9] **Economic Report to Congress.** President Nixon's Economic Report to Congress, delivered Jan. 27, stressed that wage and price controls would be continued until "reasonable price stability can be maintained without controls." The President predicted that such stability could be maintained, but "how long it will take, no one can say." He pledged that his Administration would "persevere" until stability was reached and that controls would not be kept "one day longer than necessary." The duration of controls was the major topic of the brief Economic Report, as it was of the accompanying annual report of the President's Council of Economic Advisers (CEA). The CEA report also predicted: that the GNP would increase by about 9.5% to $1,145 billion in 1972 (see [2]), with a 6% increase in constant dollars; that inflation would decline in 1972 to "around 3.25%" from the 4.6% 1971 inflationary rise in the GNP price index; that consumer spending would increase by about 8% from the $662.2 billion 1971 total; that the business-inventory accumulation would increase fourfold over 1971 to an $8 billion total; that business-fixed investment would rise 8%; and that the foreign trade balance would "probably be close to zero" for 1972 as a whole. The report also favored a free-trade policy and stressed the importance of the Federal Reserve Board (FRB) in the planned economic stimulus for 1972.

[10] **Labor leaders quit Pay Board.** Four of the five labor members of the Pay Board resigned March 22 and 23, prompting President Nixon to revamp the 15-member tripartite (business-labor-public) board March 23 into a single unit with seven members. AFL-CIO President George Meany, United Steelworkers of America President I. W. Abel and International Association of Machinists President Floyd Smith quit the board March 22. United Automobile Workers President Leonard Woodcock quit the board March 23. Frank E. Fitzsimmons, president of the International Brotherhood of Teamsters, was the only labor member to remain on the board. The three labor leaders who quit March 22 declared that their walkout came because the Pay Board offered labor "no hope for fairness, equality or justice." Meany denounced the Administration's economic policy as unfair and accused the Administration of "flagrant favoritism" toward "big business and the banks." Citing labor's grievances with the board, Meany specifically pointed to the board's recent rejection of the West Coast longshoremen's contract (see LABOR). Meany also said the board had been neither tripartite nor independent. A statement released by the AFL-CIO Executive Council March 22 backed, without reservation, the walkout of the three labor leaders. In his resignation March 23, Woodcock said he was quitting not solely because some of the board's decisions had gone against labor, but also because of continued inflation and Administration policy. Woodcock called on Congress to investigate what he called the "scandalous and unfair" administration of the Economic Stabilization Act of 1971.

[11] *Pay Board revamped.* In reaction to the labor leaders' walkout, President Nixon March 23 issued an executive order restructuring the Pay Board. Under the new set-up, the five public members of the board (Chairman George H. Boldt, former CLC Director Arnold R. Weber, Brookings Institution President Kermit Gordon, Kenyon College President William G.

Caples and University of California professor Neil H. Jacoby) would remain. Fitzsimmons would also remain on the board, joined by one of the five business representatives now on the board. (President Nixon March 28 named Rocco C. Siciliano as the seventh member of the board.) Nixon's order indicated that the labor and business members would be regarded as public members of the revised Pay Board.

See also BUDGET; DEFENSE; ELECTIONS [17, 35]; LABOR; LATIN AMERICA; POLLUTION [1, 15]; POPULATION; SOCIAL SECURITY; SOVIET-U.S. RELATIONS [2]; SPACE [3]; TAXES

ECUADOR—Velasco overthrown. President Jose Maria Velasco Ibarra was deposed (for the fourth time since 1933) Feb. 15 in a bloodless military coup. Velasco, who was accused of "exploiting the people," was flown by the air force to Panama. A three-man junta (army Brig. Gen. Guillermo Rodriguez Lara, air force Gen. Julio Espinosa Pineda and navy Rear Adm. Reinaldo Anibal Vallejo) proclaimed a "revolutionary and nationalist" government Feb. 16 and suspended general elections scheduled for June 4. The junta's first decrees put Ecuador in a state of siege and imposed a night curfew. Schools were closed; public transportation was put under military control; and the constitution of 1945, which was drafted by leftists, was put into effect. Gen. Rodriguez announced Feb. 16 that six military officers and one civilian, none of them politicians, had been appointed Cabinet ministers in his Council of Government. The new Cabinet: health—air force Col. Raul Maldonado Mejia; interior—navy Capt. Gotardo Valdivieso; natural resources—navy Capt. Gustavo Jarrin Ampudia; production—army Col. Rodolfo Proana Tafur; defense—army Gen. Victor Aulestia; works—army Col. Rafael Rodriguez Palacios; finance—civilian Nestor Vega Moreno.

According to a report Feb. 17, the decision to remove Velasco from office was taken reluctantly after efforts to persuade him to call off the June elections had failed. Officers of the joint command were said to fear a violent campaign and to distrust the favored candidate, populist leader Assad Bucaram, head of the Concentration of Popular Forces and former provincial governor of Guayas. (Bucaram had been arrested in September 1970 on charges of subversion and subsequently had been expelled from the country. He had been permitted to return to Ecuador Jan. 8.) Military leaders had asked Velasco to disqualify Bucaram's candidacy on grounds that he was not an Ecuadorian citizen, but Velasco had refused, saying that only Congress could make such a ruling. (Bucaram was born to Lebanese immigrants; but Congress upheld his nationality in 1960, when he first ran for political office.)

Junta members resign. The members of the junta resigned from the Council of Government Feb. 19, stating that only lower-ranking officers would serve on the body, in order to avoid problems of "hierarchy and power." However, Vallejo and Espinosa also resigned from their military posts Feb. 21 and were replaced Feb. 22 by Rodriguez, who remained in sole control of the government. It was speculated Feb. 23 that the air force and navy officers had been dismissed by Rodriguez after disagreements over the organization of the ruling council. (The air force was reported particularly unhappy over its representation on the body since Maldonado, its sole representative in the new Cabinet, was a physician who had never been a fighter pilot.)

Cabinet changes. Rodriguez May 12 dismissed Interior Minister Valdivieso and Production Minister Proana and ordered them back to their posts in what he claimed was "purely a military matter." Proana was replaced May 12 by civilian economist Felipe Orellana; Valdivieso was replaced May 23 by army Col. Wilfrido Latorre. Two other officers—Capt. Raul Sorroza, the navy's representative on the Council of Government, and army Maj. Miguel Santacruz, an aide in the Production Ministry—were also dismissed, according to a report May 27. According to a report June 9, the dismissals signaled the victory of the army over the navy in an ideological struggle within the government. Valdivieso and Sorroza, aided by Proana, reportedly had sought to commit the government to leftist policies, in opposition to the more conservative approach of Rodriguez and other army officers.

Student unrest. About 25 students were arrested and an undetermined number injured Aug. 14 when security forces using tear gas, fire hoses and dogs broke up student demonstrations in Guayaquil. The incidents came a week after student disturbances had caused imposition of a curfew in the neighboring town of Babahoyo.

Judiciary crisis. Four of the 17 supreme court justices resigned Nov. 7 in protest over the Nov. 6 dismissal of several members of a military tribunal for acquitting former Natural Resources Minister Alfonso Arroyo and other defendants of irregularities during the Velasco administration. The resignations caused a crisis in the judiciary which was partially resolved Nov. 24 by the appointment of seven new justices and the announcement of plans for a complete reorganization of the body. (Capt. Valdivieso, according to a report Nov. 17, was jailed for four days for publicly supporting the justices who had resigned.)

See also ATOMIC ENERGY [13]; DRUG USE & ADDICTION [16, 20]; FOREIGN POLICY; LATIN AMERICA; TERRITORIAL WATERS

EDUCATION—Learning contracts fail. The Office of Economic Opportunity (OEO) reported Jan. 31 that a $5.6 million one-year test of performance contracts with private firms to teach low-income students reading and mathematics had failed and would be discontinued. The project had involved 1970-71 contracts with six companies, who used teaching machines, incentive payments and special classrooms to teach 13,000 children in 18 school districts, ranging from urban ghettos to rural areas. After the experiment, no significant differences were found between those in the program and a control group of 10,000 similar children. The six companies had agreed to accept compensation according to their teaching success, but five of them disputed OEO's findings and were still negotiating final payments.

[2] Commission asks states to assume full costs. The President's Commission on School Finance March 6 submitted a report to President Nixon which recommended the assumption by states of nearly all the costs of public elementary and secondary education in order to relieve localities of the growing burden of property taxes and to guarantee equal educational opportunities within each state. The report did not specify how the states should raise the 52% ($26.6 billion a year) of education costs borne locally, but suggested as possibilities statewide property, sales and income taxes. According to the report's recommendations, no district would have its budget reduced, but all districts would be prohibited from adding more than 10% over state contributions in order to conform with court decisions on equal school expenditures. As an incentive to the states, the commission proposed that the federal government supply them with about $1 billion a year over five years. (Even without considering state assumption of local contributions, the states would need an estimated $6 billion a year in new revenue to equalize spending between poor and wealthy school districts.) However, the commission emphasized that education should remain a state and local responsibility, with all new federal funds channeled through the states. A majority of the 18-member commission favored proposals to have the federal government equalize expenditures between states through subsidies and to increase aid to private and parochial schools, although a minority of the commission dissented on each proposal. The commission requested a $250 million-a-year expansion of pre-school education and about $1 million a year more in funds for inner-city schools. On the volatile integration issue, the commission supported redistricting to achieve racial and economic diversity, even if this "may require, in some cases, the use of buses." "However," the report continued, "busing to produce a uniform racial ratio in all the schools of a district may not be the best procedure." Other sections of the report called for federal assistance to improve state education agencies and for reductions "in the number of incompetent teachers." (The provision on increased aid to inner-city schools specified that the funds not be applied to salary increases.)

[3] Title I inefficiency charged. A survey prepared for the U.S. Office of Education of the Department of Health, Education and Welfare (HEW) and released April 10 said that the Title I program to improve education for poor children "has never been implemented" as intended in the 1965 Elementary and Secondary Education Act. The report, based mostly on federal and state evaluation data and audits, concluded that "there is little evidence at the national level that the program has had any positive impact on eligible and participating children." The report said that, after six years of operation, 37 states (as of June 1971) were violating Title I rules. Among the major deficiencies were the use of funds for routine school expenses, improper auditing and accounting and failure to involve parents. (HEW had requested in September 1971 that the District of Columbia and six states return $5.6 million in misspent funds. At the time of the report, only Wisconsin had complied. An HEW spokesman said April 10 that 26 more states would be asked to return $28 million-$30 million. Eight more states were requested Nov. 20 to refund Title I money.) The report uncovered "no hard evidence" to link the cost of special programs with results or indicating any "minimum necessary expenditure" as a prerequisite for success. In very few cases was the difference between achievement by poor children and the national average on standardized tests substantially narrowed as a result of a Title I program. The report recommended a maximum per-pupil aid figure, to prevent "expensive programs that deny services to many deserving children." It also recommended that such non-academic services as food, health and "cultural enrichment" should be covered by other federal programs, with Title I concentrating on reading and mathematics.

[4] U.S. panel urges nonpublic aid. The Presidential Panel on Nonpublic Education, composed of four members of the school finance commission *(see* [2]), recommended April 20 a $500 million annual program of tuition tax credits to middle-income parents of nonpublic schoolchildren and grants to poor families with such children. Construction loans for nonpublic schools and a share of direct federal education aid were also recommended. In other nonpublic aid developments: a special three-judge federal court Jan. 11 ruled unconstitutional a New York law providing $33 million in direct subsidies to parochial schools to help pay for secular educational services; the same federal panel April 27 ruled unconstitutional another New York law providing $28 million annually to reimburse nonpublic schools for the cost of services mandated by the state, such as recordkeeping and testing, and Oct. 2 struck down a New York law that would have reimbursed low-income families for part of the cost of nonpublic school tuition; a special three-judge federal panel March 6 overturned Vermont's parochial school aid law, citing a 1971 Supreme Court finding against a similar Pennsylvania law for "excessive entanglement between government and religion"; a three-judge federal panel April 6 overturned a Pennsylvania law reimbursing parents for nonpublic school tuition payments; a three-judge federal panel April 17 ruled that a 1971 Ohio law reimbursing parents for private school tuition was an unconstitutional violation of the separation of church and state; the Supreme Court Oct. 10 reaffirmed the panel's Ohio ruling without a hearing; a three-judge federal panel Dec. 29 ruled that an Ohio law granting state, sales and local tax credits to parents of nonpublic school children was unconstitutional. President Nixon April 6 told 12,000 Roman Catholic educators attending a meeting in Philadelphia that he was "irrevocably committed" to aiding nonpublic schools and pledged to submit appropriate legislation to Congress.

[5] Voucher test. The OEO announced April 24 a two-year experiment of the educational voucher system for 4,000 elementary and junior high schoolchildren in a San Jose, Calif. school district. Parents of the children—chosen as a cross-section of the mixed Mexican-American, black and white Anglo district—

would receive vouchers equivalent in value to the funds currently spent by the district for each pupil. They would turn the voucher over to any of six public schools in the district, each of which would develop a separate curriculum centered on such studies as reading, the arts, ethnic studies or bilingual studies. The OEO would provide a supplement of one-third the voucher value for each of 2,000 poor children in the district, as an incentive for the schools to develop programs attractive to poor parents. Private and parochial schools would be excluded from the experiment to conform with California law.

[6] Computer schools charged. The Federal Trade Commission (FTC) May 2 issued a proposed complaint charging that three major computer training school chains (Electronic Computer Programming Institute, Inc.; Control Data Corp.; and Lear Siegler, Inc.) had engaged in deceptive advertising practices. The FTC asked the schools to disclose the percentage of their graduates placed in computer jobs, the names of employers and starting salaries. According to the FTC, the companies had advertised that graduates of the $1,000-$2,500 courses were assured of jobs, that many graduates earned $6,500-$11,000 a year and that programming jobs did not require a college degree. In fact, the commission charged, fewer than 50% of the graduates found computer jobs and, during recession periods, the courses were "virtually worthless."

[7] Amish exempt from secondary schooling. The Supreme Court ruled May 15 that 300 years of dedication by the Amish religious sect to its simple way of life entitled it to be exempt from state compulsory education laws requiring children to attend school beyond the eighth grade. All seven justices who participated in the case agreed with the decision, but Justice William O. Douglas filed a partial dissent arguing that the Amish children involved in the case be consulted. At issue in the case was the Amish belief that education in the secondary schools taught children worldly values that were at odds with the Amish way of life. The court's decision, however, emphasized that the ruling would not automatically apply to any group or sect that opposed formal education. Although the ruling—that Wisconsin law requiring children to attend school until they were 16 violated the constitutional right of the Amish to free exercise of their religion—applied specifically to Wisconsin, the justices used language broad enough to apply to other states that had compulsory education laws. The decision marked the first time the court had exempted a religious group from compulsory school attendance laws.

[8] Higher education aid bill signed. President Nixon June 23 signed the higher education aid bill after it had been approved in its final version by the Senate May 24 and by the House June 8. *(For desegregation provisions, see* CIVIL RIGHTS [5].) The bill would authorize for the first time $1 billion annual direct all-purpose aid to colleges and universities. (90% of the funds would be allocated on the basis of the number of students at each school receiving federal scholarship aid and on the amount of such aid, and 10% would be allocated on the basis of the number of graduate students in attendance.) Special grants would be allocated to schools facing financial collapse or enrolling veterans. Current federal student aid programs were extended three years, and a new system of federal scholarships to every college student in the country would be implemented (depending on subsequent appropriations bills). Under the new system, each student would receive up to $1,400 a year according to family means, provided that no more than 60% of a student's educational costs were covered. A National Student Loan Marketing Association was established by the bill, to buy student loan paper from banks in order to encourage new loans. Present programs of federal loan guarantees and interest subsidies for needy students would be continued. Discrimination against women in any graduate school or public undergraduate college would disqualify the institution from federal aid. (Military schools and a few traditionally one-sex public colleges were exempted from the provision.) Other provisions of the bill expanded vocational education, established a National Institute of Education to conduct research, and aided local programs for Indian students.

[9]   Union ties opposed. Delegates to the annual convention of the National Education Association (NEA) voted 3,723-2,051 June 30 to expel any state or local unit that entered a merger agreement "requiring affiliation with the AFL-CIO." (State NEA units in Michigan, Illinois and Rhode Island had been considering merger.) Units that had already merged with locals of the American Federation of Teachers (AFT), an AFL-CIO affiliate, in New York State, Los Angeles, New Orleans and Flint, Mich. would be allowed to remain in the NEA.

See also CIVIL RIGHTS [1-13, 18]; ELECTIONS [6, 16-17, 21, 23, 35, 44]; HEALTH; MEDICINE; NEGROES; NIXON, RICHARD MILHOUS; POLITICS [8]; POVERTY; WOMEN'S RIGHTS

EGYPT—*See* ARAB REPUBLIC OF EGYPT

ELECTIONS—President Richard M. Nixon, elected in 1968 with less than 50% of the vote in a three-man race, won re-election Nov. 7 in a popular and electoral vote landslide with few precedents in U.S. history *(see* [36]). Democratic candidate George S. McGovern of South Dakota resisted the Nixon sweep only in Massachusetts and the District of Columbia. Nixon captured every other state. A massive display of ticket-splitting, however, enabled the Democrats to retain their majority in both Houses of Congress, gaining a net two seats in the Senate *(see* [38-39]) and losing a comparatively small 13 seats in the House *(see* [40-41]). With a large number of freshmen in the House, Democrats retained the strength to continue to exert a critical influence on legislation and domestic policy. Democrats also did well in gubernatorial races, winning 11 of 18 contests and increasing their margin of control in statehouses to 31-19 *(see* [42-43]).

[2]   The campaign leading up to the elections, both in the primaries *(see* [4-8]) and after the Democratic and Republican National Conventions *(see* [15-19, 22-24]), was one-sided, with almost all the activity on the Democratic side. President Nixon had little opposition before the Republican convention and did very little campaigning after the convention *(see* [27]). On the Democratic side, Sen. Edmund S. Muskie of Maine started out as the Democratic front runner *(see* [4-5]), but soon lost his lead to McGovern in a race which featured a number of active contenders *(see* [3]). In primary activities, Gov. George Wallace of Alabama, vying for the Democratic nomination, was shot during his campaign and paralyzed from the waist down *(see* [10]). Following the Democratic Convention, McGovern's running mate, Sen. Thomas Eagleton of Missouri, disclosed that he had been hospitalized for psychiatric treatment *(see* [30-31]). Eagleton withdrew from the Democratic ticket and was replaced by R. Sargent Shriver *(see* [29, 31]). With the absence of President Nixon from active campaigning, the McGovern-Shriver ticket was unable to muster much excitement for its issues. McGovern's opposition to the Vietnam war was undermined by advancing peace talks to end the war *(see* INDOCHINA WAR [44-51]), and little public interest seemed to be roused in response to the Watergate incident in which Democratic party headquarters were bugged *(see* POLITICS [9-12]).

Pre-Convention Activities

[3]   Candidates. A number of individuals had already declared their candidacy for the presidency in 1970 and 1971. Although several also dropped out of the race in 1971, those who maintained their candidacy into 1972 were: Democratic Sens. McGovern and Henry M. Jackson of Washington (withdrew May 2, citing "deficit financing"); former Democratic Sen. Eugene J. McCarthy of Minnesota; Walter E. Fauntroy, the District of Columbia's Democratic representative in Congress; Democratic Mayor John V. Lindsay of New York; Democratic Mayor Sam Yorty of Los Angeles; Republican Rep. Paul McCloskey Jr. of California (withdrew March 10); and Republican Sen. Robert

Taft Jr. of Ohio (withdrew as a favorite son candidate Jan. 4). The following individuals announced their candidacy for the presidency in 1972: President Nixon (announced Jan. 7); Democratic Sen. Vance Hartke (announced Jan. 3); Muskie (announced Jan. 4); Conservative Republican Rep. John M. Ashbrook (announced Jan. 6); Democratic Sen. Hubert H. Humphrey of Minnesota, the 1968 Democratic presidential candidate (announced Jan. 10); Wallace, who had campaigned as a third-party candidate in 1968 (announced Jan. 13); Democratic Rep. Shirley Chisholm of New York, the only black woman ever to serve in Congress (announced Jan. 25); and Democratic Rep. Wilbur D. Mills of Arkansas (announced Feb. 11). *(For candidates from minor parties, see* [37].) Sen. Hartke withdrew from the presidential race March 26 because the financial burdens of campaigning were "impossible." He endorsed Sen. Humphrey. Sen. Muskie withdrew from "active participation" in the primaries April 27, but retained his candidacy.

[4] Primaries single out Nixon, McGovern. The series of state primary elections which began March 7 in New Hampshire and ended June 20 in New York singled out President Nixon and Sen. McGovern as the leading contenders for the presidency. The President easily surmounted the challenge from the left offered by Rep. McCloskey and the challenge from the right offered by Rep. Ashbrook. In many of the state primaries, the President was unopposed. He won in all the primaries in which his name was entered. On the Democratic side, McGovern won primaries in Wisconsin (April 4), Idaho (April 17), Massachusetts (April 25), Nebraska (May 5), Oregon (May 23), Rhode Island (May 23), New Jersey (June 6), California (June 6), New Mexico (June 6), South Dakota (June 6) and New York (June 20). Sen. Humphrey won primaries in Pennsylvania (April 25), Ohio (May 2), Indiana (May 2) and West Virginia (May 9). Gov. Wallace won Democratic primaries in Florida (March 14), Tennessee (May 4), North Carolina (May 6), Maryland (May 16) and Michigan (May 16). Sen. Muskie won primaries in New Hampshire and Illinois (March 21). By June 25, Sen. McGovern commanded 1,378.9 votes to the Democratic convention, only 130.1 short of the 1,509 needed for nomination. The next largest bloc of votes to the Democratic convention, 493.75, was uncommitted, and 58 votes were reserved for favorite sons. The remainder of the tally: Humphrey, 386.3; Wallace, 377; Muskie, 209.1; Jackson, 53.75; Mills, 30.55; and Chisholm, 28.65.

[5] Primary highlights—New Hampshire. In the Republican primary March 7, President Nixon captured 68% of the vote and 13 of the 14 delegates to the Republican Convention. Rep. McCloskey captured 20% of the vote; and Rep. Ashbrook captured 11% of the vote. The remaining Republican delegate to the convention was favorable to Nixon. On the Democratic side, Sen. Muskie won 46.6% of the vote and 15 delegates to the national convention; but Sen. McGovern, with an active organization, made a strong showing—winning 37% of the vote and five delegates. The two candidates left far behind the other Democratic contestants—Yorty (6% of the vote), Mills (4% of the vote), Hartke (3% of the vote) and Hartford, Conn. poverty worker Edward T. Coll. By winning in New Hampshire, Muskie maintained his position as the Democratic front-runner, but McGovern's surprising strength kept Muskie from gaining additional steps on his rivals. A victory in New Hampshire, because it was a neighbor to Muskie's home state of Maine, was conceded by Muskie to be essential to his leading status among the many Democratic presidential contenders. Muskie based his campaign on his image as neighbor, which was strong enough to keep some Democratic contenders (including Humphrey) out of the primary. But a steady slippage in the polls during the final weeks of the campaign forced Muskie into some hectic moments—a tearful denunciation of the conservative newspaper, the *Manchester Union Leader,* for attacks on him and his wife, and a nervous performance during a televised debate March 5 with all of his Democratic opponents except write-in candidate Mills, who was not invited. McGovern had campaigned in New Hampshire 24 days, compared with 13 for Muskie. The well-organized

McGovern campaign, staffed with youthful volunteers, set forth his major themes: a rapid withdrawal from Vietnam and less spending for defense.

[6] Primary highlights—Florida. Gov. Wallace, as expected, won the Florida primary March 14, collecting 42% of the vote and 75 of the state's delegates to the Democratic convention in a race against 10 other contenders. The ratings for the other Democrats: Humphrey, 18% of the vote and the remaining six delegates; Jackson, 13% of the vote; Muskie, 9%; Lindsay, 7%; McGovern, 6%; Chisholm, 4%; and McCarthy, Mills, Hartke and Yorty—who together polled less than 2% of the vote. Wallace dominated the campaign as well as the voting, chiding the other candidates on the necessity of focusing on his issues—school busing, taxing the rich and cracking down on crime. Busing became the major issue. (The primary also included a straw poll, without legal effect, on busing. The results of the poll showed that 74% of the voters favored a constitutional amendment to prohibit busing and to guarantee the right of a student to attend the public school nearest his home and that 79% favored an equal opportunity for quality education for all children and opposed the return of the dual system of public schools.) Wallace flatly opposed any form of busing to desegregate schools; Humphrey opposed forced busing and busing children from good schools and neighborhoods to bad ones, but condoned busing if it improved education; Jackson proposed a constitutional amendment to prohibit mandatory busing; Muskie resisted the issue of busing, which he considered an undesirable but sometimes necessary tool to achieve desegregation; Lindsay, McGovern and Chisholm firmly supported busing as a way to desegregate until integrated neighborhoods were attained. In the Republican primary, President Nixon received 87% of the vote and all of the state's 40 delegates to the Republican convention. (The President did not campaign in the state.) Ashbrook polled 9% of the vote and McCloskey polled 4%.

[7] Primary highlights—Michigan. Gov. Wallace May 16 won a sweeping victory in Michigan with 51% of the primary vote, his first plurality in a Northern state election since he entered such competition in 1964. Sen. McGovern received 27% of the vote; Humphrey polled 16%. The remainder of the Democratic vote went to Chisholm, Muskie, Jackson and Hartke. A large part of Wallace's support was said to have come from Republican and independent voters; Michigan had no party registration. Although a sympathy vote for Wallace because of the attempt on his life *(see* [9]) could have been a factor, Wallace was the acknowledged leader in the primary campaign from the start. School busing was a dominant issue in the campaign. In the Republican presidential primary, President Nixon received 95% of the vote.

[8] Primary highlights—California. McGovern June 6 won the California Democratic presidential primary and all of the state's 271 delegates to the Democratic convention. McGovern won 47.1% of the total presidential preference vote, while Humphrey won 41.7%. (A poll had predicted a 20% McGovern margin over Humphrey.) The two candidates put forth intense efforts for California's huge delegate bloc, which was awarded on a winner-take-all basis. The McGovern campaign was well-organized—some 35,000 volunteers from more than 120 headquarters canvassed the Democratic electorate—and well financed—McGovern TV and radio messages were on the air three weeks before the first Humphrey spot appeared. One of McGovern's messages was that the public did not want "a rerun of 1968," when Humphrey unsuccessfully campaigned against Nixon. By contrast, Humphrey's campaign lacked organization and relied on organized labor's get-out-the-vote program and the candidate's personal efforts. Humphrey began his California campaign with harsh attacks on McGovern's defense and welfare proposals as too liberal. One of the highlights of the campaign came in a series of three debates. Humphrey surprised McGovern with the fierceness of his attack in the first debate May 28. The second debate May 30 was milder. The third debate June 4 was expanded, under court order, to include Chisholm, Yorty and Gen. Taylor Hardin (representing Wallace). The debate was expanded after Mrs. Chisholm obtained a federal court order requiring equal time for the first two debates. In the Republican primary, President Nixon won 90% of the vote and all the state's 96 delegates. Ashbrook won the remaining 10% of the vote.

[9] McGovern offers 'defense budget.' Sen. McGovern Jan. 19 offered an "alternative defense budget" that he said was part of "the very heart of my campaign" for the presidency. The budget called for $54.8 billion in military spending in fiscal 1973, as compared with President Nixon's budget request *(see* BUDGET) for $78.3 billion for defense spending in fiscal 1973. McGovern said his alternative budget would replace "fat" with muscle in a stronger national security system and would reduce military spending by one-third. The budget proposed: reduction of an all-volunteer armed force by one-third; withdrawal of all U.S. troops in Indochina and South Korea; reduction of U.S. troop strength in Europe by one-half; reduction of the Navy's attack carrier force from 14 to six; and the cancelation of the Safeguard antiballistic missile system, the B-1 bomber, the F-14 and F-15 fighter bombers and additional work on the multiple independently targetable re-entry vehicles (MIRVs). The last proposal was put forward, McGovern said, because the projects were unnecessary. McGovern indicated that the difference between his budget and Nixon's was the difference "between conservatism and paranoia," between a "buy what we need" approach and a "wasteful arms race." Defense Secretary Melvin Laird, in what he said was a nonpartisan view, July 6 described McGovern's proposed budget as a threat to American security. Laird called the proposal "a white flag surrender budget" that "substitutes a philosophy of give-away now, beg later, for a philosophy of strength and a willingness to negotiate throughout the world."

[10] Wallace shot in assassination attempt. Gov. Wallace was shot and seriously wounded May 15 while campaigning in the Maryland presidential primary. The assailant, firing a .38-caliber revolver at point-blank range, immediately was seized by security personnel accompanying Wallace and was later identified as Arthur Bremer *(see* CRIME [7-8]). The attack came at about 4 p.m. after Wallace had delivered his standard campaign speech before about 1,000 persons at a shopping center in Laurel, a suburb of Washington. Stepping down from his three-sided bulletproof lectern, Wallace went down to mingle with the crowd. He began shaking hands with his supporters, his retinue veering toward cries of "Hey, George! Hey, George! Over here!" which witnesses later said came from the assailant. When Wallace neared him, the assailant thrust his arm between two people in the front rank and fired at Wallace—one shot, a pause, two more shots, then more shots. Security personnel reacted immediately, hitting the assailant's gun arm and subduing him while shots from his revolver continued. Wallace, his wife Cornelia at his side, was rushed to the Holy Cross Hospital in Silver Spring, Md. with critical chest and abdomen wounds. He underwent surgery for five hours, and his condition was stabilized. He recovered sufficiently to be taken off the critical list by May 16, although he was paralyzed from the waist down, with a bullet lodged near his spinal cord. Wallace indicated May 17 that he would continue his campaign. A program of physical therapy was begun May 18, and doctors reported May 22 that there had been "some return of involuntary muscular activity to the toes of both feet" and some evidence of increasing sensation down to the level of the mid-thigh. The bullet in the governor's spinal column was removed June 18, but doctors said there was "less than a 50-50 chance" Wallace would regain full use of his paralyzed lower extremities. (Three other persons suffered bullet wounds during the Laurel shooting. Secret Service agent Nicholas Zorvas suffered a serious wound in the neck requiring surgery, but was reported in satisfactory condition May 17. Capt. Eldred C. Dothard of the Alabama State Police, a close associate and longtime Wallace bodyguard, received a wound in the abdomen. Mrs. Dora Thompson, a Wallace worker in Maryland, received a minor leg wound.)

[11] **Mitchell quits as Nixon campaign manager.** Former Attorney General John N. Mitchell resigned July 1 as President Nixon's campaign manager to "meet the one obligation which must come first: the happiness and welfare of my wife and daughter." His wife, Martha, had indicated June 25 that she was separating from her husband because she was "a political prisoner" and she "can't stand" the life she had been leading since Mitchell resigned as attorney general. Mrs. Mitchell also said she could no longer stand "all those dirty things that go on." President Nixon later July 1 named Clark MacGregor, his chief adviser on congressional relations, as his new campaign director.

[12] **Democratic telethon raises funds.** The Democratic party July 8-9 held a 19-hour telethon to raise funds for the party. The telethon, planned by Kentucky Fried Chicken Corp. board chairman John Y. Brown, cost $1.6 million to produce and raised an estimated $3.5 million in cash (over $4 million in pledges). A money dispute overshadowed the production from its planning stages until its completion. McGovern supporters wanted the funds allotted to the coming fall campaign. When that request was rejected, actor Warren Beatty, who had produced other successful money-raising extravaganzas for McGovern, refused to produce the telethon. Brown planned to use the money to pay off the 1968 campaign debts of Humphrey ($6 million) and Robert Kennedy ($2 million) and the 1968 convention costs ($1 million). Democratic party Treasurer Robert Strauss had indicated that he would allocate the money raised by the telethon on a pro-rated basis to contributers loaning money to the party in 1968.

[13] **Connally to aid Nixon.** John Connally, the Texas Democrat who had become one of President Nixon's confidantes, said July 14 he would work for the President's re-election by spending most of his time until November seeking to persuade other Democrats to support Nixon *(see* NIXON, RICHARD MILHOUS). Connally, a former Treasury secretary, said he was still a Democrat, but could not support McGovern because the candidate's ideas were "all too isolationist in character and also too radical in character."

[14] **Agnew on ticket.** President Nixon announced July 22 that Vice President Spiro T. Agnew would again be his running mate in the November election. The announcement ended months of speculation that Agnew would be dropped. Such speculation had often centered on the possibility that Connally would replace Agnew.

Conventions

[15] **Democratic National Convention.** The Democratic party convened July 10-13 in Miami Beach in its 36th quadrennial convention. Following a July 10 series of challenges to the seating of delegations, it became clear that McGovern forces were in control of the convention. The two most crucial credentials questions raised in the convention were in the seating of delegations from California and Illinois. Because of the close vote in the California primary *(see [7])*, and because of the spirit of reform sought by the party, the convention Credentials Committee had voted June 29 to ignore California's winner-take-all primary law and to take away 151 of the 271 delegates McGovern had won, splitting the seats among the other candidates in proportion to their primary vote totals. (Thus, Humphrey would receive 106 delegates, Wallace 16, Chisholm 12 and the other candidates from two to six delegates each.) McGovern reacted strongly to the committee's decision, calling it "an incredible, cynical, rotten political steal" and threatening to bolt the party if the decision were upheld by the convention. The committee June 30 also voted to oust Mayor Richard J. Daley and 58 other Chicago delegates and to seat a slate of challengers that included 40-50 McGovern supporters. The Daley delegation had been challenged on violations of the party's reform guidelines—balanced representation for women, blacks, Latin Americans and young people; and open nominating sessions for the delegate candidates. U.S. District Court

Judge George L. Hart Jr. of Washington July 3 upheld the committee on both the California and Illinois cases. On the California question, he said the issue was a question for the convention, not for the courts. On the Daley case, he reissued a ruling he had made June 20 that delegates could not be excluded solely because of race, age or sex of individual delegates or groups of delegates, but he upheld the committee's right to reject the Daley group for using closed procedures in forming the delegation. The U.S. Court of Appeals for the District of Columbia July 5 ruled against the Credentials Committee on the California case, but upheld it on the Chicago case. The Supreme Court July 7 met in special session and, by a 6-3 decision, returned both cases to the convention devoid of court rulings on the ground that court intervention in the political process immediately prior to the convention was unprecedented and not in the public interest. On the convention floor July 10, the delegates voted 1,618.28-1,238.22 to seat the entire California McGovern delegation and 1,486-1,371 to refuse to seat the Daley delegation. (Democratic National Chairman Lawrence O'Brien ruled on the floor that the 151 challenged California delegates could not participate in the California vote, thus lowering the majority needed for approval of seating the California delegation to 1,433.)

[16] *Platform accepted.* In a marathon 11-hour session July 11-12, the convention adopted with only two minor changes the liberal draft platform prepared by the 150-member platform committee two weeks before. The platform called for a broad range of liberal federal programs to meet domestic needs and a reduced reliance on military and executive power in foreign policy, although it supported an active international role for the U.S. Despite a dramatic wheelchair appearance by Gov. Wallace to support conservative minority reports, the convention rejected by large voice vote margins proposals for: a strong stand against school busing; a constitutional amendment allowing school prayers; support for the right of citizens to bear arms; a strong military establishment; and a pledge to remain in Vietnam until American prisoners were released. The convention also rejected a series of controversial minority reports to strengthen the platform's stand on tax reform, welfare, Vietnam, abortion and rights for homosexuals. The only changes accepted were a more explicit expression of support for Israel and a provision on surplus land for American Indians.

[17] *McGovern wins on first ballot.* Sen. McGovern July 12 won the presidential nomination on the first ballot, collecting 1,715.35 delegate votes to defeat four others placed in nomination. The four did not include Sens. Humphrey or Muskie, his major rivals, who withdrew from the competition July 11 when it was clear that stop-McGovern forces were in the decline. Rep. Mills and former Sen. McCarthy withdrew their candidacies the day of the balloting. Sen. Jackson, backed by organized labor after Humphrey's withdrawal, received 534 delegate votes. Gov. Wallace received 385.7 votes; Rep. Chisholm received 151.95 votes; and Duke University President Terry Sanford, a former governor of North Carolina, received 77.5 votes. The votes putting McGovern over the 1,509 needed for nomination were cast by the Illinois delegation. McGovern accepted the nomination July 14 and pledged to "dedicate" his campaign to the American people. Much of McGovern's acceptance speech dealt with the war in Indochina, but he also spoke of planned improvements in the fields of education, medicine, health, environment, law enforcement, the welfare system, employment and tax reform. He singled out for particular attention jobs and tax reform and promised "the end of a system of economic controls in which labor is depressed, but prices and corporate profits are the highest in history."

[18] *Reform compromise approved.* Convention delegates July 13 overwhelmingly endorsed proposed party reforms under compromise arrangements made by McGovern forces July 12 to avoid further antagonizing members of Congress, party regulars and labor representatives, all of whom had opposed extensive party reform. Under the compromise, approval was won

for restructuring the Democratic National Committee (DNC) to include grass-roots representatives, effective immediately, while delaying for two years adoption of a new party charter and other party reforms. The newly expanded DNC would increase in size from 110 members to 303 members, with their voting strength divided to total 237. The new representatives joining national and state committee men and women would include three governors, four members of Congress, two at-large party workers, state members elected proportionately on the basis of each state's population and Democratic voting strength, and the highest-ranking state party official of the sex opposite to that of the state chairman. The reorganized committee could call a party conference in 1974, two-thirds comprised of delegates elected at a local level, to adopt a new party charter, which would then require approval from the 1976 presidential nominating convention. The compromise which was arranged by the McGovern forces, however, prevented the convention from voting on reform measures approved by the party's Rules Committee June 24. Those measures would have extended convention rule changes (increased delegate representation for women, minority groups and young voters and abolition of the winner-take-all primary and Republican crossover votes in Democratic primaries) to the party as a whole. They also would have called for a 3,980-member party policy conference to determine party policy between election years and would have given only dues-paying and enrolled party members a vote in choosing policy conference delegates.

[19] *Eagleton nominated.* Sen. Thomas Eagleton was nominated as the Democratic candidate for vice president by acclamation of the convention shortly before 2 a.m. July 14 after accumulating more than the 1,509 votes on the first ballot. More than 1,000 votes were cast by delegates for 39 other persons, including television character Archie Bunker, CBS newsman Roger Mudd and Martha Mitchell. Seven other persons were formally nominated: former Massachusetts Gov. Endicott Peabody; Frances T. Farenthold, defeated candidate for the Democratic nomination for governor of Texas; Sen. Mike Gravel (Alaska); Hodding Carter 3rd, editor of the *Greenville* (Miss.) *Delta-Times;* Stanley Arnold, an advertising executive from New York City; Rep. Peter W. Rodino Jr. (N.J.); and Clay Smothers of Dallas, a black supporter of Gov. Wallace. The divided vote on the nomination resulted partly from resentment among some delegates that McGovern allegedly had rammed through his personal choice for the vice presidency. Party unity was restored, however, when Mrs. Farenthold withdrew her name from nomination during the balloting, followed shortly by Sen. Gravel and former Gov. Peabody. The choice of Eagleton as McGovern's running mate had been announced by Frank Mankiewicz, McGovern's national political coordinator, July 13. The only other person offered the post, according to Mankiewicz, was Sen. Edward M. Kennedy (Mass.), who had repeatedly refused it for personal reasons. The hope that Kennedy would join the ticket was kept alive, however, until immediately after McGovern won the nomination, when the two men talked by telephone. The position was offered once again at that time, and was refused. McGovern later consulted with Kennedy on his final selection of Eagleton. Gov. Reubin J. Askew (Fla.) was said to have been another personal choice of McGovern, but Askew said July 12 that he did not want the nomination. Sen. Abraham Ribicoff (N.Y.) said July 13 that he had been offered the nomination, but had refused.

[20] *Activity outside the convention.* In contrast to the 1968 Democratic Convention in Chicago, the only major demonstration outside the 1972 convention was peaceful, as 3,000 non-delegate youths and a few poor people rallied peacefully for two hours July 11, protesting U.S. imperialism, racism and sexism as a group of 700 Cubans marched nearby in opposition to Fidel Castro. Miami Beach Police Chief Rocky Pomerance was credited with maintaining amicable relations between the non-delegates and police and city officials. A 4-2 vote of the Miami Beach City Council July 5 allowed protesters to sleep at campgrounds near the convention hall. A Poor Peoples Coalition—

formed by members of the Southern Christian Leadership Conference, the National Tenants Organization and the National Welfare Rights Organization (NWRO)—established a "tent city" at the campsite for all non-delegates attending the convention and the NWRO's five-day conference in Miami Beach, which ended July 9. In the only incident during the convention, a group of 300 young demonstrators July 10 pulled down 90 feet of fence surrounding the convention hall after breaking away from a peaceful march. But security remained tight as 3,000 National Guardsmen moved into the Miami Beach area July 9 to join 1,000 law enforcement officers and 2,000 paratroopers of the 82nd Airborne Division.

[21] **American party convention.** Rep. John F. Schmitz (R, Calif.) was nominated as the presidential candidate of the American party at its convention in Louisville, Ky. Aug. 4. Schmitz, a member of the ultra-conservative John Birch Society and an unsuccessful 1972 candidate for the Republican nomination for his Congressional seat, won on the first ballot with 329.75 votes, defeating Georgia Lt. Gov. Lester Maddox (55.65 votes), Allen Greer of Florida (25.5 votes), Tom Anderson of Tennessee (23.6 votes) and Richard B. Kay of Cleveland (16 votes), a lawyer who defended Lt. William Calley (see WAR CRIMES). Anderson, former publisher of farm and ranch magazines and currently associated with *The American Way Features,* was nominated by the convention Aug. 5 as the party's vice presidential candidate. Anderson was also a member of the John Birch Society. There had been strong support at the convention, which convened Aug. 3, for the nomination of Gov. Wallace as the presidential candidate. The support did not subside, despite Wallace's stand that he "was not physically able" to run as the party's candidate, until Wallace spoke to the convention by telephone Aug. 4 and informed it "that my physical condition is such that I cannot answer the people's wish to draft me." A platform adopted by the convention Aug. 4 stressed local government, individual rights and law and order, and advocated election of federal judges, strong drug laws, voluntary school prayer and a ban against busing to achieve integration. Schmitz Aug. 4 outlined to the convention his own two-point platform: "One, foreign—never go to war unless you plan to win. Two, domestic—those who go to work ought to live better than those who don't."

[22] **Republican National Convention.** The 30th Republican National Convention, lacking the drama of the Democratic Convention, convened in Miami Beach Aug. 21-23. (The Republican National Committee had formally voted May 5 to switch the site of the convention from San Diego to Miami.) The convention Aug. 22 renominated President Nixon by a vote of 1,347-1. (The one dissenting vote was cast for Rep. McCloskey by the New Mexico delegation.) Nixon's name was placed in nomination by Gov. Nelson A. Rockefeller (N.Y.), the President's chief rival at the 1968 Republican convention. The convention Aug. 23 also renominated Vice President Agnew as Nixon's running mate. The vote for Agnew was 1,345-1, with the dissenting vote cast for NBC newsman David Brinkley. In his acceptance speech Aug. 23, President Nixon asked the nation to give him a "new majority" of support so his Administration could continue the progress of the previous four years and "the progress we have made in building a new structure of peace in the world." The President directed special appeals to the young, the elderly and disaffected Democrats. He referred to himself "not as a partisan of party which would divide us, but as a partisan of principles which can unite us."

[23] *Platform approved.* With only perfunctory debate, the convention Aug. 22 approved the party platform, written largely under White House guidance. Plank by plank, the platform reflected the President's views. It included his terms for peace in Vietnam, his strong opposition to school busing to achieve integration, his support for a strong military posture and his policies for increasing contacts with the Communist-bloc nations. Significantly, the platform included a plank incorporating the President's recent praise for organized labor. The plank was seen as an effort to woo the votes of disaffected

Democrats from the ranks of organized labor. The theme of the platform was repeated throughout: President Nixon and the Republicans had "restored reason and order and hope" to a country that had lost its way under the Democrats. The platform preamble said that the choice in 1972 was clearer than it had been in previous years—"Between moderate goals historically sought by both major parties and far-out goals of the far left." The delegates adopted the platform with only one minor change—the addition of a plank calling for preferential hiring and promotion of Indians within federal agencies which direct Indian affairs programs and recommending the passage of new legislation to improve the Indian standard of life. Another proposal that would have prohibited President Nixon from submitting deficit budgets was rejected by a voice vote.

[24] *Compromise reform plan.* The convention, by a 910-434 vote Aug. 22, rejected a delegate reform proposal to increase representation for the populous states at the 1976 convention by 400 bonus delegates. Instead, the convention adopted a complex formula which benefitted the smaller states. The formula awarded each state six bonus delegates-at-large and three bonus delegates for each congressional district. In addition, states that carried the vote for the Republican presidential nominee would receive an extra 4.5 bonus delegates plus additional bonus delegates equal to 60% of their electoral vote. Another bonus delegate would be awarded each state for each senator or governor elected between conventions and another for a Republican majority Congressional delegation. The hour-long debate over the reform plan provided the only open floor dispute of the convention. The conservative bloc, composed of Southerners and representatives of smaller states, decisively defeated the liberals, composed mainly of representatives from urban areas and larger states. The dispute carried an undercurrent of presidential politics. The conservative plan was considered more favorable to the chances of Vice President Agnew to succeed President Nixon as the party's nominee in 1976. (The bonus plan went against a U.S. District Court ruling by Judge William B. Jones April 28. Jones had held that the bonus system was unconstitutional because it unfairly discriminated against the largest, most populous states.) The convention Aug. 22 also approved, by voice vote, a Rules Committee report calling upon the Republican National Committee to take "positive action to achieve broadest possible participation by everyone in party affairs, including such participation by women, young people, minority and heritage groups and senior citizens in the delegate selection process." The report was adopted with one amendment, calling upon the party chairman to appoint a representative of "a black Republican organization" to the party's executive committee.

[25] *Activity outside the convention.* Protesters demonstrated in Miami throughout the convention. The protesters' aims were as varied as the activist groups represented, which had been organized by the Miami Conventions Coalition (MCC), an umbrella group comprised of the Youth International party (Yippies), the Peoples Coalition for Peace and Justice, the Coalition of Gay Organizations and the Miami Women's Coalition. Apart from the MCC actions were those organized by the Students for a Democratic Society (SDS) and the Zippie faction of the Yippies. Those two groups Aug. 20 sponsored a demonstration in which about 350 protesters marched on the Fontainbleu Hotel, Republican party headquarters, where a $500-a-plate gala honoring Mrs. Nixon was held. Police dispersed the crowd after 45 minutes when several persons trying to enter the hotel were roughed up by demonstrators, who also damaged cars. Members of the Vietnam Veterans Against the War (VVAW), who were consistently peaceful and well-disciplined during the convention demonstrations, joined other protesters Aug. 21 for a demonstration in front of the Miami Beach High School, which was occupied by National Guardsmen. (Florida National Guardsmen, paratroopers from the 82nd Airborne and several Marine units also were on call at the nearby Homestead Air Force Base during the convention. The Secret Service, the Federal Bureau of Investigation and local police officials brought the total force to 8,500.) Several arrests were made at the rally when demonstrators tried to climb the roof of the school. More than 200 were arrested Aug. 22 when demonstrators, led by Zippies, converged on the convention hall. They were charged with blocking traffic, damaging cars and assaulting delegates. An SDS-led group of 300 marched the same day down the center of the city, ripping flags and bunting and smashing windows in two buildings. No arrests were made. Another group of 1,200, led by the VVAW, held a peaceful afternoon rally near the Fontainbleu. That evening, 3,000 demonstrators staged a guerrilla theater performance protesting the deaths of Vietnamese, the 1970 deaths of students at Kent State University during a war protest and the 1971 prisoner deaths at Attica Prison *(see* PRISONS).

[26] Protesters staged a massive sitdown outside the convention hall Aug. 23, with the purported aim of delaying the acceptance speeches of Nixon and Agnew. However, the convention session was delayed by only seven minutes. More than 1,129 demonstrators were arrested during the day and evening as splinter groups roamed streets in the convention area trying to block traffic, slashing tires and overturning garbage cans. Members of the VVAW tried to restrain the more damage-prone members of the crowd. Protesters were prevented from gathering in large groups by extensive police use of CS or "pepper" gas, a crowd-control device. The convention hall itself was sealed off by a bus barricade. Only 38 minor injuries were reported during the disturbances as police adopted the highly mobile, low-profile tactics urged by Police Chief Pomerance. Protesters were arrested on misdemeanor charges involving, in most cases, a minimal $10 bail fee. Most demonstrators were freed on bond by Aug. 24.

The Campaign

[27] **In general.** The campaign was one of contrasts. The Republicans, whose candidate never lost a seemingly insurmountable poll lead, spent (according to preliminary estimates) almost $50 million. The Democrats spent about $25 million. The Republicans conducted a massive get-out-the-vote drive to undercut the McGovern organization that had achieved candidacy status because of its remarkable voter-contact efficiency in the primaries. Nixon did not publicly identify his opponent by name during the campaign. He played the role of an on-the-job president, delegating his campaign candidacy until the close of the campaign to numerous "surrogates," including his wife and daughters. In contrast, McGovern conducted the longest presidential campaign of the century, begun in January 1971. The President held only one news conference during the campaign and, while using radio extensively, delivered only one set campaign speech on television. McGovern July 22 challenged the President to a series of nationally televised debates, but Clark McGregor rejected the proposal the same day. Nixon rarely took to the stump. McGovern criss-crossed the country repeatedly, logging, according to airline officials, 65,000 miles in the air since Labor Day. Many Democrats seeking office tried to dodge association with McGovern. Republicans seeking office were largely abandoned by Nixon, who was courting Democratic votes.

[28] **AFL-CIO takes neutral stand.** The Executive Council of the AFL-CIO voted 27-3 July 19 to withhold its endorsement from either McGovern or Nixon. The decision to remain neutral did not extend to Congressional races, where the council said it would seek "the election of our friends." It was the first time in its 17-year history that the AFL-CIO had not endorsed the Democratic presidential candidate. The council's stand denied either candidate the federation's campaign contributions (estimated at $10 million in 1968) and campaign support of the AFL-CIO Committee on Political Education (COPE). COPE organized the 13.5 million-member federation's get-out-the-vote campaign. Following the council meeting, federation President George Meany said that he would "not support and will not vote" for either Nixon or McGovern. Meany also expressed his opposition to McGovern. The council vote

prevented federation-created units from endorsing either candidate, but did not prevent individual unions affiliated with the AFL-CIO from issuing endorsements. State AFL-CIO bodies in Colorado and Florida openly opposed the council decision and endorsed the McGovern ticket. (Meany Sept. 20 suspended the Colorado affiliate for refusing to renounce its endorsement.) Several individual unions in the 116-member AFL-CIO also endorsed the McGovern ticket.

[29] **Eagleton withdraws from ticket, replaced by Shriver.** Sen. Eagleton Aug. 1 withdrew as the Democratic vice presidential candidate. The decision was announced by Sen. McGovern July 31, and Democratic National Chairman Jean Westwood accepted the resignation Aug. 1. Eagleton was replaced Aug. 8 by R. Sargent Shriver. Shriver was nominated by the DNC on the recommendation of McGovern, who had named Shriver as his choice Aug. 5 after Sen. Muskie declined an offer to become the running mate because of his "family duties." In naming Shriver as his running mate, McGovern cited his service under President Kennedy as the first director of the Peace Corps, under President Johnson as the first director of the Office of Economic Opportunity and as ambassador to France under Presidents Johnson and Nixon. Shriver, married to President Kennedy's sister Eunice, had never tried for elective office before. In the DNC voting for Shriver, Missouri cast its vote for Eagleton and Oregon cast four votes for its former Sen. Wayne Morse. Guam did not cast its three votes, but Shriver received the rest of the committee's votes.

[30] The debate which resulted in Eagleton's withdrawal began July 25 when Eagleton revealed that he had hospitalized himself three times between 1960 and 1966 for psychiatric treatment of nervous exhaustion and fatigue. On two of these occasions, Eagleton said, he had undergone electro-shock therapy, which he termed "the prescribed treatment" for manifestations of emotional depression. Eagleton denied that alcoholism had played a part in his illness. He described himself as an "intense and hard-fighting person" who, in the past, had pushed himself beyond his limits. His first hospitalization came following the 1960 election campaign, during which he was elected the youngest attorney general in Missouri's history and had campaigned extensively for President Kennedy. He had entered Barnes Hospital in St. Louis for a month following the election, and had received electro-shock therapy. The second period of hospitalization occurred after the 1964 campaign when he was elected lieutenant governor. Eagleton said he spent several days in December at the Mayo Clinic in Rochester, Minn. for a physical examination and treatment of a "nervous stomach." In 1966, he returned to the Mayo Clinic for one month between September and October and again received electro-shock therapy. Following Eagleton's disclosures, McGovern admitted that he had known nothing of Eagleton's past illnesses when he chose him as a running mate, but said he would not have hesitated to select Eagleton if he had known of the health problem. Asked July 26 if he had made an "irrevocable decision" to keep Eagleton on the ticket, McGovern replied "Absolutely." Rumors of Eagleton's hospitalization for nervous fatigue and of a "drinking problem" had reached the McGovern staff before the vice presidential nominee was selected, but only a cursory investigation of the charges was made. According to McGovern campaign aides, checks with reporters and Missouri officials had found no substance to the rumors, although no effort was made to contact Eagleton directly. Frank Mankiewicz reportedly had asked Eagleton July 13, only 15 minutes before the deadline for filing nominations for the vice presidency, "Do you have any skeletons rattling around in your closet?" Eagleton replied "No." (He afterwards explained he did not consider hospitalization for health problems to be a "skeleton.") Eagleton reportedly had considered disclosing his health record July 16, but had decided not to. He was unable to talk to McGovern about the matter, because of lengthy Senate floor debate and McGovern's vacationing in South Dakota, but spoke July 19 with Mankiewicz and another McGovern aide. During the weekend of July 22-23, the Knight newspapers detailed for McGovern's staff a list of charges concerning

Eagleton's health which it had uncovered as a result of tips from anonymous telephone callers.

[31] The controversy over Eagleton was compounded July 27 by columnist Jack Anderson's charges that Eagleton had been arrested several times for reckless and drunken driving. Anderson said he based his charges on revelations by "a former high official from Missouri whose reliability is beyond question." Eagleton responded angrily that the charges were false and that he was determined to remain on the Democratic ticket. Eagleton said July 27 that he had been involved in only two traffic "incidents," which had "absolutely no connection with alcohol." One was a 1962 speeding ticket for which he paid a $46 fine, the other a minor accident in 1963 when he skidded on ice into a road marker. Anderson Aug. 1 publicly retracted his charges and apologized to Eagleton. Pressure on Eagleton to withdraw mounted, partially fed by fear that potential financial contributors would react badly to Eagleton's presence on the ticket. In his withdrawal Aug. 1, Eagleton said he would have preferred to remain on the ticket but was aware of the "growing pressures" both for and against it. He said he would "not divide the Democratic party, which has already too many divisions." He indicated that his withdrawal had been at McGovern's request. McGovern said Eagleton's health "was not a factor" in the decision to withdraw, but added that the public debate over Eagleton's medical history "continues to divert attention from the great national issues that need to be discussed."

[32] Dispute flares over '69 peace chance. Shriver charged Aug. 10 that President Nixon had lost an opportunity for a Vietnam peace settlement when he took office in 1969. Shriver said "Nixon had peace handed to him literally in his lap. He blew it." The remarks were taken to imply that a 1969 decrease in battlefield activity had indicated North Vietnam's willingness to negotiate a settlement of the war. The comments set off a dispute between the Administration and the Democratic ticket over the charge. Secretary of State William P. Rogers Aug. 11 called the remarks "bunk" and "political fantasy." Henry Cabot Lodge, the 1969 Paris negotiator in talks to end the war, issued a statement Aug. 13 saying he "neither was informed of any such peace opportunity nor had any reason to believe one existed." However, Averell Harriman and Cyrus Vance, the Paris negotiators in 1968, Aug. 12 issued a joint statement supporting Shriver's remarks. The State Department later Aug. 12 issued a statement that "no record of any such so-called signal" of willingness to negotiate could be found. McGovern Aug. 12 referred to a national security study assembled by presidential adviser Henry Kissinger in February 1969 which hypothesized that the 1969 decrease in battlefield activity could be a result of political as well as military considerations.

[33] Major McGovern policy statements. McGovern made several policy proposals during the campaign. The President did not respond to the proposals, and McGovern said Aug. 29 that "this may be the first national campaign in memory where we can know with greater certainty the results of electing the challenger than of re-electing the incumbent." The proposals included revised plans for tax reform and welfare reform, presented by McGovern Aug. 29. In the welfare plan revision, McGovern dropped his much-criticized proposal to provide a $1,000-per-person welfare grant and proposed instead a National Income Insurance Plan to provide: public service jobs for the employable on welfare; a $4,000 aid floor, consisting of cash and food stamps, for a family of four on welfare; and a shift of care for the aged, disabled and blind from welfare to the Social Security system. In the revised tax plan, McGovern proposed: taxing capital gains at ordinary income tax rates rather than at half or less of the regular income rate; tightening the rules regarding depreciation deductions for business; prohibiting deduction of interest on money borrowed to make investments when the interest greatly exceeded the income earned from the investments; eliminating the depletion allowances for oil, gas and other mineral industries; repealing certain tax incentives for real estate development which he contended were providing tax shelters for rich investors; permitting state and local governments to issue fully taxable bonds, with a federal subsidy for 50% of the interest cost, as an option to issuance of tax-exempt bonds; eliminating the "gentleman farmer" tax break for losses; eliminating any tax break for U.S. business income earned abroad; and reducing the maximum rate of taxation on both earned and unearned income from 70% to 48%. McGovern said the proposals would result in a net increase of $22 billion in federal revenues—$12.6 billion from individuals and $9.4 billion from corporations.

[34] McGovern delivered major foreign policy statements on "A New Internationalism" Oct. 5 and on the Vietnam war Oct. 10. The new internationalism outlined by McGovern was based on guidelines that the U.S. should: be supported "by a strong national defense"; seek "prudent" relaxation of tensions with potential adversaries; attempt to re-establish "healthy" economic and political relationships with its allies and trading partners; "avoid the kind of reflexive interventionism that has foolishly involved us in the internal political affairs of other countries"; "envision a world community with the capacity to resolve disputes among nations to end the war between man and his own environment"; and "reassert America's role as a beacon—and friend—to those millions in the human family desperately trying to achieve the elemental dignity which all men seek." As the foundation for the whole policy, McGovern said, there must be "a just and prosperous domestic society where all our people—and the people's representatives—are involved in decision-making." In the Oct. 10 statement on Vietnam, McGovern said that the Vietnam issue constituted the "most important" and "fundamental" difference between Nixon and himself. If he were elected President, McGovern said, he would: immediately order an end to "all bombing and acts of force in Indochina," a halt to all "shipments of military supplies that continue the war" and an orderly withdrawal of all U.S. forces from Vietnam, Laos and Cambodia, "along with all salvageable" U.S. military equipment, the process to be completed within 90 days; notify the enemy peace negotiators that these steps had been taken and "that we now expect that they will accept their obligation under their own seven-point proposal of 1971" *(see* INDOCHINA WAR [47]) to "return all prisoners of war and to account for all missing in action," this process to be completed within 90 days to coincide with the U.S. withdrawal; send the vice president to Hanoi "to speed the arrangements for the return of our prisoners and an accounting of our missing"; close U.S. bases in Thailand, return troops and equipment to the U.S. from Thailand and reassign ships stationed adjacent to Indochina, all to be accomplished after the return of U.S. prisoners and the accounting of missing men; "join with other countries in repairing the wreckage left by this war"; and ask Congress to expand educational and jobs programs for Vietnam veterans. McGovern also said he would favor extending an amnesty to those "who chose jail or exile because they could not in conscience fight in this war." He also said he would oppose "any so-called war crimes trials to fix the blame for the past" on any citizen or group of citizens.

[35] **Major Nixon statements.** President Nixon broadcast a series of 12 paid radio addresses during the campaign. These addresses primarily recorded the advances of the first four years of the Nixon Administration and repeated the President's previously expressed stands on foreign and domestic issues. In the third broadcast Oct. 21, the President defined the tenets of "the new American majority" and outlined "the principles which will guide me in making decisions over the next four years." Nixon upheld individualism, self-reliance and hard work as the personal characteristics he would seek to foster in the national character and cited taxation, school busing, job quotas, income redistribution and national defense as the issues which embodied these principles. He outlined the beliefs of the new majority as: "each person should have more of the say in how he lives his own life, how he spends his paycheck, how he brings up his children." The new American majority also believed, he said, "in taking better care of those who truly cannot take care of themselves," in "taking whatever action is needed to hold down the cost of living" and in "a national defense

second to none." While he would assume unpopular positions when necessary and not peg his actions to public opinion polls nor "follow the opinion of the majority down the line," Nixon said he was confident that "what the new majority wants for America and what I want for this nation are basically the same." Nixon also defended opposition to increased taxation, school busing, job quotas and income redistribution. Conceding that "some people oppose income redistribution and busing for the wrong reasons," the President said "they are by no means the majority of Americans, who oppose them for the right reasons."

Elections

[36] **Nixon re-elected to presidency.** Richard Nixon was re-elected president by an overwhelming majority Nov. 7. The Nixon-Agnew ticket won in 49 states. The McGovern-Shriver ticket won only in Massachusetts (by a 55% majority) and in the District of Columbia (by a 79% majority), with their combined total of 17 electoral votes. Needing 270 electoral votes to win, Nixon amassed 521 (517 in Electoral College voting)—97% of the total, second in margin only to Franklin D. Roosevelt's 98% in 1936. (Roosevelt had lost only Maine and Vermont.) The President's mandate for a second term came from 60.83% of the 76 million persons voting. The turnout was low, however, with only 55% of the electorate voting—the lowest turnout since 1948. The popular vote totals were: Nixon 47,168,963; McGovern, 29,169,615. Support for the President encompassed almost every sector of the electorate and every region. Nixon received 55%-60% of the urban vote, 70% of the suburban vote, 80% of the rural vote and an exceptionally strong Southern vote (rising to 79% in Mississippi). Preliminary analysis of the results indicated that Nixon picked up a majority of the Roman Catholic vote and the blue-collar vote, both unprecedented for a Republican presidential candidate. It appeared that he split with McGovern the vote from union families and the youth vote, which was cast for the fist time in a presidential election. However, the youth vote, which was one of McGovern's original sectors of support, had a much lower turnout than expected. The Nixon vote cut into normal Democratic strength from Jewish, Spanish-surname and black communities. Surveys indicated that more than a third of all Democrats voted for Nixon, compared with an average defection rate of 16% for the previous five elections. The President seemingly lacked support only among black voters and the very poor. Nixon became the first two-term vice president ever to be elected to two terms as president and the first president ever to begin two terms with an opposition Congress each time. The 1972 victory came on the 10th anniversary of Nixon's political nadir, his defeat for governor of California in 1962. McGovern conceded his defeat before midnight Nov. 7.

[37] **Minor party presidential candidates.** Also on the presidential ballot Nov. 7 in many states were these minor-party tickets for president and vice president: American party—Schmitz and Anderson (on the ballot in 33 states, polled 1,080,541 votes or 1% of the total vote cast); People's party—Benjamin Spock and Julius Hobson (on the ballot in 10 states and polled 78,801 votes); Socialist Workers' party—Linda Jenness and Andrew Pulley (on the ballot in 23 states); Communist party—Gus Hall and Jarvis Tyner (13 states); Socialist Labor party—Louis Fisher and Genevieve Gunderson (12 states); Libertarian party—John Hospers and Theodora Nathan (2 states); Prohibition party—Earl Munn Jr. and Marshall Uncapher (4 states); Universal party—Gabriel Green and Daniel Fry (Iowa only); America First party—John V. Mahalchik and Irving Homer (New Jersey only).

[38] **The Senate.** Despite President Nixon's overwhelming victory Nov. 7, the Democrats picked up a net two seats in the Senate, increasing their majority to 57-43. In 20 of the 33 Senate seats at stake in the elections, incumbent senators were re-elected. Ten of the 33 seats shifted parties, with the Democrats picking up previously Republican-held seats in Colorado, Delaware, Iowa, Kentucky,

Maine and South Dakota. Republicans won seats previously held by Democrats in Mew Mexico, North Carolina, Oklahoma and Virginia. The Republicans lost two senators holding party leadership posts in the chamber—Margaret Chase Smith (Me.), who was chairman of the Republican Senate Conference, a senator since 1949 and the only elected woman in the Senate; and Gordon Allott (Colo.), chairman of the Republican Policy Committee, who was seeking a fourth term. Of the 13 new senators (including two elected to seats held by temporary appointment to replace deceased incumbents Richard B. Russell of Georgia and Allen J. Ellender of Louisiana and one elected to fill the Idaho seat being vacated by Len. B. Jordan) included four moving from House seats (Democrats William D. Hathaway of Maine and James Abourezk of South Dakota and Republicans William L. Scott of Virginia and James A. McClure of Idaho). Another Senate newcomer, Delaware Democrat Joseph R. Biden Jr., was not 30, and thus eligible to serve in the Senate, until Nov. 20. Upon assuming his seat, he would become the youngest senator ever to be seated in the organization of a new Senate.

[39] *Senators of the 93rd Congress.* Listed below are the 100 members who make up the Senate of the 93rd Congress. Each senator is described according to his party designation (D=Democrat, R=Republican), the year in which he entered the Senate (date in parentheses) and his election status (* designates an incumbent, italics indicate that the Senator was elected or re-elected in November 1972, and † indicates that the senator's service began in the year shown but has not been continuous).

Members

State		
Ala.	*John J. Sparkman* (D) b. Dec. 20, 1899 (1946)	
	*James Browning Allen (D) term ends 1975; b. Dec. 28, 1912 (1969)	
Alaska	*Ted Stevens* (R) b. Nov. 18, 1923 (1968)	
	*Mike Gravel (D) terms ends 1975; b. May 13, 1930 (1969)	
Ariz.	*Paul J. Fannin (R) terms ends 1977; b. Jan. 29, 1907 (1965)	
	*Barry M. Goldwater (R) term ends 1975; b. Jan. 1, 1909 (1953)†	
Ark.	*John L. McClellan* (D) b. Feb. 25, 1896 (1943)	
	*J. W. Fulbright (D) term ends 1975; b. Apr. 9, 1905 (1945)	
Calif.	*Alan Cranston (D) term ends 1975; b. June 19, 1914 (1969)	
	*John V. Tunney (D) term ends 1977; b. June 26, 1934 (1970)	
Colo.	Floyd K. Haskell (D); b. Feb. 6, 1916	
	*Peter H. Dominick (R) term ends 1975; b. July 7, 1915 (1963)	
Conn.	*Abraham A. Ribicoff (D) term ends 1975; b. Apr. 9, 1910 (1963)	
	*Lowell P. Weicker Jr. (R) term ends 1977; b. May 16, 1931 (1970)	
Del.	Joseph R. Biden Jr. (D) b. Nov. 20, 1942	
	*William V. Roth Jr. (R) term ends 1977; b. July 22, 1921 (1970)	
Fla.	*Edward J. Gurney (R) term ends 1975; b. Jan. 12, 1914 (1969)	
	*Lawton Chiles (D) term ends 1977; b. Apr. 30, 1930 (1970)	
Ga.	Sam Nunn Jr. (D) b. Sept. 6, 1938	
	*Herman E. Talmadge (D) term ends	

	1975; b. Aug. 9, 1913 (1957)
Hawaii	*Hiram L. Fong (R) term ends 1977; b. Oct. 1, 1907 (1959)
	*Daniel K. Inouye (D) term ends 1975; b. Sept. 7, 1924 (1963)
Idaho	James A. McClure (R) b. Dec. 27, 1924
	*Frank Church (D) terms ends 1975; b. July 25, 1924 (1957)
Ill.	*Charles H. Percy (R) b. Sept. 27, 1919 (1967)
	*Adlai E. Stevenson 3rd (D) term ends 1975; b. Oct. 10, 1930 (1970)
Ind.	*Vance Hartke (D) term ends 1977; b. May 31, 1919 (1959)
	*Birch Bayh (D) term ends 1975; b. Jan. 22, 1923 (1963)
Iowa	Richard Clark (D) b. Sept. 14, 1929
	*Harold E. Hughes (D) term ends 1975; b. Feb. 10, 1922 (1969)
Kan.	*James B. Pearson (R) b. May 7, 1920 (1962)
	*Robert J. Dole (R) term ends 1975; b. July 22, 1923 (1969)
Ky.	Walter Huddleston (D) b. Apr. 15, 1926
	*Marlow W. Cook (R) term ends 1975; b. July 27, 1926 (1969)
La.	J. Bennett Johnston Jr. (D) b. June 10, 1932
	*Russell B. Long (D) term ends 1975; b. Nov. 3, 1918 (1948)
Me.	William D. Hathaway (D) b. Feb. 21, 1924
	*Edmund S. Muskie (D) term ends 1977; b. March 28, 1914 (1959)
Md.	*Charles McC. Mathias Jr. (R) term ends 1975; b. July 24, 1922 (1969)
	*J. Glenn Beall Jr. (R) term ends 1977; b. June 19, 1927 (1970)
Mass.	*Edward W. Brooke (R) b. Oct. 26,

1919 (1967)

Mich. *Robert P. Griffin* (R) b. Nov. 6, 1923 (1966)

*Philip A. Hart (D) term ends 1977; b. Dec. 10, 1912 (1959)

Minn. *Walter F. Mondale* (D) b. Jan. 5, 1928 (1965)

*Hubert H. Humphrey (D) term ends 1977; b. May 27, 1911 (1949)†

Miss. *James O. Eastland* (D) b. Nov. 28, 1904 (1943)

*John C. Stennis (D) term ends 1977; b. Aug. 3, 1901 (1948)

Mo. Stuart Symington (D) term ends 1977; b. June 26, 1901 (1953)

*Thomas F. Eagleton (D) term ends 1975; b. Sept. 4, 1929 (1969)

Mont. *Lee Metcalf* (D) b. Jan. 28, 1911 (1961)

*Michael J. Mansfield (D) term ends 1977; b. March 16, 1903 (1953)

Neb. *Carl T. Curtis* (R) b. March 15, 1905 (1955)

*Roman Lee Hruska (R) term ends 1977; b. Aug. 16, 1904 (1955)

Nev. *Alan Bible (D) term ends 1975; b. Nov. 20, 1909 (1954)

*Howard W. Cannon (D) term ends 1977; b. Jan. 26, 1912 (1959)

N.H. *Thomas J. McIntyre* (D) b. Feb. 20, 1915 (1963)

*Norris Cotton (R) term ends 1975; b. May 11, 1900 (1954)

N.J. *Clifford P. Case* (R) b. Apr. 16, 1904 (1955)

*Harrison A. Williams Jr. (D) term ends 1977; b. Dec. 10, 1919 (1959)

N.M. Pete V. Domenici (R) b. May 7, 1932

*Joseph M. Montoya (D) term ends 1977; b. Sept. 24, 1915 (1965)

N.Y. *Jacob K. Javits (R) term ends 1975; b. May 18, 1904 (1957)

*James L. Buckley (Conservative) term ends 1977; b. March 9, 1923 (1970)

N.C. Jesse A. Helms (R) b. Oct. 18, 1921

*Sam J. Ervin Jr. (D) term ends 1975; b. Sept. 27, 1896 (1954)

N.D. *Milton R. Young (R) term ends 1975; b. Dec. 6, 1897 (1945)

*Quentin N. Burdick (D) term ends 1977; b. June 19, 1908 (1960)

Ohio *William B. Saxbe (R) term ends 1975; b. June 24, 1916 (1969)

*Robert Taft Jr. (R) term ends 1977; b. Feb. 26, 1917 (1970)

Okla. Dewey F. Bartlett (R) b. Mar. 28, 1919

*Henry L. Bellmon (R) term ends 1975; b. Sept. 3, 1921 (1969)

Ore. *Mark O. Hatfield* (R) b. July 12, 1922 (1967)

*Robert W. Packwood (R) term ends 1975; b. Sept. 11, 1932 (1969)

Pa. *Hugh Scott (R) term ends 1977; b. Nov. 11, 1900 (1959)

*Richard S. Schweiker (R) term ends 1975; b. June 1, 1926 (1969)

R.I. *Claiborne Pell* (D) b. Nov. 22, 1918 (1961)

*John O. Pastore (D) term ends 1977; b. March 17, 1907 (1950)

S.C. *Strom Thurmond* (R) b. Dec. 5, 1902 (1955)

*Ernest F. Hollings (D) term ends 1975; b. Jan. 1, 1922 (1967)

S.D. James Abourezk (D) b. Feb. 24, 1931

*George McGovern (D) term ends 1975; b. July 19, 1922 (1963)

Tenn. *Howard H. Baker Jr.* (R) b. Nov. 15, 1925 (1967)

*William E. Brock 3rd (R) term ends 1977; b. Nov. 23, 1930 (1970)

Tex. *John G. Tower* (R) b. Sept. 29, 1925 (1961)

*Lloyd Bentsen (D) term ends 1977; b. Feb. 11, 1921 (1970)

Utah *Wallace F. Bennett (R) term ends 1975; b. Nov. 13, 1898 (1951)

*Frank E. Moss (D) term ends 1977; b. Sept. 23, 1911 (1959)

Vt. *George D. Aiken (R) term ends 1975; b. Aug. 20, 1892 (1941)

*Robert T. Stafford (R) term ends 1977; b. Aug. 8, 1913 (1971)

Va. William Lloyd Scott (R) b. July 1, 1915

*Harry F. Byrd Jr. (Independent) term ends 1977; b. Dec. 20, 1914 (1965)

Wash. *Warren G. Magnuson (D) term ends 1975; b. April 12, 1905 (1944)

*Henry M. Jackson (D) term ends 1977; b. May 31, 1912 (1953)

W.Va. *Jennings Randolph* (D) b. March 8, 1902 (1959)

*Robert C. Byrd (D) term ends 1977; b. Jan. 15, 1918 (1959)

Wis. *William Proxmire (D term ends 1977; b. Nov. 11, 1915 (1957)

*Gaylord Nelson (D) term ends 1975; b. June 4, 1916 (1963)

Wyo. *Clifford P. Hansen* (R) b. Oct. 16, 1912 (1967)

*Gale W. McGee (D) term ends 1977; b. March 17, 1915 (1959)

[40]   **The House of Representatives.** Voters throughout the country, while spurning the Democrats' national ticket, split their ballots in vast enough numbers to enable the Democrats to retain control of the House. Returns showed that the Republicans had been held to a net gain of 13 seats, far short of the 41 they needed to gain control. The new House would be composed of 242 Democrats, 192 Republicans and an independent (John J. Moakley of Massachusetts) who was expected to vote with the Democrats. While the turnover in the House was small, the House itself was expected to show a

leftward shift in ideology, principally as a result of primary election defeats and voluntary retirements earlier in 1972 of many of the House's most powerful figures. Among the absentees were six of the 21 Democratic committee chairmen and nine Republicans who were ranking minority members of House committees. Replacing those who had charted the House's course in recent years were more of the young, more blacks (16) and more of those with liberal views. There were 68 new representatives elected. Republicans defeated eight Democratic incumbents (William R. Anderson of Tennessee, Abner Mikva of Illinois, Louise Day Hicks of Massachusetts, John G. Dow of New York, John S. Monagan of Connecticut, Earle Cabell of Texas, Andrew Jacobs Jr. of Indiana and Graham Purcell of Texas), most of whom fell on issues and were not victims of President Nixon's sweep. The other six GOP gains came through elections in which incumbents were not on the ballot. Three Republican incumbents (James D. McKevitt of Colorado, Fred Schwengel of Iowa and Sherman P. Lloyd of Utah) lost their seats to Democrats. Two other Republican congressmen (John H. Kyl of Iowa and Alvin E. O'Konski of Wisconsin) were defeated by Democratic incumbents (Neal Smith and David R. Obey, respectively) in districts where they were pitted against each other. The Republicans made their biggest gains in the South, where they picked up eight seats.

[41] *Congressmen of the 93rd Congress.* Listed below are the 435 members who make up the House of Representatives of the 93rd Congress. Each representative is described according to his party designation (D=Democrat, R=Republican), the date of his birth or his age, the year in which he entered the House (date in parentheses) and his election status (* designates an incumbent and † indicates that the respresentative's service began in the year shown but has not been continuous).

Alabama: 4 D, 3 R [5 D, 3 R]
1. *Jack Edwards (R) b. Sept. 20, 1928 (1965)
2. *William Louis Dickinson (R) b. June 5, 1925 (1965)
3. *William Nichols (D) b. Oct. 16, 1918 (1967)
4. *Tom Bevill (D) b. Mar. 27, 1921 (1967)
5. *Robert E. Jones (D) b. June 12, 1912 (1947)
6. *John Hall Buchanan Jr. (R) b. Mar. 19, 1928 (1965)
7. *Walter Flowers (D) b. Apr. 12, 1933 (1969)

Alaska: 1 D [1 D]
At Large. *Nicholas J. Begich (D) b. April 6, 1932 (1971)

Arizona: 1 D, 3 R [1 D, 2 R]
1. *John J. Rhodes (R) b. Sept. 18, 1916 (1953)
2. *Morris K. Udall (D) b. June 15, 1922 (1961)
3. *Sam Steiger (R) b. Mar. 10, 1929 (1967)
4. John B. Conlan (R) age 42

Arkansas: 3 D, 1 R [3 D, 1 R]
1. *William Vollie (Bill) Alexander Jr. (D) b. Jan. 16, 1934 (1969)
2. *Wilbur D. Mills (D) b. May 24, 1909 (1939)
3. *John Paul Hammerschmidt (R) b. May 4 1922 (1967)
4. Ray Thornton (D) age 44

California: 23 D, 20 R [20 D, 18 R]
1. *Don H. Clausen (R) b. Apr. 27, 1923 (1963)
2. *Harold T. (Bizz) Johnson (D) 64 (1959)
3. *John E. Moss (D) b. Apr. 13, 1913 (1953)
4. *Robert L. Leggett (D) b. July 26, 1926 (1963)
5. *Phillip Burton (D) b. June 1, 1926 (1964)
6. *William S. Mailliard (R) b. June 10, 1917 (1953)
7. *Ronald V. Dellums (D) b. Nov. 24, 1935 (1971)
8. Fortney H. Stark (D) age 41
9. *Don Edwards (D) b. Jan. 6, 1915 (1963)
10. *Charles S. Gubser (R) b. Feb. 1, 1916 (1953)
11. Leo J. Ryan (D) age 47
12. *Burt L. Talcott (R) b. Feb. 22, 1920 (1963)
13. *Charles M. Teague (R) b. Sept. 18, 1909 (1955)
14. *Jerome R. Waldie (D) b. Feb. 15, 1925 (1966)
15. *John J. McFall (D) b. Feb. 20, 1918 (1957)
16. *B. F. Sisk (D) Dec. 14, 1910 (1955)
17. *Paul N. (Pete) McCloskey Jr. (R) b. Sept. 29, 1927 (1967)
18. *Robert B. Mathias (R) b. Nov. 17, 1930 (1967)
19. *Chet Holifield (D) b. Dec. 3, 1903 (1943)
20. Carlos J. Moorhead (R) age 50
21. *Augustus F. Hawkins (D) b. Aug. 31, 1907 (1963)
22. *James C. Corman (D) b. Oct. 20, 1920 (1961)
23. *Delwin (Del) Morgan Clawson (R) b. Jan. 11, 1914 (1963)
24. *John H. Rousselot (R) b. Nov. 1, 1927 (1961)†
25. *Charles E. Wiggins (R) b. Dec. 3, 1927 (1967)
26. *Thomas M. Rees (D) b. Mar. 26, 1925 (1965)
27. *Barry M. Goldwater Jr. (R) b. July 15, 1938 (1969)
28.

*Alphonzo Bell (R) b. Sept. 19, 1914 (1961)
29. *George E. Danielson (D) b. Feb. 20, 1915
30. *Edward R. Roybal (D) b. Feb. 10, 1916 (1963)
31. *Charles H. Wilson (D) b. Feb. 15, 1917 (1963)
32. *Craig Hosmer (R) b. May 6, 1915 (1953)
33. *Jerry L. Pettis (R) b. July 18, 1916 (1967)
34. *Richard T. Hanna (D) b. June 9, 1914 (1963)
35. *Glenn M. Anderson (D) b. Feb. 21, 1913 (1969)
36. William M. Ketchum (R) age 50
37. Yvonne Brathwaite Burke (D) age 40
38. George E. Brown Jr. (D) b. Mar. 6, 1920 (1963)†
39. Andrew J. Hinshaw (R) age 49
40. *Bob Wilson (R) b. Apr. 5, 1916 (1953)
41. *Lionel Van Deerlin (D) b. July 25, 1914 (1963)
42. Clair W. Burgener (R) age 50
43. *Victor V. Veysey (R) b. Apr. 14, 1915 (1971)
   Colorado: 3 R, 2 D [2 D, 2 R]
1. Patricia Schroeder (D) age 32
2. *Donald G. Brotzman (R) b. June 28, 1922 (1963)†
3. *Frank Edwards Evans (D) b. Sept. 6, 1923 (1965)
4. James T. Johnson (R) age 42
5. William L. Armstrong (R) age 35
   Connecticut: 3 D, 3 R [4 D, 2 R]
1. *William R. Cotter (D) b. July 18, 1926 (1971)
2. *Robert Steele Jr. (R) b. Nov. 3, 1938 (1970)
3. *Robert N. Giaimo (D) b. Oct. 15, 1919 (1959)
4. *Stewart B. McKinney (R) b. Jan. 30, 1931 (1971)
5. Ronald A. Sarasin (R) age 37
6. *Ella T. Grasso (D) b. May 10, 1919 (1971)
   Delaware: 1 R [1 R]
At Large. *Pierre S. duPont IV (R) b. Jan. 22, 1935 (1971)
   Florida: 11 D, 4 R [9 D, 3 R]
1. *Robert L. F. Sikes (D) b. June 3, 1906 (1941)
2. *Don Fuqua (D) b. Aug. 20, 1933 (1963)
3. *Charles E. Bennett (D) b. Dec. 2, 1910 (1949)
4. *William V. Chappell Jr. (D) b. Feb. 3, 1922 (1967)
5. William D. Gunter Jr. (D) age 38
6. *C. W. Young (R) b. Dec. 16, 1930 (1971)
7. *Sam M. Gibbons (D) b. Jan. 20, 1920 (1963)
8. *James Andrew Haley (D) b. Jan. 4, 1899 (1953)
9. *Lou Frey Jr. (R) b. Jan. 11, 1934 (1969)
10. L. A. Bafalis (R) age 43
11. *Paul G. Rogers (D) b. June 4, 1921 (1955)
12. *J. Herbert Burke (R) b. Jan. 14, 1913 (1967)
13. William Lehman (D) age 58
14. *Claude Denson Pepper (D) b. Sept. 8, 1900 (1963)
15. *Dante B. Fascell (D) b. Mar. 9, 1917 (1955)
   Georgia: 9 D, 1 R [8 D, 2 R]
1. Ronald B. Ginn (D) age 38
2. *Dawson Mathis (D) b. Nov. 30, 1940 (1971)
3. *Jack Thomas Brinkley (D) b. Dec. 22, 1930

(1967)
4. *Ben B. Blackburn (R) b. Feb. 14, 1927 (1967)
5. Andrew J. Young (D) age 40
6. *John James Flynt Jr. (D) b. Nov. 8, 1914 (1954)
7. *John William Davis (D) b. Sept. 12, 1916 (1961)
8. *Williamson Sylvester Stuckey Jr. (D) b. May 25, 1935 (1967)
9. *Phillip Mitchell Landrum (D) b. Sept. 10, 1909 (1953)
10. *Robert Grier Stephens Jr. (D) b. Aug. 14, 1913 (1961)
   Hawaii: 2 D [2 D]
1. *Spark Masayuki Matsunaga (D) b. Oct. 8, 1916 (1963)
2. *Patsy Takemoto Mink (D) b. Dec. 6, 1927 (1965)
   Idaho: 2 R [2 R]
1. Steven D. Symms (R) age 34
2. *Orval Hansen (R) b. Aug. 3, 1926 (1969)
   Illinois: 10 D, 14 R [12 D, 12 R]
1. *Ralph H. Metcalfe (D) b. May 29, 1910 (1971)
2. *Morgan F. Murphy Jr. (D) b. April 16, 1932 (1971)
3. Robert P. Hanrahan (R) age 38
4. *Edward J. Derwinski (R) b. Sept. 15, 1926 (1959)
5. *John C. Kluczynski (D) b. Feb. 15, 1896 (1951)
6. *Harold R. Collier (R) b. Dec. 12, 1915 (1957)
7. *George W. Collins (R) b. March 5, 1925 (1971)
8. *Dan Rostenkowski (D) b. Jan. 2, 1928 (1959)
9. *Sidney R. Yates (D) b. Aug. 27, 1909 (1949)†
10. Samuel H. Young (R) age 49
11. *Frank Annunzio (D) b. Jan. 12, 1915 (1965)
12. *Philip M. Crane (R) b. Nov. 3, 1930 (1969)
13. *Robert McClory (R) b. Jan. 31, 1908 (1963)
14. *John N. Erlenborn (R) b. Feb. 8, 1927 (1965)
15. *Leslie C. Arends (R) b. Sept. 27, 1895 (1935)
16. *John B. Anderson (R) b. Feb. 15, 1922 (1961)
17. George M. O'Brien (R) age 55
18. *Robert H. Michel (R) b. Mar. 2, 1923 (1957)
19. *Thomas F. Railsback (R) b. Jan. 22, 1932 (1967)
20. *Paul Findley (R) b. June 23, 1921 (1961)
21. Edward R. Madigan (R) age 36
22. *George Edward Shipley (D) b. Apr. 21, 1927 (1959)
23. *Charles Melvin Price (D) b. Jan. 1, 1905 (1945)
24. *Kenneth J. Gray (D) b. Nov. 14, 1924 (1955)
   Indiana: 4 D, 7 R [5 D, 6 R]
1. *Ray J. Madden (D) b. Feb. 25, 1892 (1943)
2. *Earl F. Landgrebe (R) b. Jan. 21, 1916 (1969)
3. *John Brademas (D) b. Mar. 2, 1927 (1959)
4. *J. Edward Roush (D) b. Sept. 12, 1920 (1959)†
5. *Elwood Hillis (R) b. Mar. 6, 1926
6. *William Gilmer Bray (R) b. June 17, 1903 (1951)
7. *John Thomas Myers (R) b. Feb. 8, 1927

134 ELECTIONS

(1967)
8. *Roger H. Zion (R) b. Sept. 17, 1921 (1967)
9. *Lee Herbert Hamilton (D) b. Apr. 20, 1931 (1965)
10. *David W. Dennis (R) b. June 7, 1912 (1969)
11. William H. Hudnut 3rd (R) age 39
Iowa: 3 D, 3 R [2 D, 5 R]
1. Edward Mezvinsky (D) age 35
2. *John C. Culver (D) b. Aug. 8, 1932 (1965)
3. *H. R. Gross (R) b. June 30, 1899 (1949)
4. *Neal Smith (D) b. Mar. 23, 1920 (1959)
5. *William J. Scherle (R) b. Mar. 14, 1923 (1967)
6. *Wiley Mayne (R) b. Jan. 19, 1917 (1967)
Kansas: 1 D, 4 R [1 D, 4 R]
1. *Keith G. Sebelius (R) b. Sept. 10, 1916 (1969)
2. *William R. Roy (D) age 45 (1971)
3. *Larry Winn Jr. (R) b. Aug. 22, 1919 (1967)
4. *Garner E. Shriver (R) b. July 6, 1912 (1961)
5. *Joe Skubitz (R) b. May 6, 1906 (1963)
Kentucky: 5 D, 2 R [5 D, 2 R]
1. *Frank A. Stubblefield (D) b. Apr. 5, 1907 (1959)
2. *William H. Natcher (D) b. Sept. 11, 1909 (1953)
3. *Romano L. Mazzoli (D) b. Nov. 2, 1932 (1971)
4. *Marion Gene Snyder (R) b. Jan. 26, 1928 (1963)†
5. *Tim Lee Carter (R) b. Sept. 2, 1910 (1965)
6. John B. Breckinridge (D) age 59
7. *Carl D. Perkins (D) b. Oct. 15, 1912 (1949)
Louisiana: 7 D, 1 R [8 D]
1. *F. Edward Hebert (D) b. Oct. 12, 1901 (1941)
2. *Hale Boggs (D) b. Feb. 15, 1914 (1947)
3. David C. Treen (R) age 44
4. *Joe D. Waggonner Jr. (D) b. Sept 7, 1918 (1961)
5. *Otto Ernest Passman (D) b. June 27, 1900 (1947)
6. *John R. Rarick (D) b. Jan. 29, 1924 (1967)
7. John B. Breaux (D) age 28
8. Gillis W. Long (D) b. June 16, 1928 (1963)†
Maine: 1 D, 1 R [2 D]
1. *Peter N. Kyros (D) b. July 11, 1925 (1967)
2. William S. Cohen (R) age 32
Maryland: 4 D, 4 R [5 D, 3 R]
1. *William O. Mills (R) b. Aug. 12, 1924 (1971)
2. *Clarence D. Long (D) b. Dec. 11, 1908 (1963)
3. *Paul S. Sarbanes (D) b. Feb. 3, 1933 (1971)
4. Marjorie S. Holt (R) age 52
5. *Lawrence J. Hogan (R) b. Sept. 30, 1928 (1969)
6. *Goodloe E. Byron (D) b. June 22, 1929 (1971)
7. *Parren J. Mitchell (D) b. April 29, 1922 (1971)
8. *Gilbert Gude (R) b. Mar. 9, 1923 (1967)
Massachusetts: 8 D, 3 R, 1 Ind. [8 D, 4 R]
1. *Silvio O. Conte (R) b. Nov. 9, 1921 (1959)
2. *Edward P. Boland (D) b. Oct. 1, 1911 (1953)
3. *Harold D. Donohue (D) b. June 18, 1901

(1947)
4. *Robert F. Drinan (D) b. Nov. 15, 1920 (1971)
5. Paul W. Cronin (R) age 34
6. *Michael J. Harrington (D) b. Sept. 2, 1936 (1969)
7. *Torbert Hart Macdonald (D) b. June 6, 1917 (1955)
8. *Thomas P. O'Neill, Jr. (D) b. Dec. 9, 1912 (1953)
9. John Joseph Moakley (Ind.) age 45
10. *Margaret M. Heckler (R) b. June 21, 1931 (1967)
11. *James A. Burke (D) b. Mar. 30, 1910 (1959)
12. Gerry E. Studds (D) age 35
Michigan: 7 D, 12 R [7 D, 12 R]
1. *John J. Conyers Jr. (D) b. May 16, 1929 (1965)
2. *Marvin L. Esch (R) b. Aug. 4, 1927 (1967)
3. *Garry Brown (R) b. Aug. 12, 1923 (1967)
4. *Edward Hutchinson (R) b. Oct. 13, 1914 (1963)
5. *Gerald R. Ford (R) b. July 14, 1913 (1949)
6. *Charles E. Chamberlain (R) b. July 22, 1917 (1957)
7. *Donald W. Riegle, Jr. (R) b. Feb. 4, 1938 (1967)
8. *James Harvey (R) b. July 4, 1922 (1961)
9. *Guy Adrian Vander Jagt (R) b. Aug. 26, 1931 (1966)
10. *Elford A. Cederberg (R) b. Mar. 6, 1918 (1953)
11. *Philip E. Ruppe (R) b. Sept. 29, 1926 (1967)
12. *James G. O'Hara (D) b. Nov. 8, 1925 (1959)
13. *Charles C. Diggs Jr. (D) b. Dec. 2, 1922 (1955)
14. *Lucien Norbert Nedzi (D) b. May 28, 1925 (1961)
15. *William David Ford (D) b. Aug. 6, 1927 (1965)
16. *John D. Dingell (D) b. July 8, 1926 (1955)
17. *Martha W. Griffiths (D) b. Jan. 29, 1912 (1955)
18. Robert J. Huber (R) age 50
19. *William S. Broomfield (R) b. Apr. 28, 1922 (1957)
Minnesota: 4 D, 4 R [4 D, 4 R]
1. *Albert Harold Quie (R) b. Sept. 18, 1923 (1958)
2. *Ancher Nelsen (R) b. Oct. 11, 1904 (1959)
3. *William E. Frenzel (R) b. July 31, 1928 (1971)
4. *Joseph E. Karth (D) b. Aug. 26, 1922 (1959)
5. *Donald MacKay Fraser (D) b. Feb. 20, 1924 (1963)
6. *John M. Zwach (R) b. Feb. 8, 1907 (1967)
7. *Bob Bergland (D) b. July 22, 1928 (1971)
8. *John A. Blatnik (D) b. Aug. 17, 1911 (1947)
Mississippi: 3 D, 2 R [5 D]
1. *Jamie L. Whitten (D) b. Apr. 18, 1910 (1941)
2. David R. Bowen (D) age 39
3. *Gillespie V. Montgomery (D) b. Aug. 5, 1920 (1967)
4. Thad Cochran (R) age 34
5. Trent Loft (R) age 31

Missouri: 9 D, 1 R [9 D, 1 R]
1. *William L. Clay (D) b. Apr. 30, 1931 (1969)
2. *James Wadsworth Symington (D) b. Sept. 28, 1927 (1969)
3. *Leonor Kretzer Sullivan (D) age 69 (1953)
4. *William J. Randall (D) b. July 16, 1909 (1959)
5. *Richard Bolling (D) b. May 17, 1916 (1949)
6. Jerry Litton (D) age 35
7. Gene Taylor (R) age 44
8. *Richard Howard Ichord (D) b. June 27, 1926 (1961)
9. *William Leonard Hungate (D) b. Dec. 14, 1922 (1965)
10. *Bill D. Burlison (D) b. Mar. 15, 1931 (1969)
Montana: 1 D, 1 R [1 D, 1 R]
1. *Richard G. Shoup (R) b. Nov. 29, 1923 (1971)
2. *John Melcher (D) b. Sept. 6, 1924 (1969)
Nebraska: 3 R [3 R]
1. *Charles Thone (R) b. Jan. 4, 1924 (1971)
2. *John Y. McCollister (R) b. June 10, 1921 (1971)
3. *David Thomas Martin (R) b. July 9, 1907 (1961)
Nevada: 1 R [1 D]
At Large. David Towell (R) age 35
New Hampshire: 2 R [2 R]
1. *Louis Crosby Wyman (R) b. Mar. 16, 1917 (1963)†
2. *James C. Cleveland (R) b. June 13, 1920 (1963)
New Jersey: 8 D, 7 R [9 D, 7 R]
1. *John E. Hunt (R) b. Nov. 24, 1908 (1967)
2. *Charles W. Sandman Jr. (R) b. Oct. 23, 1921 (1967)
3. *James J. Howard (D) b. July 24, 1927 (1965)
4. *Frank Thompson Jr. (D) b. July 26, 1918 (1955)
5. *Peter H. B. Frelinghuysen (R) b. Jan. 17, 1916 (1953)
6. *Edwin B. Forsythe (R) b. Jan. 17, 1916
7. *William Beck Widnall (R) b. Mar. 17, 1906 (1950)
8. *Robert A. Roe (D) b. Feb. 28, 1924 (1969)
9. *Henry Helstoski (D) b. Mar. 21, 1925 (1965)
10. *Peter Wallace Rodino Jr. (D) b. June 7, 1909 (1949)
11. *Joseph George Minish (D) b. Sept. 1, 1916 (1963)
12. Matthew J. Rinaldo (R) age 41
13. Joseph J. Maraziti (R) age 60
14. *Dominick V. Daniels (D) b. Oct. 18, 1908 (1959)
15. *Edward James Patten (D) b. Aug. 22, 1905 (1963)
New Mexico: 1 D, 1 R [1 D, 1 R]
1. *Manuel Lujan Jr. (R) b. May 12, 1928 (1969)
2. *Harold L. Runnels (D) b. March 17, 1924 (1971)
New York: 22 D, 17 R [24 D, 17 R]
1. *Otis G. Pike (D) b. Aug. 31, 1921 (1961)
2. *James R. Grover Jr. (R) b. Mar. 6, 1919 (1963)
3. Angelo D. Roncallo (R) age 45
4. *Norman F. Lent (R) b. March 23, 1931

(1971)
5. *John W. Wydler (R) b. June 9, 1924 (1963)
6. *Lester Lionel Wolff (D) b. Jan. 4, 1919 (1965)
7. *Joseph Patrick Addabbo (D) b. Mar. 17, 1925 (1961)
8. *Benjamin S. Rosenthal (D) b. June 8, 1923 (1962)
9. *James J. Delaney (D) b. Mar. 19, 1901 (1945)†
10. *Mario Biaggi (D) b. Oct. 26, 1917 (1969)
11. *Frank James Brasco (D) b. Oct. 15, 1932 (1967)
12. *Shirley Anita Chisholm (D) b. Nov. 30, 1924 (1969)
13. *Bertram L. Podell (D) b. Dec. 27, 1925 (1968)
14. *John J. Rooney (D) b. Nov. 29, 1903 (1944)
15. *Hugh L. Carey (D) b. Apr. 11, 1919 (1961)
16. Elizabeth Holtzman (D) age 30
17. *John M. Murphy (D) b. Aug. 3, 1926 (1963)
18. *Edward I. Koch (D) b. Dec. 12, 1924 (1969)
19. *Charles B. Rangel (D) b. June 11, 1930 (1971)
20. *Bella S. Abzug (D) b. July 24, 1920 (1971)
21. *Herman Badillo (D) b. Aug. 21, 1929 (1971)
22. *Jonathan Brewster Bingham (D) b. Apr. 24, 1914 (1965)
23. *Peter A. Peyser (R) b. Sept. 7, 1921 (1971)
24. *Ogden Rogers Reid (D) b. June 24, 1925 (1963)
25. *Hamilton Fish Jr. (R) b. June 3, 1926 (1969)
26. Benjamin A. Gilman (R) age 49
27. *Howard Winfield Robison (R) b. Oct. 30, 1915 (1958)
28. *Samuel S. Stratton (D) b. Sept. 27, 1916 (1959)
29. *Carleton James King (R) b. June 15, 1904 (1961)
30. *Robert Cameron McEwen (R) b. Jan. 5, 1920 (1965)
31. Donald J. Mitchell (R) age 49
32. *James Michael Hanley (D) b. July 19, 1920 (1965)
33. William F. Walsh (R) age 60
34. *Frank Horton (R) b. Dec. 12, 1919 (1963)
35. *Barber B. Conable Jr. (R) b. Nov. 2, 1922 (1965)
36. *Henry P. Smith III (R) b. Sept. 29, 1911 (1965)
37. *Thaddeus J. Dulski (D) b. Sept. 27, 1915 (1959)
38. *Jack F. Kemp (R) b. July 13, 1935 (1971)
39. *James F. Hastings (R) b. Apr. 10, 1926 (1969)
North Carolina: 7 D, 4 R [7 D, 4 R]
1. *Walter B. Jones (D) b. Aug. 19, 1913 (1966)
2. *L. H. Fountain (D) b. Apr. 23, 1913 (1953)
3. *David Newton Henderson (D) b. Apr. 16, 1921 (1961)
4. Ike F. Andrews (D) age 47
5. *Wilmer David Mizell (D) b. Aug. 13, 1930 (1969)
6. *Lunsford Richardson Preyer (D) b. Jan. 11, 1919 (1969)
7. Charles G. Rose 3rd (D) age 33

8.　*Earl B. Ruth (R) b. Feb. 7, 1916 (1969)
9.　James G. Martin (R) age 36
10.　*James Thomas Broyhill (R) b. Aug. 19, 1927 (1963)
11.　*Roy A. Taylor (D) b. Jan. 31, 1910 (1960)
　　North Dakota: 1 R [1 D, 1 R]
At large. *Mark Andrews (R) b. May 19, 1926 (1963)
　　Ohio: 7 D, 16 R [7 D, 17 R]
1.　*William J. Keating (R) age 45
2.　*Donald Daniel Clancy (R) b. July 24, 1921 (1961)
3.　*Charles W. Whalen Jr. (R) b. July 31, 1920 (1967)
4.　Tennyson Guyer (R) age 58
5.　*Delbert L. Latta (R) b. Mar. 5, 1920 (1959)
6.　*William H. Harsha (R) b. Jan. 1, 1921 (1961)
7.　*Clarence J. Brown (R) b. June 18, 1927 (1965)
8.　*Walter E. Powell (R) b. April 25, 1931 (1971)
9.　*Thomas Ludlow Ashley (D) b. Jan. 11, 1923 (1955)
10.　*Clarence E. Miller (R) b. Nov. 1, 1917 (1967)
11.　*John William Stanton (R) b. Feb. 20, 1924 (1965)
12.　*Samuel L. Devine (R) b. Dec. 21, 1915 (1959)
13.　*Charles Adams Mosher (R) b. May 7, 1906 (1961)
14.　*John F. Seiberling, Jr. (D) age 52 (1971)
15.　*Chalmers Pangburn Wylie (R) b. Nov. 23, 1920 (1967)
16.　Ralph S. Regula (R) age 47
17.　*John Milan Ashbrook (R) b. Sept. 21, 1928 (1961)
18.　*Wayne L. Hays (D) b. May 13, 1911 (1949)
19.　*Charles J. Carney (D) b. April 17, 1913 (1971)
20.　*James V. Stanton (D) b. Feb. 27, 1932 (1971)
21.　*Louis Stokes (D) b. Feb. 23, 1925 (1969)
22.　*Charles A. Vanik (D) b. Apr. 7, 1913 (1955)
23.　*William E. Minshall (R) b. Oct. 24, 1911 (1955)
　　Oklahoma: 5 D, 1 R [4 D, 2 R]
1.　James R. Jones (D) age 33
2.　Clem Rogers McSpadden (D) age 46
3.　*Carl Bert Albert (D) b. May 10, 1908 (1947)
4.　*Tom Steed (D) b. Mar. 2, 1904 (1949)
5.　*John Jarman (D) b. July 17, 1915 (1951)
6.　*John N. Happy Camp (R) b. May 11, 1908 (1969)
　　Oregon: 2 D, 2 R [2 D, 2 R]
1.　*Wendell Wyatt (R) b. June 15, 1917 (1964)
2.　*Al Ullman (D) b. Mar. 9, 1914 (1957)
3.　*Edith Green (D) b. Jan. 17, 1910 (1955)
4.　*John Dellenback (R) b. Nov. 6, 1918 (1967)
　　Pennsylvania: 13 D, 12 R [14 D, 13 R]
1.　*William A. Barrett (D) b. Aug. 14, 1896 (1945)†
2.　*Robert N. C. Nix (D) b. Sept. 9, 1905 (1958)
3.　*William Joseph Green (D) b. June 24, 1938 (1964)
4.　*Joshua Eilberg (D) b. Feb. 12, 1921 (1967)
5.　John H. Ware III (R) b. Aug. 29, 1908

6.　*Gus Yatron (D) b. Oct. 16, 1927 (1969)
7.　*Lawrence G. Williams (R) b. Sept. 15, 1913 (1967)
8.　*Edward G. Biester Jr. (R) b. Jan. 5, 1931 (1967)
9.　E. G. Shuster (R) age 40
10.　*Joseph Michael McDade (R) b. Sept. 29, 1931 (1963)
11.　*Daniel J. Flood (D) b. Nov. 26, 1903 (1945)†
12.　*John Phillips Saylor (R) July 23, 1908 (1949)
13.　*Lawrence Coughlin (R) b. Apr. 11, 1929 (1969)
14.　*William S. Moorhead (D) b. Apr. 8, 1923 (1959)
15.　*Fred B. Rooney (D) b. Nov. 6, 1925 (1963)
16.　*Edwin D. Eshleman (R) b. Dec. 4, 1920 (1967)
17.　*Herman T. Schneebeli (R) b. July 7, 1907 (1960)
18.　*H. John Heinz 3d (R) b. Oct. 23, 1938 (1971)
19.　*George A. Goodling (R) b. Sept. 26, 1896 (1961)†
20.　*Joseph M. Gaydos (D) b. July 3, 1926 (1969)
21.　*John H. Dent (D) b. Mar. 10, 1908 (1958)
22.　*Thomas E. Morgan (D) b. Oct. 13, 1906 (1945)
23.　*Albert Walter Johnson (R) b. Apr. 17, 1906 (1963)
24.　*Joseph Phillip Vigorito (D) b. Nov. 10, 1918 (1965)
25.　*Frank M. Clark (D) b. Dec. 24, 1915 (1955)
　　Rhode Island: 2 D [2 D]
1.　*Fernand Joseph St Germain (D) b. Jan. 9, 1928 (1961)
2.　*Robert Owens Tiernan (D) b. Feb. 24, 1929 (1967)
　　South Carolina: 4 D, 2 R [5 D, 1 R]
1.　*Mendel J. Davis (D) b. Oct. 23, 1942 (1971)
2.　*Floyd Spence (R) b. Apr. 9, 1928 (1971)
3.　*William Jennings Bryan Dorn (D) b. Apr. 14, 1916 (1947)†
4.　*James Robert Mann (D) b. Apr. 27, 1920 (1969)
5.　*Thomas Smithwick Gettys (D) b. June 19, 1912 (1964)
6.　Edward L. Young (R) age 52
　　South Dakota: 1 D, 1 R [2 D]
1.　*Frank E. Denholm (D) b. Nov. 29, 1923 (1971)
2.　James Abdnor (R) age 49
　　Tennessee: 3 D, 5 R [5 D, 4 R]
1.　*James H. (Jimmy) Quillen (R) b. Jan. 11, 1916 (1963)
2.　*John James Duncan (R) b. Mar. 24, 1919 (1965)
3.　LaMar Baker (R) b. Dec. 29, 1915
4.　*Joe L. Evins (D) b. Oct. 24, 1910 (1947)
5.　*Richard Harmon Fulton (D) b. Jan. 27, 1927 (1963)
6.　Robin L. Beard Jr. (R) age 33
7.　*Ed Jones (D) b. Apr. 20, 1912 (1969)
8.　*Dan H. Kuykendall (R) b. July 9, 1924 (1967)
　　Texas: 20 D, 4 R [20 D, 3 R]
1.　*Wright Patman (D) b. Aug. 6, 1893 (1929)
2.　Charles Wilson (D) age 39

3. *James M. Collins (R) b. Apr. 29, 1916 (1968)
4. *Ray Roberts (D) b. Mar. 28, 1913 (1962)
5. Alan Steelman (R) age 30
6. *Olin E. Teague (D) b. Apr. 6, 1910 (1946)
7. *W. R. (Bill) Archer (R) b. March 22, 1928 (1971)
8. *Bob Eckhardt (D) b. July 16, 1913 (1967)
9. *Jack Brooks (D) b. Dec. 18, 1922 (1953)
10. *J. J. (Jake) Pickle (D) b. Oct. 11, 1913 (1963)
11. *William Robert (Bob) Poage (D) b. Dec. 28, 1899 (1937)
12. *James C. Wright Jr. (D) b. Dec. 22, 1922 (1955)
13. *Robert Dale (Bob) Price (R) b. Sept. 7, 1927 (1967)
14. *John Young (D) b. Nov 10, 1916 (1957)
15. *Eligio de la Garza (D) b. Sept. 22, 1927 (1965)
16. *Richard Crawford White (D) b. Apr. 29, 1923 (1965)
17. *Omar Burleson (D) b. Mar. 19, 1906 (1947)
18. Barbara C. Jordan (D) age 36
19. *George H. Mahon (D) b. Sept. 22, 1900 (1935)
20. *Henry B. Gonzalez (D) b. May 3, 1916 (1961)
21. *O. Clark Fisher (D) b. Nov. 22, 1908 (1943)
22. *Robert (Bob) Randolph Casey (D) b. July 27, 1915 (1959)
23. *Abraham Kazan Jr. (D) b. Jan. 17, 1919 (1967)
24. Dale Milford (D) age 46
     Utah: 2 D [1 D, 1 R]
1. *K. Gunn McKay (D) b. Feb. 23, 1925 (1971)
2. Wayne Owens (D) age 35
     Vermont: 1 R [1 R]
At large. *Richard W. Mallary (R) b. Feb. 21, 1929 (1972)
     Virginia: 3 D, 7 R [4 D, 6 R]
1. *Thomas N. Downing (D) b. Feb. 1, 1919 (1959)
2. *G. William Whitehurst (R) b. Mar. 12, 1925 (1969)
3. *David Edward Satterfield III (D) b. Dec. 2, 1920 (1965)

4. Robert W. Daniel Jr. (R) age 36
5. *W. C. (Dan) Daniel (D) b. May 12, 1914 (1969)
6. M. Caldwell Butler (R) age 47
7. *James Kenneth Robinson (R) b. May 14, 1916 (1971)
8. Stanford E. Parris (R) age 43
9. *William Creed Wampler (R) b. Apr. 21, 1926 (1953)†
10. *Joel T. Broyhill (R) b. Nov 4, 1919 (1953)
     Washington: 6 D, 1 R [6 D, 1 R]
1. Joel M. Pritchard, (R) age 47
2. *Lloyd Meeds (D) b. Dec. 11, 1927 (1965)
3. *Julia Butler Hansen (D) b. June 14, 1907 (1960)
4. *Mike McCormack (D) b. Dec. 14, 1921 (1971)
5. *Thomas Stephen Foley (D) b. Mar. 6, 1929 (1965)
6. *Floyd V. Hicks (D) b. May 29, 1915 (1965)
7. *Brock Adams (D) b. Jan. 13, 1927 (1965)
     West Virginia: 4 D [5 D]
1. *Robert H. Mollohan (D) b. Sept. 18, 1909 (1953)†
2. *Harley O. Staggers (D) b. Aug. 3, 1907 (1949)
3. *John Slack (D) b. Mar. 18, 1915 (1959)
4. *Ken Hechler (D) b. Sept. 20, 1914 (1959)
     Wisconsin: 5 D, 4 R [5 D, 5 R]
1. *Les Aspin (D) b. July 21, 1928 (1971)
2. *Robert William Kastenmeier (D) b. Jan. 24, 1924 (1959)
3. *Vernon Wallace Thomson (R) b. Nov. 5, 1905 (1961)
4. *Clement J. Zablocki (D) b. Nov. 18, 1912 (1949)
5. *Henry S. Reuss (D) b. Feb. 22, 1912 (1955)
6. *William A. Steiger (R) b. May 15, 1938 (1967)
7. *David R. Obey (D) b. Oct. 3, 1938 (1969)
8. Harold V. Froelich (R) age 40
9. *Glenn R. Davis (R) b. Oct. 28, 1914 (1947)†
     Wyoming: 1 D [1 D]
At Large. *Teno Roncalio (D) b. Mar. 23, 1916 (1965)†

[42] Governorships. Democrats increased their statehouse majority with a net gain of one governorship, continuing a trend begun in 1970. Of the 50 states, 31 had Democratic governors and 19 had Republican governors. Of the 10 Democratic and eight Republican statehouses at stake in 1972, five changed hands, with Democrats defeating incumbents in Illinois and Delaware and picking up the Vermont seats. Republicans won in North Carolina, which elected its first Republican governor since 1901, and Missouri, which had not had a Republican governor since the mid-1940s. Seven of nine incumbents won their re-election races. Local issues and personalities dominated most of the races.

[43] *State Governors.* Listed below are the governors of the 50 states. Each governor is described according to his party designation (D=Democrat, R=Republican), the year in which he became governor (date in parentheses) and his election status (* designates an incumbent, italics indicate that the governor was elected or re-elected in November 1972 and † indicates that the governor's service began in the year shown but has not been continuous). Unless indicated, the governor serves four years, with his term ending in January of the year shown for holdover governors.

Ala.   *George C. Wallace (D) term ends 1975; b. Aug. 25, 1919 (1963)†

Alaska *William A. Egan (D) term ends 1975; b. Oct. 8, 1914 (1959)†

Ariz.   *Jack Williams (R) term ends 1975; b. Oct. 29, 1909 (1967)

Ark.   (2-yr. term) *Dale Bumpers (D) age 47 (1971)

Calif. *Ronald Reagan (R) term ends 1975; b. Feb. 6, 1911 (1967)

Colo.   *John A. Love (R) term ends 1975; b. Nov 29, 1916 (1963)

Conn.   *Thomas J. Meskill (R) term ends 1975; b. Jan. 30, 1928 (1971)

Del.   Sherman W. Tribbitt (D); age 49

Fla.   *Reubin Askew (D) term ends 1975; b. Sept. 11, 1928 (1971)

Ga.   *Jimmy Carter (D) term ends 1975; age 46 (1971)

Hawaii *John A. Burns (D) term ends 1975; b. March 30, 1909 (1963)

Idaho *Cecil D. Andrus (D) term ends 1975; age 40 (1971)

Ill.   Daniel Walker (D); age 49

Ind.   Otis R. Bowen (R); age 54

Iowa   (2-yr. term) *Robert D. Ray (R) b. Sept. 26, 1928 (1969)

Kansas (2-yr. term) *Robert B. Docking (D) b. Oct. 9, 1925 (1967)

Ky.   *Wendell Ford (D) term ends 1975; age 48 (1971)

La.   *Edwin W. Edwards (D) term ends 1976; age 45 (1972)

Me.   *Kenneth M. Curtis (D) term ends 1975; b. Feb. 8, 1931 (1967)

Md.   *Marvin Mandel (D) term ends 1975; b. April 19, 1920 (1969)

Mass.   *Francis W. Sargent (R) term ends 1975; b. July 29, 1915 (1969)

Mich.   *William G. Milliken (R) term ends 1975; b. March 22, 1922 (1969)

Minn.   *Wendell R. Anderson (D) term ends 1975; b. Feb. 1, 1933 (1971)

Miss.   *William Waller (D) term ends 1976; age 47 (1972)

Mo.   Christopher S. Bond (R); age 33

Mont.   Thomas L. Judge (D); age 38

Neb.   *James J. Exon (D) term ends 1975; b. Aug. 9, 1921 (1971)

Nev.   *Mike O'Callaghan (D) term ends 1975; age 42

N.H.   (2-yr. term) Meldrim Thomson Jr. (R); age 60

N.J.   *William T. Cahill (R) term ends 1973; b. June 25, 1912 (1970)

N.M.   *Bruce King (D) term ends 1975; age 45

N.Y.   *Nelson A. Rockefeller (R) term ends 1975; b. July 8, 1908 (1959)

N.C.   James E. Holshouser Jr. (R); age 37

N.D.   Arthur A. Link (D); age 58

Ohio   *John J. Gilligan (D) term ends 1975; b. March 22, 1921 (1971)

Okla.   *David Hall (D) term ends 1975; age 41 (1971)

Ore.   *Tom McCall (R) term ends 1975; b. March 22, 1913 (1967)

Pa.   *Milton J. Shapp (D) term ends 1975; age 57 (1971)

R.I.   (2-yr. term) Philip W. Noel (D); age 41

S.C.   *John C. West (D) term ends 1975; b. Aug. 27, 1922 (1971)

S.D.   (2-yr. term) *Richard F. Kneip (D) b. Jan. 7, 1933 (1971)

Tenn.   *Winfield Dunn (R) term ends 1975; age 43 (1971)

Tex.   (2-yr. term) Dolph Briscoe (D); age 49

Utah   *Calvin L. Rampton (D); b. Nov. 6, 1913 (1964)

Vt.   (2-yr. term) Thomas P. Salmon (D); age 40

Va.   *Linwood A. Holton (R) term ends 1974; b. Sept. 21, 1923 (1971)

Wash.   *Daniel J. Evans (R); b. Oct. 16, 1925 (1964)

W. Va.   *Arch A. Moore Jr. (R); b. April 16, 1923 (1969)

Wis.   *Patrick J. Lucey (D) term ends 1975; b. Mar. 21, 1918 (1971)

Wyo.   *Stanley K. Hathaway (R) term ends 1975; b. July 19, 1924 (1967)

[44] California referendum results. California voters were faced with 22 ballot propositions. In response to California and U.S. Supreme Court rulings curbing capital punishment (see CRIME [10-11]), they passed, by a 2-1 margin, a state constitutional amendment to restore the death penalty for treason, train wrecking, murdering a prison guard while under life sentence, or perjury during a capital case. A proposal to end state penalties for growth or use of marijuana by adults was defeated by a 3-1 margin. A severe anti-pornography measure was defeated, as was a proposal to slash property taxes in favor of increased sales taxes and other measures to be decided by the legislature. Voters curbed school busing for integration by a 2-1 margin and approved a proposal for state and regional shoreline planning. (The planning proposal had been the target of a heavy television campaign by the oil and real estate industries, who opposed the measure.)

[45] Colorado defeats Olympic bid. Colorado voters rejected a $5 million bond issue to supplement a $20 million proposed federal outlay for financing the 1976 Olympic Winter Games, which were to be held in Denver. (Another $10 million was to have been raised through licensing, television revenue and other sources.) Opposition to the Olympics had coalesced in previous weeks over the issue of what the Games would do to Colorado's environment. Denver Nov. 8 withdrew its bid to host the 1976 Winter Games, but a U.S. court in Denver Nov. 9 issued a restraining order to bar the Denver Olympic Committee from officially withdrawing its bid for the games.

Campaign Funding & Spending Developments

[46] **Curb passed, signed.** The House, by a 334-19 vote Jan. 19, approved the Federal Election Campaign Act of 1971, passed by the Senate Dec. 17, 1971. The bill, signed by President Nixon Feb. 7, limited for the first time the amount presidential and congressional candidates could spend on election campaigns. (Nixon had vetoed a similar bill in October 1970.) Under the bill, effective April 4, campaign spending by candidates for federal office was limited to 10¢ per constituent, with not more than 60% of the total to be spent in any one media (radio, television, newspapers, magazines, billboards or mass telephoning). Spending by presidential candidates and their running mates was limited to no more than $8.4 million on radio and television during the post-convention campaign. The legislation also limited the amount of a candidate's own money that could be spent during a campaign: $50,000 for the presidency or vice presidency; $35,000 for the Senate; and $25,000 for the House. Candidates and committees receiving and spending more than $1,000 were required to report contributions and expenditures of more than $100. Reports were required three times a year and six times during election years. The legislation did not call for repeal of the equal-time provision for broadcasts, did not establish an overall ceiling on campaign spending and did not limit individual contributions except for those from the candidates themselves.

[47] **Early Nixon drive nets $10 million.** Fund-raising committees June 10 reported collecting $10.1 million for the Nixon presidential campaign in early 1972, before the April 7 effective date of the Federal Election Campaign Act. The citizens' group Common Cause June 10 deplored the failure of the committees to disclose the names of donors to the $10.1 million fund. Common Cause Sept. 6 filed suit against the Finance Committee to Re-Elect the President, the fund-raising branch of the Committee to Re-Elect the President, to force the disclosure of the names of those donors. In an out-of-court settlement of the case Nov. 1, the finance committee agreed to release a partial list of the donors—those who had made donations from January 1971 to March 9, 1972. Those who had made donations from March 10 to April 7 were not listed. Donors lists published Nov. 3 and Nov. 5 disclosed the names of 1,573 individuals and groups who had donated approximately $5,462,338. (Republicans had previously said that the records of all donations made before April 7 had been destroyed.) The March 9 cutoff date was chosen because it was the final date for filing under the 1926 Federal Corrupt Practices Act, which was the basis for the Common Cause suit. The Republicans had argued that they could ignore the 1926 act, which was superseded by the 1971 act April 4, since Nixon was not a candidate until nominated by the GOP convention in August *(see* [22]). Under the out-of-court settlement, the trial for the Common Cause suit was postponed until after the Nov. 7 elections.

[48] **Union contributions backed.** The Supreme Court ruled 6-2 June 22 that the provision of the Taft-Hartley Act outlawing political contributions from labor groups in connection with "any election" for federal office did not apply to unions making campaign gifts with money from voluntary donations of its members. The ruling apparently also would permit corporations to set up similar political funds and seek voluntary donations from employees. The decision overturned the convictions of a St. Louis Pipefitters Union local and three of its officials for collecting political money from union members.

[49] **Impeachment committee sued, cleared.** The Justice Department Aug. 17 filed a civil suit against the National Committee for Impeachment and two of its principal officers (Randolph Phillips and Elizabeth A. Most), charging them with violations of the Federal Election Campaign Act. The suit charged

that the committee, which called for the impeachment of President Nixon, had failed to file a report of its campaign contributions in connection with a two-page advertisement placed in the *New York Times* May 31. (The Justice Department announced Sept. 13 that it would not press criminal charges against the *Times* for publishing the ad.) The suit also charged that the ad did not include a notice of where the financial reports could be obtained by the public and did not state that the candidates mentioned in the ad had authorized the use of their names. The ad had featured a reprint of an impeachment resolution introduced in the House May 10 by Rep. John J. Conyers Jr. (D, Mich.). Seven other Democrats, who had endorsed the House resolution, and Rep. McCloskey, who had not, were listed in the committee's "honor roll." The committee was enjoined from further political actions Sept. 5, but a federal appeals court ruled Oct. 30 that the committee was not a "political committee... soliciting contributions or making expenditures, the major purpose of which is the nomination or election of candidates" and therefore was not covered by the Election Campaign Act.

See also CIVIL DISORDERS; CIVIL RIGHTS [17]; CONGRESS; CRIME [7]; FEDERAL BUREAU OF INVESTIGATION; INDOCHINA WAR [24]; NIXON, RICHARD MILHOUS; POLITICS; POLLUTION [3]; PUERTO RICO; SOVIET-U.S. RELATIONS [9]; TAXES; VOTING RIGHTS

ELIZABETH II —*See* AUSTRALIA [7]; GREAT BRITAIN [12]

ELLSBERG, DANIEL—*See* PENTAGON PAPERS

EL SALVADOR—Molina elected. Following the failure of any candidate to gain an absolute majority in elections Feb. 20, the National Assembly met Feb. 25 and proclaimed Col. Arturo Armando Molina, candidate of the ruling National Conciliation party (PCN) and winner of the popular balloting by a margin of 9,844 votes, as the next president of El Salvador. Losing candidate Jose Napoleon Duarte, an ex-mayor of San Salvador who ran on a center-left coalition ticket headed by the Christian Democratic party, Feb. 26 charged the government with election fraud and threatened to organize a national strike to protest election irregularities. (Duarte had won heavily in San Salvador, where over 30% of the country's voters live.) Strikes, shootouts and arson followed the Feb. 20 elections, but Molina was inaugurated with his Cabinet July 1. The new Cabinet: foreign affairs—Mauricio A. Borgonovo Pohl; interior—Col. Juan Antonio Martinez Varela; justice—Jose Enrique Silva; economy—Salvador Sanchez Aguillon; education—Rogelio Sanchez; defense—Col. Carlos Humberto Romero; agriculture and livestock—Enrique Alvarez Cordova; health—Julio Astario; public works—Antonio Jorge Seaman; presidential private secretary—Lt. Col. Anibal Velarde; special secretary—Rodrigo R. Pineda Rodriguez.

Congressional, municipal elections. The ruling PCN won an overwhelming victory in Congressional and municipal elections March 12, taking 38 of the 52 seats in Congress and 206 of the 261 municipal mayoralties. The National Opposition Union (UNO) took seven Congressional seats and 54 mayoralties; the Popular Salvadorean party (PPS) won six Congressional seats and one mayoralty; and the United Democratic Independent Front (FUDI) took one Congressional seat. According to a report March 9, FUDI leader Gen. Jose Alberto Medrano, a candidate in the presidential elections, had withdrawn his party prior to the balloting, charging that the "public will again be mocked by the government."

100 die as army coup fails. More than 100 soldiers and civilians were killed and 200 others were wounded March 25 as rebel troops under the command of Col. Benjamin Mejia tried unsuccessfully to overthrow the government of outgoing President Gen. Fidel Sanchez Hernandez. The revolt reportedly began early March 25 when Col. Mejia sent soldiers from San Salvador's El Zapote barracks to arrest Sanchez at the presidential palace.

Sanchez and two guards held off the soldiers with gunfire for two hours until the three ran out of ammunition and the president and his daughter were taken into custody. The rebels, joined by troops from the San Carlos barracks, took over the country's communications system and sealed El Salvador's borders. Loyal troops from garrisons at Sonsonate, 30 miles west of San Salvador, and San Miguel, 70 miles southwest, advanced against the rebels during the afternoon of March 25, supported by air force planes. The rebels surrendered early in the evening, and Sanchez and his daughter were released unharmed. Sanchez immediately proclaimed martial law and a state of siege and set a 6 p.m.-6 a.m. curfew. Unsuccessful presidential candidate Duarte, who had urged the nation in a radio broadcast March 25 to support the uprising, was arrested the same day in the home of the first secretary of the Venezuelan embassy (where he had sought political asylum) for his part in the plot. The arrest brought a protest from the Venezuelan embassy, which charged that the diplomatic immunity of its members had been violated; but the government replied that no one could seek asylum in the home of an embassy attache. The government officially sanctioned Duarte's exile, and Duarte March 29 set out for Venezuela, by way of Miami and Guatemala. The government's decision avoided temporarily a politically explosive trial for the popular leader and eased the developing diplomatic crisis over his arrest. (In a press conference April 4, Duarte said he had not participated in planning the rebellion, but had supported it because of what he felt to be fraud in the presidential elections.) Duarte was brought to trial in absentia, along with 10 other persons, but was acquitted of involvement in the coup Dec. 1. Only Mejia and Manuel Reyes Alvarado were found guilty. Both were in exile. Mejia was sentenced Dec. 8 in absentia to 25 years in prison; Alvarado was sentenced to 15 years.

State of siege imposed. Congress April 3 voted (36-0 with 18 abstentions) to impose a month-long state of siege to help the government regain full control of the country after the abortive coup. The measure said siege regulations were necessary because coup leaders had distributed large numbers of firearms among civilians during the short revolt and civilians had not turned the weapons over to authorities. The state of siege was finally lifted June 3.

University occupied. The National University was occupied by troops July 19 and closed for two months on orders from President Molina, who claimed the school had "fallen into the hands of Communists." Molina added that the school had become a center for planning robberies and kidnapings and distributing subversive literature, and that university authorities had permitted "sexual abuses" and the consumption of drugs. (Military sources announced July 26 that troops searching the university had found a series of secret cellars and tunnels, a few of which contained automobiles fitting descriptions of cars used in bank robberies. Other authorities investigating the university's files reportedly found that a student fund had been used to send students to Prague, Moscow and Havana.) University Rector Rafael Menjivar and the five other members of the board of regents were arrested July 19 and subsequently expelled to Nicaragua.

According to reports July 21, the occupation of the university followed a crisis in the medical school, whose professors, lecturers and directors had recently been expelled by the university's superior council for "inciting students to rebellion." Medical students had broken away from the university and formed their own faculty after a dispute with central university authorities over the number of students to be admitted to medical studies. Authorities had told the school to accept 1,200 new students, but the faculty had wanted to maintain the existing level of 700 students and raise the quality of medical education. The situation had been aggravated by recent elections for new university leaders, which embodied reforms declared unconstitutional by the Salvadorean Supreme Court.

See also TERRITORIAL WATERS

EMERGENCY BROADCAST SYSTEM (EBS)—*See* TELEVISION & RADIO [5]

EMMY AWARDS—*See* TELEVISION & RADIO [8]
ENERGY—*See* ATOMIC ENERGY; CIVIL RIGHTS [16]; ENVIRONMENT; OIL
& NATURAL GAS; POLLUTION [3]; POPULATION

ENVIRONMENT—Nixon's message. President Nixon sent his third annual environmental message to Congress Feb. 8. The message had few new proposals, but urged Congress to act on a backlog of ecological legislation left over from 1971. Nixon promised to submit legislation for a tax on sulphur dioxide emissions in polluted areas, which had been discussed in the 1971 message. The 1972 message also proposed legislation: penalizing states that failed to adopt landuse plans concerning roads and airports; denying tax depreciation write-offs for construction on coastal wetlands, which would be designated as environmentally critical areas; outlawing the harming of the over 100 species on the endangered species list; protecting water supplies by providing for Environmental Protection Agency (EPA) guidelines for state programs to control the disposal of toxic wastes; controlling sediment runoff from construction sites into waterways, with state regulation and ultimate federal control; creating a 24,000-acre Golden Gate National Recreation Area on San Francisco Bay; and adding 18 parcels totaling 1.3 million acres to the wilderness system. The message also proposed executive orders immediately banning the poisoning of predators on all federally owned lands, with emergency exceptions, and requiring control of off-road vehicles (motorcycles, snowmobiles and dune buggies) on federal lands. Nixon also announced that 20 additional parcels would be provided for parks near urban areas and that the Department of Health, Education and Welfare (HEW) had established grants to combat lead poisoning of slum children by examinations and educational programs. He also proposed that the United Nations (U.N.) set up a five-year $100 million environmental fund *(see below)* and pledged to ask Congress for support "on a matching basis."

U.N. conference. About 1,200 delegates from 112 nations and about 400 international agencies were present June 5 at the opening of the U.N.-sponsored World Conference on the Human Environment in Stockholm, Sweden. The Soviet Union, Poland, Hungary, Czechoslovakia and Bulgaria boycotted the conference to protest the exclusion of East Germany, which was denied full participation because it did not belong to the U.N. or to any of its ancillary organizations. Among the measures approved by the delegates were: an appeal to all countries (approved June 6) to minimize the release of toxic metals and chemicals into the environment; committee reports (approved June 7) urging the establishment of an early warning system to monitor water, air and food contamination and asking government programs to prevent pollutants from crossing international borders; a proposal (approved June 7) to set up a network of 110 stations to monitor changes in the world's climate and air pollution; a U.S.-sponsored recommendation for a 10-year ban on commercial whaling (approved June 9); a call for the halt of all tests of nuclear weapons, "especially those carried out in the atmosphere" (approved June 12); a proposal for a global program, called Earthwatch, to monitor the habitability of the earth (approved June 14); a proposal (approved June 15) to establish a new permanent organization in the U.N. to coordinate environmental activities; a proposal (approved June 15) to establish a fund of at least $100 million to be used by the U.N. over the next five years to stimulate efforts to protect the environment; and proposals (approved June 16) to establish an international referral system for pooling and distributing environmental data and to establish a strengthened system to collect and safeguard the planet's animal and plant resources.

The conference ended June 16 after delegates endorsed a much-debated declaration of principles designed to serve as a guide for an international campaign against pollution. The declaration went to the U.N. General Assembly for approval. The document, called Declaration on the Human Environment, contained 26 principles, including a call for efforts toward "the elimination and complete destruction" of nuclear weapons and other instruments of mass destruction. Four principles—two dealing with wildlife and ocean protection, one with helping developing countries maintain stable prices amid environmental outlays, and one assuring nations of autonomy on internal environmental standards—had been added to the conference's original draft declaration, which had been disclosed March 16 after two years of planning by a 27-nation body. The delegates June 8 had unanimously approved a Chinese proposal to open the draft declaration for revision. (China had argued that it and other nations had not had an opportunity to express their views on the draft.) The document was presented to the conference June 16 after an all-night committee debate which also produced additions to six of the principles. Three additions—including a denunciation of environmental projects "designed for colonial and racist domination"—were apparently introduced by China, and an addition condemning apartheid was apparently added by African delegates. Other developing countries reportedly added phraseology regarding technical assistance and exemption from undue "economic burden."

Alaska pipeline stay lifted. U.S. District Court Judge George L. Hart Aug. 15 lifted an injunction he had issued in April 1970 against construction of the trans-Alaska oil pipeline. Hart ruled in Washington that the Interior Department's environmental impact statement—a six-volume report issued March 20—had adequately considered alternatives, and that all right-of-way and landuse permits had been legally issued. He said he had issued a final ruling to expedite the appeals process, since "it can be confidently anticipated that the final decision in this matter rests with the Supreme Court." The Interior Department's impact statement had conceded that any method of transporting oil from Alaska's North Slope would pose a potential threat to the environment, but said that recovery of the oil was "an important national security objective" and that the proposed 789-mile Prudhoe-Valdez pipeline was the earliest feasible route. According to the report, oil spillage would be the major environmental threat from the pipeline, since it was considered almost certain that at least one large-magnitude earthquake would strike the region traversed by the pipe during its lifetime. Once the oil was loaded on tankers in Valdez, "persistent low-level discharge from the ballast treatment facility and tank-cleaning operations" might endanger salmon and other fishing industries even more than major one-shot spills. The report said that a proposed route across northwest Canada to the Midwest would incur less danger from earthquakes and, if it followed the same route as a proposed natural gas pipeline, would avoid the double damage that two separate routes would entail. However, the report said, engineering studies for a Canadian route were not advanced, and Canadian environmental legislation could require still further delays for detailed impact consideration.

Environmental and energy experts from the U.S. and Canada had testified June 9 before the Congressional Joint Economic Committee that the Interior Department had not given adequate consideration to the cross-Canada route. David Anderson, a Canadian parliamentary environment expert, had reported in the hearing that Canada had spent $43 million on 30 economic and environmental studies of the trans-Canada route, but that U.S. Interior Secretary Rogers C. B. Morton had ignored this information. Anderson warned that the Canadian government might not approve the natural gas pipeline if the oil was not moved through the same corridor. Economist Richard Nehring, who had resigned from the Interior Department to protest attitudes on the Alaska pipeline, told the committee that the department's impact statement had concluded that the Canadian route would cause less environmental damage, but that the conclusion had been dropped from the published version of the statement. Nehring also said that most department economists believed the Canada route would be economically more practical, since the need for oil was expected to be greater in the East and Midwest than on the West Coast. Interior Secretary Morton appeared before the committee June 22 to explain his opposition to the Canada route. Morton claimed that the route would "produce more environmental damage in the long run," largely because it would pass through longer sections of permafrost and over 12 major rivers as opposed to one river on the Alaska route. As for the possibility of laying the oil pipeline in the natural gas corridor, Morton claimed that gas transported underground at sub-freezing temperatures and hot oil transported through an elevated pipe required different terrains "a considerable distance apart." Morton also claimed that the Canada route would be more expensive and would cause a delay of "as much as seven years" in oil deliveries.

U.S.-Soviet environment projects. The U.S. and the Soviet Union Sept. 21 ended three days of talks in Moscow by agreeing to set up about 30 projects as a means of protecting the environment of both countries. The agreement, an extension of one signed by President Nixon during his May visit to the U.S.S.R. *(see* SOVIET-U.S. RELATIONS [4]), was reached by the Joint Committee on Cooperation in the Field of Environmental Protection. The joint studies were to deal with such problems as air and water pollution, urban environment, pest management, atmospheric pollution, problems found in permafrost regions and earthquake prediction methods. They would involve transfer of Soviet and U.S. specialists to research sites in each other's countries for periods of several months.

See also ATOMIC ENERGY [1-5]; CONSERVATION; ELECTIONS [17, 45]; EUROPEAN ECONOMIC COMMUNITY [10]; JUDICIARY; NIXON, RICHARD MILHOUS; PESTICIDES; POLLUTION; POPULATION; POVERTY; PUBLIC LAND; SOVIET-U.S. RELATIONS [1, 4]; STATE & LOCAL GOVERNMENTS

ENVIRONMENTAL PROTECTION AGENCY (EPA)—*See* CONSERVATION; ENVIRONMENT; PESTICIDES; POLLUTION [1, 4-8, 11-16]
EPIDEMICS—*See* HEALTH
EQUAL EDUCATIONAL OPPORTUNITIES ACT—*See* CIVIL RIGHTS [2-3]
EQUAL EMPLOYMENT OPPORTUNITIES COMMISSION (EEOC)—*See* CIVIL RIGHTS [1, 14, 16]; WOMEN'S RIGHTS
EQUAL RIGHTS AMENDMENT—*See* MILITARY [5]; WOMEN'S RIGHTS
EQUATORIAL GUINEA—*See* GABON

ESPIONAGE—Diplomats expelled. Information supplied by the Soviet defector, Oleg Lyalin, whose disclosures had led to the ouster of 105 Soviet officials from Great Britain in 1971, reportedly led to the expulsion from France Feb. 13 of three members of the Soviet embassy on charges of espionage. Among those ordered out of the country was Alexei Krokhine, third in command at the embassy. Italy March 12 expelled four East European diplomats (Konstanty Janowski, a first secretary in the Polish embassy's consular section in Rome; Milos Dospiva, a first secretary at the Czechoslovakian embassy; and Dimcho Vavov and Borislav Balchev, Bulgarian trade representatives) on espionage charges. The four, ordered to leave Italy by March 13, were charged with spying on the activities of the North Atlantic Treaty Organization (NATO) in Malta and elsewhere in the Mediterranean. The Soviet ambassador to Denmark agreed to recall three unnamed members of the embassy's staff after the Danish Foreign Ministry April 7 accused the three of engaging in intelligence work. Frantisek Korisko, third secretary in the Czechoslovak embassy in Paris, was caught receiving confidential documents April 7. Expulsion proceedings against him were begun April 13, but Korisko had already returned to Czechoslovakia. The Czechoslovak government April 12 retaliated with the expulsion of Georges Vaugier, third secretary in the French embassy in Prague, for allegedly receiving secret documents.

Soviet aide charged in N.Y. Valery Markelov, a Soviet citizen employed as a translator at United Nations headquarters in New York, was arraigned Feb. 17 by a federal grand jury in Brooklyn for trying to obtain classified documents on the U.S. Navy's new supersonic F-14A jet fighter and for failing to register as a Soviet agent. Markelov had been arrested Feb. 14 by Federal Bureau of Investigation (FBI) agents after allegedly receiving secret documents about the plane from an unidentified engineer employed by the aircraft's manufacturer, Grumman Aerospace Corp. The engineer, in cooperation with the FBI, had allegedly held 11 separate meetings with Markelov since 1970. Markelov pleaded innocent to the charges. He was authorized by a federal judge in Brooklyn May 19 to return to the U.S.S.R. while his case was pending. The decision was made on the eve of President Nixon's departure for summit talks in the Soviet Union (see SOVIET-U.S. RELATIONS [1-6]), but U.S. officials refused comment on whether the release was connected with the visit.

British naval officer sentenced. Sub-Lt. David James Bingham, a British torpedo expert, was sentenced March 13 to 21 years in prison for selling naval secrets to the Soviet Union. Bingham, who pleaded guilty, had been paid $5,980 for transmitting information to a Soviet assistant naval attache, Lori Kuzmin, who had since left Britain. Attorney General Sir Peter Rawlinson charged that the information, on fleet movements and the strength and firepower of Western navies, "had a value to a potential enemy almost beyond price." Bingham had spied for an 18-month period ending with his arrest in August 1971. He confessed to having sought out the Russians at his wife's urging to supplement the household income. His wife, Maureen, was charged March 17 with violating the Official Secrets Act in connection with the case. She had told reporters that she had "nagged him into becoming a spy" and had acted as an intermediary in passing the information to the Russians. Mrs. Bingham was sentenced Nov. 15 to 2.5 years in prison for her role in the espionage activities.

Challenge to Army surveillance dismissed. The Supreme Court, in a 5-4 decision June 26, ruled that the Army could not be brought into court to defend the mere existence of its surveillance of civilian political activities against charges that the surveillance discouraged freedom of speech. The justices held that to permit such a trial of the Army would make federal courts "virtually continuing monitors of the wisdom and soundness of executive judgment." The majority opinion said that surveillance by the Army could be challenged in court only if and when individuals could demonstrate "actual or threatened injury" by having been watched by Army agents. In other instances, control of such surveillance must be left in the hands of Congress and the executive branch. Chief Justice Warren E. Burger wrote the majority opinion. He was joined by Justices Harry A. Blackmun, Lewis F. Powell Jr., William Rehnquist and Byron White. Justices William J. Brennan Jr., William O. Douglas, Thurgood Marshall and Potter Stewart dissented on grounds that the plaintiffs had judicial precedents to take the Army to court over the surveillance issue. At issue in the case was a lawsuit filed by Arlo Tatum, executive director of the Central Committee for Conscientious Objectors, and 12 other individuals and groups who said they were targets of the Army's surveillance. The plaintiffs had sought an injunction to prevent further surveillance and a court order to require the Army to destroy the dossiers compiled by its agents.

See also CHINA, COMMUNIST; DISARMAMENT; FEDERAL BUREAU OF INVESTIGATION; KOREA, SOUTH; PENTAGON PAPERS; POLITICS [1, 9-12]; RUMANIA; SECURITY, U.S.;SPACE [21-22]

ETHIOPIA—Students expelled. It was reported May 7 that nearly half the students at the national university in Addis Ababa had been expelled by Emperor Haile Selassie's government during the previous three months following student agitation to secure reform of the university and the city's high schools. The report said that Mara Larsen, a U.S. lecturer at the university, and Patrick Gilkes, a Briton and former lecturer, had been expelled from the country in April for attempting to organize a faculty meeting to discuss the unrest.

See also HEALTH; HIJACKING [7]; INTERNATIONAL MONETARY DEVELOPMENTS [9]; OLYMPICS [3]

EUROPEAN ATOMIC ENERGY COMMISSION (EURATOM)—*See* ATOMIC ENERGY [8]; EUROPEAN ECONOMIC COMMUNITY [12]

EUROPEAN ECONOMIC COMMUNITY (EEC or COMMON MARKET)—The six members of the EEC (France, Belgium, West Germany, Italy, the Netherlands and Luxembourg) moved during 1972 toward greater union in economy *(see* [3, 10-11]), money *(see* [10]) and politics *(see* [5, 10]). The community also approved a plan to modernize the agriculture of Common Market members *(see* [4]). The community was enlarged Jan. 22 when Great Britain, Ireland, Denmark and Norway signed the Treaty of Accession which was the first formal step toward their membership in the EEC *(see* [12]). Ireland *(see* [14]), Great Britain *(see* [15-16]) and Denmark *(see* [18]) approved membership in the EEC; but the people of Norway rejected Norwegian membership in a national referendum *(see* [17]).

[2] **U.S. trade pact.** The EEC Council of Ministers Feb. 11 formally approved the terms of a trade agreement reached with the U.S. Feb. 4. The pact gave the U.S. short-term trade concessions on its agricultural imports in return for a U.S. agreement not to plant 26 million acres of wheat and feed grains during the 1972-73 crop year. The concessions won by the U.S. were EEC agreements: to add 1.5 million tons of surplus wheat during the 1972-73 crop year to its wheat stockpile, rather than sell it in competition with the U.S.; to lower tariffs on certain citrus fruit imports in 1972 and 1973; to apply export subsidies to grains to prevent "trade diversions" favoring the EEC; and to make proposed taxes on tobacco "neutral" as between domestic tobacco and imports and to consult with the U.S. before putting the taxes into effect. The EEC's acceptance of the pact had been held up by France's insistence Feb. 7 that the pact be made contingent on future concessions from the U.S. The other EEC countries persuaded France to accept a compromise by which the EEC would orally request U.S. concessions on certain EEC exports when the pact was signed. (In another development in U.S.-EEC relations, the EEC July 31, acting in response to a protest by the U.S., abolished its system of "compensatory levies" on most agricultural products from nonmember countries. The levies had been introduced in May, 1971 to compensate EEC farmers for price disadvantages resulting from changes in world currency exchange rates.)

[3] **Economic union plans approved.** Foreign and finance ministers of the six EEC members March 21 formally approved a plan aimed at economic and monetary union. (The plan had been agreed upon by the finance ministers March 7.) The plan provided for the reduction, effective July 1 on an experimental basis, of fluctuation rate margins among EEC currencies from the present 2.25% to 1.125% above or below the parity rate. A wider margin of 4.5% that was agreed upon in December 1971 would remain in effect between European and foreign currencies. As part of the economic package, the ministers also agreed to create a high-level committee, composed of a representative from each member state, to coordinate short-term economic policies. The six central bank governors of the EEC members April 10 agreed to reduce the fluctuation margins effective April 24, instead of July 1. *(See also* [10].)

[4] **Agricultural accord reached.** The EEC agricultural ministers March 20 began a stormy negotiating session on a farm program. Agreement was reached March 22 on the thorny issue of agricultural border taxes that were used to compensate farmers for losses resulting from the 1971 currency changes. West Germany and France had clashed sharply March 21 over the issue. France had demanded that West Germany set a firm timetable for abolition of the border tax, and West Germany charged that France had reneged on a March 16 agreement in which the EEC agricultural ministers authorized Germany to continue its border taxes and to begin a new program of tax rebates in exchange for an agreement in principle to abolish the border

taxes gradually. The crisis was resolved when France agreed to drop its demand in return for a West German agreement to accept slightly lower price increases for grains. The agricultural ministers March 24 agreed on a program to boost farm prices and implement the Mansholt plan on modernization of the farming system. Under the accord, the guaranteed prices for the 1972-73 crop year would rise 4%-5% for grain and 8% for dairy products. Beef prices would rise 4% immediately, with additional increases to be worked out later. (The ministers agreed July 17-18 on an additional 4% rise, effective Sept. 15.) The increases largely followed a compromise recommended by the EEC Commission, but were lower than the average 8% rise in cereal prices and 12% rise in milk product prices demanded by farmers' organizations. The major price dispute was between France and Germany, with France urging higher prices for beef than for crops to encourage animal production, and Germany seeking to protect its grain farmers with higher grain prices. The EEC ministers March 24 also agreed on proposals to increase farm efficiency, but allocated only $285 million a year for this purpose. As a concession to Italy, the ministers agreed that farmers leaving the land could receive a pension at age 55 in Italy and 60 in the other member nations.

[5] **Report urges stronger Parliament.** The EEC Commission April 5 published a report calling for the direct election of the European Parliament and for stronger legislative powers for the body. The report, which was to be used by the Commission in its formation of proposals for reform of EEC institutions, urged the introduction of the principle of co-decision, in which the European Parliament would be empowered to approve or veto the decisions of the Council of Ministers. Co-decision would be applied at first only to negotiation of trade pacts with nonmember countries, with only a suspensive veto (requiring a second reading in the council) permitted in the areas of agriculture, transport, industrial competition and short-term economic and monetary policy. The report set 1976 as the target date by which ratification by the Parliament would be required in the latter sectors and 1978 as the date by which its approval would be mandatory in all council decisions. The report also proposed that a timetable for introducing universal suffrage in the election of the Parliament should be approved at the same time the Parliament's powers were strengthened.

[6] **VAT delay approved.** The Council of Ministers April 24 approved Italy's request for a six-month postponement of introduction of the value-added tax (VAT) until Jan. 1, 1973. (The VAT was a levy imposed at each stage of the production and distribution of goods. All EEC members except Italy already had introduced the tax.) In return for the delay—Italy's third—Rome agreed to cut the export rebate in its present turnover tax system by 10%-15% July 1. Italy sought the VAT postponement on the grounds that the premature legislative elections (see ITALY [4]) and continuing administrative difficulties made it impossible to implement the scheduled July 1 introduction. (The Italian Cabinet Oct. 17 adopted a decree to introduce the VAT, effective Jan. 1, 1973.)

[7] **Trade preferences extended to 12.** The EEC foreign ministers agreed June 27 to extend generalized trade preferences to 12 developing nations in addition to the 91 already covered. The nations to be included, effective Jan. 1, 1973, were Cuba, Bhutan, Fiji, Bangla Desh, Bahrain, Qatar, Union of Arab Emirates, Oman, Sikkim, Nauru, Western Samoa and Tonga. A decision on requests from Israel, Spain and Rumania for inclusion in the plan was postponed until fall. France opposed their requests because of the relatively higher level of development of the three.

[8] **EFTA trade pacts signed.** The six present and four candidate members (see [12-18]) of the EEC July 22 signed preferential trade pacts, effective Jan. 1, 1973, with the five members of the European Free Trade Association (EFTA) not seeking EEC membership: Switzerland, Sweden, Austria, Portugal and Iceland. The pact with Switzerland also applied to the principality of Liechtenstein, which maintained a 50-year-old customs union with Switzerland

but was not an EFTA member. (Liechtenstein signed the pact.) Finland, the sixth EFTA nation not seeking EEC membership, did not sign its negotiated treaty because of the recent resignation of its government over the accord *(see* FINLAND). The treaties linked about 300 million people in an industrial free trade zone that accounted for more than 40% of the world's trade. (Agriculture was generally excluded from the treaties, although Portugal won special arrangements for its fruits, vegetables, cork, wine and tomato paste.) The key provision of the agreements was the reduction of tariffs on most industrial goods traded among the 17 nations by 20% annually from April 1, 1973 to July 1, 1977, when they would disappear. The transitional timetable for Iceland and Portugal would be extended to Jan. 1, 1980, and tariff reductions on "sensitive" products (e.g. special steels and paper) would be subject to slower timetables. Iceland's treaty provided for the duty-free sale of fish and fish products to the EEC, conditional on a satisfactory solution to the dispute over Iceland's unilateral extension of its fishing limits to 50 nautical miles *(see* TERRITORIAL WATERS). (Iceland did not sign final documents on the pacts Dec. 21 when the other nations did.) Rules of origin under the treaties would be comparable to those already applied by EEC member states and in the community's preferential agreements with other states. Under the rules of origin, there were limitations on the extent to which components from third countries could be present in the goods traded.

[9] Egyptian trade pact signed. The EEC Oct. 5 signed a five-year preferential trade pact with Egypt, effective upon its ratification by the Council of Ministers and the Egyptian government. (It was ratified by the council Oct. 9.) Negotiations between the EEC and Egypt had been delayed for two years because of Egypt's at least nominal acceptance of the Arab League's boycott of firms dealing with Israel. The stalemate was circumvented by an ambiguous formula in which Egypt would declare that the pact would not affect its national security regulations and at the same time would promise that these regulations would conform with the trade agreement. The last obstacle to signing of the accord had been eliminated July 20 when the EEC foreign ministers agreed to a 20% reduction of tariffs on rice imports from Egypt. The major details of the accord had been worked out April 27-28. Under the accord, the EEC would grant a 45% tariff reduction to Egyptian industrial exports Jan. 1, 1973 and a further 10% cut a year later. The tariff reductions would apply to Egyptian oil products and cotton textiles, but annual quotas for those products would remain in effect. Egyptian agricultural exports to the EEC would be given tariff cuts of between 20% and 50%; citrus fruit tariffs would be cut 60%. In return, Egypt would cut tariffs 30% on some EEC industrial exports in 1973 and 10% in each of the following two years.

[10] Summit reaffirms 1980 union goal. Leaders of the six members of the EEC, Ireland, Great Britain and Denmark Oct. 21 committed themselves to a tentative schedule for achieving economic, monetary and some degree of political union by 1980. The commitment came following two days of summit talks among EEC heads of state and foreign ministers in Paris. As the next step toward economic and monetary union, the nine approved April 1, 1973 a previously decided agreement to create a European monetary cooperation fund. The fund, to be run by central bank governors, would be designed initially to coordinate operations in the maintenance of currency fluctuation margins among members. The summit also asked for a report from central bank governors by Sept. 30, 1973 on increasing short-term resources of the fund and for another report by Dec. 31, 1973 on the pooling of central bank resources. Jan. 1, 1974 was envisaged as the target date for commencing the scheduled second phase of European economic and monetary union. Among other points of the summit communique: a report would be prepared by 1975 on what European union should entail, with another summit held that year to consider the report; a fund of undetermined size would be created by the end of 1973 to aid the EEC's economically underdeveloped regions; EEC finance ministers were authorized to adopt short-term concrete measures to curb inflation *(see* [11])*; and the nine countries agreed to maintain a "common attitude" in forthcoming international monetary and trade talks. In a declaration of political intentions accompanying the communique, the leaders pledged to: raise living standards without pursuing expansion at the needless expense of environmental and nonmaterial human needs; develop more social programs; coordinate foreign policy objectives; and increase aid to developing nations.

[11] *Anti-inflation plan adopted.* The six finance ministers of the EEC, meeting in Luxembourg Oct. 30-31, adopted a nonbinding anti-inflationary program aimed at reducing price increases from an average 6% annually to 4%. (The ministers of Britain, Denmark and Ireland associated themselves with the objectives of the plan, but said they would decide on how to enact the plan only after taking into account their respective internal situations after entry.) The ministers also agreed to: restrict the growth in money supplies to the increase in the real gross national products (GNPs) of each state, plus the allowed 4% price rise; hold government spending rises to the GNP rates of increase; and urge "concerted action" against inflation between government, labor and industry in each nation. The ministers also halved the tariffs on beef until Feb. 1, 1973; abolished import quotas on potatoes for a year, effective Dec. 15; and decided in principle to stimulate competition and attack concentrations of industrial power. (The EEC Commission had proposed total abolition of beef tariffs; and across-the-board 15% tariff reduction on other products for a six-month period, effective Jan. 1, 1973; and a 20% increase in industrial import quotas except textiles, to last six months. The French had opposed the across-the-board cut, arguing that it would weaken the EEC position in world trade negotiations.)

Membership

[12] **Treaty of Accession signed.** The six EEC members and four applicants for membership (Great Britain, Ireland, Denmark and Norway) Jan. 22 signed the Treaty of Accession to create an enlarged EEC. The occasion represented a successful outcome to nearly 19 months of intensive negotiations. The documents comprising the treaty were: the brief treaty providing for the entry of the four applicants into the EEC and the European Atomic Energy Community; a decision made earlier Jan. 22 by the Council of Ministers on the entry of the applicants into the European Coal and Steel Community; and the draft accord setting out conditions of entry and the transitional arrangements by which the four would adapt to the EEC rules. The treaty was to go into effect Jan. 1, 1973, subject to ratification by the applicant nations, including approval by the Norwegian and Danish parliaments *(see* [17-18]), passage of enabling legislation by the British and Irish Parliaments *(see* [14-16]) that would adapt their laws to the EEC rules and approval in referendums slated for Ireland, Norway and Denmark *(see* [14, 17-18]).

[13] **Enlarged EEC backed.** The French electorate approved the planned enlargement of the EEC in a referendum April 23. The final results of the referendum were: 10,601,645 "yes" votes (67.86% of the valid votes cast); 5,020,683 "no" votes (32.14% of valid votes cast); 11,619,070 abstentions (39.64% of registered French voters); and 2,071,239 blank or spoiled ballots (7.07% of registered voters). The abstention rate was the highest recorded in France since the introduction of universal suffrage in 1848. The combined number of abstentions and spoiled ballots meant that only 36.4% of registered voters had voted "yes" on the referendum question. The results were an apparent rejection of French President Georges Pompidou's frequent appeals during the referendum campaign for a "massive yes" vote. (Pompidou had announced the referendum March 16, in a surprise announcement. He had declared that Britain's entry into the market went "well beyond a simple

widening" of the EEC to the creation of a new Europe. Because of the significance of enlargement of the market, Pompidou said, he felt it his responsibility to ascertain the will of the French people through a referendum.)

[14] **Irish entry approved.** Ireland, by a margin of nearly 5-1, approved entry into the EEC in a national referendum May 10. The final results showed that 1,041,890 (83%) of the 1,253,768 ballots cast favored entry, while about 211,888 (17%) opposed it. About 70% of the registered voters participated in the poll. In the referendum campaign, Prime Minister John Lynch's ruling Fianna Fail party and the major opposition party, Fine Gael, had supported EEC entry. The Labor party, some leaders of the Irish Congress of Trade Unions and the "official" and "provisional" factions of the Sinn Fein—the political branch of the outlawed Irish Republican Army—had opposed entry. Lynch said May 11 that Ireland would work for a strong regional policy within the EEC, implementation of which would transcend the border between the Irish Republic and Northern Ireland. (The Irish Parliament still had to enact enabling legislation to amend the constitution in line with EEC rules. Both houses of Parliament Sept. 26 approved the VAT, effective Nov. 1.)

[15] **English Parliament approves entry.** The House of Lords Sept. 20 approved the bill enabling Britain to enter the EEC, thereby completing the required parliamentary process. The legislation was to be enacted after it received the royal assent. The bill, which adapted British law to EEC rules, had been given final approval by the House of Commons July 13 after stormy conflict between the ruling Conservative party and the opposition Labor party over its adoption. The Commons approval came on the third reading of the bill. The Conservatives had won an unexpectedly close (309-301) Commons vote on the second reading of the bill Feb. 17. The second reading victory had followed a warning by Prime Minister Edward Heath that his government would resign and new elections would be held if the bill were defeated. Labor opposition to EEC membership had led April 10 to the resignation of Roy Jenkins, a firm supporter of Britain's entry, as the Labor party's deputy leader. The resignation of Jenkins (who was replaced by Edward Short April 25) was followed April 10 by the resignations of Harold Lever and George Thomson as the party's spokesmen on power and fuel and on defense, respectively. Lord Chalfon resigned April 11 as foreign affairs and defense spokesman in the House of Lords; Dick Taverne resigned April 11 as a lower echelon spokesman on financial affairs; David Owen resigned April 11 as spokesman on the navy; Dr. Dickson Mahon resigned April 12 as spokesman on Scotland; and Robert MacLennan resigned April 13 as defense spokesman. The resignations plunged the Labor party into its most serious crisis in years.

[16] The bill enabling entry excluded many explicit details of the transition to EEC rules, which would be covered by subsequent orders issued directly by the government. However, the government was barred from issuing orders that would increase taxes, create new criminal offenses or confer new powers on the executive branch of the government. Orders with retroactive effect also were prohibited. The key provision of the bill, Clause 2, stated that EEC "rights, powers, liabilities, obligations and restrictions" would prevail over existing British law "without further enactment" and would be "enforced, allowed and followed accordingly." Among other provisions, the bill repealed and amended a long list of Britain's customs and farming rules and provided for establishment of an agricultural intervention board which would implement EEC agricultural policy in Britain and oversee the collection of EEC agricultural levies. (The Commons April 18 had defeated an amendment to the bill which called for a referendum on Britain's entry to the EEC.)

[17] **Norway vetoes entry.** The Norwegian electorate decisively rejected entry into the EEC in a national referendum held Sept. 24-25. While the referendum was technically nonbinding, parliament was likely to abide by the poll when it made the final decision on entry. The vote plunged the nation into a political crisis, and Premier Trygve Bratteli announced Sept. 27 that his minority government would resign Oct. 6 *(see* NORWAY). The government had campaigned hard for entry. Official results of the referendum indicated that 53.6% (1,094,950 voters) had opposed entry, while 46.4% (949,489) had supported it. Slightly more than 75% of those eligible voted. The campaign leading up to the referendum had been bitter, with the electorate sharply divided. Pro-market forces (including industrialists, bankers and almost all labor leaders, major political parties and newspapers) had even enlisted West German Chancellor Willy Brandt, who had campaigned in Oslo Sept. 14 for Norwegian membership. Those opposed to entry included fisherman who feared it would insure EEC members access to Norwegian waters, farmers who thought they would lose income with EEC pricing policies, conservative nationalists, young radicals who opposed capitalist domination and left-wing trade unionists who wanted closer ties with Communist East Europe. The EEC Commission Sept. 26 rejected Norway's request for immediate negotiation of a free trade agreement similar to those signed with the EFTA nations *(see* [8]). The Commission said that talks on such an accord could not start before 1973. Norway Dec. 4 formally asked the EEC for a free trade agreement on industrial goods. The request called for elimination of tariffs on the same schedule as negotiated for Norway's membership in the community.

[18] **Denmark approves membership.** Danish voters overwhelmingly approved EEC entry in a binding national referendum Oct. 2. (The Danish Parliament had approved entry Sept. 8.) The victory for pro-market forces was unexpectedly strong, particularly in light of the Norwegian rejection the previous week. The final count was 1,955,932 (63.5%) in favor of membership and 1,124,106 (36.5%) opposed. 89.8% of those eligible voted. Danish farmers voted massively in favor of entry, primarily because they did not want to be cut off from their biggest customer, Great Britain. Other pro-market groups included industrialists, financiers and most newspapers. Membership foes included small farmers, radical intellectuals, youth organizations, rightist and leftist splinter groups and the two largest unions—the metal workers and semi-skilled workers. The referendum campaign was unusually bitter for Denmark, splitting the Federation of Danish Trade Unions and the ruling Social Democratic party as well as other parties. The government had warned of economic hardship, stern austerity policies and devaluation of the kroner if membership were rejected.

See also FINLAND; FRANCE [1]; GERMANY, WEST [9]; GREAT BRITAIN [2-3]; INTERNATIONAL MONETARY DEVELOPMENTS [6]; NORWAY

EUROPEAN FREE TRADE ASSOCIATION (EFTA)—*See* EUROPEAN ECONOMIC COMMUNITY [8, 17]

EUROPEAN SECURITY—Helsinki talks. Representatives of 34 nations (including the U.S. and Canada) met in Helsinki, Finland Nov. 22-Dec. 15 for talks designed to prepare the way for holding a European security conference in June 1973. (The talks were adjourned for one month Dec. 15.) Fifteen North Atlantic Treaty Organization (NATO) members and seven Warsaw Pact states sent representatives to the opening session of the talks. Twelve other countries—including Switzerland, San Marino, Malta, Liechtenstein, Cyprus and the Vatican—also sent representatives. The conference was expected to formulate a European policy on such matters as economic and political relations and the freer movement of people and information. Dr. Richard Totterman, secretary general of the Finnish Foreign Ministry, was elected chairman of the talks Nov. 22. Substantive discussions were held up for the following few days by the Rumanian delegation's insistence on settlement of procedural questions—including decision-making by consensus, election of a vice-chairman on a rotating basis and a declaration that countries were participating in the talks "irrespective of membership in military alliances."

(Delegates agreed Nov. 28 to state that the talks were being held "outside military alliances.") Delegates made general policy statements Nov. 29-Dec. 7 and then turned to planning the security conference. Although there was no agreement by adjournment on the manner in which a full-scale conference should be organized, there were indications of support for a conference in three stages: a meeting of foreign ministers, detailed work by appointed commissions and a second foreign ministers' meeting to approve the results.

Invitations sent for troop reduction talks. The U.S. and other NATO countries Nov. 16 sent invitations to the Soviet Union and its Warsaw Pact allies to attend exploratory talks Jan. 31, 1973, with a view to holding a full conference between August and October of that year on the mutual and balanced reduction of forces in Central Europe. The NATO foreign ministers, at a meeting May 30-31, originally had wanted to hold force reduction talks either before or parallel to the European security conference. The NATO Council Oct. 23 had accepted the timetable for the force reduction talks reflected in the invitations sent in November. (The timetable had been worked out by U.S. Presidential adviser Henry Kissinger during a visit to Moscow in September.)

See also FOREIGN POLICY; GERMAN CONSULTATIONS; NORTH ATLANTIC TREATY ORGANIZATION; POLAND; SOVIET-U.S. RELATIONS [6]

EUROPEAN SPACE RESEARCH ORGANIZATION (ESRO)—*See* SPACE [24]
EUROPEAN STEEL & COAL COMMUNITY—*See* EUROPEAN ECONOMIC COMMUNITY [12]; TARIFFS & WORLD TRADE
EXPLO '72—*See* CHURCHES
EXPORT-IMPORT BANK (EXIMBANK)—*See* SOVIET-U.S. RELATIONS [12]
EXTORTION—*See* AVIATION; HIJACKING [1-13]; MIDDLE EAST [29]; OLYMPIC TERRORISM

FAMINE—*See* AFGHANISTAN; FOREIGN POLICY; INDIA [6]
FAULKNER, BRIAN—*See* NORTHERN IRELAND [3, 10, 18]
FAUNTROY, WALTER E.—*See* ELECTIONS [3]
FEDERAL AVIATION ADMINISTRATION (FAA)—*See* HIJACKING [14]

FEDERAL BUREAU OF INVESTIGATION (FBI)—Stolen papers printed. "A virtually complete collection" of 271 documents on political surveillance stolen from the FBI's Media, Pa. office in March 1971 was printed in the March issue of *Win,* an antiwar magazine, which received the documents from the secret Citizens' Commission to Investigate the FBI. The documents, some of which had been released earlier, detailed FBI surveillance of peace, student and black groups. According to a statement by the commission in the *Win* article, over 200 documents concerned "left or liberal" groups, while only two referred to "right-wing" groups (the Philadelphia branches of the Ku Klux Klan and the Jewish Defense League). Responding to Justice Department charges that the documents previously released overemphasized the proportion of FBI activity devoted to political surveillance, the commission said that about half the substantive documents from among the 800 stolen pertained to this area, equal to the attention paid all criminal activities and military desertion together.

    Informer charges use as provocateur. Robert W. Hardy, an informer who aided the FBI in August 1971 draft office raids in Camden, N.J., said in an affidavit filed March 15 in U.S. District Court in Camden that he had been used by the bureau as a "provocateur," without whom the raid could never have taken place. Hardy's affidavit was filed in support of a pretrial motion to dismiss charges against 20 defendants, for breaking and entering federal property and stealing and destroying federal records, and against eight others charged with conspiring and abetting the crimes. The affidavit said the plot had been abandoned before Hardy first reported it to the FBI and that the FBI had paid him about $60 a day plus expenses thereafter to keep the agency posted, to help plan the raid and to provide tools, instructions and supplies. Hardy's purchases, reimbursed by the FBI, included groceries and the van and gasoline used in the raid. They also included "90% of the tools necessary for the action," which the defendants couldn't afford. According to Hardy, he also trained the defendants in the use of some of the tools and provided them with diagrams of the draft office and the entire federal building in which the draft office was located. In explaining why he was filing the affidavit, Hardy said the FBI had first told him that arrests would take place before the building was

153

actually entered, limiting the charges to conspiracy and ruling out jail terms. He was later told by the FBI that "the higher-ups, someone at the Little White House in California," which Hardy "took to mean someone high in the FBI or in the Justice Department, then in California, wanted it to actually happen."

Hoover dies. J. Edgar Hoover, 77, the first and only director of the FBI, died in his Washington home May 2 of the effects of high blood pressure. At the time of his death, Hoover was in his 48th year as director of the FBI. Under his aegis, the bureau had become one of the most efficient and controversial organizations in America's law enforcement history. During his tenure, Hoover served eight presidents and 16 attorneys general. Hoover's body lay in state in the Capitol Rotunda May 3, marking the first time a civil servant had been honored in a way generally reserved for presidents, military heroes and congressmen. Hoover's body was removed May 4 to the National Presbyterian Church, where he was a lifelong member, for a funeral service. Following the service, Hoover's body was taken to the Congressional Cemetery for burial.

Gray named interim director. President Nixon May 3 named Patrick Gray 3rd, the No. 2 man in the Justice Department and a long-time friend of Nixon, to serve as acting director of the FBI until Nov. 7, after the Presidential elections. The White House attributed Nixon's decision to a desire to keep the appointment apart from politics in an election year. The President's decision, however, evoked some displeasure from Senate Democrats, who had expected to have a chance to confirm a new FBI director. (As interim director, Gray did not need Senate confirmation.) The White House said that Gray would function in two roles—as acting FBI director and as assistant attorney general in charge of civil division. Gray had been nominated to replace Richard G. Kleindienst as deputy attorney general when the latter was selected to be attorney general *(see* NIXON, RICHARD MILHOUS; POLITICS [3-7]). With his new FBI assignment, Gray's nomination as deputy attorney general was withdrawn.

Bureau to recruit women. Gray announced May 11 that, for the first time in the bureau's history, it would recruit women for positions as special agents. (Under Hoover's directorship, the only women in the bureau were employed in secretarial and clerical capacities.) Gray also said that decisions had been made on efforts to recruit more minority group members, a liberalization of dress codes, establishment of a "director's consulting group" (made up of educators, congressmen, law enforcement personnel, social scientists and others—all from outside the bureau) and establishment of a "director's staff group" to plan short- and long-range policy.

See also CIVIL DISORDERS; CRIME [1, 4]; ELECTIONS [25]; ESPIONAGE; HIJACKING [2-7]; INDIANS, AMERICAN; ISRAEL; MINES; OLYMPIC TERRORISM; POLITICS [6, 8-9]; SECURITY, U.S.

FEDERAL BUREAU OF PRISONS—*See* SECURITY, U.S.
FEDERAL COMMUNICATIONS COMMISSION (FCC)—*See* BUSINESS; SPACE [23]; TELEVISION & RADIO [3, 7, 9, 11]
FEDERAL CORRUPT PRACTICES ACT OF 1926—*See* ELECTIONS [47]
FEDERAL ELECTION CAMPAIGN ACT OF 1971—*See* ELECTIONS [46-47, 49]
FEDERAL HOUSING AUTHORITY (FHA)—*See* HOUSING; STATE & LOCAL GOVERNMENTS
FEDERAL POWER COMMISSION (FPC)—*See* CIVIL RIGHTS [1, 16]
FEDERAL RESERVE BOARD (FRB)—*See* BANKS; ECONOMY [9]
FEDERAL TRADE COMMISSION (FTC)—*See* BUSINESS; CONSUMER AFFAIRS [1, 6]; EDUCATION [6]; HEALTH
FEDERATION OF ARAB REPUBLICS—*See* MIDDLE EAST [17, 33]; SYRIA
FIJI—*See* EUROPEAN ECONOMIC COMMUNITY [7]; INTERNATIONAL MONETARY DEVELOPMENTS [8]
FINANCE COMMITTEE TO RE-ELECT THE PRESIDENT—*See* ELECTIONS [47]

FINLAND—Legislative elections. Legislative elections Jan. 2-3 marked slight gains for leftist parties, but still gave non-Socialist parties a 108-92 majority in parliament. The election results (previous parliamentary representation in parentheses): Social Democrats 25.8% of the vote, 55 seats (52); Communists 17.1%, 37 seats (36); Centrists 16.5%, 36 seats (36); Conservatives 17.5%, 34 seats (37); Country party 9.2%, 18 seats (18); Liberals 5.1%, 7 seats (8); Christian party 2.5%, 3 seats (1); Swedish People's party 5.3%, 10 seats (12). The elections had been called after the center-left government resigned in October 1971 because of a dispute over agricultural policy.

Paasio forms minority government. Rafael Paasio, a former premier and leader of the Social Democrats, Feb. 22 formed a minority government composed only of his party. The Cabinet was sworn in Feb. 23 to replace the caretaker government of Teuvo Aura, which had governed since the government resigned in 1971. Negotiations to form a coalition government had begun in January, but faltered over a dispute between the Social Democrats and the Centrists about agricultural policy, with the Centrists backing farmers' demands for more money. President Urho Kekkonen Feb. 9 had asked Paasio to form a five-party center-left government, but this effort also faltered when the Communists withdrew from the negotiations Feb. 16 on the grounds that they could not accept the proposed coalition program. The effort was given the final death blow Feb. 21 when Paasio said his party could not accept the "new demands" of the Centrists. Kekkonen then asked him to form a minority government. The new Cabinet: premier—Paasio; foreign affairs—Kalevi Sorsa; interior—Martii Viitanen; finance—Mauno Koivisto; agriculture and forestry—Leo Happonen; labor—Veikko Helle; education—Ulf Sundkvist; justice—Pekka Paavola; industry—Seppo Lindblom; defense—Sulo Hostila; trade—Jussi Linnamo; communication—Valde Nevalainen; social affairs and health—Osmo Kaipainen; head of the Chancellery—Matti Louekoski.

Cabinet resigns. The five-month-old Cabinet resigned July 19, calling for the formation of a majority government to sign the recently negotiated free trade accord with the European Economic Community *(see* EUROPEAN ECONOMIC COMMUNITY [8]). Paasio declared that a minority regime should not have responsibility for such a momentous decision. He said the resignation was also prompted by a domestic political stalemate.

New coalition Cabinet. Former Foreign Minister Sorsa, secretary general of the Social Democrats, was sworn in Sept. 4 as premier of a four-party coalition Cabinet composed of the Social Democratic, Centrist, Liberal and Swedish People's parties. The major stumbling block in the negotiations for a new government had been resolved Aug. 29 when the Centrists accepted Sorsa's compromise offer on financing a general increase in pensions. The same day, President Kekkonen had named Sorsa to form a new coalition. The new Cabinet retained Education Minister Sundkvist and Trade Minister Linnamo. Communications Minister Nevalainen became labor minister, and Head of the Chancellery Louekoski became justice minister. The other members of the Cabinet (party initials in parentheses): foreign affairs and deputy premier— Ahti Karjalainen (C); finance—Johannes Virolainen (C); interior—Heikki Tuominen (non-political); industry—Grels Teir (SP); agriculture—Erkki Haukipuro (C); defense—Kristian Gestrin (SP); transport—Pekka Tarjanne (L); social affairs and health—Seija Karkkinen (SD).

See also EUROPEAN ECONOMIC COMMUNITY [8]; EUROPEAN SECURITY; POLLUTION [13]; TERRITORIAL WATERS

FIRES—See CONSUMER AFFAIRS [10]; DRAFT & WAR PROTEST; EARTHQUAKES; MINES; SHIPS & SHIPPING; STUDENT UNREST
FISCHER, BOBBY—See CHESS
FISHING—See CONSERVATION; ENVIRONMENT; PERU; TERRITORIAL WATERS
FLANIGAN, PETER—See POLITICS [5]

FLOODS—107 die in West Virginia. Coal mine waste waters Feb. 26 burst through a 200-foot-high pile of coal mine wastes serving as a makeshift dam and enveloped a valley in Logan County, W. Va. containing 14 mining communities. President Nixon Feb. 27 declared the valley a major disaster area. The death toll reached 107 March 6, with 57 persons still missing. The waste pile, accumulated since 1955 and cited constantly as a source of danger, had given way after three days of torrential rains. Otto Mutters, a deputy sergeant in Man (one of the 14 towns in the valley), attempted to warn residents after he received an anonymous telephone call that the dam was about to give way, but his warnings went unheeded. Ben Tudor, assistant superintendent of the Buffalo Mining Co., a subsidiary of the New York-based Pittston Co., which owned the mine, said Feb. 28 that his firm had made attempts for a year to get permission from the West Virginia Department of Natural Resources, to drain water from the dam. The requests, he said, were refused because "they were too concerned about the trout downstream." (Several investigations of the dam's collapse took place. Among charges made during the investigations: William R. Waymont, the head of an Interior Department investigating team, said May 11 that the U.S. Bureau of Mines had been negligent in failing to inspect the dam regularly as required by federal regulations and could have acted to prevent the use of waste accumulations as a dam; Hollis M. Dole, the Interior Department's assistant secretary for mineral resources, testified March 15 at a House subcommittee hearing that the dam was built and maintained in violation of both state and federal statutes; and a report by the Army Corps of Engineers, released May 29, said the dam "should never have been built.")

Rapid City flooded. A flash flood swept through Rapid City, S.D. June 10 after 10 inches of rain fell June 9-10 and two earth dams between the city and the Black Hills resort area to the west collapsed. Two waves of water swept through the city in the worst flood disaster since 1937, causing 226 deaths and $120 million in damage to the city and nearby towns. The damage included the destruction of over 600 homes and 300 mobile homes. By July 3, 124 persons were still missing. President Nixon June 10 declared Rapid City a disaster area. The Agriculture Department the same day announced that food stamps would be available to flood victims. The Department of Housing and Urban Development June 13 began setting up temporary trailer housing for some 2,000 homeless families.

Flood relief bills. President Nixon Aug. 20 signed a $1.6 billion flood relief bill which he said was the "largest single appropriation for disaster relief in our history." The bill—passed unaminously by the House Aug. 15 and by the Senate Aug. 16 on a voice vote—provided $1.3 billion for Small Business Administration (SBA) loans and $17.5 million for construction projects and flood control activities undertaken by the Army Corps of Engineers (an amount the President had not requested). The Senate, on a voice vote Aug. 11, and the House, by a 359-1 vote Aug. 14, had approved a bill reducing the interest rate and loosening restrictions on SBA loans. The bill, signed by the President Aug. 17, would permit 30-year loans at 1% interest with the first $5,000 of the principal forgiven.

30 die in Peruvian floods. An estimated 30 persons were killed and more than 150,000 were injured in floods and avalanches that swept along Peru's Pacific coastline, according to a report March 23. The floods followed torrential rains in the Andes Mountains. Hardest hit was the northern state of Piura, on the Ecuadorian border, which was declared an emergency area and placed under military rule. The cities of Chimbote (Peru's largest fishing port), Canete, Catacaos and Palpa were flooded. The Pan American Highway was closed in several areas north and south of Lima, leaving some cities virtually isolated and cutting off their supplies of food and gasoline.

37 killed in Mexico. A thunderstorm accompanied by flash flooding May 3 killed at least 37 people and left 100,000 homeless in Mexico City. More victims were feared buried under mud and rocks which had swept down from hills surrounding the city.

See also INDOCHINA WAR [23]; STORMS

FOOD & DRUG ADMINISTRATION (FDA)—*See* CONSUMER AFFAIRS [1-4, 7, 9, 11-14, 16-17]; DRUG USE & ADDICTION [8]
FOOD PRICES—*See* ECONOMY [5]; POPULATION
FOOD STAMPS—*See* BUDGET; ELECTIONS [33]; FLOODS; WELFARE

FOOTBALL—College. *Bowl Games.* Jan. 1: Orange Bowl (Miami)—Nebraska 38, Alabama 6; Rose Bowl (Pasadena, Calif.)—Stanford 13, Michigan 12; Cotton Bowl (Dallas)—Penn State 30, Texas 6; Sugar Bowl (New Orleans)—Oklahoma 40, Auburn 22.

NCAA removes freshman ban. The National Collegiate Athletic Association (NCAA), in a surprise move at its convention in Hollywood, Fla., voted Jan. 8 to give major colleges permission to let freshmen play varsity football, effective Aug. 1. The new rule was permissive and not mandatory. It did not affect NCAA members with small-school status, since they already were allowed to use freshmen in their football programs.

Professional. *Dallas wins Super Bowl.* The Dallas Cowboys pierced the Miami Dolphins' defense Jan. 16 to score a 24-3 triumph in the sixth Super Bowl game before 81,023 fans in Tulane Stadium in New Orleans. It was the second consecutive Super Bowl appearance for the Cowboys, who had lost to Baltimore in 1971. Dallas, coached by Tom Landry, had captured the National Football League's (NFL) National Conference title Jan. 2 in Irving, Tex. by defeating the San Francisco 49ers, 14-3. The Dolphins, coached by Don Shula, had won the NFL's American Conference crown Jan. 2 in Miami by shutting out the Baltimore Colts, 21-0.

Pro Bowl. The American Conference all-stars defeated the National Conference all-stars, 26-13, Jan. 23 in the 22nd annual NFL Pro Bowl game in Los Angeles. The American Conference's victory evened the series at 1-1 since the format of the game was changed in 1971 to pit American Conference stars against National stars.

Cowboys trip All-Stars. The Dallas Cowboys July 29 thoroughly outplayed a team of collegiate players in the annual All-Star game in Chicago. The Cowboys won 20-7. The Cowboys' defense dominated the game, allowing the collegians only a fourth-quarter touchdown.

Owners swap Colts, Rams. In a deal unprecedented in professional team sports, Carroll Rosenbloom, the owner of the Baltimore Colts, July 13 traded his entire team to Robert J. Irsay, the owner of the Los Angeles Rams, for his club. The personnel of both the clubs were to remain the same; only the ownerships were to change. Rosenbloom would save $4.4 million in capital gains taxes by the swap. Irsay first bought the stock of the Rams for $19 million. He then swapped his Rams to Rosenbloom for the Colts in a no-cash transaction.

FOREIGN AID—Authorization bill. The House of Representatives Jan. 25 approved and sent to the President by a 203-179 vote a bill authorizing a foreign aid program at the $2.752 billion level ($1.518 billion for military assistance) for fiscal 1972 (July 1, 1971 through June 30, 1972). The bill, which authorized about $800 million less than the Administration had requested, also authorized $984 million in fiscal 1973 for economic aid. President Nixon Feb. 7 signed the bill into law, but protested that Congress had set the funding authorizations "below minimum acceptable levels" and had attached to the bill an "unprecedented number of restrictive and nongermane amendments, some of which raise grave constitutional questions." Foreign aid financing for fiscal 1972 had been stymied by a Senate vote in October 1971 to reject the foreign aid program. Congress later enacted a temporary financing arrangement, at an annual rate of $2.4 billion, that would expire Feb. 22.

Amendments. The amendments to the bill included: a ban against aid to Pakistan except for food and humanitarian assistance through international agencies; a $341 million ceiling on aid to Cambodia; the earmarking of $250 million for relief of East Pakistani refugees; a curb against aid to Greece without a presidential declaration that it was in the national interest; a 15% cut in U.S. military missions abroad; an obligation on a recipient nation to pay 10% of the value of aid in its own currency, to be used for educational and cultural exchange purposes; notification of Congress if the Administration shifted funds from one country to another; and the release of some $2.8 billion in impounded funds for domestic programs by April 30 or a withholding of the foreign aid funds. President Nixon Feb. 14 notified Congress that the restriction against aid to Pakistan no longer applied since conditions in Pakistan were returning to normal and since Pakistan was no longer responsible for conditions in Bangla Desh (formerly East Pakistan).

Appropriations bill. The House Feb. 24 (by a vote of 213-167) and the Senate March 2 (by a 45-36 vote) passed a conference bill appropriating $2,618,221,000 for the fiscal 1972 foreign aid program. The bill, signed by the President March 9, provided $1.45 billion for military aid programs—$500 million for military grant aid, $550 million for security-supporting assistance ($50 million earmarked for Israel) and $400 million for military credit sales funds ($300 million earmarked for Israel). The bilateral economic aid program was funded with a total of $1,168,221,000. With $571,216,000 appropriated for related international programs, the bill's total appropriations were $3,189,437,000—$1.2 billion less than the Administration's fiscal 1972 budget request.

Fiscal 1973 funding. Both houses of Congress Oct. 17 passed a foreign aid appropriations bill in the form of a resolution allowing a temporary funding of the aid program until Feb. 28, 1973 at an annual level of $3.65 billion. The total funding was $1,510,323,000 less than the Administration had requested, $542,454,000 less than the House had voted Sept. 21, but $828,804,000 more than the Senate had voted Sept. 28. (The Senate had acted only to appropriate economic aid.) The appropriations bill had been stalled in conference by House and Senate differences over a foreign aid authorization bill. The differences, based on two Senate Foreign Relations Committee amendments proposed by Sen. Clifford Case (R, N.J.), resulted Oct. 11 in the conferees abandoning their efforts to pass the authorization bill in the current congressional session. The two amendments dealt with the long-standing debate between Presidential prerogatives and the Senate's role in foreign policy-making. One amendment would have barred appropriations for a 1971 U.S.-Portugal agreement, signed by the President, which permitted establishment of an Air Force base in the Azores Islands. Case sought to have the executive agreement considered a treaty, requiring Senate approval. The second proposal would have denied funds to implement any future foreign agreement for military base rights without Senate approval of the pact. (President Nixon Oct. 28 signed a bill allowing continuing emergency appropriations to the foreign aid program and to all government units whose regular fund bills had not passed Congress or had been vetoed.)

See also ARMAMENTS, INTERNATIONAL; DRUG USE & ADDICTION [15]; FOREIGN POLICY; MALTA; PAKISTAN [2-4]; PESTICIDES; TERRITORIAL WATERS; UGANDA [10, 12]

FOREIGN POLICY—Tougher stand on expropriations. President Nixon Jan. 19 announced that the U.S. would follow a tougher policy against nations that expropriated U.S. property without paying adequate and swift compensation. He said that, in most cases except in overriding interests of national policy, the U.S. would grant no new economic aid to those countries and would oppose loan grants by international lending agencies. The new policy, which would not be retroactive, would not apply to aid for "humanitarian assistance," such as earthquake or famine relief. To carry out the policy, the President established an inter-agency group under the Council on International Economic Policy to review each case and recommend courses of action. The policy statement appeared to be directed largely at Latin American countries—including Chile,

Peru, Ecuador and Bolivia—which had expropriated U.S. holdings estimated by their owners to be worth $500 million-$1 billion. The policy was said to represent a compromise between the Treasury Department, which had consistently pressed for a tougher stand against expropriating countries, and the State Department, which had said that no U.S. action could stop a nation bent on expropriation.

State of World message. President Nixon's third annual State of the World message, delivered to Congress Feb. 9, viewed 1971 as a "breakthrough" year in which U.S. initiatives constituted "a profound change in America's new world role." "The heart of our new conception of that role," he said, "is a more balanced alliance with our friends—and a more creative connection with our adversaries." The major focus of the report was on U.S. relations with its "two principal adversaries," the Soviet Union and China. The report also dealt extensively with the arms race, the Soviet role in the Middle East, Japan, the Indian-Pakistani war and international monetary and trade practices. Although the prevailing tone of the report was optimistic—that the U.S. was "once again acting with assurance and purpose on the world stage"—the President listed numerous "disappointments" in the foreign policy area in 1971. The greatest, he said, was the failure to negotiate a Vietnam settlement. Others were the inability: to prevent the Indian-Pakistani war; to "make a breakthrough toward peace" in the Middle East; to "work out with our friends" in Latin America "a solution of the conflict between their desire for our help and their determination to be free of dependence upon us"; to assist adequately, because of Congressional cuts in aid appropriations (see FOREIGN AID), in development of the African nations; and to preserve a United Nations seat for Nationalist China.

In his remarks on the Soviet Union, the President cautioned that competition would likely be "the hallmark of our relationship" for a long time. Despite progress toward arms control, the continuing buildup of Soviet military power was an "obvious source of deep concern," he said. The President also said that the failure of the U.S.S.R. to play a restraining role in the Indian-Pakistani war until late in the war held "dangerous implications for other regional conflicts." However, Nixon also said that there was evidence "that on both sides there is an increasing willingness to break with the traditional patterns of Soviet-American relations." The President also listed "tasks ahead" of the U.S. in dealing with the Soviet Union: an accord on an initial arms limitation agreement (see DISARMAMENT) or on the issues to be discussed in the second stage of SALT negotiations; a discussion of the problems of the Middle East; a discussion of European security and the identification of mutually shared objectives which would provide a basis for further normalization of intercourse between Eastern and Western Europe; an exploration of U.S. and Soviet policies in other areas of the world; and an examination of the possibility of additional bilateral cooperation.

The President also listed the "unfinished business" of the U.S. in foreign affairs: proof, "through additional concrete accomplishments," of the benefits to the U.S. and the U.S.S.R. of self-restraint and accommodation; continuance of the "process of creating a better relationship" with the People's Republic of China; control of the arms race; discovery of "the most effective way to help the poorer nations"; completion, "with our partners," of the construction of a reformed trade and monetary system; continuance of the construction of an international system; and realistic treatment of the fact that the United Nations is facing "a crisis of confidence."

International agreement bill passed. The House of Representatives Aug. 14 passed by a voice vote a measure requiring the President to submit to both houses of Congress the texts of all international agreements. The Senate had approved the measure Feb. 16 by an 81-0 vote. President Nixon signed the bill Aug. 22.

See also BANGLA DESH [1, 13]; CHILE [1, 11]; DRUG USE & ADDICTION [19]; ELECTIONS [16, 23, 34-35]; FOREIGN AID; INDOCHINA WAR; MIDDLE

EAST [31, 34]; NIXON, RICHARD MILHOUS; PAKISTAN [1-3]; POLITICS [8]; SINO-U.S. RELATIONS; SOVIET-U.S. RELATIONS; UGANDA [12]

FRANCE—The government of Premier Jacques Chaban-Delmas was rocked during 1972 by allegations of scandal involving government and Gaullist party members *(see* [7-9]). The allegations, combined with the failure of the government to muster strong support during a referendum for enlarging the European Economic Community *(see* EUROPEAN ECONOMIC COMMUNITY [13]), resulted in the resignation of Chaban-Delmas and his Cabinet *(see* [10]) and the appointment of Pierre Messmer as premier *(see* [10-11]). Despite the change of government, however, allegations of scandal continued *(see* [13]).

[2] **Economic measures.** The Cabinet Jan. 12 announced expansionary measures to stimulate France's lagging economy and halt the growth of unemployment (reportedly up 39% during the preceding 14 months). The measures authorized about $234 million in accelerated reimbursements of the value-added tax (VAT—a tax at each stage in production on the value increased by that stage) to industrial, commercial and agricultural enterprises; the allocation of about $200 million in loans to aid housing construction and a faster expenditure of about $900 million on public works projects. The measures did not entail budget increases. In a later anti-inflationary measure, Finance Minister Valery Giscard d'Estaing announced March 14 a new price program to replace the previous plan, under which industries restricted their price rises to 1.5% over the previous six months. Under the new policy, effective April 1, companies with fewer than 20 employees (accounting for 97.7% of all French companies and 20% of production) would recover total freedom to set their own prices. Other industrial firms would be restricted to 3% annual price increases. The government would increase rates in the public sector in proportion to the private sector increases. The government June 15 exempted from the price controls certain industries subject to stiff international competition. D'Estaing warned industrialists Aug. 30 that they should adhere to the voluntary price control program or they would face stiff mandatory controls. D'Estaing also announced new anti-inflationary measures Aug. 30, including a freeze on prices in the state-controlled sector of the economy until March 31, 1973, a requirement that banks increase their deposits with the Bank of France and plans to ask members of the European Economic Community (EEC) to develop a common anti-inflationary policy and to ease controls to encourage meat imports. In another attack on France's economic problems, d'Estaing Dec. 7 announced that the 7% VAT on meat would be dropped for six months, the VAT on manufactured goods would be cut by 2%, the VAT on pharmaceutical goods would be cut by 3% and the VAT on pastry would be cut by 10%. The potential inflationary effect of the cut in taxes was to be offset by the sale of a 15-year state bond issue worth approximately $1 billion and by a .25% increase in interest rates on savings accounts.

[3] **Prison reforms announced.** In the wake of several devastating prison riots, Justice Minister Rene Pleven Jan. 19 announced a series of prison reforms. The measures included improvement of prison inspection boards, an increase in the staff of judges assigned to follow prisoners throughout their imprisonment, better job training and work payments, social security for prisoners' families, simplification of procedures for probation and work outside prisons, and a definition of prisoners' status to give less discretion to prison wardens. The government also removed the entire staff of the Toul prison, where riots in December 1971 had sparked subsequent outbursts in other jails.

[4] **Barbie extradition sought.** French President Georges Pompidou Feb. 11 sent a personal letter to Bolivian President Hugo Banzer Suarez asking for the extradition of a man thought to be Klaus Barbie, former head of the Nazi Gestapo in Lyons during World War II. (Barbie had been tried in absentia in France for the execution of Jews deported from Lyons, for torturing to death the leading martyr of the French Resistance and for other Nazi crimes.) The accused, known as Klaus Altmann, a German-born naturalized Bolivian

businessman, had been identified as Barbie by Mrs. Beate Klarsfeld, a member of the Central Committee against Anti-Semitism and Racism. Altmann had been identified while he was in Peru. The French government had asked Peru Jan. 28 to arrest and extradite Altmann, who then slipped back to Bolivia. (France had no extradition agreement with Bolivia.) The Bolivian government Aug. 20 announced that it had rejected Pompidou's request for extradition of Altmann. (In an interview published May 20, Altmann had admitted to heading a special command of the German SS Elite Guard in Lyons under the name of Klaus Barbie, but denied French charges of leading the Lyons Gestapo and of responsibility for the murder of French Resistance fighters and Jews.) Bolivia Oct. 18 halted its own prosecution of Barbie, allegedly because of lack of funds for translation of six volumes written in French and German.

[5] **Maoist killed in Renault plant.** Rene-Pierre Overney, a Maoist and former Renault worker dismissed for political activism, was fatally shot Feb. 25 by Jean-Antoine Tramoni, a plainclothes security guard at a state-owned Renault plant in the Paris suburb of Boulogne-Billancourt. The killing, which Tramoni termed accidental, occurred when company guards tried to stop a group of Maoists, including Overney, from forcing their way into the plant. The Maoists were protesting dismissals of workers and distributing pamphlets urging workers to join a protest against discrimination of foreign workers. The incident sparked sharp repercussions among leftist political and trade union circles, all of whom denounced the shooting and the presence of armed security guards at the factory in apparent violation of Renault regulations. However, the Communist party, fearing the impact of extreme leftist violence in 1973 elections, denounced the shooting as a Maoist provocation exploited by the government and the plant management.

[6] Some 10,000-30,000 demonstrators participated in a Paris march staged by leftist extremist groups Feb. 28 to protest the shooting. After the march, police clashed with several hundred young Maoists who had constructed street barricades and set them on fire. The funeral procession for Overney March 4 resulted in the biggest extreme leftist demonstration in Paris since the strikes and protests in May 1968. Police estimated the number of marchers at 18,000, but most estimates set the figure at 50,000-100,000. The march, boycotted by the Communist party and the Communist-dominated General Confederation of Labor (CGT), remained peaceful. In another protest at Overney's death, the Maoist New Popular Resistance March 8 kidnaped Robert Nogrette, a Renault personnel officer. Nogrette was released unharmed March 10 despite government rejection of the group's demands for release of all their comrades arrested since the shooting and the rehiring by Renault of all persons fired in connection with the incident. Every political party and trade union denounced the kidnaping.

[7] **ORTF scandal.** Jean-Jacques de Bresson and Pierre de Leusse resigned May 13 as director general and chairman of the board, respectively, of ORTF, the state-controlled radio and television organization. The resignations came amid a growing scandal over alleged corruption and the use of clandestine advertising by the ORTF. The two officials had been defended May 10 by Premier Chaban-Delmas, who said they had "reacted wisely" to charges of ORTF irregularities disclosed in reports by commissions of the Senate and the National Assembly. Following its own inquiry, the broadcasting system had ordered minor sanctions against nine unidentified producers and executives. The Senate commission report April 26 had charged the government with negligence and accused (by name) leading ORTF producers of arranging free commercial plugs of products and services on a number of popular programs in exchange for illicit payoffs by advertisers. Other abuses mentioned by the report included production of shows for the sole purpose of promoting certain services or places and the increased programming of quiz shows as vehicles to plug the merchandise awarded as prizes. The report suggested that corruption in broadcasting was due to the close tie between the ORTF and the

government. The high cost of official advertising on ORTF programs was cited as a cause for the resort to clandestine advertising. The National Assembly report April 28 had charged the ORTF organizational structure with responsibility for management slack and recommended that ORTF be divided into two separate groups—one responsible for conception and programming of shows, and the other for the technical production and broadcasting.

[8]   In the wake of the scandal, the National Assembly June 16, by a 363-100 vote, and the Senate June 27, by a 176-96 vote, approved a new charter reorganizing the ORTF. The reform, prepared by State Secretary for Civil Service Philippe Malaud (assigned May 4 to investigate ORTF improprieties), involved a decentralization of the organization, with strong control by a newly expanded post of president. However, the state retained its monopoly over the networks. Changes in the charter provided for the appointment of a president-director general (Arthur Conte, named July 12), named by the Cabinet to a three-year term, who would assume direct control of news programs. The board of directors, previously dominated by the government, would be composed of an equal number of government officials on one hand and representatives of the public, the press and ORTF personnel on the other. The ORTF would be broken up into separate administrative authorities, which would run the two existing television channels and a third planned to start in 1973; run the radio network; assume technical responsibility; and produce special programs ordered by the channels. (ORTF personnel had struck June 14 to protest the proposed charter.)

[9]   In other exposures of scandals connected with the government, Andre Rives-Henrys, a Gaullist parliamentary deputy connected with a 1971 real-estate scandal, was sentenced Feb. 12 to a four-month suspended sentence and a fine for using his parliamentary title in advertisements for the Garantie Fonciere real estate firm. Rives-Henrys resigned his parliamentary seat May 15 in the face of threats that his resignation would be demanded. Philippe Dechartre resigned as secretary of state for labor, employment and population May 15 in the wake of his conviction April 13 for his role in a plot to extort money from a building contractor in exchange for issuing a construction permit. *(see also* [10, 13].)

[10]   **Chaban-Delmas dropped.** President Pompidou July 5 accepted the resignation of Premier Chaban-Delmas and replaced him with Messmer, an orthodox member of the Gaullist party, the Union for the Defense of the Republic (UDR), and minister of overseas departments and territories in the outgoing Cabinet. Pompidou indicated that he had, in effect, dismissed Chaban-Delmas and his Cabinet, but gave no detailed explanation. The surprise action was thought to be intended to revitalize the UDR in preparation for legislative elections to be held in March 1973. Many party members were known to have become increasingly hostile to Chaban-Delmas as overly liberal, and Pompidou was known to have been shaken by the government's poor showing in an April referendum on the enlargement of the EEC *(see* EUROPEAN ECONOMIC COMMUNITY [13]). Despite a resounding victory by Chaban-Delmas in a parliamentary confidence vote May 24, the premier's prestige had been tarnished by the recent series of scandals *(see* [7-9]), which included charges that Chaban-Delmas was guilty of tax evasion. (The premier Feb. 15 had denied the charges as "pure and simple invention.")

[11]   *New Cabinet appointed.* Messmer July 6 formed a Cabinet that retained the top ministers in the outgoing Cabinet. The new 30-member Cabinet was composed of 20 ministries (two more than the previous government) and 10 junior ministries (reduced from 18). Retained at their posts were d'Estaing, Pleven, Maurice Schumann (foreign affairs), Raymond Marcellin (interior), Michel Debre (defense), Jacques Duhamel (cultural affairs) and Robert Poujade (environment). The most prominent newcomer was Edgar Faure, a former premier known for his liberal Gaullist orientation, who was appointed head of the new combined Ministry for Social Affairs, Labor and Health. His

appointment was apparently designed to reassure progressive Gaullists in the face of a shift to the orthodox Gaullism represented by Messmer. Other ministerial changes were: education—Joseph Fontanet; supply—Oliver Guichard; agriculture and rural development—Jacques Chirac; minister attached to the Foreign Ministry—Andre Bettencourt; industrial and scientific development—Jean Charbonnel; public health—Jean Foyer; posts and telecommunications—Hubert Germain; trade and small businesses—Yvon Bourges; ex-servicemen—Andre Bord; transport—Robert Galley; parliamentary relations—Robert Boulin.

[12] **Social reform program presented.** Messmer Sept. 6 outlined a social reform program aimed at spreading the benefits of France's growing prosperity. The program provided for an 850-franc increase in old-age and handicapped pensions to 4,500 francs (nearly $900) annually, effective Oct. 1; a lowering of the age at which widows could receive pensions from 65 to 55, effective Jan. 1, 1973; and an end to the differences in rates on family allowances between different locales. The program also envisaged that social security pensions would be reckoned in the near future on the basis of an individual's 10 highest earning years, rather than on the last ten years of earnings, and that supplementary pensions would be extended to more than 600,000 workers, such as domestics, not yet covered by the system. The last two measures would require parliamentary approval. The program, developed by Social Affairs Minister Faure, would cost an estimated 2.5 billion francs (nearly $500 million) and reportedly would be financed without additional taxation. Messmer also promised an increase in the national minimum wage and hinted that the government would encourage faster salary rises for the lowest wage groups than for the average income earners.

[13] **Ex-aide charges corruption.** Gabriel Aranda, press spokesman for former Housing and Equipment Minister Albin Chalandon until both were removed in the July Cabinet shuffle, Sept. 21 submitted to an examining magistrate photocopies of 136 ministry documents that he contended proved 48 politicians were corrupt. The action followed eight days of disclosures by Aranda to the press on alleged corruption. Aranda had warned Sept. 13 that he would expose corruption of leading members of the UDR unless the government halted delivery of Mirage jets to Libya. This demand was later dropped. An examining magistrate Sept. 18 charged Aranda with theft of government documents and then freed him on his own recognizance. Aranda denied that he had stolen the documents, asserting he had merely copied them in accordance with a law prohibiting concealment of crimes. The disclosures produced a storm of controversy and led to demands for government action. In response to charges of corruption made against him by Aranda, Gerard Sibeud, a UDR deputy, resigned from the party Sept. 27. (Two other UDR deputies also resigned from the party in response to charges of scandal, although the scandals were unrelated to the Aranda disclosures. Edouard Charret resigned from the UDR Sept. 10 following accusations of his involvement in a chain of brothels in Lyons. Henri Modiano resigned under strong pressure Oct. 10 following accusations against him for minor offenses in connection with a commercial bankruptcy in 1970.)

[14] **Strike actions.** A series of strikes swept France in October and November. The CGT and the Socialist-dominated French Democratic Confederation of Labor (CFDT) organized a march in Paris Oct. 26, joined by about 20,000 persons, to demand a national minimum wage of 1,000 francs a month and retirement at age 60 with a minimum pension of 800 francs a month. Parades also were staged in Lyons, Marseilles, Bordeaux and other industrial cities. Mine workers and dock workers stopped work for 24 hours in other parts of the country the same day. Railway unions staged a series of rotating strikes throughout France Nov. 14-17 to support demands for higher wages following a breakdown in annual contract talks. A strike of post office and telecommunications workers called by the CGT and CFDT branches of the

Post Office workers' unions was staged Nov. 15. About 10,000 Paris hospital and municipal workers staged a march Nov. 16 to demand wage parity with other national sectors.

See also ARMAMENTS, INTERNATIONAL; ATOMIC ENERGY [8, 13]; AVIATION; CONSERVATION; CONSUMER AFFAIRS [14]; DISARMAMENT; DRUG USE & ADDICTION [13, 18]; ESPIONAGE; EUROPEAN ECONOMIC COMMUNITY [1-2, 4, 7, 11, 13]; GERMAN CONSULTATIONS; HIJACKING [17]; INDOCHINA WAR [25]; INTERNATIONAL MONETARY DEVELOPMENTS [2, 4-6, 9]; LATIN AMERICA; MALAGASY REPUBLIC; MIDDLE EAST [35]; OIL & NATURAL GAS; POLLUTION [13]; RAILROADS; SWITZERLAND

FRANCO, GENERALISSIMO FRANCISCO—*See* SPAIN
FROEHLKE, ROBERT F.—*See* WAR CRIMES
FUEL—*See* OIL & NATURAL GAS
FUNGICIDES—*See* HEALTH; PESTICIDES

GABON—Cabinet shuffles. Paul Moukambi replaced Augustin Boumah as finance minister in a Cabinet reorganization disclosed Feb. 8. Boumah became minister delegate to the presidency in charge of planning. In a Sept. 20 Cabinet shuffle, Minister of Justice Jean-Remy Ayoune left the government and was replaced by Valentin Obame. Minister of Mines Jean-Baptiste Obiang-Ekomie became minister of agriculture and was replaced as minister of mines by Edouard-Alexis Mbouy-Boutzit.

Equatorial Guinea dispute. Gabon Aug. 23 occupied the uninhabited islands of Mbanie and Cocotiers in the Bay of Corisco in a move said to be aimed at protecting Gabonese fishermen. Equatorial Guinea, which laid claim to the islands, Sept. 12 asked for a United Nations Security Council meeting on the seizure and charged Gabon with the occupation of three more Equatorial Guinean islands—Corisco, Elobey Grande and Elobey Chico. Both nations agreed Sept. 18 to a peaceful settlement of the dispute Gabonese President Albert-Bernard Bongo and Francisco Macias Nguema, the Equatorial Guinean leader, met with the leaders of Zaire and the Congo Republic in Brazzaville. The meeting, held under the auspices of the Organization of African Unity, appointed a four-nation commission to determine ownership of Mbanie and Cocotiers. Bongo said Oct. 10, however, that Nguema had "flouted" the decisions taken at Kinshasa.

GAMBIA—Elections. In elections for the House of Representatives held March 29, the first elections since Gambia became a republic in 1970, the People's Progressive party, led by President Sir Dauda Kairaba Jawara, won 28 seats, with the opposition United party gaining three and an independent one. Jawara appointed a new nine-man Cabinet April 6, New ministers were Sir Alhaji Jack, formerly speaker of the House, and Alhadji Momodou Cham, who became minister of information. Howsoon Sennega Janneh, formerly minister of agriculture, was dropped; and three ministers changed portfolios.

Cabinet shuffle. Vice President S. M. Dibba resigned his post Sept. 16, reportedly because of the involvement of a member of his family in a smuggling incident, but retained the finance portfolio. Dibba was replaced as vice president by Foreign Minister Andrew Camara.

See also INTERNATIONAL MONETARY DEVELOPMENTS [8]

GANDHI, INDIRA—*See* BANGLA DESH [4, 11]; INDIA [2-3, 9]; PAKISTAN [12]
GENERAL ACCOUNTING OFFICE (GAO)—*See* DEFENSE; HEALTH CARE; PAKISTAN [3]; SOVIET-U.S. RELATIONS [8]

GENERAL AGREEMENT ON TARIFFS & TRADE (GATT)—*See* TARIFFS & WORLD TRADE
GENEVA CONFERENCE ON DISARMAMENT—*See* ATOMIC ENERGY [13]; DISARMAMENT
GENEVA CONVENTION—*See* VIETNAM, NORTH

GERMAN CONSULTATIONS—East German visits allowed. The East German Communist party Politburo and the Council of Ministers announced Feb. 22 that West Berliners would be allowed to visit East Germany for periods of one week each at Easter and Whitsunday (Pentecost). It was the first time such visits had been allowed since 1966. The visiting periods were March 29-April 5 and May 17-24.

Traffic agreement. West German State Secretary Egon Bahr and his counterpart on the East German Council of Ministers, Michael Kohl, April 26 reached agreement in East Berlin on a treaty governing traffic between the two German states. The Treaty on Transport Questions, initialed in Bonn May 12 and signed in East Berlin May 26, went into effect Oct. 17. The document followed a precedent established in a recent Soviet-West German trade agreement by including West Berlin within the area represented by Bonn *(see* GERMANY, WEST [8]). It regulated all traffic between East and West Germany, except air traffic, and allowed West Germans to visit East Germany as tourists or to see friends and relatives. East Germans were allowed to travel to West Germany "in pressing family matters." Permission to travel between the two countries could be obtained under the pact repeatedly during a year—not just once annually as had been the previous practice. There were no age limits imposed on travel. Kohl remarked April 26 that the pact was the first "state treaty" between East and West Germany that "accords with international usage." (Although the agreement specified that West Berliners wishing to visit the eastern part of the city be given immediate entry for periods of up to 30 days in a year, East German officials in practice required such travelers to stipulate dates for their visits and apply for each trip as long as two days in advance. However, officials of the East German government and the West Berlin city government issued an agreement Oct. 2, effective Oct. 3, enabling West Berliners to obtain visas on request. The agreement also provided for special visiting permits which would allow up to eight one-day trips to East Berlin during a three-month period.)

Four-power accords signed. The foreign ministers of Britain, France, the U.S. and the Soviet Union—the countries with responsibility for the status of Berlin—signed June 3 in West Berlin a comprehensive agreement affecting relations between portions of the divided city. Signing of the "final protocol," which consisted of a main accord and two supplementary pacts negotiated in 1971, had been made the condition for the ratification of West Germany's Eastern treaties *(see* GERMANY, WEST [5-7]) and for progress toward a European security conference *(see* EUROPEAN SECURITY). The full Berlin agreement was not a treaty and did not change the legal status of Berlin. However, it was expected to bring a major improvement in the conditions of travel to and from the city and in the frequency of visits allowed there. Representatives of the four countries Nov. 5 completed work on a declaration affirming their rights and obligations for Berlin and the two German states. The one-paragraph agreement emphasized that the prerogatives of the four powers would not be affected by the expected applications of East and West Germany for United Nations membership.

General treaty completed. Bahr and Kohl Nov. 6 reached agreement on a treaty preparing the way for diplomatic relations between the two Germanys and for eventual admission to the U.N. The two negotiators signed the pact Dec. 21 in East Berlin. The treaty authorized the exchange by the two governments of diplomats who would have the function, but not the rank, of ambassadors. An appendix to the agreement provided for border visits along the frontier; joint control of fire-fighting, drainage and canal traffic; and establishment of new crossing points. The treaty's preamble left open the question of German reunification, declaring only that the two states proceeded "from the historic facts and without detriment to the differing views of" each on "the national question." However, a West German note deposited at the signing of the treaty expressed hope that the two states eventually could join by peaceful means. Other sections of the treaty pledged the two states to "develop normal good-neighborly relations," refrain from "the threat or the use of force" and respect their common border.

See also GERMANY, WEST [6-7, 12]; SOVIET-U.S. RELATIONS [6]

GERMANY, EAST (GERMAN DEMOCRATIC REPUBLIC)—Social reform approved. Government approval of an extensive social reform program was reported April 30. The program involved government expenditures of $2.5 billion through 1975 and called for an increase in pensions and social assistance for 3.4 million citizens and a decrease of rent in modern apartments for families earning less than 2,000 marks (about $700) annually. The plan also provided 600 million marks for child allowances and financial aid to newly married couples and reduced the work week of working mothers with three or more children from 45 to 40 hours.

Administrative reform adopted. The Volkskammer (People's Chamber) Oct. 16 approved a bill introduced by Premier Willi Stoph increasing the power of the Council of Ministers (headed by Stoph) at the apparent expense of the Council of State (headed by former Communist party chief Walter Ulbricht). Among the bill's provisions: the Council of Ministers was made accountable to the Volkskammer alone, instead of to both the Volkskammer and the Council of State as previously; and the chairman of the Council of Ministers was empowered to represent East Germany under international law, a role formerly held by the chairman of the Council of State.

Cabinet appointments. The Volkskammer Oct. 16 approved the appointment of Hans-Joachim Heusinger as minister of justice to replace Kurt Wunsche, who resigned. The Volkskammer Dec. 16 also approved the replacement of Johann Wittik, light industry minister, and Gunter Sieber, trade and supply minister, by Werner Greiner-Petter and Gerhard Briksa, respectively. Margarete Wittkowski also was named to the Cabinet.

See also ATOMIC ENERGY [6]; CUBA; ENVIRONMENT; GERMAN CONSULTATIONS; GERMANY, WEST [5-7, 12]; OLYMPICS [6]; POLAND; UNITED NATIONS

GERMANY, WEST (FEDERAL REPUBLIC OF GERMANY)—Nazi trials. A West Berlin court April 11 sentenced Friedrich Bosshammer, a senior officer in the Nazi SS (Elite Guard), to life imprisonment for responsibility in the murder of more than 3,000 Italian Jews during World War II. Bosshammer had been charged with deporting the Jews to the Auschwitz concentration camp in Poland in 1944. A Frankfurt court June 6 acquitted Kurt Born, a former doctor, of charges that he had helped in killing thousands of the incurably mentally ill during the Nazi period. The court upheld the possible validity of Born's contention that he had acted from humane considerations. Born, who had taken charge of the "killing service" at the National Socialist Institute of Euthanasia in Saxony in 1940, said he had acted out of a belief he was helping to solve the problem of incurable insanity.

[2] Brandt defeats CDU ouster move. The ruling coalition of the Social Democratic party (SDP) and the Free Democratic party (FDP) April 27 defeated by two votes a Christian Democratic Union (CDU) motion of constructive no confidence that would have ousted Chancellor Willy Brandt and replaced him with CDU chairman Rainer Barzel. The motion of constructive no confidence, which provided for the nomination of a new chancellor rather than the simple ouster of the chancellor as would a regular no confidence motion, was used for the first time in West Germany's 23-year history. It received 247 votes in favor—two short of the required absolute majority of the Bundestag's (lower house of parliament) 496 deputies. The motion was directed against the government's general record, but the major issue was the opposition CDU's attempt to scuttle nonaggression treaties with the Soviet Union and Poland *(see* [5-7]). Ten deputies voted against the motion, while three cast abstaining votes. The Social Democrats remained in their seats during the vote and refrained from casting ballots in a move designed to pinpoint possible defectors. Some Free Democrats followed suit, but others voted—including two FDP deputies who announced that they had voted for Barzel and would resign their parliamentary seats. It was reported that Barzel had been forced to back the no confidence motion by his rival, Helmut Kohl, governor of the state of Rhineland-Palatinate, and Franz Josef Strauss, leader of the CDU's sister party in Bavaria, the Christian Social Union (CSU).

[3]   **Terrorist activities.** A wave of terrorist bombings swept through West Germany May 11-24, killing four U.S. servicemen and wounding 34 other persons, 12 of them seriously. Interior Minister Hans-Dietrich Genscher said May 24 that suspects sought in the attacks were linked to the Baader-Meinhof gang, a group of leftist anarchists which engaged in terrorist attacks in what they termed their revolutionary fight against imperialism. (The group had also been linked to six or more bank robberies in recent years and had been connected by the police with five deaths—three of policemen and two of alleged gang members.) The Petra Schelm Command of the Red Army Faction (a self-proclaimed identification of the gang) May 15 claimed responsibility for a series of explosions May 11 at the headquarters of the 5th U.S. Army Corps in Frankfurt. A letter allegedly from the group said that the bombing was in retaliation for the "bomb blockade of the U.S. imperialists in North Vietnam" and demanded an end to the mining of North Vietnamese harbors and immediate withdrawal of all U.S. troops from Indochina. Other bombings occurred May 12 (two bomb explosions at police headquarters in Augsburg and one at the Munich criminal police headquarters), May 15 (one bomb explosion in the car of Mrs. Gerta Buddenberg, the wife of Judge Wolfgang Buddenburg, who had been investigating the activities of the Baader-Meinhof gang), May 19 (two bomb explosions at the Hamburg headquarters of the right-wing Axel Springer newspaper and magazine publishing concern) and May 24 (two explosions inside the U.S. Army's European headquarters in Heidelberg). It was reported May 12 that the bombs used in the first explosion were unknown in Germany, but familiar to Vietnam veterans, leading security authorities to suspect that a U.S. army deserter was responsible for the bombings.

[4]   In later developments, state and federal police June 1 captured Andreas Baader, one of the organizers of the Baader-Meinhof gang, and two other leading members of the group (Holger Meins and Jan-Carl Raspe) after a brief gun battle. Baader, who had been hunted by police since 1970 when masked gang members freed him in a spectacular jail break in Berlin while he was serving a sentence for setting fire to a department store in 1968, was shot by police in the gun battle. The shootout occurred when police surrounded a garage used as the gang's hideout. Another allegedly "hard-core" gang member, Gudrun Ensslin, was arrested by police June 7 in a downtown shopping center in Hamburg. Ulrike Meinhof, the other organizer of the gang, was arrested in a suburb of Hanover June 15, along with Gerhard Mueller. Weapons and ammunition were seized in the apartment where Meinhof was arrested. Police June 19 arrested another member of the group, Siegfried Hausner.

[5]   **Eastern treaties approved.** Following a three-week parliamentary impasse, the Bundestag May 17 approved Bonn's nonaggression treaties with the Soviet Union and Poland by votes of 248-10 (238 abstentions) for the Soviet treaty and 248-17 (231 abstentions) for the Polish treaty. Both treaties were approved by the Bundesrat (upper house of parliament) May 19 by a 20-0 vote with 21 abstentions, and signed by President Gustav Heinemann May 23. The treaties, negotiated in 1970, recognized existing European frontiers, including

the Oder-Neisse border between Poland and East Germany, and renounced the use of force to settle disputes between the signatories. Chancellor Brandt owed passage of the treaties to massive abstention of the CDU and the CSU, which marked a last-minute turnabout by Barzel. He directed CDU members to abstain after previously authorizing them to vote freely. Barzel, who had tried to rally his party in favor of the treaties, had opted for abstention in an attempt to preserve party unity in the face of a threat by many CSU members to vote against the treaties. The vote, however, showed that the coalition government had lost its working majority in parliament. (Herbert Hupka, an SDP deputy in the Bundestag, had resigned from the party Feb. 29 in disagreement with the government's support of the treaties. Wilhelm Helms, an FDP deputy, had resigned April 23 for the same reason. The resignations brought the coalition's parliamentary strength down to 249 votes.)

[6] In conjunction with voting on the treaties, the Bundestag approved, by a vote of 491-10 (5 abstentions), an all-party declaration on foreign policy hammered out during three weeks of negotiation. The 10-point declaration said that nothing in the treaties would be a barrier to the self-determination of the German people and the reunification of the two Germanies. A bipartisan commission had drafted the declaration May 9 with the participation and conditional approval of the Soviet ambassador to West Germany, Valentin Falin. (Polish Premier Pyotr Jaroszewicz said May 14 that Poland regarded the text of its treaty alone as binding.)

[7] The two treaties took effect June 3 when instruments of ratification were deposited at the Foreign Ministry in Bonn. (The Presidium of the Supreme Soviet of the U.S.S.R. had unanimously approved the Soviet treaty May 31. The Polish Council of State had ratified the Polish treaty May 26.) A threatened delay in the ceremony had been averted June 2 when a compromise was reached over the status of two West German diplomatic notes, one expressing Bonn's wish for eventual unification of Germany and the other acknowledging four-power responsibility for Germany as a whole. Ambassador Falin had rejected a German demand that the notes be included in a certificate listing the documents making up the Soviet friendship treaty. It was finally decided to include the notes as part of the instruments of ratification.

[8] *Soviet trade pact signed.* A commercial agreement initialed April 7 was signed July 5 by West German Economics and Finance Minister Karl Schiller and Soviet Foreign Trade Minister Nikolai S. Patolichev. The document was to run until the end of 1974 and to increase substantially the more than $750 million worth of trade conducted in 1970. The most notable aspect of the pact was the inclusion of West Berlin within the trading zone represented by Bonn.

[9] **Schiller resigns.** Chancellor Brandt July 6 accepted the resignation of Economics and Finance Minister Karl Schiller. Schiller had reportedly submitted the resignation July 2 but held it in abeyance pending the conclusion of Franco-German summit talks. Schiller said that his resignation stemmed from a variety of differences with the government over economic policy, including the introduction of foreign exchange controls. He said he also intended to quit the SDP, of which he had been a member for 26 years. He resigned his two posts in the SDP Aug. 21 and gave up membership in the party in late September. Schiller was replaced as minister July 7 by Defense Minister Helmut Schmidt. (Brandt also named George Leber, minister of transport and posts, to succeed Schmidt at the Defense Ministry. Lauritz Lauritzen was temporarily assigned the Transport and Posts Ministry in addition to retaining responsibility for housing and town planning.)

[10] *Two junior Cabinet members resign.* Joachim Raffert, parliamentary state secretary in the Education and Science Ministry and an SDP member, and Wolfram Dorn, undersecretary of the Interior Ministry and an FDP member, resigned Aug. 29, one day after disclosures that they had served while in office as paid consultants to the right-wing antigovernment publishing firm Bauer Verlag. The expired contracts of the two had been found by police

during controversial raids by state police on the offices of *Quick* magazine, a weekly published by Bauer Verlag. The raids on *Quick,* staged Aug. 9-10, allegedly had been made to seek evidence of tax evasion and the leakage of secret government papers. *(Quick* had published Schiller's confidential resignation letter in which he sharply criticized the government's new financial policies. *Quick* also had published alleged notes on the negotiation of the Soviet nonaggression treaty.) Current West German laws did not bar government officials from receiving private remuneration while in office, but the publishing firm's sharp opposition to the government raised the possibility of a conflict of interest.

[11] **1973 budget adopted.** The Cabinet Sept. 7 adopted the broad outline of the 1973 budget and medium-term economic plan. Expenditures were estimated at DM 120.4 billion ($37.3 billion), a 10% increase over 1972. The deficit was estimated at DM 4.9 billion, compared with a DM 5.9 billion estimated deficit in 1972. Minor cuts in tax allowances and minor tax increases were planned, but specific details were not worked out. The largest budget increase was slated for agriculture, with spending to rise 21% to DM 5.4 billion. Education and science expenditures would be increased by 16.6% and defense spending would rise by 6.2% to DM 22.2 billion.

[12] **Brandt coalition wins in federal elections.** Chancellor Brandt's coalition government won an unexpectedly large margin of Bundestag seats in federal elections Nov. 19. The election marked the first time that Brandt's SDP won a higher vote percentage (45.9% of the total vote) than the CDU and the CSU (44.8%). The FDP increased its vote percentage to 8.4%; and other parties won less than 1% of the vote, falling short of the 5% required for Budestag representation. A recount Dec. 2 resulted in the loss of one FDP seat to the CDU, making the Bundestag seat totals (1969 election results in parentheses): SDP—230 (224); CDU/CSU—225 (242); FDP—41 (30). A record 91.2% of the electorate voted in the elections, which had been dominated by the issues of signing a treaty with East Germany *(see* GERMAN CONSULTATIONS) and of inflation. Chancellor Brandt was re-elected chancellor by a 269-223 vote of the Bundestag Dec. 14 and was sworn in for his second term the same day.

[13] The elections had been held 10 months ahead of schedule as a result of parliamentary maneuvering by Brandt, who had sought elections to end an even split in the Bundestag between the government coalition and the CDU opposition. The deadlock, caused by defections from the government ranks *(see* [5, 9]), had paralyzed parliament since April. Brandt Sept. 22 had deliberately lost a Bundestag confidence vote to necessitate the calling of elections. To assure the government's defeat in the vote, Brandt and his 13-member Cabinet did not vote—resulting in a vote of 248-233, with one abstention, against the confidence motion. Immediately after the vote, President Heinemann formally dissolved parliament and called for new elections. It was the first time in West German history that parliament had been dissolved prematurely and the first time that a chancellor had engineered his own defeat.

[14] *Cabinet sworn in.* A new coalition Cabinet of 12 Social Democrats and five free Democrats was installed Dec. 15. The only significant Cabinet changes involved the separation of the Economics and Finance Ministry. The new Cabinet (party in parentheses): vice chancellor and foreign—Walter Scheel (FDP); finance—Schmidt (SDP); defense—Leber (SDP); research and technology—Horst Ehmke (SDP); interior—Genscher (FDP); economics— Hans Friderichs (FDP); justice—Gerhard Jahn (SDP); labor—Walter Arendt (SDP); nutrition, agriculture and forests—Josef Ertl (FDP); urban construction and planning—Hans-Jochen Vogel (SDP); education and science—Klaus von Dohnany (SDP); intra-German relations—Egon Franke (SDP); transport—Lauritzen (SDP); youth, family and health affairs— Katharina Focke (SDP); overseas development aid—Erhard Eppler (SDP);

without portfolio—Egon Bahr (SDP); without portfolio—Werner Maihofer (FDP).

See also AVIATION; DRUG USE & ADDICTION [18]; EUROPEAN ECONOMIC COMMUNITY [1, 4, 17]; GERMAN CONSULTATIONS; GREECE [9]; HIJACKING [7-8, 10]; INTERNATIONAL MONETARY DEVELOPMENTS [2, 5-7, 9]; IRELAND; MALTA; MIDDLE EAST [28]; OLYMPICS [3, 5-11]; OLYMPIC TERRORISM; PERU; POLAND; POLLUTION [13]; SOVIET-U.S. RELATIONS [6]; SPACE [24]; SWITZERLAND; TERRITORIAL WATERS; UNITED NATIONS

GERMICIDES—See CONSUMER AFFAIRS [14]

GHANA—**Busia ousted.** A group of Ghanian army officers led by Col. Ignatius Kutu Acheampong seized power in a bloodless coup in Accra Jan. 13, deposing the government of Prime Minister Kofi A. Busia, who was in London for treatment of an eye ailment. Acheampong's men cut off communication with the outside world, closed the airport in Accra, withdrew the constitution and dissolved parliament. Acheampong Jan. 13 said that the years of Busia's rule had been marked by the same "corruption, arbitrary dismissals, economic mismanagement and a host of other malpractices" as had characterized the rule of Kwame Nkrumah, deposed by elements of the army in 1966 (see OBITUARIES [Kwame Nkrumah]). He specifically accused Busia of pushing his austerity program to the extent of taking over many of the "amenities and facilities" of the army, whose officers became too demoralized to exert "any meaningful influence over their men." (Busia Jan. 21 attributed the coup to his government's attempt to limit free housing, water and electricity for army officers.) Acheampong also charged that the Trade Union Congress (TUC) had been "disorganized" by Busia's actions. Among recent actions of the Busia government that would be "looked into," Acheampong said, were the abolition of the Workers Brigade and state farms (originally set up by Nkrumah), devaluation of the cedi by 44% and the expulsion of foreign businessmen.

Acheampong announced that Ghana would be run by a National Redemption Council, made up of representatives from "various walks of life." (Expanded Jan. 16 to 11 members, the council included seven officers from the army, one each from the navy, air force and police, and a civilian attorney general.) The commanders of Ghana's six army battalions and one mortar regiment were to act as regional military governors.

Countercoup defeated. Acheampong's strength was tested Jan. 15 when he defeated an attempt to restore Busia to power. The countercoup reportedly was led by Lt. Gen. Akwasi A. Afrifa, who had headed the military government in 1969 shortly before power was returned to civilian hands, and assisted by the commander of the army brigade at Kumasi and by a civilian administrator in that area.

Monetary policy. Col. Acheampong announced Feb. 5 that he had nullified the revaluation of the cedi which had taken place in December 1971 and that he was revaluing the cedi upward by 42% so that it would be exchanged at the rate of one for 78 U.S. cents. Acheampong also said that Ghana was repudiating $94.4 million worth of debts incurred with four British firms prior to the 1966 ouster of Nkrumah. He described the debts as being "tainted and vitiated with corruption." A further $72 million in interest on the debts was "emphatically rejected"; one-third of the principal was "repudiated outright"; and the rest would be paid only if validly contracted and if the projects themselves were economically viable. Long-term debts owed the International Development Association (IDA), a World Bank affiliate, and the U.S. government would be repaid according to the agreed terms.

Busia plot thwarted. The government announced July 16 that it had smashed a plot to restore former Prime Minister Busia to power. All those connected with the planned rebellion were said to have been seized. The National Redemption Council said Busia had engineered a plan with some businessmen and officials of the outlawed Progress party to overthrow the council July 14. Busia was to return to Ghana the following day if the dissidents succeeded—bringing with him foreign troops in the event Ghana's armed forces resisted. According to the council, the plotters planned to remain in power 14 days, after which the Progress party was to have been restored to office. Busia July 16 derided the plot story as "imaginary." (A military tribunal in Accra Nov. 14 condemned to death three civilians for their role in the coup. The three were: George Ofosu-Amah, a university law lecturer and former director of Busia's intelligence service; Emil Wilson Kofi Adzima, former press secretary to Busia; and Daniel Owusu Daokes Atakora, an executive in a fish company owned by Busia's brothers. David Afful Bimpong, a banker, was sentenced to 25 years for concealment of subversion.)

Supreme Court abolished. The National Redemption Council announced Sept. 13 the abolition of the Supreme Court and the establishment of the Appeals Court as the country's highest tribunal. The decree said the continued existence of the Supreme Court was unjustified because the constitution establishing the court had been suspended *(see above).*

See also INTERNATIONAL MONETARY DEVELOPMENTS [8]

GIBRALTAR—New government formed. Sir Joshua Hassan, leader of the Gibraltar Labor Party-Association for the Advancement of Civil Rights (GLP-AACR), was appointed chief minister June 25 and authorized to form a new government to replace the coalition Cabinet of Maj. Robert Peliza, leader of Gibraltar's Integration with Britain party. The formation of the new government followed June 23 general elections to the House of Assembly in which the GLP-AACR won eight seats and the Integration with Britain party won seven. Peliza had requested the dissolution of the House May 22, a year ahead of schedule, ostensibly because of his lack of confidence in Maj. Alfred Gache, minister for commercial economic development and one of three independents with whom Peliza had formed a coalition in 1969. However, news reports speculated that Peliza had actually called the election to challenge Hassan's views on the future of Gibraltar's status in the face of Spanish pressure for Great Britain to relinquish sovereignty. During the campaign, Peliza accused Hassan of willingness to accept a compromise settlement that would recognize Spanish sovereignty over Gibraltar in exchange for a Spanish grant to Britain of a 1,000-year lease on Gibraltar and the removal of restrictions confining residents on the Rock. The GLP-AACR denied any intention of abandoning support for British sovereignty over the Rock.

General strike. Trade unions Aug. 22 launched a general strike to protest an order by Gibraltar's governor, Admiral Sir Varyl Begg, dispatching troops to run the main electrical generating station. (The operations of the station had been affected by a limited strike begun Aug. 20 by government-employed industrial workers.) The general strike ended Aug. 26 after the unions accepted a wage offer from employers increasing the weekly minimum salary to $34 for blue-collar workers and $42.70 for white-collar workers.

See also MOROCCO

GOLD—*See* INTERNATIONAL MONETARY DEVELOPMENTS [1-3, 8, 11]

GOLF—Nicklaus ties Jones record. Jack Nicklaus June 18 joined the late Bobby Jones as the only golfer to have won 13 major titles. Nicklaus had won two U.S. Amateurs, three U.S. Opens, four Masters, two Professional Golfers Association (PGA) titles and two British Opens. Nicklaus scored his fourth Masters victory April 9 at the Augusta National Golf Club course in Augusta, Ga. Nicklaus had led the tournament from the first day—only the third time that a golfer had led the Masters field from start to finish. Nicklaus scored 68-71-73-74 in four rounds for a 72-hole total of 286, three under par. Bruce Crampton, Tom Weiskopf and Bobby Mitchell tied for second place with 289s. Nicklaus won his third U.S. Open June 18 at Pebble Beach, Calif. by three strokes with a 290. Crampton finished behind Nicklaus with a 293.

Trevino wins British Open. Lee Trevino ended Nicklaus's chances in 1972 of becoming the first golfer in history to sweep golf's grand slam—the U.S. and British Opens, the Masters and the PGA title. Trevino, defending champion in the British Open, again won the tourney July 15 in Muirfield, Scotland with a 278. Trevino carded a closing-round 71 to finish a stroke ahead of Nicklaus, who closed with a 66. The Muirfield tournament marked the fourth time Nicklaus had been the British Open's runner-up.

Mrs. Berning takes Women's Open. Mrs. Susie Maxwell Berning July 2 regained the U.S. Women's Open championship she had won in 1968 with a score of 299 in the 72-hole tournament in Mamaroneck, N.Y. Mrs. Berning posted rounds of 79, 73, 76 and a closing one-under-par 71 to win the title by a stroke over Kathy Ahern, Pam Barnett and Judy Rankin.

Player wins PGA. Gary Player, a native of South Africa and the only non-U.S. citizen ever to win the PGA title, captured it a second time Aug. 6 by carding a final-round 72 over the Oakland Hills Country Club course in Birmingham, Mich. Player finished at 281, with earlier rounds of 71, 71 and 67.

GONORRHEA—*See* HEALTH
GOVERNORS—*See* ELECTIONS [1, 42-43]
GRAMMY AWARDS—*See* RECORD INDUSTRY
GRAVEL, SEN. MIKE—*See* ELECTIONS [19]; PENTAGON PAPERS

GREAT BRITAIN—The British government attempted to cure Britain's sluggish economy—the result of inflation and unemployment—by several actions *(see* [2]), including the imposition of a temporary wage, price freeze *(see* [7]). Attempts at ordering the economy were hampered, however, by serious labor disputes during the year. A coal miners' strike in January and February caused an energy emergency and a severe shortage of electrical power *(see* [8-9]). Rail unions pitted themselves against the government for two months beginning in April, with drastic slowdowns in rail service *(see* [11]). Disputes with dock workers over the unloading of containerized cargo resulted in the proclamation of a state of emergency throughout Britain *(see* [12-14]). The government passed the Industrial Relations Act as an attempt to restrict the actions of labor in disputes with management, but the bill roused bitter opposition from labor *(see* [10]). Unions and management representatives later created independent conciliation and advisory machinery to resolve industrial disputes without resorting to the act *(see* [15]).

[2] '73 budget slashes taxes. In an attempt to spur Britain's sluggish economy, Chancellor of the Exchequer Anthony Barber March 21 announced tax cuts of $3.14 billion in his annual budget message for the 1973 fiscal year (April 1, 1972-March 31, 1973). Barber said that the budget was aimed at defeating "the twin evils of inflation and unemployment." The budget estimated expenditures at $43.1 billion and revenues at $43.6 billion. The tax reductions provided for an increase in the income tax exemption for single persons from $745 to $996 and for married couples from $1,209 to $1,560. The effect would be to exempt 2,750,000 persons from all income taxes and to reduce the taxes of the remaining 21 million taxpayers by about $2.60 weekly. The major tax benefits to business would be a 100% depreciation allowance for investment in capital equipment and extra incentives for investments in economically depressed areas. (Barber also announced that a value-added tax— a levy imposed at each stage of the production of goods—would be introduced in April 1973 and would probably be set at a 10% rate, the lowest rate of any of the members of the European Economic Community.) The budget also provided for a 12.5% increase in old age pensions; a revision in the purchase tax (a form of sales tax), with the top two rates reduced from 30% and 45% to 25%; the imposition of the surcharge on incomes beginning at $7,800 annually instead of at $6,500; tax deductions for interest payments above $91; and other benefits for charity contributions and inheritances.

[3] Cabinet changes. Prime Minister Edward Heath shuffled his Cabinet April 7. The changes included appointment of Robert Carr, secretary of state for employment, as majority leader of the House of Commons and Lord President of the Council. Carr replaced William Whitelaw, who had previously been named secretary of state for Northern Ireland. Maurice MacMillan, son of former Prime Minister Harold MacMillan, was named secretary of employment. Five junior ministers, including Aerospace Minister Frederick Corfield, were dropped from the government, and 11 new ministers were appointed. In a later development, Home Secretary Reginald Maulding resigned July 18 and was replaced by Carr, who retained his other posts. Maulding's resignation came as a result of his past connection with a bankrupt company under police investigation for possible corruption. A Cabinet shuffle involving 19 junior and senior ministerial changes was announced Nov. 5. Peter Walker, secretary of state for the environment, was named secretary of trade and industry. He replaced John Davies, who w~s appointed chancellor of the Duchy of Lancaster with special responsibi.;ty for European Economic Community affairs, a post formerly held by Geoffrey Rippon. Rippon replaced Walker as secretary of state for the environment. Solicitor General Sir Geoffrey Howe was given the newly created post of minister for trade and consumer affairs. Joseph Godber, minister of state at the Foreign Office, was promoted to agriculture minister, replacing James Prior. Prior was named Lord President of the Council and majority leader in the House of Commons. Carr remained as home secretary.

[4] New commercial radio-TV agency. The establishment of a new Independent Broadcasting Authority (IBA), with power to license some 60 commercial radio stations was reported July 16. The IBA would replace the Independent Television Authority. A bill creating the commercial radio network had been enacted June 12 following parliamentary approval.

[5] Fixed bank rate abolished. Chancellor of the Exchequer Barber announced Oct. 9 that the government would abolish the fixed bank discount rate effective Oct. 13, replacing it with a minimum lending rate that would be fixed each Friday on the basis of the average prevailing discount rate on treasury bills at the end of the preceding week. The purpose of the move reportedly was to control the growth of the money supply without halting economic expansion. The fixed rate had been the fulcrum of British monetary policy for 270 years, signaling the government's desire to expand or contract the money supply. Barber said he hoped the fluctuating rate would eliminate the wider economic significance associated with the fixed rate. He said the nation needed "a rate that could respond more flexibly to the changing conditions of the money market and one whose week-to-week movements were not interpreted as signaling major shifts of monetary policy.

[6] Tax, welfare reform plan proposed. The government Oct. 10 proposed a major reshaping of the tax and welfare system that would result in a form of negative income tax for low-income families and pensioners. The scheme would replace the existing system of family allowances, family income supplements and personal income tax deductions by tax credits against a single 30% tax rate imposed on all taxpayers. The credits would be allotted for dependents or for those with special status, such as pensioners. The government would pay the difference when tax credits exceeded the tax due, resulting in a negative income tax for the poor. The system would cover all employees earning at least about $19 a week, the level at which wage-earners begin to contribute to the compulsory national insurance system. It would also cover national insurance beneficiaries, such as the sick and invalid, unemployed, widows and retired pensioners. The Green Paper outlining the proposal said the plan would eliminate up to 15,000 civil service jobs because of the simplification of the welfare and tax system, including elimination of the welfare means test in certain cases. The government estimated it would pay an additional $3.2 billion to taxpayers as a result of the scheme.

[7] Wage, price freeze imposed. Prime Minister Heath Nov. 6 imposed an immediate 90-day freeze on wages and most prices, rents and dividends (exempting prices on fruit, vegetables, meat, fish and imported raw materials and rent increases already ordered for public housing and rents in furnished apartments). A bill to make the freeze statutory, called the Counter-Inflationary (Temporary Provisions) Bill, was published the same day. (It was given final approval in the House of Commons Nov. 20.) It provided for the freeze to become effective immediately and to last for 90 days after Parliament passed the legislation and the Queen gave her assent. It also gave the government the option to extend the freeze for an additional 60 days if the government failed to reach agreement with labor unions on voluntary curbs. The bill did not set up any new watchdog authority, but left monitoring to government ministers, who were empowered to fine any firm or union disobeying government orders to roll back unauthorized increases in prices or wages. The bill authorized $930 fines for summary convictions and unlimited fines for offenders convicted by the higher courts. In announcing the wage, price freeze, Heath said he had been forced to take the action following the collapse of talks between the Trades Union Congress (TUC), the Confederation of British Industry (CBI) and the government on voluntary anti-inflation measures. (The talks collapsed Nov. 2 when the TUC rejected government proposals for voluntary wage and price controls. The labor leaders had insisted on a higher ceiling on wage increases than the $4.90 proposed by the government and had demanded that key retail prices should be controlled by law, while wage restraints should remain voluntary.) Heath said the freeze was the first stage of his anti-inflationary program, and he indicated that it would be followed by a more   sophisticated set of controls if the government failed to reach agreement with the unions on voluntary curbs.   The TUC Nov. 8 refused to hold new talks   with the government until the freeze was removed.

Labor Developments

[8]   **Coal strike.** Coal miners went on strike throughout Britain Jan. 9, after talks between the miners' unions and the state-owned National Coal Board broke off in December 1971. The talks had broken off after the unions rejected a board offer to raise wages by an average 7.9% annually. The unions wanted an 11% increase. (Miners' basic salaries, including overtime, ranged from about $47 weekly for surface workers to $78 for underground workers.) The picketing miners blocked delivery of coal to power stations in many areas, causing the government to declare a state of emergency Feb. 9 in order to conserve power. The first emergency measure, a ban on the use of electricity for advertising and display, went into effect Feb. 11. Further emergency regulations went into effect Feb. 14, closing down 20,000 medium-sized factories for four days a week, imposing 50% cuts in electricity consumption for the nation's biggest companies and causing blackouts of up to nine hours daily on a staggered basis for homes, offices and stores. The government also imposed a total ban on the use of electric heat in stores, offices, public halls, restaurants and buildings used for recreation or entertainment. (The emergency measures won approval in the House of Commons Feb. 14 by a 315-276 vote.) The number of workers laid off as a result of the power restrictions reached 1.4 million—a twentieth of the working population—by Feb. 16.

[9]   The miners voted Feb. 25 to end their strike and returned to work Feb. 28. Acting on a recommendation of the National Union of Mineworkers, the miners had voted by a 96% majority to accept the recommendations of a special government-appointed court of inquiry, headed by Lord Wilberforce, for a strike settlement. The accord recommendations, involving a 16-month pay package retroactive to Nov. 1, 1971, provided that surface miners would get a $13-a-week raise, underground workers a $15.60-a-week raise and underground workers at the coal face an $11.70 raise. The settlement meant an average pay increase of nearly 20%, considerably higher than the government's unofficial wage increase ceiling of 8%. The Wilberforce report, released Feb. 18, had acknowledged the government's concern in avoiding inflationary pay increases, but concluded that the miners deserved "special treatment" because of the

"combination of danger, health hazard, discomfort in working conditions, social inconvenience and community isolation." It found that the "fall in the ranking of coal mining pay has been quite unwarranted" and ruled that the government should provide the funds if the National Coal Board could not afford the pay raises. (A 7.5% increase in coal prices, effective March 26, was announced March 6 as a means of providing for part of the increases in wages. To meet the rest of the cost, the government would increase the board's accumulated deficit and would make an emergency $260 million grant to the board. The government Dec. 11 announced a grant of $1.792 billion in coal subsidies over the next five years and a write-off of the accumulated deficit of the National Coal Board).

[10] **Labor bill in force.** The most comprehensive labor relations bill in British history went into effect Feb. 28. Among other provisions, the Industrial Relations Act banned wildcat strikes, the closed shop and union action against a third party outside a labor dispute. It also established a national industrial relations board and authorized 60-day cooling-off periods and a secret strike ballot in disputes deemed a threat to the national interest. The TUC suspended 32 affiliated unions for registering under the act. (A TUC order had forbidden such registration.)

[11] **Rail unions, government clash.** The government and state-run railways were pitted against Britain's three rail unions for two months, beginning in April, as the government sought to use the new Industrial Relations Act to halt wildcat strikes and the unions bitterly resisted the attempt to curb their freedom of action. The confrontation erupted April 17, when the unions rejected a mediator's compromise wage offer of a 12% wage rise and instructed members to work to rule, a procedure in which every railroad work rule was followed to the letter, causing serious delays. (The British Railways Board originally had offered an 11% increase in wages; the unions had demanded a 16% rise.) The National Industrial Relations Court (NIRC), created by the labor relations act, April 19 ordered a 14-day cooling-off period, to start from the resumption of normal services, to allow an opportunity for resumed wage negotiations. The unions April 20 decided, "with the greatest reluctance," to obey the order; but militant railwaymen, defying the court order and their own union instructions, continued the slowdown until April 25, when the government informed the court that the normal working schedule was back in force. The government notification paved the way for the resumption of talks between the unions and the British Railways Board. With the expiration of the cooling-off period, the three unions resumed their overtime ban and work to rule at midnight May 11. In response, British Railways closed down for 32 hours May 13-15. The unions called off their job action May 14-15 under a new court order, pending a government-requested compulsory ballot of the union's membership on the mediator's wage offer. (The court had ordered the ballot May 13.) The balloting May 31 marked a serious defeat for the government as the railway workers voted, by a 5-1 margin, to back further union-ordered job actions. Agreement on a new wage pact was finally reached June 12 in the face of a resumption of the work slowdown threatened for midnight that day. The settlement provided for wage increases equivalent to about 13.5%. The settlement was ratified June 13 by the three rail unions.

[12] **Dock strike.** Leaders of the Transport and General Workers Union voted 38-28 (18 abstentions) July 27 to call an official dock strike effective July 28 after rejecting a special committee report recommending measures to ease growing unemployment among longshoremen. The report, issued July 24, had proposed higher severance pay for dockers to encourage them to leave the industry and had suggested measures to give the dockers more work with container trucks. The underlying issue in the dispute was the dockers' demand that they, and not lower-paid warehousemen, load and unload container trucks at inland depots. The growing use of container trucks had contributed to the decline of dock jobs from 60,000 in 1967 to 40,000 in 1972. The strike July 28

idled an estimated 500-600 ships at British ports and cut off imports of food and other supplies. In response to the strike, Queen Elizabeth II proclaimed a state of emergency Aug. 3, effective at midnight for 28 days, authorizing emergency standby powers. The government reportedly acted because of a critical shortage of imported foodstuffs for animals. Under the proclamation, the government was authorized to fix prices for scarce goods; requisition ships, trucks, fuels, food and medical supplies; and use troops to unload strikebound ships. Private aircraft began an emergency airlift of feed grains to the Orkney and Shetland Islands off the coast of Scotland Aug. 9, while Royal Air Force aircraft flew foodstuffs there Aug. 11. The government described the military airlift as a humanitarian gesture and not as implementation of emergency powers.

[13] Delegates of the dock workers voted Aug. 16, 53-30, to end the strike Aug. 20 after accepting an improved offer on job security. The job security proposals had been worked out by a special labor-employer committee jointly chaired by Jack Jones, leader of the union, and Lord Addington, chairman of the Port of London Authority. The proposals guaranteed full pay for all union-registered dockers, whether or not there was work, and provided that dockers working for employers who went out of business would be reassigned to other employers. The program also promised severance pay of up to $10,000 for dockers voluntarily leaving the industry; pledged that port authorities would rebuild old, unused port areas and create new jobs there; promised that port authorities would ask container-handling companies to give preference to dockers for future jobs and to move part of their business into union dock labor areas; and provided for imposition of higher port dues and shipping charges on container trucks not loaded by union dock labor. The offer also promised further study of shop stewards' demands to extend union agreements to small ports and private wharves. The outlook for settlement clouded later Aug. 16 when militant shop stewards in eight ports decided to disregard the call to return to work, but dockers rejected the stewards' position and nearly all returned to work Aug. 21. (At Liverpool, however, a separate strike by 800 clerical workers on the Merseyside docks interfered with a full resumption of dock operations.)

[14] *Background.* Leaders of the dock workers had threatened a nationwide strike, scheduled to begin June 16, to protest pay and the jurisdictional dispute over unloading containerized cargo. However, the strike was called off June 14 following a new pay and working conditions offer by the port employers. (The offer, scheduled to go into effect June 26, provided for an immediate guaranteed weekly wage of about $60 and a guaranteed daily payment of about $12 if no dock work was available. If a docker chose to leave the industry voluntarily, he would receive up to $7,358 in compensation.) Despite abandonment of the official strike, an unofficial strike June 14 involved about 30,000 of Britain's 42,000 dockers and almost completely tied up the ports of London, Liverpool, Hull and other, smaller harbors. About 35,000 dock workers again began a wildcat strike June 16 to protest the anticipated arrest of five dock workers. Most of the strikers returned to work June 19-20, but the arrest of the five dock workers led to five days of mounting wildcat strikes in many sectors of the economy July 21-26—including a dock strike July 21. (The NIRC had ordered the arrests because the five had refused to obey its order to stop picketing an East London Container depot. An appeals court had overturned the arrest order; but the House of Lords, Britain's highest judicial authority, July 21 upheld the earlier NIRC ruling. NIRC President Sir John Donaldson had jailed the workers July 21.) In the face of a threat by the TUC to call a general strike for July 31, the NIRC freed the five men following an independent intervention by Norman Turner, Britain's official solicitor charged with safeguarding personal liberties. (The men had refused to appeal themselves because they did not recognize the jurisdiction of the NIRC.)

[15] **CBI, TUC create conciliation service.** The TUC and the CBI Aug. 2 signed an agreement creating independent conciliation and advisory machinery for the resolution of industrial disputes. The service, effective Sept. 1, was operated initially with part-time, unpaid personnel who eventually would be replaced by full-time experts. The aim of the agreement was to encourage settlement of industrial disputes without recourse to the Industrial Relations Act.

See also ARGENTINA [3]; ATOMIC ENERGY [8]; AUSTRALIA [7, 11]; AVIATION; BAHAMAS; BAHRAIN; BANGLA DESH [13]; CEYLON; CHEMICAL & BIOLOGICAL WARFARE; CHINA, COMMUNIST; CONSERVATION; DISARMAMENT; ESPIONAGE; EUROPEAN ECONOMIC COMMUNITY [1, 10-13, 15-16, 18]; GERMAN CONSULTATIONS; GILBRALTAR; GRENADA; HIJACKING [15, 17]; INTERNATIONAL MONETARY DEVELOPMENTS [2, 5-9]; IRELAND; LATIN AMERICA; MALTA; MIDDLE EAST [35]; NORTHERN IRELAND; OIL & NATURAL GAS; OLYMPICS [3]; PAKISTAN [7]; POLLUTION [13]; RHODESIA; SPACE [24]; SWITZERLAND; TARIFFS & WORLD TRADE; TERRITORIAL WATERS; TURKEY; UGANDA [1, 7-13]

GREECE—Relations between the U.S. and Greece improved during 1972 with the establishment in Pireaus of home-port facilities for the U.S. 6th Fleet *(see* [5]) and the beginning of negotiations between the two countries for the sale of arms to Greece *(see* [6]). In domestic developments, Premier George Papadopoulos assumed the Greek regency in March *(see* [7]) and ended martial law in Salonika during December *(see* [14]).

[2] **Government reorganized.** Premier Papadopoulos Jan. 14 ordered a government reorganization and a minor Cabinet shuffle, both designed to overcome administrative problems stemming from the creation of the Ministry of National Economy out of the 1971 merger of several economic and trade ministries. Sotirios Agapitidis, a professor, was appointed alternate minister of national economy to replace Ioannis Stavropoulos, whose resignation had been reported Jan. 13. A new undersecretary of national economy and four deputies were also appointed to streamline the new economic ministry's operations. Responsibility for foreign trade relations was switched to the Foreign Ministry. Other changes included the appointments of Undersecretary for Foreign Affairs Christian Xanthopoulos-Palamas as alternate foreign affairs minister and the appointment of Constantine Panayotakos, ambassador to Cyprus, as undersecretary of foreign affairs with particular responsibility for political and commercial affairs.

[3] Papadopoulos again shifted his government July 31, appointing 10 new members (all former military men). The government reorganization had been preceded July 10 by the resignation of Education Minister Gerasimos Frangatos, Public Order Minister Spyridon Velianitis and Deputy National Economy Minister George Carter—all of whom resigned for "private reasons." The new ministers were: Constantine Papadopoulos (the premier's brother), appointed minister to the premier on questions of planning and government policy; Gen. Vassilios Tsoumbas, former chief of the army until retired in May, who was named minister of public order; Nikolaos Gantonas, a former colonel responsible for northern Greece, who was named education minister; Ioannis Ladas, who was named social services minister; Nikolaos Efessios, who was named national economy minister; and Emmanuel Fthenakis, who was named minister of marine, transport and communications.

[4] **New loyalty oath.** The government decided Feb. 1 to require prospective civil servants and employees of state-controlled bodies to answer a 10-point questionnaire on the applicant's loyalty to the nation. (According to a report May 5, candidates for the Greek Orthodox priesthood also would be required to take the test.) The questionnaire, which replaced loyalty certificates that had been abolished late in 1971, would require the applicant to state (among other things) whether he had ever joined a subversive or Communist party or other type of anti-government organization and whether he had ever participated in social or other activities organized by these groups. The applicant would also have to repudiate the views of any immediate relative linked to a subversive group. The questionnaire ended with a pledge of loyalty to the government and to "national ideals."

[5] Home port for U.S. The U.S. State Department announced Feb. 5 that the U.S. and Greece had reached an agreement in principle on establishment of home-port facilities at the Greek port of Piraeus for units attached to the U.S. 6th Fleet. The accord was being negotiated, according to the State Department, to reduce the fleet's maintenance costs and to counter the Soviet naval buildup in the eastern Mediterranean. (When moves toward the accord were first disclosed Jan. 21 by Adm. Elmo R. Zumwalt Jr., U.S. chief of naval operations, Zumwalt had said the Navy wanted to house about one-third of the families of officers and enlisted men attached to the 6th Fleet in an attempt to boost Navy morale. Zumwalt March 7 reiterated his belief that the establishment of the home-port facilities was crucial to morale of the 6th Fleet.) The accord was opposed by U.S. congressmen, who feared a greater involvement of the U.S. with the Greek government, and by the Soviet Union, which criticized the escalation of U.S. involvement in the Mediterranean. The first phase of the home-port plan began Sept. 1, with the move of six 6th Fleet destroyers into Phaleron Bay. The squadron had a complement of 1,700 men. About 300 families, with 681 dependents, arrived in Piraeus Sept. 5 to join the men of the squadron. Eventually, Piraeus would accommodate the six destroyers, an aircraft carrier, 6,600 crewmen and about 3,100 dependents.

[6] U.S. to sell arms. The State Department announced March 3 that negotiations were under way for the sale to Greece of about $70 million worth of arms for the fiscal year ending June 30. Congress had banned such assistance to the military government of Greece except in cases of "overriding" security interest to the U.S., but President Nixon had determined the aid to be of such interest. Nixon Feb. 17 had signed a memo to Congress citing the Soviet naval buildup in the Mediterranean as justification for the aid. The State Department announced March 29 the signing of an agreement under which the U.S. would sell 36 Phantom jets to Greece.

[7] Papadopoulos assumes regency. Premier Papadopoulos March 21 took over the post of regent after dismissing Gen. George Zoitakis, who had held the largely ceremonial office since King Constantine's flight from Greece in December 1967 following an abortive counter-coup against Papadopoulos's regime. The changeover was accomplished through a Cabinet decree relieving Zoitakis of his post for "unjustified interference in the government's legislative work." (He reportedly had refused to sign a law increasing the police force and fire brigade.) Citing a "climate of dissonance," caused by Zoitakis, the decree named Papadopoulos "to exercise the royal authority in the name of the king," while continuing in his other offices of premier and minister of defense, foreign affairs and government policy. Papadopoulos was administered the oath of regency the same day by Archbishop Hieronymos Kotsonis, head of the Greek Orthodox Church. Zoitakis's ouster was thought by observers to be a step toward abolition of the monarchy and establishment of a presidential regime under Papadopoulos. It followed a campaign in late February by pro-government newspapers favoring a referendum on the future of the monarchy. (In mid-July, pro-government papers again featured editorials proposing that Papadopoulos be made premier for life or that Constantine abdicate in favor of his five-year-old son, Paul, and allow Papadopoulos to continue as regent until 1985, when Paul would come of age.)

[8] Rival parties form joint opposition. The Center Union and the National Radical Union, former rival parties which had won 85% of the vote in the last Greek election in 1964, joined March 24 in signing a manifesto pledging their support for any government that would restore democracy to Greece. The manifesto, signed by 167 former parliamentary members of the two parties, accused the current regime's leaders of "openly exercising power as an end in itself" and announced a joint program to restore "the Greek people's sovereignty and liberties, real freedom of the press, free trade unionism and justice."

[9] Mangakis 'escape.' Prof. George-Alexander Mangakis, a prominent law professor sentenced in 1970 to an 18-year prison term for alleged sedition, and his wife flew to Bonn, West Germany April 15 aboard a West German Defense Ministry jet, which took off from the U.S. air base at Athens International Airport. The departure of the two, both of whom lacked required Greek travel papers, came a few hours after an Athens court had granted Mangakis an eight-month remission of his sentence to enable him to get medical care for a serious eye ailment. Following the departure, the Greek government accused West German Ambassador Peter Limbourg, who saw the couple off at the airport, of violating Greek sovereignty by "organizing" the "escape" of Mangakis. The West German Foreign Ministry April 22 rejected the Greek charges, but announced that Limbourg would be recalled from Athens at the request of the Greek government. There were reports that Greece and West Germany had actually reached a prior agreement on Mangakis's departure and that Greece's subsequent denunciation stemmed from displeasure at the unorthodox manner in which the departure was carried out or at the publicity accorded the incident. (In a related incident, Greek complaints that the use of the U.S. base for Mangakis's departure violated a 1953 agreement authorizing the U.S. to maintain bases in Greece led to the signing Oct. 2 of a protocol reaffirming respect for Greek laws and sovereignty at U.S. military installations.)

[10] Student protests. Following a week of mounting student agitation, about 400 striking physics students from Athens University staged a silent, illegal march April 27 through downtown Athens to the University senate building, where they were dispersed by police without violence. The students were demanding changes in examination procedures and the right to elect leaders of student bodies to replace officials appointed by the government following the 1967 coup in which it came to power. (The government Nov. 20 allowed students at the Universities of Athens, Salonika and Ioannina to vote for student organization leaders.) The demands were also the cause of a strike by 2,600 engineering students in Athens and Salonika the previous week. In an attempt to curb the student agitation, the government May 2 enacted a decree authorizing police to use firearms at their own discretion to break up illegal demonstrations "in case of immediate threat to public order and human life." The police also arrested 10 students at Athens University and 5-20 students at Salonika during late April. Six Greek Cypriot students were expelled from Greece, according to a government announcement May 13, for inciting others to break laws. The government charged the six students had "illegally taken over the Athens section of the Cypriot National Student Federation" to issue a communique demanding student elections. Athens newspapers May 14 published a statement by the federation's former president declaring that the expelled students had been lawfully elected.

[11] Armed forces shuffled. Premier Papadopoulos May 31 reshuffled the command of the armed forces, promoting Lt. Gen. Dimitrios Zagorianakos, former commander of the 3rd army corps of Salonika, to the post of chief of army. Papadopoulos also raised Maj. Gen. Thomas Mitsanas from deputy chief to commander of the air force. Several other officers were retired. (The Ministry of National Defense June 20 charged that recurrent reports of large-scale purges in the armed forces misrepresented routine retirements and promotions. The government said that 2,590 officers had retired in the five years since the 1967 coup, compared with 1,751 in the preceding five years.)

[12] Alleged terrorist plot foiled. The government announced July 15 the arrests in June of eight Greeks whom it charged with conspiracy to stage robberies, kidnap prominent persons and bomb foreign embassies in Athens as part of a plot to overthrow the existing political system. The intended kidnap victims allegedly included the labor minister, chief of the armed forces, foreign ambassadors, Thomas A. Pappas (a wealthy Greek-born U.S. businessman) and John F. Kennedy Jr. (Kennedy, son of the late President, frequently vacationed on the Greek island of Skorpios, owned by his stepfather, Aristotle Onassis.) An Athens court Aug. 4 acquitted three of the alleged terrorists and sentenced the five others to prison terms ranging from seven to 39 months. Seven of the defendants had denied the charges of setting up an urban guerrilla band and plotting violence to overthrow the government. The eighth, Christos Ramadanis, the alleged leader of the group, had admitted on the first day of the trial Aug. 3 that robbery, bombing and kidnaping plans had been discussed, but he dismissed this as "idle, romantic talk." He denied charges that the group had planned to kidnap Kennedy. Ramadanis was sentenced to 39 months in prison; and Georgios Boussiotis, described as his lieutenant, was sentenced to 18 months. The sentences of the other three convicted were subsequently suspended.

[13] 15-year economic plan announced. The government Sept. 11 published a brief summary of a 15-year plan for economic and social development. The summary promised to increase the average citizen's annual income from the 1972 level of $1,100 to $2,600 by 1987 and to "achieve material prosperity without sacrificing the nation's spiritual values." It forecast a 7% annual economic growth to nearly $27 billion by 1987, with industry to contribute 43% of the gross national product rather than the current one-third, and agriculture to contribute just under 10% rather than 17%. The summary also envisaged an increase in annual imports from the 1972 $2.25 billion to $12 billion in 1987, and a rise in exports from $800 million to $6 billion. It also predicted that the country would become a capital-exporting nation by 1987. Government expenditures for education would total $3.5 billion over the 15-year period. (In a related development, the Cabinet Nov. 30 approved a 1973 budget which estimated expenditures at $3.46 billion and revenue from taxes at $2.65 billion, with the deficit to be covered by domestic loans of $674 million and foreign loans of $133 million. The budget allocated a 41% increase in education spending and a 17% hike in public health spending.)

[14] Martial law ended in Salonika. Premier Papadopoulos, in his annual year-end message, announced Dec. 16 the abolition of martial law in Salonika. He said, however, that martial law would remain in effect in Athens and Piraeus. Papadopoulos also said that the cases of about 250 convicted political prisoners would be reviewed by a military appeals court; that nine persons who had been banished to remote villages as "security risks" would be freed soon (released Dec. 19); and that five foreigners sentenced as "importers of revolution" would be permitted to appeal to a civilian court for deportation. The premier also barred a return to parliamentary government in the near future.

[15] Anti-inflation program. The government Dec. 24 announced an anti-inflation program and plans for stricter policing of the Athens stock exchange. The government action followed a 5% increase in the cost of living in 1972 and a leap in security sales. The economic program provided for a six-month freeze on bank loans for housing, imposition of more stringent wage and price controls and introduction of a ceiling on credit card sales. In an effort to curb stock speculation, the government also ordered all commercial banks to liquidate 45% of their security portfolios within one year and announced plans for legislation to tighten stockbrokers' practices.

See also ATOMIC ENERGY [6]; CYPRUS; DRUG USE & ADDICTION [18]; FOREIGN AID

GRENADA—Premier Eric Gairy's United Labor party Feb. 28 won 13 of 15 seats in the island's legislature to remain in power for another five years. The government also received a mandate to move Grenada toward independence from Great Britain.

GROSS NATIONAL PRODUCT (GNP)—*See* ECONOMY [2, 9]; POLLUTION [1]
GROUP OF 77—*See* INTERNATIONAL MONETARY DEVELOPMENTS [5]
GROUP OF 10—*See* INTERNATIONAL MONETARY DEVELOPMENTS [5]
GUAM—*See* CONGRESS; ELECTIONS [29]; POLLUTION [8]

GUATEMALA—Officials assassinated. Olivero Castaneda Paiz, a leader of the ruling National Liberation Movement (MLN) and first vice president of Congress, was shot to death in Guatemala City June 25 by two young men who presumably were left-wing guerrillas. The two escaped. Castaneda reportedly had been accused of being a leader of the White Hand, a right-wing terrorist organization. His assassination ended a period of relative political peace among the country's various terrorist groups. Four other leaders of the MLN— Cayetano Estrada, Juan Barrientos, Jose Duarte and Miguel Angel Espin— were reported killed July 12 by gunmen in different parts of the country. However, the government allegedly denied the reports.

Defense minister resigns. Gen. Leonel Vassaux Martinez, frequently mentioned as a possible presidential candidate in the 1974 elections, resigned as defense minister, according to a report July 14. He was replaced by the army chief of staff, Gen. Eugenio Kjell Laugerud Garcia.

See also LATIN AMERICA

GUINEA—Government changes. President Sekou Toure April 27 announced creation of the post of premier, to be filled by Economics Minister Lansana Beavogui, who would also control the army, foreign affairs and information. The other members of the new government: economic and financial affairs— Ismael Toure; trade and communications—Barry Alpha Oumar; social affairs—Nfamara Keita; education—Mamadi Keita; interior—Moussa Diakite.

Sekou Toure June 9 announced a reform of the government which expanded the Cabinet to 29 ministerial posts, grouped under seven "domains" and five "superministries." Those in charge of the superministries had all been members of the old Cabinet, with Oumar moving to social affairs and Nfamara Keita taking over responsibility for exchanges. Saifoulaye Dially was named minister delegate to the presidency and Fily Sissoko became foreign minister.

See also CUBA

GUN CONTROL—*See* CRIME [9]

GUYANA—Cabinet changes. Prime Minister Forbes Burnham Aug. 2 shuffled and expanded his Cabinet following the resignation of all ministers Aug. 1. Only one member of the old Cabinet—Information and Culture Minister Edwin McDavid—was replaced. Seven ministers shifted portfolios, and Burnham himself gave up several portfolios while remaining defense minister and head of the Cabinet. Three technocrats were brought in, raising the Cabinet's membership to 18. A communique Aug. 2 said that the Cabinet changes were aimed at "streamlining the Cabinet and government in terms of greater effectiveness in the context of the philosophy of cooperativism and the maximum involvement of the people, at the same time making the fullest possible use of the expertise and professionalism available."

Elections postponed. Parliament Dec. 22 postponed for two years local elections scheduled for December.

See also INTERNATIONAL MONETARY DEVELOPMENTS [8]; LATIN AMERICA; TERRITORIAL WATERS

HAITI—Dominique dismissed. It was reported Jan. 3 that President Jean-Claude Duvalier had fired his brother-in-law, Max Dominique, as ambassador to France. It was also reported that Dominique's cousin, Michel Bernardin, had been recalled as Haitian consul in Le Havre, France. Dominique's dismissal was linked Jan. 6 to a power struggle between Dominque's wife, Marie-Denise (sister of the president), and President Duvalier and his close associate, Defense Minister Luckner Cambronne.

Cambronne dismissed. President Duvalier Nov. 15 dismissed Cambronne. No reason was given for the action, but observers cited Cambronne's rivalry with Marie-Denise and Dominique. Cambronne took refuge in the Colombian embassy outside Port-au-Prince for over a week before being allowed to leave Haiti. He arrived in Colombia Nov. 27 on a Haitian passport, not under political asylum. Cambronne was to be replaced as interior and defense minister by Roger Lafontant, Haitian general consul in New York, a close confidant of the Duvaliers. Finance and Economics Minister Edouard Francisque would assume Cambronne's duties as head of the Cabinet. (In announcing Cambronne's dismissal, Duvalier also announced the dismissal without explanation of Justice Minister Andre Rousseau.)

Aftermath of dismissal. Following Cambronne's dismissal, the government decreed a number of reforms. A controversial 10-year contract which permitted a U.S. firm to export blood plasma taken from Haitians for sale in the U.S. was canceled by the government Nov. 21. (The pact had been made by Cambronne with Hemo-Caribbean of Haiti.) The government Nov. 25 decreed that all future divorce applications from non-Haitians be submitted to a council of lawyers and that all government fees from the divorce court be placed in a special fund to be administered by the Defense and Justice Ministries. (In the past, most of the revenue from non-Haitian divorces had gone to Cambronne.) Some observers said the decree could put an end to Haiti's quick-divorce business. The government Nov. 28 granted full pardons to 60 political prisoners and reduced the sentences of 29 others, including key figures in the 1968 Cap-Haitien invasion. Seventy-two other political prisoners were freed Dec. 19. The government Nov. 28 also moved against some of Cambronne's extensive economic interests, placing most of them under the temporary direction of the Bank of Haiti. A reorganization also was ordered in the national security service, where Cambronne had built up a personal following that officials said amounted to his own informal armed force.

See also LATIN AMERICA

183

HANRAHAN, EDWARD V.—See BLACK MILITANTS
HARDIN, CLIFFORD—See POLITICS [2]
HARRISBURG 7—See SECURITY, U.S.
HARTKE, VANCE—See ELECTIONS [3, 5-7]
HASSAN II, KING—See MOROCCO
HEAD START—See POVERTY

HEALTH—Polio epidemics. Epidemics of poliomyelitis broke out during 1972 in Mexico and in Trinidad and Tobago, spurring campaigns of massive inoculations against the disease. In Mexico, 110 polio cases were reported between Jan. 1 and April 10, spurring a campaign to inoculate 85% of the population. One out of every four cases of polio reportedly occurred in Mexico. In Trinidad and Tobago, the epidemic affected 173 persons and killed 10 between Dec. 25, 1971 and Feb. 8, closing schools and forcing the cancellation of carnival celebrations scheduled for Feb. 14-15. The epidemic virtually halted tourism and caused financial losses estimated at $2 million. The government reportedly started an intensive vaccination program in early February with the assistance of the Pan American Health Organization. U.S. agencies sent 50,000 doses of oral vaccine, three respirators and an iron lung to aid in combatting the epidemic. Newspapers in Trinidad and Tobago reportedly criticized the government for the outbreak, attributing it to failure to clean up Port of Spain, particularly the smoldering municipal dump located near the city's center.

Smallpox cases rise. The number of smallpox cases recorded in the first three months of 1972 surged 94% compared to the same period in 1971, the World Health Organization (WHO) reported April 8. Some 15,200 cases were reported in such areas as Ethiopia, India, Pakistan, Nepal and the Sudan. In Bangla Desh, reportedly 7,000 deaths during the two-month period ending April 11 had been attributed to smallpox. In Syria, the number of cases rose to 47 April 13. Yugoslavia April 9 unofficially reported 33 smallpox deaths over a three-week period.

Cholera outbreaks. It was reported Feb. 3 that at least 27 persons had died from cholera in Angola during January. Ninety cases of the disease were found, mostly at Luanda, Porto Amboim, Benguela and Gabela. Half a million persons were vaccinated. Cholera broke out in Australia and New Zealand during November. A meal prepared at the Bahrain airport for the economy class of a Qantas Airlines jet was considered to be the probable source of the disease. The plane had arrived in Sydney Nov. 4. By Nov. 14, 40 cholera cases were confirmed in Australia. In New Zealand, an elderly passenger on the flight died of cholera Nov. 9.

Intensified VD drive urged. The National Commission on Venereal Disease, a federal health panel of 16 physicians and an osteopath, reported April 4 that the federal campaign against venereal disease, although intensified by a $16 million drive against gonorrhea announced Feb. 8, was still inadequate to control a situation described as having reached epidemic proportions. (Officials in the Department of Health, Education and Welfare had estimated April 4 that there would be 1,000 new cases of infectious syphilis and a record 2.5 million new cases of gonorrhea in 1972. The rise in syphilis would be the largest since antibiotic drugs began 20 years ago to control the disease.) The panel cited an "alarming increase" of reported venereal disease cases, "woefully inadequate efforts" in research, inadequate VD education, the failure of doctors to report new cases and a lack of federal funds. At the same time, the group recommended a series of steps to make more effective the federal effort against VD, including measures for increased testing, better education, more money and stricter reporting of VD cases. The testing recommendation included a proposal for a voluntary VD education program for schoolchildren in the 7th grade. It would also provide for mandatory enforcement of existing tests for VD that would result in the testing of some 40 million Americans in fiscal 1973. The panel recommended that over $300 million in federal funds be spent over the next five fiscal years to fight VD, including $46.1 million which the panel said should be spent in the fiscal year beginning July 1. The budget of the Nixon Administration had earmarked $31 million for fighting VD in fiscal 1973.

Syphilis project revealed. The Associated Press (AP) July 25 made public details of a U.S. syphilis study involving 600 Alabama black men that dated back to 1932. According to the report, the U.S. Public Health Service (PHS) conducted the study in which 400 black men with syphilis went untreated, even after a cure for the disease (penicillin) was known, in order to determine from autopsies what untreated syphilis did to the human body. The other 200 men, who had no syphilis, were monitored as a control group. The men used in the study were induced to join the program with promises of free lunches, free transportation, free medicine for any disease other than syphilis and free burial after autopsies were performed.

Mercury poisoning in Iraq. The worst outbreak of mercury poisoning on record killed hundreds of people in Iraq over a two-month period ending May 5. Reports March 8 said hospitals were "jammed" with poisoning cases. The poisoning apparently stemmed from grain imported from Canada and coated with a mercury-based fungicide. The grain, intended for planting, had been used as cattle fodder or ground into flour. The Kirkuk region, about 150 miles north of Baghdad, was cited as the source of the outbreak. The government March 10 denied that hundreds had died and said that strict controls had brought the outbreak under control. The controls were lifted May 5.

Typhoid fever epidemic in Mexico. Mexico City health authorities, according to a report June 14, claimed that an outbreak of typhoid fever in the central states of Hidalgo, Tlaxcala, Mexico and Puebla had been brought under control. Several thousand cases had reportedly occurred since January in the largest epidemic of the disease in several decades. Health authorities had reported June 6 that the strain of typhoid bacterium causing the epidemic had become resistant to chloramphenicol, the drug generally used to treat the disease, and to three other antibiotics. Doctors said the infection could be treated adequately by other antibiotic drugs.

Smoking and Health

Cigarettes also endanger nonsmokers. U.S. Surgeon General Jesse L. Steinfeld Jan. 10 reported to Congress that persons who did not smoke cigarettes faced some of the same health hazards of smoking that imperiled smokers. Steinfeld placed new emphasis on carbon monoxide as a hazard in cigarette smoke, for the first time listing the gas as among the "most likely" contributors to the hazards of smoking cigarettes. He cited studies showing that the levels of carbon monoxide in a room or automobile with persons smoking could rise above the occupational guideline of 50 parts per million in effect in the U.S., endangering nonsmokers as well as smokers. As he did in his 1971 report to the Congress, Steinfeld recommended banning smoking in public places.

Ads to have warning. The Federal Trade Commission (FTC) said Jan. 31 that the nation's six largest cigarette manufacturers (American Brands, Inc.; the Brown & Williamson Tobacco Corp.; Liggett & Myers, Inc.; the Lorillard Division of Loews Corp.; Philip Morris, Inc.; and the R. J. Reynolds Tobacco Co.) had agreed to use a "clear and conspicuous" health warning in their cigarette advertisements. During 1971, advertisements by all the companies except American Brands had included pictures of cigarette packages which carried the statement required by federal law: "Warning: the Surgeon General has determined that cigarette smoking is dangerous to your health." The FTC had said that the warnings displayed voluntarily were not sufficiently conspicuous and had warned the companies in July 1971 that it would start court action unless the six companies agreed to display health warnings. Under the consent order, the six companies—who accounted for 99% of all cigarette production in the U.S. and virtually all cigarette advertising—agreed to display the package warning in a black bordered space at the bottom of each advertisement.

See also ATOMIC ENERGY [1]; BRAZIL; EARTHQUAKES; ELECTIONS [17]; HEALTH CARE; MINES; PESTICIDES; POLLUTION [3]; STATE & LOCAL GOVERNMENTS; STORMS

HEALTH CARE—Free hospital care ordered. Health, Education and Welfare (HEW) Secretary Elliot L. Richardson, acting in response to five class action suits filed against HEW, April 18 announced new regulations, effective May 18, to enforce requirements that all hospitals and health care facilities that have received federal aid provide a minimum amount of free services to poor people. Under the rules, any institution that had ever accepted funds under the Hill-Burton Act would have to provide free services to poor people equivalent to at least 5% of its operating cost and at least 25% of its net income. Failure to comply with the rules would invoke penalties ranging to revocation of the facility's license. Institutions in financial difficulties or in areas of few poor people would be exempt.

Landmark mental health decision. In what was regarded as a landmark decision, U.S. District Court Judge Frank M. Johnson Jr. April 13 ordered Alabama to meet detailed guidelines for psychiatric treatment and custodial care in its institutions for the mentally ill and retarded. The decision set minimum professional and nonprofessional staff-patient ratios, as well as minimum educational-time and class-size limits for a school for the retarded. An "individual treatment plan" for each patient was required, and federal minimum wages were ordered to be paid for any work performed. (The decision also said that work could not be compulsory.) Seven-member "human rights committees," with a patient on each, were named for each facility, to review all programs and aid patients who claimed rights abuses. If the Alabama legislature did not provide funds for the remedial action, or if the Alabama Mental Health Board failed to abide by the specific standards within six months, the court pledged to appoint a master to oversee operations. The decision came in a suit brought by patients and staff members at two mental hospitals and a school for the mentally retarded.

Health Services Corps inaugurated. The newly organized National Health Services Corps May 23 assigned its first 288 professional personnel to 122 communities with inadequate services in 39 states and the District of Columbia. The volunteers, who would be fulfilling their draft obligation, would be paid with federal money, with doctors receiving $12,000-$15,000 annually. The 152 doctors, 72 nurses, 20 dentists and 44 other personnel included in the first assignment began serving in rural and urban slum areas in July. (Patients involved in the program were to be billed according to their ability to pay.)

U.S. emergency care criticized. A National Research Council report Sept. 17 charged that "thousands of lives" were lost in the U.S. each year "through lack of systematic application of established principles of emergency care." The report also charged that HEW and the Executive Office of the President had failed to mobilize existing resources to develop a nationwide emergency treatment system. The council asked the Executive Office of the President to organize implementation of a program which would include: establishment of a nationwide "911" emergency telephone number staffed by informed operators; replacement of 80% of the nation's 25,000 ambulances as inadequate; establishment of emergency communications centers and special radio frequencies; nationwide training of emergency personnel; classification of hospitals according to their specialized emergency resources; upgrading of hospital emergency staffs and an increase in emergency residencies; more responsibility for nurses; and increased research funds.

Health facilities study. The General Accounting Office (GAO—the auditing arm of Congress) Nov. 22 released a report stating that billions of dollars could be cut from the costs of health care in the U.S. by better construction planning, more attention to preventive medicine and better use of current facilities. The report focused principally on better construction planning. The report recommended: reuse of hospital designs rather than a search for architectural originality; establishment of a central data bank for hospital planners to obtain information about construction techniques, operating systems and materials; adoption of a common set of new construction requirements under federal building programs; and use of systems analysis in design and construction. The report also recommended: a sharing of hospital services to reduce the demand for new facilities; expanded home health care programs; and use of out-patient clinics and nursing homes to handle services generally provided in the hospital room. (The study found that one of every four patients was receiving more care than necessary in hospitals and that health insurance coverage promoted such unnecessary care.) The report also noted a deficiency in planning on the part of hospitals, reflected in the fact that "less than 50% of the 163 health planning agencies responding to our inquiries...provided data showing they had knowledge of 1972 needs for various types of in-patient, extended and ambulatory care facilities and beds."

See also ABORTION; NIXON, RICHARD MILHOUS

HEATH, EDWARD—See GREAT BRITAIN [3, 7]; NORTHERN IRELAND [9-10]
HEINEMANN, GUSTAV—See GERMANY, WEST [5, 12]; OLYMPICS [5]
HERBICIDES—See PESTICIDES
HEROIN—See DRUG USE & ADDICTION [1-2, 8-9, 11-14, 16-18]
HEXACHLOROPHENE—See CONSUMER AFFAIRS [14]
HIGHWAY TRUST FUND—See TRANSPORTATION

HIJACKING—Aircraft hijackings continued through 1972 (see [2-13]), with hijackers claiming ransoms as high as $2 million (see [6]). The continued terrorism led to harsher countering actions from authorities. The U.S. issued orders for stricter airport screening of passengers and detection of possible hijackers (see [14]). Airline pilots around the world struck during June to press demands for more stringent international sanctions against hijacking and sabotage of aircraft (see [15]). The United Nations issued a strongly worded consensus statement condemning hijacking and calling for preventive and punitive measures (see [16]). The U.S. and Cuba began talks in November to stop the hijacking of U.S. airliners to Cuba (see [19]).

[2] **U.S. hijackings.** An unidentified couple with an infant Jan. 7 hijacked a Pacific Southwest Airlines jet en route from San Francisco to Los Angeles, forcing the plane to fly to Cuba when they found it did not have the range to fly to Africa. The 132 passengers on the plane were permitted to disembark at Los Angeles, but seven stewardesses were kept aboard as hostages. Former Army paratrooper Richard C. LaPoint was arrested Jan. 20 near Sterling, Colo. hours after he parachuted with $50,000 ransom from a plane he had commandeered on a flight from Las Vegas to Reno. LaPoint had taken over the plane by telling a crewman that he had a bomb. Jose Luis Lugo, who had used banker Jose Luis Carrion as a hostage to collect $290,000 ransom from a San Juan, Puerto Rico bank, hijacked a plane April 7 to take him and his hostage to Cuba. Richard F. McCoy Jr., a former Green Beret and a Brigham Young University student majoring in law enforcement, April 7 commandeered a United Airlines jetliner en route to Los Angeles from Newark, N.J. After collecting $500,000 ransom in Los Angeles, McCoy ordered the plane aloft, with five crew members aboard, and later parachuted out near Provo, Utah. He was arrested April 9 by the Federal Bureau of Investigation (FBI), and was sentenced July 10 to 45 years in prison for the hijacking. Stanley H. Speck, a cabdriver, April 9 took over a Pacific Southwest Airlines jet on its way to San Diego from Oakland. He demanded parachutes and a $500,000 ransom when the plane landed in San Diego, but was seized by FBI agents when he left the plane to pick up maps.

[3] Ricardo Chavez-Ortiz, a Mexican, April 13 hijacked a Frontier Airlines jet en route from Albuquerque, N.M. to Phoenix and forced it to land in Los Angeles, but surrendered to the FBI after he had decried injustices suffered by

the poor and minorities in a two-hour interview with newsmen. During the interview, Chavez-Ortiz held the plane's crew at gunpoint, but his gun later was found to be empty. The FBI and Chicago police April 17 arrested William Herbert Green 3rd, who had sought to extort $500,000 after hijacking a Delta Air Lines jet en route from Miami to Chicago with 91 persons aboard. Michael Lynn Hansen used a pistol to hijack a Western Airlines plane to Cuba May 5. Hansen had originally demanded that the plane, en route from Salt Lake City, Utah to Los Angeles, be flown to Hanoi, but changed his mind when told that the plane could not travel that far. A pistol-armed hijacker May 5 commandeered an Eastern Airlines jet en route from Allentown, Pa. to Miami and ordered it flown to Washington, D.C. At Dulles Airport in Washington, he demanded and received $303,000 in ransom and let the 48 passengers get off the plane. The plane took off but, after circling Dulles for an hour, landed again. On the second landing, the hijacker exchanged the ransom, mostly in $100 bills, for an equal amount in $500 and $1,000 bills. He then ordered the plane to New Orleans for a refueling stopover which turned into a five-hour delay when airport officials told him the plane was no longer operable. Using the crew as hostages, he climbed aboard a substitute plane that took him to Honduras, where he bailed out over jungle area. Frederick W. Hahneman, who was suspected of being the hijacker, surrendered at the U.S. embassy in Tegucigalpa, Honduras June 2. He was charged June 3 in a federal court in Alexandria, Va. with three counts of air piracy, kidnaping and assault. He pleaded not guilty. The ransom money was not recovered.

[4]   Robb D. Heady, a Vietnam veteran, took over a United Air Lines jet June 3, while it was on the ground at Reno before going on to San Francisco, and held three stewardesses and two pilots hostage while he collected $200,000 in ransom and had a second jet made ready for his escape. Shortly after the second jet was in the air, Heady parachuted into the Nevada hills near Reno. He was arrested by police five hours later. Police and FBI agents later recovered all the ransom money. Heady was sentenced Aug. 25 to 30 years in prison for the hijacking. William Holder and Catherine Kerkow June 2 took over a Western Airlines jet as it began its descent in Seattle. The two ordered the plane to New York where Holder picked up $500,000 in ransom and exchanged 36 hostages for a navigator to take the jet to Algiers. The two were taken into custody by the Algerian government on their arrival in Algiers. Martin Joseph McNally, an unemployed veteran, June 23 commandeered an American Airlines jet en route from St. Louis to Tulsa and forced it to return to St. Louis, where he demanded a $502,200 ransom, a parachute and a shovel. He allowed 80 of the 93 passengers to disembark at St. Louis, but ordered the plane aloft before he collected his ransom. He ordered the plane to Fort Worth, but ordered it back to St. Louis just before landing at Fort Worth. In St. Louis, he received the ransom and released 12 more passengers and two of the seven crew members. The commandeered jet was disabled on an airport apron at St. Louis when an automobile crashed into its underbelly. Changing planes, the hijacker took off from St. Louis June 24 and later bailed out near Peru, Ind. $502,000 of the ransom money was found by a farmer in a bean field in Peru June 26. The same day, another farmer found the machine gun used in the hijacking in a field five miles away. McNally was arrested by the FBI June 29 and charged with extortion and hijacking. Walter J. Petilkowsky of Detroit was arrested by the FBI June 30 and charged with helping McNally plan the hijacking.

[5]   Charles Smith surrendered to police at the Greater Buffalo International Airport July 5 after holding his infant daughter at knifepoint aboard an empty jetliner and threatening to kill her unless he was flown to a foreign country. Smith had earlier stabbed his estraged wife and another man in a Buffalo apartment. He was arraigned later July 5 on a federal charge of attempted hijacking. Spec. 4 Francis M. Goodell, an Army mechanic absent without leave from his post, July 7 hijacked a plane en route from Oakland to Sacramento and ordered it to land at San Diego. In San Diego, he collected $455,000 in

ransom and freed 52 of the 57 persons aboard. He then ordered the plane to Oakland, where he said he wanted a helicopter ready for his use. One of his hostages persuaded Goodell to surrender to the FBI in Oakland July 8. Melvin Martin Fisher, who used an empty revolver July 12 to hijack an American Airlines jet bound for Dallas from Oklahoma City, surrendered to a stewardess on the plane July 13. Fisher had ordered the plane back to Oklahoma City, where he had collected $200,000 of a demanded $550,000 ransom and had allowed the 51 passengers to deplane. He ordered the plane back into the air and then surrendered. He was sentenced Sept. 28 to life imprisonment for air piracy. Michael Stanley Green and Lulseyd Tesfa July 12 commandeered a National Airlines jet en route from Philadelphia to New York and forced the plane to return to Philadelphia. The two freed 113 passengers in Philadelphia in return for a $501,600 ransom, part of it in Mexican pesos. They forced the crew aboard another jet, which they ordered to take a southwest course. In landing at a small airfield in Lake Jackson, Tex., the crew deliberately swerved the plane, bursting the jet's tires and immobilizing the aircraft. Shortly afterward, the two armed hijackers surrendered to an FBI agent. A group of black hijackers (George Edward Wright, George Brown, Melvin McNair, Jean Carol Allen McNair and Joyce T. Burgess), later identified as sympathizers of the Black Panthers, July 31 hijacked a Delta Airlines jet en route to Miami from Detroit, directing the plane to Algeria after collecting a record $1 million ransom. The 101 passengers were allowed to disembark at Miami before the plane flew to Boston for refueling and for the boarding of a trans-Atlantic navigator. Upon their arrival in Algiers Aug. 1, the hijackers were taken into custody and the ransom was impounded. The hijackers were released Aug. 4; but the Algerian government continued to hold the ransom, despite a request by American Black Panthers exiled in Algeria that the money be turned over to them. (The Algerian government Aug. 23 turned the money over to Delta Airlines.)

[6] Charles A. Tuller, his sons Bryce and Jonathan, and William W. Graham Oct. 29 hijacked an Eastern Airlines jet to Havana after killing a ticket agent during the seizure of the plane at Houston International Airport. The four had been charged with murder, attempted murder and attempted bank robbery in connection with a bank holdup Oct. 24 in Arlington, Va. in which a bank manager and guard were killed. The four were taken into custody by Cuban officials upon their arrival in Havana and were indicted by the U.S. on air piracy and kidnaping charges Nov. 16. Henry D. Jackson and Lewis D. Moore (both suspected rapists) and Melvin C. Cale (Moore's half-brother and an escapee from a Tennessee penitentiary) took over Southern Airways Flight 49 after it departed Birmingham, Ala. Nov. 10. The three were armed with pistols and hand grenades. On board the DC-9, destined for Memphis, were 27 passengers and a crew of four. Under the hijackers' control, the plane was diverted to Jackson, Miss. for refueling. It then flew north and the hijackers radioed ahead for Detroit officials to meet them to negotiate demands for a $10 million ransom. Instead of landing in Detroit, however, the plane flew to Cleveland for refueling and then flew to Toronto, where it landed after circling for three hours. The hijackers then took the plane south. While circling Knoxville, Tenn., the hijackers demanded an official document stating that the $10 million would be a "U.S. government grant." They threatened to crash the plane into the Atomic Energy Commission's installation in nearby Oak Ridge if their demands were not met. The hijackers then ordered the plane flown to Lexington, Ky., where it was refueled, and then returned to circling over Knoxville. At 1 p.m. Nov. 11, the plane headed for Chattanooga, where the hijackers took aboard a reported $2 million ransom and ordered the jet to Havana. Negotiations between the hijackers and Cuban officials broke down in Havana, however; and the plane took off for Key West, Fla., where it was refueled and flew off to McCoy Air Force Base in Orlando, Fla. During a servicing stopover at McCoy, one of the hijackers shot co-pilot Billy H. Johnson in the shoulder. As the plane taxied for takeoff, FBI agents shot out

the plane's tires in hopes of keeping the DC-9 at the base—a move which later stirred debate that it had impaired the safety of the passengers and crew. Despite the punctured tires, the plane successfully took off to Key West, where it circled while the hijackers unsuccessfully demanded to talk to President Nixon, who was at his Key Biscayne home. The gunmen then ordered the plane back to Havana, where it circled to burn off fuel and successfully landed on a foam-covered runway. The three hijackers were seized by Cuban authorities, who also took the ransom. Two passengers and the co-pilot were hospitalized. The passengers and crew of the hijacked jet returned to Miami Nov. 12. Cuba announced Nov. 20 that the hijackers would be tried for offenses committed during their first Cuban landing. The three also were indicted Nov. 21 by a U.S. grand jury on charges of air piracy, kidnaping and obstruction of interstate commerce.

[7] *Hijackers shot.* An FBI agent Jan. 27 killed Heinrich vonGeorge with a shotgun blast at close range after vonGeorge had received a $200,000 ransom. VonGeorge had taken over the Mohawk jet, en route from Albany, N.Y. to a suburban airport, with a track starter's pistol and a fake bomb. An FBI agent posing as a Trans World Airlines crewman Jan. 29 shot and captured Garrett Brock Trapnell, a former mental patient who had hijacked a Los Angeles-to-New York TWA jet. Trapnell was shot at New York before any of the $300,000 ransom he had demanded was turned over. An armed passenger July 2 shot and killed Nguyen Thai Binh, a South Vietnamese student who had sought to commandeer a Pan American Airways jet, en route from San Francisco to Saigon. Binh was killed in Saigon. He had said his hijacking was an "act of revenge" for American bombing of North Vietnam. FBI agents, one of them disguised as a pilot, July 5 shot and killed Dimitr Alexiev and Michael Dimitrov Azmanoff, who had taken over a Southwest Airline flight from Sacramento to Los Angeles and had held the passengers and crew at gunpoint at the San Francisco International Airport while they waited for an $800,000 ransom. One passenger (E. H. Stanley Carter) was killed and two others wounded in the gun battle between the hijackers and the FBI. The hijackers had demanded that they be flown to Siberia. In related actions in other countries: an armed teenager who had tried to hijack an Italian plane on a domestic flight was found shot to death aboard the plane Oct. 7, the apparent victim of a gunfight with police the night before; a West German sharpshooter Nov. 25 shot to death Victor Widera, a German citizen who had held a stewardess hostage for almost 24 hours aboard an Air Canada DC-8 jet at Frankfurt Airport; seven hijackers were killed by Ethiopian security guards Dec. 8 when they tried to take over a national airlines plane bound for Paris from Addis Ababa.

[8] **Arab guerrilla actions.** Five Palestinian guerrillas, self-identified as members of the Organization for Victims of Zionist Occupation but later identified as members of the Popular Front for the Liberation of Palestine, Feb. 21 hijacked a West German Lufthansa jumbo jet airliner, en route from New Delhi to Athens, and diverted the plane to Aden, Southern Yemen Feb. 22. According to the plane's pilot, the guerrillas did not say they wanted to fly to any specific country, but submitted compass readings that would have brought them to the desert along the Red Sea on the coast of the Arabian peninsula. They were persuaded to fly to Aden instead. On landing, the hijackers wired the doors of the jet with explosives and threatened to blow it up. All 172 passengers held hostage—including Joseph P. Kennedy 3rd, son of the late Sen. Robert F. Kennedy—were released Feb. 22. The 16 crew members were freed Feb. 23 and the hijackers surrendered to Yemeni authorities. The guerrillas' motives for seizing the plane were not clear, according to Yemeni and West German officials who questioned them. West German Transport Minister Georg Leber said Feb. 25 that the hijackers had demanded $5 million in ransom Feb. 22 for the release of the plane and crew. The money reportedly was paid. The hijackers were released by Yemeni authorities Feb. 27 and left Aden for an unknown destination.

[9] *Hijackers thwarted at Lod.* Israeli paratroopers, disguised as aircraft repairmen, May 9 broke into a hijacked Belgian airliner at Lod Airport in Tel Aviv, killing two of four Palestinian commandos and rescuing all 90 passengers and 10 crewmen. (A woman passenger, accidentally wounded by the Israelis, died May 18.) The plane, operated by Sabena Airlines, had been seized May 8 by the two male and two female Arabs after taking off from Vienna en route to Tel Aviv. The hijackers, armed with guns and grenades, were identified as members of the Black September Organization, a splinter commando group. On landing at Lod, the Arabs, using International Committee of the Red Cross (ICRC) representatives as intermediaries, began negotiating with Israeli authorities in the field's control tower. The guerrillas demanded the release of 317 Palestinian commandos in Israeli prisons in exchange for the safety of the plane and its passengers and crew, and threatened to blow up the aircraft with all its hostages if the demands were not met. According to Lt. Gen. David Elazar, Army chief of staff, the negotiations with the commandos were merely a ploy to gain time for preparing a plan to take over the plane. Both negotiations and the takeover were directed by Defense Minister Moshe Dayan. Witnesses said that Israelis crawled under the aircraft during the night of May 9 and damaged the plane, making it unable to take off. They offered to repair the plane so that it could fly on to Cairo with the hostages, as the hijackers later demanded. The 18 disguised paratroopers then were driven to the airliner in an airlines service vehicle, opened two emergency doors and burst into the jet. A 10-second exchange of gunfire with the Arabs followed, killing the two male hijackers and wounding one of the female hijackers. An Israeli military court Aug. 14 convicted and sentenced both female hijackers (Therese Halasseh and Rima Issa Tannous) to life imprisonment for their role in the hijacking. The two women, both members of Al Fatah, could have received the death penalty for two of the four counts on which they were convicted—carrying weapons and explosives.

[10] **Czechoslovak miners hijack flight.** Two Czechoslovak miners, later identified as Antonin Lerch and Karel Dolezal, hijacked a domestic airliner on a flight from Prague to Marienbad April 18 and forced it to land in Nuremberg, West Germany, requesting political asylum. Lerch shot and slightly wounded the pilot, Robert Pfleger, who flew the plane back to Czechoslovakia later in the day. Lerch and Dolezal, who said they had hijacked the plane because of opposition to Czechoslovak political conditions, were convicted July 31 by a court in Nuremberg to seven years in prison for the hijacking. In a related development, 10 Czechoslovaks June 8 forced a domestic airliner on a flight from Marienbad to Prague to land in Weiden, West Germany. The hijackers—seven men, two women and a child—seized the plane shortly after takeoff and ordered the pilot to fly to Nuremberg. According to a report June 10, the pilot, who refused the order, was shot and killed when a crewman tried to subdue one of the hijackers.

[11] **Turkish hijackers free passengers, plane.** Four armed Turkish guerrillas May 3 hijacked an Ankara-to-Istanbul flight and forced the plane to fly to the airport in Sofia, Bulgaria, where they threatened to blow up the plane and everyone aboard unless the Turkish government agreed to their demand for the release of condemned guerrillas Deniz Gezmis, Yusef Aslan and Huseyin Inan (*see* TURKEY). Later reports said the hijackers had also demanded the release of at least three other imprisoned guerrillas. The Turkish government refused to bargain with the hijackers—who extended their ultimatum deadline several times—but said it would agree to asylum for the guerrillas in Bulgaria if they released the passengers and crew. The four abandoned their demands May 4 and released unharmed the 68 passengers and crewmen. They were granted political asylum in Bulgaria after their surrender, but were each sentenced to three years in prison by a Bulgarian court Nov. 3. (Four armed hijackers, reportedly Turkish students, Oct. 22 hijacked an Istanbul-to-Ankara flight and forced the pilot to fly to Sofia. The hijackers

threatened to blow up the plane and 60 hostages if the Turkish government did not release 12 leftist prisoners, abolish a strike ban in martial law areas, provide greater freedom in the universities, present a program of land reform and end "anti-democratic" articles in the constitution. The four surrendered to authorities in Sofia Oct. 23 after the Turkish government refused to grant their demands. Bulgaria granted political asylum to the hijackers.)

[12] **South African jet hijacked to Malawi.** Two Lebanese men (Fyad Abdul Camil, a South African resident, and A. Yaghi, a Lebanese resident) May 24 seized a South African Airways jet on a flight from Salisbury, Rhodesia to Johannesburg, South Africa and diverted it to the airport at Blantyre, Malawi. The Lebanese reportedly hoped to extort "an amount of money" from Harry Oppenheimer, chairman of the Anglo-American Mining Co., one of the world's largest diamond concerns. Shortly after the plane landed in Blantyre, technicians let the air out of its tires. The five passengers remaining on board (53 were released in Salisbury during a refueling stop) and four crewmen escaped from the plane while the hijackers were inspecting the contents of a box of ransom money that had been brought on board. Malawi government troops then rushed the plane and captured the two Lebanese. The two were sentenced Sept. 18 by a Malawi court to 11 years in prison.

[13] **Croats surrender in Spain.** Three Croatian gunmen, believed to be members of the Yugoslavian Utashi terrorist movement, Sept. 15 hijacked a Scandinavian Airlines System (SAS) plane bound from Guteborg to Stockholm and forced it to land at Malmo, Sweden. The hijackers demanded the release of seven Croatian prisoners, including two men convicted for the 1971 murder of the Yugoslav ambassador to Sweden, in exchange for the lives of the plane's 79 passengers and four crewmen. They threatened to blow up the plane unless the demand was met. After an emergency Cabinet session, Swedish Premier Olaf Palme ordered the prisoners taken to the Malmo airport, where Justice Minister Lennart Geijer conducted negotiations with the hijackers. After three prisoners had been exchanged for 30 passengers, the terrorists refused to go on with the exchange until they were paid about $200,000. The Croats settled for half that amount, however, and the exchange was completed. (One prisoner refused to join the hijackers.) Following the exchange, the Croats flew to Madrid, Spain, where they surrendered to authorities Sept. 16 within hours of their arrival. The surrender followed three hours of negotiations with Spanish authorities and reportedly was partly caused by the terrorists' belief that few countries would accept them. Although there was no extradition treaty between Spain and Sweden, Sweden Sept. 19 made a formal request for the return of the three hijackers and the six exchanged prisoners. The Spanish Aviation Ministry announced Sept. 23 that the three hijackers would be put on trial in a military court and the six prisoners would be turned over to civilian authorities. The $100,000 ransom was returned to Sweden.

Anti-Hijack Measures

[14] **U.S. government actions.** The Federal Aviation Administration (FAA) announced Feb. 1 an order, effective Feb. 5, that required the nation's scheduled airlines to begin screening all passengers and their baggage to prevent hijackings and sabotage. Most domestic airlines had voluntarily been using an FAA-approved screening system, but the new order made screening mandatory for all domestic and foreign flights by U.S. scheduled airlines. Under the system, airline employees would use a "behavioral profile" devised by the FAA to detect passengers displaying behavioral traits common to many hijackers. All passengers going through boarding gates would also pass through magnetometers that detect the presence of a metal object that could be a weapon or explosive device. In later action, presidential adviser John D. Ehrlichman disclosed July 7 that President Nixon had ordered the FAA to require all commuter airlines to follow the same anti-hijacking measures prescribed for the commercial air carriers. The FAA also announced Sept. 2

that it would require 54 foreign airlines operating in the U.S. to meet the same security regulations as required for U.S. airlines.

[15] **Pilots stage 24-hour strike.** Airline pilots around the world staged a one-day work stoppage June 19 to press for more stringent international sanctions against hijacking and sabotage of aircraft. The strike, organized by the International Federation of Air Line Pilots' Associations (a blanket group of national pilots' unions), was the first strike by international pilots on the world's carriers. Specifically, the pilots were seeking to have the United Nations Security Council direct the U.N. International Civil Aviation Authority to begin setting up the necessary machinery to enforce anti-hijacking accords. While it was virtually impossible to determine exactly how many travelers were affected by the walkout, some reports put the number at 200,000—about 20% of the million passengers who would normally fly on a Monday in mid-June. The strike had the most impact in Europe. In almost all Western Europe, except Great Britain, air traffic was at a virtual standstill. In the U.S., most pilots obeyed court orders barring them from joining in the stoppage. Only about 10% of operations of U.S. airlines was disrupted, and only two major U.S. carriers (Eastern and Northeast) suspended flight operations entirely when the strike began at 2 a.m. EST June 19. Of the Communist-bloc nations, only pilots of Yugoslavia and Czechoslovakia showed support for the strike. Yugoslavian pilots stayed on the ground, while Czechoslovak pilots took part in a one-hour work stoppage. Among the major non-Communist nations whose pilots were nonparticipants in the strike were Australia, countries of the Arab world, the Philippines and Japan.

[16] **Security Council condemnation.** The U.S. Security Council June 20 issued a strongly worded consensus statement condemning aircraft hijacking and calling on all nations to deter and prevent such acts and "to take effective measures to deal with those who commit such acts."

[17] **Conference fails to adopt treaty.** A special 15-member conference on aircraft hijacking ended two weeks of meetings in Washington Sept. 15 without agreeing on the terms of a new international treaty against air piracy and sabotage. The new treaty had been fashioned by the U.S., Canada, Great Britain and the Netherlands as a compromise measure after the Soviet Union, Great Britain and France sharply opposed the terms of the original draft. The rewritten treaty outlined the machinery under which signatory nations could investigate whether another nation had improperly failed to punish or extradite hijackers or airline saboteurs. Under the original treaty, proposed when the conference opened Sept. 4, much stronger sanctions would have been imposed against nations failing to punish or extradite airplane terrorists. While the 15 nations could not agree on the terms of the revised treaty, the delegates agreed to submit proposed language for a new treaty to the Legal Committee of the International Civil Aviation Organization. The conference delegates emphasized, however, that they were sending the document on only for consideration and were not endorsing its specific terms.

[18] **Nixon signs accord.** President Nixon Nov. 1 signed an international agreement to curb hijackings by requiring the extradition or prosecution of persons who commit sabotage against international civil aviation. The agreement, known as the Montreal Sabotage Convention, was concluded in September 1971 and was the third in a series of such agreements aimed at providing an international groundwork for dealing with hijackers and terrorists. The agreement extended the two earlier accords on aircraft piracy to include a broader category of criminal acts such as sabotage and bomb threats as acts requiring extradition or prosecution.

[19] **U.S., Cuba talks begin.** The U.S. State Department announced Nov. 27 that negotiations on an accord to halt the hijacking of airliners to Cuba had begun in Havana Nov. 25. The Swiss ambassador to Cuba, who normally represented U.S. interests in Havana, was representing the U.S. (The U.S. and Cuba did not maintain diplomatic relations.)According to a report Dec. 5, the

U.S. and Cuba had agreed in principle that the proposed accord should cover ships as well as airplanes.

See also ARGENTINA [1, 12]; OLYMPIC TERRORISM

HOCKEY—All-Star game. Phil Esposito of the Boston Bruins scored against Minnesota's Gump Worsley early in the final period to give the East a 3-2 victory over the West Jan. 25 in the National Hockey League's (NHL) All-Star game in Bloomington, Minn. Esposito's goal gave the East a record of 2-1-1 since the NHL changed the All-Star game format in 1969 to pit East against West. Al MacNeil, the former coach of the Montreal Canadiens, coached the East. Billy Reay of the Chicago Black Hawks coached the West.

Boston U. wins NCAA title. Boston University won its second consecutive National Collegiate Athletic Association (NCAA) hockey title March 18 by shutting out Cornell, 4-0, in Boston. It was the first time that Cornell had been held scoreless in 225 games.

Czechs win amateur title. Czechoslovakia's national hockey team defeated the Soviet Union club, 3-2, April 20 in Prague to capture the world amateur hockey title. It was the first time in nine years that the Soviets had not won the championship in the round-robin competition.

Boston wins Stanley Cup. The Boston Bruins, anchored on defense and led on offense by all-star defenseman Bobby Orr, scored a 3-0 victory over the New York Rangers May 11 at New York's Madison Square Garden to win the championship round of the Stanley Cup playoffs four games to two. It was the Bruins' second Stanley Cup victory in the past three years. Boston, coached by Tom Johnson, had gained the final round by eliminating Toronto in five games and St. Louis in four. Under coach Emile Francis, the Rangers had stopped Montreal in six games and Chicago in four.

Canada edges Soviets. Canada's leading players in the NHL, skating together as Team Canada, recovered from a humiliating opening-game loss to the Soviet Union's national hockey team to capture an eight-game series, the first meeting between Canada's pros and the Soviet Union's perennial world amateur champions. The record for the series was four victories for Canada, three for the Soviets and one game tied. The game-by-game scores: Game One (Sept. 2 in Montreal)—Soviet Union 7, Canada 3; Game Two (Sept. 4 in Toronto)—Canada 4, Soviet Union 1; Game Three (Sept. 6 in Winnipeg)—tied 4-4; Game Four (Sept. 8 in Vancouver)—Soviet Union 5, Canada 3; Game Five (Sept. 22 in Moscow)—Soviet Union 5, Canada 4; Game Six (Sept. 24 in Moscow)—Canada 3, Soviet Union 2; Game Seven (Sept. 26 in Moscow)—Canada 4, Soviet Union 3; Game Eight (Sept. 28 in Moscow)—Canada 6, Soviet Union 5.

NHL to add 2 new clubs. The NHL's board of governors June 8 voted league franchises to Washington, D.C. and Kansas City, Mo. The Washington franchise went to Abe Pollin, a builder who also owned the Baltimore Bullets of the National Basketball Association. The Kansas City club, which would actually play its games in suburban Overland Park, Kan., would be operated by a group of businessmen headed by Edwin G. Thompson. The new clubs, the league's 17th and 18th, would begin league competition in 1974.

HODGSON, JAMES D.—*See* CIVIL RIGHTS [17]; NIXON, RICHARD MILHOUS
HOFFA, JAMES R.—*See* INDOCHINA WAR [40]
HOFFMAN, JULIUS J.—*See* CIVIL DISORDERS
HOLLAND—*See* NETHERLANDS
HOMOSEXUALITY—*See* CRIME [5]; ELECTIONS [16, 25]

HONDURAS—Teachers' strike. According to a report Aug. 25, a teachers' strike had closed most of the country's 4,000 schools. The strike, reportedly called to demand the dismissal of an Education Ministry official, also resulted in violent clashes in Tegucigalpa between rival groups of students and teachers as a pro-government teachers' association, supported by the extreme right-wing group Mancha Brava, tried to break up the strike.

Cruz ousted in military coup. President Ramon Ernesto Cruz and his civilian government were overthrown Dec. 4 in a bloodless coup led by Gen. Oswaldo Lopez Arellano, the armed forces commander. It was the 22nd coup in Honduras's 151-year history and the third led by Lopez Arellano, who had turned over the presidency to Cruz in June 1971. (Lopez Arellano had ruled Honduras as head of a military junta in 1956-57 and 1963-65, and as congressionally elected president in 1965-71. He had also been the strongman under the Cruz regime, with the constitutional right to dispute or ignore orders from the president.) An armed forces communique said that Cruz was under house arrest with "all necessary guarantees," and that the government had been replaced in view of the "situation of chaos and weakness the nation is suffering" under the ruling coalition of the Nationalist and Liberal parties. The possibility of a military coup had been rumored in October and November as the government coalition, originally organized by Lopez Arellano, continued to break down. Liberals claimed that the Nationalists prevented their Cabinet ministers from operating effectively and that the civil service was so packed with Nationalists that all Liberal measures were blocked. Cruz also had removed two Liberal ministers in 1971 and replaced them with Nationalists, upsetting the Cabinet balance accorded in the coalition pact. Nationalists had met in a special convention Oct. 25, following a Liberal demand that they formally declare support for a second coalition agreement, signed after the 1971 elections to further define the obligations and political assignments of each party. However, the convention adjourned without a declaration, and the way was paved for a return to power by Lopez Arellano, who, as armed forces commander, was sworn to uphold the pact.

New Cabinet appointed. Lopez Arellano Dec. 5 named a new Cabinet which included two military officers, four Nationalists, three Liberals and two members from the newly formed Innovation and Unity party. Some members of the Cabinet had served in previous Lopez Arellano governments and others in the Cruz government. The new Cabinet: government and justice—Col. Juan Alberto Melgar Castro; national defense—Col. Raul Galo Soto; foreign affairs—Cesar Batres; finance—Manuel Acosta Bonilla; economy—Abraham Ramos Benaton; labor—Gautama Fonseca; education—Napoleon Alcerro Oliva; public health—Enrique Aguilar Paz; natural resources—Raul Edgardo Escoto; communications, public works and transport—Miguel Angel Rivera; economic planning council—Manglio Martinez. Roberto Ramirez, ex-president of the Central Bank, was appointed Supreme Court president Dec. 5.

See also HIJACKING [3]

HONG KONG—*See* CHINA, COMMUNIST; INTERNATIONAL MONETARY DEVELOPMENTS [9]

HOOVER, J. EDGAR—*See* FEDERAL BUREAU OF INVESTIGATION

HORSE RACING—Riva Ridge wins Derby, Belmont. Riva Ridge, ridden by Ron Turcotte, won the 98th running of the Kentucky Derby May 6 at Churchill Downs in Louisville and the Belmont Stakes June 10 in New York. Riva Ridge won the Derby by a 3¼-length lead over No Le Hace. He was never headed during the race, the first gate-to-wire triumph since Kauai King's victory in 1966. Hold Your Peace finished third in the 1¼-mile race. Riva Ridge won the 1½-mile-long Belmont seven lengths ahead of Ruritania. Cloudy Dawn finished third.

Bee Bee Bee wins Preakness. Long-shot Bee Bee Bee won the 1³⁄₁₆-mile Preakness May 20 at Pimlico Race Track in Baltimore, Md. The victory prevented Riva Ridge from becoming the first winner of racing's Triple Crown (Derby, Preakness, Belmont) since Citation in 1948. Bee Bee Bee scored a 1¼-length lead over No Le Hace. Key to the Mint was third. (Riva Ridge finished fourth.)

Dancer's Image loses '68 Derby purse. The Kentucky Court of Appeals April 28 ruled that Dancer's Image, who crossed the finish line first in the 1968 Derby, would not get the $122,600 first-place prize money. Dancer's Image had been disqualified after the race when a test showed traces of a banned drug in the colt's system at the time of the race. The victory and the purse had been awarded to Forward Pass, the horse who had finished second. A Circuit Court had held in 1970 that Dancer's Image was the rightful winner of the Derby and therefore entitled to the winner's prize money. In the appeals court ruling, the court held that the prize money should go to Forward Pass, but it did not upset the lower court's decision that established Dancer's Image as the winner of the 1968 Derby.

Fixer testifies on druggings. Bobby Byrne (an alias), a self-described swindler with a prison record, June 13 told the House Select Committee on Crime how he had drugged hundreds of race horses at East Coast and Midwest tracks to fix the outcome of races. According to Byrne, the drug he most often used was a tranquilizer known as H Primazene—and none of the hundreds of horses he had drugged had ever finished in the money. Byrne testified that his drugging activities took place in 1968-70 at tracks including Churchill Downs, Pimlico, Aquaduct in New York, Garden State Park in New Jersey and Hialeah in Florida. Byrne said that, after he and his associates had won on a rigged race, they would move on to another state and another track to avoid attracting the attention of track security agents. He said that, when the fixing operations had begun, he and his associates had relied partly on "friendly" trainers, grooms and jockeys; but later, when those people became more greedy, the fixers relied more on tranquilizers to rig the races. Byrne had been giving state's evidence before state and federal committees investigating crime since April 1971, when he was arrested while trying to enter the stable area at a track outside Boston.

HOSPITALS—*See* HEALTH CARE
HOUSE OF REPRESENTATIVES—*See* CONGRESS; ELECTIONS [1, 40-41, 46]
HOUSING—**Dispersal set.** The Department of Housing and Urban Development (HUD) Jan. 16 published regulations, effective Feb. 7, on site selection for subsidized housing. The regulations were expected to curtail most construction in urban renewal and model cities areas, in order to promote housing opportunities for moderate-income families outside the central cities. They allowed an "adequate" (though not a "superior") priority rating for urban renewal and model cities areas, but required that the rating be given only in a housing market area with few minority residents, in an integrated area in which the new project would not alter the population balance or in a minority area whose minority residents had access to adequate housing outside the area. "Overriding housing needs" in an area, if they were not caused by discrimination, would merit an exception from the regulations. A former provision was eliminated which would have allowed minority area projects "if prospective residents of the project or residents of the project area express a desire for it." The provision was eliminated because HUD feared the provision was unworkable and would have been abused.

HUD concedes subsidy abuses. An audit by HUD of federal mortgage subsidy programs under the direction of the Federal Housing Authority (FHA), released by HUD Secretary George Romney Feb. 27, confirmed earlier reports of widespread financial and construction abuses. According to the audit, cost per unit in the "section 236" (apartment house mortgages) program of the 1968 Housing Act had run substantially higher than in privately financed housing because of excessive fees and land markups and other fraudulent practices inadequately policed by the FHA. Rents under the program were consequently higher than for comparable apartments on the private market. Vacancy rates, resulting partly from locations near junkyards, factories, power lines and former lake beds, were high enough to cause or threaten frequent defaulting of section 236 mortgages. Romney reported that

HUD had fired seven employees for "wrongdoing" under the program. In the "section 235" (new and used private home mortgages) program, some 26% of a sample of 700 new houses and 43% of a sample of used homes contained serious property, safety, health or "livability" deficiencies. HUD referred 362 alleged section 235 violations for Justice Department investigation.

Detroit scandal. Secretary Romney March 27 acknowledged a major housing scandal in which the FHA had become entangled in Detroit. According to Romney, real estate speculators in Detroit had purchased run-down houses in poor neighborhoods for a few thousand dollars and then had them valued by the FHA at sometimes quadruple the original purchase prices. The speculators then sold the houses to the poor, who could not keep them up; and further deterioration resulted, blighting entire blocks and neighborhoods in Detroit's inner city. The House Government Operations Committee revealed June 22 that HUD had purchased, under the Detroit program, 8,000 homes guaranteed by the FHA on which mortgages had been defaulted. According to the committee, another 18,000-20,000 homes were in default and likely to be purchased by HUD, which was losing as much as $10,000 each on houses it attempted to resell. The committee said that HUD had allowed FHA appraisers to overvalue "structurally unsound houses," had not sufficiently advised poor home buyers and had not turned over enough cases for prosecution.

New York scandal. A federal grand jury March 29 named 40 persons and 10 corporations in indictments filed in U.S. district court in New York. The defendants were charged with 500 counts of bribery, conspiracy and filing false statements in a scheme to defraud the FHA. The pattern of the scheme was similar to that used in Detroit (*see above*). According to the indictments, some of the defendants procured false credit records and false appraisals which were used to obtain FHA insurance for excessively high mortgages on houses in the boroughs of Brooklyn and Queens. The houses were then said to have been sold to low-income families. One of the firms named as defendants was the credit investigating firm of Dun and Bradstreet. (HUD announced April 2 that it had ordered its regional offices not to do business with Dun and Bradstreet. Most of Dun and Bradstreet's contract with HUD was resumed by late April, but the contract part dealing with the office involved in the indictments was kept in suspension.) Another firm indicted was Eastern Service Corp., one of the largest mortgage-lending concerns in the East. The other eight corporations were all local real estate firms. Of the 40 persons named, eight were present or former FHA employees accused of having accepted bribes to participate in the fraud. The other 32 defendants were mostly real estate speculators, brokers, lawyers and appraisers—all from the New York area. The assistant U.S. attorney who presented the case to the grand jury, Anthony Accetta, said the scheme would probably result in a $200 million loss to the government in foreclosed mortgages. It was estimated that 2,500 homes went into default on mortgages, totaling $100 million in 1968, and that a similar loss had been incurred for 1970-71.

Chicago scandal. Four FHA officials were indicted in Chicago July 27 on charges of bribery and submitting false inspection statements in connection with federal housing programs for the poor. Seven Chicago builders and two real estate brokers were also indicted for bribery, false statements and conspiracy.

Congressional critique. The Congressional Joint Economic Committee Nov. 1 issued a report calling for an overhaul of federal housing programs and suggesting the use of direct housing subsidy payments to poor families. The report pointed to inflated costs and lack of coordination in present programs and charged that the total federal housing effort benefitted middle- and upper-income families (through home-owner tax benefits), contractors and investors far more than poor people. As one solution, the report suggested a $3.2-$4.1 billion program of grants to 6.8 million households with annual incomes below $7,500. The families would apply the grants to housing of their choice. (HUD

already had begun such a program on an experimental basis in Kansas City and other areas.)
    See also POLITICS [8]; STATE & LOCAL GOVERNMENTS

HUBBARD, FRED—*See* CIVIL RIGHTS [19]
HUGHES, HOWARD R.—*See* BOOKS; SPACE [17]
HUMPHREY, HUBERT H.—*See* ELECTIONS [3-8, 12, 15, 17]

HUNGARY—1971 economic development figures. The Central Statistical Office Jan. 29 announced the results of the 1971 economic development plan. Measured against the figures for 1970, the following major increases were reported: national income 7%; industrial production 5%; agricultural production 9%; exports 8%; imports 19%; per capita real income 5%-6%; and retail trade 9%. The report said that the 1971 wheat crop was "particularly outstanding" but that sugar beets, fruit, rough fodder and "the yields in certain vegetables" had "lagged behind earlier years."
    Student protest march. Government officials April 13 confirmed Western press reports that a student demonstration had occurred in Budapest the previous month—the first such event since the 1956 Hungarian revolt. According to a report April 15, the disturbance occurred March 15 when a group of students described by Budapest officials as "a small minority with no political background" broke away from a rally, staged by the Communist party youth organization Kisz, to commemorate the 124th anniversary of the war of independence against the Hapsburg empire. The dissidents were said to have shouted down a speaker in Heroes' Square and several thousand were said to have marched along a route taken by the 1848 rebels. Officials would not confirm reports that the students clashed with police and that a number were arrested.
    See also CHESS; CUBA; ENVIRONMENT; INDOCHINA WAR [52]; RUMANIA; SPACE [22]

HUNGER—*See* AFGHANISTAN; BANGLA DESH [14]; INDIA [6]
HUNTING—*See* CONSERVATION
HURRICANES—*See* POLLUTION [11]; STORMS
HUSSEIN—*See* JORDAN; MIDDLE EAST [1, 17, 19-20]
HYDROGEN BOMB—*See* ATOMIC ENERGY [13]

ICELAND—President re-elected. Kristjan Eldjarn, president of Iceland since 1968, was re-elected for a new term, according to a report Aug. 8.

See also CHESS; CONSERVATION; EUROPEAN ECONOMIC COMMUNITY [8]; INTERNATIONAL MONETARY DEVELOPMENTS [8]; POLLUTION [13]; TERRITORIAL WATERS

IMMIGRATION, U.S.—See POPULATION

INDIA—Northeast region reorganized. India created three new states (Meghalaya, Tripura and Manipur) and two union territories (Arunachal Pradesh and Mizoram) in the northeast region, it was reported Jan. 22. The reorganization move increased the number of Indian states to 21 and union territories to eight. Meghalaya had been a substate administered by Assam State. Tripura and Manipur, formerly princely states, had been administered as federal territories since India's independence in 1947. Union territories also were administered by the central government, but they elected their own advisory councils. The northeastern region was to continue to have a common governor and a common high court for its five states and two union territories. A proposed North-Eastern Council was to be composed of representatives of each of the seven political entities who would discuss common problems and coordinate development problems.

[2] Tamil Nadu seeks autonomy. The Dravidian Advancement Party (DAP) launched a campaign Feb. 12 to obtain autonomy for the state of Tamil Nadu in southern India. The party's conference passed a resolution calling for total self-government except in defense, foreign relations, currency and communications. (Before attaining control of the state government in 1967, the DAP had advocated complete independence along with three other Dravidian states in the south—Andhra, Mysore [renamed Karnataka July 28] and Kerala. Failure to rally support for the idea prompted the DAP to campaign for autonomy instead.) A week after the party congress, Indian Prime Minister Indira Gandhi's governing New Congress party announced the end of its political alliance with the DAP, which held 25 seats in the central parliament. Mrs. Gandhi warned May 21 against granting more autonomy to Tamil Nadu. (In another event, Tamil Nadu political parties opposed to the DAP organized a farmers' demonstration July 5. Fourteen persons were killed by police in breaking up the demonstration.)

[3] Congress party wins elections. Mrs. Gandhi's Congress party won absolute majorities in 14 of 16 states and in one of two union territories in

199

assembly elections held March 5-12. Manipur and Meghalaya were the only states where the party failed to win enough seats to govern without coalition parties. No balloting was held in the states of Kerala, Uttar Pradesh, Tamil Nadu and Orissa, whose assemblies' five-year terms had not yet expired. (However, the Congress party came into control of Orissa June 14 after the state's non-Congress government collapsed. The collapse came when a group of former dissident Congress members withdrew from the ruling coalition alliance and pledged their allegiance to Mrs. Gandhi.) The most significant victory for the Congress party in the elections was registered in West Bengal State, where the party wrested absolute control from the militant, pro-Peking Communist party of India, Marxist, which had dominated the state assembly for nearly 10 years. The Congress party and the pro-Moscow Communist party's chapter in West Bengal had signed an agreement Jan. 1 to form a Democratic Alliance, merging their efforts to defeat the pro-Peking Communists.

[4]   Uttar Pradesh riots. Rioting in at least five major cities in Uttar Pradesh State June 16-18 resulted in the deaths of 24 persons—five killed by police bullets and the others in battles between Moslems and Hindus. The violence began when a group of Moslems staged a march to protest a law adopted in May by the central parliament opening Aligarh University, a Moslem institution, to teachers and students of all denominations. The law had gone into effect June 15.

[5]   Cabinet changes. Changes in the Indian Cabinet were announced July 22. Moinul Haque Choudhury resigned as minister of industrial development and was replaced by C. Subramaniam. K. Hanumanthaiya resigned as minister of railways and was replaced by T. A. Pai. D. P. Dhar was appointed minister in charge of planning, and Jagannath Pahadia was transferred from the Agriculture Ministry to the Communications Ministry as deputy minister.

[6]   Government combats drought. The government was reported Aug. 6 to have ordered emergency relief measures to prevent famine in 13 drought-stricken states. An expenditure of $130 million was authorized for relief. The government also planned to distribute 10 million tons of wheat in the drought areas. The drought had been caused by the absence of monsoon rains which normally come in mid-July. (The rains came in September, saving most of the grain crops in northern and central India.) The states hardest hit were Bihar and Rajasthan, where cases of malnutrition deaths of humans and dying cattle were reported.

[7]   Naga organizations outlawed. The government Aug. 31 decreed the outlawing of rebel Naga tribesmen organizations. Nagaland State Governor B. K. Nehru announced that henceforth members of the Naga National Council, the Naga Federal Government and Naga Federal Army would be subject to prosecution. Nehru also announced resumption of military operations against the rebels, suspended since a 1966 cease-fire.

[8]   Student unrest. Student riots in Bihar Sept. 7 resulted in the death of one student, reportedly caused by police. Mobs of students Sept. 9 protested the police action by burning railway stations, storming police outposts and stoning policemen in various parts of the state. Bihar Chief Minister Medar Nath Pandey asserted Sept. 9 that the disturbances had been fomented by the pro-Moscow Communist party. Similar riots were reported in Kerala, Tamil Nadu, Orissa, Gujarat and Rajasthan, according to a report Sept. 13. A district in New Delhi had been the scene of four days of student riots the previous week. The Congress party accused four opposition parties of fomenting the New Delhi unrest. The parties' leaders denied the charges Sept. 13 and accused the Congress party of failing to cope with India's economic ills, which they claimed were to blame for the unrest. New Congress President Shandar Dayal Sharma had also accused the U.S. Central Intelligence Agency (CIA) of being involved in India's civil disturbances in an attempt "to sour relations between India and Bangla Desh." The U.S. embassy in New Delhi denied the charges Sept. 21.

[9] Economic controls set. Prime Minister Gandhi decided at a meeting of the Congress party Oct. 9-11 to impose greater government control of the economy to cope with increasing prices, growing unemployment and a scarcity of essential commodities. The party's policy-making body, the All India Congress Committee, approved two resolutions to deal with the problems. One called for the takeover of wholesale trade in the food grains and strict government control of the distribution of essential goods. The second resolution would give the government a dominant role in "core sector" industries, limiting the role of private entrepreneurs. Under the plan, the government would establish publicly owned plants to produce more steel, chemicals, cement and oil.

[10] Andhra Pradesh riots. At least 14 persons were killed Nov. 21-22 in riots in a number of cities in Andhra Pradesh State. Further violence erupted Nov. 23 in the state capital of Hyderabad, where police opened fire on demonstrators who stoned police and set fire to buildings. The city was shut down by a general strike Nov. 23. (Another strike by civil servants in the city Dec. 6 paralyzed the state, shutting down courts, schools, colleges and most government offices.) The unrest stemmed from a recent Supreme Court ruling upholding a 50-year-old law which provided residents of the former princely state of Hyderabad with preference for state government jobs and admission to educational institutions in the city. Residents of the state's nine western districts (called the Telengana Region) denounced the law as discriminatory and engaged in violent protest to express their resentment. The demonstrators called on Mrs. Gandhi either to abolish the law or to accept the principle of dividing the state.

[11] U.S. military flights banned. The U.S. embassy in New Delhi disclosed Nov. 25 that the Indian government had banned flights into India by the U.S. Military Airlift Command. (The command transported diplomats and other officials as well as military personnel.) Under the new ruling, U.S. officials were required to use commercial flights unless the American embassy could show it had a special need for a military plane to land in India. The Indian government said Dec. 21 that the ban was aimed at adopting a uniform policy toward all foreign counties.

See also BANGLA DESH [1-2, 4, 7, 9, 11-13]; DRUG USE & ADDICTION [12, 18]; FOREIGN POLICY; HEALTH; INDOCHINA WAR [25]; INTERNATIONAL MONETARY DEVELOPMENTS [8-9]; MIDDLE EAST [30]; PAKISTAN [1-4, 6, 8, 12, 15, 17]; PULITZER PRIZES; SINO-U.S. RELATIONS [5]; UGANDA [1, 7, 9]; UNITED NATIONS; VIETNAM, NORTH

INDIANS, AMERICAN—Navajo self-rule offered. Anthony Lincoln, director of Navajo affairs in the Bureau of Indian Affairs (BIA), July 17 offered to turn over to the Navajo control of all BIA operations in its area, including the $110 million annual Navajo budget. The offer was seen as a victory for the self-determination forces within the bureau, led by Commissioner Louis Bruce. Only two tribes had previously acquired complete control of all programs affecting their reservations—the Miccosukee of Florida and the Zuni of Arizona. Neither compared in size with the 25,000-square-mile Navajo reservation covering parts of Arizona, Utah and New Mexico, with a 1970 population of 134,000.

Militants occupy BIA. About 500 Indians, most of them young, arrived in Washington Nov. 2 after a cross-country "Trail of Broken Treaties" for a planned week of demonstrations to promote reform of the BIA and Congressional action on a program of 20 demands—including treaty adjustments, land policy changes and social and economic programs. The protesters were led by activists of the American Indian Movement (AIM), composed largely of urban Indians. The protesters met with government officials Nov. 2 to negotiate for temporary lodgings, food and money, and for plans to hold memorial services for Indians buried at Arlington National Cemetery. (The U.S. Court of Appeals for Washington ruled Nov. 5 that the Arlington services could take place.) An agreement to lodge the demonstrators in certain government buildings was reached, but collapsed after scuffles took place between demonstrators and Washington police attempting to lock the doors of the BIA building. The protesters barricaded themselves inside the building and remained there despite a Nov. 3 district court order directing them to leave. Further discussions between Indians and Interior Department aides failed, and U.S. District Court Judge John H. Pratt Nov. 6 found the protesters guilty of contempt of court for ignoring the earlier evacuation order. However, the Court of Appeals stayed the order until Nov. 8, by which time the Indians had reached agreement with government negotiators including Leonard Garment (presidential consultant for minority affairs), Frank Carlucci (deputy director of the Office of Management and Budget) and Commissioner Bruce. The accord provided for a federal study group, to include representatives of 13 departments and agencies, to submit recommendations to President Nixon by June 1, 1973. The panel would accept testimony from all segments of the Indian community and would address itself to questions concerning the balance of government help between reservation and urban Indians, the adequacy of governmental organizational structure in programs for Indians, the effectiveness of federal government programs and of Indian self-government institutions, and the need for further legislation.

Administration negotiators agreed to recommend that no Indians be prosecuted for occupying the BIA building; but, after the building was evacuated Nov. 8, BIA officials found extensive damage to the building and furniture and massive theft of art works and artifacts. (It was estimated that 1,000-2,000 pounds of BIA documents and over $700,000 worth of art work and artifacts had been removed.) Interior Department officials estimated Nov. 10 that the government had suffered losses of $2.28 million from the occupation. A White House spokesman said Nov. 9 that the no-prosecution recommendation did not cover theft and vandalism, and that the Justice Department was investigating the case. Another White House spokesman said Nov. 13 that the inter-agency study panel would not meet "until all questions regarding stolen government property are settled." Thirty-one of the 600-700 stolen paintings were returned Nov. 11, through the mediation of the Young Men's Christian Association, which refused to reveal the names of those involved. According to a report Nov. 20, the Federal Bureau of Investigation (FBI) recovered a number of stolen paintings, artifacts and books at Haskell Junior College, an Indian institution in Lawrence, Kan. Oklahoma officials Nov. 23 arrested three Indians who were found on a state highway in an overturned van which contained two BIA office machines and miscellaneous BIA documents. The three and two others were indicted Nov. 22 by a federal grand jury in Oklahoma City on charges of possessing government property taken from the BIA building.

3 BIA aides lose power, posts. Interior Secretary Rogers C.B. Morton Dec. 2 removed "all present authority for Indian Affairs" from Bruce, Assistant Secretary Harrison A. Loesch and Deputy BIA Commissioner John O. Crow as a "short-run" measure to restore orderly functioning of the BIA. Morton said "personality and administrative conflicts" had complicated consideration of any long-term changes in Indian programs or in the BIA structure. (Crow Nov. 30 had publicly criticized Bruce as incompetent, and both Crow and Loesch had denounced Bruce for his attitude during the BIA occupation. Bruce had expressed support for some of the protesters' goals. Militant Indian groups had demanded the ouster of Crow and Loesch for allegedly opposing attempts to extend Indian control over BIA programs.) The resignations of all three officials were announced Dec. 8.

See also BRAZIL; ELECTIONS [16, 23]; LATIN AMERICA

INDOCHINA WAR—Despite an intensification of military activity in Indochina, the war was drawing to a close as the U.S. continued to withdraw its men from South Vietnam and the U.S. and North Vietnam moved close to a diplomatic agreement on ending the fighting. Still, no agreement was reached during 1972. In fighting, the Communists launched a major offensive in South Vietnam March 30 and scored significant victories. Meanwhile, the U.S. was accelerating the air war with large-scale bombing raids over North Vietnam. For details on: fighting in Cambodia, *see* [2-7]; fighting in Laos, *see* [8-10]; peace negotiations in Laos, *see* [11-12]; fighting in Vietnam, *see* [13-34]; allied withdrawal moves, *see* [35-38]; prisoner of war developments, *see* [39-40]; and moves toward peace, *see* [41-54].

Cambodia

[2] **Eastern sector.** *South Vietnamese actions.* A force of 10,000 Vietnamese troops began pulling out of the Krek area of southeastern Cambodia Jan. 2 in a move to bolster the defenses around Saigon for a possible Communist Tet (lunar new year) offensive in mid-February. The pullback was followed by a similar Cambodian withdrawal in the area and the reported desertion Jan. 12 of an entire 2,400-man Cambodian brigade. While South Vietnamese troops were withdrawing in the southeast, an 1,800-man Saigon force carried out a limited operation in the northeastern part of the country Jan. 7 to destroy Communist bases and capture supplies being massed for the expected Tet offensive. The South Vietnamese and Cambodian forces Jan. 12 opened another offensive outside Antgassom, 42 miles south of the capital of Pnompenh, but reportedly made no contact with the enemy. South Vietnam carried out three separate drives into southeastern Cambodia Feb. 1, 23 and 27 in an attempt to block Communist infiltration into South Vietnam and to smash suspected Communist preparations for attacks on South Vietnam's Mekong Delta. South Vietnamese troops with American air support launched other drives into eastern Cambodia March 10, 11 and 22 in an attempt to prevent enemy attacks on the approaches to Saigon. A force of about 2,000 South Vietnamese troops July 31 launched a drive near Kompong Trabek in the Parrot's Beak of Eastern Cambodia to thwart a possible North Vietnamese offensive aimed at cutting Route 4, linking Saigon with the Mekong Delta. Cambodian troops Dec. 21 joined South Vietnamese troops in a joint operation aimed at clearing a Communist-occupied area in southeast Cambodia, 55 miles south of Pnompenh.

[3] **Fighting.** Communist troops were reported April 25 to have taken effective control of all Cambodian territory east of the Mekong River along the border with South Vietnam, except for government strongholds, such as the provincial capital of Svayrieng. (Svayrieng itself came under heavy Communist attack May 25-28.) Communist forces broke through government positions along Route 1 April 20, seizing a 50-mile stretch of the highway. The collapse of the government positions began with the fall of the market town of Kompong Trabek, 50 miles southeast of Pnompenh, where 450 of the town's defenders were either killed or captured. (Kompong Trabek was recaptured by Cambodian and South Vietnamese forces July 24, but again captured by the North Vietnamese Sept. 9 after bitter fighting which had begun Aug. 6. All three government battalions in the town moved out and headed in the direction of Pnompenh. A fourth Cambodian battalion that had been defending a nearby position was reported to have "disappeared.") Communist troops April 23 occupied the town of Kompong Trach near the South Vietnamese border. A joint Cambodian-South Vietnamese garrison there had been under heavy pressure for 17 days, and the town had been occupied briefly by 1,500 rebel troops April 9. The fall of Kompong Trach was followed by the fall of 11 Cambodian positions between April 30 and May 12.

[4] **Angkor Wat.** Cambodian forces totaling about 6,000 men were reported Feb. 12 to have launched a major drive against North Vietnamese troops around the ancient Buddhist temples at Angkor, seized by the North Vietnamese in June 1970. A force of 4,000 enemy troops were dug into heavily wooded areas west and south of the perimeter walls surrounding the temples, while government units were based in the nearby town of Siemreap. In further

fighting at the temple city: Cambodian troops Feb. 18 reportedly captured a temple in the western sector of the city; heavy clashes broke out within three miles of Angkor Feb. 21, and 11 government soldiers were killed and 39 wounded; rebel forces April 17 cut off and surrounded 1,000 government troops near the temples; a force of 4,000 Cambodians launched another drive May 16 to recapture the temple ruins at Angkor. The government disclosed Sept. 29 that its forces had abandoned efforts to dislodge North Vietnamese troops from the temples at Angkor.

[5] **Attacks on Pnompenh.** Communist artillery and rockets pounded the capital of Pnompenh and its outskirts March 21 in the heaviest attack on the city since the beginning of the war in Cambodia in 1970. More than 100 civilians were killed and 280 others wounded. The enemy launching sites were believed located about five miles southwest of the city limits. The shelling was followed by a Communist ground attack with the largest assault centered on Takhmau, six miles southeast of Pnompenh, where a force of 500 Communists entered and killed at least 25 civilians. Communist demolition squads carried out three attacks on Pnompenh in late March—blowing up a 5,000-ton cargo vessel and two fuel-bearing barges in the Bassac River on the southern end of the city March 23, knocking out a bridge over the Tonle Sap River March 24 and setting off an explosion inside Pnompenh March 28. Viet Cong forces sent about 25 rocket shells into Pnompenh May 6, killing two persons and wounding 44. The rocket attack was followed by an unsuccessful ground attack against the city's only bridge across the Bassac leading to Route 1, the main road to Saigon. Government defenders drove the Communists back, fighting them from house to house. Pnompenh came under daylight artillery shelling June 5, for the first time during the war. The attacks, directed at the Defense Ministry building and an area near Cambodian President Lon Nol's residence, killed six persons and wounded 11 others. A force of about 200 Vietnamese Communists Oct. 7 carried out one of the heaviest raids inside Pnompenh since the start of the war, killing 36 Cambodian soldiers and civilians and themselves suffering losses of 28 men. The raiders, attacking with mortars and rockets, blew up a bridge over the Tonle Sap, less than two miles from the center of Pnompenh. Four or five infiltrators entered the French embassy compound with armored personnel carriers they had seized from the Cambodians and machinegunned the buildings. Eight persons were wounded Nov. 29 by North Vietnamese rockets, which hit Pnompenh's international airport. Two rockets struck a government building in the city Dec. 1, causing extensive damage.

[6] **Khmer Rouge left with burden of Communist fighting.** According to reports Oct. 31, several thousand North Vietnamese and Viet Cong troops were moving out of Cambodia into South Vietnam's Mekong Delta and Saigon areas, leaving the burden of fighting Cambodian government troops to the Khmer Rouge, the Cambodian rebel guerrillas. The Vietnamese move was believed connected with the Communists' determination to expand their control of South Vietnamese territory before a truce went into effect (*see* [10, 49]).

[7] **Trapeang Kraleng.** Communist forces Nov. 1 captured Trapeang Kraleng, 35 miles west of Pnompenh, but Cambodian troops retook the town Nov. 15. In seizing Trapeang Kraleng, the Communists temporarily had cut Route 4, which connected Pnompenh with the country's deep water port of Kompong Som. Government forces Nov. 16 reoccupied the last remaining stretch of Route 4. The road had been closed for two weeks, halting the flow of imported food and U.S. military supplies to the capital and aggravating the food shortages caused by the Communist capture of part of Route 5 in August. (Cambodian troops reopened Route 5 Nov. 17.) Trapeang Kraleng was placed under Communist siege Dec. 7; but the seige was lifted Dec. 8 by Cambodian reinforcements, who broke through a ring of Communist forces and rescued two trapped battalions. The Communists also captured a 2.5-mile stretch of Route 4 Dec. 8, but three Cambodian battalions recovered the area Dec. 9.

Laos

[8] **Long Tieng.** The government base at Long Tieng, under heavy North Vietnamese artillery attack since Dec. 31, 1971, was largely evacuated by Meo tribal forces of the Laotian government, according to a report Jan. 3. The troops pulled out were said to have been deployed in nearby villages and on high ground around the strongpoint. Long Tieng itself was downgraded to a forward operations base, although its airstrip was still in use. North Vietnamese forces Jan. 11 captured two government positions on high ground overlooking the base. Laotian and Thai reinforcements were flown into Long Tieng and were reported Jan. 15 to have partially eased the siege of the base by recapturing Skyline Ridge, high ground two miles to the north. North Vietnamese and pro-Communist Pathet Lao forces seized a ridge overlooking Long Tieng in heavy fighting Jan. 20-21. Government forces, however, recaptured the high ground (used as helicopter landing zones) Jan. 25. More than 500 men on each side were reported to have died in the January fighting for Long Tieng. A North Vietnamese force of 4,500-6,000 men threatened to capture Long Tieng March 11 after seizing Sam Thong, a village seven miles to the northwest. (Sam Thong, defended mainly by 4,000 Thai troops, was first attacked March 10.) The airstrip at Long Tieng was closed March 12 because of a heavy artillery barrage. The Communists followed up their capture of Sam Thong by taking control March 14 of a ridge overlooking Long Tieng. One key position overlooking Long Tieng was reported March 21 to have been recaptured by Thai and Laotian troops, but the base itself was said to have come under heavy North Vietnamese mortar attack from two other positions.

[9] *Plaine des Jarres.* In an attempt to relieve pressure on Long Tieng, about 4,000 Laotian troops (aided by American air strikes) launched a drive Feb. 7 against North Vietnamese forces occupying the Plaine des Jarres in northern Laos. The plain, 18 miles northeast of Long Tieng and Sam Thong, had been captured by the North Vietnamese Dec. 20, 1971. The Communists occupying the area responded to the Laotian drive by a counterattack Feb. 22 which drove government troops from a hillside overlooking the southeast corner of the plain. Increasing North Vietnamese attacks were reported March 6 to have forced the Laotians to call off their offensive. Several thousand Laotian soldiers and Meo tribesmen were said to be in full retreat toward Long Tieng, but Laotian government sources said the drive had succeeded in relieving pressure around Long Tieng. Meo tribesmen launched another offensive operation around the Plaine des Jarres in mid-August, but were forced by North Vietnamese fire to withdraw from positions in the area Sept. 5. The tribesmen suffered heavy losses and were evacuated by U.S. helicopters. The North Vietnamese launched their own offensive on the western edge of the plain Sept. 25, reportedly forcing Meo tribal forces to withdraw toward Long Tieng. The government launched another drive to recapture the plain area, but the effort received a serious setback Oct. 27 when strong North Vietnamese counterattacks drove them off the plain into surrounding high ground. The North Vietnamese began another attack in the area Nov. 4, and succeeded Nov. 13 in driving several Meo battalions from the southern edge of the plain. The Communists overran two government defensive positions in the plain Dec. 8 and 9.

[10] **Activity increases.** Communist and government forces in Laos stepped up their fighting in October in an effort to gain ground advantage in expectation of an Indochina cease-fire *(see* [6, 49]). Government troops began a drive for Saravane in the south Oct. 22. The village, which had been in Communist hands almost continuously since May 1970, was reoccupied by the Laotians Oct. 28. (The town was retaken by the Communists Nov. 14, by government forces Nov. 22, by the Communists Dec. 1 and again by government troops Dec. 4.) Pathet Lao and North Vietnamese soldiers went on the offensive in many parts of Laos Oct. 28, capturing a number of towns and large amounts of territory. Communist troops Nov. 1 overran the garrison town of Namthorn Buk Kwang, about 90 miles east of the capital of Vientiane,

killing an estimated 200 government troops. The remaining 300 base defenders joined 1,000 civilians in fleeing the town and crossing the border into Thailand. Communist forces Nov. 13 bombed the airport of the royal Laotian capital of Luang Prabang for the first time in nearly a year. Rockets damaged two T-28 fighter-bombers and three light observation planes.

[11] **Souvanna agrees to peace talks.** Laotian Premier Souvanna Phouma July 7 accepted an offer from the Lao Patriotic Front (Pathet Lao) leader, Prince Souphanouvong, for a resumption of talks aimed at ending the fighting between government and Pathet Lao Forces. Preliminary talks—led by Pheng Phongsavan for the government and Gen. Phoun Sipraseuth for the Pathet Lao—began Oct. 17 in Vientiane. The two groups met again throughout the rest of the year, but the talks remained deadlocked over the procedural issues of the Laotian flag's presence in the meeting room (to which the Pathet Lao objected) and Pathet Lao insistence that the Vientiane delegation had no right to call itself representatives of a Laotian government.

[12] *Peace plans exchanged.* The Pathet Lao offered an immediate cease-fire and proposed the formation of a new government at the peace negotiating session Dec. 12. Government representatives made a counter-proposal at the Dec. 19 meeting, but it was rejected by the Pathet Lao. The Pathet Lao plan provided that: U.S. and other foreign troops would withdraw from Laos within 90 days of a truce and all their bases in the country would be dismantled; all military operations, repression, arrests and reprisals would be barred "in the zone provisionally controlled" by the Laotian government; neither the Pathet Lao nor the government would be permitted to introduce into their respective zones any foreign troops, advisers, new weapons or war materiel, but worn-out equipment could be replaced on a one-to-one basis with the permission of both sides; both zones would permit free elections and freedom of speech and assembly; and the truce would be supervised by a mixed commission of the two sides, assisted by the existing International Control Commission. As for the political aspects of the plan, the Vientiane government and its National Assembly would be dissolved; but the country, four-fifths of which the Pathet Lao claimed to control, would continue to be administered as at present until a new government and assembly were chosen. A Political Council of Coalition and a new provisional government of national union would be formed prior to the holding of national elections and within 30 days of the signing of the agreement. The council would be composed of four equal delegations of the Pathet Lao, the Vientiane government, the neutralists (who supported the Pathet Lao) and representatives named by King Savang Vatthana. The new three-part regime would be equally divided among the Pathet Lao, the neutralists and the Vientiane government. The council would control Vientiane, which would become a neutral zone. The government rejected the Pathet Lao proposal on the ground that it was unconstitutional. Vientiane's own peace proposal was similar to the Pathet Lao plan in that it stressed the neutralization of Laos and the need to form a new coalition government. (The contents of the Vientiane plan were not reported to the press.)

Vietnam—Fighting

[13] **Air war intensifies.** The air war over Indochina intensified at the start of 1972, reportedly in order to neutralize Communist preparation for a possible offensive during Tet. The intensification was marked by a step-up of American bombing of Communist supply lines in Laos and the Central Highlands of South Vietnam and by continued U.S. protective reaction strikes on missile sites, antiaircraft batteries and radar installations in North Vietnam. Between Jan. 1 and Feb. 1, U.S. jets made nearly one-third as many protective reaction strikes on North Vietnam as in all of 1971. The U.S. Feb. 9 launched a series of over 100 air strikes on suspected North Vietnamese troop buildups and infiltration trails in the Central Highlands, and Feb. 16 launched a "limited-duration" bombing offensive against North Vietnamese artillery positions in the southern province of North Vietnam and in the northern section of the

demilitarized zone (DMZ). By March 19, U.S. aircraft had carried out 100 protective reaction strikes against North Vietnam during 1972. Hanoi radio reported March 7 that the U.S. had launched a major, widespread bombing offensive against the North, striking "many populated areas."

[14] Communists launch major drive across DMZ. An estimated 20,000 North Vietnamese troops launched a major offensive March 30 across the DMZ. (An enemy offensive had been expected during Tet, but had not materialized.) By April 1, the Communist ground and artillery attacks had forced defending South Vietnamese troops to abandon a number of base camps near the DMZ, and the enemy was pushing the government forces in disarray toward their rear bases in the biggest Communist offensive since the 1968 siege of the allied bases of Conthien and Khesanh. U.S. advisers believed the objective of the enemy drive was to seize Quangtri, capital of Quangtri Province. Its fall would pose a serious threat to Hue and Danang further south. The enemy troops were artillery units and antiaircraft units equipped with surface-to-air missiles. The North Vietnamese launched the offensive March 30 by firing more than 5,000 rockets, long-range artillery shells and mortar shells on 12 South Vietnamese positions just below the DMZ. (According to South Vietnamese reports, 285 enemy soldiers and 31 government troops were killed in the first two days of fighting.) Six South Vietnamese outposts (fire support bases Fuller, Mailoc, Holcomb and Pioneer and two other small camps) near the DMZ were abandoned March 31. Heavy cloud cover restricted U.S. air support for the retreating government troops.

[15] *U.S. reacts with air strikes.* In an effort to stem the Communist offensive, hundreds of U.S. planes and Navy warships launched heavy sustained attacks April 6 on North Vietnamese missile sites and troop concentrations above and below the DMZ. The U.S. decision to carry out reprisal air and naval strikes against North Vietnam was authorized by President Nixon following meetings in Washington April 3-5 of the Special Action Group, a panel which met during periods of emergency. American jets had been striking sporadically at North Vietnam since the start of the offensive, but bad weather had limited the raids. The emergence of clear weather April 6 permitted systematic strikes. The early strikes (225 missions between April 6 and 9) were limited to the area south of the 18th Parallel, but U.S. B-52s April 10 began bombing deep inside North Vietnam for the first time since November 1967. The U.S. command refused to disclose the targets of the April 10 raids, but B-52s reportedly struck the Vinh area, 145 miles north of the DMZ. U.S. planes penetrated even further into North Vietnam April 16. On that date, 18 B-52s and about 100 Navy and Air Force jet fighter-bombers carried out bombing raids on supply dumps near the harbor of the port of Haiphong. A second wave of 60 fighter-bombers hit petroleum storage areas on the outskirts of Hanoi seven hours later, and a third wave hit the storage areas again later in the afternoon. A North Vietnamese report April 18 said 60 civilians had been killed in the attacks—13 in Hanoi and 47 in Haiphong. The Soviet Union April 16 protested that four Soviet ships had been struck and damaged during the air strikes on Haiphong, and demanded that the U.S. "immediately adopt strict measures to prevent similar provocations in the future." An American reply to the Soviet protest declined to accept blame for the alleged attacks on Soviet ships, but pledged "to continue to make every effort to avoid damage to international shipping." (U.S. Administration officials disclosed May 2 that a Soviet freighter had been sunk during the raids on Haiphong. Neither Moscow nor Hanoi had mentioned any ship sinking.)

[16] *Major ground fighting during the offensive. Quangtri.* South Vietnamese forces abandoned the northern half of Quangtri Province April 2 as North Vietnamese soldiers pressed their drive southward. Only three major bases in the northern part of the province remained in government hands— Quangtri city, the Quangtri combat base and Dongha, all under heavy enemy attack. The South Vietnamese commander moved his division staff out of

Quangtri combat base to Quangtri city after the base was struck by more than 1,000 rocket and artillery shells. Dongha was reportedly in flames April 3 after being hit by thousands of North Vietnamese shells. The Communist menace to Quangtri city was heightened April 4 as South Vietnamese troops abandoned one of their remaining defense points on the northern bank of the Cua Viet River (the South Vietnamese northern line of defense in the province). Government troops were forced to pull out of Fire Base Anne, a small artillery position eight miles southwest of the city. Enemy activity in the province eased somewhat April 7 as U.S. planes bombed North Vietnamese positions. The North Vietnamese launched a massive assault against South Vietnamese positions west of Quangtri city April 9, but were thrown back with a heavy loss of life. Allied commanders reported that 1,000 of the enemy had been slain and 30 tanks destroyed. The exact number of government casualties was not given, but the losses were believed heavy. An unknown number of enemy troops broke through Quangtri's northern defenses April 27 and penetrated to within two and a half miles of the city. The North Vietnamese April 28 captured Dongha, seven miles north of Quangtri city, thus tightening the Communist ring around the provincial capital and allowing heavy shelling which left many sections of Quangtri city in flames. The Communists May 1 captured Quangtri city itself, thus gaining control of the entire province. An estimated 8,000 South Vietnamese troops abandoned the city after putting up little resistance. North Vietnam claimed May 2 that its forces had killed, wounded or captured nearly 10,000 South Vietnamese and other allied troops in the battle for Quangtri city. The Viet Cong May 4 announced the establishment of a provisional revolutionary administration in Quangtri city. (For later Quangtri developments, *see* [27].)

[17] *Binhlong.* The Communists April 5 launched a drive into Binhlong Privince from eastern Cambodia. Initial reports said several hundred men of a 1,000-man attacking force cut Highway 13 between Anloc and Saigon, only 37 miles north of the capital. The Communists, equipped with tanks, increasingly expanded their operations and were reported April 7 to be in control of the northern section of the province. The North Vietnamese April 7 captured Locninh, a district capital of the province. Some 15,000 South Vietnamese troops retreated from Locninh to Anloc, several miles south, and were immediately surrounded by enemy soldiers. Heavy fighting broke out around Anloc April 8 and some engagements were fought within the city as advance enemy elements made their way into the town. In a move at rescuing the beleaguered garrison, the Saigon command April 9 ordered the 21st Division shifted from the Mekong Delta, but the relief column was blocked by enemy resistance 15 miles from Anloc. The enemy April 13 launched a major assault on Anloc with a force of 3,000 men, spearheaded by 40 tanks. After more than 24 hours of close combat, the Communists captured half of Anloc. Heavy B-52 raids April 12-13 on enemy troops west of the city and fighter-bomber attacks in the area failed to slow the Communist advance. Fierce fighting continued in the city through the end of April, with the defenders of Anloc coming under increasing attacks by North Vietnamese and Viet Cong forces. U.S. planes pounded enemy troops around the city April 15, reportedly killing 200. North Vietnamese tanks pushed into Anloc April 18, but were driven out by defenders. The government relief column on Route 13 tried to move closer to Anloc May 5, but was beaten back by the North Vietnamese, who overran a fire base supporting the South Vietnamese push. (For later Anloc developments, *see* [29].)

[18] *Hue.* Communist pressure spread to Thuathien Province, the province south of Quangtri, April 5 as two government bases south of Hue (the provincial capital) came under enemy fire. Fire Base Bastogne, a government strongpoint 20 miles west of Hue, came under enemy siege, with heavy fighting April 11. Bastogne was resupplied April 16 by parachute and by some government troops who slipped through enemy forces surrounding the strongpoint. (The base's 500 defenders had been running low on food, water

and ammunition.) Bastogne was captured April 28 after enemy commandos penetrated the camp's barbed-wire defenses. The defenders withdrew to Fire Base Birmingham, four miles to the east, but continued to come under heavy ground and artillery fire. Following the fall of Quangtri and the subsequent threats to Hue, an estimated 80% of Hue's 200,000 residents fled the city to Danang. (Hue's population had been swollen to more than 300,000 by refugees fleeing Quangtri.) (For later Hue area developments, see [28].)

[19]   *Central Highlands.* Enemy activity in the Central Highlands erupted April 8 for the first time during the offensive. U.S. officers reported April 8 that Communist troops had cut the main highway between Kontum and Pleiku in several places. Ten government positions near Kontum were shelled by the enemy April 11, but B-52 strikes in the area apparently thwarted any bolder move against the city. The Communists April 15 drove government troops out of Fire Base Charlie, 20 miles northwest of Kontum, and April 20 cut strategic Route 19 at the Ankhe Pass between Pleiku and the coastal city of Quinhon. (A government force was reported April 26 to have succeeded in fighting its way through the block on Route 19. South Korean troops reportedly cleared the Ankhe Pass, with a loss of 51 men.) An estimated 20,000 North Vietnamese soldiers were reported converging on Kontum by April 28. Enemy forces had cut Route 14 on both the north and south sides of the city. As enemy troops closed in around the city, an estimated 10,000 persons, including military men, were removed by plane and helicopter to Pleiku April 29-30. Route 14 was reopened briefly by the South Vietnamese May 4, but was closed again by Communist troops May 5 as they repelled a government paratrooper attack supported by American air strikes. Government bases and positions around Kontum came under North Vietnamese ground and artillery attack May 7-8. (For later Kontum area developments, see [30].)

[20]   **Nixon orders mining, interdiction.** President Nixon May 8 announced that he had ordered the mining of North Vietnamese ports and interdiction of land and sea routes to North Vietnam in a move to prevent delivery of war supplies to that country. "Rail and all other communications will be cut off to the maximum extent possible," the President said; and "air and naval strikes against military targets in North Vietnam will continue." The President stressed that the actions were not directed against other nations, such as allies of North Vietnam. "Their sole purpose," he said, "is to protect the lives of 60,000 Americans who would be gravely endangered in the event that the Communist offensive continues to roll forward and to prevent the imposition of a Communist government by brutal aggression upon 17 million people" of South Vietnam. Nixon said the interdiction and bombing would cease if the following conditions were met: the return of all U.S. prisoners of war and an internationally supervised cease-fire throughout Indochina. Once those conditions were met, Nixon said, "we will stop all acts of force throughout Indochina" and "proceed with a complete withdrawal of all American forces from Vietnam within four months." In making his decision to interdict the enemy's supplies, Nixon said he rejected the alternatives of immediate withdrawal and continued reliance on negotiation to end the war. "By simply getting out," he said, "we should only worsen the bloodshed. By relying solely on negotiations, we would give an intransigent enemy the time he needs to press his aggression on the battlefield.... There is only one way to stop the killing. That is to keep the weapons of war out of the hands of the international outlaws of North Vietnam." The North Vietnamese delegation to the Paris peace talks May 9 assailed Nixon's decision as a violation of the 1954 Geneva agreements and of a 1968 U.S. pledge to end air attacks on the North. The Viet Cong May 10 rejected Nixon's offer to end the interdiction and bombing in return for a release of U.S. POWs and an internationally supervised cease-fire. The Nixon decision was scored by the Soviet Union, China and eastern European countries. It was met with mixed criticism by Western European nations.

[21] *Haiphong harbor mined.* U.S. Navy planes May 9 dropped mines into the port of Haiphong and six other harbors of North Vietnam (Thanhhoa, Hongai, Campha, Vinh, Donghoi and Quangkhe) to block the arrival or departure of North Vietnamese and foreign ships. Seven or eight ships left Haiphong before the mines were activated May 11. About 25 ships, half of them Soviet, had been headed for Haiphong when the first mines were dropped, but none entered the port. Twenty-eight or 29 ships remained in Haiphong harbor. The U.S. disclosed May 15 that North Vietnamese rivers and canals also had been mined. The U.S. claimed May 12 that the mining of the North Vietnamese ports was "100% effective," but a report from Haiphong May 17 said the mines were being cleared out as planes dropped them and that ships were moving in and out of the harbors.

[22] *New air war phase.* U.S. planes launched heavy attacks May 8 in the opening phase of the interdiction ordered by Nixon. Attacks in this new phase of the air war were aimed at storage facilities, barracks, troop training facilities, rail lines leading to China, bridges, petroleum pipelines, electrical power plants and oil storage tanks. The air war was widened May 23 with the U.S. announcement that more industrial sites and other non-military targets would be subject to bombing. Most of the raids centered on rail lines and in and around the Hanoi-Haiphong area, but U.S. planes June 5-6 bombed targets only 15 miles away from the China border. (U.S. officials June 26 announced the establishment of a 25-mile bomb-free buffer zone south of the China border, but some strikes continued within the zone to destroy railroad bridges.) Bombing raids in the Hanoi area were suspended June 15-18 while Soviet leader Nikolai V. Podgorny conferred with North Vietnamese leaders in Hanoi. The U.S. Oct. 23 ordered a temporary halt to bombing north of the 20th Parallel in North Vietnam to signal U.S. recognition of concessions made by North Vietnam in secret peace negotiations *(see* [49-51]). Bombing missions continued only below the 20th Parallel until Dec. 18, when the U.S. resumed massive strikes on the northern part of the country. The renewed raids were launched in the wake of a breakdown in the private peace negotiations in Paris *(see* [52-53]). A White House statement Dec. 18 warned that the bombings "will continue until such a time as a settlement is arrived at." The targets in the renewed raids included "such categories as rail yards, ship yards, command and control facilities, power plants, railway bridges, railroad rolling stock, truck parks, MiG bases, air defense radars and gun and missile sites." The decision to resume heavy bombing north of the 20th Parallel evoked strong criticism Dec. 19-20 from foreign governments, including the Soviet Union and China. The governments of Italy, the Netherlands and Sweden officially condemned the intensified American air war. The bombing above the 20th Parallel was again halted Dec. 30 on orders from President Nixon. The White House statement on the bombing curb was coupled with an announcement that secret peace discussions would resume in January 1973 *(see* [53]).

[23] *Hanoi charges dikes bombed.* North Vietman throughout the period from May to July charged that U.S. planes and naval vessels had damaged dikes used in the North to control flooding during the rainy season (lasting from the end of June till October). Hanoi charged that the bombings of dikes were deliberate and repeated, but the U.S. Defense Department repeatedly denied any deliberate or inadvertent attacks against the dikes. United Nations Secretary General Kurt Waldheim said July 24 that he had received "private" and "unofficial" information that U.S. planes had deliberately bombed dikes in North Vietnam. He appealed to the U.S. "to stop this kind of bombing, which could lead to enormous human suffering, enormous disaster." Waldheim's charges were denied by President Nixon and U.S. Secretary of State William P. Rogers. The U.S. State Department July 26 said that any American air strikes on the dikes were accidental, and the resultant damage was minimal. Nixon said July 27 that the controversy over the dikes was "a deliberate attempt on the part of the North Vietnamese to create an extraneous issue, to

divert attention from one of the most barbaric invasions of history." The Nixon Administration July 28 issued a Central Intelligence Agency (CIA) report conceding that U.S. bombing had damaged North Vietnam's dike system at 12 points, but asserting that the hits were unintentional and the damage minor. North Vietnam July 31 disputed the Administration report and said that 173 strikes had been made against the dikes since April, with direct hits in "149 places."

[24] *Clark visit stirs controversy.* A visit by former U.S. Attorney General Ramsey Clark to North Vietnam July 29-Aug. 12 to inspect the effects of U.S. bombing generated widespread controversy on the U.S. political scene. Clark visited North Vietnam with other members of the Stockholm-based International Commission of Inquiry into alleged U.S. war crimes in Indochina. The group was investigating charges of the bombing of non-military targets. In recorded interviews broadcast by Hanoi radio, Clark reported seeing evidence of bomb damage to dikes, hospitals, schools and civilian areas. Clark said Aug. 14 that some American prisoners of war would be released by North Vietnam if Sen. George McGovern were elected President *(see* ELECTIONS [1-2, 36]), and that all of the POWs would be released within three months after that. Clark had interviewed POWs in North Vietnam and said they "were unquestionably humanely treated, well treated."

[25] *French mission bombed in Hanoi.* A U.S. air raid on the Hanoi area Oct. 11 heavily damaged buildings of the French diplomatic mission. Hanoi radio reported that a member of the French delegation and four North Vietnamese employees were killed, and the French delegate general and a visiting Albanian diplomat were injured. (Delegate General Pierre Susini died Oct. 19.) The air strike was reported also to have caused lesser damage to the Algerian and Indian missions nearby. The French government formally protested the attack, as did the Algerian and Indian governments. The U.S. Navy, whose planes had been involved in the attack, said the intended target of the bombs was the Gialam railroad yard and repair shop, three miles northeast of the French mission. The U.S. Defense Department said that the damage to the French mission might have been caused by North Vietnamese antiaircraft fire and not by American bombs, but the U.S. formally admitted Oct. 20 that the mission had been "accidentally struck" by U.S. planes.

[26] **Saigon forces counterattack.** South Vietnamese forces May 13-14 launched a series of counterattacks in Quangtri Province and in the Central Highlands around Hue. Government forces also began an advance to relieve besieged Anloc.

[27] *Quangtri fighting.* The government thrust into Quangtri Province was the first counterattack since the start of the Communist offensive *(see* [14]). About 1,000 marines, accompanied by six American advisers, were landed by 17 U.S. helicopters behind Communist lines southeast of Quangtri city May 13 and reportedly killed more than 300 North Vietnamese before returning to friendly soil May 14. Another 500-man government unit that served as a blocking force for the assault troops was reported May 14 to have rescued "a number of civilians from enemy-held territory and brought them back behind friendly lines." No government losses were reported in the fighting. An estimated 20,000 South Vietnamese troops launched a major drive June 28 to retake Quangtri Province. The Saigon troops pushed into the province in force across the Mychanh River. The South Vietnamese push was preceded and accompanied by the war's biggest concentration of firepower, nearly all of it American. Seventeen U.S. cruisers and destroyers offshore and more than 100 B-52s were said to be pounding Communist positions in Quangtri almost continuously. Another 1,000 South Vietnamese marines were flown into Quangtri Province June 29 to join the main government force there. More government troops were airlifted into the province by helicopter June 30. Although slowed by heavy Communist shelling and bad weather, some advance government units penetrated the southeastern limits of Quangtri city July 4,

capturing the Mailinh section. The South Vietnamese troops were stalled by fierce North Vietnamese resistance at the edge of Quangtri city July 7-15, but pushed into the city July 15 and advanced toward the Citadel, a large walled enclave in the center of the town. The Citadel reportedly was taken July 25, but fighting continued in and around the city. The government troops abandoned the Citadel July 27, and the fortress was occupied by 400 North Vietnamese. South Vietnamese forces were reported Aug. 10 to have cleared North Vietnamese troops from the southern part of the city. South Vietnamese troops again stormed the Citadel Sept. 11 and engaged in heavy combat with the North Vietnamese defenders. The Citadel and the city were recaptured by the South Vietnamese Sept. 15. The retreating North Vietnamese defenders fled to the outskirts of the city, deploying around the Thachan River, where they continued to put up fierce resistance. According to the South Vietnamese, 8,135 North Vietnamese and 977 South Vietnamese had been killed in the battle for Quangtri city. Following the recapture of the city, the South Vietnamese tried to extend their hold on Quangtri Province. The offensive bogged down Dec. 2, however, in bad weather.

[28] *Hue area.* Government troops May 14 launched a second thrust of their counterattack, pushing out from two points southwest of Hue and reoccupying Fire Base Bastogne May 15. The assault force, ferried in by five helicopters, encountered no Communist fire as they landed at the base, the North Vietnamese having abandoned the strongpoint. The recapture of Bastogne was aimed at disrupting Communist preparations for an expected attack on Hue. Communist forces, however, July 2 began shelling Hue, using long-range 130-mm. guns against the city for the first time. The shelling of Hue was accompanied by shelling of Bastogne. The 600 defenders of Bastogne abandoned the base July 26 in the face of intense Communist shelling and heavy infantry assaults, but Bastogne was reoccupied by South Vietnamese troops Aug. 2 after the Communists abandoned it.

[29] *Anloc.* South Vietnamese forces May 17 were transported by helicopter to within two miles of Anloc in an advance supported by five B-52 strikes south of the city. Meanwhile, the relief column moving up Route 13 advanced to within six miles of the city May 18, and some units reached to within two miles of the city May 19. A heavy North Vietnamese attack May 20, however, forced the relief forces to halt. The relief column was reported June 7 to have made contact with a rear element of the Anloc garrison less than a mile from the city, and part of the column finally succeeded in reaching the town June 9. The main force of the relief column was relieved June 22 of the task of lifting the siege. The troops were replaced by soldiers of the 25th Division from nearby Tayninh Province, which also came under heavy Communist assault and remained stalled 10 miles from Anloc.

[30] *Kontum.* North Vietnamese commandos slipped into the besieged Central Highland city of Kontum May 25 and remained in control of scattered pockets of the town. (Earlier attempts to capture the city May 14 and May 18-21 had failed, as North Vietnamese were driven back by U.S. jet strikes and artillery fire.) The North Vietnamese force, totalling about 100 men, seized houses near Kontum's airport May 25, isolating the city from its only means of supply. About half the Communist force was said to have been killed or driven out of the city the same day, but the rest clung to sniper positions while more North Vietnamese apparently made their way into Kontum. The entire North Vietnamese force was reported June 7 to have been virtually driven out of Kontum. Only a handful of Communist troops reportedly remained in the city. Heavy fighting around the city continued, however.

[31] *Binhdinh Province.* South Vietnamese troops July 19 opened a counteroffensive in coastal Binhdinh Province in an attempt to retake the area captured by the Communists in their offensive. Some 8,000-10,000 government troops pushed north toward the Communist-held district capital of Hoainhon Bongson, and an element of about 500 men was airlifted to positions less than a

mile south of the city. The city was taken by the South Vietnamese July 21, but the North Vietnamese were reported July 29 to have seized control over the western half.

[32] Communists attack near Saigon. The Communists during August began a series of attacks on the Saigon area. South Vietnamese forces suffered heavy losses Aug. 7-8 in Communist attacks 17 miles east of Saigon. Communists Aug. 10 closed three major supply highways to the capital (Route 1 to the east, Route 4 to the southwest and Route 13 to the north) at points 25-60 miles from Saigon. Government forces Aug. 11 launched a drive to reopen the roads and reported success Aug. 20. However, Route 4, Saigon's link to the rice-producing areas of the Mekong Delta, was cut again Aug. 26 in heavy fighting 50 miles southwest of the capital. Fighting again erupted along Route 13, 20 miles north of Saigon, Oct. 6 as Communist attackers seized a number of hamlets. (Five of the captured hamlets were retaken by the South Vietnamese in fighting Oct. 7-11.) Route 1 was cut 30 miles from Saigon Oct. 13. It was reopened to civilian traffic Oct. 16, but clashes continued within sight of the road. Route 12 was severed Oct. 9 and was reopened only to military convoys Oct. 16. Route 1 was severed again both east and west of Saigon Oct. 29. All highways to Saigon were reported open Nov. 2. In other attacks around Saigon, South Vietnam's two big airports near the capital—Tansonnhut and Bienhoa—came under Communist shelling attack Sept. 10 and received heavy damage to planes and helicopters. Bienhoa was again struck by Communist rockets Oct. 22 and Dec. 15-16. Tansonnhut received its worst shelling attack in four years Dec. 6.

[33] Communists capture Queson. Communist forces Aug. 19 captured the district town of Queson and a nearby defense base (Base Camp Ross) in northern Quangnam Province after a major assault that routed the South Vietnamese defenders. The enemy force launched a heavy ground and shelling attack Aug. 18 against Queson and Ross, using 130-mm. artillery in the sector for the first time. Government troops, aided by heavy air support, drove the attackers out of Queson Aug. 19, but the enemy resumed the attack after a few hours and forced the government defenders to pull out. The South Vietnamese withdrew to Base Camp Baldy, about two miles southeast, in what was believed to be a rout. The defenders and hundreds of civilians were said to have fled Queson, abandoning artillery, tanks and other heavy weapons. South Vietnamese forces launched heavy counterattacks Aug. 22-23 in an attempt to recapture Queson, but strong North Vietnamese resistance thwarted their efforts. South Vietnamese forces succeeded during September in retaking Queson, but the Communists again captured the district capital Oct. 31. South Vietnamese troops retook Queson Nov. 3 after suffering heavy casualties.

[34] Communists open Quangnai drive. The North Vietnamese Sept. 16 opened a new drive in Quangnai Province, 150 miles south of Quangtri city, and were reported making steady progress. The attackers concentrated on five of the province's 10 district capitals. (The five capitals were Bato, Moduc, Ducpho, Binhson and Tunghia.) Bato was taken Sept. 18 but recaptured by the South Vietnamese Oct. 12. Bato was again taken by the Communists Oct. 31. Moduc and Ducpho were put under Communist siege, and Binhson and Tunghia were also under attack. In other action in the province, Communist forces Sept. 22 pressed their assaults on Quangnai city, forcing government defenders to abandon two small bases to the east and west.

Allied Withdrawal Developments

[35] Nixon ties total pullout to POWs. President Nixon said Jan. 2 that U.S. troop withdrawals from Vietnam would continue, but that a force of 25,000-35,000 troops would be retained in Vietnam unless all U.S. prisoners of war were released. He said the issue of release of the POWs in return for a pullout deadline had been discussed in Paris with the peace negotiators, but that the North Vietnamese had "totally rejected it." In response to charges from

Sen. George McGovern (Nixon's opponent for the presidency in November elections) that U.S. negotiators had never discussed with the North Vietnamese the question of total U.S. withdrawal in return for the release of POWs, the White House Jan. 3 provided a clarification of Nixon's original statement. The White House statement said that the U.S. had pressed in September 1971 for a clarification on the issue of whether a pullout deadline would lead to release of the POWs. The statement also said that the Administration was not conditioning a pullout solely on release of the POWs.

[36] **Withdrawals set.** President Nixon announced that 70,000 more U.S. troops would be withdrawn from South Vietnam over the following three months, reducing the authorized troop ceiling to 69,000 by May 1. Nixon's goal of reducing the American troop force to 69,000 men by May 1 was exceeded by 2,700 men. The U.S. command reported May 1 that, as of midnight April 30, U.S. troop strength in South Vietnam had dropped to 66,300. Nixon announced April 26 that 20,000 more troops would be withdrawn from Vietnam during May and June. The President further announced June 28 that 10,000 more troops would be withdrawn by Sept. 1, reducing the size of the U.S. force in Vietnam to 39,000. (At the same time, the President announced that draftees would not be sent to Vietnam in the future, unless they volunteered for duty there.) The withdrawal announced in June included the departure from South Vietnam Aug. 12 of the last units of American combat troops—members of the 3rd Battalion, 21st Infantry and G Battery, 29th Field Artillery. Nixon announced a further withdrawal of 12,000 men Aug. 29. The withdrawal was to be completed by Dec. 1. Actual U.S. withdrawals by the end of 1972 had reduced the American force in Vietnam to 24,200—2,800 below the authorized troop level—by Dec. 25. Nixon's announcements of withdrawals during 1972 were the 7th through 10th since the President assumed office in January 1969. The authorized troop level at that time had been 549,500.

[37] **Shift to Thailand.** The U.S. command in Saigon June 26 completed a shift of more than 2,000 American pilots and up to 150 American planes from Danang air base in South Vietnam to bases in Thailand 500 miles west. The Defense Department reported June 21 that the "driving factor" of the withdrawal was the decision June 17 to pull out the 19th Infantry Brigade, which provided security for the airmen at Danang. A department statement said: "We are not going to leave these Air Force people there without American security." According to a July 3 report, Thailand would soon replace South Vietnam as the major U.S. military base in Southeast Asia. Thailand itself announced Dec. 16 that it had given the U.S. approval to move its military headquarters from Saigon to Thailand in the event that a cease-fire went into effect in Vietnam.

[38] **Other Allied withdrawal moves.** The last members of Thailand's 12,000-man force in South Vietnam left the country Feb. 4. The Thai contingent of 824 soldiers withdrew without any ceremony. South Korea completed the first phase of the withdrawal of part of its 48,000-man force from Vietnam Feb. 29, when the last contingent of a marine brigade landed in the port of Pusan. The South Korean Foreign Ministry disclosed Sept. 7 that the country's remaining 37,000 troops in South Vietnam would be withdrawn starting in December. The South Korean troops ended their combat operations Nov. 8 and retired to rear bases. Australia ended its military involvement in the Vietnam war Dec. 18, when the country's last contingent (about 60 military advisers) left Saigon. (Australia also announced Dec. 27 that it was halting military assistance to South Vietnam and abandoning its program for training Cambodian troops.)

Prisoners of War

[39] **Hanoi frees 3 POWs.** The North Vietnamese government announced Sept. 2 that it would release three American prisoners of war, the first to be freed since 1969. However, it warned the U.S. government not to use the freed POWs to "slander" North Vietnam, an action it said would be against "the

interests of the families of other captured U.S. pilots." (Hanoi also said it had "temporarily suspended" the release of POWs after 1969 because the three prisoners released then had been "compelled" by the U.S. government to "put forward distortions about the humane policy" shown by Hanoi to POWs.) The three captured pilots—Navy Lts. (j.g.) Markham L. Gartley and Norris A. Charles and Air Force Maj. Edward K. Elias—were released in Hanoi ceremonies Sept. 17. The three arrived in the U.S. Sept. 17 after stopovers in Peking, Moscow and Copenhagen. They were accompanied by members of an antiwar group—the Committee for Liaison with Families of American Servicemen Detained in North Vietnam—that had arranged for their release. The trip home was marked by a sharp controversy between U.S. authorities, who sought to take custody of the men and fly them back to the U.S. in a military plane, and representatives of the antiwar group. The three were immediately sent to hospitals for medical examinations. (Gartley and his mother, soon after landing in New York, engaged in a heated discussion with a Defense Department official who told Gartley that his previous request for at least two days to visit with his family upon his return home would not be approved.) The North Vietnamese Sept. 22 had announced four conditions for the release of the prisoners: that the three pilots were to do nothing to further promote the U.S. war effort in Indochina; that they were to proceed home with the American peace activists and with their own families (Gartley's and Charles's families had flown to Hanoi for the release ceremonies) in a civilian plane; that they were to be given 30-day furloughs if they wished; and that they were to receive medical checkups at the hospital of their choice, military or civilian.

[40] **Hoffa Hanoi trip dropped.** James R. Hoffa, former president of the International Brotherhood of Teamsters, reported Sept. 7 that he was canceling, at least for the time being, a private trip to Hanoi to negotiate the release of American POWs. Shortly thereafter, the State Department reported that Hoffa's passport validation to travel to North Vietnam had been improperly granted by a "low-level official" without such authority and would be immediately revoked on orders of Secretary of State Rogers. Hoffa said he had been invited by North Vietnamese trade unions and had planned to set out Sept. 7. Certain undisclosed problems had caused him to postpone the trip, which had been damaged, he said, by news disclosures. Hoffa's attorney, William L. Taub, had claimed Sept. 7 that Presidential adviser Henry A. Kissinger had approved the trip in a meeting between Taub, Kissinger and a Teamster official. The White House Sept. 8 denied the claim, saying that Kissinger aides had told Taub that the Administration opposed the plan. Attorney General Richard G. Kleindienst Sept. 8 said that his deputy, Ralph Erickson, had rejected an Aug. 28 offer from Taub that Hoffa be allowed to resume union activities if he obtained the release of some POWs. (Hoffa had been barred from such activities when paroled in 1971 after serving nearly five years in prison for jury tampering and fraud.)

Moves Toward Peace

[41] **Paris peace talks.** The Paris peace talks resumed Jan. 6 after a month's suspension, but were plagued throughout 1972 by frequent cancellations and suspensions of meetings. The talks opened Jan. 6 with the Communist delegations restating the conditions for the release of American POWs. Nguyen Van Tien, the Viet Cong delegate, said freeing the captives was contingent on the pullout of American forces and the withdrawal of American support of the South Vietnamese government of President Nguyen Van Thieu. North Vietnam's chief negotiator, Xuan Thuy, added another condition for the release of U.S. POWs—that the U.S. "stop the 'Vietnamization' of the war." The talks continued weekly until Feb.10, when the U.S. delegation to the talks refused to agree to a date for the next meeting in order to protest a three-day anti-war rally scheduled to open in Versailles Feb. 11. The talks resumed Feb.

24, but came to an abrupt halt when the North Vietnamese and Viet Cong delegations walked out only a few minutes after the meeting had convened. The Communist walkout was in protest over American air raids on North Vietnam. The North Vietnamese had attempted to stop the Feb. 24 meeting and set March 2 as the next session, but the U.S. and South Vietnamese delegation refused to grant immediate consent. The U.S. and South Vietnam announced Feb. 25 that they would not attend meetings March 2 or March 9. Instead, the allies proposed March 16 as the date for the next meeting. The Communists accepted the date March 15, and the talks reopened March 16 with discussions on the POW issue.

[42]   The U.S. delegation, acting on the personal orders of President Nixon, March 23 announced an indefinite suspension of the talks. In announcing the decision, chief U.S. delegate William J. Porter said there would be no further meetings until the North Vietnamese and Viet Cong representatives entered into "serious discussions" on concrete issues determined beforehand. The Communists rejected Porter's contention, asserting that he was posing unacceptable conditions. Porter disclosed April 13 that President Nixon April 1 had proposed the resumption of the peace talks, but that the Communists' "only response to this overture came in the form of a mushrooming invasion of South Vietnam by North Vietnamese troops, and a classic prevarication in the Viet Cong statement that North Vietnamese troops were not involved in the military operation." (The State Department April 13 indirectly confirmed that Nixon's message to the Communists contained the stipulation that the conference could resume only if the Communists halted their offensive in the South.) The North Vietnamese delegation to the talks asserted April 15 that it had accepted Nixon's offer, but that Washington had canceled the proposal four days later. The North Vietnamese and Viet Cong delegations formally proposed resumption of the talks April 20, indicating they would agree to meet whether or not the U.S. halted its current bombing campaign over North and South Vietnam. (Hanoi previously had demanded an end to the bombing as a condition for resumption of the talks.) The U.S. replied April 25 that the U.S. and South Vietnam would resume negotiations provided the first order of business was discussion of measures to put an end "to the flagrant North Vietnamese invasion of South Vietnam." The talks resumed April 27, but the session was fruitless.

[43]   The U.S. and South Vietnam May 4 called an indefinite halt to the Paris peace talks because of, according to Porter, "a complete lack of progress in every available channel." The North Vietnamese and Viet Cong May 16 proposed a resumption of the talks, but the proposal was rejected by the U.S. delegation May 18. The U.S. and South Vietnam June 14 also rejected a North Vietnamese-Viet Cong statement June 13 that asked the U.S. to halt its acts of war and "participate in the work of the Paris conference each Thursday as usual." President Nixon June 29 disclosed that the talks would resume July 13 "on the assumption that the North Vietnamese are prepared to negotiate in a constructive and serious way." The talks resumed July 13, but remained deadlocked until Dec. 21, when the Communist delegations walked out in protest over American raids on North Vietnam.

[44]   **Nixon reveals new offer, discloses secret talks.** President Nixon Jan. 25 announced that he had submitted to the Communists through secret channels an eight-point program to end the war in Vietnam. (South Vietnamese President Thieu supported the program in a statement Jan. 26.) The President also disclosed that Henry Kissinger had privately discussed peace prospects with two North Vietnamese diplomats in Paris on 12 occasions between Aug. 4, 1969 and Aug. 16, 1971. Those talks ended before Kissinger was able to submit Nixon's new plan in its entirety, but the eight-point formula had been sent to the North Vietnamese delegation in Paris in a private communication from the President Oct. 11, 1971. Among the major elements of the plan, which was formally rejected by the North Vietnamese delegation Feb. 5: all U.S. and

foreign allied troops would be withdrawn from South Vietnam within six months of a peace agreement with the Communists, and the Communists would remove their forces from South Vietnam, Cambodia and Laos; all military and civilian prisoners of both sides would be released "in parallel with the troop withdrawals"; a cease-fire was to go into effect when the agreement was signed; military aspects of the agreement would be subject to "international supervision"; and new presidential elections were to be held in South Vietnam, organized and operated by an "independent body" comprised of all political forces, including the Viet Cong, with President Thieu and Vice President Tran Van Huong resigning one month before the balloting. The plan did not mention withdrawal of U.S. planes stationed aboard aircraft carriers off the coast of Vietnam or in bases in Thailand.

[45] *Secret talks.* In announcing his new plan, the President said that he had decided, after 10 months in office, to end the impasse at the Paris conference by entering into secret talks with the Communists. The disappointing results of those private contacts, Nixon said, prompted him to make them public to the American people in a further "try to break the deadlock at the negotiations." According to the President, Kissinger, during the course of his meetings with the two North Vietnamese diplomats (seven meetings with Le Duc Tho and five meetings with Xuan Thuy), had advanced several proposals which Democratic critics of the President had accused him of not making. One of those proposals, submitted May 31, 1971, called for total American withdrawal in exchange for release of all prisoners and a cease-fire *(see* [35]). The North Vietnamese had rejected the proposal June 26, 1971 and had presented their own nine-point plan, "which insisted that we overthrow the government of South Vietnam." Following three fruitless 1971 meetings July 12, Aug. 16 and Sept. 13, the President Oct. 11 "sent a private communication to the North Vietnamese that contained new elements that could move negotiations forward" and requested that they be discussed with Kissinger Nov. 1. The North Vietnamese agreed to such a meeting, to be held Nov. 20, but canceled it Nov. 17, claiming that Le Duc Tho was ill. After that, the Communists expressed no further interest in meeting to discuss the Nixon plan. Kissinger himself Jan. 26 revealed more details of his secret meetings. He said that there were two points in Hanoi's nine-point plan that prevented an agreement in the talks: North Vietnam's insistence that the U.S. end all of its support to the South Vietnamese government; and the Communists' conception of the word "withdrawal," which they interpreted to mean the removal of all American equipment, economic aid and all American arms held by the South Vietnamese army. Kissinger said that the Communists' withdrawal would mean the collapse of the Saigon government. (For details on further secret peace talks, *see* [48-53].)

[46] **Hanoi discloses its plan to end the war.** North Vietnam Jan. 31 made public a nine-point plan to end the war. The plan, reportedly the same one submitted to the secret talks in 1971, was published along with a communique released by the North Vietnamese delegation to the Paris peace talks in response to President Nixon's Jan. 25 disclosure. In addition to making known their plan, the North Vietnamese presented their own version of the U.S. eight-point plan, the seven-point plan submitted by the Viet Cong in 1971 and the texts of an exchange of messages between the U.S. and North Vietnam on the private meeting set for Nov. 20, 1971. There were two principal differences between the U.S. and North Vietnamese positions as outlined in their respective programs: President Nixon called for withdrawal of all foreign forces from the territory of South Vietnam, conditioned on an agreement in principle on a final settlement, while the North Vietnamese demanded the withdrawal of U.S. and allied troops from all Indochinese countries, with such withdrawal set without conditions; the American plan called for elections to be held by a commission, with the South Vietnamese government resigning one month before the elections, while the North Vietnamese wanted the immediate resignation of the

South Vietnamese government, with elections to be held by a tri-partite (North Vietnam, South Vietnam and Viet Cong) replacement government. The communique issued with the North Vietnamese plan asserted that President Nixon and Kissinger had "unilaterally divulged the substance" of the secret talks and had "even distorted the facts." The communique also charged the U.S. with causing the impasse in the secret talks and with canceling the Nov. 20, 1971 meeting. The North Vietnamese said they had informed the U.S. Nov. 17 that Tho was ill and suggested that Thuy take his place in the talks, but that the U.S. had called off the meeting Nov. 19. (The U.S. Feb. 1 released its own version of the North Vietnamese nine-point plan, which differed from the Communist version only in minor grammatical variations. In releasing the text, the U.S. also acknowledged that Kissinger had turned down a proposal to meet alone with Thuy. The refusal reportedly had been based on the belief that the private talks could not produce results unless a representative of North Vietnam's political leadership were present. Tho was a member of the North Vietnamese Politburo.)

[47] **Viet Cong issue revised plan.** The Viet Cong Feb. 3 presented a new version of their 1971 seven-point peace plan. The new plan called for the immediate resignation of President Thieu before negotiations on a coalition government in South Vietnam could start, but, unlike the original proposal, did not ask the U.S. to oust Thieu and did not restate earlier demands for a new administration in Saigon prior to coalition talks. Another new aspect of the plan was a call for "a precise date for the complete withdrawal from South Vietnam of all troops, military advisers and personnel, arms, war equipment of the United States and of other foreign countries in the American camp without putting any condition whatever." The Viet Cong previously had suggested a withdrawal date for the U.S. to accept, generally with the proviso that the U.S. could select a "reasonable" date of its own if the deadline were not acceptable. The new Viet Cong plan did not mention a cease fire, in contrast to the first point of its 1971 proposal. Unlike the old formula, it also failed to mention parallel releases of war prisoners as troops were withdrawn. The plan's stand on a political settlement differed widely from the 1971 version. According to the original plan, there would be a "new administration favoring peace, independence, neutrality and democracy," with which the Viet Cong would negotiate to form a coalition. The revised program demanded, in addition to Thieu's resignation, that Saigon must abandon "its bellicose policy, abolish its apparatus of repression and coercion against the population, put an end to the policy of pacification, liberate persons arrested for political reasons and guarantee the democratic freedoms stipulated by the 1954 Geneva accords on Vietnam." South Vietnam immediately rejected the revised Viet Cong plan.

[48] **Secret talks resume.** Secret meetings between Kissinger, Tho and Thuy resumed May 2 in Paris. The meeting (rumored at the time and confirmed by the White House May 5) was, according to Kissinger, six months in the making. Kissinger said May 9 that the meeting was the result of "innumerable exchanges." Kissinger also said that the meeting was unproductive, that Tho had refused to negotiate and had presented previously published demands. Kissinger and Tho met again in Paris July 19, Aug. 1, Aug. 14, Sept. 15, Sept. 26-27 and Oct. 8-11. No details on the meetings were released. A flurry of speculation that the meetings were rapidly approaching agreement on a settlement of the war was roused after the Aug. 14 meeting when Kissinger visited Saigon for talks with President Thieu Aug. 17-18 and Tho departed for Hanoi Aug. 16. The trips by the two negotiators led to rumors that an agreement had been reached and that Tho was informing his government of it, while Kissinger was giving the South Vietnamese government the same information. Rumors that an agreement had been reached surfaced again after the Sept. 26-27 and Oct. 8-11 meetings because of the unprecedented length of the conferences.

[49] 'Peace is at hand.' Kissinger Oct. 26 said that he believed "peace is at hand" in all of Indochina. Reporting on the secret talks in public for the first time, Kissinger said a final agreement on a truce and a political settlement could be worked out in one more conference with the North Vietnamese, "lasting no more than three or four days." Kissinger confirmed a Hanoi statement broadcast earlier Oct. 26 that the U.S. and North Vietnam had reached a breakthrough in private talks Oct. 8, when, Kissinger asserted, the North Vietnamese for the first time submitted proposals "which made it possible to negotiate concretely." At that meeting, Kissinger said, the Communist side came around to accepting the American position of concentrating "on bringing an end to the military aspects of the war" and then agreeing "on some very general principles within which the South Vietnamese parties could then determine the political evolution of South Vietnam." According to Kissinger, the North Vietnamese Oct. 8 dropped their demands for a coalition government absorbing all existing authority and for a veto over the personalities and the structure of the existing government. Kissinger said the North Vietnamese also agreed for the first time to a formula which permitted simultaneous discussion of Laos and Cambodia. Kissinger said that "six or seven concrete issues" remained to be ironed out before a final agreement could be drawn up. He cited possible temptations by South Vietnamese and Viet Cong forces to make "a last effort to seize as much territory as possible" before a truce went into effect. He also said that the U.S. wanted to take up with the North Vietnamese measures that a proposed international supervisory body could take "to avoid the dangers of the loss of life," and the matter of speeding up separate peace talks in progress in Laos and Cambodia so that a truce could go into effect through Indochina at the same time. Kissinger also cited "linguistic problems" that had arisen between the English and Vietnamese texts of the U.S.-North Vietnamese agreement.

[50] *Hanoi report on agreement.* In its broadcast Oct. 26, the North Vietnamese government gave its version of the nine-point Indochina peace plan it said had been drawn up by its representatives and Kissinger. The North Vietnamese statement detailed the agreement for scaling down and eventually halting U.S. military activities against North Vietnam and a timetable for signature of the agreement. According to the statement, the two parties to the talks had agreed Oct. 9 that the U.S. would stop the bombing and mining in North Vietnam Oct. 18, that the text of the agreement would be initialed in Hanoi Oct. 18 and that the agreement would be formally signed Oct. 26 in Paris by the "foreign ministers of the two countries." The statement also said that the U.S. Oct. 11 had proposed changing the three deadlines to Oct. 21, Oct. 22 and Oct. 30, respectively, and that the North Vietnamese had agreed to the change. The Communist statement said that the U.S. Oct. 20, "on the pretext that there still remained a number of unagreed points," changed the three dates to Oct. 23, Oct. 24 and Oct. 31. The North Vietnamese, according to their own account, had accepted the U.S. changes "while stressing that the U.S. side should not, under any pretext, change the agreed schedule"; but the U.S. Oct. 23 again demanded that negotiations be continued for resolving new problems. The North Vietnamese and Viet Cong Oct. 26-Nov. 1 demanded that the U.S. sign the agreement on Oct. 31, but the deadline passed without signing. (In his Oct. 26 statements, Kissinger said there was a "misunderstanding" about signature of the agreement by Oct. 31. He said the U.S. had agreed it would "make a major effort to end the negotiations by Oct. 31," but had made it clear that it could not set a definite date to conclude the talks.) The North-Vietnamese-U.S. agreement was supported by the Viet Cong Oct. 28, but President Thieu Oct. 27 expressed reservations about a political settlement as expressed in the agreement. Thieu Nov. 1 also denounced the draft agreement as "a surrender of the South Vietnamese people to the Communists" and as "only a cease-fire to sell out Vietnam."

[51]   *The 9-point plan.* In its broadcast Oct. 26, the North Vietnamese gave the following summary of the U.S.-North Vietnamese draft agreement. According to the summary, the North Vietnamese "proposed a cessation of the war throughout Vietnam, a cease-fire in South Vietnam, an end to all U.S. military involvement in Vietnam, a total withdrawal from South Vietnam of troops of the United States and those of the foreign countries allied with the United States and with the Republic of Vietnam, and the return of all captured and detained personnel of the parties. From the enforcement of the cease-fire to the installation of the government formed after free and democratic general elections, the two present administrations in South Vietnam will remain in existence with their respective domestic and external functions. These two administrations shall immediately hold consultations with a view to the exercise of the South Vietnamese people's right to self-determination, achieving national concord, insuring the democratic liberties of the South Vietnamese people and forming an administration of national concord which shall have the task of promoting the South Vietnamese parties' implementation of the signed agreements and organizing general elections in South Vietnam within three months after the cease-fire comes into effect. Thus the Vietnam problem will be settled in two stages in accordance with the often-expressed desire of the American side: The first stage will include a cessation of the war in Vietnam, a cease-fire in South Vietnam, a cessation of the United States military involvement in South Vietnam and an agreement on the principles for the exercise of the South Vietnamese people's right to self-determination; in the second stage the two South Vietnamese parties will settle together the internal matters of South Vietnam. The DRVN side proposed that the Democratic Republic of Vietnam and the United States sign this agreement by mid-October, 1972." In his statements Oct. 26, Kissinger said he had "no complaint with the general description" of the plan outlined by Hanoi.

[52]   **Talks resume.** The White House Nov. 17 announced that secret talks in Paris to resolve remaining differences would resume Nov. 20. Talks were held Nov. 20-21, Nov. 23-25, Dec. 4, Dec. 6-9 and Dec. 11-13. No agreement was reached on the major issues dividing the two sides. Kissinger Dec. 16 said that the secret talks had failed to reach what President Nixon regarded as "a just and fair agreement" because Hanoi had reneged on earlier accords negotiated by the two sides. Kissinger warned that the U.S. would not be "blackmailed," "stampeded" or "charmed" into an agreement "until its conditions are right." He said that the negotiations were now at "a curious point," where "we have an agreement that is 99% completed," but required a major decision by North Vietnam on the remaining 1%. Kissinger implied that there were at least two stumbling blocks to an agreement—the proposed four-nation (Canada, Hungary, Indonesia and Poland) supervisory team that was to observe the truce and the question of South Vietnam's sovereignty. He said the U.S. envisioned an observer force of "several thousand people...to monitor the many provisions of the agreement." North Vietnam, he said, insisted that the number of truce inspectors be limited to "no more than 250, of which nearly half should be located at headquarters," and that their movement and means of communication be severely restricted. On the question of South Vietnam's sovereignty, Kissinger said the U.S. sought to include in an agreement a statement that "the two parts of Vietnam would live in peace with each other." He contended that North Vietnam had accepted this "fundamental point" in negotiations two weeks before, but rejected the idea in subsequent talks. (According to other Administration officials, Kissinger was talking about the acceptance by Hanoi of the re-establishment of a DMZ, which would, in effect, mean that Vietnam was two countries, with Saigon having sovereignty over all of South Vietnam. President Thieu had insisted on such sovereignty as a principal condition for his acceptance of any peace agreement.) Kissinger said that the North Vietnamese Dec. 4 had switched their position on every major point agreed to by Nov. 20. By Dec. 9, the differences were worked out and both sides were so close to an agreement that Nixon had ordered Kissinger's

deputy, Gen. Alexander M. Haig Jr., to prepare to take the proposed pact to South Vietnam. At a meeting of technical experts Dec. 11, however, the North Vietnamese, according to Kissinger, brought in "17 new changes in the guise of linguistic changes." (The technical talks to work out problems envisaged under the new agreement had begun Dec. 10.) Kissinger said that Hanoi negotiators would raise a new proposal as soon as one problem was solved. At that point, according to Kissinger, Nixon decided to suspend the talks.

[53]   Hanoi and the Viet Cong Dec. 16 and 19 disputed Kissinger's version of the failure of the secret talks. The Viet Cong delegation to the regular Paris peace talks Dec. 16 released a statement assailing the "double-crossing attitude" of the U.S. and accusing it of "schemes to revise the contents" of the Oct. 26 draft accord. The Viet Cong asserted that the U.S. had blocked final agreement by raising the questions of North Vietnamese troop withdrawal from South Vietnam and restoration of the DMZ. Thuy Dec. 19 said that the U.S. was to blame for the impasse in the talks. He claimed that Kissinger had returned to Paris Nov. 20 and had brought with him 126 changes in the October draft accord. "Except for a very small number that were details or technicalities," Thuy said, the changes affected points of "fundamental importance." The U.S. Dec. 19 denied Thuy's charges. Despite the suspension of the secret talks, however, the technical talks between North Vietnam and the U.S. continued until Dec. 20, when North Vietnam called off the talks to protest renewed U.S. bombing above the 20th Parallel (see [22]). In conjunction with his Dec. 30 announcement halting bombing above the 20th Parallel, Nixon also issued an announcement that Kissinger and Tho would resume their secret talks Jan. 8, 1973 and that lower-echelon technical talks would be resumed Jan. 2, 1973.

[54]   **Thieu proposes truce, POW exchange.** President Thieu Dec. 12 proposed a truce between North and South Vietnam, that would start before Christmas and continue at least until Jan. 1, and an exchange of prisoners between Hanoi and South Vietnam if Hanoi released all the American captives it held. Thieu's offer was rejected by Viet Cong spokesmen in Paris and by the U.S. Dec. 14. In making his proposal Dec. 12, Thieu also reiterated his opposition to the Oct. 26 peace draft's failure to provide for the withdrawal of North Vietnamese troops from South Vietnam and to the proposed administration of national concord, which Thieu charged would pave the way for a coalition government that would include Communists.

See also CHINA, NATIONALIST; CUBA; DEFENSE; DRAFT & WAR PROTEST; DRUGUSE & ADDICTION [2]; ELECTIONS [2, 5, 9, 16-17, 23, 25, 32, 34]; FOREIGN POLICY; GERMANY, WEST [3]; HIJACKING [7]; MILITARY [5, 6-9]; NIXON, RICHARD MILHOUS; PENTAGON PAPERS; PULITZER PRIZES; SELECTIVE SERVICE SYSTEM; SINO-U.S. RELATIONS [5]; SOVIET-U.S. RELATIONS [6]; THAILAND; UNITED NATIONS; VIETNAM, NORTH; VIETNAM, SOUTH; WAR CRIMES

INTERNATIONAL AMATEUR BASKETBALL FEDERATION (FIBA)—*See* OLYMPICS [11]

INTERNATIONAL ATOMIC ENERGY AGENCY (IAEA)—*See* ATOMIC ENERGY [6, 8]

INTERNATIONAL BANK FOR RECONSTRUCTION & DEVELOPMENT (IBRD OR WORLD BANK)—Reorganization announced. IBRD President Robert S. McNamara Aug. 11 announced the first operational change in the World Bank's 20-year history. Under the reorganization, effective Oct. 1, five regional vice presidents would oversee activities for Asia, Latin America and the Caribbean, East Africa, West Africa and a grouping of European, Middle Eastern and North African countries. Spokesmen said the changes resulted from the expanding number of bank operations, which totaled nearly $3 billion during fiscal 1972 for the 117-member bank and its affiliate, the International Development Association.

Rumania joins World Bank, IMF. Rumania Dec. 15 joined the IBRD and the International Monetary Fund, becoming the first Soviet-bloc nation to apply for membership in the international finance organizations.

See also GHANA; LATIN AMERICA

INTERNATIONAL BROTHERHOOD OF TEAMSTERS—*See* INDOCHINA WAR [40]; LABOR

INTERNATIONAL CIVIL AVIATION AUTHORITY—*See* HIJACKING [15, 17]

INTERNATIONAL COFFEE ORGANIZATION (ICO)—*See* TARIFFS & WORLD TRADE

INTERNATIONAL COMMITTEE OF THE RED CROSS (ICRC)—*See* BURUNDI; HIJACKING [9]

INTERNATIONAL CONTROL COMMISSION (ICC)—*See* INDOCHINA WAR [12]; VIETNAM, NORTH

INTERNATIONAL COURT OF JUSTICE—*See* ARGENTINA [3]; SOUTH AFRICA [7]; TERRITORIAL WATERS; UNITED NATIONS

INTERNATIONAL DEVELOPMENT ASSOCIATION (IDA)—*See* GHANA; INTERNATIONAL BANK FOR RECONSTRUCTION & DEVELOPMENT

INTERNATIONAL FEDERATION OF AIR LINE PILOTS' ASSOCIATIONS—*See* HIJACKING [15]

INTERNATIONAL LAWN TENNIS FEDERATION (ILTF)—*See* TENNIS

INTERNATIONAL LONGSHOREMEN'S & WAREHOUSEMEN'S UNION (ILWU)—*See* LABOR

INTERNATIONAL LONGSHOREMEN'S ASSOCIATION (ILA)—*See* LABOR

INTERNATIONAL MONETARY DEVELOPMENTS—SDR allocation. The International Monetary Fund (IMF) Jan. 2 made its third allocation of Special Drawing Rights (SDRs or paper gold), equivalent to $2,951.5 million credited to the 112 participants in the IMF's Special Drawing Account. (The two earlier allocations had been made Jan. 1, 1970 in the amount of $3,414 million and Jan. 1, 1971 in the amount of $2,949 million.) The 1972 allocation was computed at 10.6% of each participant's quota in effect Dec. 31, 1971. The U.S. allocation was $710.2 million. (SDRs were used for international payments as if they were gold or convertible currency.)

[2]   Britain repays IMF debt. The IMF announced April 27 a complex arrangement by which Great Britain would repay in full its debt of just over 1.15 billion SDRs to the fund. The repayment, made April 28, marked the first time since 1964 that Britain owed no short- or medium-term debts to the IMF. The debt repayment restored Britain's automatic drawing rights to borrow the equivalent of 292 million pounds from the fund. The repayment formula provided for eight nations (Austria, Belgium, Canada, France, West Germany, Italy, Japan and the Netherlands) to make 500 million SDRs ($543 million) available to Britain in exchange for U.S. dollars, which Britain had in surplus. (The IMF would not accept dollars because of U.S. indebtedness to the fund and because of the U.S. refusal to convert dollars into gold.) The plan also provided for the U.S. to draw 200 million SDRs worth of pounds sterling from the IMF; and for Britain to repurchase from the fund 425.2 million SDRs, of which 400 million were from Britain's own SDR reserves and 25 million were provided by Canada, and 25 million SDRs worth of gold. (At the request of the fund, Canada would transfer 25 million SDRs worth of gold and 25 million SDRs to Britain in exchange for British pounds. Britain would convert the gold and SDRs into U.S. dollars.)

[3] **Nixon signs gold bill.** President Nixon April 3 signed into law a bill devaluing the dollar 7.89% by raising the price of gold from $35 to $38 an ounce. The bill had been passed by an 86-1 Senate vote March 1 and by a 342-43 House vote March 21. The U.S. had committed itself to devalue the dollar in the Smithsonian currency accord reached Dec. 18, 1971. The devaluation became official May 8 after the IMF formally announced the reduction in the parity of the U.S. dollar to 0.818513 grams of fine gold from 0.888671 grams. (The U.S. Treasury had officially notified the IMF of the reduced official parity of the dollar May 5. The U.S. announcement had been delayed until after Senate approval May 5 of a House-passed bill appropriating $1.6 billion to compensate the IMF and other international financial institutions for the loss in the value of their dollar holdings stemming from devaluation.) Despite the official U.S. parity of $38 dollars for an ounce of gold, the price of gold on the international market remained well above that parity throughout 1972. In London trading Aug. 1, the price of gold reached $70 an ounce.

[4] **French exchange controls eased.** French Finance Minister Valery Giscard d'Estaing May 7 announced the relaxation of French foreign exchange controls, effective May 8. The relaxation broadened the scope of the commercial franc market in France's two-tier monetary exchange system and authorized the outflow of more francs abroad. The range of the franc in the more advantageous commercial market was extended to include overseas services, such as transport and insurance. (Previously, the commercial franc market, in which the government intervened to support the official exchange rate, was reserved for export-import business transactions.) The financial franc market, in which the franc was permitted to fluctuate freely, would be limited to direct overseas investments, investments in foreign securities, currency exchanges by tourists and transfers of wages and salaries abroad.

[5] **UNCTAD III fails to act.** The third United Nations Conference on Trade and Development, which had begun April 13 in Santiago, Chile, ended May 21 with little substantive action by the 140 nations represented. Few resolutions were passed, to the frustration of the "Group of 77," which represented 97 developing countries in Asia, Africa and Latin America. The group had arrived at the conference with a long list of demands—including trade preferences for poorer countries, a voice in world monetary reform and debt relief. Its failure to gain major concessions was attributed to the group's inability to maintain unity among its members as well as to the intransigence of developed countries. The conference reportedly reached a climax May 21 after two days of all-night sessions and backroom negotiations on world monetary reform. The developing countries demanded a voice in reorganization of the world monetary system, arguing that their international reserves and the costs of imports in relation to exports had been damaged by the devaluation of the dollar (see [3]) and the December 1971 changes in parities between the currencies of the industrial nations. The developing nations also demanded that the Group of 10—the Western industrialized nations that managed world finances—agree at the UNCTAD conference on allocations to the developing nations of a special quota of SDRs from the IMF. After the U.S. balked at endorsing a special SDR allocation, the issue was settled by the adoption May 21 of a resolution (supported by the Group of 77) urging the IMF to complete work on proposals for a link between SDRs and the provision of resources for development financing. The measure was passed by a 71-0 vote, with 14

abstentions (including the U.S., Great Britain, West Germany, France, Japan and other capital-exporting countries).

[6]   Britain floats pound. The British Treasury announced June 23 that it was freeing the pound sterling from its official parity rate of $2.6057 and letting it float temporarily in the international money market to a new level determined by supply and demand. The Treasury simultaneously announced the extension of exchange controls to capital transactions in the overseas sterling area, a move designed to prevent British citizens from circumventing controls over capital movement of the pound. Chancellor of the Exchequer Anthony Barber said that the immediate cause of the government's surprise decision to float the pound was massive speculation against sterling that had forced Britain to use its reserves and had led to intervention by Europe's central banks to maintain the official parity rate set out in the Smithsonian Agreement. (Britain July 31 repaid the central banks $2.607 billion they had expended to support the pound during the speculation.) The British action constituted a de facto devaluation and ended Britain's efforts to maintain the pound to within 2.25% above and below the fixed parity rate. It also cut Britain loose from the European Economic Community's (EEC) policy of adhering to a narrower 1.125% margin above and below the parity rates among present and future members' currencies. The speculation crisis that had led to the float of the pound had been caused by rumors of an imminent devaluation as a result of Britain's widening trade deficit and the threat of a national dock strike, scheduled to begin June 16. Immediately following the announcement that the pound would float, Britain, Italy, Denmark, the Netherlands and Belgium closed their foreign exchange markets. France, West Germany and Switzerland opened their markets, only to experience a speculative run on the dollar, forcing the central banks to intervene in support of the official parity rates. The deluge of dollars caused all the remaining West European markets and most of the Middle East, Asian and South African exchanges to close within a few hours. The London foreign exchange market reopened June 27, and markets in West Europe reopened June 28. There were declines in the value of the pound and the dollar, but no discernible sharp trend. (Britain Nov. 23 paid $150 million to compensate nations whose international currency reserves fell in value because of the pound's decline.)

[7]   *Bonn sets exchange controls.* The West German Cabinet June 29 decided to impose foreign exchange controls to prevent an inflow of unwanted speculative currencies in the wake of the floating of the pound. The measures, effective July 1 along with previously decided increases in domestic reserve requirements held by banks, were passed over the opposition of Economics and Finance Minister Karl Schiller, an advocate of unrestricted monetary flows who repeatedly threatened to resign if the controls were passed (*see* GERMANY, WEST [9]). Under the measures, the basic minimum reserve requirements in commercial banks on incoming new capital would be raised to 60% from 40%, while the minimum reserve requirements on existing foreign term deposits and special-term liabilities would be raised by 9% and 13%, respectively. Other measures stipulated that non-interest bearing deposits that banks must keep with the Central Bank would be raised from 40% to 50% of the amounts borrowed abroad. The amount a bank would be allowed to borrow abroad without such a deposit would be reduced from $620,000 to $155,000. Sales of fixed-interest German securities to nonresidents would be subject to approval from the Central Bank. The measures were decided to reduce German banks' liquidity by the $2.5 billion worth of foreign currency that had flowed into West Germany since June 1.

[8]   *Currency exchange rate changes.* The IMF announced July 31 that 15 countries in the sterling zone would follow the British lead and allow their currencies to float. The countries were: Barbados, Botswana, Fiji, the Gambia, Guyana, India, Ireland, Jamaica, Lesotho, Malawi, Mauritius, Sierre Leone, South Africa, Swaziland and Trinidad and Tobago. Twelve countries in the sterling zone (Australia, Ghana, Iceland, Jordan, Kenya, New Zealand, Nigeria, Pakistan, Tanzania, Uganda, Western Samoa and Zambia) maintained a previously existing peg to gold or the dollar. Cyprus, Kuwait, Malaysia, Oman and Singapore discontinued their pegs to sterling and maintained parity with gold or the dollar. Iraq, though not a formal member of the sterling zone, discontinued its June 1972 tie to sterling. Hong Kong maintained a temporary tie to the dollar. Sri Lanka, previously pegged to the dollar, was pegged to sterling and thus floated its currency.

[9] Committee of 20 formed. The IMF announced June 26 the formation of a "Committee of 20" to negotiate world currency reform and "related issues." The scope of the committee's proposed negotiations included international trade issues, capital flow, investment, development assistance and preferential trade pacts. The inclusion of trade rules in the currency negotiations was considered a victory for the U.S., which had maintained that international trade issues could not be isolated from reform of world monetary systems. The 20 member nations of the committee were chosen Sept. 28. They were: Great Britain, France, West Germany, the U.S. and Japan—who would represent only themselves; and India, Brazil, Morocco, Sweden, Ethiopia, Argentina, Italy, Mexico, the Netherlands, Zaire, Austria, Canada, Belgium, Indonesia and Iraq—each representing a "cluster" of countries.

[10] New IMF members. The Persian Gulf states of Bahrain and Qatar joined the IMF Sept. 7 and 8, bringing the total membership to 123 nations.

[11] IMF annual report. The IMF Sept. 10 released its 1972 annual report, after extensive study of the impact of the 1971 Smithsonian Agreement. The report concluded that there would be little improvement in the worldwide balance of payments problem during 1973, but that "it can be expected that the realignment will, in due course, lead to the restoration of international payments equilibrium—unless [the Smithsonian Agreement's] intended effects are blunted or frustrated by inappropriate national policies." The report also found that underdeveloped countries, with the exception of the oil-producing nations, were not adversely affected by the 1971 currency realignment. It also recommended that the U.S. raise its short-term interest rates as an interim measure to attract capital and realign its foreign trade imbalance (*see* [1]) and that Japan and those European countries with large payment surpluses, economic slack and unemployment adopt expansionary monetary policies aimed at bringing down interest rates. The IMF had earlier (Sept. 6) issued a separate report on money reform which concluded that any future currency system should be more "symmetrical" than the old, in which the dollar was the dominant influence. The Sept. 6 report also recommended that: the U.S. settle its future balance of payments deficits by paying out reserve assets (gold, foreign currency holdings, SDRs and the U.S. quota in the IMF) rather than by financing the deficit through the issuance of more dollars; parity changes be subject to clearer criteria; SDRs play an increased role in international monetary affairs; the U.S. have greater freedom to change the value of its currency; and changes in currency values be smaller and more frequent.

See also ARGENTINA [1, 4]; BOLIVIA; BRAZIL; CHILE [1, 11, 13]; DRUG USE & ADDICTION [16]; ECONOMY [2]; EUROPEAN ECONOMIC COMMUNITY [2-5, 10-11, 18]; FOREIGN POLICY; GHANA; GREAT BRITAIN [5]; INTERNATIONAL BANK FOR RECONSTRUCTION & DEVELOPMENT; JAPAN [8]; KOREA, SOUTH; OIL & NATURAL GAS; TARIFFS & WORLD TRADE

INTERNATIONAL MONETARY FUND (IMF)—*See* ARGENTINA [4]; INTERNATIONAL BANK FOR RECONSTRUCTION & DEVELOPMENT; INTERNATIONAL MONETARY DEVELOPMENTS [1-3, 8-11]

INTERNATIONAL OLYMPIC COMMITTEE (IOC)—*See* OLYMPICS; OLYMPIC TERRORISM

INTERNATIONAL TELECOMMUNICATIONS SATELLITE CONSORTIUM (INTELSAT)—*See* SPACE [23]

INTERNATIONAL TELEPHONE & TELEGRAPH CORP. (ITT)—*See* CHILE [1, 11-13]; POLITICS [1, 3-7]
INTERNATIONAL WHALING COMMISSION—*See* CONSERVATION
INTERPOL—*See* DRUG USE & ADDICTION [20]
INTERSTATE COMMERCE COMMISSION (ICC)—*See* RAILROADS

IRAN—Iraqi ouster moves protested. Iran, according to a Jan. 4 report, filed a protest with United Nations Secretary General Kurt Waldheim over the deportation of 60,000 Iranians from Iraq in the previous three months. The Iranian protest said that 36,000 Iranians had been rounded up Dec. 31, 1971, had their homes and possessions seized and identity papers destroyed, and were then put across the border. Many of the expellees were said to have been beaten and tortured by the Iraqi police. According to Iran, those expelled had lived in Iraq for many years, having settled there after visiting the Moslem Shiite shrines in the Iraqi border cities of Najaf and Karbala. Talib el-Shibib, Iraq's chief delegate to the U.N., Jan. 4 denied that 36,000 Iranians had been deported. He declined to say how many had been expelled, but said his government had ejected only those who had entered the country illegally and posed a security risk.

    Guerrillas executed. Six guerrillas were executed by a firing squad in Teheran March 1, after a military tribunal had sentenced one to death Jan. 31 and the other five to death Feb. 1. The six were among 23 defendants accused of anti-state activities, bank robbery, illegal possession of arms and membership in the outlawed Communist party. The 17 other defendants received sentences ranging from one year to life imprisonment.

    Nixon visit. Following his visit to the Soviet Union (*see* SOVIET-U.S. RELATIONS [1-6]), President Richard Nixon stopped in Iran May 30 for talks with Shah Mohammed Riza Pahlevi. The following day, terrorists exploded three bombs. One bomb exploded at the tomb of the Shah's father, delaying for nearly an hour a ceremony in which Nixon was scheduled to lay a wreath there. (Nixon was preparing to drive to the tomb during the time when the bomb exploded.) A second device went off under the car of Brig. Gen. Harold L. Price, U.S. advisor to the Iranian air force, breaking both his legs, injuring his driver and killing an Iranian woman who had been standing nearby. The third blast took place at the U.S. Information Service building in Teheran, causing property damage but no injuries. A communique issued May 31 said that meetings between the Shah and the President had been "warm and cordial," in keeping with the "close and friendly relations that exist between the two countries."

    See also AVIATION; DRUG USE & ADDICTION [12, 18]; EARTHQUAKES; IRAQ; MINES; OIL & NATURAL GAS; SOVIET-U.S. RELATIONS [2]

IRAQ—30 arrested in Egyptian plot. The Egyptian government Feb. 26-29 arrested 28 Iraqis believed involved in a Baghdad-led assassination plot aimed at Iraqi political refugees living in Cairo. The arrests were set off by the attempted assassination Feb. 26 of former Col. Erfan Khader Wagi. The colonel, who had been commandant of the Iraqi military academy, was shot and wounded. Three Iraqis were seized soon after the incident; 11 more were arrested Feb. 28 as they attempted to leave Egypt by way of Alexandria; and Cairo security police picked up 14 others Feb. 29. Interrogation of the prisoners revealed that two groups of Iraqi security men had been sent to Egypt Feb. 18 and 20. They were given weapons by the Iraqi military attache in Cairo and by an officer sent to the Iraqi embassy to supervise the operation. Eighteen refugees in opposition to the Baathist regime of Iraqi President Ahmed Hassan al-Bakr were listed as assassination targets.

    Iranian border clashes. Baghdad radio reported April 14 that Iraqi forces had clashed with Iranian forces April 11-14 and had inflicted heavy losses on the Iranians "in lives and material." Iraqi casualties were listed as one soldier and two policemen slightly wounded. The fighting reportedly erupted

April 11 after Iranian border guards opened fire on an Iraqi police vehicle at Khanaqin in eastern Iraq. The police allegedly came under Iranian fire again April 12 when they attempted to tow the vehicle away. The Baghdad radio report said that Iraqi troops intervened when Iranian soldiers moved into Iraqi territory and "our forces were able to drive the enemy out and establish control of the area" by April 14. An Iranian report April 15 claimed that Iraqi troops had attacked six Iranian border posts in the previous five days and were waging "aggressive actions." According to Iran, the Iraqis had kidnaped three Iranian policemen April 14 and had made daily border assaults with artillery support.

Cabinet shuffle. In a reshuffle of the Cabinet announced May 14, three ministers were dropped and nine new ministers appointed—including two highranking officials of the Iraqi Communist party. The two CP members—Amer Abdullah, deputy secretary general of the party, named minister of state without portfolio, and Makram Talabani, of the party's Central Committee and Politburo, appointed minister of irrigation—were the first appointed to the Cabinet since 1963.

See also ATOMIC ENERGY [6]; HEALTH; INTERNATIONAL MONETARY DEVELOPMENTS [8-9]; IRAN; JORDAN; MIDDLE EAST [17]; OIL & NATURAL GAS

IRELAND (REPUBLIC OF IRELAND)—IRA prison riot.

Inmates at the Mountjoy Prison in Dublin rioted May 18 against prison conditions and the holding of political prisoners for up to four months without trial. About 30 political prisoners—those charged with offenses connected to activities of the outlawed Irish Republican Army (IRA)—had begun the riot by breaking out of their cells and freeing the other inmates. The rioters seized control of the prison wing and held three hostages, including the chief prison officer. The riot was ended early May 19 by more than 200 armed soldiers called in to reinforce 100 policemen.

Special court created. The government May 26 announced the creation of special criminal courts of three judges to try without jury suspected members of the IRA. The courts were established to overcome the refusal of juries to convict IRA suspects. The militant IRA Provisional wing June 2 denounced the government action and the increase in arrests of IRA members since Feb. 23, accusing Prime Minister John Lynch of "outright collaboration with the British government." The Provisionals vowed to continue their campaign against the British army in Northern Ireland.

Weapons surrendered. Police reported Aug. 6 that almost 1,500 handguns and high-caliber rifles had been surrendered to them in compliance with an Aug. 2 government order. The government hoped that 2,000 military-type guns would be turned in by civilian owners.

Ulster relief funds reportedly misused. The Dail (parliament) Committee of Public Accounts reported Aug. 23 that less than £30,000 (about $73,000) of a £105,000 government grant was used for its intended purpose of aiding Catholic victims of the 1969 rioting in Northern Ireland (Ulster). The report said that almost £35,000 had been "possibly spent" in Ulster on undetermined purposes and that almost £41,500 was "not spent on the relief of distress." The report also stated that the government was seeking the return of £35,000 paid to a West German arms dealer for weapons and ammunition. News reports speculated that the arms had been delivered to the IRA, not to the republic.

MacStiofain jailed. The long threatened crackdown on the IRA was put into effect Nov. 25 as a special Dublin criminal court sentenced Sean MacStiofain, reputed leader of the IRA's Provisional wing, to six months imprisonment for belonging to an illegal organization. The three-judge court convicted MacStiofain after accepting the identification of a voice on a radio tape recording as that of MacStiofain. (Earlier Nov. 25, the court had jailed Kevin O'Kelley, the interviewer on the radio tape, for refusing to reveal the person interviewed. The Irish government Nov. 24 also had dismissed the nine-member executive board of the state radio and television network on the ground that the interview had violated a directive prohibiting publicity about activities of an illegal organization. The network was closed down the following day when a hundred broadcast commentators staged a protest strike.) MacStiofain was taken to a Dublin hospital after being sentenced. (He had collapsed during the trial as the result of a hunger strike begun immediately after his arrest Nov. 19.) Eight armed gunmen, disguised as priests and doctors, made an abortive attempt to rescue him from the hospital Nov. 26. A policeman, two gunmen and two civilian bystanders were wounded in the ensuing gunfight. (Four of the gunmen were sentenced Dec. 19 to seven years in prison for their participation in the escape attempt.) MacStiofain was transferred from the hospital to a military hospital at Curragh Nov. 27 because of security risks in Dublin. MacStiofain's conviction resulted in serious protest demonstrations. A bomb exploded in a Dublin motion picture theater Nov. 26, injuring at least 25 persons. About 3,000 persons marched through downtown Dublin the same day demanding the resignation of Prime Minister Lynch and shouting support for the IRA. The government Nov. 27 canceled police leaves and placed 1,000 reserve troops on standby alert to meet any fresh outbreak of violence.

Anti-terrorism bill. In its continuing crackdown on the IRA, the government Nov. 27 published an anti-terrorism bill that would admit as evidence the sworn "belief" by a senior police officer that a suspect was a member of an illegal group. The bill also provided that an individual's failure to deny a public report that he belonged to an illegal group would be admitted as evidence of his membership. The bill carried penalties of a fine of up to $2,350 and five years in prison for conviction. The bill seemed headed for certain defeat, which would have led to the dissolution of the Dail and new elections. The major opposition parties, Fine Gael and Labor, opposed the measure on the grounds it was repressive. However, the heated debate on the bill was recessed Dec. 1 after two bomb explosions in downtown Dublin killed two men and injured many others. When the Dail reconvened, the Fine Gael announced that it "had decided to put nation before party" and would withdraw its amendment to kill the measure. Patrick Cooney of the Fine Gael said that most of his party's members had decided to abstain after the perpetrators of the blast "were revealed as fellow travelers of the IRA." (The Provisional IRA denied all responsibility for the explosions.) The anti-terrorism bill was then passed by a 70-23 vote early Dec. 2. The Senate passed the bill early Dec. 3, and President Eamon de Valera signed the measure into law later the same day.

Special status of church ended. The Irish electorate Dec. 7 voted decisively to end the "special position"of the Roman Catholic Church in the Irish constitution. About 85% (721,003 persons) of the voters in the national referendum approved the repeal. (Votes against repeal totaled 133,430.) The results were marred by the fact that only 46% of the eligible voters participated in the referendum. Government officials attributed the low turnout to the fact that the result was a foregone conclusion. Prime Minister Lynch Dec. 8 hailed the results, which, he said, would "strengthen the hand of all, in North and South, who work for peace and reconciliation among all the people of Ireland." (Ulster Protestants traditionally had cited the church's special position as a major obstacle to the reunification of Ireland.) The referendum would not affect Ireland's prohibition against the import and sale of contraceptives or the constitutional ban on divorce.

See also ATOMIC ENERGY [6, 8]; EUROPEAN ECONOMIC COMMUNITY [1, 10-12, 14]; INTERNATIONAL MONETARY DEVELOPMENTS [8]; NORTHERN IRELAND [4, 18]

IRISH REPUBLICAN ARMY (IRA)—*See* IRELAND; NORTHERN IRELAND [3-7, 10, 12-14]

IRVING, CLIFFORD—*See* BOOKS

ISRAEL—Fiscal 1972 budget. The Cabinet Jan. 17 approved a record budget of $4.03 billion for the 1972 fiscal year beginning April 1. The budget included $1.2 billion for defense. The overall expenditure was 15% higher than that for the fiscal 1971 year.

Justice minister resigns. Justice Minister Yaacov Shimshon Shapiro, a senior Zionist leader and close confidant of Premier Golda Meir, resigned June 11 under fire in a domestic economic controversy. It was the first break in the governing coalition since the August 1970 withdrawal of the hard-line Gahal faction. Shapiro gave no reason for his resignation, but reports cited recent public outcries against his approval of large stipends to lawyers who participated in a judicial investigation of the Netivei Neft Oil Co., the government corporation in charge of oil exploration in the occupied Sinai Peninsula. The fees—$630 a day (more than the premier made in a month)—had been condemned by the Cabinet, despite Shapiro's contention that they were in line with what the Israeli legal profession had come to expect.

Lansky citizenship denied. The Israeli Supreme Court Sept. 11 refused Israeli citizenship to Meyer Lansky, reportedly a major U.S. crime figure, even though he was a Jew. Lansky, who had been living in Israel with his wife under a tourist visa since July 1970, was wanted in the U.S. in connection with income tax evasion charges and contempt of court. Lansky had sued for permission to remain in Israel as a citizen under the Law of Return, which gave every Jew the right to enter Israel as an immigrant. However, the court upheld a ruling by the Israeli interior minister, who had invoked a clause in the law empowering him to exclude, as liable to endanger public order, Jews with criminal pasts. The court's decision did not mean that Lansky could be extradited, since the charges against him were not extraditable offenses under the existing treaty between Israel and the U.S. After the court's decision was announced, the Israeli government said it would offer Lansky a travel document to let him go to any country that would take him. (Lansky's U.S. passport had been invalidated by Washington except for his return to the U.S.) Lansky left Israel Nov. 4 after he reportedly had offered $1 million to any country that would grant him asylum. Half a dozen South American countries refused to take him. He landed Nov. 7 in Miami, where he was arrested by agents of the Federal Bureau of Investigation.

See also ARAB REPUBLIC OF EGYPT; ELECTIONS [16]; EUROPEAN ECONOMIC COMMUNITY [7, 9]; FOREIGN AID; HIJACKING [9]; JORDAN; LATIN AMERICA; MIDDLE EAST; OLYMPICS [5]; OLYMPIC TERRORISM; POLITICS [8]; SYRIA; UGANDA [4, 13]; UNION OF SOVIET SOCIALIST REPUBLICS [8]

ITALY—Italy's 32nd government since 1946 resigned during January because of its failure to reconcile conflicts between the members of the ruling coalition (*see* [2]). A minority government was sworn in during February, but resigned only eight days later (*see* [3]). Following the collapse of the minority government, parliament was dissolved and new elections were held in May (*see* [3-4]). A new centrist coalition Cabinet was sworn in during June (*see* [5]). In other developments, the country's economy was disrupted throughout the year by widespread strike actions (*see* [7]).

[2] Cabinet resigns. The center-left government of Premier Emilio Colombo resigned Jan. 15, culminating months of growing tension between the centrist and leftist parties forming the coalition. The Colombo government had been in power for 17 months. The immediate cause of the government's resignation was a decision by the small Republican party Jan. 7 to withdraw its parliamentary support from the government. (The party had quit the coalition government in February 1971, but had continued to support it in parliament.) The coalition partners had already split sharply during the presidential elections in December 1971. Conflicts between feuding factions of the Christian Democratic party as well as between the two main coalition parties—the Christian Democrats and the Socialists—had led to a government crisis in which 16 days and 23 ballots were required to elect Giovanni Leone as president of Italy. One of the major causes of the conflict was disagreement over seeking ties with the Communist party. Leone Jan. 21 asked Colombo to reconstitute his coalition government, but Colombo was forced to abandon his efforts Feb. 1 because of bitter political differences. Leone then asked Giulio Andreotti, chairman of the Christian Democrats in the Chamber of Deputies, to form a coalition government Feb. 5.

[3] *Minority Cabinet formed, resigns.* Andreotti was sworn in Feb. 18 as premier of a minority Cabinet composed of only Christian Democrats following the collapse of his efforts to form a coalition government. His efforts, and those of Colombo, failed because of disputes over ways to revive Italy's lagging economy, push through social reforms, seek ties with the Communists and settle the dispute over Italy's controversial divorce law (*see* [6]). The new Cabinet lacked majority backing in parliament and lost a vote of confidence in the Senate Feb. 26 by a 158-151 vote. Only the conservative Liberal party and the South Tyrol People's party backed the Christian Democrats in the vote. The Cabinet resigned Feb. 26. President Leone dissolved the parliament Feb. 28—14 months before the expiration of its term of office. It was the first time in the 25-year history of the Italian Republic that parliament had been dissolved before its term expired.

[4] *New parliament elected.* In parliamentary elections May 7-8, the Christian Democrats maintained their predominant position, halting a feared electoral shift to the extreme right and left. However, no party came close to winning a majority. The neo-Fascist Italian Social Movement scored some significant gains. The Communists won seats in the Chamber of Deputies and suffered losses in the Senate, while the allied Proletarian Socialists lost all representation in the Chamber of Deputies. (The Proletarian Socialists merged with the Communists July 16.) The pro-Chinese Manifesto faction, which had broken away from the Communist party in 1970, also failed to obtain the minimum amount required for representation. The composition of the new 630-member Chamber of Deputies (1968 seats in parentheses): Christian Democrats 267 (266); Communists 179 (177); Socialists 61 (62); Social Democrats 29 (29); Italian Social Movement and the allied Monarchists (the two merged July 15) 56 (30); Liberals 21 (31); Republicans 14 (9); South Tyrol People's party 3 (3); Proletarian Socialists 0 (23). Composition of the new 315-seat Senate: Christian Democrats 135 (135); Communists and Proletarian Socialists 94 (101); Socialists 33 (36); Social Democrats 11 (10); Italian Social Movement and Monarchists 26 (13); Liberals 8 (16); Republicans 5 (2); South Tyrol People's party 2 (2). The electoral campaign had been marked by street clashes between leftist and rightist extremists.

[5] *Centrist Cabinet sworn in.* Premier Andreotti June 26 formed a three-party centrist coalition government of Christian Democrats, Social Democrats and Liberals. It was the first time in 15 years that the Liberals helped form a Cabinet. The government, which had the outside support of the Republicans, commanded a majority of four in the Senate and a larger majority in the Chamber of Deputies. The search for a new government had begun May 30 when President Leone began political consultations for the designation of a new premier. He chose Andreotti to form a new government June 4. Andreotti's choice of the Liberals over Socialists for third position in the Cabinet aroused strong opposition among the left wing of the Christian Democrats. The new Cabinet (party initials in parentheses): deputy premier and defense—Mario Tanassi (SD); foreign affairs—Giuseppe Medici (CD); interior—Mariano Rumor (CD); justice—Guido Gonella (CD); budget, economic planning, the South—Pado Emilio Taviani (CD); finance—Athos Valsecchi (CD); treasury—Giovanni Malagodi (L); education—Oscar Scalfaro (CD); public works—Antonino Gullotti (CD); agriculture—Lorenzo Natali (CD); transport and civil aviation—Aldo Bozzi (L); posts—Giovanni Gioia (CD); industry and trade—Mauro Ferri (SD); labor—Dionigi Coppo (CD); foreign trade—Matteo Matteotti (SD); merchant navy—Giuseppe Lupis (SD);

state participation in industry—Mario Ferrari Aggradi (CD); health—Remo Gaspari (CD); tourism—Vittorio Badini Confalonieri (L); ministers without portfolio—Fiorentino Sullo (CD), Giorgio Bergamasco (L), Pier Lugi Romita (SD), Silvio Gava (CD), Giulio Caiati (CD) and former Premier Colombo (CD). The Cabinet won votes of confidence in the Chamber of Deputies by a 329-288 vote July 7 and in the Senate by a 163-155 vote July 13.

[6] **Court approves divorce referendum.** The constitutional court Jan. 26 upheld the constitutionality of a request for a referendum on the divorce law passed in 1970. (Conservative Roman Catholics opposed the law as a violation of Italy's 1929 Concordat with the Vatican, which gave the church jurisdiction over dissolving marriages.) The date for the referendum was to be set by the Cabinet and the President unless a way to avoid the referendum was found. Most politicians were anxious to halt the referendum because of the bitterness such a campaign would arouse. The referendum was scheduled for June 11, but was automatically postponed for a year by the dissolution of parliament Feb. 28 (*see* [3]).

[7] **Strike actions.** A 24-hour general strike in Rome Feb. 3—called by unions to support their demands for full employment and social reforms—halted trains and buses and shut down factories, theaters, newspapers and most offices, shops and restaurants. From 5.5 million to 8 million workers staged strikes or temporary work stoppages March 21 to support 1.7 million farm workers in a 24-hour strike for a new labor contract. The major trade unions called a labor truce prior to the national elections in May (*see* [4]), but a three-month wave of strikes followed the truce. Strikes in that wave included: a strike May 18-19 by about 300,000 lower-level civil servants protesting raises given their superiors; a strike June 8 by about 300,000 workers in the chemical industry after a breakdown in contract negotiations; a strike June 15 by about 100,000 doctors aimed at stimulating medical services and hospital reform and at showing support for 3,500 doctors who were protesting the conditions of their employment by various health insurance bodies; a second and third strike June 23-24 and July 12 by the nation's agricultural workers; a 24-hour strike June 23 by pilots of Alitalia Airlines and its domestic subsidiaries to back demands for higher pay and shorter work hours; and a four-day strike the week of June 25 by journalists protesting a decision by newspaper publishers to cease publication of Monday morning papers because of high publication costs. (The publishers agreed Aug. 1 to resume the Monday editions.) Italy's more than 200,000 railway workers staged 24-hour strikes Aug. 3-4 and Sept. 4-5 to back their demands for an across-the-board wage increase of $25 a month, staff increases, improved working conditions and the modernization of the railway system. Butchers and other retailers Sept. 4 began a week-long strike to protest a 60-day freeze on retail food prices imposed in Rome Aug. 28. The strikers contended that the price freeze belonged on wholesale, not retail, prices. (Food prices had soared by 8% in Rome since July.) Nearly 1.5 million construction workers staged 24-hour strikes Sept. 27 and Oct. 31 to demand higher wages. Teachers from the elementary to the university level struck Oct. 13-14 and Oct. 30-31 to protest what they termed the "shameful" condition of the schools. More than 4 million workers struck in the Lombardy industrial region around Milan Oct. 31 to demand social reforms, full employment and consolidation of democratic forces "against the drift to the right and the danger of fascism." Banks closed Nov. 3 when 150,000 bank clerks staged a strike to demand higher pay and shorter hours. Three million workers—including metal and construction workers, civil servants and bank employees—struck Nov. 22. Government ministries remained closed Nov. 23 in further strikes, while 350,000 farm workers struck the same day for a renewal of contracts and agricultural reforms. More than one million civil servants, bank employees and teachers staged strikes Dec. 6-10 to demand pay raises and educational and administrative reforms.

[8] Regional units given wide powers. The central government April 1 transferred broad administrative powers and 14,000 civil servants to 15 new regional administrations in a far-reaching decentralization move. The new regional responsibilities covered local police operations, welfare, agriculture, public works, education, health, transportation and other fields. Three of the new regions—Emilia-Romagna, Tuscany and Umbria—were controlled by the Communists. Christian Democrats dominated the other 12: Piedmont, Liguria, Lombardy, Venetia, Marche, Latium (including Rome), Campania, Abruzzi, Molise, Basilicata, Apulia and Calabria. Five other regions had previously been set up: Sicily, Sardinia, Val d'Aosta, Tentino-Alto Adige (South Tyrol) and Friuli-Venezia Giulia.

[9] Pieta damaged. Michelangelo's Pieta, one of the world's sculptural masterpieces, was severely damaged May 21 when a Hungarian-born emigre to Australia, Laszlo Toth, attacked it with a hammer in St. Peter's Basilica in Rome. The attack on the Pieta, which lasted approximately two minutes, shattered the left arm of the Virgin Mary and chipped her nose, left eye and the veil covering her head. An official in charge of St. Peter's technical services reported that the sculpture of the Madonna holding the dead Christ had suffered "severe damage" and that restoration work, particularly on the eyelid, would pose severe problems. Toth had pushed through a crowd of worshippers and tourists, jumped onto the altar where the Pieta was on display and rained hammer blows on the sculpture until he was finally subdued by an Italian fireman and other onlookers. Toth had shouted during the attack, "I'm Jesus Christ." He was turned over to the police for criminal proceedings. The attack stirred sharp controversy about protection of Italy's art treasures. An Italian newsman, Sandro Mazzerioli, May 22 staged a mock hammer attack on Michelangelo's sculpture of Moses, located in the Church of St. Peter in Chains in Rome, to show that other art masterpieces remained virtually unprotected.

[10] Record deficit budget approved. The Cabinet July 31 approved a budget for fiscal 1973 which had a record deficit (including subsidies to the railroad and postal services) estimated at about $7.8 billion—43.9% higher than the projected 1972 overall deficit. (The deficit minus the subsidies was set at $6.2 billion—51.8% above the 1972 budget deficit.) Revenues were estimated at $25.8 billion (a 12.6% increase), with expenditures projected at $32 billion.

See also DRUG USE & ADDICTION [18]; ESPIONAGE; EUROPEAN ECONOMIC COMMUNITY [1, 4, 6]; HIJACKING [7]; INDOCHINA WAR [22]; INTERNATIONAL MONETARY DEVELOPMENTS [2, 6, 9]; MALTA; OIL & NATURAL GAS

IVORY COAST—See AFRICA; TARIFFS & WORLD TRADE

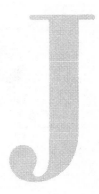

JACKSON, HENRY—*See* DISARMAMENT; ELECTIONS [3-4, 6-7, 17]

JAMAICA—Government upset in elections. The opposition People's National party (PNP) upset the ruling Jamaica Labor party (JLP) in general elections Feb. 29, taking 36 of the 53 seats in the House of Representatives. Michael Manley, head of the PNP and president of the Caribbean Bauxite and Mine Workers Federation, was sworn in as prime minister March 2 and named a Cabinet March 11. Manley had campaigned during the elections on the issues of favoritism, corruption, unemployment, violence and neglect of youth. (Unemployment and underemployment were reported to be as high as 40%, and armed assaults were said to have increased from 217 in 1957 to 2,142 in 1971.) The JLP, which had been in power since Jamaica's independence in 1962, had claimed that under its administration tourism had increased, industry had expanded, the gross national product had risen rapidly and education and technical training had improved. The party also charged that the PNP was Socialist and that it intended to nationalize major industries, such as the bauxite-alumina complex run by five U.S. companies and one Canadian firm. Manley refused during the campaign to discuss nationalization of the bauxite or sugar industries or federation with other British Commonwealth countries in the Caribbean.

There had been numerous incidents of violence during the campaign. Shots had been fired at political rallies, bombs had been thrown and partisans beaten. One PNP supporter had been shot and killed, and Manley himself had been fired at Feb. 24 while speaking in a crowded Kingston market. Shops and offices in central Kingston were closed and barricaded on election day. They were opened March 1, only to be closed again when snipers fired on PNP victory marches and buses and shops were ransacked.

Cabinet named. In naming his Cabinet March 11, Manley took for himself the defense and foreign economic policy posts. He was also to preside over the Planning and Economic Council. The new Cabinet: public utilities—Eric Bell; local government—Rose Leon; housing, youth and community development—Eli Matalon; consumer protection—Keble Munn; education—Florizel Glasspole; finance—David Coore; industry and tourism—P.J. Patterson; mining and natural resources—Allan Isaacs; labor and employment control—Ernest Peart; home affairs—Noel Sivera; commerce—Wills Isaacs; pension and social security—Howard Cooke; works—Winston Jones; special duties in the prime minister's office—Dudley Thompson.

See also INTERNATIONAL MONETARY DEVELOPMENTS [8]; TERRITORIAL WATERS

JAPAN—Cabinet approves budget. The Cabinet Jan. 12 approved a $37.2 billion budget for the 1972-73 fiscal year beginning April 1 (*see also* [8]). The budget was 21.8% higher than the previous budget. Defense expenditures totaled $2.6 billion, a 19.2% boost over the previous year. The defense appropriation precipitated a suspension of parliament Feb. 7-26. The suspension was caused by a parliamentary boycott by four opposition groups aroused by the size of the expenditure. The suspension ended with acceptance of a compromise which called for: the removal of an $11 million budget appropriation for new aircraft; the submission of a new budget the following week; and the freezing of the entire aircraft program pending National Defense Council approval of the overall $1.7 billion five-year defense plan.

[2] Rebel followers murdered. Tokyo police disclosed March 11 that members of the ultra-left Rengo Sekigun (United Red Army or URA) had killed 12 of their rebel followers after mock trials ordered by their commander, Tsuneo Mori. Mori confessed to the killings and was placed under arrest with 13 other URA members. It was believed that the 12 slain radicals, nine of whose tortured bodies had been recovered in graves through March 12, were executed because of their opposition to the URA's revolutionary policies. (Police said the organization had planned an armed attack on government leaders in April with the aim of establishing a "provisional revolutionary government.")

[3] Dock strike. The 160,000 members of the All-Japan Seaman's union walked off their jobs April 11 to press demands for an average monthly increase of $72 plus fringe benefits. (Basic pay averaged $197-$230 a month.) Ocean-going seamen April 14 joined the fishing-vessel seamen in the strike, and coastal ship workers followed the next day. The strike tied up Japanese and foreign shipping and resulted in a pileup of cargo at major Japanese ports. The coastal ship workers returned to work June 7 following a tentative agreement between labor and management to submit the main issues of employment security and underemployment compensation to collective bargaining talks. (The dock workers were demanding improvements in working conditions and guaranteed minimum wages of $333 a month.) The ocean-going seamen ended their strike July 12 with the acceptance of a government mediation plan which provided for an average monthly increase of $37.50 plus fringe benefits. (In another strike action, Japan's 1.6 million transportation workers went on strike April 26, virtually paralyzing the country's trains and subways and disrupting airline and taxi service in Tokyo. The strike ended April 27 when the workers were granted a pay increase of more than $30 a month.)

[4] Okinawa returned. The U.S. May 15 formally returned Okinawa and other Ryukyu Islands to Japan after 27 years of American rule. (The date was a compromise between April 1, favored by the Japanese, and July 1, favored by the U.S.) Agreement on the return of the islands had been made in talks between President Nixon and Japanese Premier Eisaku Sato Jan. 7, and documents ratifying the agreement had been exchanged March 15. The May 15 return ceremonies in Tokyo were attended by Vice President Spiro Agnew (representing President Nixon), Premier Sato, Emperor Hirohito and other U.S. and Japanese officials. The ceremonies were also marked by the exchange of greetings between Nixon and Sato over a newly opened "hot line" between the White House and the premier's office in Tokyo and by the release of a letter from U.S. Secretary of State William P. Rogers assuring Japanese Foreign Minister Takeo Fukuda that the U.S. was turning over the islands free of nuclear weapons. Okinawa leaders had rejected invitations to attend the ceremonies to protest the treaty clause that provided for continuation of the American military base on Okinawa and for plans to establish Japanese installations there. The Ryukyu Islands were to become a Japanese prefecture.

[5] *Documents leaked.* Takichi Nishiyama, a newspaper reporter, and Mrs. Kikuko Hasumi, a secretary in the Foreign Ministry, were arrested April 4

under a law that prohibited disclosure of government secrets and were charged with leaking secret documents relating to the negotiations over Okinawa. Three Foreign Ministry officials (Assistant Deputy Foreign Minister Takeshi Yasukawa, for whom Mrs. Hasumi had worked, Deputy Foreign Minister Haruki Mori and Deputy Foreign Minister for Administration Shoji Sato) took responsibility for the document leakage and offered to resign. Nishiyama allegedly persuaded Mrs. Hasumi to give him copies of secret cables sent in June 1971 dealing with the Okinawa negotiations. The messages reportedly disclosed that Japan had agreed with the U.S. to pay $4 million to Okinawan landowners for the damage caused to their property by the U.S. military occupation. Premier Sato's critics assailed this as an unreasonable concession to Washington. The alleged secret deal was publicly disclosed by Takahiro Yokomichi, a Socialist member of parliament. It was not clear how he came into possession of the documents.

[6] Sato resigns; Tanaka elected premier. Premier Sato, Japan's longest-serving postwar premier, resigned June 17 at a meeting of the parliamentary members of the ruling Liberal Democratic party. Sato's office term had been due to expire in October, but he resigned earlier because of his declining popularity. His prestige had suffered sharply when President Nixon failed to consult Japan in advance about his visit to China and when the U.S. introduced economic measures that eventually forced revaluation of major world currencies, including the Japanese yen, during 1971. Sato was succeeded by Kakuei Tanaka, minister of international trade and industry. Tanaka was elected president of the Liberal Democratic party—a position tantamount to premiership since the party held a majority in parliament—at a special caucus of party leaders July 5. Tanaka defeated Foreign Minister Fukuda in a runoff election, 282-190, after four votes had been declared invalid. The runoff was required after the first-round balloting involving four candidates (Tanaka, Fukuda and former Foreign Ministers Masayoshi Ohira and Takeo Miki) failed to produce the necessary majority for any of the candidates. Tanaka had received 156 votes, Fukuda 150, Ohira 101 and Miki 69. Tanaka was confirmed as premier by a special session of the parliament July 6. He named a new Cabinet July 7. The Cabinet: foreign affairs—Ohira; minister without portfolio—Miki (appointed deputy premier Aug. 29); international trade and industry—Yasuhiro Nakasone; finance—Koshiro Ueki; director general of the Defense Agency—Kekichi Mashuhara; health and welfare—Shunji Shiomi; labor—Hajime Tamura; posts and telecommunications—Makoto Miike; and director general of the Economic Planning Agency—Kiichi Arita. Miike and Arita originally refused to accept their posts, but July 12 agreed to serve. The two were members of a Liberal Democratic faction led by Fukuda, who reportedly had demanded four positions for his group.

[7] End state of war with China; resume diplomatic relations. Premier Tanaka and Communist Chinese Premier Chou En-lai Sept. 29 signed a joint communique ending the legal state of war that had existed between the two countries for 35 years and agreeing to establish diplomatic relations. The communique was signed at the conclusion of a Peking summit meeting that had begun Sept. 25. Among other principal points of the joint statement were Japanese acceptance of China's position that "Taiwan is an inalienable part" of the People's Republic of China (Communist China), Chinese renunciation of war indemnities from Japan and an agreement to negotiate a "treaty of peace and friendship" and accords on trade and other bilateral arrangements. Following the signing of the accord, Japan immediately notified Nationalist China of its decision to recognize China and broke relations with the Taiwan government. Nationalist China followed suit and severed ties with Tokyo Sept. 29. (Japan and Nationalist China Nov. 11 agreed to establish a liason office in Tokyo to maintain trade and other nondiplomatic ties. The two countries Dec. 26 signed an agreement to continue diplomatic relations on an unofficial level.

Tanaka's visit to China, made at the invitation of Premier Chou, also included a 90-minute nonpolitical meeting with Chairman Mao Tsetung Sept. 27.

[8] Anti-surplus bills passed. The House of Representatives Nov. 13 approved two trade measures and a $3.8 billion supplementary budget aimed at reducing Japan's growing trade surplus. The trade bills provided for a 20% reduction in tariffs on industrial and processed agricultural products (resulting in an estimated $300 million cut in Japan's international payments surplus), a lowering of exports, an increase in the liberalization of quantitative curbs on imports and a hike of more than 30% in annual quotas for imports. The supplementary budget provided for a $2.2 billion outlay in the general account and $1.2 billion in loan and investment programs. It was expected to reduce the international payments surplus to $500 million by March 31, 1974.

[9] Soviet peace treaty talks. Japan and the Soviet Union Oct. 23 began formal talks aimed at the negotiation of a peace treaty officially terminating the state of hostilities which technically had existed between the two states since World War II. The talks immediately became deadlocked over four Soviet-held Kurile Islands taken from Japan in 1945. The Japanese demanded the return of the islands as a condition for the peace treaty. The talks were postponed until 1973.

[10] Tanaka's party wins elections. Premier Tanaka's Liberal Democratic party retained power in nationwide elections Dec. 10, but had its margin reduced by 15 seats in the 491-member House of Representatives, while the opposition Socialist and Communist parties made impressive gains. (Tanaka had dissolved the House Nov. 13 and announced the elections in an attempt to obtain a new mandate from the electorate and to seek an increase in the number of Liberal Democratic house seats.) Final election results (1969 seats in parentheses): Liberal Democrats 282 (297); Socialists 118 (87); Communists 38 (14); Komeito party 29 (47); Democratic Socialists 19 (29); independents 3 (3); minor parties 2 (0). In the popular vote, the Liberal Democrats dropped slightly to 46.7% from the 47.6% they received in 1969. The Socialists increased their popular poll from 21.5% to 21.9%, and the Communists showed an increase to 10.5% from 6.8%. For the first time, the Communist party attained the 20-seat minimum that gave it a right to submit legislation and to sit in the House Steering Committee.

[11] *Tanaka forms new Cabinet.* Premier Tanaka Dec. 22 formed a new 20-member Cabinet that included virtually all his political rivals in the Liberal Democrats. The new Cabinet replaced one that had resigned earlier the same day to make way for a new government in the wake of the parliamentary elections. Tanaka kept five posts for his faction of the Liberal Democrats, gave two each to the Ohiro and Fukuda wings, one each to the Miki and Kakasone factions, and distributed other Cabinet jobs to minor factions of the party. Ohira was appointed foreign minister; Fukuda was named director general of the Administrative Management Agency; Nakasone was reappointed minister of international trade and industry; Miki was given the additional post of head of the Environment Agency; former Foreign Minister Kiichi Aichi was appointed finance minister; and Zentaro Kosaka was named economic planning minister.

See also ATOMIC ENERGY [6, 13]; AVIATION; CHINA, COMMUNIST; CONSERVATION; FOREIGN POLICY; HIJACKING [15]; INTERNATIONAL MONETARY DEVELOPMENTS [2, 5, 9, 11]; MEXICO; MIDDLE EAST [22-23]; OLYMPICS [1-2]; PERU; SINO-U.S. RELATIONS [5, 8]; SPACE [24]; TARIFFS & WORLD TRADE

JARRING, GUNNAR—*See* MIDDLE EAST [30]
JEHOVAH'S WITNESSES—*See* MALAWI
JET PROPULSION LABORATORY (JPL) —*See* SPACE [20]
JEWISH DEFENSE LEAGUE (JDL)—*See* FEDERAL BUREAU OF INVESTIGATION; MIDDLE EAST [27]; UNION OF SOVIET SOCIALIST REPUBLICS [8-9]

JEWS—*See* AUSTRIA; ELECTIONS [36]; GERMANY, WEST [1]; ISRAEL; MIDDLE EAST; NETHERLANDS; UNION OF SOVIET SOCIALIST REPUBLICS [8-11]

JOHNSON, LYNDON BAINES—*See* ELECTIONS [29]; PENTAGON PAPERS

JORDAN—Commando campaign opens. A Jordanian soldier and three civilians were killed March 31 when their vehicle struck a land mine near the Syrian border. The Palestinian commando organization, Al Fatah, April 1 claimed responsibility for the incident, saying it was the first blow in a new campaign launched March 27 to overthrow King Hussein for his plan to federate the East and West Banks of the Jordan River under his sovereignty (*see* MIDDLE EAST [17]). According to Amman's account of the mine incident, the four persons were killed when their vehicle struck a mine "planted by subversive elements operating from Syrian territory."

National Council plans Hussein ouster. The Palestinian National Council, a loosely organized federation of commando groups, April 7 established a Jordan Affairs Committee to map plans for the overthrow of Hussein. A council statement April 10 appealed to the Arab states to recognize the committee as the official representative of Jordan instead of the embassies of Hussein's government. The council also urged that Hussein be tried by a special court on charges of conspiring against the rights of the Palestinian people, an Arab economic boycott of Jordan, the abrogation of all financial subsidies paid to Jordan by the oil-producing Arab states and the ouster of Jordan from the Arab League. The council, meeting in Cairo, also approved April 15 a suggestion by Al Fatah leader Yasir Arafat that Arabs who cooperated with Israeli occupation authorities or "adopted a lenient attitude toward the rights of the Palestinian people" should "become one of the targets of the revolution."

Cabinet shift. King Hussein Aug. 21 ordered changes in Prime Minister Ahmed Lawzi's Cabinet. The changes: Salah Abu Zeid, Hussein's political adviser, replaced Abdullah Salam as foreign minister; Ahmed al-Taruneh, head of the Royal Household, was appointed to the newly established post of deputy prime minister and replaced Ibrahim Habasneh as interior minister; Sen. Rashid al-Khatib was appointed to the newly established post of minister of state at the prime minister's office; and former Ramallah Mayor Nadim al-Zarru was named transport minister.

Plot against Hussein crushed. King Hussein Nov. 27 confirmed press reports that his government during the weekend of Nov. 18 had thwarted a Libyan-backed Palestinian commando plot to assassinate him, overthrow his regime and proclaim a republic. According to Hussein, Arafat had taken part in the conspiracy, and Arafat's deputy, Salah Khalef, had made the contacts with the Jordanian plotters. Hussein said that Maj. Rafeh Hindawi, commander of Jordan's 4th Armored Brigade, was the only military man arrested and that Hindawi had confessed that Khalef had given him $60,000 to finance the uprising. The monarch also said that Hindawi had quoted Khalef as saying that, when the time came to launch the coup, Libyan leader Col. Muammar el-Qaddafi was to arrive in Damascus to put pressure on the Syrian and Iraqi governments to send planes to bomb the royal palace, radio station and military installations in Amman. Hindawi, Said Dajani (president of the bank of Jordan) and Mohammed Khalili (vice president of the bank) were convicted Dec. 14 of involvement in the plot. Their sentences were not announced at the time of conviction, but were later reported to be death sentences. King Hussein Dec. 24 commuted the three death sentences and those of three others convicted to death for their role in the plot.

See also INTERNATIONAL MONETARY DEVELOPMENTS [8]; MIDDLE EAST [1, 17, 19-20, 26, 37]; OLYMPIC TERRORISM; PAKISTAN [4]

JUDICIAL CONFERENCE, U.S.—*See* JUDICIARY

JUDICIARY—State of the Judiciary address. Supreme Court Chief Justice Warren E. Burger Aug. 14 addressed the convention of the American Bar Association in his third annual State of the Judiciary address. Burger called on Congress to do away with the three-judge federal district courts, which he said were taxing the judicial system with additional work. (The courts, created by Congress in 1910 as a states' rights measure so that a single judge could not overrule the laws of state legislatures, were composed of one member from a circuit's Federal Court of Appeals and two district judges—all drawn by lot in any federal suit in which a constitutional question was raised about a state or federal law. Under the system, the loser in a district court suit could appeal directly to the Supreme Court rather than to the Circuit Court of Appeals.) Burger said that the reasons for the existence of the district courts, "whatever their validity at the time" they were created, no longer were valid. Burger also urged Congress to give more attention to the effects of legislation that added more work to the federal courts' case load. To that end, he recommended that Congress refuse to pass any laws creating new federal crimes or civil actions without first preparing a "court impact statement" showing how many more judgeships would be needed to handle the new work. Such an impact statement could be patterned along the lines of the environmental reports required of federal agencies before they were allowed to approve projects that might affect the environment. Burger also listed internal reforms that U.S. courts were testing in an effort to contend with "the crisis of confidence" that had been created by a heavy backlog of cases. A major improvement, Burger said, would be to increase the number of U.S. judges from the current 620 to 900 by 1980.

Canons of ethics revised. In other action at the ABA convention, the delegates Aug. 16 approved a strong new code of conduct for the nation's 15,000 state and federal judges. The code—the ABA's first major revision of the canons of judicial conduct since 1924—dealt with the conduct of judges on and off the bench. It required judges to report publicly any income from outside activities, except private investments, and to disqualify themselves in any case in which they had a financial interest, even if it was no more than owning a share of stock in a company being sued or suing. (The National Conference of State Trial Judges had voted 60-31 Aug. 11 to oppose adoption of the new code because of the income-disclosure provision.) Included in the code were provisions requiring judges to report gifts worth $100 or more, to disqualify themselves if their relatives or their wives' relatives were directly involved in a case or had an interest in it, and to disqualify themselves if they had formed "fixed beliefs" about a case or had personal knowledge of the facts involved. State legislatures and state supreme courts would see that the code was implemented. For the federal courts, the code would be imposed by the U.S. Judicial Conference. It would not be binding on justices of the Supreme Court.

See also BUDGET; CIVIL DISORDERS; CIVIL RIGHTS [1-5]; CRIME [10-12]; ELECTIONS [21]; POLLUTION [2]; SECURITY, U.S.; SUPREME COURT

JUPITER—*See* SPACE [5-6]

**KOREA, NORTH (PEOPLE'S REPUBLIC OF KOREA)—New charter
announced.** North Korea Oct. 30 announced the draft of a new constitution,
which it said had been drawn up in preparation for the reunification of the two
Koreas (*see* KOREAN RELATIONS). The announcement gave no details of the
new charter, which had been worked out at a meeting Oct. 23-26 of the Central
Committee of the ruling Workers party, but said the document would "become
a powerful legal guarantee for consolidating the historic cause of national
reunification by defining in the most revolutionary way and correctly all
principles governing the political, economic, cultural and military spheres."

See also KOREAN RELATIONS; KOREA, SOUTH; SINO-U.S.
RELATIONS [2, 5, 7]; SOVIET-U.S. RELATIONS [11]

KOREAN RELATIONS—Thai force quits South. Thailand's 157-man unit left
South Korea June 21, marking the end of Bangkok's troop contribution to the
United Nations Command. The Thai departure left Americans as the only non-
Korean combat force under U.N. leadership.

North and South agree on reunification negotiations. North and South Korea July 4 released a joint communique announcing that the two had agreed on principles to hold negotiations to reunite the divided country. The communique disclosed that the agreement had been reached in secret talks between Lee Hu Rak, director of the South Korean Central Intelligence Agency, and Kim Yong Ju, director of the Organization of the North Korean Workers (Communist) party, in Pyongyang, North Korea May 2-5 and between Lee and Pak Sung Chul, North Korea's second deputy premier, in Seoul, South Korea May 29-June 1. (It was the first time the two Koreas had held direct bilateral talks on reunification since the country was divided at the end of World War II in 1945.) The joint declaration said the two Koreas agreed to refrain from "armed provocations," to take "positive measures to prevent inadvertent incidents," to carry out "varied exchanges in many fields," to prevent the outbreak of "unexpected military incidents" and "to install a direct telephone line between Seoul and Pyongyang." The telephone "hot line" was established one hour after the joint declaration was announced.

The joint statement said that reunification would be based on three principles: it would be "achieved through independent efforts without being subject to external imposition or interference"; it would be "achieved through peaceful means"; and it would transcend "differences in ideas, ideologies and systems." The communique further said that both sides would "not slander or defame each other" and would "cooperate positively with each other to seek early success of the South-North Red Cross talks on humanitarian problems growing out of the Korean war." (The Red Cross talks formally began Aug. 30.) The communique also said that the two Koreas had agreed to establish a "South-North Coordinating Committee [jointly headed by Lee and Pak] to solve the various problems existing between the South and North and to settle the unification problem on the basis of the agreed principles." Both the North and the South warned, however, that the dialogue between the two would not be easy and said that further defense efforts would be necessary to back up the dialogue. South Korea also warned July 5 that the opening of the discussions did not mean that Seoul was granting "de facto or de jure" recognition of North Korea. (The two Koreas opened political talks Oct. 12.)

Political cooperation agreement. North and South Korea agreed Nov. 4 to broad political and economic cooperation as a step toward eventual reunification. The pact was signed by Lee and Pak. It fixed the composition and functions of the North-South Coordinating Committee and halted propaganda broadcasts and leaflet distributions effective Nov. 11. The committee (formally organized Dec. 1) would be composed of five members from each side, including a co-chairman, a deputy co-chairman, an executive officer and two other members—all with the rank of Cabinet minister or deputy minister. Lee and Kim Yong Ju of North Korea's ruling Workers party would serve as co-chairmen. The committee was charged with: working toward "independent and peaceful unification"; arranging political exchanges between political parties, social groups and individuals in the two Koreas; negotiating "economic, cultural and social exchanges and joint cooperative projects"; ending the "state of military confrontation"; and developing programs of "joint...activities abroad in order to enhance the national pride as an homogeneous people." The committee was to establish a joint secretariat at Panmunjom to handle routine affairs and to conduct full meetings "once in every two or three months." (Its officers were to convene every month.) It was to have separate subcommittees on political, military, diplomatic and cultural matters.

See also KOREA, NORTH; KOREA, SOUTH; UNITED NATIONS

KOREAN WAR—*See* SELECTIVE SERVICE SYSTEM

KOREA, SOUTH (REPUBLIC OF KOREA)—Spy activity. The South Korean Army Security Command Jan. 29 announced the smashing of a North Korean espionage ring aimed at organizing a popular revolt against the South Korean regime, assassinating ROK leaders, infiltrating the armed forces and gathering military information. The army said that nine spies and 14 collaborators had been seized in Seoul and two other cities. The army March 27 announced the smashing of another North Korean spy ring and the arrest of 12 more spies and 10 more suspected collaborators. According to the announcement, the ring had been led by Chung Ki Ryong, who held the rank equivalent to a deputy Cabinet minister in North Korea. Chung was said to have been sent to the South by the North in 1955. He reportedly had been conducting espionage activities since that time in Seoul, Pusan and Taegu. (In a related development, former ROK National Assembly Deputy Kim Kyoo Nam was executed by hanging July 13, and South Koreans Park No Su and Chung Tae Mook were executed by hanging July 28. Kim and Park had been condemned in 1970 for operating a spy ring based in East Berlin and Japan. Chung had been convicted in 1969 for involvement in an espionage ring based on an offshore island.)

Cuban ship ban lifted. The Transportation Ministry March 17 announced that Cuban ships were now permitted to visit South Korean ports. The ban was lifted as of March 11 after the Seoul government decided to regard Cuba as a nonhostile Communist state. The government still banned from its ports ships of North Korea, North Vietnam and Communist China.

Emergency economy decree. President Chung Hee Park Aug. 2 issued an emergency decree aimed at stabilizing the country's recessionary economy. The measures included a three-year moratorium on all usurious private loans to businesses and a reduction in bank interest rates from 19% a year to 15.5% for general loans and from 16.8% to 12% for one-year time deposits. The decree also stabilized foreign currency rates at around the level of 400 won to the U.S. dollar.

Martial law declared. President Park Oct. 17 declared martial law throughout Korea—suspending part of the constitution, dissolving the National Assembly, imposing press censorship and closing all universities and colleges. Park said that the measures were "fundamentally designed to reform the political structure" of the country to meet the "rapidly changing international situation around us" and to facilitate dialogue with North Korea on reunification (*see* KOREAN RELATIONS). The president noted that the legality of the reunification talks had been questioned on the ground that the constitution stated that the South Korean government had sole jurisdiction over all of Korea. As a result, Park said, the constitution would have to be amended to provide a legal basis for the negotiations. The charter proposals would be put into a referendum. If the referendum were rejected, Park said, the government would "seek another new approach to the task of national reunification." Presidential spokesman Kim Sun Jin said new presidential and parliamentary elections would be held on the basis of a new constitution before martial law could be lifted. He said the situation would return to normal "in about two months." (The South Korean action aroused strong disapproval by the U.S.)

In the wake of the declaration of martial law, the government Oct. 23 published three special statutes implementing the declaration. The first statute invested legislative power in a special state council composed of Cabinet members, to be chaired by Park. The council was to deal with all bills pending before the dissolved National Assembly. The second statute established new procedures for a national referendum on a new constitution. It barred campaigning by individuals or the media for amendments to the charter, but made provision for official management committees and "persons of learning and virtue" named by the committees "to guide and enlighten" the voters on the contents of the proposed amendments and on voting procedures. The third law called for appointment of members to the election management committees.

The committees previously had included some members recommended by major political parties.

Park wins unlimited power. The new constitution, granting virtually unlimited power to Park, was approved in a national referendum Nov. 21 by 91.5% (13,186,556 persons) of those who cast ballots. The new constitution provided for Park's re-election to a six-year term by a "National Conference for Reunification" consisting of 2,359 delegates picked by popular vote Dec. 15. (Park Nov. 25 barred all politicians from running for the conference.) It also permitted Park to abolish the two-term limit (and run for president indefinitely) and to dissolve parliament at any time, while putting through "emergency measures" to temporarily limit civil liberties. The constitution also provided that: two-thirds of the National Assembly's members would be chosen by popular vote, with assembly terms increased from four to six years; the assembly would convene 150 days a year at most, unless the president called for special sessions; the assembly would be empowered to oust Cabinets or individual ministers; the president and other top government leaders could be impeached by a constitutional commission that would rule on the motions of the assembly; and the president would be permitted to call national referendums on major policy decisions. The National Conference for Reunification Dec. 23 re-elected Park as president by a vote of 2,357-2. (The two ballots were declared invalid.) Park was inaugurated Dec. 23, the same day that the new constitution went into effect.

Martial law ends. President Park Dec. 13 removed martial law. In announcing the decision, however, Presidential spokesman Kim said the ban on political activities would remain in effect "for the time being." (Martial law had been eased Nov. 28 when schools and universities were allowed to reopen.)

See also ELECTIONS [9]; INDOCHINA WAR [38]; KOREA, NORTH; KOREAN RELATIONS; SINO-U.S. RELATIONS [5, 7-8]

KOSYGIN, ALEKSEI N.—*See* BANGLA DESH [10]; SOVIET-U.S. RELATIONS [1-3, 6]; UNION OF SOVIET SOCIALIST REPUBLICS [10]
KU KLUX KLAN—*See* FEDERAL BUREAU OF INVESTIGATION
KUWAIT—*See* INTERNATIONAL MONETARY DEVELOPMENTS [8]; OIL & NATURAL GAS; YEMEN

LABOR—East Coast dock strike. Longshoremen in the American Federation of Labor-Congress of Industrial Organizations (AFL-CIO) International Longshoremen's Association (ILA) Jan. 6 reached agreement on a tentative contract settlement, contingent on approval by the federal Pay Board, for six north Atlantic ports between Boston and Hampton Roads, Va. (The ILA had ended a 58-day strike in 1971 under a Taft-Hartley injunction barring a strike until Feb. 14.) The settlement called for a total package increase of 41% over three years—16.9% in the first year. Basic pay would rise 32.6% from $4.60 to $6.10 an hour over the three years. The total for wages and fringe benefits would go from $5.745 an hour to $6.72 in the first year and to $7.45 and $8.12 in the other two contract years. The Pay Board voted 6-1 May 8 to trim the wage increase to 9.8% to 12.1%, depending on the area in which longshoremen worked. East Coast dockers would get a 35¢ hourly raise, plus the fringe benefits negotiated with the shippers, for a 9.8% raise. New Orleans dockworkers would get the 12.1% boost, and dockers working in Gulf ports further west would get an 11.4% raise. The variation in raises resulted in differences in current salary scales among East and Gulf port dockworkers. The ILA appealed the wage ruling, but the Pay Board June 6 refused the appeal. The board voted to accept the negotiated second and third year raises of the contract, however.

West Coast dock strike. The International Longshoremen's and Warehousemen's Union (ILWU) Jan. 17 resumed its strike on West Coast docks after new contract talks had broken down over the issues of a work guarantee for the 13,000 dockers and of the handling of containerized cargo. (A 100-day strike by the ILWU in 1971 had been interrupted by a Taft-Hartley injunction. After its expiration, the longshoremen had agreed to work under the old contract until Jan. 17.) President Nixon Jan. 21 submitted to Congress legislation proposing that a three-man arbitration panel, appointed by the secretary of labor, be authorized to investigate the issues in the dispute and present binding findings for a settlement within 40 days. The proposal also called for an 18-month ban against a strike or lockout by the ILWU or the Pacific Maritime Association, representing the shippers. Congress Feb. 9 cleared a bill incorporating the major aspects of the President's bill, but a tentative settlement ending the strike had already been reached Feb. 8. President Nixon signed the bill Feb. 21 as a symbolic gesture after the ILWU had ratified the contract Feb. 19 and strikers had returned to work Feb. 21. (The signing of the bill was delayed to encourage voluntary agreement.) The new contract, extending until July 1, 1973, provided for a total increase in the

243

wage base from $4.28 to $5.40 an hour. It also called for a guarantee of 36 hours' weekly pay for more than 4,000 part-time workers. Another key item in the pact was a $1 "tax" paid by the employers for every ton of containerized dock cargo handled by non-ILWU members. (The ILWU had a jurisdictional dispute with the International Brotherhood of Teamsters over handling containerized cargo. Under the agreement, the Teamsters would perform the work.) The Pay Board March 16 voted 8-5 to sharply cut the wage and benefit increases in the contract, which the board said amounted to a 20.9% increase in the first year of the contract. The board, however, approved a 10% raise in pay and fringe benefits and a 4.9% raise in fringe benefits not covered by the board's controls. The ILWU first threatened a strike to protest the reduction of the wage settlement, but May 15 accepted the Pay Board's decision.

Alliance dissolved. Leonard Woodcock, president of the United Automobile Workers of America (UAW), announced Jan. 24 that he and Frank E. Fitzsimmons, president of the Teamsters, had agreed to dissolve the Alliance for Labor Action. The alliance had been formed by the two unions in 1969 to channel union activity into social problems and toward organizing lower-paid workers. Woodcock said the dissolution was caused by the UAW's poor financial condition as a result of the two-month auto-workers' strike in 1971. The UAW was forced to end financial support of the alliance in July 1971, which prompted similar action by the Teamsters. The end of the venture was not caused by a deterioration of relations between the two unions, which, Woodcock said, "have never been better."

Florida agricultural pacts. The AFL-CIO United Farm Workers Organizing Committee (UFWOC) and the Coca-Cola Co., food division, which markets Minute Maid orange juice, Feb. 29 signed a three-year labor agreement covering 1,200 agricultural workers in Florida. It was the first collective-bargaining agreement for the Florida citrus industry and the first in the southeast for UFWOC. (Led by Cesar Chavez, the UFWOC had organized California grape workers after a long dispute involving national product boycott efforts.) The union had been selected as the bargaining agent by Minute Maid employees in December 1971, and negotiations had begun in January. In a later development, H. P. Hood and Sons, a major processor and distributor of dairy and citrus products in the northeast, agreed March 21 to recognize the UFWOC's representation of the company's 300 Florida grove workers. (In a related development, the Teamsters Dec. 14 announced the end of a jurisdictional accord with the UFWOC on unionizing lettuce workers in California.)

Workmen's compensation evaluated. The National Commission on State Workmen's Compensation, a special federal commission established to study state workmen's compensation laws, said in a report July 30 that the laws generally were "inadequate and inequitable." The report charged that coverage offered under the state programs were too low. The report said that only 85% of all workers were protected by workmen's compensation, and "those not covered usually are those most in need of protection... non-union, low-wage workers such as farm help, domestics and employees of small firms." While work-related injuries were compensable, it added, "the status of work-related diseases is less satisfactory." According to the report, 31 states provided benefits equivalent to less than the federal poverty level. Benefit inadequacies were attributed to the veto power of employers, who feared cost increases, and to trade unions unwilling to give up "disproportionate awards" for minor injuries. The report urged states to broaden coverage, liberalize benefits and improve medical and rehabilitation services. It called on Congress to compel states to take action by 1975 by setting minimum workmen's compensation standards to guarantee compliance. The report, however, rejected the "alternative of a federal takeover" of the workmen's compensation system.

Blue collar wage hike approved. President Nixon Aug. 21 signed a bill which would permit a 4% pay raise for many of the government's blue collar workers by April 1973. (Nixon had vetoed a smaller wage hike in 1971 as inflationary.) The bill—approved by voice votes in the Senate Aug. 7 and the House Aug. 15—would create a fourth and fifth wage level in the blue collar job ladder of the Civil Service Commission (CSC) and would add an estimated $181 million to the federal payroll. It also established a Federal Prevailing Rate Advisory Commission to study the system and report to the CSC.

Minimum wage bill dies. Both the House and the Senate voted increases in the minimum wage, but the House refused Oct. 3 to send its bill to a conference committee where differences could be worked out between it and the Senate bill. The House move was sponsored by Republicans and the Administration, who feared that House Democratic liberals (the majority of House conferees) would abandon the more conservative House bill in favor of the more generous Senate version. The House bill, passed May 11 by a 330-78 vote, would have raised the minimum wage for most manufacturing and retail workers from $1.60 an hour to $1.80 in 1972 and to $2 in 1973. It would have set a $1.70 minimum wage, rising to $1.80 in 1973, for most employees of schools, colleges, laundries, hotels and restaurants, and would have increased the $1.30 agricultural minimum wage to $1.50, rising to $1.70 in 1973. For persons under 18 and students under 21, the minimum would have been $1.60 on nonagricultural jobs and $1.30 in farm jobs. Under the Senate version of the bill, passed July 20 by a 65-27 vote, the minimum wage would have been raised to $2 an hour for most manufacturing and retail workers in 1972 and to $2.20 an hour in 1974. The bill would also have extended coverage to 7.5 million additional workers, including domestics and Civil Service employees. The only agricultural workers who would have been covered by the Senate bill would have been those on large farms, whose wages would increase to $2.20 an hour by 1974.

Job-safety deadline deferred. The Labor Department Nov. 30 extended the deadline for state job-safety programs set under the 1970 Federal Occupational Safety and Health Act, but a U.S. district court judge Dec. 29 invalidated the extension. Under the department's order, the deadline for states to submit plans to the department would have been extended from Dec. 28 until June 30, 1973. If such plans were not "at least" as effective as the federal standards set under the 1970 law, the federal program was to be enforced in the state. If the plans were accepted, the state was to apply its own program and receive federal assistance for it. (Montana and South Carolina had submitted approved plans. Plans from 26 other states were being considered.)

See also ARGENTINA [1, 7, 13-18]; AUSTRALIA [3]; BANGLA DESH [8]; BASEBALL; BELGIUM; BOLIVIA; CANADA [8-13]; CHILE [1, 15, 18-22]; CIVIL RIGHTS [1, 3, 14-19]; COLOMBIA; CONSUMER AFFAIRS [5]; COSTA RICA; DOMINICAN REPUBLIC; ECONOMY [1, 7-11]; EDUCATION [9]; ELECTIONS [8, 17-18, 23, 28, 35-36, 48]; FRANCE [14]; GIBRALTAR; GREAT BRITAIN [1, 7-15]; HIJACKING [15]; HONDURAS; INDIA [10]; IRELAND; ITALY [1, 7]; JAPAN [3]; MEXICO; MINES; NETHERLANDS; NIXON, RICHARD MILHOUS; NORTHERN IRELAND [4, 10, 16]; PAKISTAN [11]; PERU; POLICE; POLITICS [14]; PUERTO RICO; RAILROADS; RHODESIA; SHIPS & SHIPPING; SOUTH AFRICA[6]; SPAIN; TERRITORIAL WATERS; TRINIDAD & TOBAGO; UNEMPLOYMENT; URUGUAY [4, 10, 14-17]; WELFARE; WOMEN'S RIGHTS

LAIRD, MELVIN R.—*See* ARMAMENTS, INTERNATIONAL; DISARMAMENT; ELECTIONS [9]; MILITARY [8-9]; NIXON, RICHARD MILHOUS; PUERTO RICO; SELECTIVE SERVICE SYSTEM; WAR CRIMES
LANSKY, MEYER—*See* ISRAEL
LANUSSE, ALEJANDRO—*See* ARGENTINA [2, 6, 13-15, 18]

LAOS—New political group. A new political group, aimed at forcing the resignation of the government of Premier Prince Souvanna Phouma and ending the ruling three-party coalition, was formed May 8. The organization, called the Group for the Protection of the Constitution, was made up of National Assembly members and was headed by the assembly president, Phoui

Sananikone, a former right-wing premier. The group had 32 members, a majority in the 60-seat assembly.

Cabinet change. Souvanna Phouma July 12 announced a sweeping change in the tripartite government. Four ministers were dismissed; eight new members were appointed; and three current ministers were promoted or shifted. The premier said the Pathet Lao (Communist) ministers absent from the government since 1963 would retain their posts even though their duties had been taken over by secretaries of state.

See also DRUG USE & ADDICTION [18]; ELECTIONS [34]; INDOCHINA WAR [1, 8-13, 44, 49]; SINO-U.S. RELATIONS [8]; THAILAND

LASER —*See* SCIENCE

LATIN AMERICA—OAS admits 'observers.' The Organization of American States (OAS) Feb. 2 extended "permanent observer" status to Canada, Israel, Spain and Guyana. Canada—which could have applied for full membership but chose not to—and Israel were admitted unanimously. Mexico voted against admission for Spain, with which it had not had diplomatic relations since 1939. Venezuela abstained from the vote on Guyana, with whom it had a border dispute. (The OAS Oct. 15 also granted permanent observer status to France.)

OAS parley. The OAS held its second General Assembly April 11-21 in Washington. After heated debate, a majority of the 23 member nations agreed April 21 that the OAS had the authority to send an observer to Belize (British Honduras)—which was not a member of the organization—to assess Britain's military strength there and determine whether it constituted a threat to Guatemala, which claimed sovereignty over Belize. The assembly also reaffirmed a 1967 resolution urging limitations on military spending and a redirection of defense funds into national development. (A 15%-20% increase in OAS members' military spending was expected in 1972. *See also* ARMAMENTS, INTERNATIONAL.) Peru proposed a motion calling for an end to sanctions imposed on Cuba by OAS member nations in 1964, but the resolution failed April 21. The entire OAS meeting was marked by criticism of the United States and its policies in Latin America.

Economic growth cited. A report by the Inter-American Development Bank (IDB), released May 8, said that Latin America experienced another year of generally high economic growth in 1971, despite lagging farm production, a declining share of world trade and rising foreign debts. The report, presented at the opening session of the IDB's annual meeting in Quito, Ecuador, said that Latin America's gross domestic product rose by approximately 6.6% during 1971, about the same as the annual average increase for 1968-70. Behind the expansion, the IDB said, were a rise in investment and savings, better fiscal policies and incoming foreign capital. Manufacturing represented the region's most important sector, generating 25% of the gross domestic product, compared with 15% for agriculture. Industry's share of total national output ranged from less than 15% in Venezuela and Haiti to over 30% in Chile and Argentina. Agricultural production, however, was failing to keep pace with population growth. Output in 1971 was as low as in 1952-56, and the farm sector still employed about 40% of the region's labor force—making the unemployment problem particularly serious. Although Latin America's foreign debt (estimated at over $20 billion) continued to rise, it was not growing as fast as in recent years, according to the report. The region's international balance of payments was again favorable, as reserves grew by $885 million, with the largest gains in Brazil, Mexico and Venezuela. Brazil led the region in growth with an 11% gain, and at least 11 other nations recorded growth of 5% or more.

IDB meeting. The IDB met in Quito May 8-12. The meeting was marked by a climate of anger and frustration over the future of the institution—second only to the World Bank among international lending agencies and the prime source of development seed money in Latin America. Latin American delegates to the meeting denounced the U.S., which held two-fifths of the bank's shares, for backing down on promises to increase the IDB capital and for attempting to get Western European countries and Japan more deeply involved in the bank. (Most Latin American delegates felt that the admission of "outsiders" would dilute their role in the bank.) U.S. representatives to the meeting were reportedly frustrated by their inability to convince Latin Americans that economic problems confronting the U.S. precluded further massive injections of capital. The delegates ended the convention May 12 by approving the admission of Canada as the bank's 24th member; and provisions for lower interest rates and longer repayment periods on loans to Haiti, Ecuador, Bolivia and Paraguay, the region's least-developed countries.

Indian conference. The seventh Inter-American Indian Congress, sponsored by the Inter-American Indian Institute of the OAS, met in Brasilia Aug. 7-12. The delegates—from 15 Latin American nations, the U.S. and Canada—approved 31 resolutions and a pledge to "continue fighting for the economic and social development of Indians without detriment to their property, culture, languages and customs." The congress also agreed to increase Indian representation at future congresses. Fewer than a dozen of the 150 persons attending the conference were Indians, and only one of those was an official delegate.

IDB reorganization. IDB President Antonio Ortiz Mena of Mexico Sept. 15 announced a sweeping structural reorganization of the bank. Projected changes included: restructuring and restrengthening of bank operations in Latin America to insure more effective participation at the beginning stages of projects as well as in the administration of loans and supervision of works in progress; establishment of an accounting office at bank headquarters, directly responsible to the president and vice president; merger of the loans and loans administration departments of the IDB's operations department; and organization of a separate project analysis department to strengthen independent evaluation of projects under consideration.

See also ARMAMENTS, INTERNATIONAL; CHILE [11]; DRUG USE & ADDICTION [1, 20]; FOREIGN POLICY; INTERNATIONAL MONETARY DEVELOPMENTS [5]; TERRITORIAL WATERS

LAVELLE, JOHN D.—*See* MILITARY [6-8]
LAW ENFORCEMENT ASSISTANCE ADMINISTRATION (LEAA)—*See* CRIME [2]
LEAD POISONING—*See* CONSUMER AFFAIRS [3]; ENVIRONMENT

LEBANON—Parliamentary elections. Three-stage elections April 16, 23 and 30 left the 99-seat unicameral parliament dominated by conservative and traditionalist deputies, but leftist candidates made significant gains. The balloting was marked by clashes between followers of rival candidates. Three policemen were killed and 10 others wounded May 2 at Aitat (10 miles west of Beirut), prompting Premier Saeb Salam to declare martial law later the same day in the Mount Lebanon area. Salam extended the martial law to the entire country May 3, authorizing troops to shoot armed civilians on sight and without warning and continuing a ban on the issuance of arms licenses in effect during the elections.

New government formed. Salam resigned as premier May 1 and his resignation was accepted May 22 by President Suleiman Franjieh. (The resignation was customary following parliamentary elections.) Salam agreed to continue as premier and formed a new Cabinet May 27. Its members: vice president—Albert Moukheiber; foreign affairs—Khalil Abou Hanad; post office, telephone and telegraph—Jamil Kebbe; agriculture—Suleiman Ali; health—Nazih Bizri; education—Edouard Honein; finance—Fouad Naffah; public works and transport—Sabri Hamade; social affairs and labor—Kazem El Khalil; economy—Anouar Sabah; defense—Majid Arslane; justice—Bechir Awarl; tourism—Michel Sassine; resources—Joseph Skaff; and state minister in charge of petroleum and industry—Pierre Helou.

Clash with commandos. Palestinan commandos and Lebanese army troops clashed in the Arkoub section of southern Lebanon Dec. 8 and 9. Two soldiers and four guerrillas were killed in the first incident and five soldiers and five commandos wounded. One commando was killed and five wounded in the second engagement. The Lebanese Defense Ministry blamed the commandos for the outbreak of fighting, saying that an army patrol had come under guerrilla fire after the Pakestinians had entered prohibited military zones. A commando statement said the Lebanese had first shelled their positions and they had fired back. (Beirut had ordered the guerrillas to leave the Arkoub region by Dec. 8.)

See also MIDDLE EAST [1-10, 23, 26]; OIL & NATURAL GAS; OLYMPIC TERRORISM; YEMEN

LEDAIN COMMISSION—*See* DRUG USE & ADDICTION [1, 6]

LESOTHO—*See* INTERNATIONAL MONETARY DEVELOPMENTS [8]

LIBERIA—Cabinet changes. President William Tolbert reorganized his government Jan. 10. The major Cabinet changes: state—Rochefort L. Weeks replaced Joseph Randolph Grimes; treasury—Stephen Tolbert, the president's brother, succeeded J. Milton Weeks; justice—Clarence L. Simpson took over from J.A.A. Pierce; health—Mai Padmore, the only woman in the government; commerce, industry and transportation—William E. Denis took over responsibility from Magnus Jones; information and cultural affairs—Henry Andrews replaced E. Reginald Townsend (Andrews was dismissed Dec. 9); land and mines—James Y. Babia (dismissed Dec. 9); labor and youth—Jenkins Field. Former Director of Information and Cultural Affairs Townsend moved to the newly created post of minister of state for presidential affairs.

See also UGANDA [10]

LIBERTARIAN PARTY—*See* ELECTIONS [37]

LIBYA—New Cabinet. The ruling Revolutionary Command Council July 16 announced the formation of a new Cabinet amid reports that the council's premier, Col. Muammar el-Qaddafi, had been ousted from power and possibly arrested by his opponents. In order to quash the reports, the Cabinet's first meeting July 17 was televised, showing Qaddafi greeting the new ministers. Qaddafi, who had been president, premier of the council and defense minister, gave up the premiership. In the listing of the new Cabinet—formed by the new premier, Maj. Abdul Salam Jallud—there was no mention of the post of defense minister. Jallud had been deputy premier under Qaddafi. The 18-member Cabinet retained eight ministers of the outgoing government. Its only two military men were Jallud and Interior Minister Maj. Abdul Moneim el-Huni (replaced without explanation Nov. 3 by Maj. Khoweildi Harmidi). U.S. State Department officials said July 17 that they believed the government shakeup was the result of about 10 days of sharp dispute within the council over Qaddafi's leadership. Many council leaders were said to feel that Qaddafi's stress on foreign affairs had led to neglect of domestic problems.

See also JORDAN; MIDDLE EAST [1, 26, 33]; OIL & NATURAL GAS; OLYMPIC TERRORISM; PAKISTAN [4]; PHILIPPINES [3]; SYRIA; UGANDA [4]

LIECHTENSTEIN—The Landtag (parliament) May 9 unanimously approved a constitutional amendment increasing its own size from 15 to 21 members and requiring a party to obtain a minimum of 8% of the total votes in an election to qualify for representation. Implementation of the amendment would be subject to popular ratification in a referendum.

See also EUROPEAN ECONOMIC COMMUNITY [8]; EUROPEAN SECURITY; PERU

LINDSAY, JOHN V.—*See* ELECTIONS [3, 8]; WELFARE
LIN PIAO—*See* CHINA, COMMUNIST
LITERATURE—*See* BOOKS; NOBEL PRIZES
LON NOL—*See* CAMBODIA; INDOCHINA WAR [5]

LOYALTY OATHS—*See* SECURITY, U.S.
LUNA 20—*See* SPACE [4]
LUTHERAN CHURCH—*See* CHURCHES

LUXEMBOURG—The Chamber of Deputies Jan. 13 approved, by a 54-0 vote (two abstentions), a constitutional amendment lowering the minimum voting age from 21 to 18 and the qualifying age for election from 25 to 21.

Cabinet minister resigns. Mrs. Madeleine Frieden-Kinnen, minister of public health, family and youth affairs, resigned Sept. 16 to fight a scandal arising from a newspaper report that she had witnessed a Roman Catholic priest and a young man swimming in the nude. Mrs. Frieden-Kinnen had denied the report and had won a libel suit against the newspaper. However, a subsequent court ruling against the validity of the young man's testimony reopened the controversy. Following Mrs. Frieden-Kinnen's resignation, the Cabinet was shuffled. Agriculture Minister Jean-Pierre Buchler was appointed family minister. He was replaced as agriculture minister by Camille Ney, secretary of state in the Agriculture Ministry. The youth affairs post was given to Education Minister Jean Dupong, and the Cultural Affairs Ministry was assigned to Jacques Sauter, secretary of state for labor.

See also EUROPEAN ECONOMIC COMMUNITY [1]; PERU

LYNN, JAMES T.—*See* NIXON, RICHARD MILHOUS

MACAO—*See* CHINA, COMMUNIST
MacGREGOR, CLARK—*See* ELECTIONS [11, 27]; POLITICS [12]
MacSTIOFAIN, SEAN—*See* IRELAND
MADAGASCAR—*See* MALAGASY REPUBLIC
MAFIA—*See* CRIME [4]; POLICE
MAKARIOS, ARCHBISHOP—*See* CYPRUS

MALAGASY REPUBLIC—Tsiranana re-elected. President Philibert
Tsiranana, running unopposed, was re-elected Jan. 30 by more than 99% of
those voting.
  Tsiranana yields power. President Tsiranana May 18 handed over full
power to Army Chief of Staff Gen. Gabriel Ramanantsoa, giving him the title
of premier and a mandate to "lead the country and form a government." The
move came after several weeks of violence in Tananarive, led by a coalition of
students and workers, and after France declined to intervene in the internal
affairs of its former colony.
  Student protest had begun April 24 with a student strike aimed at causing
the government to reform the republic's educational system (making it more
relevant to the country's needs and less dependent on France) and to change
cultural agreements with France. Tsiranana had declared a state of emergency
May 13. The same day, students and security police clashed in Tananarive, and
fires were started in several public buildings and in the offices of the country's
largest newspaper, the *Madagascar Courier.* According to unofficial reports, 25
persons were killed in violence May 13-15, 160 injured and more than 400
arrested, among them leaders of the student strike. In an apparent move to
pacify the students, Tsiranana May 14 accepted the resignation of Cultural
Affairs and Education Minister Laurent Botokeky and replaced him with
Norbert Ranohavimanana, who was believed to be popular with the students.
Some 100,000 students, workers and civil servants marched on Tsiranana's
residence May 15, demanding that he free the student leaders arrested during
the violence. The demonstrators withdrew when the government agreed to
consider their demands, particularly those requesting limits on security forces.
Tsiranana May 16 released the arrested students, appointed Gen. Giles
Andiamahazo as military governor of Tananarive and ordered the confinement
of the Republican Security Force to their barracks. He reopened the university
at Tananarive May 17.

Gen. Ramanantsoa May 27 appointed a government of four army officers and six civilians. Capt. Didier Ratsiraka was named foreign minister and Ramanantsoa himself took over the portfolios of national defense and planning.

Martial law declared. Citing "grave economic problems" and the need for the government to operate "in a peaceful climate," Gen. Ramanantsoa proclaimed martial law Aug. 29. Ramanantsoa Sept. 1 announced that voters would be invited to participate in a national referendum to confirm the military government for five years.

Ramanantsoa assumes full control. Following the national referendum Oct. 7, Gen. Ramanantsoa assumed full control of the country. The referendum, which had called for Tsiranana's departure from office and the closure of both legislative chambers as well as for confirmation of the military government, had won 96% support from the voters.

Tamatave riots. Secondary students from the black coastal tribes of Tamatave Dec. 13 launched a protest against reforms instituted earlier in the year which they said would establish a national Madagascar language at the expense of the Tamatave dialect. The protests set off three days of rioting in which some 50 people were believed to have been injured. The Tamatave courthouse, the jail and a hotel were burned, as were a number of Indian and Chinese shops. The government declared a state of siege in the province Dec. 14.

MALAWI—Cabinet changes. President Hastings Banda made the following Cabinet changes during 1972 (date of announcement of change in parentheses): Watson Deleza was appointed minister of labor (Feb. 28) and took over responsibility for transport and communications (April 4); John Gwengwe became minister of agriculture (Feb. 28), but lost the portfolio to Banda and replaced Deleza as minister of labor (June 26); John Msonthi was named minister of education (Feb. 28); Richard Matenje became minister of finance (April 4); Aaron Gadama was named minister of community development and social welfare (April 4); Aleke Banda was named to head the newly created Ministry of Trade, Industry and Tourism (April 4).

Jehovah's Witnesses flee. According to a report Oct. 21, some 10,000 Jehovah's Witnesses had fled Malawi and were encamped in eastern Zambia. Members of the religious sect allegedly fled because of violent attacks on them by the Young Pioneers (members of the Malawi Congress party's youth wing) after President Banda denounced the sect as "devil's" witnesses in September. Deacon Dulani Mwale, a leader of the refugees, said he was told that at least 60 Jehovah's Witnesses had been killed in Malawi. By Dec. 19, the number of refugees to Zambia reportedly had mounted to 19,000, and 342 of them reportedly had died in their Zambian encampments because of "lack of good drinking water." Lewis Changufu, Zambian home affairs minister, said Dec. 6 that arrangements had been made for the return of the refugees to Malawi. The repatriation to Malawi ended Dec. 21.

See also HIJACKING [12]; INTERNATIONAL MONETARY DEVELOPMENTS [8]

MALAYSIA—Indonesian subversion and smuggling agreement. Deputy Prime Minister Tun Ismail Aug. 7 announced a Malaysian-Indonesian agreement under which both countries would patrol the Malacca Straits to curb subversion and smuggling activities. The patrol would be carried out by naval ships of the newly created bilateral Western Regional Border Committee. Ismail also said that an Eastern Regional Border Committee had been created to conduct antisubversion operations along the border areas between the Malaysian state of Sarawak and West Kalimantan in Indonesia.

See also ATOMIC ENERGY [6]; INTERNATIONAL MONETARY DEVELOPMENTS [8]; SINO-U.S. RELATIONS [8].

MALI—A military court in Bamako Aug. 1 sentenced former Premier Yoro Diakite to life imprisonment for his part in the March 1971 effort to overthrow the government. The same sentence had been given July 31 to another former army captain and a sergeant major. A fourth soldier and a civilian received five years' imprisonment each for their role in the coup attempt.

See also AFRICA

MALTA—Base accord signed. Maltese Prime Minister Dom Mintoff and British Defense Secretary Lord Carrington March 25 signed a new seven-year defense treaty for Britain's continued use of the military facilities on Malta. The agreement, signed in London, came only five days before Mintoff's latest deadline for evacuation. The pact provided for payments of about $37 million in rent. Britain would pay about $14 million of the sum, slightly higher than its payments before the accord; the U.S. would reportedly pay $9 million; and West Germany and Italy would provide most of the remainder, according to a formula worked out by the members of the North Atlantic Treaty Organization (NATO). The rental figure exceeded Britain's original $26 million offer, but fell far short of Mintoff's first demand for nearly $78 million, a figure he later cut to $47 million. Mintoff had originally rejected the British-NATO offer, but then accepted it because of a U.S. promise to study further economic foreign aid to Malta. Moreover, Mintoff gained $18.2 million in bilateral aid from NATO nations over seven years, plus an additional immediate cash grant of $6.5 million from Italy. The accord provided for an increase in the British troop level (reduced to 1,000 as part of evacuation moves) to 3,000. Approximately 6,000 dependents would be returned, and the British agreed to slow their plans to reduce civilian employees on the base from 4,900 to 3,600. The accord also included a pledge not to use the Malta bases against Arab states. The accord specifically barred the use of any Maltese military facilities by the U.S.S.R. (The U.S.S.R. was still allowed by a 1971 pact to use the island's drydock facilities.) The U.S. and other NATO allies were to negotiate individually with Malta for use of the Valleta harbor and of the military facilities. (Access was not authorized in the pact.)

Malta had abrogated its defense treaty with Great Britain in 1971 and had stated that new arrangements would have to be made if British troops were to remain on the island. Britain had announced at the end of 1971 that it would withdraw its forces from Malta rather than pay the amount demanded by Mintoff for use of military facilities. Mintoff had originally set Dec. 31, 1971 as the deadline for agreement with Britain on renting the military facilities, but extended the deadline to Jan. 15. The deadline was again extended Jan. 15.

See also ESPIONAGE; EUROPEAN SECURITY

MANUFACTURERS AIRCRAFT ASSOCIATION, INC.—*See* BUSINESS

MAO TSETUNG—*See* CHINA, COMMUNIST; JAPAN [7]; SINO-U.S. RELATIONS [1, 4]

MARCOS, FERDINAND E.—*See* PHILIPPINES

MARIJUANA—*See* DRUG USE & ADDICTION [1, 4-6]; ELECTIONS [44]; MEDICINE

MARINE CORPS, U.S.—*See* DRUG USE & ADDICTION [2]; ELECTIONS [25]; MILITARY [4, 7]

MARINER 9—*See* SPACE [20]

MARS—*See* SPACE [20]

MASS TRANSIT—*See* POLLUTION [8]; STATE & LOCAL GOVERNMENTS; TRANSPORTATION

MAURITANIA—*See* AFRICA

MAURITIUS—*See* ATOMIC ENERGY [6]; INTERNATIONAL MONETARY DEVELOPMENTS [8]

McCARTHY, EUGENE J.—*See* ELECTIONS [3, 6, 17]

McCLOSKEY JR., PAUL—*See* ELECTIONS [3-6, 22, 49]

MEDICINE—New cancer links. Scientists working under Dr. Sol Spiegelman at Columbia University in New York were reported Jan. 14 to have found chemical links between three types of human cancer (breast cancer, sarcoma and leukemia) and viruses known to cause comparable types of cancer in animals. Spiegelman emphasized that the team's findings did not prove the link between viruses and human cancer. He said, however, that the experiments came as close to that link as one could now get. The work of Spiegelman's group was sponsored by the special virus cancer program of the National Institutes of Health.

Nuclear heart pump used. An artificial heart pump powered by a nuclear engine implanted in the chest of a calf kept the animal's heart beating for five hours Feb. 14. The experiment at Boston City Hospital was the first time nuclear energy had been used to drive a mechanical heart pump in a living animal. During its five-hour test, the heart pump replaced the function of the left ventricle, pumping blood through the arteries to the body. The pump was connected to a six-pound cylindrical canister which contained a tiny steam engine powered by a plutonium-238 energy source. Energy came from heat caused by the release of atomic alpha particles as the plutonium decayed. The engine was controlled by a miniature computer that would monitor the heart's function. The plutonium-drive device was expected to last at least 10 years. Dr. Theodore Cooper, director of the National Heart and Lung Institute, which sponsored the experiment, said that much research work remained, but that nuclear-powered heart devices might be available for use by man by the end of the decade.

'Artificial brain' used. A Stanford University (Calif.) research team, headed by Dr. Lawrence R. Pinneo, said Feb. 9 that it had developed an experimental "artificial brain" that helped restore some movements in the limbs of partly paralyzed monkeys. The artificial brain was not a "thinking" brain, but helped replace a lost function of the brain by altering the way the brain operates. (The researchers used electrodes to stimulate the subcortical structures of the monkeys' brains to prompt skeletal motor activities.) The technique, if it could be extended to humans, was thought to be a possibly significant step in helping stroke victims overcome paralysis.

Salt water replaces blood. Air Force doctors disclosed April 28 that, presumably for the first time, a human being had been kept alive by salt water introduced into his circulatory system while his entire blood supply was removed. The salt water was in the body of Sgt. Tors Olson for more than eight minutes March 31. Olson was in a coma when the exchange was made at the Wilford Hall Air Force Medical Center in San Antonio. His blood was removed, to be replaced by salt water and ultimately new blood, in order to purge his system of poisons that had built up because of a malfunctioning liver. As in other operations involving a stoppage of the blood's flow, Olson was chilled to 85° Fahrenheit, slowing his body functions and enabling doctors to suspend blood circulation to the brain for more than eight minutes.

AMA begins modernization. The American Medical Association (AMA) acted at its annual convention in San Francisco June 18-22 to modernize its 125-year-old constitution. However, it deferred for at least a year taking any action on a 1971 proposal for drafting a new constitution. The convention also left for further study the issue of "peer review," under which doctors could check the performance of other doctors. The AMA did, however, move to give younger doctors a greater role in determining AMA policies by electing a 27-year-old resident to the 241-member House of Delegates, which sets AMA policy. The convention also: voted to create an 18-member committee to supervise graduate medical education; installed Dr. Charles A. Hoffman of Huntington, W. Va. as the AMA's 127th president; proposed that tax incentives be used to induce doctors to take their practices into the nation's inner cities and rural areas, places where they were most needed; and adopted a resolution indicating the AMA's support for the recommendation by the National Committee on Marijuana and Drug Abuse *(see* DRUG USE & ADDICTION [5]) that felony penalties for the possession of "insignificant" quantities of marijuana be abandoned.

  See also ELECTIONS [17]; HEALTH; HEALTH CARE; NOBEL PRIZES; SOVIET-U.S. RELATIONS [4]

MEIR, GOLDA—*See* ISRAEL; MIDDLE EAST [10, 17-18, 23, 34-35]; OLYMPIC TERRORISM
MENTAL HEALTH—*See* HEALTH CARE
MERCURY POISONING—*See* HEALTH; POLLUTION [13]
METHADONE—*See* DRUG USE & ADDICTION [1, 8]
METHAMPHETAMINES—*See* DRUG USE & ADDICTION [10]
METHODIST CHURCH—*See* CHURCHES

MEXICO—Bank security increased. The government Jan. 18 ordered banks to tighten security measures in the wake of robberies and shootouts by urban guerrillas in the northern cities of Chihuahua, Monterrey and Aguascalientes. The guerrillas reportedly took $24,000 from a Monterrey bank Jan. 14 and $40,000 from three Chihuahua banks Jan. 15. Three persons allegedly were killed in a shootout between guerrillas and police outside one of the Chihuahua banks. Two persons reportedly were killed in a similar battle in Aguascalientes Jan. 16. The Chihuahua state government Jan. 17 offered a $12,000 reward for information leading to the capture of the robbers of its three banks. Throughout the year, terrorists in Mexico carried out robberies, bombings and kidnapings.

  Japanese relations. President Luis Echeverria Alvarez flew to Tokyo March 9 for a five-day visit and talks with Japanese Premier Eisaku Sato and leading Japanese industrialists and bankers. Echeverria returned to Mexico March 14 after receiving promises of Japanese loans and increased imports of Mexican products. As a result of the visit, Japan reportedly was considering a joint venture to manufacture telephones in Mexico. Mexico's need was estimated at 2 million telephones, and Japan reportedly was interested in penetrating the Latin American phone market. (In apparent response to growing Japanese and European economic activity, the U.S. had opened a $450,000 trade center in Mexico City Feb. 14.)

  U.S. border pact. Mexico and the U.S., according to a report April 20, signed a treaty aimed at settling existing boundary disputes and establishing a mechanism for resolving future territorial disputes. The accord provided for the restoration and maintenance of the Colorado River and the Rio Grande as continuous natural boundaries and incorporated procedures to guard against future loss of territory by either country from shifts in river flow. It also established maritime boundaries between Mexico and the U.S. in the Pacific Ocean and the Gulf of Mexico.

  Echeverria on U.S. tour. President Echeverria toured the U.S. June 14-21, conferring with President Nixon in Washington June 15-16 and then visiting New York, Chicago, San Antonio and Los Angeles. In a joint communique issued June 17, the two countries pledged to study the problems of Mexican migrant workers who entered the U.S. for seasonal employment and to continue efforts to halt the international narcotics traffic. The U.S. also agreed to take steps to improve the quality of water flowing from the Colorado River into Mexico. (Mexico had complained that irrigation works in southern Arizona resulted in such high saline content of river water crossing the border that it damaged agriculture and fishing in the Mexicali valley, causing losses estimated at $240 million a year.)

Student unrest. Violent student disturbances throughout the early part of the year resulted July 25 in the imposition of strict security measures. There reportedly was no connection between the disturbances in various parts of the country. Among the major incidents of student unrest: two students were killed and others wounded April 7 when police in the northern city of Culiacan fired into a crowd of student demonstrators protesting a proposed university law and demanding the resignation of the Sinaloa University rector; an effort by police and a right-wing paramilitary group to restore the rector in early August resulted in the death of two students, the injury of others and the arrest of over 200; students in Culiacan also burned down the offices of the ruling Revolutionary Institutional party in late July to protest the murder of two peasants; Culiacan students paralyzed the city's public transportation beginning Oct. 6 with their demands for compensation to the family of a worker run over by a bus; two persons were killed and several wounded in Mexico City June 13 when a gun battle broke out between left-wing and right-wing students who had been struggling for several months for control of the campus of the University of Mexico; students from the National University in Mexico City in late July seized a number of buses and held them as security for compensation they demanded from the city's bus company on behalf of the family of another worker run over by a bus; students, teachers, peasants and workers demonstrated in Puebla, near the capitol, during late July to protest the murder, apparently by right-wing terrorists, of Joel Arriaga Navarro, a left-wing architect and headmaster of the local university's preparatory school; student riots were also reported during late July in Monterrey and in the southeastern city of Oaxaca.

National University rector resigns. Pablo Gonzalez, the rector of the National University, resigned Nov. 18 after failing to curb continuing student unrest and to find a solution to a strike by the university's non-academic employees. (The strike, begun in October for recognition of the employees' union, was joined early in December by workers at other Mexican universities.) Gonzalez's resignation followed exposure by the government of the "Pancho Villa" group, a band of right-wing thugs trained by police officers in violent tactics to be used against "progressive" students. The National University's director of information and public relations and the dean of the law faculty were among officials linked to the group.

Estates expropriated. According to a report July 28, President Echeverria had decreed the expropriation of several large estates, totaling some 222,000 hectares, and their distribution among 941 peasant families. Seizure of the land, owned by some of Mexico's leading families, reportedly underscored Echeverria's determination to press political and economic reforms.

Telephone company controlled. The government Aug. 16 purchased 51% of the stock in Telefonos de Mexico, the national telephone company. It was the largest privately owned corporation in the country, and most of its stockholders were Mexican. Government control of the company reportedly caused concern among U.S. investors in Mexico, who feared nationalization along Chilean lines (*see* CHILE [7-10, 12]). However, National Patrimony Minister Horacio Flores de la Pena asserted that the government had not nationalized the phone company. Flores added that the government would control, but not administer, the system and that stockholders would be able to retain their equity. He also said that dividends would not be reduced.

See also CONSERVATION; DRUG USE & ADDICTION [1, 10, 16, 18]; FLOODS; HEALTH; INTERNATIONAL MONETARY DEVELOPMENTS [9]; LATIN AMERICA; RAILROADS

MIAMI CONVENTIONS COALITION (MCC)—*See* ELECTIONS [25]

MIAMI WOMEN'S COALITION—*See* ELECTIONS [25]

MICRONESIA—U.S. severs talks. The U.S. Oct. 7 broke off negotiations with Micronesian nationalists that had begun Sept. 28. The American action followed a Micronesian request that the discussions be widened to include independence as a possible alternative to association with the U.S., which administered the U.N. trust territory in the Central Pacific.

MIDDLE EAST—The cease-fire accepted in 1970 still prevailed between governments within the Middle East area, but military and terrorist attacks by Palestinian guerrillas continued to build tension between Israel and the Arab states. Israeli troops carried out attacks against Lebanon *(see* [2-10]) and Syria *(see* [11-14]) in retaliation for commando raids made against Israel from the territory of the two Arab countries. Terrorist actions during 1972 took on a more international aspect with the shooting attack on Israel's Lod International Airport *(see* [22-23]), the murder of members of the Israeli Olympic team in Munich *(see* OLYMPIC TERRORISM) and an international letter-bomb campaign *(see* [25]). In developments concerning the areas occupied by Israel after the six-day war, King Hussein of Jordan proposed a merger of Jordan and the Israeli-occupied West Bank *(see* [17]) and a program of joint Jordanian-Israeli rule in Jerusalem *(see* [20]). In the Arab world, Egypt expelled Soviet "military advisers and experts" during July *(see* [31]). Egypt and Libya also announced a political merger of their two countries by Sept. 1, 1973 *(see* [32]). Efforts to find a peaceful settlement of the Middle East situation continued during the year, but reached no resolution *(see* [33-36]).

Fighting—Lebanon

[2] **January Israeli raids.** Israeli forces crossed into southern Lebanon Jan. 10 and 13 to carry out retaliatory attacks against Palestinian commando bases just north of the Israeli border. The Jan. 10 attack against the towns of Bint Jbail and Kfar Hamam reportedly was in retaliation for four separate guerrilla raids on Israel Jan. 6-10. (Israel's northern border region was shelled from Lebanon Jan. 6. An Israeli engineer driving on a road in the Golan Heights was shot to death by commandos the same day. The Israeli town of Kiryat Shmona was shelled Jan. 8 and 10. Palestinian infiltrators fired rockets at Safad Jan. 9.) According to Israel, two Israeli soldiers were killed in the Jan. 10 attack, which also resulted in the death of "a number of terrorists" and the destruction of four buildings. According to the Lebanese government, a number of buildings were blown up and three commandos and a civilian were killed. A commando statement reported that the Israelis had lost 20 killed and wounded, while the commandos had suffered losses of two killed and two wounded. The Jan. 13 attack against the town of Kafra reportedly was in retaliation for Jan. 12 guerrilla shelling of Kiryat Shmona. The attackers blew up two houses allegedly used by guerrillas. (Lebanon claimed that four houses were blown up and a Lebanese woman seriously wounded.)

[3] **February raids.** Israeli air and ground forces carried out heavy reprisal operations against commandos in southeast Lebanon Feb. 25-28, pulling out after the United Nations Security Council adopted a resolution demanding the withdrawal. The Israeli thrust against guerrilla strongholds in the Arkoub Valley, where an estimated 2,000-5,000 guerrillas were believed deployed, was reportedly in retaliation for recent infiltration of commandos into Israel from Lebanon. (Three Israeli soldiers and a civilian couple were killed and several others wounded in guerrilla ambushes Feb. 22-23.) The Israelis claimed that the raids had resulted in the death of 60 guerrillas (over 100 wounded), the capture of large quantities of equipment and the destruction of buildings, installations, base camps and headquarters. Israel placed its own losses at 11 slightly wounded. The guerrillas admitted that 20 of their men were killed and 36 wounded. Following the Israeli withdrawal Feb. 28, Lebanese troops quickly moved into the commando areas. A high-ranking Lebanese officer was quoted as saying: "This time we intend to occupy the guerrilla positions and keep them."

[4] **March raids.** Israeli forces renewed raids on Lebanon March 9, allegedly in retaliation for Lebanon-based guerrilla attacks on Israel March 8. (An undisclosed number of shells fell in empty fields near the Israeli villages of Sasa and Baram, but no casualties were reported.) Jerusalem authorities said Israeli artillery first responded with bombardment in the central area of the front. This was followed by air strikes on guerrilla encampments in the village of Kfar Azait, seven miles inside Lebanon. A Lebanese military spokesman reported that two civilians were injured and nine buildings destroyed in an Israeli air attack in the Hasbaya region, west of Mt. Hermon.

[5] **June attacks.** Following a June 20 resumption of guerrilla attacks across the border (after a four-month lull), an Israeli force June 21 struck into southern Lebanon simultaneously with an Israeli air and artillery attack against a suspected commando base at Hasbaya. During the armored force attack, Israel captured five Syrian officers, a Lebanese officer and three military policemen. An Israeli military spokesman said that the capture of the Syrians came as a surprise and was "evidence of joint Syrian-Lebanese planning against Israel." Israeli planes and artillery again struck at suspected commando bases June 23, inflicting heavy casualties. The attack followed the commando shelling earlier the same day of Kiryat Shmona. Israeli gunboats operating off the coast of Lebanon June 23 fired on a commando vessel and set it ablaze. Lebanon reported another naval clash June 24 in which Israeli warships sank a Lebanese fishing boat and fired machine guns at a Lebanese army post. The Lebanese returned the fire and forced the Israeli ships to withdraw. A commando communique said an Israeli ship was sunk June 24 by a guerrilla vessel after the Israelis tried to attack a Palestinian refugee camp at Rashiya.

[6] *Commandos agree to curb raids.* Lebanese Premier Saeb Salam and guerrilla leader Yasir Arafat June 27 reached a formal agreement barring commando raids on Israel from Lebanon. Neither side gave details of the accord, which reportedly was reached in order to spare Lebanon from Israeli reprisal attacks. Informed sources reported, however, that the commandos had agreed to pull back from a number of Lebanese towns and villages near the Israeli border and that the guerrillas had acceded to a Lebanese request to establish a unified information office in Beirut that would not be permitted to issue its own military communiques. The Popular Front for the Liberation of Palestine, General Command, a splinter commando group which had broken away from the PFLP in 1968, announced June 28 that it would not freeze raids against Israel, but would carry out continued raids "in the depth of enemy territory" and not near the cease-fire lines.

[7] **September attacks.** Following clashes on Israeli territory Sept. 6 and 7 in which two Arabs and an Israeli were killed, an Israeli armored patrol, supported by helicopters, struck more than a mile inside southern Lebanon Sept. 7 in search of commandos. Military sources in Lebanon also said that three formations of Israeli military planes flew sorties as far north as Tyre and Marjioun in Lebanon. An estimated 50-80 Israeli planes Sept. 8 carried out a damaging attack against Arab guerrilla bases and naval stations deep in Lebanon and Syria in retaliation for the slaying of Israeli Olympic athletes in Munich *(see* OLYMPIC TERRORISM). The raids, lasting 17 minutes, were the heaviest by Israel since the 1967 war. The planes dropped bombs and fired rockets on what Israel described as troop concentrations, training centers, supply depots and headquarter units of Al Fatah—which Israel regarded as the parent unit of the Black September Organization responsible for the Munich slayings. In Lebanon, the following targets were attacked: the Al Fatah naval training base of Nahar el Bard; a regional Al Fatah headquarters at Rashiya el Wadi; and the Al Fatah maintenance base at Rafid. (There reportedly were heavy civilian casualties in the Rafid attack.) Among the targets struck in Syria were: El Hameh, regarded as the principal Al Fatah base in Syria; and three Al Fatah naval installations, including the chief naval base at Burj Islam.

Israeli authorities reported that, in other action Sept. 8, one of their navy missile boats sank a small commando attack vessel off the southern Lebanese coast.

[8] Israeli forces carried out a major ground attack against commando bases in southern Lebanon Sept. 16-17 in retaliation for the Sept. 15 killing of two Israeli soldiers by Arab raiders. An estimated 3,000 troops, spearheaded by about 50 tanks and other armored vehicles and supported by about 25 jets, thrust 15 miles across the border in the deepest penetration of Lebanon to date. Israeli authorities reported that "at least 60" guerrillas were killed in the 33-hour operation, 16 villages were searched for terrorists and more than 150 houses believed to have quartered the commandos were destroyed. Israel placed its losses at three killed and six wounded. The Lebanese army, as well as the guerrillas, put up strong resistance. Arab sources said the Israelis killed at least 35 guerrillas, 18 Lebanese soldiers and 23 Lebanese civilians. A Beirut communique said Israeli jets had destroyed two major bridges over the Litani River.

[9] *Beirut curbs commandos.* In the aftermath of the Israeli foray, Lebanon Sept. 17 ordered the commandos to evacuate all villages in southern Lebanon, effective the same day. The Palestine Liberation Organization (PLO) was reported Sept. 20 to have acceded to the Beirut government's demands following mediation moves by Mahmoud Riad, secretary general of the Arab League. Premier Salam announced Sept. 25 that the commandos had agreed to accept the government's restrictive measures against their movements. According to Arab informants, the following restrictions were imposed against the commandos: in the Arkub sector, on the southeastern flank, they were prohibited from moving south on the Chebaa-Hasbaya road and into villages or within a mile and a quarter of them; they were barred from the vicinity of villages in the Rashiya administrative region; no new commandos were permitted to enter the central part of the southern border region; those who were already in the center border region were to evacuate villages and remain a mile and a quarter from them. The Lebanese government also reportedly restrained the guerrillas from wearing battle dress and carrying arms until their command and the Lebanese army were coordinated. In other action to curb the guerrillas, the Lebanese government announced Sept. 18 that the army had established roadblocks in the southern part of the country "to prevent the Palestinian forces from returning" to their regular positions.

[10] **Israel attacks without provocation.** Israeli planes Oct. 15 bombed Al Fatah commando bases in Lebanon and Syria without immediate provocation. In explaining the new Israeli policy, Chaim Herzog, former chief of staff, said: "We are not engaged in reprisal, but a war against terror. The very presence of terrorists in the area between the border and the Litani River is a provocation" and Israel, therefore, considered itself "free to act against them." Israeli Premier Golda Meir said the attacks were carried out because guerrillas in Syria and Lebanon had planned the killing of Israeli athletes in Munich *(see* OLYMPIC TERRORISM), the Tel Aviv airport massacre *(see* [22]) and the mailing of letter bombs to Jews *(see* [25]). In describing the attacks, Israeli military authorities said that about 20 planes bombed four guerrilla installations in Lebanon and one in Syria. The targets in Lebanon were a naval base at Ras Naba Muhiliv, a command post north of Bafika, the Deir Ashayer base on the principal road leading from Lebanon to Syria, and a central motor pool for vehicle repairs near Saida on the coast. The target struck in Syria was the Al Fatah training camp one mile east of Masyaf. (Israeli forces again clashed with Lebanese forces Nov. 23 and with a Palestinian commando unit in Lebanon Nov. 24.)

Fighting—Syria

[11] **January attack.** In the first Israeli air strike on Syrian territory to be reported since June 24-26, 1970, Israeli planes Jan. 24 bombed commando

concentrations north of Dera, in southwestern Syria. The attack reportedly was in response to increased guerrilla attacks from Syria on civilian areas in Israel since September 1971, including a Jan. 23 incident in which three infiltrators crossed the cease-fire line but were killed by an Israeli patrol. Syria confirmed the Israeli jet strike, but claimed its air defenses had driven off the attackers. Damascus said there were no casualties or property damage.

[12] **Golan Heights clash.** Israeli forces, reportedly retaliating for mortar attacks on Israeli settlements Feb. 29, made air and artillery strikes March 1 on suspected guerrilla bases in the southern and central part of the Golan Heights. Syrian planes retaliated later in the day with raids on Israeli settlements about two miles inside the heights. A Damascus broadcast said the Syrian raids were in retaliation for Israeli shelling of three Syrian villages in the heights and an air raid on a guerrilla camp near Dera.

[13] **September-October clashes.** In air clashes over the Golan Heights Sept. 9—the first since June 26, 1970—Israel claimed that three Syrian jets were shot down and another damaged, while all Israeli planes returned safely to base. Syria conceded the loss of three planes, but claimed that three Israeli planes were also shot down by Syrian air and ground fire. Syria's armed forces were placed on the alert Sept. 9 after the Israeli air strikes *(see also* [7]). Israeli jets Oct. 30 bombed four Arab guerrilla bases near Damascus and returned later to attack a Syrian army camp at Tel Kalakh, 100 miles north. *(See also* [10].) At the same time, Syrian forces shelled Israeli positions in the Golan Heights. Syrian authorities reported that more than 60 civilians had been killed and 70 wounded in the first Israeli air strike, which they claimed included the bombing of Palestinian refugee camps. Palestinian commandos placed their losses at 15 dead.

[14] **November-December clashes.** Israeli jets raided Syria Nov. 9 following two clashes in the Golan Heights Nov. 8 and 9. An Israeli civilian was wounded in the northern section of the heights Nov. 8 when his tractor hit a commando-planted mine. An Israeli patrol Nov. 9 clashed with a group of 18 commandos attempting to set up an ambush position in the southern part of the heights. Israeli jets retaliated by striking at two Syrian army positions near the Golan truce line where the infiltrators had passed through. The Syrian army responded with a three-hour artillery barrage against two Israeli settlements in the heights, killing one soldier and causing considerable property damage. Israeli jets then attacked Syria for the second time, striking at four army forward positions, two artillery concentrations and a surface-to-air missile battery on the northern part of the truce line. Israel claimed its pilots shot down two Syrian MiG-21 fighters before returning safely to base. Damascus claimed the downing of four Israeli planes. Israel Nov. 10 sealed off the Golan Heights and placed its forces on full alert there. Israeli and Syrian armed forces fought an eight-hour battle along the Golan Heights truce line Nov. 21, using planes, artillery and tanks. The clash, the most serious between the two countries in more than two years, followed Israeli air strikes in retaliation for commando attacks from Syria. Brief fighting erupted again Nov. 25 along the Golan Heights truce line. Damascus radio claimed that Syrian artillery shelled Israeli positions at Kafr Naffakh and El Quneitra after the Israelis had fired at Syrian positions earlier in the day. Israel claimed that the Syrian attacks were made without provocation. According to a report Dec. 9, Syria ordered the Palestinian commandos to stop using Syrian territory for raids against Israel. In later fighting, Irsaeli jets Dec. 27 attacked guerrilla bases and army positions in retaliation for recent guerrilla attacks in the Golan Heights. In retaliation for the Dec. 27 strikes, Syrian forces Dec. 30 shelled Israeli civilian settlements and army positions in the Heights. The Syrian assault was followed quickly by an Israeli air raid on a Syrian army camp.

Fighting—Egypt

[15] Israel, Egypt claim jets shot down. Israel and Egypt June 13 gave conflicting reports of an air battle over the Mediterranean in which each nation claimed to have shot down two of the other's aircraft. It was the first such clash since the Suez Canal ceasefire of August 1970. An Israeli military spokesman said two Egyptian MiG-21s were shot down over international waters about 25 miles north of Port Said when the MiGs intercepted a patrol of Israeli F-4 Phantoms. Two Egyptian pilots were seen parachuting into the sea, but all Israeli aircraft returned safely from the area, according to the spokesman. An Egyptian statement released after the Israeli report claimed eight Egyptian interceptors shot down two Israeli Mirage jet fighters when 16 Israeli planes invaded Egyptian airspace about 35 miles west of the Suez Canal, near the seaside resort of Ras el Bar. The statement acknowledged that two Egyptian planes had been hit, but did not indicate whether they had crashed.

[16] Israeli jets attacked. Israel reported that two of its jets flying over the Sinai Peninsula July 24 were the targets of four Egyptian surface-to-air missiles fired from the western bank of the Suez Canal. The planes were not hit or damaged and returned safely to base, according to the Israelis. Egypt claimed that one of four Israeli jets that crossed over the canal in the Qantara-Ismailia area was shot down by its air defenses on the waterway.

Occupied Areas Developments

[17] Hussein proposes West Bank merger. King Hussein of Jordan proposed March 15 the creation of a new federated Arab State comprised of two autonomous regions—Jordan and Jordan's former West Bank, occupied by Israel since the 1967 war. Under the plan, East Jerusalem would be the capital of the West Bank region, while Amman would be the capital of the entire new nation (to be called the United Arab Kingdom) as well as of the Jordan region. Hussein said the kingdom would also include "any other Palestinian territories to be liberated," an apparent allusion to the Gaza Strip, also occupied by Israel. (Hussein did not specify how he would regain control of the West Bank, the Gaza Strip and East Jerusalem.) Among other aspects of the king's proposal: the king would be chief of state and would assume the central executive authority with the aid of a council of ministers; legislative power would be held by the king and a national assembly in which each region would have equal representation; each region would be under the rule of a governor general, named by an elected people's council and assisted by a regional Cabinet. Hussein's plan was denounced by Mrs. Meir March 16 as an assumption of territory by Hussein over which he had no control. It was denounced March 15 by Iraq as a threat to Arab unity. The PLO March 16 rejected the plan "categorically and conclusively." The Presidential Council of the Federation of Arab Republics also denounced the plan March 18. Al Fatah March 17 called for a "removal of the Jordanian regime" because of the proposal. Egypt April 6 severed diplomatic relations with Jordan in opposition to the Hussein plan.

[18] U.N. scores Israeli occupation. The U.N. Human Rights Commission March 22 adopted a resolution accusing Israel of committing "war crimes" in the occupied Arab territories and calling on Israel to rescind and desist from all practices affecting the population composition and physical character of the occupied areas and the rights of their inhabitants. A three-nation (Yugoslavia, Somalia and Sri Lanka) U.N. investigating committee formed by the General Assembly in 1968 Oct. 18 accused Israel of continued violation of Arab rights in the occupied territories. The committee charged that Israel had displaced 11,000 Arabs in 1972, particularly in Gaza and the Sinai Peninsula, and that Israel had established 43 settlements in the territories since the war. The three nations warned that Israel would "make the occupied territories socially, economically, politically and juridically part of Israel unless some form of supervision of the occupation is put into effect immediately to arrest such a trend." The committee conceded that Israel had relaxed security measures in the preceding year, but said that prisons were overcrowded and interrogation practices "very frequently involved physical violence." The U.N. General Assembly Dec. 8 approved a compromise resolution urging governments not to recognize changes carried out by Israel in occupied territories and to "avoid actions, including actions in the field of aid, that could constitute recognition of that occupation." The vote was 86-7, with 31 abstentions. An earlier version of the resolution had included a call for sanctions against Israel, prompting Israel to warn that approval would lead it to ignore future U.N. peace-making efforts in the Middle East. (In a related incident, Israeli Defense Minister Moshe Dayan pledged July 9 to impose tighter control of the military after receiving complaints from Mrs. Meir of "painful irregularities" by Israeli army authorities in the occupied areas.)

[19] **West Bank elections.** Arabs voted March 28 in elections for municipal councils in 10 towns in the West Bank area. Defying demands by Hussein and by commandos for a boycott of the balloting, 84% of the 16,000 eligible voters went to the polls in the first West Bank election since the 1967 war. A second round of elections in 12 other towns was held May 2. In the March elections, incumbent leaders, committed to continued union with Jordan, were re-elected in five towns. New leaders opposed to Hussein and in favor of an independent Palestinian state were elected in five towns. In the May elections, only three of 10 incumbent mayors were re-elected.

[20] **Hussein asks joint Jerusalem rule.** King Hussein March 29 proposed that a final Middle East peace settlement include an agreement on joint administration by Jordan and Israel of Jerusalem as "a unified, open city—a meeting place for the three great religions of the world." Hussein insisted that the eastern part of Jerusalem taken by Israel in the 1967 war be returned to Jordan. He proposed that the city become "the capital of Israel and the capital of the Palestinian portion of Jordan."

[21] **Gaza Arabs may enter Israel.** The 35,000 Arabs living in the Gaza Strip were allowed to work in Israel without permits beginning April 30, although they were still barred from staying overnight in Israel without official permission. The Israeli Cabinet had approved the free movement plan, put forward by Defense Minister Dayan, April 23. Dayan declared April 25 that Israel considered itself the only authority in the strip "and must therefore treat the local residents as Israelis." He insisted that Israel was not annexing the territory, but was creating "a new reality which the people of Gaza will not oppose."

Terrorism

[22] **Terrorists attack Lod.** Three Japanese gunmen hired by the PFLP attacked the Lod International Airport near Tel Aviv the night of May 30, killing 24 persons and wounding 76 others. A 25th person died June 1. One of the attackers (later identified as Ken Torio) was killed by his own grenade; another (later identified as Jiro Sugizaki) was shot to death, apparently by bullets shot by his own companions; and the third (originally identified as Daisuke Namba, but later identified as Kozo Okamoto) was captured by an El Al airliner mechanic. Those killed by the three included eight Israelis (including Dr. Aharon Katzir-Katchalsky, one of the country's leading scientists), an unidentified Canadian and 16 Puerto Ricans on a pilgrimage to Christian holy places. (The slaying of the Puerto Ricans touched off strong anti-Japanese and anti-Arab feelings in Puerto Rico. The government of Puerto Rico May 31 put into effect security measures designed to protect Japanese businesses after a Puerto Rican group warned it would "kill two Arabs and one Japanese" for every Puerto Rican who died in the attack.) The three Japanese had debarked with 116 other passengers from an Air France flight from Paris and Rome. (They had boarded at Rome.) Entering the passenger lounge at the Lod Airport, the three picked up two valises from a conveyor belt, unzipped them and whipped out machineguns and grenades. They then began firing and

lobbing grenades indiscriminately at a crowd of about 300 in the waiting room. One of the terrorists fired at aircraft on the runway from an opening in the baggage conveyor, and Okamoto raced out to the tarmac shooting at everyone in sight and at jets parked near the terminal. The attack lasted 3-4 minutes. The PFLP announced May 31 that it had recruited the three members of "the Army of the Red Star," but said that it had instructed the three not to fire on Air France passengers. According to the PFLP, the terrorists were told to attack those debarking from an El Al flight due to arrive 10 minutes later and those waiting for them. Okamoto was convicted and sentenced to life in prison by a three-man Israeli military tribunal for his role in the airport attack. Okamoto was found guilty on three counts of possessing and discharging firearms and grenades and on one count of "serving an unlawful organization." He could have received the death penalty for each of the first three charges.

[23] *Reaction to attack.* Prime Minister Meir assailed the raid May 31, but absolved the Japanese government and people of responsibility. Mrs. Meir denounced the guerrillas for recruiting the gunmen and linked Lebanon to the incident. In anticipation of a new terrorist attack, Lod was put on military alert June 1, but the alert was lifted June 2. The Israeli government warned June 2 that it would retaliate for the attack and announced that eight international airlines (Air France, Sabena, Lufthansa, Canadian Pacific Air, Japan Airlines, Swissair, Alitalia and Olympic) had agreed to Israeli demands for tighter security measures on flights to Israel.

[24] **Plane bombers arrested.** Police in Rome Aug. 19 arrested Ahmad Zaid of Iraq and Ahmad Mojammed Ali Hashan of Jordan as suspects in a bomb explosion aboard an Israeli passenger plane Aug. 16. The bomb, contained in a record player stored in the baggage compartment of an El Al airliner, exploded 10 minutes after the plane's takeoff from Rome for Tel Aviv. The damaged airliner returned safely to Rome after the explosion, with four passengers slightly injured. The two Arabs had been traced as a result of information given to Italian police by two British women who said they had been given a package containing the record player as a farewell gift from the two men. Zaid and Hashan were identified from pictures taken by the two women. (Judicial authorities in Rome Aug. 18 declared the two women innocent of involvement in the bombing.)

[25] **Letter bomb campaign.** Dr. Ami Shachori, a counselor for agricultural affairs in the Israeli embassy in London, was killed Sept. 19 by an explosive device in a letter postmarked Amsterdam and apparently mailed by Arab guerrillas. Dr. Theodore Kaddar, who had arrived at the embassy to replace Shachori, was slightly injured by the explosion. (Commandos had sent 13 explosive packages to Israeli officials Jan. 2-9. Those packages, most sent from Vienna, had resulted in the injury of a bomb disposal expert in Tel Aviv.) A postal clerk in a New York post office was seriously injured Oct. 14 when a letter bomb bearing a Malaysian postmark exploded. The letter was addressed to an unidentified former national officer of Hadassah, the women's Zionist organization. A large number of other letter bombs were found during September through November—addressed to Israeli embassy officials in London, Paris, the U.S., Canada and Belgium; to members of American Zionist circles; to Israeli government officials; to U.S. officials, including President Nixon; and to Jewish firms, organizations and individuals. Except for those which exploded Sept. 19 and Oct. 14, all were defused or failed to explode.

[26] *Letter bombs sent to Arabs.* A Jordanian government spokesman said Sept. 23 that the Amman post office that day had intercepted and defused four letter bombs—all bearing Amsterdam postmarks and all addressed to Jordanian officials. Letter bombs bearing Belgrade, Yugoslavia postmarks were received Oct. 25 in Lebanon, Algeria, Libya and Egypt. A letter, addressed to a Palestinian partner in a Beirut trading company known to have arranged arms deals with Arab countries, exploded and injured the company's secretary. A Beirut postman was blinded after one of the letters he was sorting exploded in

his face. PLO official Abu Khalil was injured in Algiers when he opened a booby-trapped parcel. PLO Libyan secretary Mustafa Awad Abu Zeid was blinded by a parcel bomb opened in Tripoli. Two other persons received less serious injuries. Egyptian authorities intercepted a bomb addressed to a PLO official, but three other letter bombs exploded at the Cairo airport Oct. 26, seriously injuring an Egyptian security officer examining the envelopes after intercepting them. A bomb intended for the Beirut office of the PFLP was intercepted and defused at the city's post office Oct. 27. A letter bomb received by the Egyptian embassy in London Oct. 31 was defused.

[27] *Israel opposes anti-terror groups.* Following the letter bomb explosion Sept. 19, the Israeli branch of the Jewish Defense League (JDL) announced the formation of an anti-terrorist organization to combat Arab guerrilla groups in Europe and the U.S. The Israeli government immediately cracked down on the JDL and on individuals attempting to take action on their own. Israeli authorities Sept. 21 arrested JDL member Abraham Hershkowitz and Amihai Paglin, a former leader in the underground struggle against British rule in Palestine, in connection with a secret shipment of arms that had been intercepted at Lod Airport. The weapons, including machine guns and grenades, were meant for use against Arabs abroad. Police Sept. 22 raided the JDL's Jerusalem headquarters, seized documents connected with the alleged arms smuggling operation and arrested JDL Secretary Joseph Schneider, charging him with illegal possession of weapons. The government Sept. 22 also issued an injunction against 20 JDL members (including the group's leader, Rabbi Meir Kahane), ordering them to stay out of the West Bank and the Gaza Strip. The order was said to be aimed at preventing the JDL from conducting "any activities liable to disrupt order or endanger security in those areas." Police Oct. 1 also arrested Rabbi Kahane in connection with the arms smuggling plot.

[28] **U.S., West Germany act against commandos.** The U.S. government announced Sept. 27 that all foreigners in transit through the U.S. would be required to have transit visas. (Previously foreign visitors had been permitted to remain in the U.S. for up to 10 days without a visa on condition that they presented evidence to airlines or shipping lines that they would leave the country by that time.) The move reportedly was prompted by the increasing threat of terrorist activities, especially those possibly planned to disrupt the U.N. General Assembly in session in New York. It was reported Oct. 4 that the government had also begun a major effort to identify Arabs in the U.S. suspected of planning terrorist acts against Israeli citizens in the country, and to carry out a more careful check of travelers from Arab countries. All federal agencies were involved in the operation of surveillance and interrogation. In West Germany, the government Oct. 4 outlawed the General Union of Palestinian Students and the General Union of Palestinian Workers after receiving "concrete evidence that new terrorist acts are being planned for Germany." *(See also* OLYMPIC TERRORISM.) Police started a nationwide search for followers of the groups.

[29] **Arabs seize Israelis in Thailand.** Four armed Palestinian commandos, members of the Black September Organization, Dec. 28 seized the Israeli embassy in Bangkok, Thailand and held its six Israeli occupants hostage for 19 hours before releasing them after negotiations with Thai officials. The commandos had held the Israelis at gunpoint, theatening to kill them and blow up the embassy unless 36 Palestinian prisoners held in Israel were freed by 8 a.m. Dec. 29. Thai Armed Forces Chief of Staff Marshall Dawee Chullaspaya and Deputy Foreign Minister Chartichai Choonhavan entered the embassy after the seizure and conferred with the guerrillas while hundreds of Thai soldiers and police surrounded the building. Egyptian Ambassador Mourtafa el-Essaway assisted in the negotiations. Following the negotiations, the commandos, the negotiators and the hostages left the embassy by bus for Bangkok airport. The commandos, the two Thais and the Egyptian

ambassador boarded a Thai plane and flew to Cairo. The six hostages (including Nitzan Hadass, the embassy's first secretary; Hadass's wife; embassy staff members Dan Beeri and Pinhas Lavie; and Shimon Avimor, Israel's ambassador to Cambodia, who was visiting Bangkok) remained in the bus at the Bangkok airport. Thai officials said the guerrillas had been shamed into releasing their captives.

Arab World Developments

[30] **Cairo students demand war.** Cairo University students demonstrated violently Jan. 16-18 to back demands for immediate war with Israel as the only means of resolving the Middle East crisis. The student outbursts were in reaction to President Anwar Sadat's Jan. 13 disclosure that Egypt had reversed a decision to go to war against Israel in December 1971 because of the outbreak of the conflict between India and Pakistan *(see* PAKISTAN [1-4]). The protesters were calling for a war policy against Israel, nationalization of U.S. oil interests in Egypt, a two-month closure of universities to permit students to obtain military training and a fixed date for the "arming of the masses." The students also opposed resumption of peace talks under the guidance of U.N. mediator Gunnar V. Jarring. Government officials met with student delegations, but President Sadat declared Jan. 19 that he would not bow to the demonstrators' demands. Sadat charged Feb. 17 that Israeli agents were responsible for instigating the student demonstrations.

[31] **U.S. asked to cut Cairo mission.** American diplomats in Cairo reported May 18 that President Sadat had demanded that the U.S. reduce its diplomatic mission in the city from 20 to 10 staff members within a month. Egypt had also instructed its mission in Washington to be cut in half. Cairo's decision reportedly was made to protest U.S. policy of "consolidating the continued Israeli aggression through occupation of Arab territories."

[32] **Sadat asks Soviet military to leave.** President Sadat announced July 18 that he had ordered the immediate withdrawal of Soviet "military advisers and experts" from Egypt. Sadat also directed that Soviet bases and equipment in the country be placed under exclusive control of Egyptian forces. He indicated that his decision was based on difficulties Egypt encountered in getting all the Soviet arms it wanted for its confrontation with Israel. (Sadat complained that arms necessary to launch an invasion of Israel in December 1971 did not arrive on "the agreed dates" and that the Soviets had attempted to impose conditions on the use of their equipment—presumably to prevent Egypt from launching an attack.) A Soviet government statement July 19 confirmed Sadat's surprise withdrawal announcement, but said the Soviet soldiers were being taken out by mutual agreement because their task of training Egyptian soldiers was complete. The Soviet force—consisting of military advisers, pilots and missile crews—was originally said to total 5,000; but 15,000-20,000 Soviets were withdrawn from Egypt by Aug. 6, when officials of the two governments announced the withdrawal was complete. At that time, less than 3,000 Soviet missile technicians and other instructors reportedly remained in Egypt.

[33] **Merger of Egypt and Libya.** Libyan leader Col. Muammar el-Qaddafi and President Sadat agreed Aug. 2 to establish by Sept. 1, 1973 a "unified political leadership." The agreement emphasized that the process of unity would require a public referendum in each state and could be vetoed by national authorities, who would approve the "final version of the unity plan." Before announcing the accord, the two leaders telephoned Syrian President Hafez al-Assad to tell him about the agreement. (Syria, Libya and Egypt had formed the Federation of Arab Republics in 1971.)

Peace Developments

[34] **Israel approves U.S. proposal.** Israel Feb. 2 announced acceptance of an American proposal for indirect talks with Egypt on reopening the Suez Canal. The proposed discussions would probably be held in the same or nearby

hotels in New York, with U.S. Assistant Secretary of State Joseph J. Sisco acting as a go-between, shuttling between Israeli and Egyptian representatives. Israeli approval of the proposal followed two weeks of discussion between Israel and the U.S. During the talks, Washington agreed to supply Israel with more planes and military equipment and assured Israel that Secretary of State William Rogers, in an Oct. 4, 1971 appeal for an interim agreement, had not intended to "impose" his views on future Israeli-Arab talks. These two positions overcame Mrs. Meir's two principal objections to the American proposal—that Washington's failure to sell Israel additional Phantom jets put her government at a disadvantage in future negotiations with Egypt, and that specific ideas outlined by Rogers in his 1971 statement differed from some of Israel's positions. Despite Israel's agreement to the talks, however, the U.S. was unable to secure Egyptian acceptance of indirect negotiations. President Sadat March 30 assailed the U.S. efforts to promote proximity talks, saying: "The Americans are not only liars but are also given to cryptic equivocations. They twist words and they twist everything."

[35] **Egypt rejects Israeli offers.** Mrs. Meir's office disclosed Feb. 15 that Egypt had recently turned down an Israeli offer to hold high-level talks. The discussions were to have been arranged by an unidentified mediator through Nahum Goldmann, a former president of the World Jewish Congress. Mrs. Meir's office said she had asked Goldmann to establish the contact, but that Cairo had spurned the proposal. Goldmann Feb. 15 denied that he had been designated as the go-between. He said another person, whom he refused to identify, had been involved in the projected meeting, but that Cairo said the time was not yet ripe for such talks. Mrs. Meir July 26 seized on the departure of Soviet military officials from Egypt *(see* [31]) as a fresh opportunity for Egypt and Israel to negotiate their differences. However, President Sadat July 27 rejected the renewed offer for direct talks. Sadat denounced Mrs. Meir's offer as "propaganda" and reportedly insisted that any Israeli-Egyptian discussions must be held in the presence of the U.S., Britain, France and the Soviet Union, who were not to act as mere "observers."

[36] **Israel proposes Sinai truce line.** Defense Minister Dayan Aug. 17 offered an interim peace agreement with Egypt based on a truce line dividing the Sinai Peninsula. Dayan noted that his suggestion represented a pullback from Israel's previous insistence that it would exchange the current truce lines only for "secure, recognized and agreed borders, determined under a peace treaty." Now, he said, Israel was prepared for interim settlements "by stages" in the absence of an overall agreement. Dayan was not specific as to where the proposed truce line would be drawn, or as to whether Israel and Egypt would be allowed to station troops along the buffer strip. Dayan also said that Israel had no intention of giving up all the former Arab territories it had occupied during the 1967 war. He warned that, if the Egyptians "refuse to meet us part way, we will have to go on acting in the way we have adopted for the five years" since the war.

[37] **Israel backs talks with Jordan.** Israeli Foreign Minister Abba Eban said Dec. 2 that Jordan would benefit from negotiations with Israel. Such talks, Eban stressed, could provide the Amman government with "peace, population, territory and a special status for the Moslem places of Jerusalem." According to Eban, Israel was not prepared to yield on the sovereignty or unity of Jerusalem, but this did not mean that it claimed "exclusive jurisdiction or unilateral responsibility over the holy places of Islam." The foreign minister added that, although it would be logical for Israel to conclude a peace pact with Egypt first, his government would not rule out an initial accord with Jordan if such an agreement were attainable. However, Eban expressed doubt that the Amman government had "the strength and stability of policy necessary" to reach a compromise settlement.

    See also ARAB REPUBLIC OF EGYPT; BAHRAIN; DRUG USE & ADDICTION [16]; ELECTIONS [16]; EUROPEAN ECONOMIC COMMUNITY

MIGRANT WORKERS—*See* MEXICO

MILITARY—Army to tighten basic training. The Army's one-year-old experiment in giving new recruits an easier time in basic training (in order to make military life more attractive to volunteers), according to a report Jan. 18, was going to be replaced by a return to the more rigid eight-week course used in the past. Among the changes to be made were the removal of beer machines from the recruits' barracks and elimination of the private cubicles which had given new soldiers their own small living quarters within the big barracks. Some of the 1970 reforms, including the abolition of reveille formation for recruits, would be kept. Brig. Gen. Ira Hunt, who was in charge of the Army's training command, said that "we've taken a long look at things, experimented around, and now we've decided that the relatively Spartan environment is the best for recruits."

[2] Chafee resigns; replaced by Warner. Secretary of the Navy John H. Chafee resigned April 3 without giving specific reasons for his resignation. President Nixon April 7 named John W. Warner, a Navy and Marine Corps veteran and undersecretary of the Navy since 1969, to replace Chafee as secretary of the Navy.

[3] USO inquiry under way. The Defense Department April 14 acknowledged that it had opened an investigation into the worldwide operations of the United Service Organization (USO) after receiving reports from Gen. Creighton Abrams, commander of U.S. forces in Vietnam, on charges of fraud and black market profiteering by USO personnel. Pentagon spokesmen declined to elaborate on the USO inquiry, but one report said that the Pentagon inquiry was centering on the alleged black-market sale of U.S. currency and the defrauding of servicemen by USO personnel in South Vietnam. (The USO, a 31-year-old organization, had a budget of about $6 million, most of it from private sources.) The government's investigation was strengthened by the disclosure April 18 by the USO president, retired Gen. Francis L. Sampson, that the "preliminary findings" of an internal investigation begun by the USO in March indicated that four or five former USO employees had been involved in alleged financial irregularities. According to Sampson, the "alleged irregularities have to do principally with certain individuals allegedly using certain USO clubs in Vietnam as a conduit for converting black market money into U.S. dollars." However, Sampson denied that U.S. soldiers had been defrauded by USO personnel. Alleged black market activities by USO personnel also came under Congressional scrutiny April 19 when Rep. Les Aspin (D, Wis.) made public the text of purported interviews with two unidentified former USO employees. The interviews gave details of alleged fraud and financial wrongdoing, including the alleged diversion of cigarettes to the black market and the theft and black-market sale of USO equipment. The interviews also charged that alleged black market activity was common knowledge among USO personnel. The final version of the USO internal investigation report, released June 15, said that evidence had been found of currency manipulations, black-market activities, mail-order fraud and other corrupt activities.

[4] Combat bonus offered. The Army and Marine Corps June 1 began to offer a $1,500 cash enlistment bonus to recruits who signed up for duty in the services' combat units—the infantry, artillery and armor. The new combat bonus would be paid only after the volunteer had completed basic training and had been accepted in a combat unit. In order to qualify for the bonus, the recruit would also have to enlist for four years. (The present tour of duty for combat service was two years.) The new bonus system was in effect between June 1 and Aug. 31.

[5] Army to double WAC force. Brig. Gen. Mildred C. Bailey, director of the Women's Army Corps (WAC), said Aug. 7 that the Army planned to double the size of the WAC force by 1978 and give it almost any type of assignment except combat. The Army's intention to use more women in more roles was seen as a move to ease the problems in achieving an all-volunteer Army by mid-1973. Gen. Bailey said that the 13,320-WAC force would be increased to 15,900 by June 1973 and to 24,000 by June 1978. (During World War II, the corps had 100,000 members.) WACs were currently allowed to fill only 139 of the 484 Army assignments open to men. Under the new program, only 48 would be forbidden to them. In a related development, Adm. Elmo R. Zumwalt Jr., chief of naval operations, announced Aug. 8 that women in the Navy soon would be able to get assignments for general ship duty. At present, Navy women enlistees had been allowed on board only hospital and transport ships as nurses and doctors. Zumwalt linked the beginning of the policy to ratification by Congress of the equal rights amendment *(see* WOMEN'S RIGHTS). Zumwalt also ordered the Navy to accept application from women officers who wanted to serve as chaplains or civil engineers, to "open paths of progression to flag rank within the technical, managerial spectrum" in "essentially the same manner" as for men, to assign women to "the full spectrum of challenging billets [posts]" and to consider women for selection to the joint war colleges of the armed forces. Revising its policy to coincide with the other armed services, the Air Force said Nov. 22 that it would allow its women to hold virtually any noncombatant job.

[6] Abrams confirmed as Army chief of staff. After weeks of delay, the Senate Oct. 12 approved, 84-2, the nomination of Gen. Abrams as Army chief staff. Abrams, commander of U.S. forces in Vietnam since mid-1968, had been nominated by President Nixon June 20, but consideration of his nomination had been sidetracked while Senate hearings were under way into unauthorized bombing raids against North Vietnam ordered by Gen. John D. Lavelle.

[7] *Lavelle probe.* Gen. Lavelle, a former four-star general and former commander of U.S. Air Force Units in Vietnam, testified before the House Armed Services Committee June 12 that he had been relieved of his post in March and later demoted after ordering repeated and unauthorized bombing strikes against military targets in North Vietnam. (Lavelle said he had been offered the opportunity to remain in the Air Force as a two-star general, but instead accepted nomination for retirement as a three-star general. He was the only four-star general in modern U.S. history to be demoted upon retirement.) In his testimony before the committee, Lavelle said that, between November 1971 and March 1972, he had ordered his planes to make "in the neighborhood" of 20 unauthorized raids on military targets (most of them in an area 11-15 miles north of the demilitarized zone between North and South Vietnam) and had reported them to command headquarters as "protective reaction" missions. (Protective reaction designated offensive or defensive actions taken by U.S. pilots when they were fired upon or pinpointed by enemy radar controlling surface-to-air missiles.) Lavelle said he had taken full responsibility for the false bombing reports. He stated: "I think Gen. Abrams knew what I was doing. But I'm positive that Gen. Abrams had no idea what the reporting requirements were. He never worried about or sat down and debated on rules of engagement before we did it." Following the House investigation into the Lavelle case, the Senate Armed Services Committee Sept. 11 opened a full-scale investigation to determine if others shared the responsibility for the unauthorized raids. Lavelle's testimony conflicted with testimony he had given in June. In his Senate testimony, Lavelle said that he had "committed no wrong" in connection with the raids and that he had received permission from Abrams and Adm. Thomas H. Moorer (chairman of the Joint Chiefs of Staff) for a number of the bombing raids under investigation. Abrams Sept. 13 denied Lavelle's allegations and testified that he did not know the raids were unauthorized. The Senate Committee ended its investigation into the Lavelle case Oct. 6 with the general conclusion that the responsibility for the unauthorized raids lay solely upon Lavelle and with the decision to retire Lavelle with two-star rank. However, Lavelle himself, in a letter published Oct. 5, said that his officers had been told that "in the event of adverse publicity" from the raids, "we could expect full backing" from the joint chiefs. Lavelle conceded that he had not been specifically instructed to plan bombing strikes in the guise of protective reaction missions, but maintained that he began the practice because of what he took to be private encouragement from his superiors.

[8] *Court martial asked.* Air Force 1st Lt. Delbert R. Terrill Jr. June 21 swore out court-martial charges against Gen. Lavelle and said he would ask Defense Secretary Melvin Laird to investigate "the propriety of the conduct" of Lavelle's superiors. Terrill said he had acted because no fellow or superior officer had done so and because "any oath of allegiance requires that I at least speak out." He said that military discipline could not be maintained if "commanders are relieved and retired while others for like offenses are court-martialed and given dishonourable discharges." Terrill charged that Lavelle willfully disobeyed a lawful order and falsified official documents, and he asked Air Force Secretary Robert C. Seamans Jr. to initiate a formal probe. He also asked Laird to set up a court of inquiry to examine how Lavelle's alleged misconduct was handled by Abrams, Moorer, Air Force Chief of Staff Gen. John D. Ryan and Navy Pacific commander Adm. John S. McCain. The Air Force Oct. 24 dropped Terrill's charges, saying it had made a "thorough investigation of all facts and material" and had dropped the charges because the "interests of discipline" had already been served. Sgt. Lonnie Franks, the officer who first had reported the unauthorized bombing strikes, Nov. 3 filed new court martial charges against Lavelle and 23 other officers; but the Air Force dropped those charges Nov. 21 because "no new information was presented which would warrant further action."

[9] **Command procedures revised.** Faced with growing congressional concern over the unauthorized bombing of North Vietnam, Defense Secretary Laird Oct. 19 described new steps he said were aimed at "further strengthening" civilian control of the military. Among the new steps was creation of a new group of inspectors general in unified command headquarters to conduct regular checks of procedures to insure that orders from Washington were scrupulously carried out. The new group was to report to Laird through the Joint Chiefs of Staff. In another change, the Army, Navy, Air Force and Marine inspectors general would now report to their civilian service secretaries as well as to their respective military chiefs. Under the new setup, the defense secretary also had authority to direct the work of the newly established Defense Investigative Service, an agency which centralized the investigative units of each of the armed services. (The authority previously had been in the hands of the chiefs of the individual services.) Another step would direct a second deputy secretary of defense—a post just approved by Congress—to concentrate on maintaining operational control of forces in the field.

Navy Racial Disorders

[10] **46 hurt in Kitty Hawk brawl.** Racial brawls involving more than 100 men aboard the aircraft carrier Kitty Hawk off North Vietnam Oct. 12-13 resulted in injuries to 46 black and white crewmen. Three men seriously injured in the fighting were evacuated to a base hospital in the Philippines. The Navy said Oct. 17 that the clash began as a fight between black and white crewmen in the ship's mess deck and then spread to other parts of the Kitty Hawk. The Navy announced Oct. 22 that 21 black crewmen aboard the ship had been charged with assault and rioting and were to face courts-martial on the Kitty Hawk. (The trials were postponed until the ship returned to San Diego, where civilian lawyers could be provided.)

[11] 123 seamen shifted in Constellation dispute. The Navy Nov. 9 reassigned 123 crewmen aboard the aircraft carrier Constellation after the seamen, most of them black, refused to reboard the ship before resolution of grievances over alleged discrimination in assignments, ratings and discharges. (Capt. J. D. Ward Nov. 4 had placed the men, plus 14 others, on shore leave at the North Island Naval Air Station near San Diego after they refused to report for scheduled duty during a sit-down demonstration. Ward had ordered the men to return to the ship Nov. 9, but the 123 refused the order. Some of the dissidents said that the tense racial situation on board before the incident made them "fear for their lives" unless the dispute were settled on shore.) The 123 men were reassigned to three installations in the San Diego area—reportedly by direct order of the Bureau of Navy Personnel. Six of the 123 were discharged "under honorable conditions," according to a Navy announcement Nov. 18. Two were given honorable discharges, and the other four general discharges. In addition to those six, 23 other crewmen were reported Nov. 25 to have received administrative discharges for inability to adjust to Navy life or because of "personality problems." Most of the other protesters were punished in the form of fines and loss of pay, extra work duties and reduction in rank. (All of the punishments and the discharges were based on the findings of captain's mast hearings Nov. 10-18.)

[12] New clashes reported. Two other clashes between black and white seamen were reported by the Navy. One clash involved 130 sailors at the naval station on Midway Island in the Pacific Nov. 25. Four white sailors and a black sustained minor injuries in the incidents, which reportedly began with a dispute between blacks and whites at a recreation area. A second clash was reported Nov. 26 at the Navy Correctional Center in Norfolk, Va. Navy officials said that 33 sailors (32 blacks and one white) remained confined at the center as the result of the fighting. According to the Navy, the 32 black sailors burned mattresses, smashed a door and defied Marine guards trying to confine four demonstrators.

See also BUDGET; CRIME [9]; DEFENSE; DRAFT & WAR PROTEST; DRUG USE & ADDICTION [1-2]; EDUCATION [8]; GREECE [5]; SELECTIVE SERVICE SYSTEM; SPACE [3]; WAR CRIMES; WOMEN'S RIGHTS

MILLS, WILBUR D.—*See* ELECTIONS [3-6, 17]

MINES—Pension suit award. U.S. District Court Judge Gerhard A. Gesell Jan. 7 announced an $11.5 million damage award against the United Mine Workers of America (UMW), the National Bank of Washington, former National Bank President Barnum Colton and Josephine Roche, the former neutral trustee for the UMW Welfare and Retirement Fund. (Gesell had upheld charges of mismanagement and conspiracy concerning the fund in April 1971. The charges had been made by a group of miners, widows and disabled and retired miners, who said that substantial amounts of the fund had been left in noninterest-bearing accounts at the bank, in which the union owned 75% of the stock.) The suit award was to be paid into the fund for distribution to its 70,000 beneficiaries.

Yablonski case. The trial for the 1969 murder of Joseph A. Yablonski, his wife and daughter—all killed three weeks after Yablonski had lost a controversial election for president of the UMW *(see below)*—revealed during 1972 the alleged involvement of officials in the UMW. In the events of the Washington, Pa. trial: Paul E. Gilly, a Cleveland house painter, was found guilty of first-degree murder March 1 and was sentenced March 2 to death in the electric chair; Mrs. Paul Gilly April 11 pleaded guilty to charges of murder and conspiracy in exchange for a state offer to spare her life; Mrs. Gilly's confession, produced in court April 13, implicated in the murder UMW President W.A. (Tony) Boyle, UMW Vice President George J. Titler, UMW Secretary-Treasurer John Owens, UMW District 19 Secretary-Treasurer Albert Pass and UMW Tennessee field representative William J. Prater; Silous Huddleston, a former UMW official in Tennessee and father of Mrs. Gilly,

May 3 confessed that he had orchestrated the murder and pleaded guilty to three counts of murder in exchange for a state offer to spare his life; Huddleston's confession said that he had received payoff money, which he believed was union money, for the murder from Pass and Prater. Prater was arrested by agents of the Federal Bureau of Investigation (FBI) April 12 in Lake City, Tenn. on the basis of federal grand jury indictments that charged him with conspiracy to violate federal laws prohibiting interference with the rights of a union member, obstruction of justice and obstruction of an investigation. Pass, a member of the UMW's 26-man international executive board as well as secretary-treasurer of District 19, was arrested May 2 by the FBI in Middlesboro, Ky. on the basis of federal grand jury indictments charging him with the same crimes. Both men were also indicted July 17 by a Washington County, Pa. grand jury on charges of murder, and Aug. 23 by a federal grand jury in Cleveland on charges of conspiracy to influence witnesses to give false testimony concerning the slayings. Also indicted on the latter two charges were District 19 field representatives Chester Philpot and Ernest Stults. Named as co-conspirators were Corwin E. Ross, George W. Hall and Noah Doss. (Doss and Hall Sept. 1 had also pleaded guilty to embezzlement charges involving $1,135 of union funds.) The four conspirators in the federal indictment were charged with having distributed $19,970 in checks drawn from union funds to miners, including Hall and Doss, who were told to cash them and return the cash to the officials. The indictment also charged that Prater had given $15,000 in cash to Silous Huddleston.

Boyle convicted. Tony Boyle was convicted by a federal court jury in Washington March 31 of conspiracy and making illegal political contributions with union funds. The indictment against Boyle had charged that $49,250 had been illegally channeled to political campaigns, most of it through the union's legislative arm. Two other union officials indicted with Boyle—Owens and lobbyist James Kmetz—were acquitted. Boyle June 27 was sentenced to five years in prison and fined $130,000. The total assessment against Boyle, including the $49,250 illegally contributed, was $179,250. U.S. District Court Judge Charles R. Richey imposed the maximum sentence on two counts against Boyle, but provided that the two five-year prison terms should run concurrently. On each of 11 other counts, he imposed maximum fines but suspended imposition of a jail sentence, requiring instead a two-year probation period and payment of the $49,250 from Boyle's own funds.

Boyle election voided. U.S. District Court Judge William A. Bryant in Washington May 1 overturned the 1969 election victory of Boyle over Yablonski. Bryant said that the evidence of wrongdoing by Boyle and other UMW officials in the election was "too strong to resist." He specifically described examples of the improper use of union funds and apparatus to promote Boyle's campaign. The case had been initiated by the U.S. Department of Labor, which had sought to have the election overturned and a new election under federal supervision ordered.

New election ordered. Bryant June 16 ordered a new election to be held in December, and put the internal affairs of the UMW under the direct supervision of the secretary of labor until after the election. The Labor Department June 20 named Ronald T. Weakley as its overseer at the union. Bryant's decision also set other strictures upon governance of the union until the election. Among other actions, he: authorized opponents to the current UMW leadership to put observers in the union headquarters in Washington and in district and sub-district offices; ordered all union employees to account for their time and expenses; and curbed the union's ability to make loans and to hire new employees.

UMW ousts Boyle leadership. Boyle was defeated for re-election as president of the UMW in a court-supervised election Dec. 1-8 closely watched by the Department of Labor. The winner was Arnold Miller, a partly disabled coal miner suffering from black lung *(see below)* who was supported by rank-and-file insurgents rallying under the banner of Miners for Democracy. Boyle resigned as president Dec. 18 and was voted a pension of $50,000 a year. Leonard J. Pnakovich, incumbent vice president defeated in the voting, became interim president after Boyle's resignation. The final tally in the elections, completed Dec. 16: Miller 70,373 votes; Boyle 56,334. Miller's running mates—vice presidential candidate Mike Trbovich and secretary-treasurer candidate Harry Patrick—also were victors. Miller's election as president was certified by a federal court Dec. 22, and he was sworn into office the same day. Miller immediately removed 20 members of the UMW executive board appointed by Boyle, retaining only four board members who had been elected. Miller filled 14 of the board vacancies on an "interim" basis and called for elections for board members and all other district posts.

91 die in silver mine blaze. A smoldering blaze at the 3,700-foot level of the Sunshine Silver Mine (the largest and richest such facility in the U.S.) near Kellogg, Ida. erupted savagely May 2, releasing flames, smoke and carbon monoxide fumes that blocked crucial exit routes for miners working in a large shaft. At least 35 were killed immediately, 108 escaped and many others were missing. A week-long rescue effort was undertaken by state and federal officials who hoped that some of the miners might have been able to reach air pockets in the 88-year-old mine. However, only two miners were found alive May 9. The dead totaled 91. The blaze was thought to have begun through either spontaneous combustion or electrical failure. Sunshine officials said the fire was a "1 in 50 million shot" and that elaborate safety precautions had been taken. However, a report of the Bureau of Mines, made public May 3, showed that the mine had failed to correct numerous hazards found during a November 1971 inspection. Byron Schulz, the last miner out of the mine when the fire was discovered, May 15 told a hearing of the House Select Subcommittee on Labor that there were an insufficient number of respirators in the mine, that many men did not know how to use the safety equipment and that some of the equipment was defective. Spokesmen from the United Steelworkers Union, also testifying the same day, charged Sunshine with a "callous and serious" disregard for safety. J. Davitt McAteer, an associate of Ralph Nader who conducted a three-day study of the disaster scene, testified May 18 that fire escape plans at the mine were outdated, escape routes were inadequately marked, and few men knew of their location. Assistant Secretary of the Interior Hollis M. Dole said May 16 that the Sunshine Company did not keep an adequate check of the number of men in the mine. Union officials had charged earlier that rescue attempts were thwarted because there was no way to determine the number of men in the shafts.

Other disasters. An explosion in the Wankie Colliery Co. coal mine in northwest Rhodesia June 6 trapped 468 men in a sloping shaft hundreds of feet below the surface. Rescue efforts were halted entirely June 7 by two small explosions and escaping poisonous gas. The final death toll was reported July 4 as 427. A fire, started by a machine striking an electrical cable, July 22 trapped nine miners more than a mile underground in a Blacksville, W.Va. mine operated by the Consolidation Coal Co. Despite two days of intensive rescue efforts, an explosion July 24 ended all hope of finding the men alive; and the mine was sealed. Seventeen miners who attempted to extinguish a blaze in a coal mine in Ipswich, Australia July 31 were killed by two gas explosions. An underground explosion Oct. 21 in a coal mine northeast of Teheran, Iran trapped 34 of 38 miners. At least 16 coal miners were reported killed Oct. 23 by two underground explosions near the Black Sea town of Zonguldak, Turkey. Leaking coke gas was believed to have caused a Dec. 16 explosion at a newly built Weirton Steel Co. coke plant in Weirton, W.Va. in which 19 men were killed.

Black lung bill liberalized. A bill liberalizing the eligibility provisions of legislation to aid coal miners afflicted with black lung disease (pneumoconiosis) was approved by the Senate May 4 and the House May 10. In a statement announcing that he had signed the bill, President Nixon noted May 30 his "mixed emotions" about approval "because of the precedent it tends to establish" for federal authority in the area of workmen's compensation normally assumed by the states. The bill extendeᴄ federal assumption of costs from Dec. 31, when it was due to expire, to July 1, 1973 and set Jan. 1, 1974 as the date the cost responsibility would fall to coal mine operators. In liberalizing eligibility standards, Congress authorized disability benefits to orphans or to dependent parents, brothers or sisters of a deceased miner, as well as to miners and widows. It also included any respiratory ailment under coverage of total disability payments and barred denial of claims solely on the basis of a negative chest X-ray, which often failed to detect black lung.

See also CHILE [1, 7-9, 15]; FLOODS; GREAT BRITAIN [1, 8-9]

MINIMUM WAGE—*See* LABOR
MITCHELL, JOHN N.—*See* ELECTIONS [11]; NIXON, RICHARD MILHOUS; POLITICS [3-4, 7, 9, 12]
MITCHELL, MARTHA—*See* ELECTIONS [11, 19]
MODEL CITIES—*See* HOUSING; STATE & LOCAL GOVERNMENTS
MONGOLIA—*See* SPACE [22]
MOON—*See* SPACE [4, 8-19]

MOROCCO—Coup trial. A total of 1,081 army officers and men went on trial Jan. 31 in Kenitra, north of Rabat, for their part in the 1971 attempted coup against King Hassan II. In what was considered a surprise verdict, the military court Feb. 29 acquitted all but 73 of the defendants. The court gave one death sentence and 72 sentences ranging from one year to life imprisonment.

New constitution. King Hassan announced Feb. 17, and Moroccans overwhelmingly approved March 1, a new constitution by which Hassan hoped to achieve a reform of the administration, the distribution of wealth "in a manner compatible with the spirit of socialism in Islam", and "impartial justice." Under the constitution, two-thirds of the members of the Chamber of Deputies were to be elected by direct universal suffrage and one-third was to be named by local political and economic groups. (In the previous assembly, these proportions had been reversed.) Hassan retained the power to name the entire government, to dissolve the assembly and to rule by decree in case of emergency.

Cabinet resigns. King Hassan March 3 accepted the resignations of the Cabinet headed by Premier Mohamed Karim Lamrani. Premier Lamrani formed a new government April 12. The post of deputy premier was created, to be filled by Justice Minister and Secretary General of the Government Hadj M'Hammed Bahnini. Six of the 19 officials were new appointees. (In a later development, Hassan Nov. 2 appointed his brother-in-law and chief administrative aide, Ahmed Osman, as the new premier and instructed him to form a government.)

Coup fails. King Hassan Aug. 16 escaped an attempt on his life Aug. 16 when Moroccan Air Force jets fired on his plane as he was returning from a trip to France and Spain. Three of the five jets sent to escort Hassan's Boeing 727 began firing when the royal airliner crossed into Moroccan territory at Tetuan. Hassan's plane was badly damaged. According to Hassan's brother, Prince Moulay Abdullah, the king broadcast a radio appeal to the attackers, claiming he was the mechanic and asking them to stop firing since the king had been "mortally wounded" and other lives might be spared. The jets retired, but continued escorting the plane to Rabat airport. Upon landing, Hassan went ahead with scheduled welcoming ceremonies, during which as many as eight jets carried out a second attack which reportedly killed eight persons and wounded 47, including four government ministers. Hassan escaped by taking refuge in a nearby grove of trees. Later he was driven to the city, where jets fired on the guest house adjoining the royal palace.

Most of the planes returned to their base at Kenitra, but one was ditched at sea off Rabat. The pilot of the abandoned plane was picked up by ship, and two other air force officers were returned to Morocco by British authorities at Gibraltar after a helicopter they had commandeered landed there. Defense

Minister Gen. Mohamed Oufkir Aug. 16 sent troops against the Kenitra base, which surrendered without a fight. Oufkir, long believed to be the strongest of Hassan's followers, committed suicide Aug. 17 when he was informed that the king had been told by two officers implicated in the plot that Oufkir had led the coup. Hassan said Aug. 19 that Oufkir had planned to rule the country through a 10-man regency council that would have been established to govern on behalf of Crown Prince Sidi Mohamed, Hassan's nine-year-old son. Hassan said Oufkir had no plans to declare a republic or to share power, since no other officer of his rank had been involved in the plot. The king also announced that he was abolishing the posts of defense minister and army chief of staff (also held by Oufkir), and was taking direct control of the armed forces himself. The post of defense minister was reinstated Sept. 14, and Justice Minister Bahnini was appointed to fill the position.

11 doomed for plot. Eleven officers of the Moroccan air force were sentenced to death Nov. 7 for their part in the unsuccessful coup. The 11 included: seven persons who had piloted the planes which strafed Hassan's jetliner; Col. Mohamed Amigrane, who directed the attack against the king's jetliner; Maj. Kouera el-Ouafi, who had led the jet fighters against the plane; 2nd Lt. Lyazid Midaoui, in charge of security at the Kenitra air base; and Capt. Larbe Bel Hadj, responsible for operations at the base's control tower. Prison terms of 3-20 years were given to 32 other defendants, while 177 soldiers attached to the Kenitra base were acquitted.

See also ATOMIC ENERGY [6]; INTERNATIONAL MONETARY DEVELOPMENTS [9]

MORPHINE—*See* DRUG USE & ADDICTION [18]
MORSE, WAYNE—*See* ELECTIONS [29]
MORTON, ROGERS C. B.—*See* CONSERVATION; ENVIRONMENT; INDIANS, AMERICAN; NIXON, RICHARD MILHOUS; POLLUTION [10]

MOTION PICTURES—Academy awards. The 44th annual awards of the Academy of Motion Picture Arts and Sciences were presented in Los Angeles April 9. *The French Connection,* a crime drama about international narcotics smuggling, captured five "Oscars," including best picture, best actor (Gene Hackman), best director (William Friedkin), best script from another medium (Ernest Tidyman) and best film editing. The other winners: **best actress**—Jane Fonda *(Klute);* **supporting actress**—Cloris Leachman *(The Last Picture Show);* **supporting actor**—Ben Johnson *(The Last Picture Show);* **foreign language film**—*The Garden of the Finzi Continis;* **original score**—Isaac Hayes (theme from *Shaft);* **cinematography**—Oswald Morris *(Fiddler on the Roof);* **special visual effects**—Danny Lee, Eustace Lycett, Alan Maley *(Bedknobs and Broomsticks);* **sound**—Gordon K. McCallum, David Hildyard *(Fiddler on the Roof);* **documentary feature**—David L. Wolper Productions *(The Hellstrom Chronicle);* **costume design**—Yvonne Blake, Antonio Castillo *(Nicholas and Alexandra);* **art direction**—John Box, Ernest Archer, Jack Maxsted, Gil Parrondo *(Nicholas and Alexandra,* Vernon Dixon, set direction); **original song score**—John Williams *(Fiddler on the Roof);* **original dramatic score**—Michel Legrand *(Summer of '42);* **screenplay based on material not previously published or produced**—Paddy Chayefsky *(The Hospital);* **short subject** (animated)—Maxwell-Petok Productions *(The Crunch Bird);* **short subject** (live action)—Producciones Concord *(Sentinels of Silence);* **documentary** (short subject)—*Sentinels of Silence.* A special Oscar was given to silent-screen star Charlie Chaplin, 82, for the "humor and humanity he brought to films." The audience gave the comedian a standing ovation.

See also TELEVISION & RADIO [6]

MOTORCYCLES—*See* AUTOMOBILES
MOZAMBIQUE—*See* BRAZIL; CHURCHES; PORTUGAL
MUJIBUR RAHMAN, SHEIK—*See* BANGLA DESH [1, 3-6, 8, 10, 14, 16]
MUSIC—*See* PULITZER PRIZES; RECORD INDUSTRY

MUSKIE, EDMUND S.—*See* ELECTIONS [2-7, 17, 29]; POLITICS [12]
MYLAI MASSACRE—*See* WAR CRIMES

NATIONAL SECURITY—*See* SECURITY, U.S.
NATIONAL SECURITY COUNCIL (NSC)—*See* SECURITY, U.S.
NATIONAL STUDENT ASSOCIATION (NSA)—*See* DRAFT & WAR PROTEST
NATIONAL TENANTS ORGANIZATION—*See* ELECTIONS [20]
NATIONAL WARNING SYSTEM—*See* TELEVISION & RADIO [5]
NATIONAL WELFARE RIGHTS ORGANIZATION (NWRO)—*See* ELECTIONS [20]
NATURAL GAS—*See* POLLUTION [3]
NAURU—*See* EUROPEAN ECONOMIC COMMUNITY [7]
NAVY, U.S.—*See* DEFENSE; DRUG USE & ADDICTION [2]; ELECTIONS [9]; GREECE [1, 5]; MILITARY [2, 5, 9-12]; PUERTO RICO; SOVIET-U.S. RELATIONS [1, 4]
NAZIS—*See* AUSTRIA; GERMANY, WEST [1]; NETHERLANDS

NEGROES—Census reports nonwhite data. In an annual report on the social and economic status of Negroes, released July 13, the Bureau of the Census reported that 31.8% of black families were headed by women in 1971, a rise from 28% in 1970, and that median black family income continued to be about 60% of white family income in 1971. The report found no significant change in the number of black or white families living below the poverty level ($4,137 a year for a nonfarm family of four), with 7.4 million blacks in that category in 1971. Unemployment among nonwhites averaged 9.9% in 1971, while the rate for whites was 5.4%. Among families in the North and West in which both husband and wife worked, black income reached 104% of white income in 1971, partly because more black women worked year-round. The high school dropout rate for blacks 14-19 years old declined to 11.1% in 1971 from 14.6% in 1970, while the white rate of 7.4% remained unchanged.

World black unity meeting held. About 2,500 American, African and West Indian blacks met in San Diego Sept. 3 at the Second International Congress of African People. The meeting, boycotted by the U.S. Congressional Black Caucus and the National Association for the Advancement of Colored People (NAACP), called for the creation of a black political party in the U.S., which would merge into a worldwide black party.

See also AUSTRALIA [1]; BLACK MILITANTS; CHURCHES; CIVIL RIGHTS; CONGRESS; ELECTIONS [3, 15, 24, 36, 40]; HEALTH; HIJACKING [5]; MILITARY [10-12]; OLYMPICS [3]; POLITICS [1, 8]; RHODESIA; SOUTH AFRICA [3-5, 10]

NEPAL—*See* HEALTH

NETHERLANDS—Wildcat strikes. About 20,000 shipbuilding workers staged wildcat strikes Feb. 4 in Rotterdam and Amsterdam following a court injunction prohibiting a 24-hour strike organized by unions against 16 metal-working companies. The unions were involved in a wage dispute with the industry.

Plans to release Nazis abandoned. Premier Barend Biesheuvel and Justice Minister Andreas Van Agt announced March 4 that the government would abandon plans to release the last three Nazi war criminals still serving life sentences in Dutch prisons. The announcement came after the Tweede Kamer (second chamber of the lower house of parliament) March 1 approved, by an 85-61 vote, a Socialist motion urging the government to reject clemency for the three prisoners. The three—in jail for 27 years—were Franz Fischer and Ferdinand Aus der Fuenten, both responsible for the deportation of over 80,000 Jews who died in concentration camps during World War II, and Joseph Kotaella, convicted of extreme cruelty to Jewish prisoners.

Cabinet resigns. Premier Biesheuvel's Cabinet resigned July 20 after Transport Minister Willem Drees Jr. and Scientific Research Minister Jonkheer Mauritz L. de Brauw resigned July 17 and the five-party coalition lost its majority in the Tweede Kamer. Queen Juliana asked the government to remain in a caretaker capacity pending her decision on whether to accept the resignations. She asked Biesheuvel July 22 to form a new government. Drees and de Brauw, who both belonged to the Democratic Socialist '70 party (DS '70, a right-wing Socialist splinter group), resigned in protest against the government's proposals to deal with an expected $1 billion deficit in the 1973 budget. The two had proposed an immediate wage and price freeze and cuts in defense spending to curb inflation, but the Cabinet had rejected their proposal. The two ministers charged that their ministries were being forced to bear an unfair share of the government's planned anti-inflationary budget cuts. Their defection from the government reduced the coalition's representation from 82 to 74 in the 150-seat Tweede Kamer.

Cabinet crisis resolved. Following talks with Queen Juliana, Biesheuvel announced Aug. 9 that the ministers of four parties of the former coalition would remain in office as a minority Cabinet until new general elections were held in November. The Liberals and the three confessional parties—the Calvinist Anti-Revolutionary party, the Catholic People's party and the Protestant Christian Historical Union—had agreed Aug. 8 to constitute a minority government under Biesheuvel and to prepare for elections. The DS '70 refused to rejoin the Cabinet.

Elections show left gains. General elections Nov. 29 resulted in a gain for a four-party left-wing coalition at the expense of the center-right parties that formed the outgoing Cabinet. The parliamentary representation of the original five-party coalition government was 76, reducing their majority in the Tweede Kamer to one. The election results (1971 strength in parentheses): Catholic People's—27 (35); Christian Historical Union—7 (10); Anti-Revolutionary party—14 (13); Liberals—22 (16); DS '70—6 (8); Labor—43 (39); Democracy '66—6 (11); Radical Political party—7 (2); Communist—7 (6); Farmers—3 (1); others—8 (8). The failure of any one group to emerge with a substantial majority pointed to another long government crisis. Queen Juliana began consultations Dec. 1 with the leaders of the parties that had won parliamentary seats. The outgoing Cabinet was to remain in a caretaker capacity until a new government was installed.

Rotterdam riots. Tensions caused by the influx during recent years of 150,000 foreign laborers erupted in violence Aug. 9 as Dutch youths fought with Turkish workers in Rotterdam. The riots began after a Turkish boarding house evicted a Dutch tenant and her three children. Neighbors who went to the woman's aid were stabbed by the landlord. Skirmishes between the two communities continued for five days, with gangs of Dutch youths smashing windows of Turkish-owned buildings. More than 40 persons were arrested and many were hospitalized with knife wounds.

Price controls imposed. The Cabinet Nov. 21 imposed statutory price controls, backdated to Aug. 15, in an attempt to curb spiraling prices. The controls replaced an early warning system instituted Oct. 27 and came shortly before industry and labor planned to sign a "social contract" on wages and prices. (Certain industries refused to sign the pact, which would have voluntarily frozen profit margins for a year, because of the imposition of the statutory controls. However, the pact was signed Dec. 7. It provided for a 3.5% maximum wage rise, plus compensation for cost-of-living increases; a price hike limit of 5.75%; and the freezing of profit margins.)

See also ATOMIC ENERGY [6]; CHESS; EUROPEAN ECONOMIC COMMUNITY [1]; HIJACKING [17]; INDOCHINA WAR [22]; INTERNATIONAL MONETARY DEVELOPMENTS [2, 6, 9]; OIL & NATURAL GAS; PERU; POLLUTION [13]; ROMAN CATHOLIC CHURCH; SPACE [24]

NEW GUINEA—*See* AUSTRALIA [5-6, 11]

NEWSPAPERS—Right to silence curbed. The Supreme Court June 29 ruled 5-4 that journalists had no constitutional right to refuse to testify before grand juries about information they obtained in confidence. In the majority opinion, Justice Byron White, joined by the four Nixon appointees to the court, said that "the public interest in pursuing and prosecuting those crimes reported to the press" took precedence over the public interest in some future news that might not be divulged to reporters if confidentiality were compromised. White wrote that establishing a First Amendment "newsman's privilege" would require still further rulings about pamphleteers, lecturers, pollsters and scholarly researchers. Only bad faith attempts by prosecutors to harass reporters could come under constitutional censure, White said. In response to a dissenting opinion by Justice Potter Stewart warning that governments might try "to annex the journalistic profession as an investigative arm of government," Justice Lewis Powell wrote in a separate opinion that "the solicitude repeatedly shown by this court for First Amendment freedoms" should dispel such fears. The ruling was made in three cases of conviction for civil contempt: the 1970 refusal by New York Times reporter Earl Caldwell to enter a grand jury room where the Black Panther party was under investigation; the refusal by New Bedford, Mass. television newsman Paul Pappas to reveal to a grand jury what transpired at a Panther headquarters he had visited; and the refusal by Louisville (Ky.) Courier-Journal reporter Paul M. Branzburg to testify before grand juries about illegal drug use he had witnessed. Laws in 18 states, as well as pending Congressional legislation, gave journalists some protection against disclosing confidential information.

See also ARGENTINA [18]; BRAZIL; CANADA [10]; ELECTIONS [46]; KOREA, SOUTH; PENTAGON PAPERS; PERU; PHILIPPINES [5-6, 9]; PORTUGAL; PULITZER PRIZES; SINO-U.S. RELATIONS [10]; UNITED NATIONS; URUGUAY [4-6]; VIETNAM, SOUTH

NEW YORK STOCK EXCHANGE (NYSE)—See STOCK MARKET

NEW ZEALAND—Holyoake resigns; Marshall installed. Sir Keith Holyoake, prime minister of New Zealand for nearly 12 years, Feb. 2 formally announced his resignation at a caucus of his ruling National party. The caucus then chose Deputy Prime Minister John Marshall as the new prime minister and Finance Minister Robert Muldoon, Marshall's only opponent for the post, as deputy prime minister. The changes were designed to revitalize the party's image for federal elections in November. Marshall assumed the post of prime minister Feb. 7 and carried out a major government reorganization Feb. 9. In the reorganization: Holyoake retained his post as foreign affairs minister; Education Minister Brian Talboys was appointed overseas trade minister, a post previously held by Marshall; Allan McCready, postmaster general, was named defense minister to replace David Thomson, who was switched to the Labor Ministry; Sir Roy Jack, speaker of the House of Representatives, was named justice minister and attorney general; Duncan MacIntyre, lands and forests minister, was named to also head the newly created Environment Ministry; George Gair was named customs minister; Leslie Gandar was named minister of science, electricity and mines and to head the new Ministry of Fuel and Power; Eric Holland was named housing minister; and David Highet was named internal affairs minister.

Anti-inflationary program. Prime Minister Marshall March 27 announced an economic stabilization program that would freeze profit margins, restrict wage and price increases to cover cost of living rises only, and authorize incentives to stimulate industry. The plan, said to contain the strictest anti-inflationary measures since World War II, would provide for a new enforcement authority that would make spot checks on accounts. The Federation of Labor, the nation's largest trade union, said it would not cooperate in the implementation of the program, which was to be in effect for at least a year.

1973 budget. The government June 22 presented to Parliament a budget for fiscal 1973. The budget, designed to spur economic growth, called for a 16% increase in government expenditures to an estimated record of $NZ2.16 billion ($US2.61 billion), including a $NZ100 million rise in spending on social services. Measures designed to stimulate the economy included a 10% reduction in personal income tax, the doubling of family allowances for each child to $NZ3 a week, substantial increases in welfare benefits to pensioners, higher and more widely applied investment allowances, improved export incentives and plans to make the payroll tax levy deductible.

Labor party returns to power. The opposition Labor party won an unexpected sweeping victory Nov. 25 in general elections. The victory, giving the Labor party its third period in office, ended the 12-year rule of the National party. With a gain of about 4.8% of the vote over the previous election in 1969, Labor won 55 seats in Parliament, while the National party won 32 seats. In the earlier, smaller Parliament, Labor held 40 seats and the National party 44. Labor's impressive victory surprised most observers. In his concession statement Nov. 25, Prime Minister Marshall indicated that the Labor victory might be attributed to the fact that the National party government had been obliged to follow unpopular policies in the previous three years to restrain wages and prices. Labor's Norman E. Kirk was designated to succeed Marshall.

Cabinet sworn in. A new 20-member Cabinet assumed power Dec. 8 following the Labor victory. The new ministers included: prime minister and foreign—Kirk; deputy prime minister and labor—Hugh Watt; finance—William Rowling; foreign trade and deputy foreign minister—Joseph Walding; trade and industry—W. W. Freer; justice—A. M. Finlay; defense—A.J. Faulkner; transport—Sir Basil Arthur; education—P.A. Amos; agriculture and fisheries—C. J. Moyle; Maori affairs—Matiu Rata (a Maori); and tourism—Whelu Tirikatene-Sullivan (a Maori).

See also ATOMIC ENERGY [6, 13]; AUSTRALIA [4]; CONSERVATION; HEALTH; INTERNATIONAL MONETARY DEVELOPMENTS [8]; PAKISTAN [7]

NICARAGUA—Liberals win elections. President Anastasio Somoza Debayle's National Liberal party (PLN) swept constitutional assembly elections Feb. 6. According to a pact between the PLN and the opposition Conservatives, the winning party received 60 and the loser 40 of the 100 seats in a constituent assembly which was to meet April 15 to draft a constitution and to name a triumvirate which would rule Nicaragua between May 1, when Somoza was to step down, and presidential elections in September 1974. The parties' agreement also provided that two positions in the triumvirate would go to the winning party and one to the losing party.

A third of the electorate abstained from the elections. Three small opposition groups—the Liberal Constitutionalist Movement, the Christian Socialist party and the Independent Liberal party—had urged voters to remain away from the polls, calling the elections "a falsification of the electoral process" because of the pact. Opponents of the pact (including the three parties and the Roman Catholic Church) had charged the agreement would perpetuate the rule of the Somoza family, which had ruled Nicaragua directly and indirectly for 43 years. They noted that the new constitution would allow Somoza to run again for the presidency and charged that the PLN members of the triumvirate would still answer to the ex-president as head of their party. Somoza, moreover, was to remain as head of the National Guard, Nicaragua's only armed forces.

Somoza steps down. Somoza resigned as president May 2, yielding power to the triumvirate, which consisted of Defense Minister Roberto Martinez Lacayo (PLN), Agriculture Minister Alfonso Lobo Cordero (PLN) and Conservative leader Fernando Aguero. In its first session May 2, the triumvirate named five Liberals to Cabinet posts. Lorenzo Guerrero became foreign minister (replaced Oct. 25 by prominent jurist Alejandro Montiel Arguello); Jose Antonio Mora became education minister; Gen. Gustavo Montiel became finance minister; Juan Jose Martinez became economics minister; and Leandro Marin Abaunza became government minister.

See also EARTHQUAKES; EL SALVADOR

NIGER—Cabinet changes. President Hamani Diori Aug. 17 shuffled his Cabinet, naming Sabo Boukari as minister of foreign affairs to replace Barcourgne Courmo. Leopold Kaziende became minister of state for national defense, giving up his post as minister of public works, transport and urban affairs—a position taken by Harou Kouka.

See also AFRICA

NIGERIA—New budget announced. Maj. Gen. Yakubu Gowan, Nigerian head of state, March 31 announced the federal budget for the 1972-73 fiscal year. The budget was to include a capital expenditure of $723 million. Gowan said that progress during 1971 had been "most encouraging" and that the final phase of the government's civil war rehabilitation program, involving resumption of normal economic activities and repair of damaged public utilities, had "virtually been completed." In order to protect local industries and "induce a rapid increase in the employment level," a 65% super tax on the import of raw materials, levied during the war years, was being abolished. Import duties on raw materials were being reduced 5-10% and excise duties by an average of 50%.

Universities placed under federal control. The military government Aug. 24 placed the country's four state universities (Benin, Ife, Ahmadu Bello University at Zaria and the University of Nigeria at Nsukka) under federal control, making their status equal to that of Ibadan and Lagos, which had always been under national jurisdiction. The Supreme Military Council declared the move had been made in order to insure "a national direction in education so as to promote uniformity in content and standard." Other factors believed to have affected the takeover were a desire to train personnel for the country's development programs and a need to make Nigeria less dependent on foreign universities.

See also INTERNATIONAL MONETARY DEVELOPMENTS [8]

NIXON, PATRICIA—*See* ELECTIONS [25, 27]

NIXON, RICHARD MILHOUS—State of the Union message. President Nixon Jan. 20 presented to Congress a two-part State of the Union message—the first part verbal and the second part, a longer and more detailed treatment, written. The major thrust of the President's speech was that the Congress should enact his legislative proposals despite the political pressures of a presidential election year. Nixon asked Congress to make 1972 "a year of action" on his past legislative proposals. Among the 90 major proposals before Congress, the President cited programs to improve life for the aging, combat crime and drug abuse, improve health services, protect workers' pension rights, promote equal opportunity, expand consumer protection, improve the environment, revitalize rural America, "help the cities," launch new initiatives in education, improve transportation and "put an end to costly labor tie-ups in transportation." Nixon said he was presenting "only vital programs which are within the capacity of this Congress to enact, within the capacity of the budget to finance and...should be above partisanship." The only major new programs which Nixon discussed were: (1) a "revolutionary" proposal, to be presented later in 1972 after further Administration study, to "cope with the gathering crisis of school finance and property taxes"; and (2) a proposal, also to be explained in detail later in 1972, for some form of federal partnership with private industry in technological research to develop projects "to improve our everyday life."

The President cited one major budget thrust upward for more defense spending. "We must maintain the strength necessary to deter war," he emphasized; and increased defense spending was mandated by rising research and development costs, increased personnel wages and "the need to proceed with new weapons systems." Within that context, Nixon stated the goals of his foreign policy: to maintain a nuclear deterrent "adequate enough to meet any threat" to the U.S. or its allies; to help other nations develop defensive capability; to honor all treaty commitments; to "act to defend our interests whenever and wherever they are threatened"; to have a "limited" role wherever U.S. interests or treaty commitments were not involved; to "use our influence to prevent war"; to stop war if it came and, once the war was over, to "do our share in helping to bind up the wounds" of the participants. As part of the policy, the President said unequivocally that "we will not intervene militarily."

In other segments of his speech, Nixon was optimistic about the progress the nation had recently made and the strength of the American character. As "significant progress in these first years of the '70s," he cited the absence of civil disorders in the cities and colleges and universities, a beginning on environmental protection and a slowing of the rate of increase in crime. And, "because of the beginnings that have been made," he looked forward to 1972 as "the year in which America may make the greatest progress in 25 years toward achieving our goal of being at peace with all the nations of the world."

Democratic rebuttal. A team of 11 Congressional Democrats Jan. 21 appeared on television to rebut President Nixon's State of the Union message in what was billed as their own party's view of the state of the nation. The Democratic spokesmen charged that the President was prolonging the war in Indochina and neglecting problems at home. One of the spokesmen, House Speaker Carl Albert (Okla.), said that the Democratic-controlled Congress would pass in some form some of Nixon's major domestic proposals for welfare reform, revenue sharing and tougher water pollution curbs. However, Albert added, "cooperation is a two-way street. We are going to cooperate with the President on everything that is in the national interest. We simultaneously call upon the President to stop vetoing bills that are in the national interest." The Democrats came up with a new format to present their response to the President's message. Congressmen took turns criticizing the Administration and answering questions from a live studio audience and from telephone callers across the U.S. Sen. Thomas F. Eagleton (Mo.) was the moderator of the broadcast. Also appearing were Sens. William Proxmire (Wis.), Frank Church (Idaho), and Lloyd Bentsen (Tex.) and Reps. John Brademas (Ind.), Martha W. Griffiths (Mich.), Leonor K. Sullivan (Mo.), Ralph H. Metcalfe (Ill.) and John Melcher (Mont.) and House Majority Leader Hale Boggs (La.).

Appointments & Resignations

Stans, Mitchell resign for campaign posts. Secretary of Commerce Maurice Stans resigned Jan. 27 to head the fund-raising apparatus for President Nixon's re-election campaign. Nixon accepted Stans's resignation and nominated Peter G. Peterson, White House assistant for international affairs, to succeed him. (White House aide Peter M. Flanigan was also named to replace Peterson as assistant for international affairs.) Attorney General John N. Mitchell resigned Feb. 15, effective March 1, to head the President's campaign for re-election. (Mitchell had directed Nixon's 1968 presidential campaign.) The President Feb. 15 named Deputy Attorney General Richard G. Kleindienst to succeed Mitchell *(see* POLITICS [3-7]) and L. Patrick Gray 3rd, an assistant attorney general in charge of the Justice Department's Civil Division, as the new deputy. Kleindienst was approved as attorney general June 8 by a 64-19 vote in the Senate.

Connally leaves Cabinet. President Nixon May 16 announced the resignation of John B. Connally Jr. as Treasury secretary. Both men said the resignation, which came as a surprise to others, was the result of a private agreement between them that Connally would remain in the Treasury post only one year, later extended six months at the President's insistence. Nixon said that Connally would undertake "some temporary assignments" for the Administration. (Connally Aug. 9 announced formation of a Democrats for Nixon committee, with himself as national chairman.) Nixon also announced that George P. Shultz, director of the Office of Management and Budget (OMB), would succeed Connally and would be replaced at his OMB post by his deputy, Caspar Weinberger. Both Schultz and Weinberger were sworn in June 12.

Major staff revision. In his first White House statement following his re-election as President *(see* ELECTIONS [1-2, 36]), Nixon said Nov. 8 that he was planning a "significant" revision of his staff and the executive department. White House Press Secretary Ronald L. Ziegler, who made the Nixon announcement, said that Nixon expected to have all presidential appointees submit resignations so the President would feel free to undertake the revision. (While it was traditional for those at the highest levels of government to submit pro-forma resignations between terms, a public reminder from the White House was unusual, as was the extension of the custom to lower levels. Ziegler said that the President had requested resignation statements from some 2,000 officials, including 1,400-1,800 employees appointed to federal posts by agency heads.) The President began his major revision Nov. 28. Among the many changes (date of announcement in parentheses): Health, Education and Welfare (HEW) Secretary Elliot L. Richardson was appointed secretary of defense (Nov. 28), replacing Melvin R. Laird, who earlier had announced his intention to resign; OMB Director Weinberger was appointed to replace Richardson at HEW (Nov. 28); Roy L. Ash, president of Litton Industries, Inc., was appointed director of the OMB (Nov. 28); New York construction union leader Peter J. Brennan was nominated as secretary of labor (Nov. 29), replacing James D. Hodgson; the President accepted the resignations of Robert H. Finch as counselor to the President, Robert J. Brown as special assistant to the President and Harry S. Dent as special counsel to the President (Dec. 2); Cost of Living Council Director Donald Rumsfeld was named as U.S. representative to the North Atlantic Treaty Organization (Dec. 4), replacing David M. Kennedy, who was to remain available to the Administration for special assignments; Commerce Undersecretary James T. Lynn was nominated as secretary of housing and urban development (Dec. 5), replacing George W. Romney, who had resigned Nov. 27; South Carolina textile manufacturer Frederick Baily Dent was named commerce secretary (Dec. 6), replacing Peterson, who would undertake a special study for the President on coordinating U.S. economic policy with American trading partners; Claude S. Brinegar, a senior vice president of Union Oil Co. of California, was named transportation secretary (Dec. 7), replacing John A. Volpe, who was named U.S. ambassador to Italy; and Alexander P. Butterfield, a deputy assistant to the president, was named administrator of the Federal Aviation Administration (Dec. 19), replacing John H. Schaffer who planned to return to private life.

Nixon also made significant changes at lower levels in the federal government. However, he retained at their posts: Secretary of State William P. Rogers (announced Nov. 30);   Treasury Secretary Shultz, who also became an assistant to the President and head of a new Cabinet-level Council on Economic Policy (announced Dec. 1); Council of Economic Advisers Chairman Herbert Stein (announced Dec. 1); Presidential Assistant Flanigan (announced Dec. 1); National Security Affairs Adviser Henry Kissinger (announced Dec. 2); Presidential Assistant for Domestic Affairs John D. Ehrlichman (announced Dec. 2); Presidential Assistant H. R. Haldeman (announced Dec. 2); Secretary of Interior Rogers C. B. Morton (announced Dec. 5); Agriculture Secretary Earl G. Butz (announced Dec. 6); Attorney General Kleindienst (announced Dec. 8); and Environmental Protection Agency Administrator William D. Ruckelshaus (announced Dec. 20).

See also ABORTION; AUTOMOBILES; AVIATION; BUDGET; BUSINESS; CANADA [3]; CHINA, NATIONALIST; CIVIL RIGHTS [1-5, 13-14, 17]; CONGRESS; CONSUMER AFFAIRS [16]; CRIME [8]; DISARMAMENT; DRAFT & WAR PROTEST; DRUG USE & ADDICTION [1, 3, 5, 7]; EARTHQUAKES; ECONOMY [1, 5, 9-11]; EDUCATION [2, 4, 8]; ELECTIONS [1-9, 11, 13-14, 22-24, 26-29, 32-36, 38, 40, 46-47, 49]; ENVIRONMENT; ESPIONAGE; FEDERAL BUREAU OF INVESTIGATION; FLOODS; FOREIGN AID; FOREIGN POLICY; GREECE [6]; HIJACKING [6, 14, 18]; INDIANS, AMERICAN; INDOCHINA WAR [15, 20, 22-23, 35-36, 42-46, 52]; INTERNATIONAL MONETARY DEVELOPMENTS [3]; IRAN; JAPAN [4, 6];

LABOR; MEXICO; MIDDLE EAST [25]; MILITARY [2, 6]; MINES; OIL & NATURAL GAS; PENTAGON PAPERS; PESTICIDES; POLAND; POLITICS [1-4, 10, 12, 15]; POLLUTION [3, 12, 14-16]; POPULATION; POVERTY; RAILROADS; SECURITY, U.S.; SHIPS & SHIPPING; SINO-U.S. RELATIONS [1-5, 7-9, 11]; SOCIAL SECURITY; SOVIET-U.S. RELATIONS [1-4, 6-8, 12]; SPACE [1-2]; STORMS; TARIFFS & WORLD TRADE; TAXES; TELEVISION & RADIO [4-5, 10]; TERRITORIAL WATERS; UGANDA [3, 12]; WELFARE; WOMEN'S RIGHTS

NOBEL PRIZES—The 1972 Nobel Prizes, each worth about $100,000, were awarded Oct. 12-25 by the Swedish Royal Academy of Science in medicine, literature, chemistry, physics and economics. The Nobel Committee had announced Sept. 27 that the peace prize would not be awarded. (It was the 19th time since inception of the awards, and the first time since 1967, that the peace prize was not awarded.) The winners:

Medicine. The Royal Caroline Institute announced Oct. 12 that Dr. Gerald M. Edelman, a molecular biologist at Rockefeller University in New York, and Dr. Rodney R. Porter, a professor of biochemistry at Oxford University in Britain, had won the 1972 Nobel Prize for Physiology or Medicine. Both scientists had worked separately since 1959 on investigations of the basic structures of antibodies, the key to the defense mechanisms of the body. Their work, the institute said, had spurred research in all aspects of immunology, which led to practical applications in treating disease. They were to share the $101,000 prize.

Literature. The Swedish Academy announced Oct. 19 that West German novelist and playwright Heinrich Boll had won the 1972 Nobel Prize for Literature for his contribution to "a renewal of German literature" in the post-World War II years.

Chemistry. The Royal Academy Oct. 20 awarded the 1972 Nobel Prize in Chemistry to Dr. Stanford Moore and Dr. William Howard Stein of Rockefeller University and Dr. Christian B. Anfinsen of the National Institutes of Health in Bethesda, Md. for their explanation of the structure of enzymes (particularly ribonuclease, a catalyst in the digestive process). Half the $98,100 prize money was given to Moore, and the other half was shared by Stein and Anfinsen.

Physics. The Academy announced Oct. 20 that the 1972 Nobel Prize in Physics had been won by Dr. John Bardeen of the University of Illinois, Dr. Leon N. Cooper of Brown University and Dr. John Robert Schreiffer of the University of Pennsylvania for their joint development of a theory of superconductivity (the tendency of certain metals to lose all resistance to electric current at very low temperatures). The prize of more than $100,000 was to be shared equally. (Bardeen had shared a Nobel Prize in 1956, and was the first person to win a Nobel Prize twice in the same field.)

Economics. The 1972 Nobel Memorial Prize in Economics was shared Oct. 25 by Sir John R. Hicks of Oxford and Prof. Kenneth J. Arrow of Harvard University for their "pioneering contributions to general economic equilibrium theory and welfare theory." The prize of about $98,000 was to be shared equally.

See also UNION OF SOVIET SOCIALIST REPUBLICS [5]

NO-FAULT INSURANCE—*See* AUTOMOBILES
NOISE POLLUTION—*See* POLLUTION [1]
NONPUBLIC EDUCATION—*See* EDUCATION [2, 4]
NORFOLK ISLAND—*See* AUSTRALIA [7]

NORTH ATLANTIC TREATY ORGANIZATION (NATO)—**Large-scale maneuvers held.** NATO held a week-long set of maneuvers in Norway, ending Sept. 21. The maneuvers were believed to be among the largest ever held by NATO. The exercise, code-named Strong Express, featured more than 65,000 men, 350 ships and about 700 aircraft from 12 nations. It was designed to determine whether NATO could reinforce northern Norway in the event of conflict and prevent its occupation by an invading force. (The Soviet Union had concentrated a large number of forces near the Kola Peninsula area of northern Norway.) The maneuvers were monitored by a force of about 50 Soviet combat vessels, including 12 submarines.

See also ESPIONAGE; EUROPEAN SECURITY; MALTA; NIXON, RICHARD MILHOUS; TURKEY

NORTHERN IRELAND (ULSTER)—The continuing intercommunal violence in Ulster (see [2-7]), which included the death of 13 civilians shot by British soldiers during a banned protest march in Londonderry (see [3-6]), led to the imposition of direct rule by Great Britain and the resignation of the Ulster government during March (see [10-11]). However, despite temporary lulls, the violence continued. There were 121 assassinations in Northern Ireland in 1972—claiming the lives of 81 Catholics and 40 Protestants. The assassinations, together with other deaths resulting from the violence, raised the death toll in fighting to 676 since the outbreak of hostilities in 1969.

[2] Soldiers to use machine guns. In an effort to curb the continuing terrorist violence, the British army Jan. 5 authorized its soldiers in Ulster to use machine guns on city streets rather than solely for the defense of police stations. The revised orders allowed a commander on the spot to order machine gun fire against identified targets, instead of the "single, aimed shots" previously authorized. Soldiers also were authorized to open fire without warning at moving cars and to shoot without warning armed persons.

[3] British troops kill 13 civilians during Londonderry march. In the most violent clash between British soldiers and Ulster Catholics since the outbreak of civil unrest, British paratroopers Jan. 30 shot to death 13 civilians participating in a banned protest march in Londonderry. (Prime Minister Brian Faulkner Jan. 18 had ordered a one-year extension of the six-month parade ban imposed in August 1971.) Between 7,000 and 20,000 persons had participated in the Londonderry march to protest the internment without trial of suspected Irish Republican Army (IRA) terrorists. When the demonstrators found themselves blocked by army barricades, they proceeded to a meeting place in the Roman Catholic Bogside area, where Bernadette Devlin, Catholic civil rights leader and a member of the British Parliament from Ulster, was scheduled to address a rally. Demonstrators began to pelt soldiers with stones, bottles and debris; and the soldiers responded with gradually escalating violence, first spraying the demonstrators with purple dye and then firing rubber bullets and riot control gas canisters. As the tension increased, the paratroopers were sent over the barricades to scatter the mob. An army statement said that more than 200 paratroopers were ordered forward and opened fire after they came under nail bomb attack and sniper fire. The army said that the soldiers fired "only at identified targets" during the 30-minute battle that ensued, while over 200 rounds were fired indiscriminately at the soldiers. Witnesses, including several leading Ulster politicians and priests, countered the army's account with charges that the paratroopers had been the first to open fire and had fired directly into the crowd.

[4] *Response to deaths.* Both the militant "Provisional" and the leftist "Official" wings of the IRA Jan. 31 vowed reprisals against the British for the deaths. In response to an IRA call, Ulster Catholics Jan. 31 began a general strike which closed hundreds of shops, offices and factories in Derry and other cities. Sitdown demonstrations and protests took place throughout Northern Ireland. Three persons were killed Feb. 1-2 in violence following the Derry deaths. In the Republic of Ireland, the Irish government Jan. 31 recalled its ambassador to Britain and declared itself "fully satisfied that there was an unprovoked attack by British troops on unarmed civilians in Derry." The Irish government also issued a statement demanding the withdrawal of British troops from Londonderry and Catholic areas in other cities, an end to "harassment" of Catholics and internment without trial, and a conference to settle the Northern Ireland crisis. Following a march through downtown Dublin, organized as part of the Irish Republic's official day of mourning for the 13 Londonderry dead, a crowd of about 25,000 Feb. 2 besieged and burned down the British embassy in Dublin. In Ulster, from 15,000 to 30,000 Roman Catholics Feb. 6 staged a silent protest march in Newry to protest British policy and the Derry deaths. About 3,000-4,000 Catholics Feb. 13 marched peacefully through the border town of Enniskillen to protest the Londonderry deaths. About 3,000-5,000 persons marched peacefully through the Bogside Feb. 27 to commemorate the Londonderry demonstration.

[5] *7 killed by bomb near London.* The IRA terrorist campaign struck England Feb. 22 when a bomb explosion at the Aldershot army base, 35 miles from London, killed five waitresses, a gardener and an army chaplain. Seventeen other persons, including 14 soldiers, were wounded. A spokesman for the IRA Official wing claimed responsibility for the blast in retaliation for the Derry deaths. The explosion ripped through the officers' mess of the parachute brigade that had been involved in the Derry shootings. The bomb, planted in a car parked in front of the kitchen, exploded while the dining room of the mess was empty, just before lunch. A British jury Nov. 14 sentenced Noel Jenkinson, an IRA explosives expert, to life in prison after Jenkinson was found guilty of the bomb explosion. Jenkinson had been found guilty on seven charges of murder and of manufacturing explosives with intent to endanger life or property. The judge recommended that he serve at least 30 years of the sentence.

[6] *Report on Derry deaths.* An official British inquiry into the Derry deaths April 19 issued a report that sought to absolve the army of responsibility for the deaths. The report was immediately denounced by Ulster Catholics as a "whitewash." The inquiry, conducted by Britain's Lord Chief Justice, Lord Widgery, concluded that an IRA sniper was responsible for the first shot fired. Widgery based his conclusion on the testimony of television newsmen present during the incident and on his own reasoning that an opening of fire would have been uncharacteristic of the soldiers and would have come to light "in the rigorous cross-examination" to which the soldiers had been subjected during the inquiry. Widgery placed a major share of responsibility for the incident on the organizers of the march for creating "a highly dangerous situation in which a clash...was almost inevitable." The army's share of the responsibility, according to Widgery, stemmed from its decision to arrest "hooligans" participating in an illegal civil rights march, rather than simply to constrain the marchers. Widgery also found no proof of the army's claim that soldiers had fired only at identified gunmen and bombers. He noted that no weapons were found by the army, that none of the photographs of the march showed a civilian holding an object that could be identified as a firearm or bomb and that there were no injuries to soldiers from firearms or bombs. However, Widgery said there was "strong suspicion" that some of the civilians killed or wounded "had been firing weapons or handling bombs" during the afternoon. The suspicion was based on paraffin tests on the hands of the victims, which revealed traces of lead particles on seven of those killed, and on four nail bombs found in the pockets of another victim. (The bombs were not discovered during two previous medical examinations.)

[7] *Minister for home affairs shot.* John Taylor, minister of state for home affairs, was shot and seriously wounded in Belfast Feb. 25 by IRA terrorists. Taylor, a right-wing hardliner in his attitude toward Catholic opponents of the government, was the first government minister to be shot by terrorists. He was attacked as he got into his car in the center of the city and suffered bullet wounds in the neck, jaw and chest. The IRA Official wing Feb. 25 claimed responsibility for the assassination attempt, saying Taylor was one of the principal architects of internment without trial and was "primarily responsible for the attitude of the British army" in the Londonderry deaths.

[8]　Parliament overturns court ruling. The High Court of Northern Ireland Feb. 23 ruled unconstitutional a regulation empowering army officers to disperse crowds and giving the army authority to search, enter homes and make arrests without warrants. The court said the powers conflicted with the 1920 Government of Ireland Act—Ulster's basic charter—which barred the provincial government from legislating "in respect of the armed forces." However, the British Parliament Feb. 24 approved, in record time, a bill overturning the court's decision and rendering soldiers immune, retroactively, for any action that would be deemed unlawful by the court decision.

[9]　Britain eases probe tactics. British Prime Minister Edward Heath March 2 barred the use of harsh interrogation methods (including subjecting detainees to continuous noise, sleep deprivation and bread-and-water diets) against detained terrorist suspects in Ulster. Heath said that the methods had been used against 14 prisoners since the inception of internment without trial in 1971. According to Heath, "interrogation in depth" would continue in the fight against terrorism, but "severe techniques will not be used" unless the government had attained prior parliamentary approval. Heath's decision followed the publication March 2 of the results of an official inquiry, headed by Lord Parker, into army interrogation methods in Ulster. The three-man committee had split 2-1 in favor of authorizing harsh methods "in cases where it is considered vitally necessary to obtain information."

[10]　Britain imposes direct rule. In an attempt to stem terrorism in Ulster, Britain March 30 suspended Northern Ireland's government and Parliament and imposed direct rule over the province for at least a year. The action ended 51 years of semi-autonomous rule by the Ulster government. Prime Minister Faulkner and his Cabinet resigned the same day, demanding restoration of the Parliament after a year or, failing that, the "complete integration" of Northern Ireland into the United Kingdom "with full and just representation in the Westminster Parliament." The new British policy, put into effect after the March 30 passage (438-18) of enabling legislation by the British Parliament, had been announced March 24. British Prime Minister Heath said the imposition of direct rule stemmed from Faulkner's March 22 rejection of British control over law and order in Ulster—a control proposed by Heath in talks with the Ulster prime minister. Under direct rule, Heath appointed William Whitelaw, leader of the House of Commons, to the newly created post of secretary of state for Northern Ireland. Whitelaw would assume all legislative and executive powers in the province and would appoint a local advisory committee composed of representatives of the Catholic and Protestant communities. In Northern Ireland, reaction to the British moves ranged from expressions of satisfaction by Catholic moderates at the end of the Protestant-dominated Faulkner regime to bitter denunciations and threats from Protestant extremists and the Official and Provisional wings of the IRA. The daily violence that had terrorized Northern Ireland was sharply reduced in the immediate aftermath of the British announcement. Militant Protestants, however, expressed their disapproval of the British measures with a two-day general strike March 27-28. The strike, organized by the Ulster Vanguard, halted air, rail, bus and postal services and sharply curtailed electricity and telephone service. Estimates on the number of strikers ranged from 180,000 to 300,000.

[11]　*Ministers, advisory committee named.* Three ministers were named March 26 to serve under Whitelaw in the new Northern Ireland Office. Lord Windlesham, a Roman Catholic serving as minister of state at the Home Office, was named minister of state for Northern Ireland. The two other appointees were Paul Channon, undersecretary of state at the Department of Environment, and David Howell, parliamentary secretary in the Civil Service Department. Whitelaw May 25 announced the appointment of seven Protestants and four Catholics to his advisory committee. Among the appointees were Tom Conaty, a leading Catholic businessman in Belfast and head of the Central Citizens Defense Committee, and Sir Robert Kinahan, a Protestant leader and former mayor of Belfast. The committee was denounced by both Catholic and Protestant extremists. (In other action, Whitelaw April 27 revoked the ban on traditional parades and declared an amnesty for the 283 persons convicted of organizing or participating in illegal marches since December 1971. The revocation of the ban applied only to traditional parades. Other parades would require organizers to give five days' notice to security authorities, who were authorized to reroute or even ban the procession.)

[12]   **Official IRA declares cease-fire.** In the face of growing demands by Catholic moderates for an end to IRA violence, the Official wing of the IRA May 29 announced the immediate suspension of all offensive guerrilla activity in Northern Ireland and ordered its members to confine themselves to "defensive" and political action. The officials said the cease-fire was necessary because of the increasing "danger of civil war which the Provisional IRA bombing campaign is threatening to provoke" between Catholics and Protestants. The Provisional IRA wing—the faction primarily responsible for the bombing campaign in Northern Ireland—rejected the cease-fire order as "surrender" May 30. The Provisionals pledged a continuation of guerrilla warfare until Britain declared an amnesty for all "pplitical prisoners," withdrew its troops from the streets and ended internment without trial. (The Provisionals had made similar demands March 11-13, during a 72-hour cease-fire declared by the Provisionals.)

[13]   **Provisional cease-fire.** The Provisional IRA June 22 announced a truce on all offensive operations, effective at midnight, June 26. The announcement followed the June 13 rejection by Whitelaw of a Provisional offer for a seven-day cease-fire in exchange for peace talks and the halting of arrests and arms searches. (Whitelaw said he could not "respond to ultimatums from terrorists.") Between the June 22 announcement of the cease-fire and its June 26 implementation, a wave of bombing and sniping violence (thought to reflect the Provisionals' determination to prove their strength) struck the province, resulting in at least eight deaths. Despite the cease-fire, 17 persons were killed in violence between July 1 and July 9. The killings baffled security officials, who reportedly thought them to be part of a chain of sectarian assassinations. The Provisional truce was halted by the IRA July 9 after charges that British troops had broken the truce "without warning" in a gun battle against Catholics. Whitelaw said that the army-Catholic confrontation had been "clearly set up by the IRA to provide justification for the resumption of terrorist activity." Whitelaw added that the troops "were fired upon and only returned the fire when under attack." The confrontation came as about 1,000 Catholics attempted to forcibly move 16 homeless Catholic families into vacant homes in the Protestant part of a public housing project. (The Whitelaw administration had been negotiating relocation of the families, but had been delayed by Protestant objections to the families' presence in the Protestant area.) When stopped by British troops, the Catholics reportedly began to throw bricks and bottles at the soldiers, who responded with rubber bullets and tear gas. Then, according to observers, snipers fired on the troops, who returned the fire, starting a three-hour battle allegedly involving Protestants, Catholics and troops. Whitelaw disclosed July 10 that he had secretly met with six Provisional leaders July 7 in an effort to maintain the truce and avoid a confrontation over the housing issue, but that agreement had not been reached at the meeting. The halt to the cease-fire set off a renewed wave of violence that claimed an estimated 41 lives by July 20. Whitelaw July 13 ordered about 700 troops to occupy the housing project site of the July 9 conflict. The order followed four days of sniping against an army post in the area. Whitelaw July 14 also announced that the British army had used rocket launchers for the first time in the area July 13.

[14]   **9 die in Belfast bombings.** Nine persons were killed and 130 injured July 21 in a mid-afternoon hour of at least 20 coordinated bombings in Belfast. The

Provisionals claimed responsibility for the attacks on what was dubbed "Bloody Friday." Bus and railway stations, hotels, truck depots, a bank and a bridge were among the targets in the most devastating attacks since civil unrest began in Ulster. About six bombs exploded at the same time in Londonderry and other places in Northern Ireland. In response to the attacks, and to other bombing violence and assassinations, the British government reversed its policy of restraint and reconciliation, intensifying military action against the renewed Provisional terrorist campaign. In the first large-scale army operation against Catholic districts since the introduction of direct rule, about 2,000 British troops July 22 moved into IRA strongholds in the Market, Lower Falls Road and other areas of Belfast to search for weapons, grenades and suspected terrorists. The troops pursued their search-and-arrest tactics throughout the week, detaining more than 100 suspects and seizing two huge arms caches. British troops, backed by armored cars and bulldozers, July 31 stormed the heavily barricaded "no go" Roman Catholic areas of Belfast and Londonderry, smashing the steel and concrete barriers that had previously barred entry to the IRA-controlled areas. Whitelaw July 30 had warned residents to remain indoors because there would be "substantial activity" by British troops. The soldiers began their three-hour assault at 4 a.m. and encountered almost no resistance from the IRA, whose members apparently had fled the areas. The operation, by nearly 21,000 troops, succeeded in dismantling the barricades throughout the province. By evening, troops and police were patrolling the previously impenetrable districts. The troops reportedly were barred from making indiscriminate house-to-house searches, a tactic which had alienated the Catholic population in the past. Instead, the troops were ordered to make "selective" roundups and security checks in specific houses where information indicated the existence of arms or terrorists. The only casualties involved in the storming of the "no go" areas were two youths killed by soldiers in the Creggan Heights area of Londonderry and three other persons wounded by soldiers in the same area. The army also dismantled the barricades in Protestant areas of Belfast, Portadown and Londonderry erected by the Ulster Defense Association (UDA), a Protestant paramilitary organization. UDA members reportedly helped the troops to demolish their barriers, which had been built to protest the existence of the IRA strongholds. The British storming action was bitterly criticized by Catholics. There was a temporary lull in violence following the storming of the "no go" areas, but the lull was broken in mid-August by incidents of bombing and sniping.

[15] **Official IRA and UDA leaders meet.** A senior officer of the Official IRA met with UDA leaders in a Protestant "no go" area of Londonderry July 29, the first such meeting between representatives of the two organizations. The IRA official was said to have proposed a future political arrangement between the two working class movements. The leaders of the two sides reportedly also reached agreement to help each other's members if they were caught in the wrong Protestant or Catholic areas.

[16] **Protestants slain in clash with army.** Amid a steady deterioration in relations between Protestants and the British army, marked by Protestant criticism of British security following the storming of the "no go" areas, two Protestant civilians were shot dead and two others wounded by paratroopers in a gun battle Sept. 7 in the Shankill Road area of Belfast. The clash came after three successive nights of violence between civilians and soldiers in the Protestant area and after the Sept. 4 UDA announcement that it had broken off "diplomatic relations" with the army because of "continual harassment" by the troops. According to the army version of the Sept. 7 battle, Protestant gunmen opened fire on army patrols attempting to prevent UDA members from setting up a command post in front of a Shankill Road police station. The paratroopers reportedly then returned the fire. The UDA, however, charged that the paratroopers had opened fire first. Protestants immediately accused the army of indiscriminate shooting and staged a series of protests. Protestant

women fought paratroopers with sticks in the Shankill Road area Sept. 8, and hundreds of shipyard workers marched through the city and staged a sitdown protest in front of the Shankill Road police station. Two Belfast power stations shut down Sept. 11 after Protestant workers walked out.

[17] **Internment without trial to end.** Whitelaw Sept. 21 announced that the government would end internment without trial of suspected terrorists in Ulster. Whitelaw said that the government would instead set up a special tribunal that could sit in secret and that would either free the remaining 241 internees or set specific jail terms for them. (Whitelaw Nov. 6 appointed Judge James Charles Leonard, Sir Ian Lewis and Sheriff John Alexander Dick to the tribunal and appointed Sir Gordon Wilmer, a former lord chief justice of appeal, to preside over a detention appeals tribunal.) Whitelaw insisted that internment could not be ended without other measures to curb the terrorists. (The British House of Commons Dec. 11 approved a bill imposing a 28-day maximum limit on detention of suspected Ulster terrorists.) He contended that terrorism posed problems that could not be met by the normal processes of law, but added that the internment tribunal would be temporary, pending establishment of a commission of lawyers and laymen who would propose a long-term program to combat terrorism. Whitelaw's Sept. 21 action apparently was designed to meet demands of the Social Democratic and Labor party (SDLP), the major Catholic opposition party, for abolition of internment as a precondition for participation in an all-party conference on a new government structure for Ulster. However, the SDLP expressed serious reservations about the new policy, calling it "an extension of internment under a different guise." SDLP leader Gerald Fitt insisted that the remaining internees must be released before his party would attend the talks.

[18] **Conference fails.** Only three of Northern Ireland's seven political parties attended the conference on the province's future form of government, held in Darlington, England, Sept. 25-27. The participating parties failed to agree on any substantial issues beyond the need for a new provincial assembly and the continuation of Ulster's union with Britain for so long as a majority of the province wanted it. The meeting was boycotted by the SDLP (which still insisted on the release of all internees as a precondition for participation), the Democratic Unionist party (headed by Protestant militant leader Rev. Ian Paisley) and William Craig (right-wing leader of the Ulster Vanguard). Craig refused to attend the talks as a member of the former ruling Protestant Unionist party delegation. The major sticking point in the conference was the insistence of the Unionist delegation, headed by former Prime Minister Faulkner, that Britain restore control of police and security forces to Northern Ireland's government. The Alliance and Northern Ireland Labor parties, both with mixed Catholic-Protestant membership, wanted the British government to control the police. Another major disagreement surfaced Sept. 26 on the structure of the future regime. Unionists favored election of a 100-member parliament—with an executive embodied in a prime minister and a cabinet— and the subsequent selection of government committees on which Catholics would be represented. The Alliance and Labor parties favored replacement of the prime minister by the committees, a move that would place executive control in the hands of both Catholics and Protestants. The two parties also favored a proportional representation electoral system. Whitelaw Oct. 30 published a green paper recapitulating the positions taken at the conference. The green paper also stated that the British government would be responsible for security within Ulster as long as the province remained inside the United Kingdom. The green paper dismissed the options of total independence for Ulster and the province's total integration with Britain.

[19] **Plebiscite announced.** Whitelaw Oct. 11 said that a plebiscite on the future status of Ulster would be held in early 1973 in order to give the British Parliament time to approve legislation necessary for the plebiscite. (Whitelaw Dec. 14 set March 8, 1973 as the plebiscite date.) The announced timing of the

plebiscite would place it after local elections scheduled for Dec. 6. However, following an increase in Protestant violence Oct. 12-18, reportedly in protest over the timing of the plebiscite, Whitelaw announced Oct. 27 that the local elections would be postponed until after the plebiscite. Protestants and some moderate Catholics wanted the plebiscite to precede the elections in the hope it would remove the issue of affiliation with the United Kingdom or the Republic of Ireland from local politics. The most serious Protestant rioting protesting the timing of the plebiscite occurred in Protestant districts of east Belfast Oct. 16-17 when British army vehicles struck and killed a man and a teen-age boy. The army termed the deaths accidental, but Protestants insisted the trucks had deliberately struck the victims. Rioters threw stones and bottles and fired more than 100 shots at the troops, injuring about a dozen soldiers. The UDA Oct. 17 accused the army of provoking the rioting by overreacting to stone-throwing by Protestants. The UDA also blamed the army for the two Protestant deaths and vowed to end all cooperation with the British forces. Army and UDA leaders conferred in Belfast Oct. 18 to halt the growing antagonism between the two groups. Following the meeting, an army spokesman said the police would investigate all complaints against soldiers, and UDA deputy chairman Thomas Herron said "our war with the British army is now over." However, Protestant youths again rioted in the Shankill Road area Oct. 18, and there was some doubt concerning UDA control over its rank-and-file members. The British government Oct. 17 announced plans to call out the volunteer Ulster Defense Regiment to deal with the Protestant violence.

See also EUROPEAN ECONOMIC COMMUNITY [14]; GREAT BRITAIN [3]; IRELAND

NORWAY—Retirement reform. The Storting (parliament) March 3 voted a reform of the retirement laws that would give people the option of retiring at age 67 instead of 70, effective in 1973. Those who opted for retirement at 70 would receive higher pensions. The reform could increase the number of retirements by 30%.

Price freeze announced. The government Sept. 15 announced a price freeze, retroactive to Sept. 7, to help reduce growing inflation. Prices had risen 7.9% since August 1971, with particularly sharp increases during the summer of 1972.

Bratteli resigns. Premier Trygve Bratteli resigned with his Labor government Oct. 7, one day after the date scheduled. His resignation followed his government's defeat in the referendum on Norwegian membership in the European Economic Community *(see* EUROPEAN ECONOMIC COMMUNITY ¿¶¿&). Later the same day, King Olav V asked Lars Korvald, leader of the small Christian People's party, to form a new minority coalition government of the Christian People's, Liberal and Center parties. (All three parties were opposed to EEC membership.) The new Cabinet would command only 47 of the 150 seats in the Storting. Bratteli headed a caretaker government until a new Cabinet was formed.

New government sworn in. King Olav Oct. 17 swore in the new Korvald nonsocialist minority coalition. The new 15-member Cabinet formally assumed power the following day. It was composed of six Centrists, five Liberals and four members of the Christian People's party. The new Cabinet included: premier—Korvald; foreign—Dagfinn Vaarik; justice—Peter Koren; municipal affairs and labor—Johan Skipnes; trade and shipping—Hallvard Eika; finance—Jon O. Norbom; defense—Johan Kleppe; consumer affairs—Eva Kolstad; industry—Ola Skjaak Braek; church and education—Anton Skulberg; agriculture—Einar Moxnes; environmental affairs—Trygve Haugland; social affairs—Bergfrid Fjose; fisheries—Trygve Olsen; transportation—John Austrheim.

See also ATOMIC ENERGY [6]; CONSERVATION; EUROPEAN ECONOMIC COMMUNITY [1, 12, 17-18]; NORTH ATLANTIC TREATY

ORGANIZATION; OLYMPIC TERRORISM; PENTAGON PAPERS; POLLUTION [13]; TERRITORIAL WATERS

NUCLEAR ENERGY—*See* ATOMIC ENERGY

OBITUARIES—Among noteworthy people who died in 1972:

Saul D. Alinsky, 63, poverty fighter and community organizer who dedicated his life to counseling poor and powerless groups throughout country. Director of Industrial Areas Foundation (1939), gained recognition as organizer of Chicago's "Back-of-the-Yards" movement; June 12 in Carmel, Calif. after a heart attack.

Sheik Abeid Amani Karume. *See* ZANZIBAR

Athenagoras I, 86, ecumenical patriarch and leader of world's 126 million Eastern Orthodox Christians since 1948. Sought to achieve reunion with Roman Catholic Church in three dramatic meetings with Pope Paul VI in 1964 and 1967. Best known and most flamboyant of Greek bishops, served as archbishop of North and South America (1930-48); July 6 in Istanbul, Turkey of kidney failure. *(See also* CHURCHES)

Erich von dem Bach-Zelewsky, 73, Nazi general who crushed 1944 Warsaw uprising by killing 100,000 Poles and leveling 90% of city, testified against Nazi leaders in Nuremberg, sentenced in 1964 to life imprisonment for murder of six Communists; March 8 (announced March 20 in Munich, West Germany).

Cristobal Balenciaga, 77, influential Spanish fashion designer whose clients included European royalty, styles noted for their classic elegance and simple innovations, retired in 1968; March 24 in Valencia, Spain after a heart attack.

John Berryman, 57, poet, taught at University of Minnesota since 1954, won 1965 Pulitzer Prize and 1969 National Book Award; Jan. 7 in Minneapolis by commiting suicide.

Warren K. Billings, 79, controversial labor organizer and agitator convicted of bombing 1916 patriotic parade in San Francisco with associate Tom Mooney, case became international cause celebre after witnesses changed testimony and fraudulent evidence was revealed, both men were released from prison in 1939; Sept. 4 in Redwood City, Calif.

Louis F. Budenz, 80, prominent American Communist (1935-45) who renounced party and served as star witness for Sen. Joseph McCarthy in 1950 exposing alleged Communists in government, managing editor of *Communist Daily Worker;* April 27 in Newport, R.I.

James F. Byrnes, 92, lawyer and politician whose public service career spanned nearly half a century as Democratic congressman from South Carolina (1911-25), senator (1930-41), Supreme Court justice (1941-42), director of war mobilization (1942-45), secretary of state (1945-47),

292

governor of South Carolina (1951-55), described by President Franklin D. Roosevelt as "assistant president" during term as economic stabilization head (1942-43) and war mobilizer, directed domestic affairs during war, intimate adviser to President Harry S. Truman, United Nations delegate (1946); April 9 in Columbia, S.C.

Thomas G. Cassady, 76, World War I flying ace who won U.S. and French honors for high-level espionage activities in France and Algiers in World War II; July 9 in Lake Forest, Ill. of cancer.

C. W. Ceram (Kurt W. Marek), 57, German author who achieved international fame in archaeology field, 1949 history *Gods, Graves and Scholars* sold more than four million copies, emigrated to U.S. in 1954 and wrote several books including *The First American* (1971); April 12 in Hamburg, West Germany.

Maurice Chevalier, 83, one of France's best known and most popular entertainers for more than half a century, popularized such songs as "Valentine," and "Louise," appeared in numerous Hollywood films in 1930s and 1940s; Jan. 1 in Paris of a kidney ailment. (Less than a thousand people turned out for the funeral in Coquette, France as Chevalier was buried near his mother Jan. 5.)

Sir Francis Chichester, 70, English adventurer who made a solo voyage around the world in 1966 aboard his ketch, Gipsy Moth IV, authored 11 books; Aug. 26 in Plymouth, England of pneumonia. (He was buried Sept. 1 in a churchyard in Plymouth.)

Richard Courant, 84, mathematician who pioneered techniques applicable to nuclear physics, organized and directed mathematics center at New York University making it world's foremost institute for research and advanced study, established and directed Germany's University of Gottingen mathematics center (1920-33); Jan. 27 in New Rochelle, N.Y. of a stroke.

Angelo Cardinal Dell'Acqua, 68, Roman Catholic vicar general of Rome, one of Pope Paul VI's closest aides. Served in Vatican diplomatic service and as undersecretary of state under Pope Pius XII. Served as Vatican's minister of finance and Pope's representative in bringing new discipline into church; Aug. 27 in Lourdes, France after a heart attack while leading a pilgrimage. (His death reduced the number of cardinals to 116 from a high of 134 in 1969.)

King Jigme Dorji Wangchuk. *See* BHUTAN

Sen. Allen J. Ellender (D, La.), 81, member of Senate for 35 years, president pro tempore of the Senate (third in the line of presidential succession behind the vice president and the speaker of the House of Representatives) since January *(see below* Carl Trumbull Hayden); July 27 at the Bethesda Naval Hospital near Washington of a heart attack following a day of campaigning for his seventh Senate term.

Adm. Sir George Elvey Creasy (ret.), 77, commander in chief of the British Home Fleet (1952-54), planned naval operations for Allied invasion of Europe in World War II; Nov. 1 in London.

Vasily G. Fesenkov, 83, Soviet astronomer, pioneered in study of zodiacal light, chairman of Soviet Committee on Meteorites, headed Institute of Astrophysics in Alma-Ata, co-authored *Life in the Universe;* March 12 in Moscow.

Ernst Fischer, 73, Austrian writer and critic, served as a leader of Austrian Communist party (1934-69), elected to National Assembly (1945) and appointed Austria's minister of culture and education. His moderate political stance led to rupture with Kremlin over 1968 Russian invasion of Czechoslovakia; Aug. 1 in village of Deutsch Feistritz, Austria after a heart attack.

Lord Fisher of Lambeth (Most Rev. Dr. Geoffrey Francis), 85, archbishop of Canterbury (1945-61) and one of the leaders of ecumenical and Christian unity movements, meeting with Pope John XXIII (1960) was the first of a Primate and a Pope since 16th century, served as bishop of Chester (1932) and London (1939); Sept. 14 in Sherborne, England.

King Frederick IX. *See* DENMARK

Joseph Gallo. *See* CRIME [4]

Paolo Cardinal Giobbe, 92, oldest member of the College of Cardinals who served 33 years as member of Vatican diplomatic corps; Aug. 14 in Rome.

Prince William of Gloucester, 30, first cousin of Queen Elizabeth II and ninth in line of succession to the British throne; Aug. 28 in London in the crash of a light plane he piloted during an air race.

Jane Grant, 80, co-founder with her first husband, Philip Ross, of the *New Yorker* magazine in 1920s, organized Lucy Stone League (1921)—a forerunner of the women's liberation movement; March 16 in Lichtfield, Conn. of cancer.

John Grierson, 73, pioneering film-maker who coined word "documentary" and helped create National Film Board of Canada (1939) making Ottawa influential filmmaking center, hosted Scottish television series *This Wonderful World* (1957-68); Feb. 19 in Bath, England.

Nubar Gulbenkian, 75, eccentric oil millionaire, one of the world's wealthiest men, life marked by opulence and grandeur; Jan. 10 on the French Riviera after a heart attack.

Franz Halder, 87, chief of German general staff in World War II, credited with engineering blitz victories against neighboring European countries, sentenced to concentration camp for estensible knowledge of 1944 plot to assassinate Hitler; April 2 in Aschau, West Germany.

Carl Trumbull Hayden, 94, Democratic senator (1927-69) and representative (1912-27) from Arizona, served in Congress longer than anyone in history, chairman of the Senate Appropriations Committee for 14 years and president pro tem of the Senate, served as acting vice president upon assassination of President John F. Kennedy, instrumental in establishing modern federal highway aid program; Jan. 25 in Mesa, Ariz.

Gil Hodges, 47, former Brooklyn Dodgers star first baseman who retired from playing in 1963, manager of the Washington Senators (1963-67), manager of the New York Mets (1968 until his death); April 2 in West Palm Beach, Fla. of a heart attack.

Prince Buu Hoi, 55, internationally renowned physicist and cancer researcher, headed National Research Center of the French Radium Institute, diplomatic troubleshooter for his native Vietnam, helped prepare 1954 Geneva Conference on French-Indochina War; Jan. 28 in Paris of cancer.

J. Edgar Hoover. *See* FEDERAL BUREAU OF INVESTIGATION

Hsieh Fu-chih, 74, Chinese minister of public security (1959-65), appointed vice premier in 1965, member of Politburo, headed Revolutionary Committee of Peking (1967), commanded 150,000 troops in Korean War, administered Szechwan Province (1948-52), played ambiguous role in Red Guard uprisings; reported March 29 from Peking.

Mahalia Jackson, 60, one of the world's foremost gospel singers, 1946 recording of "Move On Up a Little Higher" sold million copies, credited with spreading gospel from deep South to concert halls throughout world; Jan. 27 in Evergreen Park, Ill. (Thousands of people viewed the body which lay in state near Lake Michigan Feb. 1. President Nixon Jan. 27 eulogized Miss Jackson as "...an artist without peer....")

Sheik Khalid bin Mohammed al-Qasimi. *See* UNION OF ARAB EMIRATES

Dr. Louis S. B. Leakey, 69, archaeologist and anthropologist whose discoveries revolutionized contemporary theories of evolution, discovered Homo Habilis (1961-64), oldest primate with human characteristics and Zinjanthropus (1959), a close ancestor of man, theories of man's age aroused controversy in field; Oct. 1 in London after a heart attack.

Vaino Leskinen, 55, Finnish foreign minister (1970-71), interior minister (1954-56), secretary of the Social Democratic party (1946-57), played major role in shaping Finland's post-World War II anti-Communist policies, ousted from executive party posts after numerous attacks by Soviet Union; March 8 in Helsinki, Finland while skiing.

Oscar Levant, 72, composer and pianist whose sardonic wit won him fame on radio and television; Aug. 14

in Beverly Hills, Calif. after a heart attack.

Cecil Day-Lewis, 68, Britain's poet laureate since 1968, wrote poetry with revolutionary slant in 1930s while member of Communist party but after break with party his works mellowed; May 22 in London.

King Mahendra (Mahendra Bir Bikram Shah Deva), 51, leader of Himalayan kingdom of Nepal since 1955, pledged to modernize isolated nation while adhering to policy of nonalignment, instituted land reform program and attempts at democracy, abolished Hindu caste system and polygamy; Jan. 31 in Bharatpur, Nepal after a heart attack. (Mahendra's eldest son, Crown Prince Birendra, 26, succeeded to the throne.)

Dr. Maria Goeppert Mayer, 65, first woman since Madame Curie to win Nobel Price in Physics (1963) for her explanation of structure of atomic nucleus; Feb. 20 in San Diego of heart failure.

Buren H. McCormack, 62, executive vice president, director and chairman of executive committee of Dow Jones &.Co., helped shape *Wall Street Journal* into national newspaper; Feb. 28 in Irvington-on-Hudson, N.Y.

Erhard Milch, 79, Nazi field marshal who organized Luftwaffe and led German aeronautics industry in World War II, pioneered in civil aviation prior to war, helped found Lufthansa, German national airline (1926), close associate of Hermann Goering and Adolf Hitler, sentenced at Nuremberg for creation of slave labor camps and criminal medical experiments (1947); Jan. 25 in Luneberg, West Germany.

Marianne Craig Moore, 84, poetess whose awards included 1952 Pulitzer Prize and National Book Award, her verse noted for meticulous crafting of themes drawn from personal insights and observations; Feb. 5 in New York.

Charles Ndizeye (King Mioame Ntare V). *See* BURUNDI

Asta Nielsen, 90, European film and stage actress (1910-37) who appeared in 73 silent films and one talkie, created sensation in 1920 production of *Hamlet,* rebuffed Hitler

request to act in Nazi films; May 25 in Copenhagen, Denmark.

Bronislava Nijinska, 81, Russian-born choreographer and ballerina who established herself as major international dance figure in 1920s working for Serge Diaghilev's Ballets Russes, younger sister of famed dancer Vaslav Nijinsky; Feb. 21 in Pacific Palisades, Calif.

Dr. William Nkomo, prominent South African physician and spokesman for country's small black elite, critic of apartheid, first black president of South African Institute of Race Relations, member of African National Congress; March 26 in Pretoria, South Africa after a heart attack.

Kwame Nkrumah, 62, former president of Ghana deposed by a military coup in 1966, first black man to lead an African colony to independence after World War II; April 27 in Bucharest, Rumania, where he was under treatment for cancer. Nkrumah's body was returned to Ghana for burial in the former president's home town of Nkroful July 9. The transfer of the body to Ghana from Guinea followed protracted negotiations between the two countires. (Guinea President Sekou Toure had taken Nkrumah under his protection following the 1966 coup.)

Lester B. Pearson, 75, former prime minister of Canada (1963-68), winner of Nobel Peace Prize (1957) for his work during the 1956 Suez crisis; Dec. 27 of cancer of the liver.

Ezra Pound, 87, one of most influential and innovative poets of the 20th century. His works, replete with foreign phrases, mythological allusions and personal references, attempted to reform poetry with concrete images and musical rhythm. Befriended and promoted important writers including T. S. Eliot, James Joyce, William Butler Yeats and Ford Maddox Ford, after moving to Europe from U.S. He wrote epic *Cantos* of 117 volumes during most of life. Advocated fascism, anti-Semitism and became obsessed with economics in World War II, indicted for treason in U.S. (1943) and hospitalized in mental asylum (1946-58), returned to Italy after release; Nov. 1

in Venice, Italy of an intestinal blockage. (He was buried Nov. 3 in a simple ceremony in a Venice cemetery attended by several hundred mourners.)

Adam Clayton Powell, 63, controversial Democratic black congressman from New York's Harlem district (1945-69), admired by blacks for championing civil rights causes and bolting party to achieve equality for minority groups, served as chairman on House Committee on Education and Labor (1960-67), unseated in 1967 by House committee on charges of misusing public funds but re-elected in special election, maintained residence in Bahamas after 1960 law suit by woman he accused of being "bag woman" for police graft, seated in 1969 Congress but fined $25,000 and deprived of seniority, Supreme Court overruled House expulsion in 1969, defeated in 1970 by Charles B. Rangel; April 4 in Miami, Fla. from complications following surgery. (The body was cremated April 10 after the funeral and the ashes scattered over the island of Bimini in the Bahamas.)

Dr. Sandor Rado, 82, Hungarian-born physician who became one of Freud's first disciples, leader of the psychoanalytic movement, fled Germany for U.S. during Nazi era and helped established first school of psychoanalysis at Columbia University (1944), founded and presided over New York School of Psychiatry (1958-67); May 14 in New York City.

Chakravarti Rajagopalachari, (Rajaji), 94, first governor general of India (1948-50) and a leader in the nation's struggle for independence, formed own Swatantra party in 1959 after split with Congress party, joined Mohandas K. Gandhi's anti-British movement in 1919, organized right-wing coalition in 1971 in bid to defeat Mrs. Indira Gandhi but was soundly defeated; Dec. 26 in Madras, India. (The government proclaimed seven days of mourning).

Paul Ricca (Paul DeLucia), 74, leader of Chicago crime syndicate after jailing of Al Capone, termed "nation's most important criminal" by Senate subcommittee in 1958,

citizenship revoked in 1957; Oct. 11 in Chicago after a heart attack.

Jackie Robinson, 53, the first black to play major league baseball, catalyst of Brooklyn Dodger teams that won six National League pennants (1947, 1949, 1952-53, 1955-56), rookie of the year (1947), National League's most valuable player (1947), elected to baseball's Hall of Fame in 1962; Oct. 24 at his home in Stamford, Conn. after suffering a heart attack.

Jimmy Rushing, 68, blues and jazz singer considered one of finest of era, performed with Count Basie group (1935-50); June 8 in New York.

Dame Margaret Rutherford, 80, British actress who achieved stardom with comedy portrayals of eccentric Englishwomen, won 1964 Oscar for role in *The V.I.P.s,* appeared in more than 100 plays and 30 films including starring roles as heroine in Agatha Christie mysteries; May 22 in Chalfont St. Peter, Buckinghamshire, England.

Leonid M. Schevchenko, 59, chief adviser to Soviet President Nikolai V. Podgorny; July 11 in Moscow.

Rose Schneiderman, 88, pioneering female labor leader who organized Women's Trade Union League in early 1900s and served as president for many years, secretary of the New York State Labor Department (1937-44), member of President Franklin D. Roosevelt's "brain trust"; Aug. 11 in New York.

Dr. Harlow Shapley, 86, astronomer noted for his studies of the Milky Way and solar system, director of Harvard Observatory (1921-52), led humanistic movement after World War II advocating policy of coexistence, rebuffed charges by Sen. Eugene McCarthy of Communist sympathies (1950), helped found UNESCO (1945); Oct. 20 in Boulder, Colo.

Edwin Myers (Ted) Shawn, 80, known as "father of modern dance"; Jan. 9 in Orlando, Fla. of a heart ailment.

Charles H. Singer, 69, radio and electronics pioneer, directed development and installation of world-wide defense systems for NATO, vice president of U.S. Underseas Cable Corp.; March 28 in Washington, D.C.

Joseph Fielding Smith, 95, 10th president of the Mormon Church (Church of Jesus Christ of Latter-Day Saints) since 1970, named one of 12 Apostles (1910) and president of the Council of Apostles (1951). A strict fundamentalist, he authored 23 books on Mormon history and theology; July 2 in Salt Lake City, Utah. (He was succeeded as president of the Mormon Church by Harold B. Lee.)

Edgar Snow, 66, American journalist who maintained close ties with Chinese leaders since 1936 when he was first Western newsman to venture into Communist areas to interview Mao Tsetung and Chou En-lai, authored *Red Star Over China* (1937) and other books about China; Feb. 15 in Eysins, Switzerland of cancer. (Mao and other Chinese leaders paid tribute to Snow Feb. 16, citing his "important contributions" to Sino-American relations.)

Paul-Henry Spaak, 73, three-time Belgian premier regarded as one of the founders of the European Economic Community. He helped write charter of the United Nations and served as first president of the General Assembly (1946), helped create the North Atlantic Treaty Organization and served as secretary-general 1957-61. Served in 17 Belgian governments—six times as foreign minister, held presidential posts on European Coal and Steel Community, Council of Europe and Organization for European Cooperation; July 31 in Brussels of kidney failure.

Adm. Harold R. Stark, 91, chief of naval operations who was relieved of command after Japanese bombed Pearl Harbor and made commander of U.S. forces in European waters; Aug. 20 in Washington after a heart attack.

Adm. Felix B. Stump, 77, commander of the Pacific Fleet until retirement in 1958, captain of aircraft carrier Lexington sunk by Japanese in World War II, headed carrier task force in battle of Leyte Gulf which defeated Japanese navy; June 13 in Bethesda, Md. of cancer.

King Talal, 63, king of Jordan for 11 months (1951-52) who abdicated to his son, King Hussein, after being declared unfit because of mental illness. Last years spent in a Turkish sanatorium; July 8 in Istanbul, Turkey. (He was buried July 9 in the royal burial ground in Amman, Jordan.)

Dr. Viorel Virgil Tilea, 76, Rumanian minister to Britain in 1938 who refused recall by Hitler and founded Free Rumania Movement in 1940, served as under secretary of state to the Presidency of Rumanian Council of Ministers (1930-33); Sept. 23 in London.

Eugene Cardinal Tisserant, 81, dean of the College of Cardinals of the Roman Catholic Church since 1951, chief of Vatican library; Feb. 21 near Rome.

Harry S Truman. *See separate entry.*

Jan Ursiny, 75, premier of Czechoslovakia and member of Slovak National Council, served prison term for resisting Communist political line; Jan. 8 in Raksa, Czechoslovakia.

Dr. Georg von Bekesy, 73, Hungarian-born physicist who won 1961 Nobel Prize for medicine for research in hearing and the human ear, professor at University of Hawaii since 1966, immigrated to U.S. in 1947; June 13 in Honolulu.

Baron Magnus von Braun, 94, father of space pioneer Wernher von Braun. Served in Weimar Republic Cabinet as agricultural minister (1932), modernized nation's agricultural cooperative movement. Press chief for Kaiser Wilhelm; Aug. 29 in Oberaudorf, Upper Bavaria.

Ferdinand (Ferde) Rudolf von Grofe, 80, composer who, with Paul Whiteman, combined classical and popular styles into "symphonic jazz" arranged and orchestrated George Gershwin's *Rhapsody in Blue,* works concentrated on American themes; April 3 in Santa Monica, Calif.

Charles E. Wilson, 85, president of General Electric Co. (1940-42, 1944-50), resigned to serve as executive vice chairman of War Production Board in World War II, directed production of record number of military aircraft in 1944, returned to GE after internal dispute, named chairman of Office of Defense Mobilization in Korean War but resigned 15 months later in dispute with President Harry S Truman; Jan. 3 in Scarsdale, N.Y.

Edmund Wilson, 77, one of the most influential literary and social critics in 20th century, considered dean of American letters. His works spanned fields of literature, history, anthropology and economics, fashioned reading habits of millions as preeminent critic of his era. Won Presidential Medal of Freedom (1963) and National Medal for Literature (1966). Books included *Axel's Castle* (1931), *To the Finland Station* (1940) and *Patriotic Gore* (1962); June 12 in Talcottville, N.Y.

Sir Horace Wilson, 89, principal architect with Prime Minister Neville Chamberlain of attempt to appease Nazi Germany before World War II, headed British Civil Service; May 21 in London.

Walter Winchell, 74, newspaper columnist and radio commentator whose melodramatic tidbits about entertainment personalities and politicians reached millions and made him most powerful journalist in nation from 1930-50; Feb. 20 in Los Angeles.

Duke of Windsor, 77, Prince of Wales who ascended to throne as King Edward VIII of England (1936) but served only 11 months before abdicating to marry Wallis Warfield Simpson, an American divorcee, in following years lived in exile but traveled widely; May 28 in Paris of cancer. (The Duke's health deteriorated steadily since a hernia operation in February. The body laid in state in St. George's Chapel June 1-2 after being flown back to England. Some 60,000 admirers lined streets for hours to catch a glimpse. He was buried in the Royal Burial Ground at Frogmore June 5 in a private ceremony.)

Fred Wolcott, 55, oilman and world's leading hurdler in late 1930s, held four world marks, five NCAA championships and seven AAU titles; Jan. 26 in Houston.

Adm. Ivan S. Yumashev, 76, Soviet navy commander (1947-51), led Pacific fleet in World War II. Until 1957 retirement headed Voroshilov Naval Academy; Sept. 2 reported from Moscow.

Marshal Matvei V. Zakharov, 73, Soviet career military officer who joined army in 1917 and achieved second-highest ranking military post in nation, chief of staff (1960-71), deposed by Nikita Khrushchev for 20-month period in 1963-64, commanded Soviet forces in East Germany (1957-60); Jan. 31 in Moscow.

Viktor A. Zuyevsky, 53, Soviet designer of nuclear warheads and chief designer of the Scientific Research Institute of the Ministry of Medium Machine Building, awarded secret Stalin and Lenin prizes for new technology; July 5 in Moscow.

OIL & NATURAL GAS—Persian Gulf agreement. The six Persian Gulf members of the Organization of Petroleum Exporting Countries (OPEC) Jan. 20 signed an agreement with Western. oil companies to compensate the countries for devaluation of the U.S. dollar in December 1971. The accord—affecting Abu Dhabi, Iran, Iraq, Kuwait, Qatar and Saudi Arabia—went into operation immediately and would expire in 1975. It gave the six countries an 8.49% increase in the posted price of oil ($2.23 a barrel before negotiations) and would increase the annual revenue from Western companies to the six by at least $700 million to approximately $8.9 billion. The OPEC had requested an 8.57% increase in the price of oil.

Representatives of five of the Persian Gulf countries (excepting Iran) Oct. 5 reached an initial agreement with representatives of the major Western oil companies on sharing ownership of petroleum production. Details of the accord were not made public pending final approval of individual agreements that were to be worked out between the firms and the five countries.

Venezuelan oil reversion law. It was reported March 5 that the Venezuelan government had approved creation of a special fund to guarantee that oil company assets, which were to be turned over to the state in the 1980s under the 1971 Venezuelan oil reversion act, would be delivered in good condition. According to the proposal, the companies would make annual deposits to the fund on the basis of a formula used for depreciation of their assets. In a related development, the government March 31 contended that U.S. oil companies in Venezuela, which were contesting the reversion act in Venezuela's Supreme Court, were also deliberately keeping production at a minimum in order to protest the act. (1971 production had increased at a normal rate until April 13, when the law appeared in the Venezuelan Congress. Following that date, production had steadily decreased, except for a brief increase in October 1971. The year-end figure for 1971 production showed a decrease of 4.3% in comparison with 1970.) The oil companies maintained that the decline was due to the mild U.S. and European winter and the consequent drop in demand for crude oil.

Iraq, Syria seize Western firm. Iraq June 1 seized the Iraq Petroleum Co. (IPC), a Western-owned consortium of U.S., British, Dutch and French firms which produced 10% of all Middle East oil. Syria the same day nationalized all IPC assets on its territory, including a section of pipeline that passed from Iraq through Syria to Lebanon. The Iraqi nationalization move followed the collapse of negotiations between the government and IPC and the rejection of a final offer by IPC May 31. (The rejection had come on the last day of a two-week ultimatum imposed by the government May 17.) During the negotiations, the government had demanded an increase in the company's lagging oil production. In announcing the nationalization, Iraqi President Ahmed Hassan al Bakr accused IPC of an "unprecedented" cut in production, aimed at plunging Iraq into an "economic ordeal" and at forcing "the revolution to retreat from its objectives." According to Bakr, the cutback since the start of 1972 had cost his country $86 million in tax and royalty revenue. The Baghdad government also accused IPC of cutting production to force Iraq to settle a number of disputes with the firm. Iraq made agreements June 18 with France and June 19 with Italy to sell its nationalized oil to the two countries. The 10 nations of the Organization of Arab Petroleum Exporting Countries (OAPEC) agreed June 20 to lend Iraq $151 million and Syria $18 million for a three-month period to help meet exchange shortages arising from the nationalization of IPC. The money would come mainly from Kuwait, Abu Dhabi and Libya.

Moves to ease U.S. shortages. President Nixon acted Sept. 18 to increase oil imports by 35% for the remainder of 1972 in the area east of the Rocky Mountains. The action, taken on the recommendation of the Office of Emergency Preparedness (OEP), would double the daily import rates of No. 2 fuel oil. Authorities had feared that a severe winter could lead to fuel shortages in New England and the Middle West, which used No. 2 oil. The OEP Dec. 8 announced that it was suspending all import curbs on No. 2 oil for the period between January and May 1973. The OEP also announced Dec. 21 and 22 that it: was running an emergency coordinating center on fuel supplies with representatives from other government agencies; had requested additional production of heating oil by refineries; and had asked railroads to expedite shipments of propane gas.

See also ARMAMENTS, INTERNATIONAL; AUSTRALIA [3]; BRAZIL; CHINA, COMMUNIST; ELECTIONS [33]; ENVIRONMENT; EUROPEAN ECONOMIC COMMUNITY [9]; INTERNATIONAL MONETARY DEVELOPMENTS [11]; ISRAEL; JORDAN; MIDDLE EAST [30]; POLLUTION [3, 9-12]; TERRITORIAL WATERS; TRINIDAD & TOBAGO

OKINAWA—*See* JAPAN [4-5]

OLYMPICS—Winter games. Emperor Hirohito Feb. 3 formally opened the 11th Winter Olympics in the Makomanai speed-skating arena in Sapporo, Japan. Forty-five minutes after Hirohito opened the games, Hideki Takada, a 16-year-old student, lit the Olympic flame high atop the Makomanai rink. Some 1,300 athletes from 35 nations (including, for the first time, Taiwan and the Philippines) participated in the 10 days of events. It was the first time that the Winter Olympics had been held in Asia. (Sapporo was to have been the site of the 1940 Winter Games, but World War II intervened.) There were several multiple gold-medal winners at the games, including Ard Schenk of the Netherlands, who swept the 5,000-meter, 1,500-meter and 10,000-meter speed-skating titles. In the 10,000-meter, Schenk set a new Olympic record. Other Olympic standouts included Marie Therese Nadig, a 17-year-old Swiss who captured the women's downhill and giant Slalom, and Galina Koulakov and Vyacheslav Vedenin, the Soviet Union's premier long distance skiers.

[2]   Throughout the games, there was an undercurrent of bitterness among some athletes toward the International Olympic Committee (IOC), which earlier had banned Austrian skier Karl Schranz from competing because of alleged professional activities involving the use of his name and photographs. Austrian officials considered withdrawing their team to protest the IOC action, but Schranz asked his teammates to remain in the competition. A second world-class skier, France's Annie Famose, Feb. 9 was suspended from further participation in the Olympics by the International Ski Federation because of an advertisement that she would do television work for a European network during the games. The suspension of Miss Famose came five days after she finished eighth in the downhill race.

National Medal Standings, Winter Games

	Gold	Silver	Bronze		Gold	Silver	Bronze
USSR	8	5	3	Japan	1	1	1
East Germany	4*	3	7	Czechoslovakia	1	0	2
Switzerland	4	3	3	Spain	1	0	0
Netherlands	4	3	2	Poland	1	0	0
U. S.	3	2	3	Finland	0	4	1
West Germany	3	1	1	France	0	1	2
Norway	2	5	5	Canada	0	1	0
Italy	2*	2	1				
Austria	1	2	2				
Sweden	1	1	2				

*East Germany and Italy tied for the gold medal in the men's luge doubles. No silver was awarded in the event.

Gold Medal Winners, Winter Games

(Asterisk denotes new Olympic record)

Alpine Skiing

Downhill—Bernhard Russi, Switzerland, Feb. 7.
Giant slalom—Gustavo Thoeni, Italy, Feb. 11.
Special slalom—Francisco Fernandez Ochoa, Spain, Feb. 13.
Women's downhill—Marie Therese Nadig, Switzerland, Feb. 5.
Women's giant slalom—Marie Therese Nadig, Switzerland, Feb. 8.
Women's special slalom—Barbara Cochran, U.S., Feb. 11.

Nordic Skiing

30kilometer crosscountry—Vyacheslav Vedenin, U.S.S.R., Feb. 4.
Nordic combined—Ulrich Wehling, East Germany, Feb. 5.
70meter special jump—Yukio Kasaya, Japan, Feb. 6.
15kilometer crosscounty—Sven-Ake Lundback, Sweden, Feb. 7.
50kilometer crosscountry—Paal Tyldum, Norway, Feb. 10.

90meter jump—Wojciech Fortuna, Poland, Feb. 11.

40kilometer relay—U.S.S.R., Feb. 12.

Women's 10kilometer crosscountry—Galina Koulakov, U.S.S.R., Feb. 6.

Women's 5kilometer crosscountry—Galina Koulakov, U.S.S.R., Feb. 9.

Women's 15kilometer crosscountry relay—U.S.S.R., Feb. 12.

Speed Skating

5,000 meters—Ard Schenk, Netherlands, Feb. 4.

500 meters—Erhard Keller, West Germany, Feb. 5.*

1,500 meters—Ard Schenk, Netherlands, Feb. 6.

10,000 meters—Ard Schenk, Netherlands, Feb. 7.*

Women's 1,500 meters—Dianne Holum, U.S., Feb. 9.*

Women's 500 meters—Anne Henning, U.S., Feb. 10.*

Women's 1,000 meters—Monika Pflug, West Germany, Feb. 11.*

Women's 3,000 meters—Stien Baas-Kaiser, Netherlands, Feb. 12.*

Figure Skating

Women's—Beatrix Shuba, Austria, Feb. 7.

Pairs—Irina Rodnina, Aleksei Ulanov, U.S.S.R., Feb. 8.

Men's—Ondrej Nepela, Czechoslovakia, Feb. 11.

Bobsledding

Two-man—Wolfgang Zimmerer, Peter Utzschneider, West Germany, Feb. 5.

Four-man—Switzerland, Feb. 12.

Hockey

Team—U.S.S.R., Feb. 13.

Biathlon

Individual—Magner Solberg, Norway, Feb. 9.

Relay—U.S.S.R., Feb. 11.

Luge

Men's—Wolfgang Scheidel, East Germany, Feb. 7.

Women's—Anna Marie Muller, East Germany, Feb. 7.

Men's doubles—Tie between Paul Hilgartner and Walter Plaikner of Italy, and Horst Horlein and Reinhard Bredow, East Germany, Feb. 11.

[3] Rhodesia out. The IOC, by a vote of 36-31 (three abstentions), Aug. 22 voted to keep Rhodesia out of the Summer Games of the 20th Olympiad, which were to begin in Munich, West Germany Aug. 26. The IOC's action followed a week of ultimatums by black African nations that they would withdraw from the games if Rhodesia competed. Rhodesia's entry was protested because of the country's racial policies. Although the racial issue had triggered the dispute, the IOC said a technicality over the passports of the Rhodesian athletes had led to the expulsion. The reason given by the IOC was that the Rhodesians had failed to produce passports to prove they were British subjects as well as Rhodesian citizens. Rhodesia, which had been excluded from the 1968 games, had received an invitation to compete in Munich under a compromise by the Supreme Council for Sport in Africa, the sports governing body for the black African bloc. That compromise was based on Rhodesia's willingness to compete as British subjects under the British flag. When Rhodesia accepted the terms, the IOC extended an invitation and Rhodesia came to Munich with a 44-member team, including six black trackmen. Rhodesia's entry first touched off token opposition from smaller African nations, including Tanzania, Sierra Leone and Sudan. But the protest took on a new shape Aug. 15-16 when Ethiopia and Kenya, the continent's two athletic powers, joined the boycott. The threat of a boycott grew Aug. 18 when a group of black U.S. athletes pledged in an unsigned statement that, if Rhodesia were allowed to compete, "we will take a united stand with our African brothers."

[4] New IOC president. IOC President Avery Brundage announced Aug. 23 that Lord Michael John Killanin of Ireland had been elected to succeed him as president. Killanin had been a member of the IOC for 20 years, the last four as Brundage's chief deputy. He took office Sept. 12, one day after the Munich games were completed.

[5] Summer games. West German President Gustav Heinemann Aug. 26 opened the summer games of the 20th Olympiad in the Olympic Stadium in Munich, West Germany. Shortly thereafter, Gunter Zahn, a middle-distance runner on the West German team, lit the Olympic flame which had been carried by 5,976 relay runners from Olympia, Greece to Munich. It was the first time that the games had been held in Germany since the 1936 Berlin Olympics. The opening days of the competition were marked by controversial decisions and charges of poor officiating *(see below)*, but the early disputes palled when eight

Arab terrorists killed 11 members of the Israeli team Sept. 5 *(see* OLYMPIC TERRORISM). The IOC ordered a one-day halt in the games to permit a memorial service to be held for the slain Israelis. Following the halt, however,. the controversies resumed.

[6]   When the formal competition came to a close Sept. 10, the Soviet Union led with 99 medals, 50 of them gold. The U.S. won 94 medals, 33 of them gold. The games also marked the arrival of East Germany as a major Olympic power. Its athletes collected 66 medals—20 gold, 23 silver and 23 bronze. The star of the games was American swimmer Mark Spitz, who won seven gold medals—the most won by an athlete since the modern games began in 1896. Spitz's achievement eclipsed the old mark of five golds in a single Olympics, a record held by three athletes (Nedo Nadi, an Italian fencer, in 1920; Willis Lee, an American marksman, in 1920; and Anton Heide, a U.S. gymnast, in 1904). Spitz picked up a gold medal and set world record time in each of the seven events in which he was entered. He won gold medals in the 200-meter butterfly, the 400-meter freestyle relay, the 200-meter freestyle, the 100-meter butterfly, the 800-meter freestyle relay, the 100-meter freestyle and the 400-meter medley relay. In the three team relays, Spitz swam the anchor leg. Another swimming star of the games was Shane Gould of Australia. The 15-year-old girl picked up three gold medals and three world records (400-meter freestyle, 200-meter freestyle and 200-meter medley), a silver and a bronze.

[7]   *2 U.S. sprinters miss race.* Eddie Hart and Rey Robinson, two of America's fastest sprinters and favorites to win the 100-meter dash, were disqualified from competition for the dash Aug. 31 when they failed to appear for their quarter-final heats earlier in the day. Both men missed their races because U.S. sprint coach Stan Wright, using an 18-month-old schedule that had been changed, told them that the quarter-finals started at 7 p.m. The races actually went off at 4:15 p.m. Wright said later that he could not find anyone with a newer schedule. Both Hart and Robinson had equaled the world record of 9.9 seconds for the 100-meter dash. A third U.S. favorite in the event, Robert Taylor, had also been given the wrong time to appear for the quarter-finals. However, he managed to discover the error and get to the track and field stadium just as his quarter-finals began. (Taylor placed second in the finals to Russia's Valery Borzov.)

[8]   *U.S. swimmer stripped of medal.* The IOC's executive board voted Sept. 6 to strip American swimmer Rick DeMont of the gold medal for his victory in the 400-meter freestyle Sept. 1 because of the presence in his system of a banned drug during the race. The drug, ephedrine, was regarded by the IOC's medical committee as an amphetamine that could affect an athlete's performance. DeMont had taken the ephedrine as a component of Malax, an asthma medication prescribed for him since childhood. In filing his Olympic medical report before the games, DeMont listed the special medication in accordance with IOC rules. However, American team doctors apparently failed to clear DeMont's prescription with the IOC medical committee. DeMont was disqualified after a post-race urinalysis showed traces of ephedrine in his system. Because of the finding, he was also disqualified from competing in the finals of the 1,500-meter freestyle, in which he held the world record. DeMont appealed the decision Sept. 7, but the executive board rejected the appeal Sept. 8. The board's final decision made DeMont the first Olympic gold medalist in 60 years to be told to return the award. (American athlete Jim Thorpe had been ordered to give up golds for the pentathlon and decathlon after he was ruled to have been a professional because he had once played minor league baseball.) The IOC said later that silver medalist Brad Cooper of Australia would get the gold medal as the race's winner. (Iranian weight lifter Mohammed Nahesi and Australian weight lifter Walter Legel had been disqualified Aug. 29 after traces of ephedrine were found in their post-competition urinalyses.)

[9]   **Ryun out of 1,500 finals.** Jim Ryun, America's premier miler, failed to qualify for the 1,500-meter finals Sept. 8 when he and Ghana's Billy Fordjour

tangled feet and fell to the track. Ryun, who suffered spike wounds in both his ankles, resumed the race, but was too far back to make up the distance. He filed a protest against another runner after the race, but it was rejected.

[10] U.S. track stars banned from Olympics. Vince Matthews and Wayne Collett, America's gold and silver medalists in the 400-meter run, were barred Sept. 8 from all Olympic competition for what the IOC called their "disgusting display" on the victory platform after they received their medals Sept. 7. Collett had joined Matthews on the top step of the victory platform and the two had chatted briefly during the playing of the national anthem. As they stepped down from the podium, Matthews twirled his medal around his finger as the crowd booed him. Following the awards ceremony, Matthews discounted reports that he and Collett had staged an informal protest. The IOC did not take away Matthews' and Collett's medals or strike their names from the roster of Olympic medalists, but the disqualification was immediate and made the two ineligible for the U.S. 1,600-meter relay team. (Since John Smith, a third member of the relay team pulled up lame during the 400-meter run, the U.S. team was scratched from the relay.) The U.S. Olympic Committee's (USOC) administrative board asked the IOC to rescind the ban, but the committee refused. In a similar action, the IOC Sept. 11 banned 11 Pakistani field hockey players from future Olympic competitions, charging that they demonstrated disrespect during the final awards ceremony.

[11] *U.S. basketball streak ended.* The U.S., which had never lost an Olympic basketball game, Sept. 10 dropped a controversial 51-50 decision to the Soviet Union in the final seconds of the championship game. U.S. coach Hank Iba protested the game on the grounds that the Soviet Union's final basket was scored in violation of international rules, but the International Amateur Basketball Federation (FIBA) disallowed his protest. Trailing throughout the game, the U.S. pulled even and then ahead, 50-49, on a pair of foul shots with three seconds remaining on the clock. The Russians then took possession and put the ball in play under their basket. A U.S. player deflected the inbounds pass and, when time ran out, the American team and its fans poured onto the court. However FIBA representative Peter Schliesser told officials to clear the court and reset the clock at three seconds. It appeared that Schliesser had decided that the Soviet Union had called time before putting the ball in play. When the game was resumed, the Soviets scored on a full-court pass and a layup. The defeat ended the U.S. 63-game Olympic streak, which began when the sport was introduced into Olympic competition in the 1936 games. Following the game, the U.S. team voted not to accept the runner-up silver medal.

National Medal Standings, Summer Games

	Gold	Silver	Bronze		Gold	Silver	Bronze
USSR	50	27	22	Czechoslovakia	2	4	2
U.S.	33	30	31	Kenya	2	3	4
East Germany	20	23	23	Yugoslavia	2	1	4
Japan	13	8	8	Norway	2	1	1
West Germany	13	11	16	North Korea	1	1	3
Australia	8	7	2	New Zealand	1	1	1
Poland	7	5	8	Uganda	1	1	0
Hungary	6	13	16	Denmark	1	0	0
Bulgaria	6	10	5	Switzerland	0	3	0
Italy	5	3	9	Canada	0	2	3
Sweden	4	6	6	Belgium	0	2	1
Britain	4	5	9	Austria	0	1	2
Rumania	3	6	7	Colombia	0	1	2
Finland	3	1	4	Iran	0	2	1
Cuba	3	1	4	Mongolia	0	2	0
Netherlands	3	1	1	South Korea	0	1	0
France	2	4	7	Lebanon	0	1	0

	Gold	Silver	Bronze		Gold	Silver	Bronze
Turkey	0	1	0	Spain	0	0	2
Argentina	0	1	0	Ethiopia	0	0	2
Greece	0	2	0	Nigeria	0	0	1
Pakistan	0	1	0	Jamaica	0	0	1
Tunisia	0	1	0	Ghana	0	0	1
Mexico	0	1	0	Niger Republic	0	0	1
Brazil	0	0	2	India	0	0	1

Gold Medal Winners, Winter Games

(Asterisk denotes new Olympic record, two asterisks denotes new world record.)

Archery
Men's—John Williams, U.S., Sept. 10.
Women's—Doreen Wilber, U.S., Sept. 10.

Basketball
Team—U.S.S.R., Sept. 10.

Boxing
Light flyweight—Gyoergy Gedo, Hungary, Sept. 10.
Flyweight—Gheorghi Kostadinov, Bulgaria, Sept. 10.
Bantamweight—Orlando Martinez, Cuba, Sept. 10.
Featherweight—Boris Kousnetsov, U.S.S.R., Sept. 10.
Lightweight—Jon Szczepanski, Poland, Sept. 10.
Light welterweight—Ray Seales, U.S., Sept. 10.
Welterweight—Emilio Correa, Cuba, Sept. 10.
Light middleweight—Dieter Kottsych, West Germany, Sept. 10.
Middleweight—Viatchesiav Lemechev, U.S.S.R., Sept. 10.
Light heavyweight—Mate Parlov, Yugoslavia, Sept. 10.
Heavyweight—Teofilo Stevenson, Cuba, Sept. 10.

Men's Canoeing
Canadian two-man slalom—Walter Hofmann, Hans Otto Schumacher, East Germany, Aug. 30.
Kayak slalom—Siegbert Horn, East Germany, Aug. 28.
Canadian slalom—Reinhard Eiben, East Germany, Aug. 28.
Kayak singles—Aleksandr Shaparenko, U.S.S.R., Sept. 9.
Canadian singles—Ivan Patzaichin, Rumania, Sept. 9.
Kayak pairs—Nikolai Gorbachev, Victor Kratassuk, U.S.S.R., Sept. 9.
Canadian pairs—Vladas Chessyunas, Yurl Lobanoc, U.S.S.R., Sept. 9.
Kayak fours—U.S.S.R., Sept. 9.

Women's Canoeing
Single kayak slalom—Angelika Bahmann, East Germany, Aug. 30.
Kayak singles—Yulia Ryabchinskaya, U.S.S.R., Sept. 9.
Kayak pairs—Ludmila Pinayeva, Ekaterina Kuryshko, U.S.S.R., Sept. 9.

Cycling
1,000meter time trial—Niels Fredborg, Denmark, Aug. 31.
Individual pursuit—Knut Knudsen, Norway, Sept. 1.
Team pursuit—West Germany, Sept. 4.

Tandem—Vladimir Semenets, Igor Tselovainkov, U.S.S.R., Sept. 4.

Road race—Hennie Kuiper, Netherlands, Sept. 7.

100kilometer time trial—U.S.S.R., Aug. 29.

Sprint—Daniel Morelon, France, Sept. 2.

Equestrian

Individual 3-day event—Richard Meade, Britain, Sept. 1.

Team 3-day event—Britain, Sept. 1.

Individual jumping—Graziano Mancinelli, Italy, Sept. 3.

Individual dressage—Liselott Lisenhoff, West Germany, Sept. 7.

Team dressage—U.S.S.R., Sept. 7.

Team jumping—West Germany, Sept. 11.

Men's Fencing

Individual foil—Witold Woyda, Poland, Aug. 30.

Individual saber—Victor Sidiak, U.S.S.R., Aug. 31.

Saber team—Italy, Sept. 4.

Individual epee—Csaba Fenyvei, Hungary, Sept. 6.

Team foil—Poland, Sept. 2.

Team epee—Hungary, Sept. 9.

Women's Fencing

Individual foil—Antonella Lonzo Rogno, Italy, Sept. 4.

Team foils—U.S.S.R., Sept. 8.

Field Hockey

Team—West Germany, Sept. 10.

Men's Gymnastics

Parallel bars—Sawao Kato, Japan, Sept. 1.

Long horse—Klaus Koeste, East Germany, Sept. 1.

All around—Sawao Kato, Japan, Aug. 30.

Side horse—Viktor Klimenko, U.S.S.R., Sept. 1.

Rings—Akinori Nakayama, Japan, Sept. 1.

Horizontal bars—Mitsuo Tsukahara, Japan, Sept. 1.

Team competition—Japan, Aug. 29.

Floor exercises—Nikolai Andrianov, U.S.S.R., Sept. 1.

Women's Gymnastics

All around—Ludmila Tourischeva, U.S.S.R., Aug. 30.

Floor exercises—Olga Korbut, U.S.S.R., Aug. 31.

Balance beam—Olga Korbut, U.S.S.R., Aug. 31.

Uneven bars—Karin Janz, East Germany, Aug. 31.

Long horse—Karin Janz, East Germany, Aug. 31.

Team competition—U.S.S.R., Aug. 28.

Handball

Team—Yugoslavia, Sept. 10.

Judo

Lightweight—Takao Kawaguchi, Japan, Sept. 4.

Welterweight—Toyokazu Nomura, Japan, Sept. 9.

Middleweight—Shinobu Sekine, Japan, Sept. 2.

Lightheavyweight—Shota Chochoshvilli, U.S.S.R., Sept. 1.

Heavyweight—Willem Ruska, Netherlands, Aug. 31.

Open—Willem Ruska, Netherlands, Sept. 9.

Modern Pentathlon

Individual—Andras Balczo, Hungary, Aug. 31.

Team—U.S.S.R., Aug. 31.

Rowing

Coxed fours—West Germany, Sept. 2.

Coxless pairs—East Germany, Sept. 2.

Singles scull—Yuri Malishev, U.S.S.R., Sept. 2.

Coxed pairs—East Germany, Sept. 2.

Coxless fours—East Germany, Sept. 2.

Doubles scull—U.S.S.R., Sept. 2.

Eights—New Zealand, Sept. 2.

Shooting

Small bore rifle—Ho Jun Li, North Korea, Aug. 28.**

Trap—Angelo Scalzone, Italy, Aug. 29.**

Small bore rifle, 3 positions—John Writer, U.S., Aug. 30.**

Rapid fire pistol—Jozef Zapedzski, Poland, Sept. 1.

Moving target—Lakov Zhelezniak, U.S.S.R., Sept. 1.

Free rifle—Lones Wigger, U.S., Sept. 2.

Skeet—Konrad Wirnhier, West Germany, Sept. 2.

Free pistol—Ragnar Skanaker, Sweden, Aug. 27.

Soccer

Team—Poland, Sept. 10.

Men's Swimming

100meter butterfly—Mark Spitz, U.S., Aug. 31.**

200meter butterfly—Mark Spitz, U.S., Aug. 28.**

100meter backstroke—Roland Matthes, East Germany, Aug. 29.*

100meter breaststroke—Nobutaka Taguchi, Japan, Aug. 30.**

200meter freestyle—Mark Spitz, U.S., Aug. 29.**

400meter freestyle—Bradford Cooper, Australia, Sept. 1.*

400meter freestyle relay—U.S., Aug. 28.**

800meter freestyle relay—U.S., Aug. 31.**

400meter individual medley—Gunnar Larsson, Sweden, Aug. 30.*

200meter breaststroke—John Hencken, U.S., Sept. 2.**

200meter backstroke—Roland Matthes, East Germany, Sept. 2.**

200meter individual medley—Gunnar Larsson, Sweden, Sept. 3.**

100meter freestyle—Mark Spitz, U.S., Sept. 3.**

1500meter freestyle—Mike Burton, U.S., Sept. 4.**

400meter medley relay—U.S., Sept. 4.**

Women's Swimming
100meter freestyle—Sandra Neilson, U.S., Aug. 29.*

200meter freestyle—Shane Gould, Australia, Sept. 1.**

400meter freestyle—Shane Gould, Australia, Aug. 30.**

100meter butterfly—Mayumi Aoki, Japan, Sept. 1.**

200meter breaststroke—Beverly Whitfield, Australia, Aug. 29.*

400meter medley—Gail Neall, Australia, Aug. 31.

400meter freestyle relay—U.S., Aug. 30.**

100meter backstroke—Melissa Belote, U.S., Sept. 2.*

200meter medley—Shane Gould, Australia, Aug. 28.**

800meter freestyle—Keena Rothammer, U.S., Sept. 3.**

400meter medley relay—U.S., Sept. 3.**

200meter butterfly—Karen Moe, U.S., Sept. 4.**

200meter backstroke—Melissa Belote, U.S., Sept. 4.**

100meter breaststroke—Cathy Carr, U.S., Sept. 2.**

Men's Diving
Springboard—Vladimir Vasin, U.S.S.R., Aug. 30.

Platform—Klaud DiBiasi, Italy, Sept. 4.

Women's Diving
Threemeter springboard—Micki King, U.S., Aug. 28.

Platform—Ulrika Knape, Sweden, Sept. 2.

Men's Track & Field
20kilometer walk—Peter Frenkel, East Germany, Aug. 31.*

100meter dash—Valery Borzov, U.S.S.R., Sept. 1.

400meter intermediate hurdles—John Akii-Bua, Uganda, Sept. 2.**

800meter run—Dave Wottle, U.S., Sept. 2.

Discus throw—Ludwik Danek, Czechoslovakia, Sept. 2.

Pole vault—Wolfgang Nordwig, East Germany, Sept. 2.*

Javelin throw—Klaus Wilfermann, West Germany, Sept. 3.*

10,000meter run—Lasse Viren, Finland, Sept. 3.**

50kilometer walk—Bernd Kannenberg, West Germany, Sept. 3.*

3,000meter steeplechase—Kipchoge Keino, Kenya, Sept. 4.*

Triple jump—Victor Saneyev, U.S.S.R., Sept. 4.

200meter dash—Valery Borzov, U.S.S.R., Sept. 4.

100meter hurdles—Rod Milburn, U.S., Sept. 7 (equaled world record).

400meter dash—Vince Matthews, U.S., Sept. 7.

Hammer throw—Anatol Bondarchuk, U.S.S.R., Sept. 7.*

Decathlon—Nikolai Avilov, U.S.S.R., Sept. 8.**

Long jump—Randy Williams, U.S., Sept. 9.

Shotput—Wladyslaw Komar, Poland, Sept. 9.*

1,500meter run—Pekka Vasala, Finland, Sept. 10.

High jump—Juri Tarmak, U.S.S.R., Sept. 10.

5,000meter run—Lasse Viren, Finland, Sept. 10.*

400meter relay—U.S., Sept. 10 (equaled world record).

1,600meter relay—Kenya, Sept. 10.

Marathon—Frank Shorter, U.S., Sept. 10.

Women's Track & Field
Long jump—Heidemarie Rosendahl, West Germany, Aug. 31.

Javelin throw—Ruth Fuchs, East Germany, Sept. 1.**

Pentathlon—Mary Peters, Britain, Sept. 3.**

800meter run—Hildegard Falck, West Germany, Sept. 3.*

High jump—Ulrika Meyfarth, West Germany, Sept. 4.**

200meter dash—Renate Stecher, East Germany, Sept. 7 (equaled world record).

Shotput—Nadezhda Chizhova, U.S.S.R., Sept. 7.**

400meter dash—Monika Zehrt, East Germany, Sept. 7.

100meter hurdles—Annelie Erhardt, East Germany, Sept. 8.*

100meter dash—Renate Stecher, East Germany, Sept. 2.

1,500meter run—Ludmila Bragina, U.S.S.R., Sept. 9.**

400meter relay—West Germany, Sept. 10 (equaled world record).

Discus throw—Faina Melnik, U.S.S.R., Sept. 10.*

1,600meter relay—East Germany, Sept. 10.**

Volleyball
Men's—Japan, Sept. 9.

Women's—U.S.S.R., Sept. 7.

Water Polo
Team—U.S.S.R., Sept. 4.

Weight Lifting
Flyweight—Zygmun Smalcerz, Poland, Aug. 27.

Bantamweight—Imre Foeldi, Hungary, Aug. 28.**

Featherweight—Norai Nurikian, Bulgaria, Aug. 29 (equaled world record).

Lightweight—Mukharbi Kirzhinov, U.S.S.R., Aug. 30.**

Middleweight—Yordan Bikov, Bulgaria, Aug. 31.**

Light heavyweight—Leif Jenssen, Norway, Sept. 2.*

Middle heavyweight—Andon Nokolv, Bulgaria, Sept. 3.*

Heavyweight—Yan Talts, U.S.S.R., Sept. 4.

Super heavyweight—Cassill Alexeyev, U.S.S.R., Sept. 6.*

Greco-Roman Wrestling
Paperweight—Gheorghe Berceanu, Rumania, Sept. 10.

Flyweight—Peter Kirov, Bulgaria, Sept. 10.

Bantamweight—Rustem Kazakov, U.S.S.R., Sept. 10.

Featherweight—Gheorghi Markov, Bulgaria, Sept. 10.

Lightweight—Shamil Khisamutdinov, U.S.S.R., Sept. 10.

Welterweight—Vitezslav Macha, Czechoslovakia, Sept. 10.

Middleweight—Csaba Hegedus, Hungary, Sept. 10.

Light heavyweight—Valery Rezantsev, U.S.S.R., Sept. 10.

Heavyweight—Nicolae Martinescu, Rumania, Sept. 10.

Super heavyweight—Antoly Roshin, U.S.S.R., Sept. 10.

Free-style Wrestling
Paperweight—Roman Dmitriev, U.S.S.R., Aug. 31.

Flyweight—Kymomi Kato, Japan, Aug. 31.

Bantamweight—Hideaki Yanagida, Japan, Aug. 31.

Featherweight—Zaga Abdulbekov, U.S.S.R., Aug. 31.

Lightweight—Dan Gable, U.S., Aug. 31.

Welterweight—Wayne Wells, U.S., Aug. 31.

Middleweight—Levan Tediashvili, U.S.S.R., Aug. 31.

Light heavyweight—Ben Peterson, U.S., Aug. 31

Heavyweight—Ivan Yarygin, U.S.S.R., Aug. 31.

Super heavyweight—Alexandr Medved, U.S.S.R., Aug. 31.

Yachting
Soling—Buddy Melges, U.S., Sept. 8.

Dragon—John Bruce Cueno, Australia, Sept 8.

Star—David Forbes, Australia, Sept. 8.

Flying Dutchman—Rodney Pattison, Britain, Sept. 8.

Tempest—Valentin Mankin, U.S.S.R., Sept. 8.

Finn—Serge Maury, France, Sept. 8.

See also ELECTIONS [45]; MIDDLE EAST [1, 7, 10]; OLYMPIC TERRORISM

OLYMPIC TERRORISM—Israeli team members killed. Arab commandos, some disguised as athletes, scaled an eight-foot-high wire fence surrounding the Olympic village in Munich at 4:30 a.m. Sept. 5, beginning a drama which ended shortly before midnight that day after the death of 11 members of the Israeli Olympic team, five commandos and a German policeman and the critical wounding of a German helicopter pilot. Inside the fence, the commandos made their way to Building 31, where the Israeli, Hong Kong and Uruguayan teams were housed. (A West German official said the commandos were familiar with the Israeli compound layout because three of the guerrillas were official employees in the village.) At about 5:30 a.m., the commandos burst into the Israeli quarters, where they were intercepted by Moshe Weinberg, the Israeli wrestling coach. Weinberg held a door against the guerrillas while shouting for the Israeli athletes to flee. (Six of the athletes managed to escape.) Seconds later, the Arabs broke in, killing Weinberg and Joseph Romano, a weight lifter. The nine athletes still trapped within their quarters reportedly fought the attackers with knives for a time, but were overpowered and seized as hostages. Once in control of the Israeli quarters, the commandos demanded the release of 200 Arab guerrillas imprisoned in Israel.

Throughout the late morning and afternoon, West German officials negotiated with the Arabs on the patio of the Israeli dormitory. Efforts by German officials to gain the release of the nine hostages were rejected by the Arabs, as was the attempt of a representative of the Arab League to break the impasse. The commandos also rejected an offer of unlimited ransom and an offer to exchange the hostages for West German Interior Minister Hans-Dietrich Genscher, Munich Police Chief Manfred Schreiber and Bavarian Interior Minister Bruno Merk. Throughout the negotiations, Munich police, some dressed as athletes, were positioned outside the Israeli dormitory. The stalemate was broken at about 9 p.m. when the West Germans succeeded in persuading the terrorists to move out of Building 31 with their hostages. As part of the bargain, the West Germans agreed to have three helicopters transport the Arabs and the hostages to the military airport at Furstenfeldbruck. Munich authorities then cleared a path around the building, from which the Arabs and Israelis emerged at about 10 p.m. Using underground passageways, the group was moved by bus out of the Olympic village to the waiting helicopters.

When the convoy arrived at the airport, two of the terrorists walked from the helicopters to inspect a Boeing 707 jet that was to take them to Cairo. As they walked back to their helicopters, West German soldiers and police sharpshooters reportedly opened fire. The Arabs, armed with automatic weapons, returned the fire. During the shootout, the hostages and five commandos were killed, as was a German policeman. Three of the Arabs were taken prisc..er. The nine hostages slain were identified as weight lifters David Berger and Zeev Friedman, wrestlers Mark Slavin and Eliezer Halfin, marksman coach Kehat Schorr, fencing coach Andre Spitzer, wrestling referee Yosef Gutfreund, weight lifting referee Yacov Springer and track coach Amitzur Shapira. The West German policeman who was killed was identified as Anton Fliegenbauer. Through much of the evening, news reports from Munich had said that the Israeli hostages had been rescued. Conrad Ahlers, the West German government's official spokesman, and Avery Brundage, president of the International Olympic Committee (IOC), had both made statements in which they said the hostages had been freed unharmed. The final word came first from the mayor of Munich, who told newsmen that all of the hostages had been killed. Interior Minister Merk said following the shooting that, although the hostages had agreed to the commandos' insistence on flying to Cairo, "we felt that it would have been a certain death sentence for the hostages."

Black September claims responsibility. In Cairo, an Arab guerrilla group called the Black September Organization Sept. 5 claimed responsibility for the attack and issued a four-page statement to foreign journalists calling for the release of Arab guerrillas held by Israel. The group grew out of a crackdown by the Jordanian government on Arab terrorist organizations in September 1970. Arab sources said the group had formally come into existence in July 1971. The Jordanian government, however, had charged that Black September was not a new terrorist group, but rather "a mask used by Al Fatah," the parent Arab guerrilla group.

World reaction. Religious and political leaders around the non-Arab world used strong language Sept. 5-6 to condemn the attack on the Israeli team. However, with the exception of the governments of Jordan and Lebanon, the nations of the Arab world kept silent over the slayings until Sept. 7. Both Jordan Sept. 5 and Lebanon Sept. 6 expressed concern and sorrow over the deaths. Egypt Sept. 7 gave responsibility for the deaths to the West German government. Israel's leadership warned the Palestinian guerrilla groups Sept. 6 that they would be held responsible for the killings and indirectly linked the governments of the Arab world to the murders. Israeli Premier Golda Meir Sept. 6 expressed her personal appreciation to the German government for its decision to "take action for the liberation of the Israeli hostages and to employ force to this end." (In the past, Israel had been the only nation to resist guerrilla actions with force. It had encouraged other nations to do likewise.) In the U.S., the Senate and the House Sept. 6 passed identical resolutions urging the U.S. and other countries to break off all contacts with nations that supported or harbored terrorists. The U.S. government also announced Sept. 8 the establishment of an intelligence committee to combat international political terrorism in cooperation with other countries. The committee was comprised of senior officials of the State Department, Central Intelligence Agency and Federal Bureau of Investigation.

Effect on Olympics. It was not until 4 p.m. Sept. 5 that IOC President Brundage ordered the Olympic games suspended. Even before the suspension was announced, however, the Egyptian basketball team forfeited a game it had been scheduled to play that day against the Philippines, because the players "were afraid for their lives." Sentiment among the Olympic teams was divided on whether the IOC should have suspended the games. Some believed the suspension indicated that the committee had bowed to protest-politics. (It was the first time since the modern games began that competition had been halted.) Others believed that the 20th Olympic world games should not be resumed because of the bloodshed. More than 80,000 persons filled the Olympic Stadium Sept. 6 for a 1½-hour memorial service for the slain Israelis. During the ceremonies, Brundage announced that the games would be resumed later in the day. Brundage said that "we cannot allow a handful of terrorists to destroy this nucleus of international cooperation and good will that we have in the Olympic movement." Following the memorial service, the Israeli team returned home. Ten members of Norway's Olympic handball team announced Sept. 7 that they were quitting the games to protest the Arab terrorist attack, but returned to the Norwegian squad when the International Handball Federation threatened to hold Norway financially responsible for lost gate receipts if the team withdrew from its remaining matches. Throughout a Sept. 7 match with Japan, the Norwegian players wore black arm bands in sympathy for the slain Israelis.

State funeral held in Israel. The bodies of 10 of the slain Israelis were flown to Tel Aviv Sept. 7 for a state funeral at Lod Airport, the site of a recent commando raid in which 28 persons were shot by Japanese mercenaries (see MIDDLE EAST [22]). The 11th victim, Berger, an emigre from the U.S., was flown to Cleveland for burial near his family's home Sept. 8.

Bonn report clears officials. A final West German report on the slayings, based on an investigation which had begun Sept. 6, was issued Sept. 20. The report, issued jointly by the federal and Bavarian state governments, cleared the police and political authorities of blame for the deaths. According to the findings of the inquiry, the deaths of the two Israelis at the Olympic village could not have been prevented by tighter security in view of the "aggressiveness and murderous intent" of the commandos. As a result of the guerrilla demands and threats and Israeli refusal to give in to them, West German authorities were left "with no other choice" than to attempt to free the nine hostages by force, the report said. The report also restated the government's contention that permitting the commandos to leave with their captives would have meant certain death for the Israelis. A preface to the report said that Bavarian officials were still investigating the incident and that the report could not be considered a "prejudgement" of their eventual findings.

Israel ousts security aides. Three unidentified security aides were dismissed by the Israeli government Oct. 16 for their failure to provide adequate protection for the members of the Israeli Olympic team. It was the first time that the Israeli government had openly acknowledged shortcomings in its own safety measures to protect the Israeli athletes. The ousted security men were later reported to be the principal "operational figures" responsible for arrangements with West German officials for protecting the Israeli athletes.

Arabs force release of slayers. Two Arab guerrillas of the Black September group Oct. 29 hijacked a West German airliner over Turkey, forcing the Bonn government to release the three commandos captured Sept. 5. The aircraft, with 13 passengers and seven crewmen aboard, was commandeered by the hijackers after it left Beirut, Lebanon for Ankara, Turkey. Threatening to blow up the plane and its occupants unless their demands were met, the commandos forced the pilot to fly to Munich with fuel stopovers at Nicosia, Cyprus and Zagreb, Yugoslavia. As the plane circled the Munich airport, the hijackers ordered it flown back to Zagreb, where it circled the airfield for an hour and landed only after a smaller jet carrying the three guerrillas released by the West Germans arrived. The three freed prisoners then boarded the hijacked airliner which flew on to Tripoli, Libya, where the plane was released to fly back to West Germany (with passengers and crew aboard) Oct. 30. The Croatian Interior minister said Yugoslav negotiators had tried to stall the hijackers when they landed in Zagreb the second time by refusing to refuel the plane in hope of freeing the hostages. The minister said that, after the hijackers threatened to blow up the plane, he consulted with the West German consul in the control tower and received written permission for refueling. The West German decision to free the three commandos to the hijackers was criticized by the U.S. State Department and sharply scored by the Israeli government. The State Department expressed "regret that known terrorists can secure their freedom as a result of extortion and blackmail and can find a safe haven." After an Israeli Cabinet meeting on the incident, Minister Without Portfolio Israel Galili assailed Bonn's decision as "shocking that no attempt was made, no real attempt, to thwart the terrorists." Israel protested the decision as "capitulation" to the Arabs.

See also MIDDLE EAST [1, 7, 10]; OLYMPICS [5]

OMAN—*See* EUROPEAN ECONOMIC COMMUNITY [7]; INTERNATIONAL MONETARY DEVELOPMENTS [8]

OPIUM—*See* DRUG USE & ADDICTION [12, 15, 18]

ORGANIZATION FOR VICTIMS OF ZIONIST OCCUPATION—*See* HIJACKING [8]

ORGANIZATION OF AFRICAN UNITY (OAU)—*See* GABON; POLITICS [8]

ORGANIZATION OF AMERICAN STATES (OAS)—*See* BAHAMAS; BRAZIL; LATIN AMERICA

ORGANIZATION OF PETROLEUM EXPORTING COUNTRIES (OPEC)—*See* OIL & NATURAL GAS

OSCARS—*See* MOTION PICTURES

PACIFIC MARITIME ASSOCIATION—*See* LABOR

PAKISTAN—Pakistan concentrated during 1972 on recovering from the December 1971 war with India and Bangla Desh (*see also* BANGLA DESH). Information was released during the early part of the year which revealed American, Arab and Soviet involvement in the 1971 war (*see* [2-4]). Pakistan withdrew from international organizations which recognized Bangla Desh (*see* [7]), but itself carried out secret talks with Bangla Desh aimed at normalizing relations between the two countries (*see* [16]). During June and July, India and Pakistan signed major agreements ending the diplomatic impasse resulting from the war (*see* [12-13]).

[2] U.S. role in 1971 war. Columnist Jack Anderson continued Jan. 3-7 and Jan. 12 to publish secret material pertaining to the Nixon Administration's policy on the Indian-Pakistani war. (He had begun publishing the material—classified as "sensitive secret"—Dec. 30-31, 1971.) Anderson released some of the material to wire services and newspapers Jan. 5, offered to make it available to a congressional subcommittee and Jan. 14 released the material in full text. The material used by Anderson was minutes of December 1971 meetings of the Washington Special Action Group (WSAG), a top-level strategy panel assembled during crises. Anderson said that his purpose in publishing the material was "to force a showdown with the Administration over their classification system," which he did not consider "in the public interest in a democracy." The published material disclosed a strong pro-Pakistan, anti-India Administration policy during the war. It purported to show that Presidential national security adviser Henry Kissinger was under Presidential pressure to take a tougher line with India than with Pakistan during the war crisis, that Kissinger told a strategy session "it is quite obvious that the President is not inclined to let the Paks be defeated in the West," that aid to India was to be cut off unless word came from the White House and that U.S. Ambassador to India Kenneth Keating had protested to the Administration its pro-Pakistan stand. The Anderson material also indicated that the Nixon Administration feared that India would carry the war to West Pakistan after the fighting in East Pakistan ended.

[3] In related developments, Indian sources charged Jan. 25 that the U.S. government had delayed by one day the transmission, from Pakistani authorities in Dacca to Indian officials in New Delhi, of the surrender message which had ended the 1971 war. According to the charges, Pakistan's commander in Dacca, Lt. Gen. A.A.K. Niazi had requested the U.S. consulate in Dacca at 6:30 p.m. Dec. 14 to transmit his acceptance of Indian surrender terms to New Delhi because his own radio equipment had been badly damaged by Indian air strikes. Indian authorities did not get Niazi's message until 3 p.m. Dec. 15. The Indian sources said the U.S. had deliberately held up the message because it was reluctant to see India defeat Pakistan. The U.S. called the charges "just plain inaccurate." The General Accounting Office (GAO, the auditing arm of Congress), in a report released Feb. 4, said that the U.S. had continued to send arms to Pakistan in July 1971 despite assurances to Congress that such shipments had stopped. In a report released June 8, the GAO also asserted that Pakistan had misused $10 million in American relief money for military purposes during the 1971 civil war. The release of the GAO study was followed by an Administration confirmation June 8 that relief aid to Pakistan had been suspended in the fall of 1971 after the discovery that the funds were being diverted for military use.

[4] *Arab, Soviet roles in war.* Libya, Jordan and the Soviet Union were reported March 28 and 30 to have shipped planes to the opposing sides in the 1971 war. Western diplomatic sources in Washington said March 30 that the Soviet union had transferred about 15 Mig-21 fighters and TU-16 bombers from Egypt to India during the December fighting. The planes were said to have been Soviet-piloted and attached to Soviet air units stationed in Egypt. According to the reports, the planes had been sent "very sparingly"—on a one-for-one basis to replace Indian planes lost in the fighting. India denied the reports March 31. Pakistani military sources disclosed March 28 (and the U.S. State Department confirmed April 18) that Libya and Jordan had provided Pakistan with American-built aircraft. The Libyan planes, F-5 jets, were said to be in the possession of the Pakistani air force. The U.S. State Department April 18 said that it had not authorized the transfer of the aircraft and that their transshipment was a violation of the U.S. Foreign Assistance Act.

[5] **Nationalization moves.** President Zulfikar Ali Bhutto Jan. 2 ordered the nationalization of the iron and steel, basic metals, heavy engineering, heavy electrical equipment, motor vehicles, petro-chemical, electricity, gas and oil refinery and cement industries in a move to break up an "undue concentration of economic power." In a separate decree announced Jan. 2, the government said it would nationalize any firm worth more than $2 million in which a single family owned more than 50% of the company's shares. The nationalization, seemingly aimed at Pakistan's 22 richest families, did not apply to foreign-owned companies or to cotton textile manufacturing, the largest single industrial group in the country and its biggest earner of hard currency. (In a related move, the government Sept. 1 nationalized 176 private colleges in the first phase of its educational reforms. The action followed a week of street demonstrations in which the country's Christian minority protested the impending takeover of four Protestant educational institutions. At least three persons were killed and several hundred injured in clashes with the police.)

[6] **Yahya arrested.** Former President Agha Mohammad Yahya Khan and former Army Chief of Staff Gen. Abdul Hamid Khan were placed under house arrest Jan. 8 on orders of President Bhutto. A government announcement said the action was taken "in the supreme interest of the state and people of Pakistan." The government was carrying out an investigation of the role of Yahya and others in Pakistan's 1971 defeat by India.

[7] **International ties broken.** President Bhutto announced Jan. 30 that Pakistan was withdrawing from the British Commonwealth as "an appropriate countermeasure" to the announcement that Britain, Australia and New Zealand planned to recognize Bangla Desh. The pullout from the loose association of 31 nations was largely symbolic and would result in few disadvantages for Pakistan. Bhutto also announced July 15 that Pakistan had withdrawn from the Southeast Asian Treaty Organization (SEATO). (The SEATO withdrawal was formalized Nov. 8.)

[8] **Pathans demand autonomy.** About 10,000 Pathans, many of then armed, demonstrated Feb. 24 for the lifting of martial law and more self-government. Other Pathan demands included the ouster of the governor of the North-West Province, who was a member of President Bhutto's Pakistan People's party. (Pathans in the North-West Province and in southwestern Baluchistan Province had been demanding complete secession from Pakistan and establishment of an independent state. The secession of the two provinces would reduce Pakistan to the provinces of Sind and Punjab.) Saeed Mohammad Ayub, president of the Peshawar City Committee of the National Awami party, had threatened war against the government unless the Pathan demands were met. He was quoted as saying that if Bhutto "lifts martial law and restores democracy, if he allows Pathans self-government, if he recognizes Bangla Desh and makes friends with India, we are ready to stay within Pakistan. Otherwise, we are armed and ready."

[9] **Military command shift.** President Bhutto March 3 dismissed Air Marshal Abdul Rahim Khan as air force commander and Lt. Gen. Abdul Gul Hassan as acting commander in chief of the army. Bhutto said that the ouster of the two men, reportedly most responsible for putting him in power, was designed to "prevent the professional soldiers from becoming professional politicians." (Both men were given ambassadorial posts March 11.) Lt. Gen. Tikka Khan, former military governor of East Pakistan and the leader of the bloody suppression of the Bangla Desh independence movement in 1971, was named army chief of staff and promoted to full general. Zafar Chowdhury, general manager of Pakistan's civil air line, was named air force commander and given the title of air marshal. In announcing the change in military leadership, Bhutto stipulated that there would be no military commander in charge of all the armed forces in the future. He also ordered the chiefs of staff of each service to remain at their posts only for a fixed period, as yet undesignated.

[10] **Interim constitution approved.** The National Assembly April 14 concluded a three-day meeting in Islamabad by approving the draft of an interim constitution and pledging to lift martial law on April 21. (President Bhutto had announced March 6 that he would lift martial law Aug. 14 and would reinstitute democratic government in phases before then. Martial law had been in effect since 1958, when Field Marshal Mohammed Ayub Khan established his military regime.) The charter and martial law abrogation were among agenda items submitted by Bhutto. The constitution permitted Bhutto to rule until August 1973. It guaranteed civil liberties and protection against arbitrary arrests, curtailed the power of detention, widened women's rights and defined provincial autonomy. Bhutto signed the interim constitution April 20. Martial law was lifted April 21, and Bhutto was sworn in as president the same day. With the lifting of martial law, all ministers and government officials automatically resigned. (A conference of 10 leaders from all the parties in the National Assembly Oct. 20 approved a draft of a new constitution. The draft document—which was to be submitted to an Assembly constitutional committee as a basis for drafting the permanent constitution—proposed a two-chamber federal parliament composed of a 210-member National Assembly and a 60-member Senate; a prime minister; and a president.)

[11] **Karachi strike violence.** Three persons were shot to death by police June 7 as Karachi industrial workers attempted to seize a textile mill on the outskirts of the city. Another 14 were killed the next day when police fired at a funeral procession for one of the victims of the first day's incident, and thousands of workers launched a protest strike June 9 in response to the killings. The workers agreed June 17, after President Bhutto agreed to accept a number of their demands, that they would end the work stoppage June 19. (In a later development, Karachi police Oct. 28 fired on strikers occupying two textile mills, killing at least 10 workers and wounding 30 others. The plants, occupied by the workers for four days in a wage dispute, were cleared by police.)

[12] **India-Pakistan summit.** Indian Prime Minister Indira Gandhi and President Bhutto June 28-July 3 held a summit in Simla, India. The summit resulted in major agreements ending the diplomatic impasse resulting from the 1971 war. (Indian and Pakistani representatives had agreed in talks April 26-29 on the agenda for the Simla summit. The agreement to have a summit meeting had followed an April 4 letter from Mrs. Gandhi to Bhutto sounding out the possibilities of holding peace talks.) An accord signed July 3 provided for the renunciation of force to settle differences between the two countries, the withdrawal of troops from their mutual borders 30 days after ratification of the agreement, the freezing of current troop positions in Kashmir until further negotiations were held on that disputed territory, a "step-by-step" normalization of Indian-Pakistani relations and efforts "to prevent hostile propaganda directed against each other." Relations between the two countries were to be improved by resumption of communications, renewal of trade and economic cooperation and exchanges in the fields of culture and science. Both sides agreed to put off for subsequent negotiations the matter of repatriating the Pakistanis held by India since the war. The summit pact was approved by the Pakistan National Assembly July 14 and by the Indian parliament July 28 *(see* [17]).

[13] Officials of both countries met in New Delhi Aug. 25-29 to resolve differences obstructing implementation of the Simla summit agreement. A joint statement issued after the talks said guidelines had been established for laying down the "line of control" in the disputed state of Kashmir and that the line would be "respected by both sides without prejudice to the recognized positions of either side." Troop withdrawals from occupied territories were to go ahead, but the deadline for completion of the move was extended from Sept. 4 (30 days after India's document of ratification of the Simla agreement was received by Pakistan) to Sept. 15. Meetings were held Sept. 3-5, 15 and 30, Oct. 1, 14 and 21-22, and Nov. 8-9 and 28 to resolve the placement of the Kashmir truce line, but no agreement was reached. The two countries Dec. 7 finally reached agreement on the delineation of the truce line in Kashmir, the site of numerous Indian Pakistani clashes during 1972. The Kashmir accord was contained in a joint statement issued by the army chiefs of both countries. The statement said that the two had been "able to compose the differences that existed" and were directing local commanders to draw up a new 500-mile cease-fire line along the positions that had existed at the end of the 1971 war. The long deadlock over negotiations was broken when Pakistan finally accepted India's contention that the Thakur Chauk area belonged to India and that Pakistan troops that had been occupying the region since the war must pull out. Both sides completed demarcation of the truce line Dec. 11, and troops from both countries began their withdrawal from each other's territory the same day. The withdrawal reportedly was completed Dec. 21.

[14] **Sindhi-Urdu riots.** The Sind Province assembly July 7 adopted a bill making Sindhi the province's official language. The bill's adoption set off violent demonstrations by Urdu-speaking residents demanding that Urdu (along with Bengali, one of Pakistan's two national languages) also be made an official language in Sind. (Urdu was the official language in the three other provinces of Pakistan.) Leaders of the Urdu- and Sindhi-speaking communities in Sind July 15 reached an agreement to resolve the language dispute, which claimed 50 lives between July 7 and 15. Under the agreement, both sides accepted the July 7 law, and the Urdu-speaking people would have 12 years to learn the language. (The government Aug. 9 arrested seven leaders of the two parties involved in the language dispute. The arrests were carried out under Defense of Pakistan rules, but the charges were not specified.)

[15] **Officers retired.** Six Pakistani army officers (Brig. Gen. R. D. Shamin, Brig. F. B. Aleem, Brig. Iqbal Mehdi, Col. Abdul Aleem Afridi, Col. Jawaid Iqbal and Lt. Col. Mohammed Khurshid) were forcibly retired Aug. 10 after being charged with planning a civil war in December 1971. The government

statement announcing the retirement said the men had taken part in an "abortive attempt to liquidate what is left of Pakistan" two days before Bhutto had taken over the presidency and after Pakistan's defeat by India.

[16] Bangla Desh talks. President Bhutto disclosed Nov. 13 that Pakistani and Bangla Desh representatives had been holding secret meetings at United Nations headquarters in New York, but that the negotiations had "drawn a blank." According to Bhutto, Pakistan had "made positive gestures, a multitude of overtures" in the secret talks, but the Dacca representatives had "not responded." Bhutto attributed the deadlock to Bangla Desh Prime Minister Sheik Mujibur Rahman, who, Bhutto claimed, demanded recognition of his regime as "a face-saving device" before agreeing to meet with Bhutto. (Bhutto repeatedly called for recognition of Bangla Desh during late November and early December, but public opinion opposed the recognition.)

[17] Prisoners freed. Pakistan and India Nov. 27 agreed to release military and civilian prisoners detained since the 1971 war. (The two countries earlier had reached agreement Feb. 17 to exchange sick and seriously wounded prisoners of the war. By May 8, 99 Pakistani prisoners had been returned to Pakistan by India.) President Bhutto the same day announced the release of 616 Indian prisoners captured on the western front of the war. In reciprocation, India Dec. 1 released all 540 Pakistani prisoners captured on the western sector. India had also announced Nov. 20 that 6,000 Pakistani women and children detained in India since the war would be released if Pakistan released all Bangla Desh nationals detained in Pakistan. President Bhutto responded Nov. 21 that he would permit 10,000 Bengalis to return to their homeland, but Bangla Desh claimed Pakistan held 400,000 of its nationals.

See also BANGLA DESH; DRUG USE & ADDICTION [18]; FOREIGN AID; FOREIGN POLICY; HEALTH; INTERNATIONAL MONETARY DEVELOPMENTS [8]; MIDDLE EAST [30]; OLYMPICS [10]; PULITZER PRIZES; SINO-U.S. RELATIONS [5]; UGANDA [1, 7, 9]; UNITED NATIONS

PALESTINE LIBERATION ORGANIZATION (PLO)—*See* MIDDLE EAST [9, 17, 26]
PALESTINIAN GUERRILLAS—*See* HIJACKING [8-9]; JORDAN; LEBANON; MIDDLE EAST [1-14, 19, 22-29]; OLYMPICS [5]; OLYMPIC TERRORISM; SYRIA
PALESTINIAN NATIONAL COUNCIL—*See* JORDAN

PANAMA—**Finance minister demoted.** The transfer of Finance Minister Jose G. Aizpu to the relatively minor post of minister of the presidency was reported June 24. No reason was given for the demotion, but Aizpu was believed to have disagreed with government economic policy following a recent increase in taxes. Aizpu's vice minister, Dora M. Roluz, was placed in charge of the ministry.

National elections. An unprecedented 88% of Panama's 525,000 eligible voters turned out Aug. 6 to elect the 505 members of the new Assembly of Community Representatives (corregidores). The elections were the first held since Gen. Omar Torrijos seized power in 1968. Reports indicated that the majority of candidates elected were from the pro-Torrijos Nouvel Panama movement. The duties of the corregidores would generally be consultative rather than legislative.

U.S. Canal payments rejected. In their first session Sept. 11, the corregidores passed a resolution charging that the Panama Canal Zone was being "occupied arbitrarily" by the U.S. and requesting Torrijos to reject the $1.93 million the U.S. paid annually for its use. Torrijos confirmed Oct. 11 that the U.S. payments would no longer be accepted. A U.S. spokesman said Sept. 12 that the U.S. would continue to make the rent payments, which were not handed over to Panama anyway but were used to repay a Panamanian loan from a U.S. bank.

Torrijos assumes legal powers. Torrijos legally assumed full civil and military powers Oct. 11 following the end of the corregidores session. The corregidores had voted full powers to Torrijos Sept. 12. Under the vote,

Torrijos's duties as "maximum revolutionary leader" for the next six years included full responsibility for public administration, appointment of Cabinet ministers and members of the legislative commission, appointment of military and police officers, designation (with the Cabinet's approval) of the attorney general and members of the Supreme Court, the agreement of contracts and loans and the conduct of foreign relations. During their session, the corregidores also approved a new constitution which was promulgated Oct. 11. The constitution, replacing that of 1946, provided for the indirect election of the president, established the National Guard as one of the country's governing institutions, required that directors of companies and members of the Roman Catholic hierarchy be Panamanian by birth, and took no formal account of the U.S.-controlled Canal Zone. Demetrio Lakas was inaugurated as president of Panama Oct. 11. Torrijos Oct. 18 shuffled his Cabinet (retaining five of the 10 Cabinet ministers) and appointed eight members to the legislative commission. The commission was to consist of the eight appointees plus Torrijos, Lakas, Vice President Arturo Sucre, Corregidores President Elias Castillo and the Cabinet.

See also CONSERVATION; DRUG USE & ADDICTION [1, 11, 20]; TERRITORIAL WATERS

PAN AMERICAN HEALTH ORGANIZATION—See HEALTH
PAPER GOLD—See INTERNATIONAL MONETARY DEVELOPMENTS [1-2, 5, 11]
PAPUA & NEW GUINEA—See AUSTRALIA [5-6, 11]

PARAGUAY—Church charges persecution. The Paraguayan Episcopal Conference, the country's highest ecclestiastical body, May 20 accused the government of carrying out "systematic persecution" of the Roman Catholic Church. The conference objected to the use of the term "subversive" against members of the church and to government attempts to discredit priests for "immorality." The charge of persecution followed the expulsion from Paraguay of eight Catholic priests, including the Rev. Jose Luis Caravias, a Spanish Jesuit, who was accused of promoting "subversive activities" among Paraguayan peasants. Caravias and the Rev. Vicente Barreto, a Paraguayan Jesuit expelled earlier, had been involved in organizing the Christian Agrarian Leagues, which had increasingly brought peasants into conflict with traditional authority, usually concentrated in the hands of the local representative of President Alfredo Stroessner's Colorado party. It was reported May 26 that Interior Minister Sabino Augusto Montanaro, who had been excommunicated from the church in 1971, had charged that the Agrarian Leagues encouraged peasants to rise up against the government and had implied that the church was in some way linked with Paraguay's main opposition party, the Liberal Radicals.

See also DRUG USE & ADDICTION [1, 13-14, 16]; LATIN AMERICA

PASSPORTS—See SECURITY, U.S.
PATHET LAO—See INDOCHINA WAR [8, 10-12]; LAOS
PAUL VI—See CHURCHES; POLAND; ROMAN CATHOLIC CHURCH; SPAIN
PAY BOARD—See ECONOMY [1, 7-8, 10-11]; LABOR
PEARCE COMMISSION—See RHODESIA
PEERS, WILLIAM R.—See WAR CRIMES
PENN CENTRAL TRANSPORTATION CO.—See RAILROADS
PENTAGON—See CIVIL DISORDERS; DEFENSE; MILITARY; PENTAGON PAPERS; PUERTO RICO; WAR CRIMES

PENTAGON PAPERS—More documents disclosed. Syndicated columnist Jack Anderson June 26 made public more secret material from the Pentagon papers, a government study of U.S. involvement in Vietnam. (Material from 43 of 47 volumes of the papers had been disclosed in 1971.) The newly released material was in volumes covering Lyndon B. Johnson Administration efforts in 1965-68 to get peace talks started. In releasing the top secret material,

Anderson said that President Nixon had made public "even more sensitive negotiations." Much of the material had already been made public by other sources, such as in President Johnson's memoirs. Some items had appeared in Anderson's columns the previous three weeks. One of the findings of the Pentagon analysis disclosed June 26 was that "it has always been clear that insofar as Hanoi is interested in negotiations, it is only as another way of achieving its objectives." The analysis also disclosed that Soviet Premier Aleksei N. Kosygin had offered in February 1967 to act as a mediator with the North Vietnamese, and that Norwegian efforts as an intermediary were highly regarded by the Pentagon analysts, but not "treated with great importance in Washington." The Pentagon analysts found the unwillingness of either side to compromise on political control of the South to be a basic cause of inability to reach a peace settlement. The North held to its objective of a· united Vietnam under a Communist form of government, the U.S. to the objective of a divided Vietnam and a non-Communist South. The study found Hanoi's diplomacy relatively consistent in private and in public efforts, with the theme of extending to the U.S. a face-saving way to pull out and deferring its long-term goal of a Communist-run South by creation of an outwardly neutral regime. The study said that U.S. public negotiations pointed diplomatically toward private evolvement of a face-saving way for Hanoi to end its war in the South in exchange for an end to the U.S. bombing and ground combat. The Communist attitude that the U.S. military power would not win out in the end was a basic difference in the two sides emphasized in the analysis.

Gravel denied immunity. The Supreme Court ruled 5-4 June 29 that Sen. Mike Gravel (D, Alaska) was not exempt from testifying before a grand jury about the publication of the classified Pentagon Papers. (Gravel had read parts of the top secret papers to a Senate committee in 1971.) However, the court also ruled that Congressional immunity, when constitutionally applicable, covered Congressional aides as well as congressmen. Gravel had challenged the right of a Boston grand jury to subpoena Dr. Leonard Rodberg, a Gravel aide, as part of an inquiry into the release of the papers. The court rejected Gravel's contention that the subpoena violated Gravel's Congressional immunity, but ruled that the immunity clause covered Congressional aides when the aides' conduct "would be immune legislative conduct if performed by the senator himself." The majority opinion said, however, that the constitutional "speech and debate" clause only applied in matters that were "an integral part of the deliberative process and communicative processes" in considering legislative actions. The court said that the clause "does not privilege either senator or aide to violate an otherwise valid criminal law in preparing for or implementing legislative acts."

Mistrial declared in Ellsberg case. Federal District Court Judge William M. Byrne Jr. Dec. 8 declared a mistrial in the Los Angeles trial for disclosure of the Pentagon Papers. Although attorneys for Daniel Ellsberg and Anthony J. Russo Jr. (the principal defendants in the case) had sought a mistrial on the ground that the use of the word "steal" by Vice President Spiro T. Agnew in referring to the publication of the papers had prejudiced the defendants' case, Byrne's decision was made because of an unparalleled lapse between the time the jury was seated and the actual opening of the trial. Mistrial was declared after Ellsberg and Russo waived their double jeopardy right. (Ellsberg was charged with 12 counts of espionage, theft and conspiracy. Russo was charged with three counts.) The delay between jury selection and trial opening had resulted from Supreme Court Justice William O. Douglas's July 29 decision to stay the trial 48 hours before opening arguments were to be heard. Douglas's action marked the first time a Supreme Court justice ever had blocked a trial after the jury was sworn in. (The jury had been sworn in July 21.) Douglas said he was "exceedingly reluctant" to stay the trial under the circumstances but that he feared the constitutional rights of the defendants might have been violated by electronic wiretapping. The stay was designed to allow attorneys for the defense to appeal to the Supreme Court their contention that the government should be required to divulge the details of a wiretapped conversation involving a defense attorney or consultant. The government had refused to make available a transcript of the conversation on the ground that the wiretap had been made in an investigation unrelated to the Pentagon Papers case and that the contents of the conversation were not relevant to the trial.

The Justice Department asked the Supreme Court to convene a special summer session to consider overturning Douglas's stay, but the court Aug. 5 refused the request. During its regular session, the court Nov. 13 refused to hear the defendants' appeal that they should have been allowed to see a transcript of the conversation. Douglas and Justice William J. Brennan Jr. dissented. The decision in effect dissolved Douglas's stay, thus clearing the way for the opening of the trial.

See also PULITZER PRIZES

PEOPLE'S COALITION FOR PEACE & JUSTICE—*See* ELECTIONS [25]
PEOPLE'S PARTY—*See* ELECTIONS [37]
PEOPLE'S REPUBLIC OF CHINA—*See* CHINA, COMMUNIST
PERON, JUAN DOMINGO—*See* ARGENTINA [1, 7, 9]
PERSIAN GULF STATES—*See* BAHRAIN; OIL & NATURAL GAS; UNION OF ARAB EMIRATES

PERU—Cabinet changes reported. Edgardo Mercado Jarrin, who had been foreign minister since the 1968 coup that installed Peru's current military government, Jan. 3 resigned his post to become army chief of staff. (He was replaced as foreign minister by Gen. Miguel de la Flor Valle.) Mercado's promotion placed him second in the government only to Gen. Ernesto Montagne Sanchez, premier and minister of war, whom Mercado was appointed Nov. 3 to replace, effective Jan. 1, 1973. The November appointment left Mercado as a likely successor to President Juan Velasco Alvarado. Two other Cabinet changes became effective Jan. 3 as Housing Minister Vice Adm. Luis Ernesto Vargas Caballero became naval minister, succeeding retiring Vice Adm. Fernando Elias. Replacing Vargas as housing minister was Rear Adm. Ramon Arrospide Mejia, former director of the Naval War College.

Foreign ownership deadline set. The government announced Jan. 14 that any company owned more than 49% by foreign interests must sign a contract with the government by Dec. 31 fixing a deadline for its transference to majority Peruvian ownership. In a related development, the government July 25 expropriated the National Telephone Co. (CNT), which handled long-distance calls and was owned by Swiss, Luxembourg and Liechtenstein interests. The action, which gave the state control of 95% of Peru's telephone service, followed the failure of negotiations for government purchase of the company.

Beltran removed. Pedro Beltran Espantoso—publisher of *La Prensa* of Lima, a leading critic of the military regime and a former economics minister and prime minister—was removed from his publishing post Jan. 14 and ordered to sell his stock in *La Prensa* within 180 days. According to the government, Beltran had violated Peru's "freedom of the press" statute by remaining abroad since July 10, 1971. Article 10 of the statute, adopted in December 1969, required that newspaper directors and shareholders live within national territory for "not less than six months per year." (Beltran had been teaching economics and international affairs at the University of Virginia in Charlottesville. He returned to Peru Jan. 21.) Beltran's ouster evoked strong protest from journalists throughout Latin America and the U.S. An appeal by the publisher's nephew, Pedro Beltran Ballen, stating that Beltran had met residency requirements by living in Peru from Jan. 1-July 10, 1971, was rejected Jan. 20 on the basis that the requirement applied to any 12-month period, not to the calendar year. Interior Minister Pedro Richter Prada agreed Jan. 26 to review the appeal, but rejected it Feb. 11. Beltran April 4 sold his 80,000 shares in *La Prensa* to the newspaper's "industrial community," which represented 508 employees. Purchase of the shares was facilitated by an interest-free loan granted to the industrial community by *La Prensa*. The majority of the paper's 314,000 shares was held by two investment companies and the younger Beltran, who had taken over as publisher from his uncle.

The younger Beltran March 15 was given a suspended six-month jail term and ordered to pay $960 in damages and a $1,500 fine for violating the freedom of the press statute. Beltran had been sued by Peruvian Ambassador to Mexico Alfonso Benavides Correa, who claimed his reputation was damaged by publication in *La Prensa* of a story about him that had appeared in a Mexican magazine. Beltran July 13 again received a suspended six-month term and a $2,320 fine for violating the press statute. Beltran and *La Prensa* editor Julio Alzola Castillo, who was also given a suspended sentence and fined, were convicted for "causing great harm to the reputation of the revolutionary government" by publishing a report that Carlos Costa Camba, editor of the small Lima newspaper *Indio,* had been deported to Argentina. Costa confirmed July 19 that he had been expelled to Argentina two months earlier for criticizing the government in *Indio.* (The sentences against Beltran and Alzola were overturned Aug. 25 but reinstituted Sept. 22.)

New education law. The government March 24 decreed a sweeping reform of education in order to create "a new Peruvian man" in a society of "justice, liberty and solidarity." The new education law, effective April 3, envisioned by 1980 bi-lingual education (Spanish and Indian dialect), equal opportunities for women, obligatory national service before graduation and student participation in university government. Radio and television, which the government had taken over in November 1971 *(see also below),* was to be used extensively for primary and secondary education in remote parts of the country. The university law allegedly was unpopular with students. Reportedly in protest over its enactment, a mob of students June 27 attacked police headquarters in the southeastern city of Puno, beginning a battle which left three civilians dead and seven policemen and five civilians wounded. Clashes occurred elsewhere in the city, but order reportedly was restored after police cut off communications with other parts of the country and imposed a curfew. The government July 3 suspended constitutional rights in Puno and declared a state of siege in apparent response to a general strike, called by a worker-student "popular front" to protest the three June 27 deaths. One person was killed and five injured July 3, when a group of students and workers tried to disarm a truck full of policemen. However, order reportedly was restored the same day. (An estimated 12,000-15,000 Lima students demonstrated July 9 to protest the Puno incidents.)

General strike ends. Members of 88 unions in Arequipa (Peru's second largest city) returned to work April 13 after the government agreed to all the strikers' demands. The four-day general strike had paralyzed the city. In other strike developments, 2,000 miners and 800 smelter workers went on strike May 22 and May 25, respectively, paralyzing the U.S.-owned Southern Peru Copper Corp., which accounted for more than half of Peru's copper production. The strikers returned to work June 7 after the company agreed to set up a tripartite commission to study workers' demands for improved social benefits and working conditions. The commission would consist of representatives of management, unions and the Justice Ministry. The Peruvian Education Workers Union (SUTEP) led nationwide teachers' strikes Sept. 14 and Nov. 29-30 to demand higher wages and the "real and effective" reinstatement of teachers dismissed "because of their syndical and ideological struggles." The union also demanded job security against "the massive transfers and repressive measures to which education workers are subjected," and an end to "intervention" in education by SINAMOS, the government social mobilization agency. SUTEP officials charged Sept. 14 that more than 300 persons had been arrested and detained following the strike and student-teacher demonstrations Sept. 14.

Farm organization dissolved. The government May 12 dissolved the National Agrarian Society (SNA), the Stockbreeders Association and the Rural Agrarian Societies. The organizations reportedly represented about 30,000 small landowners. The action came after the government decided to abolish the SNA and create new associations which would give "just and necessary representation" to socially oriented agrarian societies, peasant communities and landless laborers. According to a report May 13, the associations would be replaced by a national institution called the National Agrarian Federation.

Broadcasting reforms. The government May 17 issued two decrees setting new standards for television and radio programming and advertising. The new programming law, effective in 90 days, sharply reduced broadcasting of U.S. programs and music, which dominated Peruvian television and radio because they were less expensive than were self-produced programs. Whenever possible, the law stated, the context and themes of programs must be Peruvian. The decree further barred direct or indirect discrimination against any identifiable group and placed all broadcasting facilities "at the disposal of the state for educational and cultural purposes." The advertising decree, also effective in 90 days, also banned discrimination of any kind and allowed advertising only for "socially useful products." The advertising of products beyond the reach of the masses of impoverished Peruvians was sharply curtailed and made subject to state censorship.

Fish product exports halted. The government announced Sept. 26 that all exports of fish oil and fishmeal would be stopped indefinitely Oct. 1, confirming that the fishing industry was experiencing the worst crisis in its history. (The ban was partially lifted Dec. 4.) Sales of fishmeal abroad had been suspended indefinitely Aug. 1. A severe, unexplained shortage of anchovies along the Pacific coast reportedly had put nearly 30,000 persons who depended on the fishing industry out of work. With the September announcement, the government reportedly sought to avoid penalty clauses in contracts to deliver 400,000 metric tons of fishmeal to buyers throughout the world by the end of 1972. The crisis meant a loss to the economy of about $150 million worth of exports, and more if fishing did not resume at the normal rate by February 1973. (In an attempt to alleviate the fishing crisis, Fisheries Minister Gen. Javier Tantalean Vianini had traveled to the U.S. to ask for assistance in determining the factors affecting the behavior of ocean currents off the Peruvian coast. According to a Sept. 22 report, however, the U.S. refused such assistance until Peru signed a bilateral agreement allowing California fishing boats unlimited access to its waters. *See* TERRITORIAL WATERS.) The government Dec. 21 announced a two-year program to develop the fishing industry with financial and technical assistance from the Soviet Union, West Germany, Poland, the Netherlands and Japan.

See also ATOMIC ENERGY [13]; DRUG USE & ADDICTION [16, 20]; EARTHQUAKES; FLOODS; FOREIGN POLICY; LATIN AMERICA; TERRITORIAL WATERS

PESTICIDES—Mercury curbs. The Environmental Protection Agency (EPA) March 24 suspended registration of 12 mercury pesticides and fungicides, and initiated cancellation procedures on 750 others. Taken together, the poisons accounted for 18% of all commercially used mercury. Interstate shipment of the suspended products would immediately cease, though sales of wholesale or retail inventories could continue. (Concentration of mercury runoffs in food fish was considered a health hazard.)

Most DDT banned. EPA Administrator William D. Ruckelshaus June 14 banned nearly all agricultural and other uses of the pesticide DDT, effective Dec. 31. In banning the pesticide, widely used to protect cotton, soybean and peanut crops, Ruckelshaus overruled the recommendation of a federal hearing examiner, who, after seven months of hearings, concluded April 25 that the benefits of DDT and the risks associated with substitute chemicals outweighed the dangers. Ruckelshaus said that, while there was no proof that DDT caused cancer, the evidence that the chemical is stored in man and that it reaches higher proportions as it progresses along the food chain "is a warning to the prudent." The deadline was placed at Dec. 31 in order to allow cotton growers time to learn safe application of the highly toxic but biodegradable methyl parathion, a substitute pesticide. DDT could still be used after the deadline on green peppers, onions and sweet potatoes in certain regions, pending the development of substitutes. Public health officials could also use DDT in emergencies; and exports, mainly for malarial control through the World Health Organization and foreign aid programs, would be continued.

Pesticide bill passed. The Senate Oct. 5 and the House Oct. 12 approved a conference committee compromise pesticide control bill. President Nixon signed the legislation Oct. 21. The bill would bring the use of pesticides and herbicides under federal control for the first time and would extend existing curbs on manufacture and sale to the intrastate as well as interstate market. Violation of the law would be a federal crime subject to penalties of up to $25,000 and a year in prison. The conference bill included a House provision for indemnification of manufacturers, distributors or users caught with stocks of banned chemicals. (Manufacturers who had withheld prior knowledge of danger from the EPA would be barred from the indemnification.) Provisions in the Senate version of the bill strengthening the disclosure requirements, citizens' rights to sue and export curbs were dropped in conference.

See also CANADA [3]; CONSUMER AFFAIRS [9, 16]; POLLUTION [13]

PETERSON, PETER G.—*See* NIXON, RICHARD MILHOUS
PETROLEUM—*See* OIL & NATURAL GAS
PHILADELPHIA PLAN—*See* CIVIL RIGHTS [17]

PHILIPPINES—State of emergency lifted. According to a report Jan. 12, President Ferdinand E. Marcos in early January lifted a state of emergency imposed in August 1971 following a bomb attack at a political rally in Manila. Habeas corpus was also restored, but not to those currently under detention.

[2] Drive against Communists. Government forces July 6 clashed with armed members of the outlawed Communist New People's Army (NPA) after the government forces intercepted and boarded a North Korean ship smuggling arms to the insurgents. A police boarding party spent two days on the ship under heavy rebel fire, but abandoned the vessel July 8 when food ran out. President Marcos July 9 ordered full-scale military action against the estimated 200 armed rebels and 800 sympathizers in Palanan in Isabella Province, where the clash had taken place. Government forces July 10 launched air and naval attacks against the NPA positions. Government forces Oct. 21-22 defeated a major NPA attack in Mindanao. A force of 300 troops was flown to Marawi to lift a rebel siege of a national police camp where about 100 paramilitary policemen had been pinned down all night by guerrilla fire. About 10,000 civilians were evacuated from Marawi Oct. 22. (Thousands of other civilians had been uprooted by the armed forces in areas of NPA activity in order to deprive NPA forces of local support.) Philippine troops Dec. 28 launched a major drive against rebel strongholds in Mindanao.

[3] Drive against Moslems. Government forces intervened July 6 against Moslem attackers in Zamboanga del Sur Province, 560 miles south of Manila, following three days of Moslem assaults against Christian groups called Ilagas. A total of 73 persons were killed between July 4 and 6, including 10 slain in the July 6 clashes. The fighting erupted as a four-man fact-finding group from Egypt and Libya arrived in Mindanao to investigate local Moslem charges that the Filipino regime was waging genocide against the country's 3.5 million Moslem minority. (President Marcos had extended an invitation to the group following reports that Libyan leader Muammar el-Qaddafi had offered arms to Filipino Moslems.) The Arab investigators met with Marcos July 9 and informed him that they had found no evidence to support the charges of genocide. In a later outbreak of Christian-Moslem fighting, nearly 30 persons were killed Aug. 22-26. Government troops that intervened in the fighting also suffered casualties.

[4] Presidential rule shifted. The Philippine constitutional convention, formed to draft a replacement for the 1935 constitution written when the Philippines were a commonwealth of the U.S., July 7 voted 158-120 to change the form of government from presidential rule to a parliamentary system. During the transition period, Marcos was to become prime minister, while retaining his presidential post, with all the powers authorized by the two constitutions. The interim period would be ended when Marcos called upon an interim parliament to select the executive and parliamentary leadership for a new government. The entire draft charter was approved by the constitutional convention Oct. 20 and passed by the convention Nov. 29 on the third and final reading. A national referendum to approve the charter was set for Jan. 15, 1973.

[5] Martial law declared. President Marcos Sept. 23 declared a state of martial law to combat what he called a Communist rebellion "enjoying the active and moral support of a foreign power." By Sept. 30, over 150 prominent persons, including a number of political opposition leaders, were arrested under martial law. The emergency action, dated Sept. 21, was invoked following an unsuccessful attempt Sept. 22 on the life of Defense Secretary Juan Ponce Enrile in Manila and a series of bombing attacks throughout the city. What government leaders had described as renewed Communist subversion and terrorist activity had also occurred earlier in September. In a nationwide radio and television address announcing martial law, President Marcos said he had imposed a midnight to 4 a.m. curfew and had placed government controls on newspapers, radio stations and foreign correspondents. He also banned public demonstrations and barred Filipinos from traveling abroad except on official missions. Marcos also announced the establishment of a military commission to try and punish military offenders, banned the carrying of firearms by civilians and provided for the military takeover of three Philippine airlines and all major utilities to guard against disruption of public services. (The country's two steel mills were nationalized Oct. 16.) In a broadcast Sept. 26, Marcos also announced sweeping land reforms, declaring the entire country a land-reform area. He attributed the current crisis partly to discontent among farmers. (Marcos Oct. 21 granted each tenant farmer 12½ acres of land and limited land owner holdings to 17½ acres.) In an earlier broadcast Sept. 26, Marcos had allowed the *Philippines Herald,* one of the newspapers seized under martial law, to resume publication. Six other dailies, charged with disseminating Communist propaganda and distorting the truth, would remain out of publication indefinitely. (The government Oct. 16 authorized publication of a new newspaper, the *Times-Journal,* after the staff was found to be uninvolved in corruption and agreed "to write positive news." *See also* [9].)

[6] Marcos Sept. 27 broadened the scope of arrests by specifying 19 new categories of persons who faced arrest and indefinite detention. The classifications were largely criminal and included income tax evasion, crimes against public morals and "crimes against liberty." Strict news censorship and curbs against newsmen, including foreign correspondents, were imposed Sept. 28 under a directive requiring the press to print and broadcast what the directive termed accurate, objective news accounts of positive national value consistent with government efforts to cope with the dangers that led to the imposition of martial law. (Censorship of foreign news dispatches ended Nov. 2.) All media were barred from expressing editorial opinion or printing objectionable advertising. The directive forbade down-grading or jeopardizing the military or law enforcement authorities and banned cameras from photographing military installations, military operations or the president's palace. All high schools and universities were closed indefinitely under an order Sept. 28 in order to permit military authorities to purge them of suspected

Communist subversives. The order also provided for the establishment of special military tribunals to try and punish all martial law offenders.

[7] Marcos Sept. 29 dismissed 452 persons from state employment as part of his drive to purge government employees considered corrupt, surplus or incompetent. The president also called on all 400,000 government workers to submit their resignations by Oct. 15. The government apparently would determine by that time which resignations were to be accepted. Marcos announced in a broadcast that he had decreed new civil service regulations that provided for dismissal without hearings and review. He said he was revamping the judiciary and said he had dismissed all but two judges of the Court of Industrial Relations.

[8] **Marcos assassination plot.** The government Oct. 17 announced the arrest of at least four persons, including two foreigners, in connection with an alleged plot to assassinate President Marcos. Two of the men—a Filipino and a "non-Asian" foreigner—had been arrested Oct. 15 while trying to flee the country. The two others (one reportedly a U.S. veteran of the Vietnam war), armed with rifles, had been arrested in a car parked inside the presidential palace grounds in Manila shortly before Marcos issued his martial law declaration Sept. 23.

[9] **Media crackdown widened.** President Marcos Nov. 2 issued a decree permanently closing Manila's seven English-language newspapers, several Chinese dailies and some of the city's radio-television stations. Only three Manila newspapers continued to publish, but two others later were allowed to resume publication. Under the Nov. 2 decree, the newspapers, radio and TV stations permitted to operate would have to have their licenses renewed every six months. All mass media were required to guarantee space and time for government announcements. The decree also established a Mass Media Council, headed by Information Secretary Francisco S. Tatad. Tatad announced the same day that the ban on the publication and broadcast of editorial commentaries (see [6]) was at an end, but said that commentators would have to be approved by the government. (In another media development, the government Nov. 8 suspended all Associated Press dispatches to AP clients in the Philippines and imposed censorship on all the agency's outgoing news reports. The curb, imposed because a Manila newspaper had published an AP report of a split in the Philippine army, was lifted Nov. 14.)

[10] **Communists face trial.** President Marcos Nov. 13 issued a decree calling for military trials in absentia for leaders of the outlawed Communist party and fugitive rebels. The trials would be preceded by publication of the indictment twice, a week apart, and delivery of a copy of the charges to a relative. Death sentences would be subject to confirmation or commutation by Marcos.

[11] **Marcos's wife stabbed.** The wife of President Marcos was stabbed and seriously wounded while presenting awards for national beautification and cleanliness in Pasay City Dec. 7. Mrs. Marcos was slashed with a knife on the hands and arms; nearly 75 stitches were required to close her wounds. Her assailant, identified as Carlito Dimailig, was immediately shot and killed by guards assigned to protect Mrs. Marcos. The government Dec. 8 charged that the attack was part of a conspiracy to kill the president and his wife. According to Information Secretary Tatad, 85 persons were detained in connection with the attack on Mrs. Marcos. Tatad also said Dec. 10 that Dimailig was "apparently after Marcos" and turned on Mrs. Marcos as a "substitution."

See also CHINA, COMMUNIST; HIJACKING [15]; OLYMPICS [1]; SINO-U.S. RELATIONS [8]; STORMS

POLAND—**1971 economic results.** The official news agency PAP Feb. 1 reported the results of the 1971 economic development plan. Measured against the figures for 1970, the following major increases were announced: national income 7.5%; agricultural production 3.7% (animal production 6.5%); foreign trade 10.7% (exports 9.4%, imports 11.9%); industrial production 8%.

Concessions to church. The Finance Ministry announced Feb. 22 that the Roman Catholic Church would no longer be legally obliged to submit to the government records of its income, expenditures and assets. (In 1971, the government had given to the Catholic church title to a number of former German church buildings.) In another move of reconciliation between Poland and the church, Pope Paul VI June 28 named six Polish bishops for Polish territories bordering on the Baltic Sea, East Germany and Czechoslovakia. The action had the effect of recognizing Polish sovereignty to lands east of the Oder-Neisse line which formerly were German. Vatican officials said the appointments were made possible by West Germany's ratification of the pact with Poland acknowledging its post-World War II boundaries (*see* GERMANY, WEST [5-7]).

Parliamentary elections. About 97% of Poland's 22 million voters turned out March 19 to choose representatives to the 460-seat Sejm (parliament). The elections had been advanced one year, reportedly to facilitate passage of legislation being recommended by Communist party First Secretary Edward Gierek. Candidates sponsored by the National Unity Front, the umbrella group for all legal political organizations in Poland, received 99.53% of all valid votes. The composition of the new Sejm was the same as it had been after previous elections in 1969: 255 United Workers (Communist) party deputies; 117 United Peasant party deputies; 39 Democratic party deputies; and 49 deputies representing nonparty Roman Catholic organizations. Because there were about 50% more candidates than seats, voters could exercise a choice by crossing out the names of those they were dissatisfied with. First Secretary Gierek obtained 99.8% of the votes in his home district of Sosnowiec, Silesia, to finish at the head of the list there; but some of his associates slipped badly in their districts, many of them finishing at the bottom of the list of successful candidates. Among those who did badly in their districts were: Gen. Mieczyslaw Moczar, a former interior minister and Politburo member; Foreign Minister Stefan Olszowski; Wladyslaw Kruczek, the trade union leader; Edward Babiuch, a Politburo member in charge of security; and Interior Minister Wieslaw Ociepka. The Communist party secretaries in Gdansk, Gdynia and Szczecin, appointed since the severe food riots in those areas in 1970, all finished last.

New president named. The Sejm March 28 elected Henryk Jablonski, former minister of education, to the post of president of Poland, succeeding Jozef Cyrankiewicz, who had been removed from the premiership and named president following the 1970 disturbances. The Sejm also re-elected Pyotr Jaroszewicz as premier.

Nixon visit. President Nixon visited Warsaw May 31-June 1 for talks with Polish leaders on his way back from his trip to the Soviet Union (*see* SOVIET-U.S. RELATIONS [1-6]). In a joint communique signed by Nixon and First Secretary Gierek June 1, the U.S. and Poland agreed to establish a joint commission to expand trade through increased contacts on governmental and business levels. The two countries also agreed to develop air and sea links in view of anticipated increases in economic contacts and tourism. The communique indicated that an air transport agreement would be signed soon. Both countries also agreed that a reciprocal reduction of armaments and armed forces in Central Europe was desirable, both to insure European stability and as "an important step toward obtaining the objective of general and complete disarmament." U.S. Secretary of State William Rogers and Polish Foreign Minister Olszowski also signed an agreement May 31 regulating a wide range of consular matters, including those dealing with arrest. Each government agreed to inform the other within 72 hours of the arrest of a citizen of the other country, and Poland agreed not to bring up old charges against returning Polish-Americans.

Tito-Gierek talks. Talks between Gierek and visiting Yugoslav President Tito June 19-23 ended with a communique which declared that "differences in the ways of building socialism in the two countries" were "not an obstacle to the successful development of mutual relations." On the issue of forthcoming plans to hold a European Security conference (see EUROPEAN SECURITY), the communique said that both sides believed "favorable conditions" existed for preparing the basis of a conference that would guarantee peace "for all nations of Europe." During Tito's visit, the two countries also signed an agreement allowing Poland to open a consulate at Zagreb (Yugoslavia's second-largest city) and an agreement to increase mutual trade by 25% to $1 billion for the period ending in 1975.

Administrative reform passed. The Communist party's Central Committee Sept. 27 initiated a major administrative reform by ordering, effective Jan. 1, a decentralization of the local government apparatus. The plan would reduce the number of local government units by half, but would strengthen their autonomy from higher authorities. (Under 1972 administrative structure, the country was divided into 4,313 districts, each with an area of about 26 square miles and a population of 3,600. There would be 2,380 new units, each with an area of 48 square miles and a population of 7,000.) The new units were to have greater control over the manner in which they collected and spent tax revenues. Profits would be invested in the area and local companies established. Each district was to be run by a council, elected locally, and an executive, appointed by the chairman of the State Peoples' Council acting on the advice of the district body.

See also CUBA; ENVIRONMENT; ESPIONAGE; GERMANY, WEST [2, 5-7]; INDOCHINA WAR [52]; PERU; SOVIET-U.S. RELATIONS [2]; SPACE [22]; VIETNAM, NORTH

POLICE—24 New York officers indicted. Twenty-four New York City police officers, including three sergeants and a policewoman, were arrested May 2 in New York for allegedly taking bribes to shield Mafia-linked gamblers from the law. One New York official said each of the patrolmen allegedly involved in the operation received about $10,000 a year to protect gamblers and bookmakers. According to one report, the payoffs to the police officers amounted to $1 million in four years. The 24 were arrested one day after Lt. Fletcher Hueston, who was also under investigation and who was scheduled to be indicted, committed suicide. Hueston had been second in command of the division to which each of the indicted individuals had been assigned during some portion of their last 18 months on the force.

ABA report. An American Bar Association (ABA) committee May 19 recommended that U.S. police departments add to their staffs an "in-house" legal advisor to help them shape law enforcement policy. (About 75 police departments currently had such advisors.) The committee said that the legal advisor could help police draw up departmental policy in handling drunks and drug addicts, settling domestic disputes and landlord-tenant conflicts and controlling demonstrations. He could also assist departments in training recruits and experienced policemen and could advise legislators when criminal laws were found to be unenforceable or ambiguous. The committee also recommended that police make far fewer arrests and instead consider other methods. In another part of its report, the committee endorsed collective bargaining by the police but not the right to strike. The committee suggested compulsory arbitration as an alternative.

See also CRIME [2, 5, 9, 12]; POLITICS [8]; PRISONS

POLIO (POLIOMYELITIS)—See HEALTH

POLITICS—Various charges were made during 1972 allegedly linking business contributions for the re-election campaign of President Richard M. Nixon to Administration policy toward business. Among the charges: that political contributions from dairy producers had influenced the granting by the Administration of an increase in milk prices *(see* [2]); and that an offer by an International Telephone and Telegraph Corp. (ITT) subsidiary to help finance the Republican National Convention had influenced the Administration decision to reach an out-of-court settlement on three ITT antitrust cases *(see* [3-7]). Individuals in the President's re-election campaign also were accused of involvement in the bugging of Democratic National Committee headquarters in the Watergate building complex in Washington *(see* [9-11]) and in sabotage efforts against Democratic contenders for the presidency *(see* [12]). In another development, the first Black Political Convention met in Gary, Ind. during March *(see* [8]).

[2] **Milk price rise tied to campaign contributions.** Consumer advocate Ralph Nader, the Federation of Homemakers, the D.C. Consumers Association and the Nader-sponsored Public Citizen, Inc. Jan. 24 filed suit in U.S. district Court in Washington, charging that an increase in federal price supports for milk stemmed from "political considerations" and asking the court to rescind the increase. The suit contended that the increase had been granted "illegally" in return for "promises and expectations of campaign contributions for the re-election of the incumbent President" Nixon. The suit cited the following sequence of events, all in 1971: Agriculture Secretary Clifford Hardin March 12 decided to deny as unjustified a rise in the milk support level; milk producers contributed $10,000 to various Republican fund-raising committees March 22; a group of 16 dairy spokesmen met with Hardin and President Nixon at the White House March 23; and Hardin announced March 25 that he was reversing his decision and granting an increase of 27¢ a hundredweight (from $4.66 to $4.93) in federal price supports for milk. Other charges in the suit were that: a total of $322,500 had been donated to Republican committees by dairy producers by the end of 1971; the price support increase would cost the government an additional $126.2 million during fiscal 1972; and Hardin had "received no new information or evidence bearing upon dairy farmers' costs" during the period between the initial decision and its reversal. The lawsuit was dismissed in March on the ground that the 1971 price support increase had terminated in March 1972, rendering the legal question moot. However, an appeals court Sept. 12 reopened the case, declaring that any "improprieties" in the 1971 decision "were not negated simply by rendition of the 1972 decision" terminating the increases. (Letters written by officials of Mid-America Dairymen, Inc., a dairy co-op, were published Aug. 25. The letters appeared to substantiate the claim that the price support increases were politically motivated. They disclosed that the organization had contributed $65,000 to the Republican party in 1971, with the money channeled to GOP finance committees through Murray Chotiner, a longtime Nixon confidante, and through Marion E. Harrison, Chotiner's law firm partner.)

[3] **ITT-Republican convention debate.** Disclosures by syndicated columnist Jack Anderson Feb. 29 led to the longest Senate confirmation hearings in history—the hearings of the Judiciary Committee into the nomination of Richard G. Kleindienst as attorney general. The hearings were prolonged by an investigation into charges that the Justice Department, during 1971, had settled three antitrust cases against ITT out of court in exchange for a pledge by an ITT subsidiary to underwrite a major part of the $400,000 in private funds needed to hold the Republican National Convention in San Diego. (The site was later changed to Miami Beach. *See* ELECTIONS [22].) The charges of ties between the settlement and the convention pledge also alleged that Kleindienst, Attorney General John N. Mitchell and others, including some persons in the White House up to President Nixon, knew of the connection, and that Kleindienst had taken an active role in arranging the antitrust settlement. The

Judiciary Committee's investigation into the ITT case was a confusing one, with charges and countercharges made by various parties and doubt cast on the testimony of at least three crucial witnesses. The hearings were not completed until April 20, and a majority of the committee did not recommend Kleindienst's nomination until May 5 *(see* NIXON, RICHARD MILHOUS). Even so, a minority of the committee opposed Kleindienst's nomination in a minority report issued in summary May 9. The long and complex hearings contrasted with earlier hearings into Kleindienst's nomination. The Judiciary Committee had begun its hearings Feb. 22 and had voted unanimously Feb. 24 to release the nomination for a Senate vote. However, the committee at the same time delayed the Senate vote to give Sen. Edward Kennedy (D, Mass.) an opportunity to prepare "separate views" delineating his policy differences with the nominee. The hearings were reopened after the Anderson disclosures.

[4] The charges of connection between the out-of-court settlement of the three ITT antitrust cases (announced July 31, 1971—eight days prior to the announcement that San Diego had been chosen as the site of the 1972 Republican convention) and the offer by the Sheraton Corp. of America, an ITT subsidiary, to underwrite part of the convention costs (an offer not revealed at the time it was made) grew out of Anderson's Feb. 29 publication of an alleged ITT memo from ITT lobbyist Mrs. Dita Beard to ITT Vice President W. R. Merriam. The memo, dated June 25, 1971 and bearing a request that it be destroyed after reading, several times referred to the ITT "commitment" or "participation in the convention" and connected it to the antitrust trust actions. In particular, the memo stated that "our noble commitment has gone a long way toward our negotiations on the mergers eventually coming out as Hal [Harold Geneen, ITT president] wants them." The memo also alleged that Attorney General Mitchell, California Lt. Gov. Edward Reinecke, White House Aide Robert Haldeman, President Nixon and Rep. Bob Wilson (R, Calif.) knew that the convention commitment had come from ITT; and that "Mitchell is definitely helping us, but cannot let it be known." Anderson said that Mrs. Beard had confirmed the memo in an interview with Anderson's associate, Brit Hume, and had also mentioned that she had discussed the antitrust action at length with Mitchell during a Kentucky Derby party in 1971 and had outlined for Mitchell the settlement ITT preferred—which allegedly conformed with the eventual settlement.

[5] *The settlement and Kleindienst's role.* While Kleindienst had served as assistant attorney general during 1971, Richard McLaren, head of the Justice Department's Antitrust Division, had determined to settle three antitrust cases against ITT out of court, rather than to seek a Supreme Court decision which would have expanded the Clayton Antitrust Act to handle the conglomerate issue. McLaren said March 2 that his determination was based on three factors: an analysis, written by an outside consultant at the direction of White House aide Peter Flanigan, on the merit of an ITT economic plea; an ITT economic presentation arranged through Kleindienst; and the Treasury Department's support for the firm's position. Kleindienst March 2 "categorically and specifically" denied exerting pressure for a settlement favoring ITT or knowing at any time of plans of the Sheraton Corp. to secure the financing for the GOP convention site. Kleindienst said that he had become aware of ITT's financial commitment to the convention only in late November or December of 1971. When confronted March 3 by Sen. Kennedy with two letters hinting that Kleindienst had known of the contribution earlier, Kleindienst said he did not recall the letters, which were of the kind "routinely handled by my staff." (One of the letters, dated Sept. 22, 1971, was to Kleindienst from a Ralph Nader associate inquiring about reports of a link between the ITT settlements and the convention financing; the second was a reply, drafted by McLaren, denying the link.) The Judiciary Committee, following the hearings, May 5 released a majority report upholding Kleindienst's nomination as attorney general,

concluding that Kleindienst had "acted properly" during the settlement of antitrust cases with ITT and stating that the ITT settlement was "not the product of political influence." A minority of the committee (Democratic Sens. Kennedy, Birch Bayh of Indiana, John V. Tunney of California and Quentin N. Burdick of North Dakota) issued a minority report summary May 9. Among other charges, the minority report accused Kleindienst of playing "a determinative role" in the ITT settlement and said that there was "an inherent conflict of interest" in the Justice Department's settlement of the ITT cases at a time when the Republican party was receiving a large monetary pledge from the company for its convention.

[6] *Other testimony highlights.* Following Anderson's disclosure of the memo, Mrs. Beard disappeared. It became known March 4 that she was in a Denver hospital in serious condition with incipient coronary thrombosis. (Mrs. Beard suffered from a chronic heart condition, angina pectoris.) She was served a Judiciary Committee subpoena, but doctors said she was too ill to be moved to testify before the committee. Her doctor for nine years, Dr. Victor L. Liszka, appeared before the committee March 6 and testified about Mrs. Beard's condition, saying that she had been suffering from periodic "distorted and irrational" behavior at the time she allegedly wrote the memo and could not remember writing it. Liszka attributed Mrs. Beard's failure to remember the memo to her weak heart (causing, he said, insufficient blood flow to the brain) and to periodic heavy use of alcohol and sometimes tranquilizers. Mrs. Beard March 17 released a statement saying that she had prepared a memo at about the time attributed to the Anderson memo, but that the published letter was not the one she wrote. ITT March 20 said it had discovered the "actual" memo, which contained "absolutely no reference to the antitrust cases." Federal Bureau of Investigation (FBI) laboratory tests on the Anderson memo, however, failed to substantiate Mrs. Beard's charges that the Anderson version was a fraud. Mrs. Beard herself testified to a special panel of the Judiciary Committee March 26 from her hospital bed, but the testimony was suspended after she collapsed with severe chest pain. However, doubt was cast on the seriousness of her illness by a report April 15 by two Denver cardiologists appointed by the Judiciary Committee to examine Mrs. Beard. The report said that the examination, performed shortly after Mrs. Beard entered the hospital, found no evidence of her heart ailment by "objective tests." They said that the diagnosis of her condition was based on her "history of chest pains." Mrs. Beard's testimony that she had not written the Anderson memo was also cast into doubt April 6 by Sen. Tunney, who said that she (and Merriam and Geneen) might be guilty of perjury. The accusation was based on a newspaper interview with Rep. Wilson in which Wilson quoted Mrs. Beard as saying she had "typed up" the Anderson memo. The interview also stated that Merriam had received the memo, while he had testified to the committee that he had not received it. The interview also quoted Geneen as pledging "up to $400,000" of the expense for the Republican convention, while Geneen had told the committee that ITT's commitment was only $200,000.

[7] The Judiciary Committee also heard testimony March 14 from Mitchell, who denied that he had taken part either in the antitrust settlements or in the selection of San Diego as the Republican convention site. Rep. Wilson testified before the committee April 10 and denied any connection between the settlement and the convention funding. Peter Flanigan also testified before the committee April 20 under an agreement that he would only be asked questions about certain specific aspects of the ITT affair. (The White House had formally notified the committee April 12 that it was invoking executive privilege to bar testimony by members of the President's immediate staff.) Flanigan, a White House aide for big business, shed no new light on the controversy. He testified that he had taken no part in the decision to settle the ITT antitrust suits and had acted only as a "conduit" to obtain for the Justice Department an independent analysis on ITT's economic plea. Flanigan April

24 sent a letter to the committee touching on some points he had refused to discuss in his testimony. In the letter, Flanigan described two times he had discussed the ITT case with Kleindienst. The revelation resulted in the committee's recalling of Kleindienst, who had testified earlier that he had not discussed the case with Flanigan, or could not recall doing so. In testimony April 27, Kleindienst attributed his previous stand to hazy memory.

[8] National black convention. Some 3,000 delegates and 5,000 observers met in Gary, Ind. March 10-12 as the first National Black Political Convention. The convention failed to resolve strategy differences between those who favored working within the traditional two-party structure and those favoring separatist action. However, it did: record itself as opposed to school busing to achieve integration and to mergers of black and white public colleges in the South, refuse to back any candidate for the Democratic presidential nomination, vote to establish a permanent 427-member representative body to set the direction for black political and social actions and endorse an agenda calling for radical social and economic changes. The convention May 19 released the "black agenda" which had been approved by the Gary meeting. The group's co-chairmen, Gary Mayor Richard Hatcher, Rep. Charles C. Diggs Jr. (D, Mich) and Newark (N.J.) activist Imamu Amiri Baraka (formerly called LeRoi Jones), pledged to campaign against candidates who opposed the proposals. The agenda called for: "an independent black political movement"; the establishment of a presidential commission to explore procedures for "an appropriate reparations policy in terms of land, capital and cash" for the black community; the establishment of a $5 billion national black development agency; an urban homestead act to distribute land and housing; a constitutional amendment to guarantee black congressional representation in proportion to population; home rule for the District of Columbia; local control of police and schools; a bill of rights for black prisoners; and a shift by the FBI from "political surveillance of black people" to ending drug traffic. The agenda also called for blacks to influence American policies toward Africa and the Caribbean and criticized U.S. relations with South Africa and Rhodesia. In the published form of the agenda, opposition to busing was modified to a criticism of the Nixon Administration for "making busing an issue," a commitment to finding "supreme quality education for all our children" and a demand that blacks retain control of any busing program. The published agenda also modified a proposal condemning Israel and calling for the "dismantling" of Israel. The modified agenda endorsed Middle East resolutions by the Organization on African Unity and the United Nations Commission on Human Rights. The National Association for the Advancement of Colored People (NAACP) withdrew from the convention May 16, citing "a difference in ideology" reflected in the agenda.

[9] Democratic headquarters raided. Five men were seized at gunpoint at 2 a.m. June 17 in the headquarters of the Democratic National Committee (DNC) in the Watergate building complex in Washington. Alerted by a security guard, police apprehended the five, along with cameras and electronic surveillance equipment in their possession, after file drawers in the headquarters had been opened and ceiling panels removed near the office of Democratic National Chairman Lawrence F. O'Brien. All of those arrested and charged with second-degree burglary were reported to have had links at one time with the Central Intelligence Agency (CIA). The five were: Bernard L. Barker, alias Frank Carter, president of a Miami real estate firm who had fled Cuba during the Castro revolution; James W. McCord, alias Edward Martin, security coordinator for the Committee to Re-Elect the President at the time of the raid; Frank A. Sturgis, alias Edward Hamilton, an associate of Barker active in the anti-Castro movement; Eugenio Martinez, alias Gene Valdes, a real estate salesman in Barker's firm; and Virgilio R. Gonzalez, alias Raul Godoy, a Miami locksmith and Barker associate. President Nixon's campaign manager, former Attorney General Mitchell, said June 18 that none of those involved in the raid were "operating either on our behalf or with our consent." A full-scale investigation of the raid by the FBI was announced June 19.

[10] *Democratic suit and Republican countersuit.* O'Brien announced June 20 that the Democratic party was filing a $1 million civil lawsuit in connection with the Watergate incident. The five suspects were originally charged with burglary, but subsequent disclosures tied them to personnel and funds from the Committee to Re-Elect the President. (A newspaper report July 31 charged that a $25,000 cashier's check, apparently intended for Nixon's re-election campaign, had been deposited April 20 by Barker in his own checking account. The check was deposited along with four other checks totalling $89,000 from a lawyer in Mexico. The $25,000 check has been made out to Kenneth H. Dahlberg, the Republican's Midwest finance chairman, who had turned it over to Maurice Stans, in charge of finances for the Nixon campaign. Stans reportedly said that the check had been passed from one to another finance official on the Nixon re-election committee and had last been in the hands of G. Gordon Liddy, finance counsel of the campaign, who had exchanged the check with someone else for $25,000 in cash.) The Democrats Sept. 11 sought to amend their court action by including as defendants Stans, Liddy, Hugh W. Sloan Jr. (former treasurer of the Committee to Re-Elect the President) and E. Howard Hunt (a former White House consultant who was an intelligence agent for the committee). The broadened complaint charged that Stans and Sloan had delivered $114,000 to finance an "espionage squad," and that Liddy and Hunt led the espionage squad and were with the raiders at the Watergate, but were warned the police were coming and withdrew. The Democrats also sought to raise the amount of damages sought from $1 million to $3.2 million and added five charges: that a spy squad had broken into DNC headquarters before May 25 and stolen and photographed private O'Brien documents; that O'Brien's phone was tapped from May 25 to June 17 and a listening post set up across the street from the Watergate at a motor lodge; that Liddy, Hunt and McCord made periodic visits to the listening post and that McCord prepared confidential memoranda of the conversation; that the squad tried to break into headquarters of Democratic presidential candidate George McGovern to install wiretaps; and that the Watergate break-in was to repair existing wiretaps, establish new ones and steal and photograph documents. U.S. District Judge Charles R. Richey Sept. 20 dismissed the original suit, thus excluding the five raiders from the suit, but accepted the amended version. The Committee to Re-Elect the President Sept. 13 filed a countersuit seeking $2.5 million in damages from O'Brien. Stans Sept. 14 filed a personal suit against O'Brien, contending that he had been "falsely and maliciously" accused of "a number of criminal acts." Stans asked $2 million in compensatory damages and $3 million in punitive damages.

[11] *7 indicted in criminal case.* A federal grand jury in the District of Columbia Sept. 15 indicted seven persons (the five raiders plus Liddy and Hunt) on charges of conspiring to break into the DNC headquarters. The indictment charged that: Liddy had been in communication with Barker before the raid, and Barker with Hunt; that McCord had rented the motor lodge room used as a listening post, had met with Liddy and Hunt May 26 and on May 27 had inspected with them the McGovern headquarters; that Liddy gave McCord $1,600 in cash June 11-15; that Liddy, Hunt and the five captured raiders, having in their possession a device to intercept oral communication and another to intercept wire communication, had broken into the Watergate to steal property, tap phones and intercept telephone calls; and that Liddy, Hunt and McCord had intercepted phone calls from May 25 to June 16 in the DNC offices. The indictment alleged burglary and possession of eavesdropping devices, brought under District of Columbia law, and conspiracy and interception and disclosure of telephone and oral communications, brought under federal law. The seven men charged pleaded not guilty Sept. 19. The trial

of the seven was to begin Nov. 15, but was postponed Oct. 27 to Jan. 8, 1973 because of the health of the judge, John J. Sirica.

[12] *Other reports of sabotage.* According to a newspaper report Oct. 10, the Watergate raid was but part of a larger espionage effort against the Democrats on behalf of the Nixon re-election effort. The report cited attempts to disrupt campaigns of Democratic candidates for president, including a published letter accusing Sen. Edmund Muskie (D, Me.) of having condoned the use of the epithet "Canucks" in reference to Americans of French-Canadian background. A report Oct. 23 linked a Republican sabotage effort directly to the White House. The report said that Los Angeles attorney Donald H. Segretti, previously identified as a recruiter for an undercover spy operation against Democratic campaigns, had been hired in September 1971 by Dwight Chapin, a deputy assistant to President Nixon, and by Gordon Strachan, a White House staff assistant. The report added that Segretti had been paid more than $35,000 for his services from funds kept in Stans's safe, that Segretti said he reported to Chapin and that Segretti said he received political sabotage and spying assignments from Hunt. Another report Oct. 25 said that five persons had been authorized to approve payments from the funds in Stans's safe: Mitchell; Stans; Jeb Stuart Magruder, deputy director of the President's re-election campaign; H. R. Haldeman, the White House chief of staff; and Herbert W. Kalmbach, the President's personal lawyer. President Nixon's campaign manager, Clark MacGregor, confirmed Oct. 26 the existence of the secret funds, which he acknowledged could have amounted to as much as $350,000. MacGregor said that money from the funds had been disbursed for preliminary planning of Nixon's campaign and, in one instance, to gather information for possible organized disruption at GOP rallies in New Hampshire. However, MacGregor denied that the fund had been used to finance a sabotage effort against the Democrats. He also stated that the funds were controlled by Stans, Mitchell, Liddy, Magruder and Herbert L. Porter (an advance man for Nixon's re-election campaign).

[13] **Woman is Democrats' chairman.** The Democratic National Committee July 14 selected Utah national committee-woman Mrs. Jean M. Westwood as its new national chairman following the refusal of O'Brien to continue as chairman. Westwood, who was presidential nominee McGovern's choice, was the first woman to head either party. The committee also elected: former New York state Sen. Basil A. Paterson as vice chairman; Wall Street lawyer Donald Petrie as treasurer; and Dorothy Bush as secretary. All except Paterson were McGovern's choices. Paterson, the first black in a national party leadership post, was selected after McGovern's first choice, campaign aide Pierre Salinger, withdrew. Mrs. Westwood's selection was seen as part of an effort to conciliate feminist supporters antagonized by McGovern organization tactics during the Democratic National Convention.

[14] *Strauss new Democratic chairman.* Robert Strauss of Texas was elected chairman of the DNC Dec. 9, following the resignation of Mrs. Westwood. A move to oust Mrs. Westwood had been mounted immediately after the party's crushing defeat in the presidential elections *(see* ELECTIONS [1-2, 36]). Mrs. Westwood resigned earlier the same day after the committee defeated, by a vote of 105-100, a motion to declare the chairmanship vacant. The vote was considered symbolic, since a number of votes on Mrs. Westwood's behalf were based on her promise to resign voluntarily after the vote. Sen. McGovern made some attempt to unite the opposition to Strauss by suggesting vice presidential candidate R. Sargent Shriver as a compromise chairman; but the attempt failed. The vote for Strauss reflected support by labor officials and Southern governors, although he also received some votes from Northern party officials and blacks. Paterson was retained as vice chairman of the committee. A new vice chairmanship also was created to fulfill a committee rule requiring that the chairman and vice chairman be of opposite sexes. Oregon party chairman Mrs. Caroline Wilkins assumed the new post.

[15] **Dole resigns as GOP chairman.** Sen. Robert J. Dole (R, Kan.) announced Dec. 11 that he was resigning as Republican national chairman and that George H. Bush had been selected by President Nixon to replace him. Bush, U.S. representative to the United Nations, would retain his ambassadorial duties through the current session of the General Assembly. His assumption of the party post was conditional on ratification by the party's executive committee, scheduled to meet in January, 1973. Dole was to remain with the committee in an advisory capacity until Bush's takeover on a full-time basis. According to a Dec. 16 White House announcement, Bush would be replaced at the U.N. by John A. Scali, a presidential adviser and former diplomatic reporter.

See also ELECTIONS; ESPIONAGE; MINES; NEGROES; NIXON, RICHARD MILHOUS

POLLUTION—Cost of cleanup feasible. A report prepared for federal environmental authorities, and released March 12, concluded that scheduled national clean air and water standards could be met without "severe" economic dislocation. The study, called "The Economic Impact of Pollution Control," conceded that the costs of pollution abatement equipment, and the phasing out of antiquated industrial facilities in violation of federal pollution laws, would raise some prices, cause some unemployment, adversely affect the U.S. international trade balance by some $700 million a year in 1972-76 and cause a net decline of $6 billion in the annual gross national product in 1972-80. (Of the 200-300 plants in 14 major industries that would close because of pollution control laws, a majority were obsolete and faced shutdowns "for other reasons.") Costs of air and water cleanup to the economy would total $31.6 billion in 1972-76. The stimulating economic effect of the booming pollution control industry would be offset by the dampening effect of rising wholesale and consumer prices. Job losses might range between 50,000 and 125,000 in the 1972-76 period. The study did not include the costs of solid waste treatment or noise pollution, nor did it calculate the economic costs of current pollution, which the Environmental Protection Agency (EPA) had estimated at $16 billion a year.

[2] **Courts powers asserted.** The Supreme Court ruled 9-0 April 24 that federal courts had common law powers to curb environmental pollution even in the absence of statutory law. The court's opinion refused original jurisdiction in two pollution cases brought by state governments. The court ruled that lower federal courts had full competence to hear the suits under the federal common law of nuisance and that the lower courts could decide in each case what level of pollution was tolerable. The court also said that the "considerable interests involved" in the fight against pollution would supersede a federal requirement that most trials brought in U.S. court involve at least $10,000. The ruling was thought to allow plaintiffs to bypass administrative complaint procedures in existing antipollution law. The court's ruling came in a case brought by the state of Illinois against waste dumping into Lake Michigan by four Wisconsin municipalities, and in a case brought by 18 states charging automobile manufacturers with conspiring to delay emission-control programs. Both cases were referred to lower courts.

[3] **Air cleaner, water dirtier.** The Council on Environmental Quality, in its third annual report to the President, said Aug. 7 that progress was being made in cleaning the air Americans breathe, but that the nation's waterways were growing dirtier. The council said that, by most available measurements, "air quality on a nationwide basis improved between 1969 and 1970." Statistics showed that emission of carbon monoxide dropped 4.5% and particulates 7.4%. The drop was tied to stricter controls over smokestack emissions. However, the council found that the waterways of the nation were likely to deteriorate further as a result of the increasing use of fertilizers in both urban and rural river basins. (The fertilizers lead to an increasing presence of phosphates and nitrogen compounds in water, which caused eutrophication, or the dying of

water life because of lack of oxygen.) The council concluded its report with a chapter on costs. It estimated that the cost of solving the country's most pressing pollution problems through the 1970s would be at least $287.1 billion—nearly triple the amount the council had forecast in 1971 for the first six years of the decade. (The report had also included three chapters on energy, recycling and pollution in the Delaware River Valley, but they were deleted from the final version submitted to President Nixon. The three chapters were released Aug. 10 after Democratic presidential candidate George McGovern charged Aug. 9 that they had been suppressed to avoid political controversy. The council said the chapters had been withheld only because they required "further work." The chapter on energy reported that large amounts of energy had been wasted by inefficient extraction of fuel and by the failure to use power plant heat for productive purposes. It said that coal extraction and use were the most damaging to the environment of various sources of energy. Coal was followed by oil, natural gas and atomic energy; but atomic energy was found to possess the greatest potential for "large-scale damage to human health and the ecosystem" through accidents and radioactive waste disposal. The recycling chapter criticized current tax policies which rewarded extraction of virgin minerals and timber, placing recycled materials at a competitive disadvantage. The Delaware Basin report urged New York, Pennsylvania, Delaware and New Jersey to assume control over further economic development of the region to stop the "balkanization of authority among some 450 separate units of government.")

Air Pollution

[4] **Committee suggests delay in exhaust standards.** The Committee on Motor Vehicle Emissions of the National Academy of Sciences, in the first of its semiannual reports required by the 1970 Clean Air Act, Jan. 5 suggested a one-year delay in the application of auto exhaust curbs scheduled for the 1975 model year. (The law permitted a one-year delay if technology were unavailable and if auto manufacturing firms had made a good faith effort to meet the 1975 deadline.) The committee said that it was possible that larger manufacturers would be able to produce models that would qualify by 1975, but that the cost to consumers would include a $200-a-car price rise, increased maintenance costs, a 3%-12% increase in fuel consumption, a loss in acceleration and an increase in stalling. A one-year delay, the committee said, "would enable manufacturers to significantly improve the performance and reliability" of the cars in ordinary use. Furthermore, according to the committee, the 1975 standards, which would reduce hydrocarbons (smoke) and carbon monoxide by 90% over 1970 models, could be met only if the government took these steps: (1) allowed replacement of equipment after 25,000 rather than 50,000 miles as required in the act; (2) allowed an "averaging" of emission levels among different models; (3) guaranteed a supply of gasoline with low levels of lead and other substances which damage pollution control equipment; and (4) required "regular, periodic maintenance" by owners. The report also criticized industry and the government for inadequate research efforts into reducing nitrogen oxide emissions, which must be reduced by 90% by the 1976 model year. EPA Administrator William Ruckelshaus said Feb. 8 that the EPA would meet the four steps recommended by the committee. (The EPA Feb. 22 proposed regulations requiring all large service stations to carry low-octane "non-leaded" gasoline by 1974 and to progressively reduce the lead level of high-octane gasoline. The 1974 deadline became effective Dec. 27, but the EPA delayed for 60 days a final ruling on eliminating lead from all gasolines. The agency Nov. 6 also proposed that the catalytic converters in auto exhaust controls be replaced after 25,000 instead of 50,000 miles and that the exhaust recirculation system could be replaced three times during the first 50,000 miles.)

[5] *Delay rejected.* Ruckelshaus Jan. 19 rejected as "legally insufficient" a formal request by General Motors Corp. (GM) for a one-year delay in the

application of the auto exhaust curbs. GM said that it could not guarantee that techniques successful in test models would be workable in mass-produced cars, but that it would have to begin ordering equipment now if the 1975 deadline were retained. In rejecting the request, Ruckelshaus said that the corporation had not yet provided adequate documentation that it had made good faith efforts to meet the deadline or that the control technology would not be available by 1975. Ruckelshaus May 12 again rejected a request by auto manufacturers for a one-year delay. After 13 days of public hearings, Ruckelshaus said that the auto firms had still failed to prove that technology was inadequate to meet the goals. GM June 8 filed a request in the U.S. Court of Appeals for the District of Columbia for a review of the EPA's denial of a delay (GM announced Sept. 24 that it had developed an emission control system that would successfully meet the 1975 and 1976 deadlines. However, the system met the deadline requirements only "in experimental cars at low mileage.")

[6] *Ford test error.* The Ford Motor Co. announced May 22 that its pollution control test procedures for 1973 model lines had violated federal law. If provisions of the Clean Air Act law barring shipment and sales of new cars pending emission certification were enforced, Ford said, it might have to suspend production for a few months, putting as many as 300,000 workers out of work at Ford and its suppliers. Ford Chairman Henry Ford 2nd said that employees had made "unauthorized maintenance" on vehicles undergoing 50,000-mile tests by replacing spark plugs and adjusting carburetors. The test cars were required to meet emission requirements without any adjustments to improve engine efficiency. The 50,000-mile tests required a minimum of 100-120 days. The EPA announced June 2 that Ford would be allowed to ship its 1973 models to dealers if it successfully conducted 4,000-mile tests. Under the order, the results of the 10-14 day 4,000-mile test would be projected over 50,000 miles, taking into account deterioration rates for 1972 Ford models and 1973 models of other manufacturers. If the results indicated that the full test would be successful, the cars could be shipped, although sales would be barred until completion of the 50,000-mile run in September. (The EPA granted full approval for 11 of Ford's 12 1973 model engine families on the basis of the tests, but Sept. 6 denied certification for an engine used in most Maverick and Comet models, which Ford had expected to account for 5% of total sales.)

[7] *Truck emission curb eased.* The EPA announced Feb. 11 that it was postponing heavy-duty vehicle emissions one year to the 1974 model year and modifying the limits in the face of industry criticism. Instead of mandating separate levels of and testing for hydrocarbons and nitrogen oxide, the EPA would allow a single total measurement, which would "leave the manufacturer the option of trading off one pollutant for another," according to an agency spokesman. More stringent rules would be imposed in 1976.

[8] **State air plans.** The EPA May 31 announced its rulings on clean air plans submitted by the states. Eleven states (Alabama, Colorado, Connecticut, Florida, Mississippi, New Hampshire, North Carolina, North Dakota, Oregon, South Dakota and West Virginia) and three other jurisdictions (American Samoa, Guam and Puerto Rico) received complete approval, while 27 cities in 18 states were granted two-year extensions beyond the 1975 deadline for meeting primary health emission standards for six classes of pollutants. For the most part, EPA Administrator Ruckelshaus said, the agency was granting the additional time because it was still "having difficulty relating transportation controls to air pollution." (Beside conventional controls of existing plant emissions and waste incineration, the plans were to include methods to reduce automobile use through traffic control, parking limits and better mass transit systems.) Ruckelshaus reported that large parts of some state plans had been disapproved, and warned that the EPA had legal authority in such cases to write its own rules if revised plans were not approved by July 31. The EPA June 14 proposed tougher controls in 10 states (Georgia, Louisiana, Maryland, Massachusetts, Michigan, Missouri, New Jersey, Tennessee, Texas and

Washington) to meet federal emission standards for nitrogen oxides and hydrocarbons and proposed changes in measurement techniques, record-keeping or public access to data in 14 other states and the Virgin Islands. The EPA also announced June 14 that the effective date for the nitrogen oxide emission limit would be delayed 11 months to July 1, 1973, because of evidence that previous measurement methods had been unreliable.

Water Pollution

[9] **Gulf lease sales canceled.** The Interior Department Jan. 20 returned unopened bids for leases to over 300,000 potentially oil-rich acres on the outer continental shelf off eastern Louisiana after U.S. District Court Judge Charles R. Richey refused Jan. 19 to lift a temporary injunction against the lease sales. Richey had issued the injunction Dec. 16, 1971 after environmental groups charged that the government's environmental impact statement for the sale was inadequate because it did not discuss alternate sources of oil to avoid the danger of offshore spills. The government later had upheld the injunction. The U.S. Court of Appeals for the District of Columbia Jan. 13 wrote an addendum to its impact statement, but Richey said he needed more time for a final ruling. By federal rules, the impounded bids could not be held more than 30 days after their submission Dec. 21, 1971. (Oil companies Sept. 12 offered over $586 million for leases of tracts after the Sierra Club announced Aug. 16 that it would no longer contest the sale of leases. The Sierra Club decision was based on a new environmental impact statement, considering alternative energy sources and the possibility of reducing demand, filed by the Interior Department.)

[10] *Santa Barbara oil permits ordered.* U.S. District Court Judge Francis C. Whelan ruled in Los Angeles June 21 that Interior Secretary Rogers C. B. Morton had exceeded his powers when he suspended oil drilling operations in April 1971 on 35 leases in the Santa Barbara Channel off California, the scene of a massive oil well blowout in 1969 that caused considerable damage to wildlife and property. Morton had suspended operations to give Congress time to consider measures canceling the leases and setting up a national energy reserve. Whelan ruled that the Outer Continental Shelf Lands Act gave the interior secretary power to suspend operations only "when necessary to prevent waste or damage to personal property." The judge ordered new permits granted to Gulf Oil Corp., Mobil Oil Corp., Texaco, Inc., and Union Oil Co. of California and extended the exploratory drilling period 32 months.

[11] *Massive Pennsylvania slick.* Some 6,000,000 gallons of used crankcase oil was released from storage lagoons near the Schuylkill River in Pennsylvania, covering a 16-mile stretch of the river near Philadelphia in early July, in the aftermath of Hurricane Agnes. Massive cleanup efforts by the EPA and the Coast Guard kept the slick from entering the Philadelphia water supply system. Receding waters deposited a layer of oil on land, crops and houses, according to a July 6 report.

[12] *Tanker control bill signed.* President Nixon July 10 signed a bill to regulate construction and operation of tankers to prevent spills of oil or other harmful cargoes. The new Port and Waterways Safety Act authorized the Transportation Department, in consultation with the EPA and other federal agencies, to issue rules regulating tanker design, construction, and operation, to be effected no later than Jan. 1, 1976. The government would have increased inspection powers and could set manning requirements and tougher qualifications for officers and seamen. The transportation secretary would control ship traffic in U.S. inland and coastal waters, regulate handling of dangerous cargo on piers and set standards for waterfront equipment. Foreign flag ships would have to comply with the new regulations in American waters, and ships already in use would be covered by rules to be set by the Transportation Department.

[13] **Atlantic dumping curbs.** Britain, Norway, Belgium, France, Denmark, West Germany, Finland, Iceland, the Netherlands, Portugal, Spain and Sweden Feb. 14 signed a pact to curb the dumping of dangerous industrial wastes into the northeast Atlantic Ocean. Durable plastics, as well as potential food poisons like mercury and cadmium, would be banned, while scrap metal, pesticides, tar and other substances would be dumped only by permit. In a related action, the California State Water Resources Control Board July 7 adopted stringent new restrictions on municipal and industrial waste discharge into the Pacific Ocean. Under the California plan, to take effect after approval by the EPA, all discharges would receive primary and secondary treatment to remove 85% of contaminants. No sewer sludge could be dumped into the ocean, and other discharges would have to be conducted through pipes away from the shore. Both houses of Congress Oct. 13 passed a bill allowing waste dumping within 12 nautical miles of the U.S. coast only under special circumstances to be determined by the EPA. Violators could be fined up to $50,000 and receive one-year jail sentences. The bill also banned the dumping by U.S. citizens of any chemical, biological or radioactive warfare agents, or any highly radioactive debris, in oceans beyond the territorial limits of the U.S. President Nixon signed the bill Oct. 28. Representatives of 91 countries Nov. 13 approved a worldwide convention to curb ocean dumping of pollutants. The convention, effective after signing by 15 nations, would ban ocean dumping by ships or aircraft of oil, highly radioactive wastes, chemical or biological warfare agents, mercury or cadmium or their compounds, some pesticides and durable plastics, and other dangerous nondegradable substances. Special permits would be required to dump substances on a "gray list," which included a variety of other metals and compounds. All other substances would require a general dumping permit. The convention provided for "emergency" dumping of banned substances if the dumping country first consulted with other countries that might be affected. Each signatory to the convention would pledge "to take all practical steps" to prevent pollution that was "liable to create hazards to human health, to harm living resources and marine life, to damage amenities or to interfere with other legitimate uses of the sea." Enforcement and sanctions would be left to individual countries, although another meeting was planned for 1973 to set up an international secretariat and to discuss details of enforcement.

[14] **Court perils water program.** A May 30 ruling of the 3rd U.S. District Court of Appeals in Philadelphia threatened to block application of the 1899 Refuse Act, which President Nixon had revived in December 1970 as the major federal water pollution control program pending enactment of new legislation. The court ruled that the Justice Department could not prosecute the Pennsylvania Industrial Chemical Corp. for polluting the Monongahela River under the act unless a system of federal pollution discharge permits, provided for in the act, was in operation. The firm had been convicted for pollution discharges occurring during August 1970, four months before Nixon instructed the Army Corps of Engineers to begin issuing permits to plants certified by the EPA as in accord with state water standards. No permits had been issued since a December 1971 ruling by U.S. District Court Judge Aubrey E. Robinson Jr. in Washington that each permit had to be preceded by a detailed environmental impact statement. Only a handful of some 20,000 permit applications had been processed when the procedure was suspended.

[15] **Water bill enacted over veto.** Congress Oct. 18 overrode a presidential veto to enact the 1972 Water Pollution Control Act originally cleared by Congress Oct. 4. The vote to override the veto was 52-12 in the Senate and 247-23 in the House, well above the required two-thirds. The bill, which set into motion a 13-year effort to clean up the nation's lakes and rivers through tough curbs on industrial wastes and massive federal outlays for sewage treatment plants, had been vetoed Oct. 17, 40 minutes before it would have become law without President Nixon's approval. Nixon had delayed action until Congress acted on his request for budget-cutting power (*See* BUDGET); after the request

was denied, the veto was announced. Nixon explained his veto entirely by his opposition to the "staggering $24.6 billion three-year cost," which he said "would lead to higher prices and higher taxes." He said that, if the bill were passed over his veto, he would use its discretionary provisions to limit expenditures "as much as possible." The veto message did not refer to the Administration's opposition, at various stages of the bill's progress, to its provisions setting 1985 as a target date for a complete halt to industrial discharges and setting industry-wide standards for pollution control. The industrial goals of the bill were to be enforced through state-run permit systems, with the EPA setting guidelines (proposed Nov. 9) for the the program, setting up permit programs for states which failed to impose their own and having veto power over state permit decisions. The bill also would require private industry to install "the best practicable" pollution abatement equipment by July 1, 1977 and to install "the best available technology economically achievable" by July 1, 1983. Government sewage plants were required to meet the same deadlines for installation of secondary treatment facilities and use of the best practicable technology. The bill would also budget $18 billion over three years for 75% federal-25% local matching grants for sewage plant construction and improvement—three times the amount requested by the Administration. The remaining $6.4 billion would pay for research on the program's impact, provide low-cost pollution loans to small companies, remove toxic sludge and reimburse localities for plants built in expectation of federal aid.

[16] *Nixon cuts water funds.* EPA Administrator Ruckelshaus announced Nov. 28 that President Nixon had ordered him to cut state allocations for waste treatment plants by more than half, reducing the fiscal 1973 total to $2 billion and the fiscal 1974 amount to $3 billion. (The Water Pollution Control Act had provided $5 billion and $6 billion, respectively.) In ordering the cuts, Nixon had noted his veto warning that he would use spending discretion if Congress ignored his call for budgetary restraint *(See* [15]). Under the Water Pollution Control Act, the EPA was required to publish allotments for each state within 30 days of passage of the bill, then negotiate binding contracts with the states— committing the federal government to future funding, which would then be appropriated as needed. Theoretically, the Administration could have curbed spending by limiting contract approvals; but the bill provided that, if a state's allotment were not exhausted, the remaining authorization would return to a national pool for subsequent reallocation. By limiting the original allocations, the Administration could put a limit on all future spending under the act.

See also ATOMIC ENERGY [2, 4]; AUTOMOBILES; BUDGET; CANADA [3]; CONSUMER AFFAIRS [8]; ECONOMY [4]; ENVIRONMENT; NIXON, RICHARD MILHOUS; PUBLIC LAND; SPACE [21]

POPE PAUL VI—*See* CHURCHES; POLAND; ROMAN CATHOLIC CHURCH; SPAIN

POPULAR FRONT FOR THE LIBERATION OF PALESTINE (PFLP)—*See* HIJACKING [8]; MIDDLE EAST [6, 22, 26]

POPULATION—Indications of growth decline. Reports from the Census Bureau and the National Center for Health Statistics gave further indication during 1972 of a long-term decline in U.S. population growth. The Census Bureau Feb. 16 reported that the average number of children expected by married women between 18 and 24, surveyed in 1971, had declined to 2.4 from 2.9 in 1967 and from 3.2 in 1955. Taking into account unmarried women, the Bureau estimated an overall expectation rate of 2.2, approaching the replacement level of 2.11 (which, if maintained for 70 or 80 years, would result in zero population growth or ZPG). The Bureau attributed the decline partly to a rise since 1960 in the average age of women at marriage, from 20.3 to 20.9, and in the proportion of women ages 20-24 who were single, from 28% to 37%. The Bureau Dec. 17 issued a new set of population projections for the U.S., to take account of changes in childbearing trends. According to the projections, the population in the year 2000 would be between 251 and 300 million. Previous estimates had ranged from 271 to 322 million.

The National Center for Health Statistics reported March 1 that the 1971 fertility rate (number of births per 1,000 women) was the lowest recorded since 1940 and was nearly 50% below 1955, the peak post-World War II year. According to the report, the fertility rate had declined to 82.3, down from 87.6 in 1970. The drop in total births was 4% or 159,000 to 3,559,000. The center also reported Dec. 4 that U.S. fertility for the first nine months of 1972 had declined below the replacement level to 75.3.

Population slowdown urged. The Commission on Population Growth and the American Future, established by Congress at President Nixon's request in 1970 *(See* ABORTION*)*, March 11 and 25 issued reports calling for a national policy of limiting population growth and guiding the distribution of population between urban, suburban and rural areas. The March 11 report concluded that "the pluses seem to be on the side of slowing growth and eventually stopping it altogether," and that this goal could be achieved if unwanted births were prevented by making "freedom of choice and equality of access to the means of fertility control" a matter of government policy. (President Nixon May 5 rejected the commission's recommendation for universal access to birth control information.) The report listed the following disadvantages accompanying population growth which would result from a three-child-average family: increased bureaucratic controls, "water as a scarce resource" and a rise in food prices of at least 50% in 50 years. The report said, however, that technological progress would probably assure an adequate supply of energy and clean air. Replying to fears that a population slowdown would hamper economic growth, the report said that slower growth in the next 10-15 years would result in higher levels of per capita and national income. In addition, slower growth would "buy time for the development of sensible solutions" to environmental problems that might otherwise provoke more drastic and damaging measures.

In its March 25 report, the commission urged the government to crack down on illegal immigration by increased border surveillance and criminal sanctions against employing illegal immigrants, and recommended that legal immigration not exceed current levels. The commission also asked for creation of a federal office to develop population growth and distribution guidelines for regional, state and local goverments, and to oversee all government actions affecting population policy. Although nearly all growth was expected to take place in metropolitan areas, the commission recommended that further migration from rural areas be channeled into small cities, whose economic development would be encouraged. Counseling, health and educational aid would be provided for rural residents preparing to relocate and for those remaining behind. Within metropolitan areas, government planning would aim at controlled, balanced development, without which the growing outer cities would be confronted with the same problems of pollution and decay as the inner cities. Economic and racial integration of the suburbs should be encouraged by construction of low- and moderate-income housing, and by the breakdown of property tax barriers.

See also ABORTION; NEGROES

PORNOGRAPHY—*See* ELECTIONS [44]

PORTUGAL—Change in territories' status. The government Jan. 16 published, and the National Assembly May 2 approved, legislation designating Portugal's overseas territories as states and giving them wider autonomy "without affecting the unity of the nation." (The enclaves of Goa, Damao and Diu, which had been annexed by India in 1961, were the only Portuguese territories which previously had been designated as states.) The bill, which immediately affected the status of the African territories of Angola, Portuguese Guinea and Mozambique, implemented constitutional reforms adopted in 1971. The new law authorized the creation of an elected local assembly and advisory council for each of the states, with authority to legislate on all internal matters, to collect taxes and to draft budgets. Governors-general, to be nominated by Lisbon, would have ministerial rank. The central Portuguese government would continue to supervise the administration and economy of the overseas states, be responsible for their defense and conduct foreign relations. The government Dec. 24 officially proclaimed legal autonomy for the three African territories and called for local elections by April 1973.

New censorship law decreed. The government May 5 announced new censorship regulations enacting provisions of a press law approved in August 1971. The law, effective June 1, abolished the old board of censors and replaced it with a "commission of previous review," which would retain the right of censorship prior to publication during a state of emergency. (A state of emergency had been in effect since November 1971.) The law would impose heavy fines and prison sentences of up to two years on journalists and newspaper owners and publishers for breaking the regulations. Accused persons would have recourse to the courts.

Thomaz installed for third term. President Americo Thomaz was sworn in for a third term Aug. 9 after winning an uncontested election July 25 by a 616-29 vote in the electoral college. Several hours before the investiture ceremony, bombs had damaged power pylons in various parts of the country, reducing Lisbon's hydroelectric power supply by 30% and briefly cutting Oporto's electrical supply. No group claimed responsibility for the attacks.

Cabinet shuffle. Thomaz Aug. 10 asked Premier Marcello Caetano, who had offered to resign his position (a traditional gesture when a president took office), to remain in office. A few Cabinet changes were also announced Aug. 10: Finance Minister Joao Augusto Dias Rosas resigned, reportedly for personal reasons, and was replaced by Manuel Cotta Dias, the president of Portugal's only authorized political movement, the National Popular Action (ANP); Alexandre de Azevado Vaz Pinto was named secretary of state for commerce, replacing Xavier Pintado, a leading liberal technocrat in the previous government; and Hermes Dos Santos became secretary of state for national industry, replacing Rogerio Martins, another leading liberal technocrat.

Student killed in clash. Police Oct. 12 shot Jose Antonio Ribeiro dos Santos, a law student, to death and wounded another law student in clashes at the Lisbon University School of Economics. The students claimed that police opened fire during a scuffle that broke out after police interrupted a meeting of the student association. (School authorities claimed that police had interrupted the meeting to pick up a man who had falsely identified himself as a policeman.) Police again clashed with students at the Oct. 14 funeral for Ribeiro dos Santos. Several youths and policemen were injured. Four schools of the University of Lisbon were closed down Oct. 17 because of violence.

Security curbs eased. The government Nov. 16 published a decree abolishing the so-called "security measures" that permitted authorities to extend indefinitely the original sentence of certain political prisoners. The decree also codified relatively minor offenses and spelled out specific penalties. Prison terms of six months to three years were established for forming, subsidizing or belonging to a subversive group. Small fines were imposed on persons meeting in illegal places or causing a disturbance; and slightly higher fines were imposed on persons writing, printing or distributing subversive literature.

See also ANGOLA; AUSTRALIA [11]; BRAZIL; CHINA, COMMUNIST; EUROPEAN ECONOMIC COMMUNITY [8]; FOREIGN AID; POLLUTION [13]; ROMAN CATHOLIC CHURCH; TARIFFS & WORLD TRADE

PORTUGUESE AFRICA—See ANGOLA; BRAZIL; PORTUGAL

PORTUGUESE GUINEA—See CHURCHES; PORTUGAL

POSTAL SERVICE, U.S.—Rate increases approved. The Postal Service announced June 29 that it had accepted a unanimous June 5 Postal Rate Commission recommendation that a $1.45 billion rate increase be reduced by $78.3 million. (The increase, which became permanent July 6, had been in effect on a temporary basis since May 1971.) The 5.5% cutback would result from a 9% rate reduction in second class mail, an 8% cutback in third class mail costs, a 16% decrease in fourth class mail rates and a refusal to increase postcard rates from 6¢ to 7¢ as requested by the Postal Service. Increases on first class mail and airmail would not be decreased. The approval of the largest rate boost in U.S. history left the Postal Service with a reported fiscal 1972 deficit of $9.9 million.

POVERTY—OEO extension enacted. President Nixon Sept. 20 signed a $4.75 billion bill extending the Office of Economic Opportunity (OEO) for three years. The bill had been passed Sept. 5 by a 223-97 vote in the House and a voice vote in the Senate. A Senate-House conference, reconciling bills passed in the House Feb. 17 and in the Senate June 29, had capitulated to Administration objections by dropping entirely a provision approved by both houses establishing an independent legal services agency for the poor. The committee had earlier modified the bill to allow the President to name all agency directors, with two selected from the poor and two from among poverty lawyers. (The House bill had mandated that 11 of the directors would be chosen from lists drawn up by legal and poverty organizations. The Senate bill had provided that the President could appoint 10 directors at his own discretion.) When rumors persisted that Nixon might repeat his 1971 veto of an earlier version of the OEO extension, Sen. Gaylord Nelson (D, Wis.), chief Senate conferee, had the bill recommitted in a rare parliamentary move; and the independent agency was dropped. The legal services program thus remained within the OEO, subject to limited veto power by state governors. The bill authorized a record $71 million for the legal services program. In other provisions, the bill prohibited any charge for Head Start participation by children from families with incomes below $4,320 a year. The secretary of health, education and welfare would determine fees for other families. At least 10% of Head Start enrollment under the bill would be offered to handicapped children. The bill also authorized a new environmental works program to employ poor people, and a consumer action and education program for the poor.

See also ECONOMY [2]; EDUCATION [1, 3-4, 8]; ELECTIONS [33, 36]; HEALTH CARE; HIJACKING [3]; HOUSING; NEGROES; STATE & LOCAL GOVERNMENTS; WELFARE

POWELL, LEWIS F.—*See* SECURITY, U.S.
PREGNANCY—*See* WOMEN'S RIGHTS
PRICE COMMISSION—*See* ECONOMY [3-6]; RAILROADS
PRICES—*See* ECONOMY [2-6, 9]
PRISONERS OF WAR (POWs)—*See* ELECTIONS [16, 34]; INDOCHINA WAR [1, 20, 24, 35, 39-41, 44-45, 47, 54]; PAKISTAN [17]

PRISONS—Soledad defendants acquitted. An all-white jury in San Francisco March 27 found the so-called Soledad Brothers Fleeta Drumgo and John Cluchette innocent of the 1970 slaying of a guard at Soledad Prison. During the trial, which had lasted three months, four prisoners and several guards testified that they had seen Drumgo and Cluchette assaulting the guard, but none saw the defendants deliver a fatal blow or throw the guard over a third floor cell tier. The defense had charged that the prisoner witnesses had been promised parole in exchange for testifying. Drumgo and Cluchette denied being at the scene of the murder. It was to free the Soledad Brothers, including George Jackson (since killed during an escape attempt in August 1971), that Angela Davis had allegedly plotted the courtroom kidnaping for which she underwent trial during 1972 *(see* BLACK MILITANTS).

Maryland disturbances. Prisoners at three Maryland penal facilities rioted during mid-July. The most serious of the uprisings broke out July 15 at the Maryland House of Correction in Jessup. The riot, which ended July 16 after Gov. Marvin Mandel persuaded about 250 inmates to return to their cells, reportedly erupted after a group of convicts rushed a fence in an escape attempt. The escapees were repelled by gunfire from prison guards. At the height of the rebellion, almost 1,400 inmates were out of their cells, wandering through open cellblocks. About 25 prison guards armed with tear gas tried but failed to regain control of the prison. State officials then brought in about 175 state troopers and 25 policemen, who cleared inmates from the open cellblocks shortly before midnight. At least four prisoners and two guards were injured during the 10 hours of trouble.

The second riot broke out July 17 at the Maryland State Penitentiary in downtown Baltimore. About 75 prisoners, attempting to dramatize their demands for better conditions, rioted for six hours, seizing four hostages and setting fires throughout the old prison. They released their hostages and returned to their cells after a meeting with Gov. Mandel and Rep. Parren J. Mitchell (D, Md.). At least four persons, including three guards, were injured in the riot.

The third riot lasted 3.5 hours July 18 at the Prince Georges County Jail in Upper Marlboro. The rebellious inmates, who at one time included virtually all the 110 inmates in the building, said they wanted a meeting with county officials to discuss better medical facilities, including dental equipment, better educational materials and a public defender on duty in the jail. The prisoners had held three guards as hostages to force the grievance meeting. County officials said no criminal charges would be made in connection with the trouble.

Attica report scores Rockefeller. The New York State Special Commission on Attica (an official state investigative commission also known as the McKay Commission after its chairman, Robert B. McKay, dean of the New York University Law School) Sept. 12 concluded that N.Y. Gov. Nelson Rockefeller should have visited the scene of the Attica prison uprising in 1971 before ordering an armed assault on the prison by lawmen. (Eleven prisoners and 32 inmates had lost their lives as the result of the riot—the bloodiest in U.S. history.) In addition to criticizing Rockefeller, the report offered the following judgments: that the police attack was characterized by mass chaos, by total lack of communication between police commanders and those leading the assault and by the lack of any way for squadron leaders to tell their men to stop firing; that much of the shooting done by police was unjustified; that the inmates' grievances, by and large, were legitimate and that correction of the grievances had been pursued unsuccessfully within the system by inmates; that the uprising was spontaneous and not planned; that the highly organized society among the inmates in the captured prison yard also developed spontaneously; that there were no effective mechanisms worked out by either side, during negotiations between the inmates and a citizens' committee, to make more likely the chances of a peaceful settlement; that the police assault plan was faulty in that it could not have saved hostage lives if inmates were, in fact, set on killing; and that the police had no nonlethal weapons available to them for the assault.

D.C. inmates seize cellblock. From 30 to 40 rebellious inmates at the District of Columbia Jail in Washington Oct. 11 overpowered guards, holding them and others hostage while they bargained for their freedom. The inmates dropped their demands for freedom later in the day when U.S. District Court Judge Albert C. Bryant agreed to hold immediate hearings on their cases. Bryant heard the grievances of the first of the inmates at 6 p.m. and ordered the city to provide every inmate involved in the rebellion with an attorney and to make a psychiatrist available to the inmates. Bryant also ordered that no reprisals be taken against any of the prisoners. After Bryant's orders were issued, the other prisoners released their 10 hostages. Two of the hostages— Washington Department of Corrections Director Kenneth L. Hardy, who suffered a mild heart attack after his release, and a prison guard, who was injured during the takeover of Cellblock 1—were hospitalized after release.

See also BLACK MILITANTS; BRAZIL; ELECTIONS [25]; IRELAND; POLITICS [8]; SECURITY, U.S.

PROHIBITION PARTY—*See* ELECTIONS [37]
PROJECT ON CORPORATE RESPONSIBILITY—*See* CONSUMER AFFAIRS [5]
PROPERTY TAXES—*See* EDUCATION [2]; ELECTIONS [44]; NIXON, RICHARD MILHOUS; TAXES
PUBLIC HEALTH SERVICE, U.S.—*See* HEALTH
PUBLIC INTEREST RESEARCH GROUP—*See* CIVIL RIGHTS [15]

PUBLIC LAND—New clear-cutting policies. The U.S. Forest Service June 24 adopted a new set of policies regulating timber land in national forests, one that Service head John R. McGuire said would restrict clear-cutting (the leveling of all trees in a given area). The plan had been reported dropped Jan. 13 because of the opposition of the lumber industry. The new plan would defer clear-cutting where land would be harmed or where new trees could not be generated within five years, and would require environmental impact statements whenever land would be converted from one type of vegetation to another. Among the criteria for determining if land would be harmed were soil conditions, necessary road construction, sedimentary pollution of lakes and streams, and the effect of cutting on areas of great natural beauty. Conservationists opposed clear-cutting as wasteful and damaging to the environment, particularly on hillsides and along streams, but timber industry spokesmen and some foresters supported the practice as a means of maintaining the vitality and productivity of forests.

See also ENVIRONMENT

PUERTO RICO—Labor developments. Some 2,200 members of the Independent Telephone Workers Union went on strike Jan. 18. The workers voted Jan. 30 to accept a settlement reached by union leaders and the Puerto Rico Telephone Company and began returning to work. In other strike action, 440 members of the Newspaper Guild (representing editorial, printing, maintenance, administrative and transportation personnel) struck the San Juan daily newspaper *El Mundo* Feb. 9-Sept. 9. The paper resumed publication Sept. 19. (During the strike, *El Mundo* continued to publish a 16-page edition that was taken daily from its grounds by helicopters.) The strike came after the breakdown of eight months of contract negotiations. The central issue reportedly was the exclusion of 200 employees from the contract as supervisors. The guild had also insisted that there would be no settlement until *El Mundo* agreed to pay the same salaries as the English-language *San Juan Star.* (Reporters with five years experience earned a minimum of $203 weekly at the *Star.*) The contract approved Sept. 9 provided wage increases of nearly 50%, with the minimum for journeymen reporters rising from $168 a week to $250 a week over the following three years.

Squatter settlements increase. The wave of land seizures which began around San Juan in 1971 increased during February, creating about 50 new shanty towns in the southern and western sections of Puerto Rico. Most of the settlements had been razed by government order, however, and numerous squatters had been arrested. According to a report March 11, Gov. Luis A. Ferre had called the squatters "persons without a housing problem" who wished "to create problems for the government [and] distress and intranquility for the people of Puerto Rico." The government also charged that the land seizures had been instigated by the Popular Democratic party (PDP), which had ruled Puerto Rico until 1969 and which would oppose Ferre in 1972 elections. A spokesman for the party denied the charge, saying the seizures reflected the failure of Puerto Rico's industrializing society to provide for the unskilled poor.

Elections. PDP candidate Rafael Hernandez Colon Nov. 7 won an upset election victory over Gov. Ferre. Hernandez totaled 623,195 votes for governor to Ferre's 529,996. The PDP, which favored a continuation of Puerto Rico's commonwealth status as opposed to Ferre's statehood aspirations, also won a majority in the legislature and all but six of 78 municipal elections.

Navy to keep Culebra range. U.S. Defense Secretary Melvin Laird said Dec. 27 that the Navy would retain its controversial naval and air-gunnery training range on Culebra Island off Puerto Rico until at least 1985, despite a 1971 commitment to move it elsewhere by June 1975. The Pentagon had agreed April 1, 1971 to issue an announcement by the end of 1972 on where the Culebra range would be relocated. Laird not only reversed the commitment, but also said "air-to-ground weapons training" on rocks and keys west of Culebra were "projected to increase."

See also CONGRESS; HIJACKING [2]; MIDDLE EAST [22]; POLLUTION [8]

PULITZER PRIZES—The 56th annual Pulitzer Prizes in journalism, letters and music were presented in New York City May 1 amid sharp criticism from the board of trustees of Columbia University (sponsor of the competition). The trustees for the first time issued a statement chiding the selection panel, saying they "had deep reservations about the timeliness and suitability of certain of the journalism awards." The 23-man board added that "had the selections been those of the trustees alone, certain of the recipients would not have been chosen." The statement was believed to have been prompted by awards to *The New York Times* for public service for its publication of the Pentagon Papers detailing U.S. involvement in the Vietnam War *(see* PENTAGON PAPERS) and to columnist Jack Anderson for national reporting for his disclosures of Administration policymaking during the India-Pakistan war *(see* PAKISTAN [2]). In both cases, classified government documents were the basis for the awards.

The other winners: **LETTERS: general nonfiction**—*Stillwell and the American Experience in China, 1911-1945,* by Barbara W. Tuchman; **biography**—*Eleanor and Franklin,* by Joseph P. Lash; **fiction**—*Angle of Repose,* by Wallace Stegner; **history**—*Neither Black Nor White,* by Carl M. Degler; **poetry**—*Collected Poems,* by James Wright; **music**—*Windows,* an orchestral piece by Jacob Druckman; **drama**—none.

JOURNALISM: general local reporting—Richard Cooper and John Machacek of the *Rochester* (N.Y.) *Times-Union* for coverage of the Sept. 13, 1971 Attica prison revolt; *special local reporting*—Timothy Leland, Gerard M. O'Neill, Stephan A. Kurjian and Ann DeSantis of the *Boston Globe* for exposure of corruption in Somerville, Mass.; **international reporting**—Peter R. Kann of *The Wall Street Journal* for coverage of the India-Pakistan war; **editorial writing**—John Strohmeyer of *The Bethlehem* (Pa.) *Globe-Times;* **editorial cartooning**—Jeffrey K. MacNelly of the *Richmond* (Va.) *News Leader;* **spot news photography**—Horst Faas and Michael Laurent of the Associated Press; **feature photography**—Dave Kennerly of United Press International; **commentary**—Mike Royko of the *Chicago Daily News;* **criticism**—Frank Peters Jr. of the *St. Louis Post-Dispatch.*

QADDAFI, COL. MUAMMAR EL—*See* Jordan; Libya; Middle East [33];
Philippines [3]; Uganda [4]
QATAR—*See* European Economic Community [7]; International
Monetary Developments [10]; Oil & Natural Gas; Union of
Arab Emirates
RACIAL & MINORITY UNREST—*See* Black Militants; Hijacking [3];
Military [10-12]; Rhodesia
RADIO FREE EUROPE—*See* Television & Radio [4]
RADIO LIBERTY—*See* Television & Radio [4]

RAILROADS—Labor pacts. A new settlement between the nation's railroads
and the American Federation of Labor-Congress of Industrial Organizations
(AFL-CIO) International Brotherhood of Firemen and Oilers was announced
Feb. 11. The pact, covering 13,000 workers, would raise the $3.30 average
hourly wage a total of 97¢ over a period extending until July 1, 1973. In
addition, about 10,000 of the union members would get 1¢ or 2¢ more an hour to
make base rates more uniform. In other pact action: The Penn Central
Transportation Co. and the United Transportation Union (UTU) reached an
agreement July 21, after four days of negotiations with Assistant Secretary of
Labor William J. Usery Jr., on a formula to cut the size of train crews *(see
below)*. (President Nixon had signed an executive order March 31 blocking for
60 days a planned strike over the issue.) The UTU had threatened a strike for
July 26 and had begun court action to block Penn Central's plans to phase out
5,700 trainmen's jobs by reducing the railroad's four- and five-man crews to
two and three men. The agreement established a standing committee of two
representatives from each side and a neutral member to work out details of the
settlement by Nov. 30. The UTU and the nation's railroads July 20 announced
two agreements ending a 35-year-old featherbedding dispute. One of the
agreements stipulated that the railroads would continue to employ the 16,000
firemen presently working until their retirement, resignation, death, promotion
or dismissal for cause; the railroads also agreed to rehire 2,000-3,000 firemen
laid off due to previous arbitration rulings. Under the second agreement, a
program would be established to train firemen for the jobs of locomotive
engineers. The two agreements together permitted the elimination through
long-term attrition of the firemen's jobs on diesel freight locomotives. The
settlement provided for compulsory retirement at age 65.

Penn Central Reorganization. The trustees of the Penn Central Transportation Co. Feb. 15 filed a preliminary reorganization plan with the Philadelphia federal district court, which was overseeing the railroad's reorganization following its June 1970 filing of bankruptcy. The trustees said that the railroad could begin to show signs of financial recovery by 1974 if the government authorized: reduction of the railroad's 20,000 miles of track to 11,000 miles; elimination of $150 million in "unnecessary labor costs" by a train crew cutback of 9,800 jobs; and full compensation by federal, state and local governments for passenger service losses. If the three conditions were met, the trustees said, the railroad would be generating $220 million-$290 million in annual income to meet fixed expenses. The Interstate Commerce Commission (ICC) and the Department of Transportation (DOT) March 16, in comments filed with the court, expressed certain reservations about the preliminary plan. The ICC said that it disagreed with the trustees' projection that reorganization would be substantially completed in 1972 and 1973 as overly optimistic. DOT objected to the trustees' "implication that nationalization is the only alternative to an income-based reorganization," adding that it was premature to consider alternatives when the present plan was feasible. In other Penn Central developments, the trustees March 23 concluded an agreement with 49 banks to cancel most of a $300 million loan made to the railroad in 1969 by a consortium of 53 banks. The agreement was subject to court approval. Four banks in the group (National Bank of Detroit, First National State Bank of N.J., Rhode Island Hospital Trust National Bank and First National of Akron, Ohio) refused to go along with the original agreement in principle, announced in May 1971, whereby the trustees agreed to turn over all the common stock of the railroad's investment banking subsidiary, Pennsylvania Co. (Pennco), in return for cancellation of the loan and a pledge of an additional $150 million in equipment financing. Under the revised agreement, 95.66% of the Pennco stock would be turned over to the consortium and $287 million of the loan would be cancelled. The four banks would continue to have a lien on the remaining Pennco stock.

C&NW sale to employees. The ICC March 20 approved the proposed sale of the Chicago & North Western Railway (C&NW) to its employees. The agency ordered completion of the sale by the railroad's parent company, Northwest Industries, Inc., upon fulfillment of 10 conditions (including protection of minority stockholders and a restriction on future acquisitions by the railroad) by the parties. The group of 14,000 employees was organized in 1970 for the purchase as North Western Employees Transportation Corp. (NETCO). Under the proposed terms, NETCO would buy the railroad for about $415 million by assuming all the carrier's public debt and about $14 million in notes payable to a Northwest Industries subsidiary.

Amtrak revises fares. The National Railroad Passenger Corp. (Amtrak) May 15 announced its first major fare revisions since it went into operation a year before. Rates generally were reduced in the East and boosted in the West for an estimated 3% overall revenue gain, based on current ridership, that had been approved by the federal Price Commission. The changes were made to increase ridership and make the nationwide rail-fare structure more equitable.

Pension bill veto overridden. President Nixon Oct. 4 vetoed a bill granting a 20% increase in railroad retirement benefits, but Congress overrode the veto the same day. The original bill had been passed by the Senate Sept. 19 and by the House Sept. 20. The President had opposed the bill on the ground that the increase would bankrupt the pension fund, because no provisions for financing the higher benefits were provided in the bill. In rejecting the bill, Nixon had cited a recent government study of the railroad pension system which had stated that the program faced bankruptcy by 1988. (According to the study, only 600,000 members were contributing to the fund, while an estimated one million retired workers were deriving benefits from it.) The House voted 353-29 to override the President's veto, and the Senate voted 76-5. Congress acknowledged that the pension system was in poor financial shape, but argued that legislation would soon be introduced to reform it. In the meantime, Congress said, retired railroad workers should receive a benefit increase comparable to the recently voted Social Security increase *(see* SOCIAL SECURITY).

Crash kills 44 commuters. Forty-four Chicago commuters were killed and 320 injured Oct. 30 in a morning rush-hour collision of two trains of the Illinois Central Gulf Railroad. The accident, the worst U.S. rail crash in 14 years, occurred when a new double-decker train backed into a station as another, older train was pulling in. The two trains, both packed with passengers, crumpled into a mass of shredded steel and glass. Police and firemen worked five hours before the last victims were freed. John H. Reed, chairman of the National Transportation Safety Board, said Nov. 1 that human error "was one of the most probable causes" of the disaster. He said the conductor of the new train had failed to protect its rear as it backed up. Reed had said earlier that the agency would investigate the railroad's signal system, practice of backing up trains that overshot stations and the structural strength of the new double-deck cars.

Other crashes. Falling rocks from a tunnel under repair near Soissons, France June 17 caused a train derailment which resulted in the deaths of at least 107 people. A two-car train which entered the tunnel was derailed by the large rocks and was struck a short time later by a six-car train traveling in the opposite direction. At least 76 persons were killed July 21 when a holiday express train carrying 500 passengers crashed head-on into a local train on a sharp curve near Jerez, Spain. A passenger train crowded with more than 1,500 persons hurtled around a curve Oct. 6 at 75 m.p.h.—twice the speed permitted—and jumped the tracks at Saltillo, Mexico. At least 204 were confirmed dead and 1,098 injured Oct. 9. Six surviving crew members were charged with negligent manslaughter. According to police, blood tests indicated they were intoxicated at the time of the accident.

See also GREAT BRITAIN [1, 11]

RAS AL KHAIMA—*See* UNION OF ARAB EMIRATES

RECORD INDUSTRY—Grammy Awards. The 14th annual Grammy Awards were presented March 14 by the National Academy of Recording Arts and Sciences in 44 categories of musical achievement. The winners: **record of the year**—"It's Too Late" (Carole King); **album of the year**—*Tapestry* (Carole King); **song of the year**—"You've Got a Friend" (Carole King); **best score from an original cast show album**—*Godspell;* **best original score for a motion picture**—Isaac Hayes for *Shaft;* **best pop vocal performance by a duo, group or chorus**—The Carpenters; **best comedy recording**—Lily Tomlin in *This Is a Recording;* **album of the year, classical**—*Horowitz Plays Rachmaninoff;* **best pop vocal performance, male**—James Taylor, "You've Got a Friend"; **best pop vocal performance, female**—Carole King, *Tapestry;* **best rhythm and blues vocal performance, male**—Lou Rawls, "A Natural Man"; **best rhythm and blues vocal performance, female**—Aretha Franklin, "Bridge Over Troubled Water"; **best rhythm and blues song**—"Ain't No Sunshine"; **best country vocal performance, male**—Jerry Reed, "When You're Hot, You're Hot"; **best country vocal performance, female**—Sammi Smith, "Help Me Make It Through the Night"; **best country song**—"Help Me Make It Through the Night."

RECYCLING—*See* POLLUTION [3]
RED CROSS—*See* BURUNDI; HIJACKING [9]
REFUGEES—*See* BANGLA DESH [1-2]; BURUNDI; MIDDLE EAST [13]; UNITED NATIONS
REFUSE ACT—*See* POLLUTION [14]
REHNQUIST, WILLIAM—*See* SECURITY, U.S.
REPUBLICAN PARTY—*See* CIVIL DISORDERS; CONGRESS; ELECTIONS [1-8, 11-14, 18, 22-28, 35-36, 38-43, 47]; POLITICS [1-7, 9-12, 15]

REPUBLIC OF CHINA—*See* CHINA, NATIONALIST
REPUBLIC OF KOREA (ROK)—*See* KOREA, SOUTH
REPUBLIC OF VIETNAM—*See* VIETNAM, SOUTH
RESERVE CLAUSE—*See* BASKETBALL [14]
RESERVE OFFICERS TRAINING CORPS (ROTC)—*See* DRAFT & WAR PROTEST
RESIGNATIONS—*See* CIVIL RIGHTS [15]; INDIANS, AMERICAN; MILITARY [2]; NIXON, RICHARD MILHOUS; SELECTIVE SERVICE SYSTEM
REVENUE SHARING—*See* NIXON, RICHARD MILHOUS; STATE & LOCAL GOVERNMENTS

RHODESIA—U.S. lifts chrome ban. The U.S. Treasury Department announced Jan. 25 that restrictions on importing Rhodesian Chrome, asbestos, silver, copper and nickel (originally imposed in compliance with 1968 United Nations sanctions against trade with Rhodesia) had been officially lifted as a result of a 1971 Congressional resolution giving the President authority to import strategic materials also being imported from Communist nations. The U.S. Senate Foreign Relations Committee April 17 approved a bill that would allow reimposition of the import ban on Rhodesian chrome, but the Senate May 31 rejected the proposal. The U.S. announced June 30 that it had also purchased three shipments of nickel from Rhodesia in violation of the U.N. sanctions. (In a related development, a U.S. district court in New York June 16, levied fines totaling $311,750 against two corporations and three men who had violated Rhodesian trade sanctions.)

Pearce vetoes constitutional pact. A British government commission headed by Lord Pearce, which had investigated Rhodesians' reaction to the constitutional and racial settlement reached by the two governments in November 1971, declared that "the people of Rhodesia as a whole do not regard the proposals as acceptable as a basis for independence." The report of the commission said that most of the whites interviewed by the commission accepted the proposals for economic reasons, declaring that the country needed some 40,000 new jobs a year in order to employ blacks. The colored (mixed white and black ancestry) and Asian communities accepted the proposals "reluctantly" and "in default of anything else." An overwhelming majority of the black population rejected the settlement's terms because of mistrust of the Rhodesian government, according to the report. British Foreign Minister Sir Alec Douglas-Home announced the commission's findings to the House of Commons May 23 and said that, as a result of the Pearce report, Britain's economic sanctions against Rhodesia would remain in force. (Of five principles outlined by the British as necessary to any agreement between the two countries, the fifth principle had been the acceptability of an agreement to Rhodesians as a whole.) Douglas-Home implied that Britain would continue its efforts to reach an agreement with the Salisbury government. Rhodesian Prime Minister Ian D. Smith said May 23 that the Pearce report was characterized by "naivete and ineptness" and "many misrepresentations and misconstructions of true positions." Smith said he was offering to implement the proposals of the 1971 settlement if Britain would also do so. Britain refused the offer.

Pearce investigation. The Pearce Commission had investigated acceptability of the settlement in Rhodesia Jan. 11-March 12. Racial violence and death had accompanied their investigation and provoked speculation that the commission should withdraw from Rhodesia. The civil disorder had also provoked hints from Lord Pearce that the Smith government might be breaking its promise to allow normal political activity during the commission's visit. Following its investigation in Rhodesia, the commission had held several days of hearings in London to gather the opinions of Rhodesians living in Britain.

Racial unrest. Rioting and other disturbances rocked Rhodesia Jan. 16-20 as blacks expressed opposition to the Anglo-Rhodesian settlement. The trouble began Jan. 16 in Gwelo, where blacks in outlying townships smashed windows and burned cars and buildings. The following day, an estimated 8,000 persons were turned back by police tear gas as they attempted to march into the predominantly white center of the city. One black youth died Jan. 18 after he fell while running from police; two other blacks were injured, one by a police bayonet; and 55 persons were arrested. Violence broke out near Salisbury Jan. 19 as black youths looted shops and stoned cars, injuring at least 100 persons. Police in the black suburbs of Port Victoria, about 200 miles to the south, shot and wounded two black youths who were attempting to ransack a liquor store Jan. 19. Three blacks were killed, at least 24 wounded and 44 arrested Jan. 19 in violence in Harari, a township on the outskirts of Salisbury. Police killed eight blacks Jan. 20 in Sakubva township in Umtali as they opened fire on a crowd of some 1,000 blacks who had smashed windows and stoned a police vehicle. Authorities in Port Victoria Jan. 20 arrested 200 blacks for similar disturbances. Prime Minister Smith alleged Feb. 10 that the violence in the country had been caused by the African National Council, a black group formed to oppose the Anglo-Rhodesian settlement.

Arrests. The Rhodesian government also arrested several prominent citizens while the Pearce Commission was in Rhodesia. The government said that the arrests were not an attempt to prevent such persons from testifying before the commission. Former Prime Minister Garfield Todd and his daughter Judith were arrested Jan. 18 on charges that they were "likely to commit or incite the commission of acts in Rhodesia which would endanger the public safety or disturb or interfere with the maintenance of public order." The Todds were released from prison Feb. 22 "for health reasons and on humanitarian grounds." They were confined to their family ranch near Shabani, forbidden to use the telephone and allowed to see only immediate members of their family. Judith Todd arrived in Britain July 14 after being warned that she would again be placed in detention if she returned to Rhodesia. The government Jan. 21 also arrested Josia Chinamano, a leader of the African National Council, and his wife Ruth. The two, who were detained because of their connection with the council, were transferred April 14 to a "more suitable accommodation," adjacent to the Marandellas prison reserve southeast of Salisbury, where they would be allowed to "re-establish family life and receive visits from their children."

African Council to continue. The African National Council revealed March 10 its intention of continuing under the same name as an "organization," rather than a "political party," whose "main aim" would be the calling of a multiracial constitutional conference to negotiate a "just settlement" of Rhodesia's problems. Bishop Abel T. Muzorewa, the group's leader, announced the names of 55 members of its national executive council. There was also to be a central committee of 23 members. The government March 27 seized the first printing of an anticipated 250,000 council membership cards as an "undesirable publication" under the Law and Order Maintenance Act. In other moves against the council, the government Sept. 1 withdrew the passport of the Rev. Ganaan Banana, vice chairman of the council, and prevented him from leaving Rhodesia under terms of the Departure from Rhodesia (Control) Amendment Act (passed the same day) which gave the immigration minister power to forbid the departure of persons whose journeys were not deemed to be in the public interest. Acting under the same act, the government Sept. 8 confiscated Bishop Muzorewa's passport.

African bus strike ends. Some 400 African bus drivers in Salisbury June 26 ended a strike which had begun 13 days earlier and which had spread to Bulawayo June 21. The drivers, who had asked for extra payment for shifts operated without conductors, returned to work when an emergency public transport system run by Rhodesian army drivers went into effect. Minister of Labor Ian McLean had said June 25 that the drivers' demands could not be negotiated until after the strike ended.

Pass law introduced. The government introduced legislation Nov. 17 requiring blacks over the age of 16 to carry identity cards similar to those used by both blacks and whites in South Africa. The bill was the fourth apartheid measure put forward by the ruling Rhodesian Front since September, when Prime Minister Smith had appeared to reject more apartheid-style laws for the country. (The government also had ordered segregation of public swimming pools and had given notice that Salisbury's principal maternity hospital would not accept Asian or colored patients. The High Court Nov. 16 had struck down regulations limiting the hours during which blacks could drink at segregated bars in white areas.) The new legislation, known as the Africans Registration and Identification (Amendment) Bill, provided for fines of $152 and six months in jail for failure to carry the proper documents at all times. It also stipulated that blacks wishing to leave the country must obtain permission from government registration officers.

See also AUSTRALIA [11]; BRAZIL; CHURCHES; MINES; OLYMPICS [3]; POLITICS [8]

RICHARDSON, ELLIOT L.—See CIVIL RIGHTS [9]; CONSUMER AFFAIRS [12]; NIXON, RICHARD MILHOUS; WOMEN'S RIGHTS
RICORD, AUGUSTE-JOSEPH—See DRUG USE & ADDICTION [14]
ROCKEFELLER, NELSON—See ABORTION; ELECTIONS [22]; PRISONS
ROGERS, WILLIAM P.—See ATOMIC ENERGY [13]; ELECTIONS [32]; INDOCHINA WAR [23, 40]; JAPAN [4]; MIDDLE EAST [34]; NIXON, RICHARD MILHOUS; POLAND; SINO-U.S. RELATIONS [4]; SOVIET-U.S. RELATIONS [3-4]

ROMAN CATHOLIC CHURCH—1971 statistics. The Vatican yearbook, Activity of the Holy See, published March 13, reported that the number of Roman Catholics in the world increased in 1971 as the number of priests declined. The number of priests fell from 351,000 in 1969 to 347,481 in 1971, producing a world average of 1,535 Catholics per priest. Newly ordained priests totaled 3,500 in 1971, 532 fewer than in 1969. The number of Catholics increased from 526.5 million in 1969 to 533 million-534 million in 1971. (In a related development, the Vatican March 29 published its first figures on priests who had left the church. The figures showed that there were 6,920 defections of secular clergy and 6,520 defections by members of religious orders during the period from 1964-1970.)

Pope consecrates Dutch bishop. Spurning a petition by the liberal Dutch hierarchy that the consecration of controversial conservative Jan M. Gijsen as bishop of Roermond be held in the Netherlands, Pope Paul VI included Gijsen among 19 prelates he consecrated in Rome Feb. 13. The Dutch hierarchy's petition had viewed Gijsen as an outsider, who should have been consecrated on Dutch soil in order to better acquaint himself with his diocese. In appointing Gijsen in January, the Pope had passed over more liberal candidates proposed by the Roermond diocese. Attending the consecration ceremony at the Pope's personal request was Dutch Primate Bernard Cardinal Alfrink, who viewed the Pope's appointment of Gijsen as a severe strain on his church's relations with the Vatican. The customary delegation from the bishop's new diocese was not present at the ceremony.

Bishop selection reform. The Vatican May 12 gave national and regional hierarchies a greater role in the selection of bishops, but still kept final determination in the selection in the hands of the Pope and the Roman Curia. Under the reform, priests and laymen were allowed consultative roles in the secret nomination process. (Liberal Catholics had expected a further democratization of the selection process through the election of bishops by priests and parishioners in each diocese.) The Vatican also reminded countries such as Spain and Portugal of the Second Vatican Council's request that they voluntarily renounce concordat arrangements which permitted state nomination of bishops for the Pope's approval.

Annulment reform. The Vatican May 31 announced new rules designed to expedite annulment proceedings. Couples seeking an annulment on grounds of nonconsummation were allowed to apply in the diocese in which they lived.

Diocesan authorities were allowed to waive medical examinations and to act without further Vatican authorization. Annulment hearings would be heard in the local language rather than Latin and would take three to five months for completion—half the time required in the past. The new regulations became effective July 1.

Group confessions curbed. The Sacred Congregation of the Doctrine of the Faith, with the approval of the Pope, July 12 issued an instruction to bishops and priests condemning the growing practice of granting absolution in community rites of penance. The instruction limited such absolution to situations where penitents were in immediate danger of death or where there was a serious shortage of priests. The Vatican restated the 400-year-old doctrine of secret, individual confession and warned priests and laymen of their obligation to uphold this tenet.

Pope rules on clerical orders. Two papal "apostolic letters" published Sept. 14 re-emphasized the church ban on a ministerial role for women, reconfirmed the celibate status of priests and abolished the tonsure (a circular shaving of the crown of the head which marked a preliminary stage in the orders of priesthood). The documents also renewed the church commitment to allow married men to serve as permanent deacons. (However, widowed and unmarried deacons would be required to swear celibacy.) The Pope also abolished the minor clerical orders of porters, lectors, exorcists and acolytes, as well as the role of subdeacon. The offices of lector and acolyte were retained as ministries open to laymen and seminarians.

See also ABORTION [4]; BRAZIL; CHURCHES; DRAFT & WAR PROTEST; EDUCATION [4]; ELECTIONS [36]; EUROPEAN SECURITY; IRELAND; ITALY [6]; NORTHERN IRELAND; PANAMA; PARAGUAY; POLAND; SECURITY, U.S.; SPAIN; ZAIRE

ROMNEY, GEORGE—*See* HOUSING; NIXON, RICHARD MILHOUS
ROOSEVELT, FRANKLIN D.—*See* ELECTIONS [36]; TRUMAN, HARRY S
RUCKELSHAUS, WILLIAM—*See* NIXON, RICHARD MILHOUS; POLLUTION [4-5, 8, 16]

RUMANIA—1971 economic report. The results of the 1971 economic development plan were announced Feb. 2. Measured against the figures for 1970, increases were recorded in the following major items: national income 12.5%; industrial output 11.5%; farm output 18.2%; foreign trade 8.6%; and industrial productivity 5.9%.

General allegedly executed. A press dispatch, citing an "authoritative diplomatic source," Feb. 14 reported that Gen. Ion Serb, commander of the Bucharest military garrison and a member of the National Assembly, had been executed by firing squad in January for passing to the Soviet Union information about Rumania's defenses. No official confirmation of the report could be obtained, but the Rumanian embassy in Vienna revealed Feb. 17 that Serb was "no longer a general." Some Western press accounts said that Serb's espionage contact was Col. A. F. Musatov, the military attache at the Soviet embassy in Bucharest, and that Musatov had been asked to leave Rumania. It was reported Feb. 25, however, that Musatov had made public appearances in Bucharest that week.

Hungarian friendship treaty. Rumanian Premier Ion Gheorghe Maurer and Hungarian Premier Jeno Fock Feb. 24 signed a 20-year treaty of friendship and cooperation in which they affirmed respect for each other's territorial integrity and promised to give military assistance in the event of an attack upon either. The original friendship treaty between the two countries had lapsed in 1968.

Party conference. A three-day Communist party conference attended by some 2,500 delegates ended July 21 with resolutions asking higher wages, a shorter work week and increased pension benefits. The meeting, held in Bucharest, also voted to expand the Central Committee from 165 to 185 members and to confirm President Nicolae Ceausescu as head of the newly created Supreme Council for Economic Development (responsible for insuring that the five-year plan due to end in 1975 be finished six months ahead of schedule).

Government changes. The Communist party Central Committee's executive committee Oct. 11 recommended a series of government personnel changes intended to involve Rumania's leaders more effectively with "concrete problems that have to be solved." As a result of the recommendation, approved by the State Council Oct. 11, Paul Niculescu-Mazil, deputy chairman of the Council of Ministers, became minister of education, replacing Mircea Malita. Virgil Trofin, who was named a deputy chairman of the Council of Ministers and minister of internal trade, took the place of Nicolae Bozdog. Manea Manescu was elevated to deputy chairman of the Council of Ministers and chairman of the State Planning Committee, replacing Maxim Berghianu, who was named minister of technical and material supplies. Former Minister of Material and Technical Supplies Mihai Marinescu became first deputy chairman of the Economic Council. Emil Draganescu was appointed minister of transport and telecommunications, replacing Florian Danalache. In another development, it was reported Oct. 18 that Corneliu Manescu, foreign minister since 1961, had been released from office by a decree of the State Council and would assume "other duties." Manescu was replaced as foreign minister by Gheorghe Macovescu.

See also ATOMIC ENERGY [6]; CUBA; EUROPEAN ECONOMIC COMMUNITY [7]; EUROPEAN SECURITY; INTERNATIONAL BANK FOR RECONSTRUCTION & DEVELOPMENT; SPACE [22]

RUMSFELD, DONALD—See ECONOMY [4-5]; NIXON, RICHARD MILHOUS
RUSSIA—See UNION OF SOVIET SOCIALIST REPUBLICS
RUSSO JR., ANTHONY J.—See PENTAGON PAPERS
RWANDA—See BURUNDI
RYUKYU ISLANDS—See CHINA, COMMUNIST; JAPAN [4-5]

SACCHARINE—*See* CONSUMER AFFAIRS [4]
SADAT, ANWAR—*See* ARAB REPUBLIC OF EGYPT; MIDDLE EAST [30-35]
SALAM, SAEB—*See* MIDDLE EAST [6, 9]
SANFORD, TERRY—*See* ELECTIONS [17]
SAN MARINO—*See* EUROPEAN SECURITY
SATELLITES—*See* DISARMAMENT; SPACE [1, 21-24]
SAUDI ARABIA—*See* OIL & NATURAL GAS; YEMEN
SCHMITZ, JOHN F.—*See* ELECTIONS [21, 37]
SCHOOLS—*See* CIVIL RIGHTS [1-13, 18]; DRAFT & WAR PROTEST; EDUCATION; ELECTIONS [6, 16, 21, 23, 35, 44]; POLITICS [8]

SCIENCE—Laser 'yardstick' developed. Scientists of the National Bureau of Standards of the Commerce Department Feb. 1 announced that they had developed a potential laser "yardstick" for the measurement of space and time. Among other things, the laser measurement could improve by nearly 30-fold the present determination of the speed of light. This would probably lead to greater accuracy in space travel, since the estimates of planetary distances were based on the speed of light and of radar signals. The yardstick also could relieve badly overloaded communications circuits by opening new ones.

See also ARCHEOLOGY & ANTHROPOLOGY; NOBEL PRIZES; SOVIET-U.S. RELATIONS [4]; SPACE

SECRET SERVICE—*See* ELECTIONS [25]
SECURITIES & EXCHANGE COMMISSION (SEC)—*See* STOCK MARKET

SECURITY, U.S.—Document classification curbed. President Nixon March 8 signed an executive order limiting the practice of classifying government documents as secret and speeding the process of declassification. Under the order, no document could be restrictively classified unless its release "could reasonably be expected" to damage the national interest. The number of agencies in possession of a "top secret" stamp would be reduced from 24 to 12, with only 13 others possessing a "secret" stamp. Only 1,860 officials would have "top secret" classification power compared with about 5,100 in the past. "Repeated abuse" of classification power, such as "to conceal inefficiency or administrative error," could result in "administrative action." In general, "top secret" papers would automatically drop to "secret" status after two years; "secret" documents would be downgraded to the "confidential" category after two years, and all "confidential" material would be released after six years.

Exceptions—including documents supplied in confidence by foreign sovereignties, lawfully protected information such as atomic energy data, information damaging to spies and information "the continuing protection of which is essential to the national security"—would undergo automatic review after 10 years. An agency withholding such data would have to explain its action to anyone requesting a specific paper. After 30 years, all documents would be declassified unless countermanded in writing by the head of the originating agency. However, presidential papers would remain undisclosed unless released by the individual president. The entire procedure of declassification would be supervised by an interagency review committee under the National Security Council.

Mistrial in Harrisburg 7 case. A federal jury deliberating charges against the Rev. Philip F. Berrigan and six fellow antiwar activists April 5 reported itself unable to reach a verdict on the charges of conspiracy to kidnap Presidential adviser Henry Kissinger, blow up Washington (D.C.) heating tunnels and raid draft offices. However, the Harrisburg, Pa. jury found Berrigan and Sister Elizabeth McAlister guilty on four and three counts, respectively, of smuggling contraband letters at the Lewisburg, Pa. federal prison. Berrigan was sentenced Sept. 5 to four concurrent two-year terms in prison, and Sister Elizabeth was sentenced to a one-year-and-a-day term. Berrigan's sentence would be served concurrently with the three years remaining of a six-year term for destroying draft records in Baltimore in 1967 and in Catonsville, Md. in 1968. The Catholic priest could be released immediately if his parole application (held up by the conspiracy trial) was accepted. (Berrigan was released on parole Nov. 29.) Defense pleas that the convictions for smuggling letters be set aside were rejected by Judge R. Dixon Herman. (The Federal Bureau of Prisons had dropped restrictions on the flow of mail in its penitentiaries before the Harrisburg trial had gone to jury, and no prosecution had ever been brought in other similar letter-smuggling cases.) Following the sentencing of Berrigan and Sister Elizabeth, U.S. attorneys moved to drop all conspiracy charges against the Harrisburg Seven.

The Harrisburg Seven trial, which had begun Feb. 21, had ended after 59 hours of deliberation by the jury. During its deliberation, the jury three times requested clarification from Judge Herman of his instructions on the conspiracy law. The defense had rested its case March 24 without calling a witness after the prosecution had completed its 23 days of testimony from 64 witnesses. The defendants had decided to call no witnesses to their defense by a 4-3 vote March 23. The majority (the Rev. Joseph Wenderoth, the Rev. Neil R. McLaughlin, Mary Cain and Anthony Scoblick) concluded that an active defense would be crippled if Judge Herman denied (as he did March 24) a motion to hold a hearing before the jury on whether the government had engaged in discriminatory prosecution and another motion asking immunity for witnesses to describe non-violent, though illegal, acts by the Catholic Left. Berrigan, Sister Elizabeth and Dr. Eqbal Ahmad had dissented from the defendants' decision. Judge Herman March 27 ordered Ahmad cleared of charges that he had smuggled contraband into Lewisburg and that he had suggested Kissinger's kidnaping through the mails. The first charge had been based solely on a reference to "Eq" in one of the smuggled letters; and the second on testimony from chief prosecution witness, government informant Boyd Douglas Jr., who claimed he had identified Ahmad's voice as that of a person with whom he had discussed the kidnaping by telephone in 1970. Douglas, who had received $9,000 from the Federal Bureau of Investigation in rewards and expenses while informing on the defendants and others, had testified Feb. 21 that he had smuggled letters between Berrigan and the other defendants while he was serving a five-year term in Lewisburg for passing bad checks and resisting arrest. (Berrigan was in Lewisburg serving his sentence for draft raids.) Douglas had conveyed the letters from the prison on trips to Bucknell University, where the prison had granted him the privilege of attending classes. Douglas said he had also participated in meetings and telephone calls with the defendants and other activists in which the alleged plot was mentioned. Douglas admitted that the FBI had indicated that he would not be prosecuted for smuggling, which carried a heavy penalty, when he was requested to become an informer. Douglas had kept his smuggling activities secret until a routine search revealed one of the letters.

Massachusetts loyalty oath upheld. In a decision reversing the trend set by the Supreme Court under Chief Justice Earl Warren, the court April 18 sustained, by a 4-3 vote, a Massachusetts loyalty oath permitting the dismissal of public employees who refused to swear they would oppose the violent over-throw of the government. The Warren court had struck down a number of state loyalty oaths, upholding only the simple affirmation of support for the Constitution routinely required for government jobs. The ruling came in the case of Lucretia P. Richardson, a research sociologist hired by the state hospital in Boston in 1968. After she refused to take the oath, she was fired. A lower court had ruled the law unconstitutional on her appeal, but the case was appealed by Massachusetts officials to the Supreme Court.

Passport oath barred. U.S. District Court Judge Thomas A. Flannery June 26 ordered the State Department in Washington to remove the loyalty oath from passport applications and to cease denying passports to citizens who refuse to swear or affirm an oath of allegiance. Flannery ruled that the Fifth Amendment to the Constitution guaranteed the right to travel abroad. He said that "no serious national purpose" was served by the oath, since it would likely be ineffective against those "intent upon committing acts contrary to the country's interests" and would harm only "those persons who find a public affirmation of loyalty repugnant to their integrity and conscience." The loyalty oath, required for passports since 1861, had been made optional in 1966, but restored in November 1971 after a federal district court judged that the option "unfairly discriminates against U.S. citizens." The Flannery decision came in a case brought by the American Civil Liberties Union (ACLU) on behalf of Beverly A. Woodward and Allan Fletcher, who were denied passports after refusing the oath.

Wiretapping of radicals curbed. The Supreme Court June 19 declared unconstitutional the federal government's use of wiretapping and electronic surveillance to monitor domestic radicals without first obtaining court warrants. The court rejected the government's argument that the president's authority to protect the country from internal subversion gave the government the constitutional authority to use wiretaps on "dangerous radicals" without court approval. The 8-0 ruling (Justice William Rehnquist, who had helped shape the government's argument as a Justice Department official, did not participate) was a major legal setback for the Nixon Administration, which had argued strenuously for its position. The court decision held that "Fourth Amendment freedoms cannot properly be guaranteed if domestic surveillances may be conducted solely within the discretion of the executive branch." (The Fourth Amendment protected citizens against "unreasonable searches and seizures.") In writing the opinion, Justice Lewis F. Powell Jr. relied heavily upon the threat to free speech he saw in unchecked wiretapping of dissenters by the government. The court's ruling meant that the government would have to obtain court warrants for wiretapping of domestic radicals with no foreign ties and that any defendant in a federal prosecution had the right to see complete transcripts of any conversations monitored through warrantless taps in a domestic case so that his attorney could make certain that no illegally obtained information was being used in the prosecution. The decision came in a Justice Department appeal of a district court's ruling that transcripts of warrantless wiretaps would have to be disclosed in a case charging three members of the radical White Panther party with plotting to blow up a government building in Detroit. Following the Supreme Court ruling, the Justice Department said that it would screen all applicable cases presently under way to decide whether to release warrantless wiretap transcripts or drop the prosecutions. Attorney General Richard G. Kleindienst said July 19 that he had "directed the termination of all electronic surveillance in cases involving security that conflict with the court's opinion." The Justice Department had been using warrantless wiretaps against domestic radicals since 1968.

Grand jury curb on wiretap evidence. The Supreme Court held 5-4 June 26 that grand jury witnesses had the right to refuse to answer questions gleaned from information overheard on illegal listening devices. The government had argued that such a ruling would slow down the work of grand juries by requiring tedious searching through wiretap transcripts before questioning could begin. The ruling sustained the challenge brought by Anne Walsh and Sister Jogues Egan against their convictions for refusing to testify about the alleged plot to kidnap Kissinger *(see above)*.

See also CIVIL DISORDERS; ESPIONAGE; FEDERAL BUREAU OF INVESTIGATION; PAKISTAN [2]; PENTAGON PAPERS

SELASSIE, HAILE—*See* SUDAN

SELECTIVE SERVICE SYSTEM—Draft calls. Defense Secretary Melvin R. Laird announced Jan. 30 that no men would be called up for military duty before April. Laird attributed suspension of the draft to continuing troop withdrawals from Vietnam, the 892,000-man Army ceiling set by Congress and military pay increases which were expected to increase enlistments. In response to Laird's announcement, the Selective Service System announced Feb. 8 that it had instructed local draft boards to cancel the induction orders for the more than 11,000 men who had been scheduled to report in the first three months of 1972. Local boards were instructed to place those men and 115,000 others, who had low lottery numbers and were eligible for the draft but were not inducted in 1971, into a second priority category that virtually assured them that they would not be drafted. In another development, Laird announced May 13 that no more than 50,000 men would be called up for military service in 1972—the lowest total since 1949, just before the Korean War, when about 10,000 men were drafted. The draft calls for 1972: January through March—0; April through June—15,000; July—7,200; August—8,900; September—4,800; and October-December—15,900. In another development, the Defense Department May 26 canceled the doctors' draft for the rest of the year. (Laird announced Nov. 28 that less than 10,000 men would be drafted during the first six months of 1973 before conscription was abandoned for an all-volunteer force.)

1973 lottery held. The Selective Service System Feb. 2 held its fourth draft lottery since Congress authorized the random selection system in 1969. The drawing assigned the nearly two million men born in 1953 draft numbers to determine the order in which they would be called up for military duty. None of the men given numbers in the new lottery would be drafted before 1973. The drawing effected only those who would turn 19 in 1972.

Board appeals to resume. The Selective Service System March 10 directed local draft boards to resume hearings on deferment or exemption appeals, suspended since December 1971 by order of Selective Service Director Curtis W. Tarr. Tarr said the new instructions brought to a close a two-year overhaul of the draft system, moving it from a state-local focus to a more national system. Among the changes in the appeal procedure which were set down in the new directive: classification proceedings for a registrant whose call-up had been long postponed could be reopened if the registrant sought exemption, deferment or conscientious objector (CO) status; registrants were to be given 15 days after their classification was mailed to request a personal appearance or appeal; state and national appeals boards were required to give at least 15 days' notice when a registrant was granted a personal appearance; registrants were allowed to bring witnesses before local boards; local boards were required to give a registrant reasons for rejection of his classification request; and a quorum of board members was required to be present during a registrant's personal appearance.

Tarr resigns. Selective Service Director Tarr announced his resignation as head of the draft agency April 11. He was sworn in May 17 as the first undersecretary of state for security assistance.

See also FEDERAL BUREAU OF INVESTIGATION; HEALTH CARE; SECURITY, U.S.; WOMEN'S RIGHTS

SENATE—*See* CONGRESS; ELECTIONS [1, 38-39, 46]

SENEGAL—The government of President Leopold Sedar Senghor underwent several changes June 19: Magatte Lo, formerly president of the Economic and Social Council, became minister of state in charge of the armed forces; Amadou Karim Gaye, formerly foreign minister, took over Lo's old post; Coumba Mdoffene Diouf, formerly minister of labor, civil service and employment, replaced Gaye as foreign minister; and Amadou Ly took over Diouf's former position.

See also AFRICA

SHARJA—*See* UNION OF ARAB EMIRATES

SHIPS & SHIPPING—**Queen Elizabeth 1 burns.** The 83,000-ton luxury liner Queen Elizabeth 1, which was being refurbished to serve as a floating college campus for Chapman College of Orange, Calif., burned for 24 hours Jan. 9 and capsized while docking in Hong Kong harbor. She was believed to be a total loss, with insurance losses estimated near $8 million. A Hong Kong marine court of inquiry July 19 ruled that the fire was probably caused by arson.

Passenger ships to be sold. President Nixon May 17 signed a bill authorizing the sale of five U.S.-flag passenger ships—all out of service for at least 16 months—to foreign operators. The ships were: the Brasil and the Argentina, owned by Moore-McCormack Lines, Inc.; the Santa Rosa and the Santa Paula, owned by the Prudential-Grace Lines, Inc.; and the Constitution, owned by American Export-Isbrandtsen Lines, Inc. The legislation, which was opposed by U.S. maritime unions, was cleared by Congress May 2 when the Senate passed a bill approved by the House Dec. 1, 1971. Proceeds from the sales were to be used for new ship construction.

Bomb scare on Queen Elizabeth 2. A team of British bomb-disposal experts May 19 searched through the 13 decks of the luxury liner Queen Elizabeth 2 for six bombs that an anonymous caller said would blow up the ship unless a ransom of $350,000 was paid. (According to the call, the bombs would be detonated by two accomplices aboard the ship unless the Cunard Lines, Ltd. paid the ransom.) The demolition team found no bombs; and the ship made its way safely across the Atlantic to Cherbourg, France, where it docked May 20. Officials of Cunard said they were convinced that the bomb scare was a hoax and that the liner's 1,500 passengers and 800 crew members were never in danger.

New cargo ships ordered. President Nixon announced July 1 that five major contracts totaling $660 million had been awarded June 30 for construction of 16 merchant ships. The government would provide a $284 million subsidy for the building costs. The 43% subsidy was arranged under a declining percentage scale as an incentive to encourage more efficient construction. The total construction order more than doubled in tonnage the shipbuilding in progress in the U.S. Among the 16 ships to be built were 13 tankers—including three 265,000-ton ships, the largest ever to be built in the United States. The construction would provide 36,000 jobs and an additional 800 jobs on the completed ships, according to a Commerce Department report.

West Coast ship strike. Commercial cargo shipping on the West Coast of the U.S. was tied up Oct. 25-Dec. 4 by striking deck officers of the AFL-CIO International Organization of Masters, Mates and Pilots. The strike against five ship owners affected about 40 vessels and was not extended to ships carrying passengers or military cargo. Job security was the major issue in the action. The old contract had expired June 15. A tentative accord, subject to union ratification, was reached Dec. 4 with the help of federal mediators.

Disasters. The Greek-owned tanker Texanita Aug. 21 collided with another tanker, the Taiwan-owned Oswego Guardian, in fog 23 miles south of the Cape of Good Hope off the South African coast. An explosion sank the Texanita, killing most of the 50 people aboard. An 11,500-ton freighter, the African Neptune, rammed the mile-long Sidney Lanier Bridge near Brunswick, Ga. Nov. 7, killing at least 10 motorists waiting in cars and trucks on the span for the ship to pass. A 450-foot section of the bridge was destroyed. The captain and two crew members of the 175-ton Greek tanker World Hero were held on manslaughter charges Nov. 25 following the Nov. 15 collision of the supertanker and a Greek navy troop carrier off Piraeus, Greece. Forty-four sailors died in the collision.

See also HIJACKING [19]; LABOR; POLLUTION [12]; SOVIET-U.S. RELATIONS [4, 11]

SHRIVER, R. SARGENT—*See* ELECTIONS [2, 29, 32, 37]; POLITICS [14]
SHULTZ, GEORGE P.—*See* NIXON, RICHARD MILHOUS
SIERRA LEONE—*See* CUBA; INTERNATIONAL MONETARY DEVELOPMENTS [8]; OLYMPICS [3]
SIHANOUK, PRINCE NORODOM—*See* CAMBODIA
SIKKIM—*See* EUROPEAN ECONOMIC COMMUNITY [7]
SINAI PENINSULA—*See* ISRAEL

SINGAPORE—Parliamentary elections. The ruling Peoples' Action party won all 65 parliamentary seats in general elections Sept. 2. According to results released Sept. 4, 77 candidates of six opposition parties and two independents failed to win a seat, but drew 31% of the popular vote. Fifty-seven seats were contested, while the remaining eight were won by Peoples' Action without opposition.

See also INTERNATIONAL MONETARY DEVELOPMENTS [8]; SINO-U.S. RELATIONS [8]

SINO-SOVIET RELATIONS—Soviets bring in divisions. It was reported Sept. 10 that the Soviet Union recently had moved three mechanized divisions to the border area near China, raising the number of divisions known to be in the region to 49. The total represented one-third of the entire Soviet army. Barracks, supply and administration buildings already had been constructed for the new troops.

Border clash denied. A Chinese official Dec. 11 denied reports circulated by Western diplomats the previous day that five Soviet soldiers in Kazakhstan had been killed by Chinese intruders in November. According to the allegations, the Chinese, who were not identified as soldiers, killed the Soviet military men and a number of shepherds and took back with them a large flock of sheep. The incident was said to have taken place at the Dzungarian Gate, a mountain pass linking the Soviet republic with the Sinkiang region of China.

See also CHINA, COMMUNIST; SINO-U.S. RELATIONS [7]

SINO-U.S. RELATIONS—One diplomatic barrier to international unity was eased during February of 1972, as President Richard M. Nixon made an historic visit to the People's Republic of China for talks with Chinese officials on easing relations between the U.S. and China. (The U.S. has never extended diplomatic recognition to China.) While in China, the President spoke with Premier Chou En-lai and Chairman Mao Tsetung. The trip ended with the release of a joint Sino-U.S. communique which indicated agreement on the need for increased contacts between the two nations and for the eventual withdrawal of U.S. troops from Taiwan.

[2] Trade barriers relaxed. Three days before his departure for China, President Nixon Feb. 14 further relaxed barriers to trade with Peking. The directive on trade placed China under the same liberalized trade restrictions as those applying to the Soviet Union and removed China from an export control group which included North Korea, North Vietnam and Cuba. China would be able to buy under general licenses from U.S. firms such items as locomotives, construction equipment, industrial chemicals, internal combustion engines and rolling mills. Special licenses would still be ..eded for the purchase of items considered strategic.

[3] **Nixon trip.** President Nixon and Mrs. Nixon left the U.S. Feb. 17 on their way to China, with scheduled stops in Hawaii and Guam. In a farewell statement made during ceremonies at the White House, Nixon described himself as being "under no illusions that 20 years of hostility between the People's Republic of China and the U.S. are going to be swept away by one week of talks that we will have there." Referring to the words of a toast given by Chinese Premier Chou to Henry A. Kissinger, the President's national security adviser, during his October 1971 visit to Peking, Nixon said both the U.S. and the Chinese were "a great people" and that their separation by "a vast ocean and great differences in philosophy should not prevent them from finding common ground." He noted "that if there is a postscript that I hope might be written with regard to this trip, it would be the words on the plaque which was left on the moon by our first astronauts when they landed there. We came in peace for all mankind." The President and his party arrived at Hung Chiao Airport in Peking Feb. 21, where they were greeted with a polite but restrained welcome by Premier Chou, several other Chinese dignataries and a 500-man military honor guard.

[4] *Itinerary.* Following the welcome to Peking, Nixon and Kissinger met for one hour during the afternoon with Chairman Mao Testung at Mao's residence somewhere in the old Forbidden City. The talks, which had not been announced previously, were also attended by Chou and by Wang Hai-jung, deputy director of protocol. The discussion was described as "frank and serious." The Chinese Feb. 21 hosted a banquet the evening of Feb. 21 at the Great Hall of the People. Nixon, Kissinger and John H. Holdridge and Winston Lord of the National Security Council met with Chou, Wang, Yeh Chien-ying (deputy chairman of the Communist party Central Committee's military commission), Deputy Foreign Minister Chiao Kuan-hua, Deputy Premier Li Hsien-nien and Chang Wen-chin (head of the European, American and Australian section at the Foreign Ministry) for four hours of talks Feb. 22 and another four hours of talks Feb. 23. Secretary of State William P. Rogers and Foreign Minister Chi Peng-fei held a separate conference Feb. 22. In the evening of Feb. 22, the Nixons attended a special performance of a revolutionary opera. The Nixons Feb. 24 made excursions to the Great Wall of China, a fortification built in pre-Christian times to keep out barbarian invaders, and to the Ming Tombs, which had been constructed by members of a dynasty that ruled China from the 14th to the 17th century. Nixon again held three hours of talks with Chou Feb. 24. The session was followed by a private dinner, which was also attended by Rogers and Chi. In its last full day in Peking Feb. 25, the Nixon party visited the Forbidden City, where the Nixons viewed the palaces and courtyards of ancient Chinese emperors. Later in the afternoon, Nixon and Chou met for an hour of private talks. That night, at the Great Hall of the People, Nixon gave a banquet for Chou. The Nixons Feb. 26 journeyed to Hangchow, a resort city 100 miles southwest of Shanghai, where they were the guests of Nan Ping, chairman of the Revolutionary Committee of Chekiang Province, of which Hangchow was the capital. The following day, in the company of Premier Chou, the Nixons flew to Shanghai.

[5] *Communique issued.* Nixon and Chou Feb. 27 released a joint communique indicating that their talks had resulted in agreement on the need for increased Sino-U.S. contacts and for eventual withdrawal of U.S. troops from Taiwan, held by the Nationalist Chinese under the leadership of Generalissimo Chiang Kai-shek. The communique had been drafted after several nights of intensive negotiation and was divided into five sections: (1) a generalized account of the President's stay in China; (2) a separate statement by each nation of its views on Asian policy issues; (3) an agreement on general rules of international relations, despite "essential differences" in the "social

systems and foreign policies" of the U.S. and China; (4) separate statements on Taiwan; and (5) mention of discussion of joint contacts "in such fields as science, technology, culture, sports and journalism." In the second part of the communique, the U.S. emphasized its support for the eight-point proposal advocated by itself and the South Vietnamese in January for an end to the Indochina War (see INDOCHINA WAR [44]). The U.S. also said that: in the absence of a negotiated settlement, it envisaged "ultimate withdrawal of U.S. forces" from Indochina "consistent with the aim of self-determination for each country of Indochina"; it would "maintain its close ties with and support for the Republic of [South] Korea"; it placed "the highest value on its friendly relations with Japan"; and it favored a continuation of the cease-fire in the Indian-Pakistani war (see PAKISTAN [12-13]) and the "withdrawal of all military forces" (see BANGLA DESH [9]). In its statement, China announced its support for the revised seven-point Viet Cong proposal elaborated in February (see INDOCHINA WAR [47]) and the Joint Declaration of the Summit Conference of the Indochinese People issued in 1970. It favored North Korean proposals for the "peaceful unification" of Korea and opposed the "revival and outward expansion of Japanese militarism." The first section of the Chinese statement on the India-Pakistan dispute was virtually identical to that of the U.S., but Peking emphasized that it "firmly supported the Pakistan government and its people in their struggle to preserve their independence and sovereignty."

[6]   In the third section of the communique, China and the U.S. agreed that countries "should conduct their relations on the principles of respect for the sovereignty and territorial integrity of all states, nonaggression against other states, noninterference in the internal affairs of other states, equality and mutual benefit, and peaceful coexistence." The two sides further agreed that progress toward the "normalization of relations" between them was "in the interests of all countries"; that both wished "to reduce the danger of international military conflict"; that neither "should seek hegemony in the Asia-Pacific region and [that] each is opposed to the efforts by any other country or group of countries to establish such hegemony"; that neither "is prepared to negotiate on behalf of any third party or to enter into agreements or understandings with the other directed at other states." In the fourth section of the communique, the Chinese declared that the "Taiwan question is the crucial question obstructing the normalization of relations" between Washington and Peking. In the remainder of the passage, China reaffirmed its traditional claim to the island, emphasizing that the "liberation of Taiwan is China's internal affair." The U.S. acknowledged "that all Chinese on either side of the Taiwan Strait maintain there is but one China and that Taiwan is part of China. The U.S. does not challenge that position." The U.S. affirmed "the ultimate objective of the withdrawal of all U.S. forces and military installations from Taiwan" and the progressive reduction of such forces and installations "as the tension in the area diminishes."

[7]   *Reaction.* Reaction to Nixon's trip and to the joint communique followed generally political lines both within the U.S. and from foreign nations. Nationalist China criticized the trip strongly Feb. 21 and denounced the communique Feb. 28. North Korea Feb. 21, North Vietnam Feb. 24 and the Viet Cong Feb. 24 criticized the Nixon trip. South Korea Feb. 22 expressed fear that Nixon would be "deceived unknowingly by Communist maneuverings." Soviet reporting of the trip in late February was equivocal, leaning to criticism of the Chinese for attempts "to curry favor" with the U.S. In the U.S., the communique was generally received with favor, but conservative Republicans criticized it, objecting to the U.S. withdrawal from Taiwan and the absence in the communique of any mention of the mutual defense pact with the Nationalist Chinese.

[8]   *Green tour.* Marshall Green, assistant secretary of state for East Asian Affairs and National Security Council staff member Holdridge (see [4]) Feb. 28

began a tour of Asian countries explaining President Nixon's China visit. The two met Feb. 28 with Japanese Foreign Minister Takeo Fukuda; March 1 with South Korean Foreign Minister Kim Yong Shik; March 2 with Taiwanese officials; March 4 with Philippine President Ferdinand E. Marcos; March 6 with South Vietnamese President Nguyen Van Thieu; March 7 with Laotian Premier Souvanna Phouma and Cambodian Deputy Premier Sisowath Sirik Matak and Foreign Minister Koun Wick; March 8 with Thai Premier Thanom Kittikachorn; March 10 with Malaysian Prime Minister Abdul Razak; March 11 with Singapore Prime Minister Lee Kuan Yew and Indonesian President Suharto; and March 14 with Australian Prime Minister William McMahon.

[9] Congressional trips to China. Senate Majority Leader Mike Mansfield (D, Mont.) and Minority Leader Hugh Scott (R, Pa.) arrived in China April 18 for a trip which ended May 7. The two had received an invitation from Premier Chou following Nixon's visit in February. The two filed separate reports on their trip with the Senate May 11. House Majority Leader Hale Boggs (D, La.) and Minority Leader Gerald R. Ford (R, Mich.) also visited China June 28-July 8. Their invitation to visit China had been tendered after House leaders had protested their exclusion from the invitation to the two Senate leaders. House Speaker Carl Albert (D, Okla.) declined to make the trip.

[10] News links. The Associated Press (AP) and Hsinhua, the official Chinese press agency, agreed July 30 to an exchange of news and photographs, reportedly the first regular news contact with mainland China for a news organization since December 1949, when the last AP correspondent left the country.

[11] U.S. eases travel. President Nixon Nov. 22 lifted an injunction against travel to China by U.S. ships and planes. In announcing the policy change, the White House emphasized that such travel would continue to be subject to Chinese authorization in each instance and that there were no plans at present to establish regular commercial traffic to China. (Commerce officials were reported as saying, however, that two charter firms—World Airways and Trans International Airlines—had been given permission by the department to travel to China.) The injunction against travel to China had been established during the Korean War.

See also CHINA, NATIONALIST; FOREIGN POLICY; JAPAN [6]

SMALL BUSINESS ADMINISTRATION (SBA)—*See* FLOODS
SMALLPOX—*See* HEALTH
SMITHSONIAN AGREEMENT—*See* INTERNATIONAL MONETARY DEVELOPMENTS [3, 5-6, 11]
SMOKING—*See* HEALTH
SOCIALIST LABOR PARTY—*See* ELECTIONS [37]
SOCIALIST WORKERS' PARTY—*See* ELECTIONS [37]

SOCIAL SECURITY—Increase voted. Congress June 30 approved a 20% increase in Social Security benefits as a floor amendment to a bill extending the federal debt ceiling *(see* BUDGET). President Nixon signed the bill July 1, but termed the Social Security measure "fiscally irresponsible." Nixon argued that the benefit increase was inflationary and said he would offset the additional $3.7 billion budget deficit resulting from the hike by cutting other federal programs. The President had originally asked for a 5% increase in benefits. Funding for the 20% increase, which took effect Sept. 1, would come from a payroll tax increase of .3% to 5.5% beginning January 1973. The taxable wage base would rise from $9,000 to $10,800 in 1973 and to $12,000 by 1974. Future automatic increases in Social Security benefits would occur when the Consumer Price Index rose 3% or more, to be funded after 1974 by an upward adjustment of the wage base as general wage hikes occurred in the economy.

The Senate Finance Committee had cleared a 10% Social Security increase June 13 as part of the omnibus welfare reform legislation HR 1 *(see* WELFARE). House passage of HR 1 in June 1971 had included approval of a

5% benefit rise. After President Nixon June 22 said he would not compromise with Senate liberals over portions of HR 1, the Social Security increase was attached to the debt ceiling bill. The House June 30 approved the bill, with the Senate-added amendment, by a 302-35 vote and rejected Republican efforts to cut the increase to 10% by a vote of 253-83. The Senate June 30 approved the increase by an 82-4 vote and rejected a cutback to 10% by a 66-20 vote.

 See also BUDGET; ELECTIONS [33]; RAILROADS; WELFARE; WOMEN'S RIGHTS

SOLEDAD BROTHERS—*See* BLACK MILITANTS; PRISONS
SOLZHENITSYN, ALEXANDER I.—*See* UNION OF SOVIET SOCIALIST REPUBLICS [5]

SOMALIA—**Plotters executed.** Three army officers, found guilty by a military court of plotting against the government, were publicly executed by firing squad July 3. The three were Brig. Gen. Salad Gaviere Kedie, Brig. Gen. Mohamed Ainanshe Gulaid and Col. Abdulkadir bin Abdulla.

 See also MIDDLE EAST [18]; UGANDA [14]

SOUTH AFRICA—**Zulus vs loyalty oath.** Members of the Zululand legislative assembly voted unanimously Jan. 12 to remove from a new oath being written for the assembly all professions of loyalty to the South African government. Chief Gatsha Buthelezi, executive of the Zulu Territorial Authority, told the legislators he was "conscience-bound to disagree" with many of the laws made by the Pretoria government and that he was therefore unable to accept an oath of allegiance to it.

[2] Bantustans become operative. Another of the government's Bantustans (rural homelands where blacks were permitted partial self-government) became operative April 11 at Giyani in the Northern Transvaal when the Gazankulu legislative assembly held its first session. Gazankulu was to be the homeland of the Shangaan tribe. Leboa, the North Sotho homeland, was reported Sept. 30 to have been given self-governing status. Bophutayswana, a Bantustan comprising 19 separate areas near the Botswana border, was given self-governing status Oct. 4.

[3] Ffrench-Beytagh cleared. Gonville Aubrey Ffrench-Beytagh, the former Anglican dean of Johannesburg, convicted in 1971 of plotting to overthrow the government, was cleared April 14 by an appeals court. Ffrench-Beytagh left the country for Great Britain following the verdict. The court held that the dean had expressed his views against South Africa's policy of apartheid (racial segregation) "with consistent vigor and at times in language that would be regarded as intemperate," but that this was not the same as involvement in terrorist activity. The court was especially critical of the government's use of police informers who gave "untruthful answers."

[4] Student unrest. The expulsion April 29 of Abraham Tiro, graduation speaker at the all-black Turfloop University College of the North near Pietersburg, for his remarks opposing apartheid, apparently set off a series of protests by black and white students against apartheid. A sit-in demonstration at Turfloop protesting Tiro's ouster led May 6 to the expulsion of all 1,146 students at the college. White students at the University of Cape Town gathered June 2 for a protest in support of black college students opposing apartheid and were reportedly attacked and clubbed by police. (Government officials said police had been provoked by an assault on an officer. South African Prime Minister John Vorster said June 5 that the police methods had been necessary "to smother unrest in its infancy.") Police June 5 used billy clubs and tear gas against a Cape Town crowd of 10,000 persons, including students and church and civil leaders, who reportedly were demonstrating to affirm the right of peaceful protest. The police took their action when the crowd refused to move after being informed that a magistrate had signed a special proclamation under the Riotous Assemblies Act prohibiting the gathering. In Johannesburg June 5, police dispersed a group of 300 Witwatersrand

University students who had gathered at St. Mary's Anglican Cathedral after marching in defiance of a city council ban. In response to the student disturbances, the government June 6 announced a month-long ban on student marches and outdoor meetings. Following the announcement, police June 7 used dogs and rubber truncheons to break up student meetings at the Witwatersrand and Cape Town universities. The academic and administrative staff at the University of Cape Town June 8 voted unanimously to support the student protest, and the University applied for a temporary restraining order against police intervention in student meetings. A Supreme Court judge in Cape Town issued the injunction June 9. Police again attacked a crowd of 100 students at Witwatersrand University June 9. Prime Minister Vorster June 13 said that the student disturbances were part of a Soviet-inspired effort to bring about the overthrow of the South African government.

[5] *Interior minister resigns.* Interior Minister Theo Gerdener June 16 announced his resignation from the Cabinet. Although Gerdener said he was leaving government to promote linguistic and race relations in the country, there was speculation that he had opposed the use of force against student demonstrators. Gerdener was replaced Aug. 1 by Connie Mulder, who retained his other posts of information, social welfare and pensions. Prime Minister Vorster Aug. 1 also named five other new ministers to take the place of four retiring officials. Agriculture Minister Dirk Uys was replaced by his deputy, Hendrik Schoeman; Health Minister Carel de Wet was replaced by his deputy, Schalk van der Merwe; Minister of Community Development and Public Works Blaar Coetzee was succeeded by Deputy Minister of Finance and Economic Affairs A. H. du Plessis; Minister of Tourism, Sport, Recreation and Indian Affairs Frank Waring was replaced by Owen Horwood (Indian affairs and tourism) and P.G.J. Koornhof (recreation and sport).

Namibia Developments

[6] **Ovambo strike.** The strike by 13,000 Ovambo miners, which had begun in December 1971, continued until Feb. 1, crippling the economy of Namibia (South-West Africa). The government failed to settle the strike by its Jan. 10 announcement that it would abolish the contract labor system, to which the workers had objected, and would replace it with the Ovambo Executive Council, a government-appointed tribal authority. The strike ended after an agreement was reached between the government and the miners abolishing the South-West Africa Native Labor Association (SWANLA), the recruiting body which had administered the contract labor system. Under the agreement, recruiting would be done by a manpower body to be established under the Ovambo Territorial Authority. (The authority was to be invested with the status of a bantustan.) The agreement also provided that individual contracts would clearly set forth salaries and other job terms and that workers would be allowed to change jobs. Workers in some quarters reportedly rejected the agreement because it did not provide for miners to be accompanied to mining areas by their families while the miners were under contract.

[7] **Waldheim visit.** United Nations Secretary General Kurt Waldheim visited South Africa March 6-10 pursuant to a Security Council resolution passed Feb. 1 empowering him to seek a settlement with that country on the future of Namibia. (The U.N. and the World Court disapproved South African control of the territory.) Waldheim talked with Prime Minister Vorster and with opponents of government policy on Namibia. Waldheim said March 8 that South Africa's refusal to hand over Namibia to U.N. control did "not necessarily" render his visit fruitless. He said that: "The aim of South Africa is to grant self-determination to Namibia. The aim of the U.N. is the same. The purpose of my visit is to clarify this situation and see if it provides any basis for further discussions." The Security Council Aug. 1 approved a resolution asking Waldheim to continue his efforts to obtain independence for Namibia. The resolution also authorized Waldheim to appoint a special representative to assist him. (Prime Minister Vorster had said July 20 that his government was willing to accept and cooperate with such a representative.) Waldheim Sept. 25 named Alfred M. Escher as that representative. *See also* [10].)

[8] Caprivi Bantustan set up. The government March 23 established a Bantustan at Katima Mulilo in the Caprivi Strip area of Namibia. The region, to have its own legislative council and to be known as East Caprivi, was bordered on the East by Rhodesia, on the south by Botswana and on the north by Zambia and Angola.

[9] Ovamboland to get self-rule. The government June 26 declared its intention of granting self-rule to Ovamboland, the most populous of the tribal areas of Namibia. Enabling legislation was to be passed by the parliament in Cape Town in 1973. In a June 27 comment, Johannesburg Radio said that the move would present U.N. members "agitating for U.N. control of South-West Africa" with "the situation of an independent country ... within the disputed territory...." The report said the the Ovambo people would "certainly be very reluctant to sacrifice their status of independence on the altar of U.N. expediency" and that, if the U.N. recognized Ovambo, "the precedent would be created for recognition of other Bantu nations."

[10] Namibia report. The U.N. Nov. 16 published a report of talks between special envoy Escher and Prime Minister Vorster on the future status of Namibia. The document, which was not an agreement, reported that the "majority of the non-white population of Namibia supported the establishment of a united, independent" nation with U.N. assistance. However, the report went on, "certain sections of the non-whites and the majority of the white population supported the 'homelands' policy and approved continued rule by South Africa." In the report, Escher said that Vorster was prepared to set up an "advisory council" for Namibia, which would report to him. The council would be composed of representatives of the Bantu homelands and would have "overall responsibility for the territory as a whole, distinct from the ministries now responsible for different sectors." Vorster reportedly also agreed that there should be "legitimate political activity, including freedom of speech and the holding of meetings," and discussed the possibility of easing traffic restrictions within Namibia. In a news conference Nov. 20, Vorster said that, even if the talks with Escher failed, he would "seriously consider" granting self-government to the 10 homelands of Namibia under an advisory council made up of black and colored (mixed white and black ancestry) leaders. In a related development, the U.N. Security Council Dec. 6 extended until April 30, 1973 Secretary General Waldheim's mandate for contacts with the South African government on Namibia.

See also ANGOLA; AUSTRALIA [11]; AVIATION; BRAZIL; CHURCHES; CONSERVATION; HIJACKING [12]; INTERNATIONAL MONETARY DEVELOPMENTS [8]; POLITICS [8]

SOUTHEAST ASIA TREATY ORGANIZATION (SEATO)—*See* PAKISTAN [7]
SOUTHERN CHRISTIAN LEADERSHIP CONFERENCE (SCLC)—*See* ELECTIONS [20]
SOUTHERN YEMEN—*See* HIJACKING [8]; YEMEN
SOUVANNA PHOUMA—*See* LAOS
SOVIET UNION—*See* SOVIET-U.S. RELATIONS; UNION OF SOVIET SOCIALIST REPUBLICS

SOVIET-U.S. RELATIONS—During May, President Richard M. Nixon became the first U.S. president to visit the Soviet Union. During his visit, Nixon talked with Communist party General Secretary Leonid I. Brezhnev, Premier Aleksei N. Kosygin, President Nikolai V. Podgorny and other Soviet officials. The U.S. and the Soviet Union also signed during the visit an arms control treaty *(see* DISARMAMENT), an agreement on health cooperation, an environmental research pact, an agreement on space exploration, an agreement on technological cooperation and a naval accord *(see* [4]). The trip ended with the signing of a joint declaration of principles and the release of a joint communique *(see* [5-6]). Both documents appeared to signal an improvement in relations between the two countries. One outgrowth of the President's trip was the conclusion in July of an agreement for the sale of U.S. grain to the Soviet Union to offset the effects of a disastrous harvest *(see* [7]). The grain sale roused serious controversy in the U.S. *(see* [8-9]) and reportedly resulted in a net loss to U.S. taxpayers of $27 million.

[2] **Nixon visit.** President Richard Nixon left the U.S. May 20 to become the first President to visit the Soviet Union. At his departure from the U.S., Nixon declared that he was seeking not to "make headlines" during his trip, but to engage in "very important substantive talks." After a two-day stopover in Vienna, Austria May 20-22, the Presidential party arrived in Moscow May 22, where they were met by Premier Kosygin and President Podgorny. The President returned to the U.S. June 1, after stops in Iran *(see* IRAN) and Poland *(see* POLAND), and reported to the Congress on his trip. Nixon described the visit as "a working summit" with "a solid record" of progress on solving difficult issues. He said that the foundation had been laid "for a new relationship" between the U.S. and the U.S.S.R., but cautioned that the Soviet Union remained a dedicated political adversary and said America must maintain adequate defenses, keep its economy vigorous and its spirit confident.

[3] *Itinerary.* President Nixon held two hours of talks May 22 and five hours of talks May 23 with General Secretary Brezhnev. During morning sessions of the talks May 23, Nixon was joined by Secretary of State William P. Rogers, Presidential national security adviser Henry A. Kissinger, Assistant Secretary of State for European Affairs Martin J. Hillenbrand and U.S. Ambassador to the Soviet Union Jacob D. Beam. Brezhnev was accompanied by Podgorny, Kosygin, Foreign Minister Andrei A. Gromyko and Andrei A. Aleksandrov, Brezhnev's personal aid. Afternoon and evening talks May 23 featured only Brezhnev, Nixon, Kissinger, Aleksandrov and an interpreter. Secretary Rogers May 23 also held discussions with Soviet Foreign Trade Minister Nikolai S. Patolichev. President Nixon May 24 laid a wreath at the tomb of the Unknown Soldier in the Alexander Gardens near the Kremlin and later held a two-hour meeting with Brezhnev, Podgorny, Kosygin, Gromyko, Aleksandrov and Soviet Ambassador to the U.S. Anatoly F. Dobrynin. In the evening, Nixon retired to Brezhnev's country residence for five hours of discussions. Nixon gave a state dinner for the Soviet leaders May 26 at the American embassy in Moscow. The President visited the Piskarevska Cemetery in Leningrad May 27 and May 28 addressed the Soviet people from Moscow in a televised speech in which he discussed relations between the U.S. and the Soviet Union. He traveled from Moscow to the Ukrainian capital of Kiev May 29 and attended a dinner given in his honor that night by the Supreme Soviet Presidium and the Ukrainian government.

[4] *Pacts signed.* In addition to the arms control treaty, members of the Presidential party signed several other pacts pledging Soviet-U.S. cooperation. Secretary Rogers and Minister of Public Health Boris V. Petrovsky May 23 signed a health agreement understood to be a formalization of a Feb. 11 exchange of letters between officials of the two governments. (The agreement pledged cooperation and exchange of information on means of fighting cancer and heart disease. It resulted June 30 in the signing of another pact providing for an exchange of experimental drugs, known as antineoplastic agents, to determine their effectiveness in fighting cancer.) Presidents Nixon and Podgorny May 23 signed an environmental research pact, described as an expansion of a U.S.-Soviet cultural pact reached in April. Nixon and Kosygin May 24 signed an agreement pledging the two countries to "develop cooperation in the fields of space meteorology, study of the natural environment, exploration of near earth space, the moon and the planets, and space biology and medicine." The cooperation was to be developed partly "by means of mutual exchanges of scientific information and delegations, through

meetings of scientists and specialists of both countries. The main feature of the accord was a project to develop compatible rendezvous and docking systems for U.S. and Soviet spacecraft. Secretary Rogers and Vladimir A. Kirillin, chairman of the State Committee on Science and Technology May 24 signed an agreement on technological cooperation. It provided for a joint commission to meet once a year for the purpose of "establishing contacts and arrangements between U.S. firms and Soviet enterprises where a mutual interest develops." The exchange of scientists and of "technical information and documentation" as well as the promotion of joint research were given as further objectives. U.S. Navy Secretary John W. Warner and Adm. Sergei G. Gorshkov, commander in chief of the Soviet Navy, May 25 signed the first military agreement between the U.S. and the Soviet Union since World War II. The document recognized that the naval operations of the two nations in open waters were subject to regulation by the 1958 Geneva Convention on the High Seas, which forbade both ships and aircraft to engage in "simulated attacks by the simulated use of weapons against aircraft and ships, or performance of various aerobatics over ships, or dropping various objects near them in such a manner as to be hazardous to ships or to constitute a hazard to navigation." The risk of collision by ships was to be decreased by avoiding "maneuvering in such a manner which would hinder the evolutions of formation."

[5] *Declaration of principles.* The summit talks were concluded May 29 with the signing of a U.S.-Soviet declaration of principles and the release of a joint communique. The documents appeared to signal an improvement in relations between the two countries. The declaration of principles bound the two nations to work for "peaceful coexistence" on the basis of respect for "sovereignty, equality, noninterference in internal affairs and mutual advantage." Both sides pledged to "do their utmost to avoid military confrontations" and to practice the "renunciation of the use or threat of force." The parties also agreed to "continue their efforts to limit armaments on a bilateral as well as on a multilateral basis." They made "no claim for themselves and would not recognize the claims of anyone else to any special rights or advantages in world affairs."

[6] In their joint communique, the two countries promised to conduct their bilateral affairs on the basis of the declaration of principles and to work for the implementation of agreements concluded between them during the previous week. The remainder of the text was devoted to international issues. Both countries "took note of favorable developments in the relaxation of tensions in Europe," particularly the 1971 Berlin accord *(see* GERMAN CONSULTATIONS) and West Germany's nonaggression treaty with the Soviet Union *(see* GERMANY, WEST [5-7]). They agreed that a European security conference should be held "without undue delay" and that talks on reduction of forces in Europe should be held separately from the security conference *(see* EUROPEAN SECURITY). Both nations reaffirmed support for a peaceful settlement of the Middle East conflict under terms of United Nations Security Council Resolution 242. Each country set forth its standard position on Vietnam, with the U.S. insisting that the political future of South Vietnam be left to the South Vietnamese without interference, and the Soviet Union calling for a cessation of the bombing of North Vietnam and a withdrawal of U.S. and allied forces from South Vietnam. Both sides approved the treaty against the use of biological weapons in warfare and promised to work for a similar ban on chemical weapons *(see* DISARMAMENT), with the "ultimate purpose" being "general and complete disarmament." The communique ended with the announcement that Nixon had invited Podgorny, Brezhnev and Kosygin to visit the U.S. and that the invitation had been accepted.

[7] **Grain sale.** President Nixon July 8 announced that the U.S. had concluded a three-year agreement for the sale of at least $750 million worth of American wheat, corn and other grains to the Soviet Union. The agreement, an outgrowth of Nixon's trip to the Soviet Union, was the biggest grain

transaction in history between the two countries. Under the agreement, the U.S.S.R. would purchase grain on the commercial market from private grain dealers in the U.S. Also included in the agreement was a U.S. pledge that it would provide long-term (three-year) credits to the Soviet Union from the Agriculture Department's Commodity Credit Corporation. (The loans would be used to finance the wheat purchases.) In cash terms, the Soviet Union would purchase $200 million worth of American wheat for delivery during the first year of the agreement—Aug. 1 through July 31, 1973. The three companies later revealed to be involved in the grain sale were the Continental Grain Co., the Cargill Corp. and the Bunge Corp.

[8] *Debate over sale.* The grain sale roused debate in many quarters and resulted, by Sept. 20, in the launching of five investigations into the transaction. The General Accounting Office (GAO) announced Sept. 6 that it was beginning an investigation of charges by Rep. Pierre S. du Pont 4th (R, Del.) that exporters benefitted from the wheat sale by acquiring inside information of the transaction, thereby purchasing grains at low cost and defrauding farmers of their rightful share in profits from the Soviet transaction, and by obtaining heavy subsidies for their subsequent sales. The House Subcommittee on Livestock and Grains opened hearings on the transaction Sept. 14. According to a report Sept. 20, the Agriculture Department's Commodity Exchange Authority was trying to discover whether grain exporters profited from inside information about the trade deal before it was announced. Rep. Benjamin S. Rosenthal (D, N.Y.), according to a report Sept. 20, requested the Justice Department to begin a study of possible violations of conflict of interest laws by two Agriculture Department officials (Clarence D. Palmby and Clifford G. Pulvermacher) who had accompanied Agriculture Secretary Earl L. Butz to Moscow in April for preliminary trade talks and then had resigned from the department in June to take executive positions with two of the companies participating in the Soviet grain deal. (Consumers Union had charged Aug. 30 that Palmby, a former assistant secretary for international affairs who had joined Continental, and Pulvermacher, a former general manager of the Export Marketing service who had joined Bunge, had violated two federal conflict of interest laws. One of the laws prohibited former federal employees from representing anyone other than the U.S. in matters in which they had a personal and substantive role while in government. The second law required a one-year ban against the handling by former federal employees of private parties' matters that were under their previous official purview.) President Nixon Sept. 20 also ordered an investigation by the Federal Bureau of Investigation (FBI) to determine whether U.S. grain exporters made "illegal excess profits" from the wheat sale.

[9] Presidential candidate Sen. George McGovern Sept. 8 criticized the wheat transaction as "another example of the big business favoritism and inside deals that have come to characterize the Nixon Administration." McGovern accused Palmby and Pulvermacher of abuse of trade information gained while employed in the Agriculture Department and charged that the inside information had allowed the big grain exporters to buy up wheat during July before farmers were aware of the Soviet deal and of the fact that it would raise prices of wheat dramatically. McGovern also charged that, under a special one-week grace period between Aug. 25 and Sept. 1, exporters were able to get certification of grain subsidies on proposed sales to the Russians at the 47 ¢ a bushel rate, which was discontinued Aug. 25. In response to McGovern's charges, Secretary Butz Sept. 14 acknowledged that a report by his department's Economic Research Service, which could have driven up the domestic price of wheat by divulging evidence of the magnitude of the Soviet wheat deal, was withheld from the public because it was considered "too controversial." The Agriculture Department also announced Sept. 22 that it was eliminating the export subsidy on wheat because of "strong demand for wheat and supplies." (The subsidy had permitted the Soviet Union to buy wheat

at $1.63-$1.65 a bushel while the U.S. domestic price was climbing to $2.10 a bushel.)

[10] *Exporters seek tax benefit.* The Treasury Department Sept. 27 made public a request by Continental Grain Co. that the company receive a tax forgiveness on half the profits already made under the Russian wheat purchase. The exporters sought relief under the 1971 tax bill which encouraged companies to establish Domestic International Sales Corporations (DISCs) for the management of their export business. Under the law, taxes on half the profits earned by DISCs could be deferred as long as the profits were returned to the export business or remained in the U.S. as "producer's loans." The law provided that the secretary of the Treasury could deny DISC tax benefits if the profits derived from sales were "accomplished by a subsidy granted by the U.S. or any instrumentality thereof," but the exporters said the subsidy clause was inapplicable when a subsidy program was "designed to subsidize both domestic and foreign markets of U.S. products (such as general [farm] price support programs)." The Treasury Department Sept. 29 issued a proposed ruling which would deny the exporters the tax advantage they had requested. The regulation made exporters of agricultural commodities who received subsidies on those sales ineligible for DISC tax deferrals.

[11] **Maritime accord.** The U.S. and the Soviet Union Oct. 14 signed a three-year maritime agreement establishing premium rates for U.S. vessels carrying Soviet grain purchases and substantially increasing the number of ports in each country open to ships of the other nation. Under the shipping part of the accord, the Soviet Union was to pay U.S. shippers either $8.05 a ton from Gulf Coast to Black Sea ports or 110% of the prevailing world rate, whichever was higher. (On the basis of a complex agreement reached Nov. 22, shipping rates were set at $9.90-$10.34 per ton of grain until Jan. 25, 1973. Another pact signed Dec. 20 set the carrier rate at $10.34 a ton until July 1, 1973.) American shipowners were to receive from the Maritime Administration a subsidy covering the difference between the Soviet rate and the cost of shipping, expected to go as high as $21 a ton. The U.S.S.R. also agreed to reduce by $1.75 a ton its cost of unloading U.S. vessels. One-third of the trade would be carried out in each nation's ships, and the other third carried by ships of other countries. Forty ports in each country were to be open to the other's ships, including research and training—but not military—vessels. Four days' notice was required for use, compared with the previous 14 days for U.S. ports and 30 days for Soviet ports. Ships entering U.S. ports from Cuba, North Vietnam or North Korea (or planning to call at those destinations) would not be allowed to pick up government-financed cargoes.

[12] **Trade pact signed.** After months of intensive negotiations, the U.S. and the Soviet Union Oct. 18 reached agreement on a three-year trade pact which included settlement of the U.S.S.R.'s World War II lend-lease debt and a U.S. promise to ask Congress for most-favored-nation treatment for Soviet imports. The lend-lease agreement, which the U.S. had insisted upon before going ahead with favored tariff treatment, required that the Soviet Union should pay a total of $722 million in principal and interest by July 1, 2001. (The amount could go as high as $759 million if the Soviet Union took advantage of four postponements it was allowed if it paid interest at an additional 3% a year.) The U.S.S.R. made its first payment of $12 million Oct. 18. The principal element of the trade agreement was the U.S. promise to secure Congressional authorization for a reduction on Soviet imports "generally applicable to like products of most other countries." Such authorization was jeopardized, however, by legislative reaction to the imposition by the Soviet Union of high exit fees for its immigrants *(see* UNION OF SOVIET SOCIALIST REPUBLICS [9-10]). As another part of the trade agreement, President Nixon Oct. 18 signed an official determination stating that it was "in the national interest" for the U.S. Export-Import Bank to extend credits and guarantees for sales to the Soviet Union. Both parties to the pact also agreed that Soviet-U.S. trade in the

three years covered by the accord would reach about $1.5 billion, triple the rate of the 1969-71 period. Each country could request that the other not ship goods that "cause, threaten or contribute to the disruption of its domestic market" through unfair low pricing. Commercial disputes were to be settled under arbitration rules of a United Nations agency in a third country. The U.S. was to set up a government-sponsored office in Moscow to help U.S. businessmen arrange commercial deals, and the Soviet Union was to have a similar office in Washington. The U.S.S.R. also would expand the number of American firms (currently four) allowed to have offices in Moscow and would construct an office-hotel-apartment-trade center complex for the use of U.S. and other foreign businessmen in Moscow.

[13]   **Accord on embassies.** Representatives of the U.S. and the Soviet Union Dec. 4 ended 10 years of negotiation by signing an agreement authorizing each nation to construct a new embassy complex in the other's capital. Under terms of the accord, local builders would construct the shell of both embassies, but each country would be able to use workers of its own choice for surveillance-proof interior finishing. Each country would have "unrestricted access" to its respective job site and would have an option to do exterior facing and final roofing.

See also DISARMAMENT; ENVIRONMENT; ESPIONAGE; FOREIGN POLICY; IRAN; POLAND; SPACE [7]

SPACE—Shuttle ordered. President Nixon Jan. 5 directed the National Aeronautics and Space Administration (NASA) to start work immediately on a controversial manned space "shuttle" which could be used to make repeated space flights instead of being discarded after one flight like current carrier rockets and spaceships. NASA Administrator James C. Fletcher said he hoped to have a reusable shuttle flying by 1978. The immediate goal of the $5.5 billion program was to create two flight vehicles able to blast off from the earth like rockets, circle the earth in orbit for 30 days like spaceships and then land like airplanes. As currently designed, the shuttle proper would be 120 feet long, with a 75-foot wingspan. It would carry two crew members, be able to carry two passengers in the command cabin and have capacity for up to 12 more passengers in additional modules. The payload would be 60,000 pounds (including passengers), to be carried in a bay 60 feet long and 15 feet in diameter. The shuttles could be used to: visit and repair orbiting communications, weather and scientific satellites; place satellites in orbit; exchange crews and provide supplies for orbiting space stations and laboratories; and perform a wide variety of other space tasks—all at a fraction of the current cost for such activities. There was a possibility *(see* [3]) that even the two booster rockets, which would be jettisoned several minutes after takeoff, could be recovered and reused. According to NASA officials, shuttle flights would cost about $10 million each and would reduce the cost of putting payloads into orbit from $600-$700 a pound to about $100 a pound.

[2]   In giving his directive to NASA, the President said that the "highly complex technical nature of the project" necessitated a "contingency" fund of about $1 billion, allocated in addition to the planned $5.5 billion. The costs of launching, recovery and maintenance facilities were estimated at an additional $300 million, and it was reported that about $75 million in other supporting funds was being requested in other parts of the NASA budget. The authorized shuttle program was for a smaller and less expensive version than NASA had originally proposed.

[3]   *Two sites selected.* NASA announced April 14 that the shuttles would be launched from the Kennedy Space Center at Cape Kennedy, Fla., and the Vandenberg Air Force Base, Calif. Officials said the bases were selected to permit east-west orbits utilizing the earth's rotation for vehicles with large payloads and those headed from the moon, and north-south orbits favored by the Defense Department in military surveillance missions. (A north-south orbit from Cape Kennedy would have required more maneuvering to avoid populated

areas and thus would have reduced the total payload, replacing part of it with the additional fuel required for the maneuvering. An east-west orbit from Vandenberg was not feasible for similar reasons.) Coastal launching sites were necessitated by a decision announced March 15 to use recoverable booster engines which could be ejected on liftoff by parachutes over the ocean. Both sites would require modifications costing more than $650 million. The program would provide Cape Kennedy, economically hard-hit by the gradual phaseout of the Apollo and other programs, with a steady employment base. The choice of Vandenberg marked the military's entry into the program, once wholly civilian. The Air Force, which had not participated in the space program since 1969, was expected to share the costs of the shuttle system with NASA.

[4]   Luna 20 brings back moon rock. The unmanned Soviet space probe Luna 20, launched Feb. 14, made a successful soft landing on the moon Feb. 21, drilled into the lunar surface for a core tube of rock and soil and returned to the earth Feb. 25. Luna 20 was the second Soviet probe to accomplish the feat. (Luna 16 in September 1970 became the first successful unmanned mission to bring back lunar material from the moon.) The probe reportedly landed a mile west of the crater Apollonius in the mountainous area between the Sea of Fertility and the Sea of Crises. It was the first spacecraft to soft land in such a ruggedly mountainous area. Luna 20 remained on the moon about 27 hours and 40 minutes.

[5]   U.S. probe begins Jupiter journey. The 570-pound unmanned U.S. interplanetary probe Pioneer 10 (originally Pioneer F) was launched from Cape Kennedy March 2 on a trip designed to take it past the planet Jupiter in December 1973 and then out of the solar system. The probe was launched by means of an Atlas-Centaur rocket booster to which a third stage had been added to give the probe the speed it needed to take it to the vicinity of Jupiter (about 525 million miles from earth at the rendezvous time). Space officials reported that Pioneer 10 had been accelerated to a record speed of 31,413 m.p.h. in 16 minutes and appeared to be on the right path. Its speed was sufficient to take it past the moon's orbit in 11 hours, compared to the 2.5-3 days required by Apollo spaceships for the trip. It was expected that when Pioneer 10 approached Jupiter, the planet's gravity would accelerate the probe from its approach speed of about 24,000 m.p.h. to perhaps three times that speed. This would whip the probe part way around the planet and hurl it away with such speed that it would become, by about 1980, the first man-made object to escape from the solar system and fly out into interstellar space.

[6]   The probe was to spend four days in the vicinity of Jupiter, photographing and collecting data on the planet, whose mass is more than that of all the other planets of the solar system together and 318 times that of the earth. The swing around Jupiter would take the probe inside the orbits of all 12 Jovian moons. Pioneer 10 was to take 10 photos, covering about $\frac{2}{3}$ of the planet's visible surface and including the first photos of Jupiter's twilight side, which is always turned away from earth. Because the probe's trip would take it too far from the sun to use solar energy, Pioneer 10 was powered by four radioisotope thermonuclear unit generators using plutonium-238 to provide the electricity to run its instruments, camera and radio. The probe's 11 instruments were designed to collect data on Jupiter's atmosphere, temperature, radiation belt, magnetic field and radio emissions and on asteroid particles, the solar wind, cosmic rays and, perhaps, the area in which the solar system ends and interstellar space begins. In addition to its 65 pounds of instruments, Pioneer 10 carried a six-by-nine-inch plaque inscribed with the first message ever written by men for examination by possible nonterrestrial intelligent beings. The message depicted a nude man, a nude woman, the earth's position in relation to 14 pulsars (pulsating stars), the earth in the solar system and the difference in energy between the two basic states of the hydrogen atom. (The message was devised by Drs. Carl Sagan and Frank D. Drake of Cornell and Sagan's artist-wife, Linda.) Pioneer 10 was the first of two probes the U.S. planned to send to the vicinity of Jupiter. Pioneer 11 was scheduled for launching in 1973. The cost of the two-probe project was estimated at $135 million. (By the end of 1972, the probe was 350 million miles from earth—three-quarters of the way through the asteroid belt.)

[7] **Soviet Venus probe.** The Soviet Union March 27 launched the 2,610-pound Venera 8 on a nearly 200 million-mile flight to Venus. The probe made a soft landing on Venus's sunlit side July 22 and radioed data back to Soviet controllers for 50 minutes before the probe's communication equipment became inoperable—presumably because of the planet's intense heat. (Venera 8 was the first Venus probe to survive passage through the atmosphere of Venus. Its equipment had been redesigned from that on other probes to be more heat-resistant.) Preliminary data on the findings sent to earth by Venera 8 were made public Sept. 10. The probe revealed the following information: that some sunlight did penetrate Venus's dense atmosphere to reach the planet's surface; that atmospheric temperature at the landing site was 760 degrees C. (840 degrees F.), plus or minus 8 degrees C.; that the atmospheric pressure at the landing site was about 90 times that of the atmosphere on earth at sea level; and that the surface rock at the landing area was 4% potassium, .0002% uranium and .000065% thorium (resembling the composition of granite rock on earth). In a related development, NASA Administrator Fletcher announced June 15 that the U.S. and U.S.S.R. had agreed to coordinate their Venus missions, with the U.S. investigating the upper atmosphere and the U.S.S.R. to concentrate on the Venusian surface.

[8] **Apollo 16.** Apollo 16 commander, Navy Capt. John Watts Young, and lunar module (LM) pilot, Air Force Lt. Col. Charles Moss Duke, spent a record 71 hours and two minutes on the moon April 20-23 during the first manned mission to the mountains of the moon. They walked, worked, and drove an electric car on the moon's surface outside their spaceship for a record total of 20 hours and 14 minutes during three separate sorties. While the two were on the moon, the crew's third member, Navy Lt. Comdr. Thomas Kenneth (Ken) Mattingly 2nd, the command and service module (CSM) pilot, remained in orbit around the moon in the CSM, which he had nicknamed Caspar for the cartoon character "Caspar the Friendly Ghost." (Young and Duke had nicknamed the LM "Orion.") The mission began with a launching from Cape Kennedy April 16 and ended April 27 with a safe splash-down in the Pacific. During the journey, the three astronauts performed dozens of scientific experiments; photographed the stars, the earth, the moon, their space vehicle and themselves repeatedly with still and TV cameras; and gathered and brought back a record 214 pounds of lunar rock and soil. Young and Duke were the ninth and tenth men (all Americans) to set foot on the surface of the moon. The Apollo 16 mission was the next to the last moon-landing flight scheduled for the Apollo project.

[9] *On the moon.* Young and Duke landed on the moon at 9:23 p.m. EST April 20. Their landing site was about 500 feet west of the original mission target on Cayley Plains, a rugged valley on the western edge of Kant Plateau in the mountainous Descartes area. The mission's first extra-vehicular activity (EVA) took place April 21. After about 1½ hours of removing equipment from the LM and setting it up on the moon, the astronauts began deploying the "Apollo Lunar Surface Experiment Package" (ALSEP), a collection of instruments operated by nuclear power and designed to collect data on moonquakes, the moon's interior, magnetic fields and other phenomena. A major blow to the scientific program took place at this time. While Duke was drilling the first of two nine-foot holes for a heat-flow detector, Young tripped over and broke the wire connecting the heat-flow instruments to the scientific station. It was decided that repair of the wire would not be feasible. The $1.2 million heat-flow set-up had been the ALSEP's "highest priority experiment," according to NASA. On the first EVA, which lasted seven hours and 11 minutes, the astronauts drove their electric-powered lunar rover a total distance

of two miles and collected about 50 pounds of lunar rock and core samples. The second EVA April 22 lasted a record seven hours and 23 minutes. The astronauts traveled about six miles afoot and drove about three miles south of the LM in the lunar rover. The third and final EVA on the moon lasted five hours and 40 minutes. The astronauts drove in the lunar rover about 3.5 miles north of the LM to the crater North Ray, the largest lunar crater (3,000-foot diameter) ever visited by an Apollo astronaut. They also explored the inner slope of the crater. Young and Duke blasted off from the moon at 8:25 p.m. EST April 23. Although they left many pounds of equipment on the moon, the 214 pounds of rocks they carried made them overweight; and they had to request Mission Control's permission to bring the entire load back.

[10] *Trip to and from moon.* During docking (linking) maneuvers in space April 16, before Apollo 16 reached the moon, Duke had reported what turned out to be the flaking away of protective paint from the upper portion of the LM. After checking by Young and Duke in the LM and by technicians on earth, it was decided April 17 that nothing serious was amiss and the paint defect was not important enough to affect the mission. Some concern for the mission was caused April 18 when an erroneous computer signal locked the navigation alignment system, but the flaw was quickly detected and a procedure devised under which the computer was to ignore such a false signal if it were repeated. The actual landing on the moon was delayed by Mission Control April 20 because of a malfunction in the CSM's secondary guidance signal. The problem showed up after Young and Duke had entered the LM and had separated the LM from the CSM. The two sections of the spacecraft were in separate orbit. Mattingly in the CSM had been scheduled to fire his main rocket during the separation to elevate the CSM to the altitudes desired for the photographic and other duties Mattingly was to perform while the others were on the moon. However, Mattingly aborted the ignition because of oscillation in the secondary guidance system's yaw gimbal. Fears mounted that the landing would have to be canceled; and Mission Control ordered Young and Duke not to land, but to remain in orbit pending a study of the problem by ground technicians. The tests and calculations indicated that both guidance systems were in good order and that the flaw was in an electronic feedback loop that could be bypassed. The astronauts were told to go ahead with the landing, and Mattingly's ignition turned out to be perfect. The two astronauts in the LM went ahead with their preparations for landing despite another problem: their failure to free from position the 26-inch-diameter steerable antenna on top of the LM. All efforts to free the dish antenna—then and later—failed, and the astronauts had to rely for communication on two smaller antennas.

[11] Following the rendezvous of the LM and the CSM after the blast-off from the moon, the astronauts April 24 jettisoned the LM. Duke and Young neglected, however, to close one of the LM's switches; and the LM therefore remained in lunar orbit but tumbling out of control. This failure made it impossible for controllers on the ground to send signals to the LM ascent stage to crash into the moon to provide data for the seismometer left there by the two astronauts. The three astronauts April 24 also released an 85-pound satellite into lunar orbit to collect and radio to earth data on the gravitational and magnetic fields of the moon and on the solar wind. (The satellite had been expected to remain in orbit for about a year, but telemetry soon provided data to show that the orbit was too low for such a long life.) Another minor problem occurred when the astronauts found they could not retract a 25-foot boom carrying a device that measured radioactivity on the surface of the moon. The boom was therefore jettisoned after having operated for 62 revolutions around the moon instead of for the planned 64. The malfunction that had delayed the lunar landing caused Mission Control to reduce the time Apollo 16 was to be in lunar orbit by one day. The spaceship left orbit April 24. Once out of orbit, the three astronauts April 25 donned space suits and depressurized the cabin to allow Mattingly to step outside of the CSM to retrieve film cassettes and

conduct an experiment on the effect of unfiltered solar radiation on microbes. (The films, exposed while Mattingly was in orbit, were to be used to aid in detailed lunar mapping.) Mattingly made two trips to the rear of the CSM to collect the film, exposed the microbes to the sun's rays and re-entered the CSM. As the astronauts approached the earth April 27, a light in the cabin flashed on and off in a false warning of trouble in the guidance and navigation system; but Young reported that the false signal stopped when he kicked the panel housing the cables involved.

[12] **Apollo 17 ends lunar program.** Navy Capt. Eugene Andrew Cernan (flight commander) and Dr. Harrison Hagan (Jack) Schmitt (a civilian geologist and the first scientist to make a trip to the moon) explored a mountainous site on the moon Dec. 11-14 in the final flight of the U.S.'s $25 billion Project Apollo. While the two were on the lunar surface, Navy Cmdr. Ronald Ellwin Evans, the third member of the Apollo 17 mission, remained in lunar orbit aboard the CSM America. The concluding mission of the Apollo program started just after midnight Dec. 7 with the launching of the Apollo 17 spaceship from Cape Kennedy, Fla. It ended Dec. 19 with a safe splashdown in the Pacific. The $450 million mission was described by NASA spokesmen as the "most perfect" and "most successful" in the U.S. lunar landing program. Apollo 17 set the following records for manned space flight: distance traveled in transit and in orbit around the moon (1,486,000 miles as compared to the previous record of 1,391,550 miles set by Apollo 15); length of flight (12 days, 13 hours, 52 minutes—six hours and 41 minutes longer than the flight of Apollo 15); length of time on the lunar surface (74 hours, 59 minutes—three hours and 57 minutes longer than the Apollo 16 crew); length of time outside the LM on the lunar surface (22 hours, 5 minutes—one hour and 49 minutes longer than the Apollo 16 crew); length of time for a single excursion on the surface of the moon (7 hours, 37 minutes, 22 seconds—14 minutes and 22 seconds longer than Apollo 16 astronauts); amount of lunar material collected (249 pounds as compared to Apollo 16's 208 pounds); speed for a land rover on the moon (11.1 m.p.h. as compared to Apollo 16's 10.5-m.p.h. record); and length of time in lunar orbit (6 days, 3 hours—two hours longer than Apollo 15).

[13] **On the moon.** Cernan and Schmitt landed on the moon at 2:55 p.m. EST Dec. 11. The LM Challenger made a safe landing at Taurus-Littrow valley just southeast of the dry Sea of Serenity. A ground controller called the landing in the mountain-ringed valley "the smoothest descent in the Apollo program," including "all the simulations." The Challenger landed about 350 feet from its designated target in an area largely covered with black soil, littered with boulders coated with the same black material, and pockmarked everywhere with small craters. The valley was bounded to the south by a 7,800-foot-high mountain described as "the south massif," on the north by the 5,000-foot-high "north massif" and the Taurus mountains, and on the northeast by the Littrow Crater. The mission's first EVA took place Dec. 11 and lasted for 7 hours, 12 minutes, 11 seconds. The astronauts unpacked their equipment, assembled and loaded their lunar rover, and drove about 300 feet to set up their array of lunar surface instruments and the nuclear generator that powered them. Cernan then spent over an hour drilling two eight-foot-deep holes in the lunar surface, and the two astronauts inserted probes in the holes to determine the amount of heat coming from the moon's interior. Among the instruments deployed were instruments to: record gravitational changes in the moon and moonquakes; delineate the shape of the bedrock formations under Taurus-Littrow; detect any traces of lunar gas; measure the speed and mass of micrometeorites hitting the moon; delve into subsurface layers and boulders by means of radio waves; examine the rock layer under the landing site to the depth of a kilometer by measuring shock waves produced by explosive charges; and measure radiation from lunar soil at various depths. The work on the experimental equipment took so much time and expended so much oxygen from the astronauts' back packs that ground controllers canceled a scheduled 1.5-mile traverse to Emory

Crater and substituted a drive of less than a mile to Steno Crater. The shorter drive was hampered by the loss of part of the rover's right rear fender (accidentally knocked off by Cernan), which resulted in the right rear wheel spewing lunar dust all over the rover and the astronauts during travel. The astronauts contrived a makeshift bumper from four stiff, coated traverse maps before their second EVA Dec. 12. During the second EVA, the astronauts drove four miles to the foot of the south massif. Near a deep crater named Shorty, Schmitt announced that they had discovered what was possibly the most significant find of the mission—a three-foot-wide layer of orange- and red-colored soil, with streaks of red soil extending down the crater. (The color of the soil raised speculation that it contained iron oxide, which would raise the possibility that the moon had water and that gases occasionally spurted out from the moon's interior.) The astronauts took two core tubes as well as surface samples of the colored material. The third and final EVA of Apollo 17 took place Dec. 13-14 and lasted 7 hours, 26 minutes. In their rover, the astronauts drove two miles north to the foot of the north massif, where they accomplished a major objective by chipping rock samples off the boulders.

[14] **Lunar orbital activities.** During his three days alone in lunar orbit, Cmdr. Evans was busy with a full schedule of experiments and observations. Using a radio sounding system capable of getting readings from below the lunar surface, Evans sought data on "mascons," dense bodies of material below some of the moon's arid seas. He used an infrared scanning radiometer to measure temperature variations on the lunar surface, and cameras for mapping and to record specific lunar features. An ultraviolet spectrometer was used to analyze the lunar atmosphere and to measure its density, and a laser altimeter was used to take precise measurements. Early findings by Evans included the detection of "cold spots" and "hot spots" (deviating from the temperature of surrounding areas by an average of perhaps 18 degrees) and evidence of volcanic activity from about 20 domes in the Aitken Crater.

[15] **Trip to the moon.** The blast off of Apollo 17 was delayed for 2 hours, 40 minutes. The delay was caused by the computerized "terminal countdown sequencer," which monitored and controlled the final three minutes and seven seconds of the Apollo countdown. The sequencer halted the countdown just 30 seconds before the scheduled time for liftoff (9:53 p.m. EST) because it erroneously detected a failure of the Saturn-5 booster rocket's third-stage liquid-oxygen tank to pressurize. The tank was pressurized by hand controls, however, and launching technicians bypassed the sequencer to allow the rocket to be launched. The launching was the first for a moon-bound Apollo rocket in darkness. Nighttime was chosen for the launching in order to get Apollo 17 to the moon when the light at the landing site would be at its best for exploration purposes.

[16] **Trip from the moon.** After six days in orbit around the moon, the America was blasted out of orbit and headed earthward Dec. 16. The three astronauts donned their spacesuits Dec. 17 and depressurized their cabin in preparation for an EVA by Evans to retrieve three film casettes from two cameras and the ultraviolet spectrometer at the rear of the CSM. Evans climbed out and used hand holds to make three trips for the three casettes. The America splashed into the Pacific Ocean at 2:24 p.m. EST about four miles from the recovery ship Ticonderoga and about 1.7 miles from its target point. Preliminary medical checks showed that the astronauts had withstood the space trip without physical harm.

[17] **Moon souvenir controversy.** The astronauts of Apollo 15 (Col. David R. Scott, Lt. Col. Alfred M. Worden and Col. James B. Irwin—all of the Air Force) were reprimanded by NASA July 11 for carrying without authorization 400 specially stamped and canceled envelopes to the moon during their 1971 flight. When they returned, the three sold 100 of the envelopes to a German stamp dealer for a sum reported to be in excess of $150,000. As another part of the bargain, a trust fund was to be set up for the astronauts' children. The

astronauts later changed their minds and refused to accept the trust funds or any money from the envelopes. (According to an unconfirmed report Sept. 18, the envelopes had been ordered by a NASA official, and billed to a man then working for Howard Hughes.) A furor also arose over a 3.5-inch statuette of an astronaut left on the moon by Apollo 15 as a memorial to the 14 American and Soviet astronauts who had died. Copies of the statuette were being reproduced by the sculptor of the original and were being sold for about $750 each. Irwin had announced his resignation from the astronauts' corps and the Air Force May 23. Scott was transferred from the astronauts' corps July 26, and Worden was reassigned a week later.

[18]   In the wake of the Apollo 15 controversy, it was disclosed July 30 that the Apollo 14 astronauts had carried 200 unauthorized silver medals coined by the Franklin Mint (a private concern in Philadelphia) to the moon on their 1971 mission. The crew (Navy Capt. Alan B. Shepard Jr., Navy Capt. Edgar D. Mitchell and Air Force Lt. Col. Stuart A. Roosa) reportedly took the medals on their mission under the terms of a "private agreement" with the Philadelphia concern. According to NASA spokesmen and officials of the mint, the astronauts received no money for their action, but did receive 150 of the medals for their "private use." The mint melted down 25 of the other coins in striking "mini-coins," which it distributed as gifts to its subscribers and did not offer to the public. The other 25 coins had been locked in the mint's vaults. NASA said that no reprimand had been given to the astronauts since none of the coins had been offered for public sale. In response to the disclosures on the Apollo 14 and 15 missions, the Senate Space Committee Aug. 3 opened an official investigation into the actions of the two crews.

[19]   NASA Sept. 15 issued a report on the commercialization of the Apollo 15 trip. Included as an appendix to the report was a disclosure that 15 of the 27 Apollo astronauts had been paid $37,500 for signing stamps and postcards without authorization. According to the report, the 15 astronauts, whose names were not disclosed, were given $2,500 each by a Florida resident for 500 signatures on stamps and postcards. NASA said some of the items were now selling in Western Europe for $16.50 each.

[20]   **Mariner ends Mars job.** Mariner 9, the U.S. interplanetary probe in orbit around Mars since Nov. 13, 1971, ended its mission Oct. 27 after having transmitted to earth a total of 7,329 photos of Mars and a large amount of additional scientific data. The Mariner mission ended after the probe used up its altitude control gas and flight controllers at the Jet Propulsion Laboratory (which managed the Mariner project for NASA) directed the spacecraft to turn off its radio. JPL scientists said that the most important findings of the mission were the indications that water had helped shape much of Mars' surface. (As a result of the Mariner mission, some scientists believed that the ice cap of Mars was partly frozen water vapor rather than entirely frozen carbon dioxide, as originally supposed. Water vapor was detected in some of the clouds above volcanic mountains; and photos showed thousands of what appeared to be dry river beds possibly formed by rain, swift-moving water and floods.) Scientists said that the Mariner photos had revealed four "major geological provinces" on Mars: a volcanic province in which the peaks of Nix Olympica were the most prominent feature; a region of equatorial plateaus in which earthquakes apparently had carved deep canyons; an area of deep craters covering more than half of Mars; and a series of terraces and deep grooves radiating from the south polar region. Data from Mariner 9 revealed that the temperature at Mars's north pole was about -200 degrees F., but that temperatures rose to about 80 degrees F. in the equatorial zone. Winds reached speeds of 300 m.p.h. during the planet's long dust storms, with speeds of up to 115 m.p.h. even in relatively calm weather. (The U.S.S.R.'s two interplanetary probes, Mars 2 and Mars 3, which had been circling the planet since Nov. 27 and Dec. 2, 1971, respectively, had apparently stopped transmitting data in March.)

Satellites

[21] U.S. launchings. The U.S. Air Force March 1 launched from Cape Kennedy a "spy" satellite as part of what was unofficially described as a program to give a quick warning of missile attack on the U.S. The satellite was reported to be the third in a series designed to operate in synchronous orbit. One of the major functions of the series was to monitor Soviet and Chinese rocket tests. A 1,965-pound satellite dubbed ERTS 1 (for earth resources technology satellite) was sent into near polar orbit July 23 by means of a two-stage Delta rocket launched from NASA's Vandenberg site. Equipped with three TV cameras (each sensitive to a different color) and a multispectral scanner, ERTS 1's mission was to transmit a wide variety of data on natural resources and the earth's surface. The data it provided was to range from facts on the growth of crops, the distribution of oceanic algae and the spread of water pollution to the advance of glaciers, the inventorying of timber and the increase of certain plant diseases. The U.S. Aug. 1 launched from Cape Kennedy a 4,900-pound astronomical satellite dubbed Copernicus. Copernicus, the fourth and last satellite in the OAO (orbiting astronomical observatory) series, was to study the interstellar gas clouds and to study X-ray-emitting pulsars. (Of the three previous OAOs in the series, only one had been successful.) The 860-pound Explorer 47, a scientific satellite in the IMP (interplanetary monitoring platform) series, was sent into orbit Sept. 23 from Cape Kennedy. The satellite was designed to study the solar wind, magnetic fields and other interplanetary phenomena.

[22] Soviet launchings. The Soviet Union launched satellites in the Meteor series March 30, July 1 and Oct. 27. Their mission was to transmit data for quick weather forecasting. Two 2,350-pound Soviet-bloc (including Hungary, Rumania, Poland, Czechoslovakia and Mongolia) scientific satellites, Intercosmos 6 and 7, were launched into orbit by Soviet space technicians April 7 and June 30 to study cosmic rays and meteoric particles. Two 1,875-pound scientific satellites, Prognoz 1 and 2, were sent into highly eccentric orbits by Soviet space technicians April 14 and June 29 to investigate solar phenomena and their effect on near-earth space. The U.S.S.R.'s second, third and fourth Molniya-2 communications satellites were launched May 19, Sept. 30 and Dec. 12; and two more Molniya-1 satellites went into orbit April 4 and Oct. 14. Both Molniya series were used for long-range communications to all parts of the Soviet Union. The U.S.S.R. launched 71 satellites in the Cosmos series—Cosmos 471-541—during 1972. Among the launchings were two in which eight satellites at a time were orbited by single rockets (Cosmos 504-511 July 20 and Cosmos 528-535 Nov. 1). Western observers said that there was reason to believe that the eight-satellite launchings were used in a global military communications system, probably used primarily by the Soviet Navy. Among other Cosmos satellites presumed to be military vehicles were Cosmos 476 (March 1), 482 (June 9), 489 (June 30), 498 (July 5), 499 (July 6), 500 (July 11), 501 (July 12), 503 (July 19), 520 (Sept. 20) and 537 (Nov. 25). Cosmos 476, 498 and 500 were believed to be a new generation of electronic intelligence satellites capable of ferreting out and relaying to the U.S.S.R. any secret military radio or radar signals being transmitted in other countries as they passed overhead. Cosmos 492, 502 and 503 were presumed to be recoverable military observation satellites capable of returning to earth with data acquired in space.

[23] Communications satellites. The fourth Intelsat-4 communications satellite was launched from Cape Kennedy June 13 by NASA on contract with Comsat (Communications Satellite Corp.), U.S. member and operating manager for the International Telecommunications Satellite Consortium (Intelsat). The satellite was stationed in synchronous orbit above the Indian Ocean at the equator at 61.4 degrees East Longitude. Its task was to relay radio and TV communications between Africa, Europe, Asia and Australia. Canada's 600-pound Anik 1 was sent into orbit Nov. 9 by means of a U.S. rocket launched from Cape Kennedy. The communications satellite was put into synchronous orbit for its task of relaying phone, radio and TV signals to and from Canada's north. (In a related development, the U.S. Federal Communications Commission June 16 voted 4-3 to end a ban on domestic satellite communications by permitting entry into the field of all financially and technologically capable companies who could demonstrate that they would be serving the public interest. The satellites would be launched by NASA, but each system would be owned and operated privately.)

[24] **Other launchings.** Japan's fourth satellite, a 165-pound payload named Rex, was put into orbit Aug. 19 by means of a four-stage Mu-4S rocket launched by Tokyo University space scientists at the Uchinoura space center. The satellite's mission was to measure the earth's magnetic field. Esro 4, the seventh satellite of the European Space Research Organization (ESRO), was sent into polar orbit Nov. 22 by means of a Scout booster rocket launched by NASA from Vandenberg. The 253.5-pound scientific payload was made by West Germany, Britain, Sweden and the Netherlands. Its principal mission was to study the sun's effects on the earth's environment.

See also DISARMAMENT; SCIENCE; SOVIET-U.S. RELATIONS [1, 4]

SPAIN—Student unrest. The University of Madrid Medical school was closed Jan. 13 and nearly all of the 4,000 students of the school were suspended when students refused to end a seven-week strike against curriculum changes and an extension of the medical course of study from six to seven years. Other students at the university, protesting the suspension, clashed violently with police at the university and in the streets of downtown Madrid Jan. 17-20. Dozens of persons were reportedly injured as students threw stones at club-wielding police, blocked traffic and overturned at least two cars belonging to government and military officials. At least 147, and possibly more than 250, students were arrested in the rioting. The violence led to a sympathy strike by resident doctors at the university's clinical hospital and to mass walkouts at the university and the Autonomous Madrid University. In other student disturbances later in the year: Valencia University was closed, seven policemen were injured and 67 students were arrested Feb. 4 in a clash at the university's medical school after police broke up an unauthorized student meeting; the University of Seville's schools of medicine, sciences, law, and philosophy and letters were closed March 2 until further notice as a result of student disturbances and absenteeism; university schools across the country were closed March 2 as students staged a "day of student struggle" resulting in clashes with police at Madrid University's civil engineering school. In what was represented as a conciliatory move, the government Oct. 11 withdrew armed police from the main campus of Madrid University, occupied since January 1969.

Charters suspended. In an effort to curb student and faculty unrest, the government July 29 suspended the charters providing some university autonomy and student representation at the University of Madrid and the Autonomous Madrid University. Under a decree issued by Generalissimo Francisco Franco, all disciplinary authority was vested in government-appointed rectors, who were authorized to revise departments, dismiss department heads and college directors, refuse entry to any student suspected of bad conduct and form disciplinary committees which could summarily expel rebellious students and professors and exclude them from any other university. Professors were obligated to try to halt student disturbances in their classrooms, with police help if necessary, and were authorized to expel troublesome students. Another decree stipulated that only the Cabinet could appoint or dismiss university rectors throughout Spain. In response to the decrees, the rectors at the two Madrid universities resigned Sept. 12.

Moderate bishops consolidate power. The consolidation of power by liberal and moderate clergymen in the traditionally conservative Spanish Roman Catholic Church marked the Spanish Bishops Conference, held in Madrid March 6-11. At the final session, the 80 bishops voted by a two-thirds majority in favor of controversial liberal reforms adopted in September 1971 at an assembly of bishops and priests. The reforms called for total separation of church and state in Spain and an activist role in social questions, including issues involving political freedom. The conference—the ruling body of the Spanish church—had opened with a dramatic denunciation of church conservatives by Vicente Cardinal Enrique y Tarancon, the liberal archbishop of Madrid, who had headed the 1971 clergy meeting. He said the conservatives had "produced a climate of tension, even of scandal," by leaking to the press Feb. 22 a study conducted by the Congregation for the Clergy (a Vatican group), intended for him. The study had condemned the conclusions of the 1971 meeting. Cardinal Tarancon charged that Bishop Jose Guerra Campos, a leading conservative, had sent him a letter that said the Congregation for the Clergy had acted with "higher authorization," implying papal approval. Tarancon said he had left immediately for a trip to the Vatican, where he was received by Jean Cardinal Villot, the Vatican Secretary of State, and twice by Pope Paul. Tarancon read to the conference a letter from Villot denying papal approval of the Congregation for the Clergy's action. The letter, and an oral message from the Pope, indicated some reservations, but praised the conclusions of the 1971 meeting and wholeheartedly endorsed the reform leaders in the Spanish church. Following the disclosure by Tarancon, the conference March 8 re-elected the Madrid archbishop as its chairman and called for the resignation of Vatican conservatives who had tried to undermine his position. In later elections, the liberals and moderates swept the top conference posts, including 11 of 14 committee chairmanships. Tarancon March 10 won the conference presidency; and Jose Maria Cardinal Bueno Monreal, archbishop of Seville, won the vice presidency. Bishop Campos lost his key post as conference secretary to Msgr. Elias Yanes, auxiliary bishop of Oviedo and an outspoken reformer.

Shipyard strike. A few hundred shipyard workers staged a sitdown strike March 9 inside the state-owned Empresa Nacional Bazan shipyards in the northwestern port of El Ferrol de Caudillo to protest the dismissal of six workers who had participated in an earlier demonstration for higher pay and better working conditions and benefits. Armed with stones and iron bars, the workers resisted police efforts to clear them from the yard. Eight policemen and 17 workers were injured. The sitdown strike resumed March 10, and police killed two workers and seriously injured three others when clashing workers seemed on the verge of overrunning the police. Several thousand metalworkers in Biscay, Vigo and El Ferrol struck March 13 in protest against the shooting; and Madrid students staged demonstrations which resulted in clashes with police. The workers ended their strike March 20 after the government threatened to impose martial law. In another labor development, an estimated 3,000-4,000 workers Sept. 9 began an illegal strike at the Citroen automobile factory in Vigo to demand a 44-hour workweek. The strike spread to other factories after the authorities dismissed five of the workers and docked the pay of four of the others. Clashes between armed police and workers erupted during demonstrations staged by the strikers. The strikers returned to work Oct. 2 after all but 250 of the approximately 6,000 workers dismissed during the strike were rehired. The official trade unions agreed to submit the dispute to a mediator.

Succession process clarified. In a decree promulgated July 18—the 36th anniversary of his uprising against the Second Spanish Republic—Generalissimo Franco clarified the succession procedure to be followed after his death. The decree expanded on the organic law of 1966, which provided for the eventual separation of the powers of chief of government and chief of state, both currently held by Franco. Franco reiterated, however, that he would remain "chief of state, head of the National Movement [Spain's only legal political party], president of the Council of Ministers, caudillo and generalissimo of the armed services" for the remainder of his life. The decree would automatically promote Spain's vice president, Luis Carrero Blanco, to head of government after Franco's death, unless Franco named a head of government in the interim. The measure also provided for the Regency Council—composed of the president of the Cortes (parliament), the senior general and senior Roman Catholic prelate—to assume temporary power after Franco's death and to summon the Cortes within eight days to swear in Prince Juan Carlos as King and chief of state.

U.S.S.R. trade pact signed. Spain and the Soviet Union Sept. 15 signed a trade agreement which reportedly called for each nation to quadruple its imports and exports to $40 million. Spanish exports under the new accord—the first major pact between the two nations since the 1936-39 Spanish Civil War, in which the Soviet Union backed the losing republicans—reportedly would include wine, textiles, shoes, agricultural products and ships. The Soviet exports would include oil, machinery and farming equipment. The pact, signed in Paris after more than a year of secret negotiations there and in Moscow, also provided for the establishment of commercial missions in Madrid and Moscow. It was seen as a first step in the normalization of relations between the two countries. Before the accord, Spain and the Soviet Union engaged in trade only through the agency of third parties.

Policeman, Basques killed in clashes. An upsurge in violence and bombings by the Basque separatist movement ETA during August and September resulted in the death of three Basques and one policeman. ETA bombs Aug. 16 burned the office of the Ministry of Information and Tourism in the seaside resort of Zarauz and damaged a cinema and a chocolate factory in San Sebastian. Guerrillas bombed the house of a separatist opponent in Miravelles Aug. 18 and blew up a civil war monument in Hernani Aug. 24. A policeman was shot dead and another wounded Aug. 29 when the two tried to arrest four members of the ETA in Galdacano. The killing led to a sharp crackdown on the separatists. Police shot to death two suspected ETA guerrillas Sept. 2 in a raid on an alleged illegal arsenal in Lequeito. A third ETA member, wanted in connection with the death of the policeman Aug. 29, was shot to death by police in Urdax Sept. 20.

See also EUROPEAN ECONOMIC COMMUNITY [7]; GIBRALTAR; HIJACKING [13]; LATIN AMERICA; POLLUTION [13]; RAILROADS; ROMAN CATHOLIC CHURCH

SPASSKY, BORIS—*See* CHESS
SPECIAL DRAWING RIGHTS (SDRS)—*See* INTERNATIONAL MONETARY DEVELOPMENTS [1-2, 5, 11]
SPORTS—*See* AUTO RACING; BASEBALL; BASKETBALL; BOWLING; CHESS; CYCLING; FOOTBALL; GOLF: HOCKEY; HORSE RACING; OLYMPICS; OLYMPIC TERRORISM; SWIMMING; TENNIS; TRACK & FIELD
SPYING—*See* ESPIONAGE
SRI LANKA—*See* CEYLON
STANLEY CUP—*See* HOCKEY
STANS, MAURICE—*See* NIXON, RICHARD MILHOUS; POLITICS [10, 12]

STATE & LOCAL GOVERNMENTS—Housing bill. The Senate March 2 passed an omnibus housing and mass transit bill that incorporated the principle of revenue-sharing (sharing of federal revenue with state and local governments), but the House Rules Committee Sept. 27 refused to approve an equivalent bill for the House. Following the Rules Committee rejection, the House Banking and Currency Committee, which had reported the bill Sept. 19, voted to extend current housing programs through the end of the fiscal year (June 30, 1973), killing all chances of revenue-sharing in housing programs until 1973. The Senate bill would have distributed $5.9 billion over two years in block grants to localities, to be spent at their discretion on urban renewal, community facilities, water and sewer projects and land acquisition. The block grants would have been allocated under a formula based largely on population and the extent of poverty, with 75% going to the 267 largest metropolitan areas, none of which would receive less than under present, categorical programs. The bill also would have: granted $600 million for the Model Cities program; reserved 20% of the apartments in federally subsidized buildings for low-income families and supplemented rent payments exceeding 25% of their income; opened government-owned public housing to moderate-income families; granted $800 million in mass transit operating subsidies to supplement federal capital grants; provided operating funds for the Federal Housing Administration (FHA) home mortgages; barred kickbacks by lawyers, insurance companies and others in closing costs on FHA-guaranteed mortgages; and expanded a housing allowance experiment to subsidize families directly and permit them to choose their own dwelling units. The House bill rejected by the Rules Committee had aroused opposition from civil rights and labor groups, who opposed a provision in the bill which would have given localities veto power over federal low-income housing. The Administration had opposed the provision for mass transit operating subsidies, as well as new categorical programs to aid central cities. The Administration had not publicly commented on the bill, but a veto had reportedly been under consideration.

Revenue-sharing bill cleared. Congress completed action Oct. 13 on a compromise revenue-sharing bill which would distribute $30.2 billion over five years in almost untied aid to states and localities. The Senate approved the compromise bill by a vote of 59-19 Oct. 13, after the House had approved it by a 265-86 vote Oct. 12. President Nixon signed the bill Oct. 20. The compromise measure, cleared Sept. 15 by a joint Senate-House committee, reconciled differences between a House bill (passed June 22) and a Senate bill (passed Sept. 12). The committee had compromised between the Senate formula for allocating the funds, which favored the smaller states, and the House version, favoring the more populous states, by allowing each state to choose the more advantageous of the two. After the states made the choice, 9.4% would be deducted to remain within total spending limits, which the committee raised by some $500 million. Some $5.3 billion was authorized for the first year, retroactive to Jan. 1, an increase of $300 million over the original Administration request. The allocation would increase slightly in each of the four succeeding calendar years. Funds would be distributed within the states according to the Senate formula, with one-third going to state governments and two-thirds to localities, based on tax effort, population and per capita income. Large cities and rural areas were expected to benefit at the expense of more affluent suburbs. The funds, which could not be used by localities to meet operating costs of education or general administration needs, could be spent on almost any capital project or on operating expenses in the areas of public safety, environmental protection, transportation, health, recreation and libraries, social services for the poor or elderly or financial administration. There would be no restrictions on the state government share of the fund. Cities and states would have to publicize their intentions for each year's allocation and submit to Treasury Department audits.

The compromise bill also limited to $2.5 billion annually a separate program of social services to combat welfare dependency. The limitation—compared with a $1.6 billion limit set by the Senate and none set by the House—would curb a rapidly expanding program begun in 1962 to aid people currently, recently or potentially on welfare to become self-sufficient. Under previous law, the Department of Health, Education and Welfare (HEW) had provided unlimited funds on a 75% federal-25% state basis for a variety of services within the program. Costs had totaled $1.5 billion for fiscal 1972, but had been expected to rise to $4.7 billion in fiscal 1973 without the new limit. Under the compromise plan, the social services money would be distributed on a straight population basis and would be retroactive to July 1. The money could be spent in any proportion on child care, family planning, aid to the retarded, foster care or treatment of narcotics or alcohol victims. Other programs could be covered, with a proviso that 90% of spending in such programs be actual welfare clients. Another provision in the compromise bill would allow the

Treasury Department to collect a state's income taxes in a "piggyback" system, if the state's tax code conformed in the main with federal practice.

Checks mailed. The first revenue-sharing checks, totaling $2.65 billion and covering the first half of 1972, were mailed Dec. 8 to 35,903 state and local governments. (July-December funds would be mailed in January, 1973.) There were substantial shifts made in computations on the checks, which caused the size estimated originally in September to differ from the actual amount received. (According to Treasury Deputy Undersecretary James E. Smith, the discrepancies resulted from the use of fiscal 1966 revenues in figuring the grant estimates, while newly updated fiscal 1971 revenues were used to figure the amount of the actual grants.) Some 6,000 local governments received checks 50% below the September estimates, while downward adjustments of 10%-50% were made in another 6,100 checks. An estimated 7,000 units received checks 50% higher than expected.

See also CANADA [3]; ELECTIONS [1, 21, 33, 42-43]; NIXON, RICHARD MILHOUS; POLLUTION [8]; POPULATION

STATE OF THE JUDICIARY ADDRESS—*See* JUDICIARY
STATE OF THE UNION ADDRESS—*See* NIXON, RICHARD MILHOUS
STATE OF THE WORLD ADDRESS—*See* FOREIGN POLICY
STEEL—*See* TARIFFS & WORLD TRADE
STERLING—*See* INTERNATIONAL MONETARY DEVELOPMENTS [2, 6-8]

STOCK MARKET—Student's spree stuns Wall Street. Abraham H. Treff, a 19-year-old college student, Jan. 11 revealed a December 1971 trading spree he had carried out to test enforcement of stock exchange rules. Treff had telephoned six New York Stock Exchange (NYSE) firms, placing market orders for more than $200,000 in securities without putting up any cash. Treff had contacted at least 25 brokerage firms. The six Philadelphia firms that opened accounts for him and executed his orders were Merrill Lynch, Pierce, Fenner and Smith, Inc.; Paine Webber, Jackson & Curtis, Inc.; White, Weld & Co.; Reynolds Securities Inc.; Weis, Voisin & Co.; and Yarnall, Biddle & Co. The disclosure of the spending spree stunned Wall Street and caused major NYSE firms to alert their branches to adhere strictly to rules for checking new accounts. The NYSE May 5 announced disciplinary action against five executives and five salesmen who had executed Treff's orders. Member firms had already levied fines (which were contributed to charity) against the dealers for violation of the NYSE "know your customer" rule and of the firms' supervisory provisions. Of the $8,750 in fines levied by the NYSE, $7,450 were waived as already collected by the member firms. Three suspensions were announced, but two had already been invoked by the firms involved. Seven of the 10 brokers were censured, the mildest form of NYSE sanction.

SEC report on securities industry. The Securities and Exchange Commission (SEC) Feb. 2 issued a wide-ranging evaluation of the securities industry and the market structure of the nation's stock exchanges. The report set forth various proposals designed to further competition among the different sectors of the industry. The major proposals concerned development of a central market system, a qualified form of institutional membership and a lower ceiling on fixed sales commissions. The SEC supported the idea of a central market system, linking all markets trading in exchange-listed securities by a common communications network which would include a consolidated market disclosure stock tape to report prices and volume of each listed stock traded on any or all of the exchanges. (Under the present system, an ordinary investor trading on one exchange had no way of determining whether he could get a better price for his stock elsewhere.) Until details could be worked out, the SEC said it would order all exchanges and "third-market" firms to report daily on the volume and price ranges of all their transactions. (The SEC proposed the integration within the central market system of the third market firms—those which specialized in over-the-counter trading of exchange-listed stocks. The

SEC said that, under the new system, the firms would be subject to new regulations and reporting requirements.)

The SEC report also endorsed a limited concept of institutional membership that would permit brokerage affiliates to become members on condition that the "predominant" part of their brokerage business came from unaffiliated investors (all types of individual accounts and any institutional account where there was no contractual tie between institution and broker). The NYSE and the American Stock Exchange (Amex) both already had membership bans on brokerage firm affiliation with institutional investors (banks, pension funds, investment and insurance firms), but other exchanges permitted institutional membership. On the issue of general membership requirements, the SEC said it would require the exchanges to adopt uniform rules restricting membership to brokerage firms that did more than half their business with the public. If the exchanges refused, the SEC would decide to make the rule mandatory or to take the matter up with Congress. (Without waiting for congressional action, SEC Chairman William J. Casey May 30 formally requested the nation's stock exchanges to adopt a rule barring membership to brokers who do less than 80% of their business with unaffiliated public investors. The request was subject to challenge in hearings and court action.)

On the subject of fee-fixing, the SEC report stated that the SEC would act by April to lower the ceiling on fixed commission fees to portions of large stock transactions over $300,000. Since April 1971, fees on portions of orders above $500,000 had been negotiable by the customer and broker, with most other fees set by the NYSE and followed by the rest of the industry.

Public role increased on NYSE. In the most far-reaching revision of the NYSE's governing structure since 1938, members voted overwhelmingly March 2 to increase the public's role in the administration of the exchange. The changes closely resembled recommendations made in 1971 by William McC. Martin Jr., former Federal Reserve Board chairman. Under the reorganization, the 33-member policy-making board of governors was replaced by a 21-member board of directors, including a new, full-time, salaried chairman elected by the board. (James J. Needham, a member of the SEC, was selected as NYSE chairman July 13.) The board was comprised of 10 public representatives, who could not be brokers or dealers, and 10 securities industry representatives, who had to be members or allied members of the NYSE and principal executives of their firms. (Previously, only three members of the governing board had represented the public.) The 10 public directors, including the first black and the first woman on the board of the NYSE in its 180-year history, were nominated June 7, subject to members' approval. The Amex June 8 voted a similar reorganization plan calling for a 21-member governing board comprised half of public representatives and half of securities industry representatives. (Only four of the past 33-man governing board were public directors.) The new governing board would elect a full-time chairman. (The Amex proposed July 27 that its present president, Paul Kolton, be appointed chairman of the governing board.)

See also CHURCHES; GREECE [15]

STORMS—Hurricane Agnes. Agnes, the first hurricane of the 1972 season, swept north from Cuba and the Gulf of Mexico as rains deluged a 250-mile swath of the eastern coast of the U.S. on a 10-day spree, taking 134 lives and causing an estimated $1.7 billion in damage. President Nixon June 23 declared Florida, Maryland, Pennsylvania, New York and Virginia eligible for federal relief and recovery aid in areas where flash flooding occurred in the low-lying basins of the Susquehanna, Allegheny, Chemung, Monongahela, Ohio and James rivers. The Red Cross announced June 25 that it was caring for 112,000 persons in eight states who had been displaced from their homes by rains. In other relief developments, President Nixon June 24 ordered the Office of Emergency Preparedness to provide $92 million in federal assistance to the five major disaster areas and June 27 asked Congress for an additional $100 million in relief aid, including Small Business Association and Federal Housing Administration loans.

The hurricane, which had been downgraded to a tropical storm as it passed Florida June 20, reintensified over Georgia and the Carolinas. Robert M. White, administrator of the National Oceanic and Atmospheric Administration June 24 termed flooding from the storm the "most extensive in the country's history." The state-by-state damage in the five states hardest hit: Florida—12 persons killed, $25 million in damages; Maryland—15 persons killed, $50 million in damages; Pennsylvania—69,000 homeless; New York—14 counties in the southern part of the state devastated; Virginia—17 persons killed, 8,000 left homeless.

Typhoon Rita devastates Luzon. Six weeks of unceasing rains, triggered in late June by Typhoon Rita, caused the worst natural calamity in Philippine history. Sheets of water estimated at 80-180 inches deep covered more than 4,000 square miles of Luzon Island and affected 6-8 million people. Bursting dams, landslides and tidal waves killed at least 427 people, according to an estimate Aug. 6. A cholera epidemic in the wake of the disaster was reported Aug. 3 to have affected 6,000 people in central Luzon. President Ferdinand E. Marcos, who took personal control of the recovery effort, proclaimed a state of calamity in 14 flood-stricken provinces Aug. 13. A shortage of 500,000 tons of rice was expected, and food prices skyrocketed 37% in the month-long period beginning July 2.

See also FLOODS; POLLUTION [11]

STRATEGIC ARMED FORCES (STRAF)—*See* DEFENSE

STRATEGIC ARMS LIMITATION TALKS (SALT)—*See* DISARMAMENT; FOREIGN POLICY; SOVIET-U.S. RELATIONS [1, 4]

STRAUSS, ROBERT—*See* POLITICS [14]

STRIKES—*See* ARGENTINA [1, 7, 13-18]; AUSTRALIA [3]; BANGLA DESH [8]; BASEBALL; BELGIUM; BOLIVIA; CANADA [8-12]; CHILE [1, 15, 18-22]; COLOMBIA; COSTA RICA; DOMINICAN REPUBLIC; FRANCE [14]; GIBRALTAR; GREAT BRITAIN [1, 8-15]; HIJACKING [15]; HONDURAS; INDIA [10]; IRELAND; ITALY [1, 7]; JAPAN [3]; LABOR; MEXICO; NETHERLANDS; NORTHERN IRELAND [4, 10, 16]; PAKISTAN [11]; PERU; POLICE; PUERTO RICO; RAILROADS; RHODESIA; SHIPS & SHIPPING; SOUTH AFRICA [6]; SPAIN; TRINIDAD & TOBAGO; URUGUAY [10, 14-17]; WELFARE

STUDENTS FOR A DEMOCRATIC SOCIETY (SDS)—*See* ELECTIONS [25]

STUDENT TRANSPORTATION MORATORIUM ACT—*See* CIVIL RIGHTS [2]

STUDENT UNREST—Wisconsin bomb suspect held. Canadian authorities in Toronto Feb. 16 arrested Karleton L. Armstrong, charged in the August 1970 bombing at the University of Wisconsin at Madison, in which a graduate student was killed. Armstrong had also been charged with the attempted Jan. 1, 1970 bombing of a Baraboo, Wis. ordnance works and with three additional bombings in 1969 and 1970. Extradition proceedings were scheduled against him.

2 killed at Southern U. Student disturbances at the predominantly black Southern University in Baton Rouge, La., led to the shooting death Nov. 16 of two black university students—Denver A. Smith and Leonard Douglas Brown. The shootings occurred after East Baton Rouge Parish sheriff's deputies and state police ordered about 300-2,000 students to leave the administration building and its environs, and began shooting tear gas canisters into the crowd. Sheriff Al Amiss admitted Nov. 19 that some of his men might have fired the buckshot that killed the two students. (A bi-racial Louisiana state commission reported Dec. 16 that one of the six sheriff's deputies deployed at one section of the campus had fired the shotgun blast that killed the two students.) Louisiana Gov. Edwin Edwards declared a state of emergency Nov. 16 after the shootings (and after a fire and a bomb explosion were reported elsewhere on the campus) and sent in the National Guard to seal the campus. Edwards originally had called in the guard Oct. 31 after more than a week of demonstrations on the campus and in downtown Baton Rouge by students demanding that University President G. Leon Netterville resign, that campus food and housing be improved and that students be given a bigger voice in university decisions. Two professors—Dr. Joseph Johnson, chairman of the physics department, and George W. Baker Jr., an assistant professor of engineering—were dismissed Nov. 19 by President Netterville on charges that the two had served as advisers to dissident students. (In a related development, Gov. Edwards Nov. 8 ordered the eviction of students occupying Southern's New Orleans administration building after banks of students allegedly roamed the campus and "routed students from classes," and after reports that guns had been brought onto the campus. However, University Vice President Emmett W. Bashville, head of the campus, ended the nine-day sit-in peacefully Nov. 9 by announcing his resignation, which had been demanded by the students.)

See also ARGENTINA [16]; BANGLA DESH [8]; CAMBODIA; CHILE [14]; COLOMBIA; DOMINICAN REPUBLIC; DRAFT & WAR PROTEST; ECUADOR; ELECTIONS [25]; EL SALVADOR; ETHIOPIA; GREECE [10]; HUNGARY; INDIA [8]; MALAGASY REPUBLIC; MEXICO; MIDDLE EAST [30]; NIXON, RICHARD MILHOUS; PERU; PORTUGAL; SOUTH AFRICA [4-5]; SPAIN; TUNISIA; URUGUAY [3, 10, 16]; VENEZUELA; YUGOSLAVIA

STUDY GROUP ON THE CASELOAD OF THE SUPREME COURT—See SUPREME COURT

SUDAN—Cabinet changes. President Gaafar Mohammed el-Nimeiry Feb. 12 announced the resignation of Vice President and Defense Minister Maj. Gen. Khaled Hassan Abbas, the main force in Nimeiry's thwarting of a July 1971 coup attempt. Nimeiry said that Abbas resigned for "personal reasons," but Abbas was reported to have objected to the president's dissolution of the country's Revolutionary Command Council. In other Cabinet changes, Nimeiry announced Feb. 12 the appointment of Presidential Affairs Minister Maj. Abdul Gasim Hashim as planning minister. The president announced May 24 that Interior Minister Mohammed el-Bagir would replace Babikr Awadallah as vice president. Awadallah had resigned May 13 for reasons of health. At the request of Nimeiry, the entire Cabinet resigned Oct. 5 following elections for a People's Council, which would draft a new Sudanese constitution. A new Cabinet took office Oct. 9, with Nimeiry taking the premiership and defense portfolios. The most influential portfolios remained in the same hands.

Accord with rebels. An agreement ending 16 years of civil war between Khartoum and the Anyanya rebels of southern Sudan was reached Feb. 26 in Addis Ababa, Ethiopia and was signed March 27 in Addis Ababa in the presence of Ethiopian Emperor Haile Selassie. Talks on ending the fighting had begun Feb. 17. The pact included provisions for a cease-fire and for the organization of the three southern provinces of Equatoria, Upper Nile and Bahr el Ghazal into the autonomous region of South Sudan, with its capital at Juba. Khartoum would retain control of foreign policy, defense and economic development; but Juba would have sole responsibility for local taxation, police and administrative affairs. President Nimeiry would review nominations made by a South Sudan legislative assembly and then appoint executives to the area's government. The pact specified that elements of the Anyanya were to be absorbed into the Sudanese army and stationed in the south, making up about 50% of the troops there. Sudanese forces in the south would be commanded by a commission made up equally of northern and southern officers. The agreement also allowed the use of English for the conduct of official business in the south.

Addressing an Omdurman rally March 3, Nimeiry promulgated the Law of Regional Autonomy establishing South Sudan as an administrative entity. He also declared that a cease-fire for all government troops would take effect March 12. Maj. Gen. Joseph Lagu, leader of the Anyanya, March 6 ordered his

forces to stop firing immediately. The Khartoum government March 20 lifted the state of emergency which had applied throughout South Sudan since 1955.
See also HEALTH; OLYMPICS [3]

SUEZ CANAL—*See* MIDDLE EAST [15-16, 34]
SUPERSONIC AIRCRAFT—*See* AVIATION
SUPREME COUNCIL FOR SPORT IN AFRICA—*See* OLYMPICS [3]

SUPREME COURT—Powell, Rehnquist take seats. Lewis F. Powell Jr. and William H. Rehnquist were sworn in Jan. 7 by Chief Justice Warren E. Burger as the 99th and 100th members of the Supreme Court. The joint swearing-in ceremony marked the first time since 1911 that two justices had taken the oath of office at the same time. The court had its full complement of nine justices for the first time since the summer of 1971. Powell took the seat of the late Hugo L. Black; Rehnquist replaced the late John Marshall Harlan.

New appeals court recommended. The Study Group on the Caseload of the Supreme Court, a panel of prominent legal scholars appointed by Chief Justice Burger, Dec. 19 recommended the creation of a new "national court of appeals" to screen out nearly all the routine cases that overrun the Supreme Court's caseload. The plan called for the new court to be immediately below the Supreme Court. Under the setup, seven judges drawn from the 11 circuits of the U.S. Court of Appeals would screen the 3,600 cases a year that go to the Supreme Court. The new court could refuse to hear the cases, determine them on their merits or send the most important cases (estimated to be about 400 a year) on to the Supreme Court. If the new court refused to hear a case or adjudicated one, no appeal would be allowed to the Supreme Court, although the Supreme Court would retain the right to consider a case before a hearing in the national court of appeals. The study group also recommended that all appeals to the Supreme Court or to the new national court of appeals be eliminated and replaced with petitions for certiorari. (Under appeal, the courts would be required to consider cases. Under petitions for certiorari, the courts could use their own discretion as to whether they would hear cases.)

See also ABORTION; ATOMIC ENERGY [4]; BASEBALL; BIRTH CONTROL; CIVIL DISORDERS; CIVIL RIGHTS [2, 7, 13]; CONSUMER AFFAIRS [6]; CRIME [10-12]; DRAFT & WAR PROTEST; EDUCATION [4, 7]; ELECTIONS [15, 44, 48]; ENVIRONMENT; ESPIONAGE; JUDICIARY; NEWSPAPERS; PENTAGON PAPERS; POLITICS [5]; POLLUTION [2]; SECURITY, U.S.; VOTING RIGHTS; WELFARE

SWAZILAND—In the country's first elections since gaining independence in 1968, the ruling Imbokodvo National Movement won 21 of the National Assembly's 24 elective seats May 19. The opposition National Liberatory Congress party won the other three elective seats, obtaining parliamentary representation for the first time. Nominations to six other seats were made by King Sobhuza II, uncle of Prime Minister Prince Makhosini Dlamini.
See also INTERNATIONAL MONETARY DEVELOPMENTS [8]

SWEDEN—New budget submitted. Finance Minister Gunnar Strang Jan. 12 submitted to the Riksdag (parliament) an $11.8 billion budget for the 1972-73 fiscal year. Based on an estimated 7% rise in revenue, the new program emphasized a trend toward tighter fiscal policy and decreased expenditures. No tax increases were proposed. Education and old age pension programs totaled $4.2 billion—one-third of projected spending. Capital assistance to developing nations was increased 25% to $250 million. $1.5 billion was allocated to defense needs, a 5% increase.

Food demonstrations. About 6,000 persons in Stockholm and groups in other cities staged demonstrations Feb. 26 to protest a 17% rise in food prices over the previous 13 months. The protests were organized by housewives who had started a boycott of milk and beef Feb. 21 because of spiraling costs (a 50% increase in the price of milk over a two-year period, a 25% increase in beef prices over a two-month period). The food price increases stemmed from substantial increases in the value-added tax (VAT, a levy imposed on each stage of the production and distribution of goods) and from the government's policy of increasing farmers' incomes to the level of industrial workers. In later related action, the government Dec. 21 imposed a one-year freeze on the prices of meat and dairy products, effective Jan. 1, 1973.

Tax program adopted. The Riksdag May 31 adopted a tax redistribution program providing for cuts in income taxes for the lower- and middle-income brackets, a 10% increase in child allowances and a doubling of the employers' payroll tax to 4%. The payroll tax hike replaced the government's original funding proposal for an increase in the VAT from 17.65% to 20%, a proposal rejected by the conservative and Communist opposition parties. The Riksdag also rejected a government proposal for an increase of the tax on gasoline and fuel.

See also ENVIRONMENT; EUROPEAN ECONOMIC COMMUNITY [8]; HIJACKING [13]; INDOCHINA WAR [22]; INTERNATIONAL MONETARY DEVELOPMENTS [9]; POLLUTION [13]; SPACE [24]; TERRITORIAL WATERS

SWIMMING—Indiana retains title. The Indiana University swim team, one of the finest collections of swimmers ever assembled, March 25 joined the University of Michigan as the only schools to win five consecutive National Collegiate Athletic Association (NCAA) swimming and diving championships. During the meet at the U.S. Military Academy at West Point, N.Y., Indiana withstood a strong challenge from the University of Southern California to take the team title, 390-371. Indiana was paced by its three All-Americans, Mark Spitz, Gary Hall and John Kinsella.

See also OLYMPICS [6, 8]

SWITZERLAND—Anarchist band revealed. Attorney General Hans Walder July 14 confirmed the existence of a band of 41 young Swiss anarchists, of whom nine had been arrested. Walder said the group had links with the so-called Baader-Meinhof urban guerrilla group in West Germany *(see* GERMANY, WEST [3-4]) and with another band in Berlin. However, Walder denied a report based on information of Western intelligence services, that foreign revolutionary groups had opened a central coordinating office in Zurich in 1971. The existence of the Swiss band had first been announced May 24 when the police disclosed the arrest of seven persons in Zurich, St. Gall and Lugano since April 24. The seven were charged with membership in a "central commando for armed struggle" dedicated to urban guerrilla warfare.

Air force modernization plans shelved. Defense Minister Rudolf Gnaegi Sept. 11 announced a Cabinet decision to abandon plans for the purchase of either U.S.-built Corsair or French-built Mirage-Milan fighter bombers as part of an air force modernization project. He said the government was considering the stopgap purchase of 24 reconditioned Hawker Hunters from Great Britain pending a reappraisal of Switzerland's defense needs. The decision amounted to a rejection of a Defense Ministry recommendation for the purchase of 60 Corsairs at a cost of about $350 million. The ministry recommendation had been the cause of some controversy. The French had sent a memo in late August complaining that Swiss defense experts were biased against the Milan and had used inadequate evaluation methods. The memo, contents of which remained secret, also reportedly stressed the need for European solidarity. The Swiss government disclosed Aug. 22 that it had officially rejected the French memo. However, Heiner P. Schulthess, head of the Defense Ministry's armaments division, resigned Aug. 31, stating that the rejection of the French complaints had not been firm enough and that the Swiss government was delaying approval of the ministry recommendation for purchase of the Corsairs.

Bern proposes Jura plan. The executive council of Bern Nov. 23 proposed a plan that eventually would give a high degree of autonomy to the French-speaking Jura region in the German-speaking canton of Bern. The plan called for the gradual decentralization of the political and administrative authority held by the capital of Bern. The plan was denounced as insufficient by the Jura Rally Movement, representing the French-speaking movement of Jura. (Protests during 1972 aimed at achieving the creation of an autonomous French-speaking Jura canton had included: an illegal protest in Bern June 17 against the rejection by Bern voters of a proposal that would have enabled the Jura region to harmonize its school systems with those of French-speaking cantons; the occupation July 13 of the Swiss embassy in Paris by about 30 members of the Rams, a militant Jura separatist group; and a bomb explosion July 16 which wrecked a munitions depot in the village of Glovelier in the Jura region. Authorities attributed the July explosion to the Jura Liberation Front because the group's initials, "FLJ," were painted on the building.)

Anti-inflation program passed. Both houses of parliament adopted an anti-inflation program granting the government modified authority to control wages, profits and prices, it was reported Dec. 22. The government had requested such power only for prices. The anti-inflation bill also provided for a reduction of depreciation allowances against federal and state income taxes, maintenance of mandatory minimum reserves that all commercial banks would have to keep with the Central Bank, and a freeze on demolition and construction of non-essential buildings. The bill became effective immediately on passage, but the government did not indicate when it would use its new powers.

See also BOOKS; EUROPEAN ECONOMIC COMMUNITY [8]; EUROPEAN SECURITY; INTERNATIONAL MONETARY DEVELOPMENTS [6]; PERU

SYPHILIS—*See* HEALTH

SYRIA—National front formed. Damascus radio March 7 announced a major shake-up of the Syrian regime. Under the change, a five-party government national front was formed, headed by President Hafez al-Assad and dominated by his ruling Socialist Baath party. The front also included the other four leftist political groups of the previous coalition government: the Arab Socialist Union (pro-Egyptian); the Communist party (Soviet-oriented); the Socialist Unionists (a breakaway faction of the Baath party); and the Arab Socialist Movement (independent Socialists). The front was to be operated by a central leadership composed of a president and 17 members. The Baathists were to control the presidency and nine seats, with each other party holding two seats. Under the front's charter, the Baath party was to have sole control of the armed forces and student groups. The charter also pledged full support for the Federation of Arab Republics (Syria, Egypt and Libya) and the principle of pan-Arab unity. It spurned "negotiations with and recognition of" Israel, promised support and aid to the Palestinian commandos and stated that the Arab areas occupied by Israel "can be recovered only by force."

Cabinet changed. President Assad March 23 reshuffled his Cabinet, reducing Baathist representation so that the 30-man Cabinet was evenly divided among Baathists and non-Baathists. Maj. Gen. Mustafa Tlas, chief of staff, was appointed defense minister, replacing Mutaab Shana, a Baathist. The formation of a new 31-member Cabinet was announced by Assad Dec. 24. The Baath party assumed more than half the posts.

See also HEALTH; JORDAN; MIDDLE EAST [1, 5, 7, 10-14, 33]; OIL & NATURAL GAS; YEMEN

TAFT HARTLEY ACT—*See* ELECTIONS [48]
TAFT JR., ROBERT—*See* ELECTIONS [3]
TAIWAN—*See* CHINA, NATIONALIST
TANAKA, KAKUEI—*See* JAPAN [6-7, 10-11]; TARIFFS & WORLD TRADE

TANZANIA—Cabinet changes. President Julius K. Nyerere Feb. 17 made the following Cabinet changes: Premier—Rashidi Kawawa, second vice-president, was named to the newly created post; defense—Edward Sekoine took over Kawawa's former responsibility; foreign affairs—John Malecela took over the post formerly held by Nyerere; commerce and industry—Amir Jamal replaced Paul Bomani; finance—Cleopa Msuya replaced Jamal; economic affairs and development planning—Wilbert Chagula replaced Abdulrahman Babu; agriculture—Joseph Mungai replaced Derek Bryceson. Other new ministers were: national education—Simon Chiwanga; land and housing—Musobi Mageni; labor and social affairs—Alfred Tandau; information and broadcasting—Daudi Mwakawago. The Ministry for Rural Administration was abolished.

   See also ANGOLA; BURUNDI; INTERNATIONAL MONETARY DEVELOPMENTS [8]; OLYMPICS [3]; UGANDA [1-3, 5, 8-9, 13-14]; ZANZIBAR

TARIFFS & WORLD TRADE—Deficit for U.S. in 1971. The U.S. suffered a $2.047 billion trade deficit in 1971, the Commerce Department reported Jan. 25. It was the first time since 1888 that imports had exceeded exports. During 1971, the U.S. exported $43.56 billion in goods and imported $45.6 billion. Exports were up 2% from 1970 figures and imports were up 14%.

   Japan, Europe to cut steel exports to U.S. The White House announced May 6 an agreement by Japanese and major European steel producers to limit steel exports to the U.S. in 1972-74. The agreement, covering about 85% of steel exports to the U.S., followed nearly 18 months of negotiations between the U.S. and the heads of steel associations in Japan, the six members of the European Coal and Steel Community and Britain. (Voluntary quotas on steel exports to the U.S. had gone into effect in 1969.) The agreement would: reduce the average annual growth rate of steel exports to the U.S. from the current 5% to 2.5%; set specific limits on exports of stainless, tool and other alloyed and high-value steel products; impose greater curbs on the shifting of steel exports within the limitations; restrict geographic distribution to prevent concentration in markets; and limit for the first time exports of some fabricated structural steel and cold finished steel bars. The accord was expected to limit total steel exports to the U.S. to 16.5 million tons, approximately 10% less than in 1971. The curbs would cut the foreign steel products share of the U.S. market to about 14.5%, compared with 17.9% in 1971. (The Treasury Department May 23 directed the Customs Bureau to establish a monitorship over the steel import quotas.)

Export controls extended. President Nixon Aug. 30 signed a bill extending export controls through June 1974. (The controls had expired July 31, but Nixon had issued an executive order Aug. 2 extending controls on the export of strategic goods.) The bill, a House-Senate conference committee compromise similar to legislation originally passed in the Senate Aug. 1, was approved by a voice vote in the Senate Aug. 15 and by a 183-124 vote in the House Aug. 18. The bill liberalized export controls on U.S. products not vital to national security that could be purchased by Communist countries in trade with other Western nations. It also established the Council on International Economic Policy, to be headed by White House aide Peter S. Flanigan. In addition, the bill rescinded Commerce Department restrictions on hide imports which had been announced July 15. (The restrictions had been imposed to ease "inflationary pressures" on U.S. prices of shoes and other leather goods.)

U.S., Japanese summit. President Nixon and Japanese Premier Kakuei Tanaka ended two days of summit talks in Hawaii Sept. 1 with agreement on short-term measures to reduce the huge U.S. trade deficit with Japan (expected to total $3.8 billion in 1972). A communique issued Sept. 1 expressed the Japanese government's intention to promote imports from the U.S. and to "reduce the [trade] imbalance to a more manageable size within a reasonable period of time." The general nature of the statement indicated Nixon's failure to obtain a specific commitment for a substantial reduction of the U.S. trade deficit with Japan. The trade statement announced an agreement under which Japan would buy $1.1 billion worth of American goods over the following two years as a step toward the reduction of the trade imbalance. The accord provided for purchase of $390 million worth of U.S. agricultural, forestry and fishery products; $50 million worth of special grain purchases; $320 million in civil aircraft; $20 million worth of helicopters and aviation-related facilities; and $320 million in uranium enrichment facilities.

Coffee talks fail. The 62 members of the International Coffee Organization (ICO), unable to agree on prices and export quotas for the year beginning Oct. 1, Sept. 2 approved an interim measure fixing an export quota of 13,059,708 bags (each weighing 60 kilos or 132.6 pounds) for the first quarter of the year. No similar agreement was reached for prices. A second round of ICO talks Dec. 4-11 also failed to reach agreement, and ICO export quotas consequently were suspended for the first time in the nine-year history of the International Coffee Agreement (ICA). Following failure of the talks, about 30 coffee-producing nations Dec. 12 informally agreed to maintain current prices and set an export quota of 11 million bags for the first quarter of 1973. However, the agreement did not set rules to enforce the quota and did not set price ceilings or supplementary quotas to meet market inflation. The stalemate within the ICO was between consumer and producer nations. According to a report Sept. 5, the U.S. and other consumer countries had demanded a rollback in coffee prices, which had risen from 43¢ a pound in August 1971 to levels of 54¢-58¢ in August 1972. They had also insisted on a guarantee that producers would not hold exports to less than the agreed quota levels to drive up prices. (The 13 major coffee producers had done that earlier in 1972.) The producers sought to maintain the high current coffee prices, asserting they were needed to compensate for losses caused by changes in currency parities in December 1971 *(see* INTERNATIONAL MONETARY DEVELOPMENTS [3, 5-6, 11]). The four major producers—Brazil, Colombia, Portugal and the Ivory Coast—had met early in August and agreed to press within the ICO for measures to stabilize prices and end control of the market by the importing countries. According to many delegates, reports of further frosts in Brazil, potentially lowering its already frost-damaged crop, had strengthened Brazil's negotiating position and prevented concessions by the producers.

U.S. overhaul sought. President Nixon Aug. 7 authorized the Tariff Commission to make the first major overhaul of the tariff system since 1963 to bring U.S. regulations on 6,700 items into conformity with the 1,096 categories, known as the Brussels tariff description, used by 85 countries. (Only Canada and the U.S. among the world's major trading nations did not utilize the Brussels system.) The Tariff Commission project was scheduled for completion by Sept. 30, 1973. It would require congressional approval.

GATT meeting. The 80 nations participating in the General Agreement on Tariffs and Trade (GATT) held their 28th session in Geneva Nov. 1-14. Much of the meeting was taken up establishing plans for a new round of major trade talks, which was scheduled to begin in 1973 and end by 1975. The GATT Nov. 14 approved a Swedish proposal that a "preparatory committee" meet within several months "to define the scope and goal of the 1973 negotiations." The proposal was adopted with a proviso that underdeveloped nations as well as GATT member-nations would be allowed to participate in the talks. The GATT also approved a U.S. plan for ministerial-level talks in September, 1973 "to establish a trade negotiations committee." President Nixon's trade representative, William D. Eberle, listed five principal U.S. trade objectives for the committee: the possible elimination of tariffs for industrial goods; the elimination of nontariff trade barriers, such as health and safety regulations and customs procedures, and the establishment of "common rules and procedures" governing the use of the remaining nontariff regulations; "substantial expansion" of agricultural trade; a "multilateral safeguard system" to establish rules by which a nation would temporarily restrict imports when "abrupt changes" threatened its domestic industry; and the "revitalization of GATT, to be accomplished by establishing new decision-making procedures and rewriting trade rules." The GATT Nov. 16 also agreed that means for improving trade relations between industrial and developing nations would be a major topic for the 1973 meetings. (In another GATT development, the group announced Nov. 20 that Bangla Desh would become the 81st member of GATT, effective Dec. 16.)

See also AFRICA; ATOMIC ENERGY [6]; BANGLA DESH [10-11]; BRAZIL; CANADA [3, 12]; CHILE [11]; ECONOMY [5, 9]; EUROPEAN ECONOMIC COMMUNITY; FOREIGN POLICY; INTERNATIONAL MONETARY DEVELOPMENTS [5-6, 9]; JAPAN [8]; MEXICO; PAKISTAN [12]; PERU; POLAND; POLLUTION [1]; RHODESIA; SINO-U.S. RELATIONS [2]; SOVIET-U.S. RELATIONS [1, 7-12]; SPAIN; TERRITORIAL WATERS; UNION OF SOVIET SOCIALIST REPUBLICS [11]

TAXES—Reform postponed. John D. Ehrlichman, President Nixon's principal domestic affairs aide, informed newsmen May 12 that the President had reached agreement with Chairman Wilbur D. Mills (D, Ark.) of the House Ways and Means Committee that tax reform legislation would not be considered during the 1972 election year. Ehrlichman said that President Nixon, if re-elected, would seek major tax reform in 1973.

New audit described. Internal Revenue Service (IRS) Commissioner Johnnie M. Walters April 11 described a new IRS auditing program that was expected to identify nearly one million taxpayers who were claiming illegal deductions on their tax returns. Among the more common unlawful deductions found by the program were inaccurate claims for deductions on casualty losses, medical expenses and dividends. Walters said the special program would probably bring the government an additional $40 million in taxes. The average additional tax paid because of the new system, according to Walters, was $45. Walters also described another new program under which IRS investigators were checking into the operations of commercial tax preparation services. Walters said that the new program—under way in the IRS's Southwest region—had found that two-thirds of those commercial operations were doing sloppy or fraudulent work. Of the 300 commercial tax preparers whose work had been checked, 41 had been arrested and 44 were under indictment. The work of 192 of the preparers indicated that they had done a sufficiently poor job to warrant further investigation.

Overwithholding. Deputy Secretary of the Treasury Charls E. Walker July 26 estimated tax overwithholding, caused by a new IRS schedule, at $8 billion-$10 billion. Walker warned of the danger of inflation in returning total repayments estimated at $21 billion-$24 billion to 56 million taxpayers.

Nixon pledges no new taxes. House Minority Leader Gerald R. Ford (Mich.) and Senate Minority Leader Hugh D. Scott (Pa.) Sept. 7 reported a pledge by President Nixon to propose no new taxes during his second term, if re-elected. Following the disclosure, White House Press Secretary Ronald Ziegler called a news conference to confirm the pledge, saying "we contemplate and plan no tax increases—period—in the next term." However, Ziegler specifically excluded a value-added tax (VAT—a tax, at each successive stage in the production of an article, on the value increased by each stage) from the pledge, since it would be proposed only to offset reductions in local property taxes. In order to clarify questions raised at the briefing, Ziegler and Ehrlichman held a second news conference. Ehrlichman said that tax reform proposals, which could raise taxes for some, were being prepared, but would be deferred until after the Presidential elections. Ehrlichman admitted that federal agencies were studying a VAT, but added that the Administration was "less favorably inclined" to the tax "than to some other possibilities." He called the tax difficult to apply and possibly inequitable, but declined to rule out its eventual adoption. Ehrlichman also warned that the President's pledge not to raise taxes was "dependent on Congressional responsibility" in limiting expenditures. Nixon himself said Oct. 7 that: "My goal is not only no tax increase in 1973, but no tax increase in the next four years." He warned, however, "that excessive spending by the Congress might cause a Congressional tax increase in 1973."

See also AUSTRALIA [6]; BUDGET; CANADA [4]; CIVIL RIGHTS [20]; ECONOMY [6] EDUCATION [2, 4]; ELECTIONS [6, 16-17, 33, 35, 44]; ENVIRONMENT; GREAT BRITAIN [6]; HOUSING; MEDICINE; NIXON, RICHARD MILHOUS; POLLUTION [3, 15]; POPULATION; SOVIET-U.S. RELATIONS [10]; STATE & LOCAL GOVERNMENTS; SWEDEN; WOMEN'S RIGHTS

TEAMSTERS—See INDOCHINA WAR [40]; LABOR

TELEVISION & RADIO—**TV violence study.** The Surgeon General's Scientific Advisory Committee on Television and Social Behavior Jan. 17 released a report which said that "viewing violence on television is conducive to an increase in aggressive behavior" in at least some children. According to the report, the evidence did not "warrant the conclusion" that television violence "has an adverse affect on the majority of children." However, the report did conclude that television violence can induce "mimicking or copying by children" and can, in some circumstances, "instigate an increase in aggressive behavior." Among the factors that might predispose a child to harmful reaction to television violence were, according to the report, pre-existing levels of aggression, parental control of television viewing, parental affection or punishment, parental emphasis on nonaggression, and socio-economic status. According to one member of the advisory committee, all of the studies used as the basis for the report failed to support the thesis that televised violence might have a cathartic effect on aggressive tendencies. The report also documented the prevalence of violence on television.

[2] The report roused immediate criticism from those who charged that the commission had deferred to the broadcast industry by diluting and qualifying the evidence. The report itself included criticism of the selection process for the 12-member advisory committee. Surgeon General Jesse L. Steinfeld admitted Jan. 17 that seven potential members had been vetoed by the National

Broadcasting Co. (NBC) and the American Broadcasting Co. (ABC), which participated in the 1969 committee selection. Steinfeld justified the vetoes by the desire to escape accusation of "picking a committee slanted against the television industry." Some of those rejected by the networks had been engaged in previous research in the field. Of the 12 members finally selected, two were broadcast executives, two were network consultants, and one was a former consultant. Several scientists who had participated in the research studies that went into making the report also criticized the commission's work Feb. 19, saying that the report's use of qualifying language might have confused the press and the public. Dr. John Murray of the National Institutes of Health said the final report gives the impression "that the findings are trivial." Murray added that "there is no question in my mind that normal children watching a large amount of TV violence will become more aggressive." Other critics said the report should have noted that violence on television, although it was not the only cause of aggressive behavior, was the easiest of such causes to control. The critics also charged that the report should have emphasized that some reform was needed, even if only some children were affected by televised violence.

[3] **New cable rules set.** The Federal Communications Commission (FCC) announced Feb. 3 a series of new rules, effective March 31, designed to regulate the future extension of cable television (CATV, a system of bringing television programs into homes by coaxial cable rather than by regular broadcast transmissions). The new policy would promote the growth of cable television from rural areas into the nation's smaller cities, while restricting its encroachment into big-city viewing markets. The decision to check the spread of CATV into major metropolitan areas was deemed necessary to win approval of the overall policy by television broadcasters, who had opposed competition by CATV for five years. The new rules permitted existing broadcast stations to retain control over program material in the 50 largest market areas, with CATV companies permitted to import to those areas only programs for which local broadcasters had not purchased exclusive rights. In the next 50 largest markets, exclusive film rights were limited to one year. In still smaller viewing markets, there would be no exclusive film rights. The regulations also required CATV systems to: carry a minimum of 20 channels, some of which would have to carry all local television stations while they were broadcasting; make two channels available for five years without charge for local government and educational broadcasts; designate one channel as a free "public access" station, with air time available on a "first-come, first-served basis," without censorship except a prohibition against advertising; and provide for a system that would enable viewers to transmit signals back to a central office.

[4] **Radio Free Europe, Radio Liberty funding.** The House March 22 and the Senate March 24 approved a bill authorizing funding of Radio Free Europe and Radio Liberty until July 1. (Federal funding for the two stations had expired Feb. 22, when the bill was in a joint House-Senate conference.) The measure, signed by President Nixon March 30, was the Senate version of the funding bill for the two stations. Senate conferees, led by Foreign Relations Committee Chairman J. W. Fulbright (D, Ark.), had refused in the joint conference to accept a compromise with the Administration-backed House bill, which called for a two-year funding and an independent body to study the stations' operations. The Senate bill provided funding through June 30 administered by the State Department. Fulbright, despite the expressed support by more than half of the Senate for the stations, adamantly refused support for the stations, which he considered to be relics of the cold war and an impediment to East-West relations. Faced with the prospect of a shutdown of operation of the stations, the Administration and House conferees agreed March 14 to accept the Senate legislation with the understanding that further authorizing legislation would be considered before the short-term financing expired. A second interim authorization was passed by the House Aug. 7 and by the Senate June 16. It was signed by the President Aug. 21. The new interim measure

(pending proposals of a study commission for future financing of the stations) authorized $38,520,000 for the two stations for fiscal 1973.

[5]   EBS revamped. The White House Office of Telecommunications Policy said April 4 that the government was revamping the Emergency Broadcast System (EBS) into two separate communications systems. The restructuring followed a year-long review of the EBS (originally set up to warn the country in the event of an enemy attack) ordered by President Nixon following a 1971 incident in which a routine test was erroneously interpreted as an actual emergency broadcast. Under the new setup, one system would be for the exclusive use of the President in case of national emergency. The second linkup, to be known as the National Warning System and to be operated by the Office of Civil Defense, would be used to broadcast news of natural disasters and less extreme national defense matters.

[6]   Trust suit against networks. The Justice Department April 14 filed civil antitrust suits in federal district court in Los Angeles against NBC, ABC, the Columbia Broadcasting System (CBS) and Viacom International, Inc., a former CBS subsidiary which controls some CBS program syndication rights. The suits sought to prevent the networks "from carrying network-produced entertainment programs, including feature films, and from obtaining financial interests in independently produced entertainment programs," with the exception of first-run exhibition rights. According to the Justice Department, the networks "used their control of access to air time to monopolize prime-time television entertainment programming and to obtain valuable interests in such programming," depriving "the viewing public, independent program suppliers and advertisers" of "the benefits of free competition." In particular, the suits alleged that the networks' entry into motion picture production threatened free competition in that industry as well. The suits charged that, during 1967, ABC had ownership interest in 86% of the entertainment programs it broadcast during prime time (defined by the suits as 6-11 p.m., but considered by the networks to be 7-11 p.m.). According to the suits, during the same year, NBC had interests in 68% of its prime-time broadcasting and CBS in 73%.

[7]   The network defendants claimed that the legal actions were superfluous in the light of recent FCC rulings that already, they claimed, had sharply reduced their control of entertainment programming. Among the FCC rulings cited were a 1970 ruling requiring every station to buy at least one hour of prime-time entertainment from non-network sources, a ruling that barred network equity ownership in all shows produced or televised in 1971 or thereafter and a ruling that curbed network control over syndication (the sale of programs to individual stations). A Justice Department spokesman noted April 14, however, that changes in FCC membership could bring about a revision or reversal of the rulings. Network officials, reacting to reports of the suits published the day before they were filed, claimed that the situation had changed drastically since 1967. According to network spokesmen April 13, CBS's production accounted for only 8.2% of its prime-time schedule in the last quarter of 1971, and NBC and ABC bought from outsiders over 90% of their prime-time programs during the same period.

[8]   Emmy awards. The 24th annual Emmy award ceremonies of the National Academy of Television Arts and Sciences were held in Hollywood May 15. The winners: **comedy series**—*All in the Family* (CBS); **variety series (musical)**— *The Carol Burnett Show* (CBS); **variety series (talk)**—*The Dick Cavett Show* (ABC); **outstanding single program (variety)**—*'S Wonderful, 'S Marvelous, 'S Gershwin* (NBC); **actor (comedy series)**—Carroll O'Connor, *All in the Family;* **actress (comedy series)**—Jean Stapleton, *All in the Family;* **actress (dramatic series)**—Glenda Jackson, *Elizabeth R* (PBS); **actor (dramatic series)**—Peter Falk, *Columbo* (NBC); **director (special comedy, variety or musical)**—Walter C. Miller and Martin Charnin, *'S Wonderful, 'S Marvelous, 'S Gershwin;* **writer (special comedy, variety or musical)**—Anne Howard Bailey, *The Trial of Mary Lincoln* (PBS); **director (variety or musical)**—Art

Fisher, *The Sonny and Cher Comedy Hour* (CBS); **supporting actor (comedy series)**—Edward Ashner, *The Mary Tyler Moore Show* (CBS); **supporting actress (comedy series)**—Valerie Harper, *The Mary Tyler Moore Show,* tied with Sally Struthers, *All in the Family;* **supporting actor (drama)**—Jack Warden, "Brian's Song" on *Movie of the Week* (ABC); **supporting actress (drama)**—Jenny Agutter, "The Snow Goose" on *Hallmark Hall of Fame* (NBC); **dramatic series**—*Elizabeth R;* **single program (comedy or drama)**— "Brian's Song"; **new series**—*Elizabeth R;* **director (single program in a dramatic series)**—Tom Gries, "The Glass House" on *The New CBS Friday Night Movies;* **writer (single program in a dramatic series)**—Richard L. Levinson and William Link, "Death Lends a Hand" on *Columbo;* **director (single program in a comedy series)**—John Rich, "Sammy's Visit" on *All in the Family;* **writer (single program in variety or musical series)**—Don Hinkley, Stan Hart, Larry Siegel, Woody Kling, Rogert Beatty, Art Baer, Ben Joelson, Stan Burns, Mike Marmer and Arnie Rosen, *The Carol Burnett Show;* **writer (single program in a comedy series)**—Burt Styler, "Edith's Problem" on *All in the Family;* **writer (drama adaptation, single program)**—William Blinn, "Brian's Song"; **writer (drama, original teleplay)**—Allan Sloane, *To All My Friends on Shore* (CBS); **classical music program**—Leonard Bernstein, *Beethoven's Birthday: A Celebration in Vienna* (CBS); **actor (single performance)**—Keith Mitchell, "Catherine Howard" on *The Six Wives of Henry VIII* (CBS); **actress (single performance)**—Glenda Jackson, "Shadow in the Sun" on *Elizabeth R;* **actor (musical or variety, one-time appearance)**—Harvey Korman, *The Carol Burnett Show;* **director (single program in a drama series)**—Alexander Singer, "The Invasion of Kevin Ireland" on *The Bold Ones* (NBC); **choreography (single program)**—Alan Johnson, *'S Wonderful, 'S Marvelous, 'S Gershwin;* **documentary**—*The Search for the Nile* (NBC); sports programming—*ABC's Wide World of Sports* and the *AFC Championship Game* (NBC). The Public Broadcasting System also won a special award for *The Pentagon Papers* broadcast.

[9] *FCC curbs TV network role.* The FCC June 8 lifted a stay on rules proposed in 1970 limiting network control of television programming. (The stay had been imposed pending court tests, which were resolved in favor of the FCC.) Beginning Aug. 1, the networks were barred under the rules from acquiring any financial or proprietary rights in any program they did not exclusively produce. Beginning June 1, 1973, the networks would be barred from distributing any programs to independent stations.

[10] Public television bill vetoed. President Nixon June 30 vetoed a bill authorizing funds for the Corporation for Public Broadcasting for two more years on the grounds that the corporation was becoming too powerful and that the bill's funding procedure was faulty. The President indicated he had been influenced by the "public and legislative" debate over the bill, during which program content and the corporation's tendency to focus on public affairs had drawn much criticism. (Conservatives had complained that the corporation had concentrated on public affairs and cultural programs at the expense of educational programs, and that news programs and personnel were biased toward the liberal side.) In his veto message, Nixon said that there were "many fundamental disagreements concerning the direction which public broadcasting has taken and should pursue," and that "perhaps the most important one is the serious and widespread concern expressed in Congress and within public broadcasting itself—that an organization originally intended to serve only local stations is becoming instead the center of power and the focal point of control for the entire public broadcasting system. The vetoed bill—passed by the House June 1 on a 254-69 vote, and by the Senate June 22 on an 82-1 vote—would have authorized $65 million for the corporation in fiscal 1973 and $90 million in fiscal 1974, with an additional $10 million over the two years for improvement of station facilities. The President had requested a one-year $45 million authorization, which was $10 million more than its current funding. (The

President Aug. 30 signed a 1973 appropriations bill for the corporation which totaled $45 million.)

[11]   Bill planned to curb TV news bias. Clay T. Whitehead, director of the White House Office of Telecommunications Policy, Dec. 18 disclosed Administration plans to introduce legislation making local stations responsible for the objectivity of network news programs. The legislation would revise television station license renewal procedure to require that each station meet two criteria for renewal of license by the FCC. The criteria which would be considered were the broadcaster's demonstration of service to the community it was in, regardless of where programming was obtained, and the broadcaster's demonstration that he has afforded "reasonable, realistic and practical opportunities for the presentation and discussion of conflicting views on controversial issues." The planned legislation also would extend the license renewal period from three years to five and would require community groups to prove complaints against local broadcasters before a hearing was held. Spokesmen for network broadcasters expressed strong opposition to the proposed legislation.

See also BRAZIL; CANADA [10]; ELECTIONS [46]; GREAT BRITAIN [4]; NEWSPAPERS; PERU; PHILIPPINES [5-6, 9]; SPACE [23]; URUGUAY [5]

TENNIS—Smith wins indoor title. Army Spec. 4 Stan Smith, winner of the •1971 U.S. Open, added the U.S. indoor title to his tennis laurels Feb. 20 as he defeated Rumania's Ilie Nastase, 5-7, 6-2, 6-3, 6-4, in the finals at Salisbury, Md. After dropping the first set, Smith came back to break Nastase's service twice in the second set. Smith was in complete command in the final two sets. His victory earned him $9,000.

Rosewall keeps World Championship. Nearly four hours after they met on the court in Dallas May 14, Ken Rosewall forced Rod Laver to net a backhand service return to win for Rosewall the World Championship Tennis title and the $50,000 first-place purse. It was the second year in a row that Rosewall had defeated Laver for the richest purse in tennis. Rosewall won his marathon victory by scores of 4-6, 6-0, 6-3, 6-7, 7-6.

Wimbledon. Smith and Mrs. Billie Jean King became the first Americans to sweep the men's and women's Wimbledon singles titles in 17 years in the competition at the All England Racquet Club in London. Mrs. King July 7 dethroned defending champion Evonne Goolagong of Australia, 6-3, 6-3. Despite a shaky start, Mrs. King kept Miss Goolagong off-balance throughout the 50-minute match. The triumph made Mrs. King a four-time Wimbledon winner (1966-67-68). Smith July 9 outlasted Nastase, 4-6, 6-3, 6-3, 4-6, 7-5, in a 160-minute struggle. It was Smith's first Wimbledon singles championship. In other Wimbledon play, Bob Hewitt and Frew McMillan of South Africa won the men's doubles title July 7 by defeating Smith and Erik Van Dillen of the U.S., 6-2, 6-2, 9-7. The women's doubles title went to Mrs. King and Betty Stove of the Netherlands, who July 9 stopped Judy Dalton of Australia and Francoise Durr of France, 6-2, 4-6, 6-3. Rosemary Casals of the U.S. and Nastase won the mixed doubles crown July 9 by beating Kim Warwick of Australia and Miss Goolagong.

U.S. Open. Defending champion Mrs. King and Nastase won the 1972 women's and men's U.S. Open tennis championships, at the West Side Tennis Club in New York. Mrs. King defeated Kerry Melville of Australia Sept. 9, 6-3, 7-5, for her third U.S. Open singles crown. Unperturbed by a short downpour and tricky winds, Mrs. King took apart Miss Melville's game with workmanlike precision. In the men's finals Sept. 10, Nastase topped American Arthur Ashe, 3-6, 6-3, 6-7, 6-4, 6-3. The men's doubles title went to Cliff Drysdale of South Africa and Roger Taylor of Great Britain. They defeated Australia's Owen Davidson and John Newcombe, 6-3, 6-2, 7-5, Sept. 9. Misses Stove and Durr won the women's doubles title Sept. 10, topping Margaret Court of Australia and Virginia Wade of Great Britain, 6-3, 1-6, 6-3. Mrs. Court and American

Marty Riessen took the mixed doubles title Sept. 10 by beating Miss Casals and Nastase, 6-3, 7-5.

Davis Cup. Smith scored a five-set triumph over Ion Tiriac of Rumania Oct. 15 in Rumania to give the U.S. its fifth straight Davis Cup victory. It was the fifth year in a row that Smith had scored, or helped score, the decisive point in the cup finals. Smith topped Tiriac, 4-6, 6-2, 6-4, 2-6, 6-0, to give the U.S. an insurmountable 3-1 lead in the three-of-five series. In the final match of the series, Rumania's Nastase defeated Tom Gorman, 6-1, 6-2, 5-7, 10-8, to make the final score 3-2.

Dispute ended. The conflict over control of professional and amateur tennis ended April 26 when the two warring factions, the International Lawn Tennis Federation (ILTF) and Lamar Hunt's World Championship Tennis (WCT) group, reached an agreement so that Hunt's pros could again compete in tournaments sanctioned by the ILTF. (The ILTF had banned the WCT group in July of 1971.) Because the agreement was not ratified by the ILTF membership until a July meeting, Hunt's pros, many of whom were the world's top-ranking players, were not allowed to play at Wimbledon. Under the agreement, Hunt would no longer sign players to his WCT troupe, but would honor all existing contracts until they expired. As the contracts expired, so would the classifications setting independent pros and contract pros apart. In exchange, Hunt would have virtual control of professional tennis for the first four months of the year. During that time, he could schedule his own tournaments all over the world with all pro players free to enter. The ILTF would be in charge of tournaments from May through December.

TERRITORIAL WATERS—Tuna boats buy Ecuadorian licenses. Despite U.S. State Department requests not to do so, 15 vessels of the Southern California tuna fleet purchased licenses to fish within Ecuador's disputed 200-mile offshore territorial limits, according to a report Feb. 7. The U.S. had disputed Ecuador's claim to a 200-mile limit and had granted the country only a 12-mile limit. Since 1971, Ecuador had seized and fined numerous U.S. tuna boats for fishing within the 200-mile limit but outside the 12-mile limit. The U.S. had responded with punitive measures. The Feb. 7 report quoted August Felando, general manager of the American Tunaboat Association, as attributing the permit purchase to the fact that boat operators could no longer afford to pay the stiff fines levied when their ships were captured in the disputed waters. The U.S. government reimbursed the operators for the fines, but only after delays of up to a year. (The so-called "tuna war" between Ecuador and the U.S. was complicated, according to a report June 17, by the fact that more than half the Ecuadorean tuna fleet was U.S.-owned or U.S.-operated and that more than 50% of Ecuador's tuna industry was controlled by two U.S. companies—Del Monte Corp. and Stokely-Van Camp Inc.)

U.S.-Brazil fisheries treaty. The U.S. and Brazil May 9 signed an agreement (subject to ratification by the U.S. Senate) allowing Brazil to regulate the operations of U.S. shrimp boats within the 200-mile offshore limit claimed by Brazil. The accord, initialed by the two countries March 6, was to remain in effect through 1973. It was the first agreement signed by the U.S. with a nation claiming the 200-mile limit, but it did not recognize the 200-mile claim as legal. The treaty limited the number of U.S. boats permitted to operate within the area and allowed Brazilian authorities to tax, license, board and search the boats. Shrimp boats found to have violated catch and seasonal restrictions would be subject to seizure, but would be released after payment of fines.

U.S. enacts aid cutoff. President Nixon Oct. 27 signed a law requiring an automatic cutoff of U.S. foreign aid to nations that refused to pay back to the U.S. fines collected from captains of U.S. fishing vessels seized by other countries. The legislation was primarily directed against South American countries claiming a 200-mile offshore territorial limit. The law was denounced jointly Oct. 31 by Chile, Peru and Ecuador.

200-mile 'patrimonial' limit endorsed. In what was seen as a possible basis for a compromise on the question of territorial limits, the foreign ministers of 15 Caribbean countries June 9 announced their support for territorial waters of 12 miles and "patrimonial" waters of a maximum of 200 miles from their coastlines. In patrimonial waters, maritime states would have full sovereignty over natural resources in the sea and on the seabed, but none over navigational rights. Jamaica, Guyana, Panama and El Salvador abstained from voting on the declaration—the latter two because their laws already provided for territorial waters of 200 miles.

Iceland declares 50-mile fishing limit. Iceland July 14 published regulations extending its fishing limits from 12 to 50 nautical miles, effective Sept. 1. Talks between British and Icelandic officials had failed to reach an accord on British fishing off the Icelandic coast, which was guaranteed to the 12-mile limit by an agreement between the two nations. Britain April 14 referred the dispute over the fishing waters to the International Court of Justice (World Court) at The Hague. The court Aug. 17 struck down the 50-mile limit in a 14-1 interim decision that called for British and West German trawlers to be allowed to fish outside the 12-mile limit pending a final decision by the court. The court also ordered Britain to restrict its annual catch in Icelandic waters to 170,000 tons and West Germany to 119,000 tons. It gave all parties to the dispute the right to request a review of the interim measures before Aug. 1, 1973. The Icelandic Cabinet Aug. 18 formally rejected the World Court decision and said that the new 50-mile limit would go into effect Sept. 1.

The new limit did go into effect Sept. 1, but about 100 British, West German and Belgian trawlers defied the limit despite a threat by Icelandic Fisheries Minister Ludvik Josefsson that Iceland would "use force, if necessary" to uphold the law. For several days after the new limit went into effect, Icelandic aircraft and gunboats patrolling the coast restricted themselves to photographing the unmarked vessels. The coast guard took its first direct action Sept. 5, when the gunboat Aegir cut the trawling wires of an unmarked British trawler, which had refused to identify itself or comply with the order to quit the 50-mile zone. A second gunboat tried to cut the trawling wires of another British trawler the same day, but the trawling crew outmaneuvered it. The British government Sept. 5 protested the cutting of the wires as a dangerous practice, but Iceland rejected the protest the following day. Amid reports that the British warship Aurora was headed for the Icelandic coast, Josefsson Sept. 6 warned that Iceland would not resume negotiations with Britain if warships were dispatched to protect the fishing vessels. The Icelandic coast guard claimed Sept. 10 that its harassment tactics had forced 20 of 33 British trawlers to move out to the 50-mile limit. (In a related action, the foreign ministers of Norway, Sweden, Denmark and Finland Sept. 2 assured their Icelandic counterpart that they supported the 50-mile limit. Belgium reached an agreement Sept. 7 with Iceland allowing Belgian trawlers to fish at certain times within restricted areas of the 50-mile limit. By Sept. 7, all countries except Britain were observing the new limit.)

An Icelandic gunboat Sept. 12 cut the trawling wires of two British trawlers, which the Icelandic coast guard said were fishing within the 50-mile limit. Following those incidents, Icelandic harassment was curbed until Oct. 17, when the coast guard cut the wires of another British vessel. Britain and Iceland Oct. 18 exchanged charges of ship-ramming, and British fishermen accused Icelandic patrol vessels of firing blank shots at British trawlers Oct. 18 and Oct. 30. The Icelandic harassment activities led the British Transport and General Workers Union Oct. 21 to declare a boycott of Icelandic trawlers docking in British ports. Iceland retaliated with a boycott against British products. Icelandic patrol boats cut the trawling wires on British fishing boats again Nov. 23 and Dec. 27. (Talks between Iceland and Britain resumed Nov. 27-28, but no progress was reported.)

Australia-Indonesia seabed accord. Australia and Indonesia Oct. 9 signed an agreement establishing a permanent boundary in the potentially oil-

and gas-rich seabed in the Timor Sea between the two countries. Under the agreement, the new boundary would extend to the southern edge of the Timor Sea trough and give Australia exploration rights to about 200 miles off the northwest Australian coast. Australia originally had claimed seabed rights to about 300 miles off its coast, while Indonesia had demanded an equal division of the rights.

See also DISARMAMENT; EUROPEAN ECONOMIC COMMUNITY [8, 17]; URUGUAY [13]

TERRORISM—*See* ARGENTINA [1, 9-12]; AVIATION; BRAZIL; COLOMBIA; GREECE [12]; HIJACKING; IRELAND; JAPAN [2]; MEXICO; MIDDLE EAST [1-14, 22-29]; NORTHERN IRELAND; OLYMPICS [5]; OLYMPIC TERRORISM; TURKEY; UNITED NATIONS; URUGUAY [1, 5-7, 9-10]; VENEZUELA

THAILAND—Fighting against insurgents. Thai government forces, heavily armed with American equipment Jan. 20 launched an operation against Communist insurgents in northeast Thailand, 300 miles from Bangkok. However, the operation was reported March 22 to have made little headway. Government units totaling 12,000 men were said to be fighting a guerrilla force of 150-200 defending a mountain base at Lom Sak. Thai commanders acknowledged that government deaths in the operation had totaled at least 30, but other sources placed the number of fatalities at 60 with at least 200 wounded. Thai military officials and Western diplomats in Bangkok were reported March 22 to have said that insurgents' activity in Thailand had increased 15%-20% over the previous year-and-a-half and that the guerrillas were receiving better arms through Laos. The Thai director of the Command for the Suppression of Communists, Lt. Gen. Saiyud Kerdphol, said the guerrillas were "still in phase one, building their organization, infrastructure and secure areas,... But they are moving close to phase two—launching guerrilla offensive operations against us." The guerrilla forces were deployed in the northeast around the Phu Phan Mountains (about 1,500 men), in the northwest (an estimated 3,000 Meo tribesmen, led by Thais and ethnic Chinese born in Thailand) and near the Malaysian border to the south (about 500 rebels).

Absolute rule ended. Thirteen months of absolute rule, which had begun with the Nov. 17, 1971 coup led by Field Marshal Thanom Kittikachorn, ended Dec. 15 with the publication of a new interim constitution. The charter abrogated the National Executive Council, headed by Thanom, which had governed the country by decree since the coup. Thanom said martial law would remain in effect despite the changes. In implementing the charter, King Phumiphol Aduldet Dec. 16 appointed a new 299-member National Assembly (handpicked by the military government and composed largely of officers) and Dec. 18 appointed Thanom as premier. Thanom Dec. 19 announced the formation of a new 27-member Cabinet which had military men in the key posts. Thanom assumed the additional positions of defense and foreign affairs. Gen. Praphas Charusathien, army commander in chief, was named deputy premier and interior minister.

See also DRUG USE & ADDICTION [18]; ELECTIONS [34]; INDOCHINA WAR [8, 10, 37-38, 44]; KOREAN RELATIONS; MIDDLE EAST [29]; SINO-U.S. RELATIONS [8]

THEATER—*Fiddler* **sets record.** With its 3,225th performance June 17, *Fiddler on the Roof* became the longest running show in Broadway history. The musical, which opened Sept. 22, 1964, surpassed *Life with Father,* which had held the record since 1947. *(Fiddler* closed July 2 after its 3,242nd performance.)

Tony awards. The 26th annual Antoinette Perry (Tony) awards for distinguished achievement in the Broadway theater during the 1971-72 season were awarded April 23 by the League of New York Theaters under the auspices of the American Theater Wing in New York. The winners: **drama**—*Sticks and*

Bones; musical—*Two Gentlemen of Verona;* **dramatic actor**—Cliff Gorman, *Lenny;* **dramatic actress**—Sada Thompson, *Twigs;* **musical actor**—Phil Silvers, *A Funny Thing Happened on the Way to the Forum;* **musical actress**—Alexis Smith, *Follies;* **dramatic supporting actor**—Vincent Gardenia, *The Prisoner of Second Avenue;* **dramatic supporting actress**—Elizabeth Wilson, *Sticks and Bones;* **musical supporting actor**—Larry Blyden, *A Funny Thing Happened on the Way to the Forum;* **musical supporting actress** —Linda Hopkins, *Inner City;* **dramatic director**—Mike Nichols, *The Prisoner of Second Avenue;* **musical director**—Harold Prince and Michael Bennett, *Follies;* **scenic design**—Boris Aronson, *Follies;* **book**—John Guare and Mel Shapiro, *Two Gentlemen of Verona;* **costume design**—Florence Klotz, *Follies;* **lighting design**—Tharon Musser, *Follies;* **choreography**—Michael Bennett, *Follies;* **musical score**—Stephen Sondheim, *Follies.*

THERMAL POLLUTION—*See* ATOMIC ENERGY [2]; CANADA [3]
THIEU, NGUYEN VAN—*See* INDOCHINA WAR [41, 44, 47-48, 50, 52, 54]; SINO-U.S. RELATIONS [8]; VIETNAM, SOUTH
THO, LE DUC—*See* INDOCHINA WAR [45-46, 48]
THUY, XUAN—*See* INDOCHINA WAR [41, 45-46, 48, 53]
TITLE I—*See* CIVIL RIGHTS [3]; EDUCATION [3]
TITO, JOSIP BROZ—*See* POLAND

TOGO—Cabinet changes. In Cabinet changes announced by Gen. Etienne Eyadema Jan. 21, Barthelemy Lamboni replaced James Assila as interior minister and Louis Amega replaced Paul Eklou as rural economy minister. Koffi Mathieu was appointed to the new Ministry of Youth, Sports, Culture and Scientific Research. Two new state secretaries were named—Henri Dogo at the Presidency and Laurent Gaba at the Public Works Ministry. (Eyadema had won an overwhelming majority in a Jan. 9 national referendum to confirm him as president.)

TONGA—*See* EUROPEAN ECONOMIC COMMUNITY [7]
TONY AWARDS—*See* THEATER
TORTURE—*See* ARGENTINA [8]; BRAZIL; URUGUAY [11]; VIETNAM, SOUTH

TRACK & FIELD—U.S. tops Russians. A team of U.S. track and field stars March 17 topped a squad of athletes from the Soviet Union in the first dual indoor meet between the two countries. The most noteworthy upsets of the meet, which was held in Richmond, Va., belonged to Debbie Heald of Neff, Calif. and Wendy Koenig of Estes Park, Colo., both 16. Miss Heald won the mile run in 4:38.5, a new American women's indoor mark. Miss Koenig captured the 880-yard run by holding off Raisa Ruus of the U.S.S.R. on the final lap. The winning time was 2:11.

Penn wins IC4A titles. The University of Pennsylvania March 4 in Princeton, N.J. won the 1972 Intercollegiate Association of Amateur Athletes of America (IC4A) indoor track and field title. The Quakers finished with 26 points, the lowest victory total in seven years, and snapped Villanova's five-year domination of the championships. (Villanova was second with 24 points.) Pennsylvania May 27 in Philadelphia completed its sweep of the IC4A titles as it captured the outdoor championship with 53 points. The Quakers easily outdistanced Penn State, which finished with 40. Villanova, the defending champion, finished fourth with 23 points. It was Pennsylvania's first outdoor IC4A crown since 1920.

NCAA crowns. The University of California, Los Angeles (UCLA), June 3 in Eugene, Ore. won the National Collegiate Athletic Association (NCAA) outdoor track and field competition with 82 points, easily outscoring Southern California (USC) which finished with 49 points. In the indoor NCAA competition in Detroit March 11, USC won the team title with a score of 19 points—one point over Bowling Green and Michigan State.

See also OLYMPICS [7, 9-10]

TRANSPORTATION—Highway bill killed. The Senate Sept. 19 and the House Oct. 5 passed bills allocating money from the highway trust fund for road-building projects during fiscal 1974-75, but House-Senate conferees reconciling the two bills were unable Oct. 15 to reach agreement on a compromise measure. Pressure from building contractors and state road departments caused the conference committee to revive the measure as a simple extension of highway construction funds and operating moneys to mass transit agencies, with funding not coming from the highway trust fund. However, despite approval by the Senate of the replacement measure Oct. 18, the measure died for the current session of Congress when proponents of urban public transportation demanded a quorum call for a vote on the legislation. A quorum was not present, and the House adjourned without voting on the bill. Administration backers of aid to cities for mass transit opposed the replacement bill because they feared that an extension of highway programs would counteract pressures on the next Congress to deal with the opening of the highway trust fund for public transportation projects. (The original Senate bill had included an amendment providing for the use of the trust fund for mass transit aid. It was the first time either house of Congress had sanctioned use of the trust fund for purposes other than financing roads.)

See also AUTOMOBILES; NIXON, RICHARD MILHOUS; POPULATION [8]; RAILROADS; STATE & LOCAL GOVERNMENTS

TRINIDAD & TOBAGO—State of siege lifted. The government in late July ended a state of siege imposed in October 1971 to quell racial disturbances among industrial workers. Seventeen political detainees, including Black Power labor leaders, were released with the lifting of the state of siege. Shortly before the government action, however, the ruling People's National Movement (PNM) pushed through parliament an unpopular industrial relations bill which, in effect, made the state of siege provisions superfluous, according to a report July 21. The bill banned strikes in the country's two main industries—oil and sugar—and among prison officers, dock and electricity workers and other "essential services" employees. It also made disputes subject to compulsory arbitration, with no substantial right of appeal. The act was passed under cover of the state of siege. It reportedly had angered elements within the PNM (which controlled Parliament 36-0), as well as unions and other political parties. A junior minister, Roy Richardson, resigned from the PNM and, with congressman Horace Charles, formed the United Progressive party to be the PNM's formal opposition in Parliament. Charles had been expelled from the PNM for voting against the industrial relations bill.

Soldiers in '70 mutiny freed. The government Aug. 11 pardoned the 26 soldiers still serving jail sentences in connection with the 1970 Black Power army mutiny. Release of the prisoners followed refusal by the Privy Council in London to allow the Trinidad government to appeal a lower court ruling overturning sentences on two of the leaders of the revolt.

See also HEALTH; INTERNATIONAL MONETARY DEVELOPMENTS [8]

TRUDEAU, PIERRE ELLIOTT—See CANADA [1, 3, 7-8]

TRUMAN, HARRY S—Harry S Truman, the 33rd president of the United States, died Dec. 26 at the age of 88. Death occurred in Kansas City's Research Hospital and Medical Center, where Truman had been a patient for 22 days, fighting lung congestion, heart irregularity, kidney blockages and failure of the digestive system. Truman's body was returned to his home town of Independence, Mo., where it lay in state in the Truman Library until burial, after a state funeral, with full military honors in the courtyard of the library Dec. 28. A national memorial service for Truman was to be held Jan. 5, 1973 at the Washington Cathedral for national and world figures wishing to pay their respects. The former president was survived by his wife, Bess, and their daughter, Margaret (Mrs. Clifton) Daniel.

Truman, president from 1945 to 1953, assumed office at the death of Franklin D. Roosevelt near the end of World War II. At the outset, he was faced with the decision to employ the atomic bomb, two of which were dropped on Japan. Other foreign policy initiatives taken under Truman were the Truman Doctrine, the Marshall Plan, the Atlantic Alliance, Point Four and the Korean War effort under the United Nations flag. Truman was known as an outspoken advocate of civil rights, low-income housing and federal health care.

TUNISIA—University closed, reopened. The government Feb. 8 closed until September the faculties of law and arts at Tunis University. However, President Habib Bourguiba reopened the faculties April 18. The faculties had been closed because of demonstrations at the university against Bourguiba. Riot police used tear gas and clubs against the protesters, who included high school students. Premier Hedi Nouira told the National Assembly that the demonstrators, who first became active in October 1971 and had called a general strike Jan. 31, had been aided by pamphlets from a "Baathist country in the Middle East" and unnamed European nations.

Defense minister replaced. Bechir Meheddebi was replaced Aug. 9 as defense minister by Abdallah Farhat, formerly director of the Tunisian Cabinet. Farhat's former position was taken by Habib Chatti, formerly ambassador to Algeria.

TUPAMAROS—*See* URUGUAY [1, 5-9, 11]

TURKEY—Martial law extended. The National Assembly Jan. 24 voted to extend martial law for two months. The extension was opposed for the first time by Ismet Inonu, chairman of the Republican People's party and a highly respected figure in Turkish politics. The assembly March 26 approved another two-month extension of martial law in 11 provinces. Two-month extensions were voted again throughout the year.

10 terrorists, 3 hostages killed. Heavily armed police and soldiers March 30 killed 10 members of the Turkish People's Liberation Army (TPLA), a leftist urban guerrilla group, after the terrorists killed two Britons (Gordon Banner and Charles Turner) and a Canadian (John Stewart Law) being held hostage for the release of three leftist terrorists sentenced to death. The government reported that the hostages—all employed as civilian technicians by the North Atlantic Treaty Organization (NATO) and all kidnaped March 26—had been shot in the head with their hands tied behind their backs before police rushed the kidnapers' remote mountain shack located about 60 miles south of Unye on the Black Sea. The troops then opened fire with rockets and small arms, killing the 10 guerrillas. No police or army casualties were reported. The government had refused to bargain with the terrorists either for the release of their condemned comrades or for the kidnapers' subsequent demand for safe passage out of Turkey once the police surrounded their hideout. It was disclosed March 31 that a letter allegedly written by the kidnapers and found in their shack had said the hostages were killed because they were "English agents of the NATO forces which occupy our country, and . . . we consider it our basic right and a debt of honor to execute them."

The three TPLA members for whose release the hostages were held were hanged May 6 in Ankara's central prison. The three—Daniz Gezmis, Yusef Aslan and Huseyin Inan—had been convicted in 1971 of kidnaping three U.S. servicemen. The executions were the first since the introduction of martial law in 1971. Fifteen other TPLA members who had been sentenced to death with the three had their sentences reduced Jan. 10 to prison terms ranging from 10 years to life. The sentences of the three had been ratified by the Ankara military court of appeals Jan. 10 and by the Senate March 17. The executions had been postponed March 27 after the Constitutional Court agreed to consider appeals on behalf of the three guerrillas. The court April 6 had revoked the death sentences because of faulty drafting of the execution order. However, the military court resentenced the three to death and the order was approved April 24 by the National Assembly, May 2 by the Senate and May 3 by President Cevdet Sunay. Several bombs exploded in Istanbul and Ankara May 7, in apparent retaliation for the hangings. Four persons were injured, one reportedly a bomb-thrower.

General shot; army put on alert. Four gunmen May 4 shot and wounded Gen. Kemalettin Eken, the commander of the Turkish national police, in an apparent kidnaping attempt in Ankara. Eken and four other persons were wounded in the shootout outside the general's home. Police said one of the assailants was killed and another captured. Reports linked the shooting to the TPLA. In response to the shooting, the armed forces were placed on alert and a six-hour curfew was imposed in Ankara.

Leftists arrested. Gen. Faik Turun, military commander of Istanbul, announced May 28 that "the backbone of anarchy has been broken." He said that 1,290 persons had been investigated, 404 persons guilty of "anarchist activities" had been arrested and 153 had been sentenced to prison terms ranging from one to 35 years.

Erim resigns. Premier Nihat Erim resigned April 17 after failing to gain parliamentary backing for economic and social reforms and measures to halt political extremism. (The country's four major political groups—the Justice, Republican People's, Democratic and Reliance parties—April 7 had rejected an April 3 request by President Sunay for temporary rule by executive decree in order to combat terrorism.) Defense Minister Ferit Melen assumed the post of caretaker premier in addition to his defense portfolio. Other Cabinet members agreed to remain in office until a new government was formed. Erim's resignation had been submitted April 14, but its acceptance was delayed pending the conclusion of a visit to Turkey by Soviet President Nikolai V. Podgorny. President Sunay cited Erim's "extreme fatigue" as the reason for the stepdown.

Melen heads new government. Sunay May 15 appointed Melen as premier-designate following the president's rejection May 13 of a four-party Cabinet selected by an earlier premier-designate, Suat Hayri Urguplu (named premier-designate April 29). Sunay had objected to the membership of that Cabinet as contrary to the spirit of a 1971 armed forces memo demanding a government "above party politics." Melen announced his Cabinet May 22 after it was approved by Sunay. The government received a 262-4 vote of confidence (160 abstentions) in the 450-seat National Assembly June 5 and was sworn into office the same day. The 25-man Cabinet included eight ministers from the majority Justice party, five from the Republican People's party, and two (including Melen) from the Reliance party, as well as nine non-political technicians and one independent senator. Sixteen members were holdovers from the caretaker Cabinet. The ministerial changes: premier—Melen; ministers of state—Ismail Arar (formerly education minister) and Zeyyat Baykara; justice—Fehmi Alpaslan; defense—Mehmet Izmen; finance—Ziya Muezzinoglu; education—Sabahattin Ozbek; health and social security—Kemal Demir; agriculture—Ilyas Karaoz (formerly minister of state); power and natural resources—Nuri Kodamanoglu; housing—Turgut Toker.

Republican party quits Cabinet. The Republican People's party Nov. 4 ordered its five Cabinet members to quit the coalition government. The party said that it would not serve in a "right-wing coalition" opposed to democratic Socialist reform. (Melen still commanded a parliamentary majority with the support of the Justice and Reliance parties.) The withdrawal from the government led to a major split within the Republican People's party. Party Chairman Inonu resigned from the party Nov. 5 in protest against the withdrawal as well as the apparent leftward swing of the party's leadership. Twenty-five deputies and senators followed his lead and resigned from the party Nov. 5-6.

See also CHURCHES; CYPRUS; DRUG USE & ADDICTION [12-13, 15, 18]; HIJACKING [11]; MINES

TYPHOID FEVER—*See* HEALTH
TYPHOONS—*See* STORMS

UGANDA—Ugandan President Idi Amin issued orders during August requiring all Asians with British passports to leave Uganda within three months (*see* [7]). The order for expulsion was later extended to citizens of Pakistan, India and Bangla Desh and to persons having their origins in any of those three countries, regardless of citizenship (*see* [7-9]). The action was met with general international disfavor. In reaction, Great Britain suspended and then halted development aid to Uganda (*see* [10, 12]). In other action, an armed force entered Uganda from Tanzania during September and engaged in fighting with Ugandan troops. The invasion set off hostilities between Tanzania and Uganda, which ended with a peace treaty in October (*see* [13-14]).

[2] **Massacres alleged.** Western press sources Feb. 14 gave an account of the slaughter of 4,000-5,000 Langi and Acholi tribesmen of the Ugandan army, said to have been executed at intervals by the government since it took power in January 1971. The account was obtained in interviews with 19 Ugandan soldiers who had broken out of their country's prison at Mutukula Feb. 6 and who were being held near the northern Tanzanian town of Tabora. Four others were in a hospital at nearby Bukoba, undergoing treatment for bullet wounds received during their escape. According to the men, they and hundreds of their fellow tribesmen had been rounded up by President Amin during the course of 1971 and taken to prisons throughout Uganda, where large numbers of them were killed. The men said they believed themselves to be the only survivors of the nearly 5,000 Langi and Acholi who had been in the army at the time of Amin's coup. Amin said Feb. 6 that 15 escaped detainees had been returned by Tanzania, but Tanzania denied return of any of the fugitives to Uganda. A government report in Uganda Feb. 18 denied the charges of tribal slaughter and claimed that the men interviewed were not escaped detainees but guerrilla supporters of Milton Obote, deposed by Amin's coup d'etat.

[3] *Investigation on missing Americans.* A judicial commission under the chairmanship of Justice David Jeffreys-Jones March 15 began an investigation into the 1971 disappearance of two U.S. citizens (Nicholas Stroh and Robert Siedle) who were attempting to investigate reports of inter-tribal warfare in the Ugandan army. The commission April 12 found the automobile of one of the men in a remote and virtually uninhabited area of Uganda. The discovery of the car followed the publication in the Western press April 9 of an interview with Ugandan Lt. Silver M. Tibihika, who had fled to Tanzania. Tibihika said he had disposed of the bodies of the Americans and had taken the car to the Buranga Pass region on the orders of Lt. Col. Waris Ali, commander of the

military post where the two were last seen. Tibihika May 3 read an affadavit to the Ugandan commission repeating his charges against Ali. Tibihika said that the Americans were killed at the army barracks at Mbarara July 9, 1971. The commission's investigation was terminated by President Amin at the end of May. The report of the investigation allegedly was sent to the government during July, but was never published. President Amin Aug. 14 sent a letter to President Nixon offering to compensate the families of the two missing men.

[4] Israeli advisers leave. Most of the 70 Israeli paratroop, army and air force advisers helping train Ugandan military units were reported to have withdrawn from the country March 26. President Amin March 23 had ordered the advisers to leave the country by March 27 and had said that the Israeli embassy staff in Kampala was to be reduced from seven persons to four. Amin had accused the Israelis during February and March of spreading rumors against the government and planning subversive activities. The Israeli Foreign Ministry March 23 denied the Ugandan charges and announced the recall of all military experts from Uganda. Following the withdrawal of all military advisers and then all Israeli citizens from Uganda, Israeli Foreign Minister Abba Eban April 10 gave his government's version of the breach with Uganda. Eban said the charges of subversion were an "improvisation of the moment" made to implement a decision reached at a Feb. 13 meeting between Amin and Libyan Premier Col. Muammar el-Qaddafi. Eban said that the two had decided to end Israel's presence in Uganda "in the most demonstrative and insulting way possible." The Israeli foreign minister implied that Amin had been influenced by offers of Libyan economic assistance. (Uganda announced April 19 that Libya had offered to build hospitals in Uganda and to train army and air force personnel.)

[5] Obote reward withdrawn. Amin May 16 withdrew Uganda's offer of a reward of one million shillings ($139,200) for the return of former President Obote. Rewards of half a million shillings each were also rescinded for Akena Adoko, former head of Obote's disbanded secret police, and Oyite Ojok, former quartermaster general for the Ugandan army. Amin said the men were "free to return as citizens of Uganda and no harm will be done to them." He thanked Tanzanian President Julius K. Nyerere for having granted Obote political asylum.

[6] Cabinet shuffle. In the first major reorganization of his government since the 1971 coup, Amin announced June 7 the creation of several new ministries and the appointment of new Cabinet personnel. The Ministries of Finance and of Planning and Economic Development were combined and would be headed by Emmanuel Wakkweya, formerly the finance minister. Another ministry was divided, becoming the Ministry of Power and Communications and the Ministry of Works and Housing, headed, respectively, by former Interior Minister Lt. Col. E. A. T. Obitre-Gama and J. M. Zikusoka. Apollo Kironde, formerly in charge of planning and economic development, was named to head the newly created Tourism Ministry.

[7] Asians ousted. President Amin Aug. 5 declared that Asians with British passports would be given three months to settle their affairs and leave Uganda. Amin said there was "no room" for the Asians because they were "sabotaging the economy" and did not have "the welfare of Uganda at heart." Most shops in the main towns, he said, were controlled by Asians, who engaged in such practices as hoarding, profiteering and currency frauds. Amin declared he intended to call on the British High Commissioner in Kampala and ask him to "make arrangements and remove the 80,000 Asian British passport holders within three months." (Other estimates of the number of Asians affected ranged between 40,000 and 50,000.) Amin announced Aug. 9 that nationals of India, Pakistan and Bangla Desh would also be required to leave the country within 90 days, but non-Ugandan Asians in a range of professional categories would be allowed to stay. (These included persons employed by the government, teachers, lawyers, doctors, owners of industrial and agricultural enterprises and managers or owners of banks and insurance companies.) In an Aug. 18 interview, Amin appeared to rescind the exemption for professionals. He announced Aug. 19 that all Asians, even citizens of Uganda, would be told to leave the country. He said that the expulsion of Asian Ugandan citizens would be "carried out as a second-phase operation after the present one involving the Asians holding British passports and nationals of India, Pakistan and Bangla Desh." Amin Aug. 22 changed his policy and said that Ugandan citizens would not be expelled, but also threatened to "weed out all those who got their citizenship through corruption or forgery." Amin also announced Aug. 27 that some non-citizen Asians would be allowed to remain in the country after the Nov. 7 deadline at the invitation of the government. Those invited would remain an additional 12 months to minimize economic disruption.

[8] In a surprise directive Aug. 28, Amin insisted that Asians being expelled from the country depart on East African Airways, the carrier owned jointly by Kenya, Tanzania and Uganda. He added that, if the airline could not carry out the operation alone, it would be "free to hire airplanes from other airlines, provided that it has the approval of the Uganda government, since embarkations will be at Entebbe airport." (British Overseas Airways Corp. and six independent British lines had reached agreement Aug. 24 on a plan to airlift the Asians.) Amin Aug. 29 set forth other economic and administrative measures—reorganizing the government into nine provinces, introducing a five-day workweek, banning teenage dances, requesting every qualified Ugandan to volunteer as instructors to train Ugandans to take over former Asian businesses, requiring that all ground transport of tourists be done in Uganda-owned vehicles, requiring tourists to pay hotel bills in foreign currency and make all arrangements through the state-owned Uganda Tourist Board and requiring that all foreign investments in the country be made through "black Ugandans."

[9] In later actions, the government said Sept. 13 that British Asians remaining in Uganda past the November deadline would be put into military camps, where they would be held until Britain "allows them entry to their own motherland, which is Britain." Amin declared Sept. 22 that Asians who had already completed emigration formalities—some 8,000 persons—would be given 48 hours to leave. About 1,100 Asians left for London by plane Sept. 23-25, with Amin taking no known steps to enforce the order. Amin Oct. 19 also ordered the expulsion of all Asians with Kenyan, Tanzanian and Zambian citizenship. Amin Oct. 25 issued a directive extending the expulsion order to "any person of Indian, Pakistan or Bangla Desh origin, extraction or descent" from any country in the world.

[10] *Reaction to expulsion.* The Ugandan action was met with general disapproval by other countries, although Kenya and Liberia hailed the move as a warning to foreigners that they must support local African aspirations. In apparent retaliation for the expulsion, Britain Aug. 29 froze a $24.5 million loan that had been set aside for Uganda. (The loan was halted Nov. 30.) The U.S. revealed Sept. 14 that it was holding up a scheduled $3 million loan to Uganda. The problem of what to do with the expelled Asians also raised serious difficulties. Great Britain was already faced with problems arising from the immigration of large numbers of Asians into the British working force. Lord Hailsham, the Lord Chancellor and principal legal adviser to the British government, announced Sept. 14 that more than a dozen countries had offered to accept the expelled Asians. Sir Alec Douglas-Home, the British foreign secretary, Sept. 27 asked the United Nations General Assembly for help in dealing with the problem of the expelled Asians. (The U.N. Oct. 27 called on all Ugandan Asians of "undetermined nationality" to report to a U.N. refugee center as part of an operation to evacuate stateless Asians.)

[11] *British aide ousted.* Richard Slater, British High Commissioner in Kampala, arrived in London Oct. 15 after he was expelled Oct. 12 by Amin for "working against the interest of the country." Amin accused Slater of being

responsible for "propaganda reports against Uganda" that appeared in British media, of advising British teachers and doctors working in Uganda to send their relatives home and of telephoning Britons working in Kampala Sept. 21 and warning them to stay home because of disturbances in the city that day. Amin also withdrew Col. Sam Lukakamwa, his high commissioner in London, Oct. 13, explaining that he did not want Uganda represented in a country which conducted propaganda against his government.

[12] **British firms seized.** The Ugandan government Dec. 18 seized and nationalized 41 foreign-owned concerns—all but seven of them partly or wholly owned by British citizens. British Foreign Secretary Douglas-Home reacted to the seizure by a statement Dec. 19 that the action was a violation of international law and would be protested to the United Nations. (Gen. Amin Dec. 20 announced that his government would pay an unspecified amount in return for the nationalized British firms. He emphasized, however, that the compensation for the seizure would be paid "in installments.") The seizure apparently took place in retaliation for Britain's decision in November to halt a loan to Uganda which had been suspended in August (see [10]). One of the nationalized firms, International Television Sales, was owned by U.S. interests. A State Department spokesman declared Dec. 19 that the U.S. view on the need for compensation was "a matter of public record." News sources took the statement as a reference to a policy directive by President Nixon establishing that countries failing to compensate for nationalization might lose U.S. aid (see FOREIGN POLICY).

[13] **Uganda, Tanzania strife.** A force of some 1,000 troops, believed to be a guerrilla army composed mainly of exiles loyal to former President Obote, attacked Uganda from Tanzania Sept. 17, capturing the small towns of Mutukula, Kyotera and Kalisizo and threatening the town of Masaka and the army barracks at Mbarara. The invaders were repulsed Sept. 20. Observers explained the apparent failure of the invasion by speculating that the guerrillas had counted on large-scale defections from the Uganda army, which had never occurred, and by noting that they had launched their attack through an area populated mostly by the Baganda, a tribe that had never supported Obote. Uganda charged Sept. 18 that the attack had been carried out by regular Tanzanian troops and Uganda guerrillas supported by British and Israeli mercenaries. Tanzania denied that any Tanzanian soldiers were involved. Sources in Tanzania said, however, that about 1,000 of the country's troops had been moved to the border west of Lake Victoria and ordered "not to yield an inch of ground" in case Uganda attacked. Tanzania Sept. 18 charged that a Uganda plane had attacked Bukoba, about 20 miles south of the border, and bombed the market place, killing five civilians and wounding 20. Reports of fighting between Tanzanian and Ugandan troops continued through September.

[14] **Peace accord.** The foreign ministers of Uganda and Tanzania Oct. 5 concluded two days of talks organized by Somali President Mohamed Siad Barre and announced that they had signed an agreement ending hostilities between their nations. The agreement reportedly required both sides to withdraw their forces by Oct. 19 to a distance of not less than six miles from their common border. The operation was to be monitored by Somali observers. Each side undertook to refrain from hostile propaganda against the other, to prevent subversive forces from attacking the territory of the other and to release all captured nationals and property.

See also BURUNDI; INTERNATIONAL MONETARY DEVELOPMENTS [8]

ULSTER—See NORTHERN IRELAND

ULSTER DEFENSE ORGANIZATION (UDA)—See NORTHERN IRELAND [14-16, 19]

UNEMPLOYMENT—The Labor Department reported Jan. 7 that unemployment in December 1971 rose to 6.1% of the labor force, bringing the average jobless rate for the year to 5.9%, its highest level since 6.7% in 1961. (The 1970 unemployment rate was 4.9%.) 1972 unemployment figures, on a seasonally adjusted basis, were: 5.9% in January; 5.7% in February; 5.9% in March, April and May; 5.5% in June and July; 5.6% in August; 5.5% in September and October; and 5.2% in November and December.

Administration drops jobless target. Herbert Stein, chairman of the Council of Economic Advisers, told the Joint Economic Committee of Congress Oct. 26 that the Nixon Administration had abandoned the goal of a 4% unemployment rate. Stein said any target would be "counterproductive" because of the "wide range of opinion about what the target rate of unemployment should be in today's context." The 4% figure had been set in 1962 as an interim level, although the jobless rate did not fall below 4% until 1966.

See also BUDGET; ECONOMY [2]; ELECTIONS [33]; NEGROES; POLLUTION [1, 6]; SPACE [3]

UNION OF ARAB EMIRATES—Sharja ruler assassinated. Sheik Khalid bin Mohammed al-Qasimi, ruler of the state of Sharja, was assassinated in his palace Jan. 24 during an attempted coup. Sheik Khalid had been held hostage in the palace before he was shot to death. Rebel forces had seized the palace, but were outnumbered by police units led by Sheik Saqr bin Mohammed al-Qasimi (Sheik Khalid's youngest brother) which surrounded the royal residence. After an exchange of gunfire in which four policemen were wounded, the insurgents surrendered. The cousin of Sheik Khalid, Sheik Saqr bin Sultan, who had been deposed as ruler of Sharja, had secretly returned to the country Jan. 24 to lead the coup. He was arrested with 18 followers after Sheik Khalid's death. Sheik Saqr bin Mohammed succeeded his slain brother as ruler of Sharja Jan. 25.

States expand. The Union of Arab Emirates' supreme council Feb. 11 announced that the Persian Gulf state of Ras al Khaima had joined the union, becoming the seventh member.

Qatar ruler deposed. Sheik Ahmed bin Ali al-Thani, ruler of Qatar, was deposed Feb. 22 in a bloodless coup d'etat. The sheik had been out of the country on a hunting trip in Iran since Feb. 18. The official announcement of the coup gave no reason for the ouster of the sheik, but he reportedly had been criticized for spending more time on holidays abroad than on affairs of state. The sheik was replaced by his cousin, Sheik Khalifa bin Hammad al-Thani, who immediately announced a series of reforms, including a 20% increase in wages for civil servants and the army and police force and a cut in consumer prices.

See also EUROPEAN ECONOMIC COMMUNITY [7]

UNION OF SOVIET SOCIALIST REPUBLICS (U.S.S.R. OR SOVIET UNION)—1971 economic report. Results of the 1971 economic development plan were published Jan. 23. Measured against the figures for 1970, the following major increases were reported: national income 6%; industrial output 7.8%; capital investments 7%; industrial productivity 6.3%; agricultural productivity 2% (agricultural output was stationary); per capita real income 4.5%; foreign trade 6%.

[2] Bukovsky sentenced. Vladimir Bukovsky, a Soviet dissident, was sentenced Jan. 5 to seven years imprisonment and five years of exile on charges of giving information to Western newsmen about how the Soviet Union sent political prisoners to psychiatric hospitals. Bukovsky, who already had spent years in prison for anti-government protests, was found guilty of having tried to bring a printing press into the country, of "disseminating slanderous lies about the social and government system of the U.S.S.R.," and of trying to persuade two Red Army officers to send information abroad. Bukovsky's sentence, the strictest possible, was to be served as two years in prison and five in a labor camp. He would then be required to live in exile in a remote area for five years. The sentence was upheld Feb. 22 by the Supreme Court of the Russian Federative Republic.

[3] *Political dissidents seized.* Soviet police carried out raids Jan. 12-16 in a number of cities in what appeared to be a general drive against opponents of the government. Police arrested seven persons in the Western Ukrainian city of Lvov Jan. 12 and at least four persons in Kiev Jan. 13. All those arrested were charged with "deliberately false fabrications defaming the Soviet state." The homes of eight Moscow dissidents were searched Jan. 14 by secret police members; and materials were taken from the home of Pyotr I. Yakir, an historian and political activist. Kronid Lyubarsky, an astronomer whose home was searched, and Yuri Shikhanovich, a mathematician, were reportedly taken into police custody Jan. 16. Shikhanovich was released after being questioned.

[4] **Tass raised in status.** The Soviet news agency Tass Jan. 10 became a State Committee, a status virtually equivalent to that of a ministry; and its director, Leonid M. Zamyatin, was given ministerial rank. The agency was expected to assume control of local news agencies in the 14 non-Russian republics of the Soviet Union and to become, according to the government newspaper *Izvestia,* an "information organ of union-republican significance."

[5] **Solzhenitsyn rules out Nobel award.** Alexander I. Solzhenitsyn, the Soviet novelist awarded the 1970 Nobel Prize for Literature, April 7 abandoned his efforts for a presentation of his prize medal. Dr. Karl-Ragnar Gierow, permanent secretary of the Swedish Academy, had announced Jan. 4 that the prize would be presented to Solzhenitsyn in a private Moscow ceremony during the spring. However, the Soviet embassy in Stockholm April 4 refused without explanation to issue a Moscow travel visa to Dr. Gierow for the presentation. After hearing that the Soviet government would not allow Gierow into the country, Solzhenitsyn April 7 sent a cable to Gierow, saying: "The refusal of the visa implies that the handing over of the prize has been forbidden. Do not be upset. We can postpone it for several years." In a statement released to Swedish correspondents April 9, Solzhenitsyn said that Moscow's action in denying the visa placed "an irreversible and final ban against any kind of presentation of the Nobel Prize on the territory of my homeland." He rejected an earlier suggestion by Swedish Foreign Minister Krister Wickman that the ceremony take place in the Swedish embassy in Moscow. He called the suggestion "unrealistic and insulting" and accused Wickman of continuing to "regard the presentation of the Nobel Prize to me not as a cultural occasion but as a political event." The author concluded: "According to what I have been told about the Swedish Academy's rules, the insignia can be kept by the Academy indefinitely.... If my life is not long enough, I bequeath them to my son in my will." The speech that Solzhenitsyn would have delivered if he had been allowed to receive the prize was published Aug. 24 in Stockholm in the Nobel Foundation's yearbook. Nobel officials declined to say how they came into possession of the lecture, which reportedly was a redraft of a milder version and bore signs of hasty translation. The speech began with a denunciation of official persecution against writers in the Soviet Union.

[6] **Party card exchange.** Plans for a nationwide exchange of Communist party membership cards, reportedly the first since 1955, were announced June 24. The exchange was to implement a Central Committee order issued earlier in the month. The exchange reportedly would "not be simply a mechanical act of issuing new party cards in return for the present cards," but would eliminate "passiveness and indifference" by screening applicants.

[7] **'73 economic plan.** The economic development plan for 1973 was presented to the Supreme Soviet Dec. 18. The plan sharply reduced the rate of consumer goods production, reportedly because of a poor grain harvest in 1972 *(see* SOVIET-U.S. RELATIONS [7-11]). While the current five-year plan had provided for a 7.6% growth rate in heavy industry and an 8.1% rate for consumer goods in 1973, the revised plan for 1973 called for a 4.5% increase in consumer goods production and a 6.1% increase in heavy industry. Overall industrial output was set to increase by 5.8% instead of the 7.8% originally envisaged. Grain targets were estimated at 197.4 million metric tons. Military expenditures, according to a separate report to the Supreme Soviet the same day, would remain at about $20 billion, approximately the same level as in recent years.

Soviet-Jewish Developments

[8] **U.S. Congressman expelled.** U.S. Rep. James H. Scheuer (D, N.Y.) was expelled from the U.S.S.R. Jan. 14 and accused of "improper activities" during his visit as a member of the subcommittee on education of the House Education and Labor Committee, which was touring Soviet schools. Scheuer said Jan. 14: "I understand I am being expelled for encouraging Soviet citizens to emigrate. I did have social contacts with some who wanted to leave, but they had made up their minds long before I arrived." *Izvestia* Jan. 17 accused Scheuer and three other members of the congressional group in which he was traveling—Reps. Alphonzo Bell (R, Calif.) and Earl F. Landgrebe (R, Ind.) and Bell's assistant, Richard Blades—of subversive activities including "conspiratorial instruction meetings" between Scheuer and Bell and Soviet Jews who had been refused permission to emigrate to Israel. (Scheuer Jan. 12 had been detained for questioning by Soviet police while he was visiting the home of a Jewish family which had been refused permission to emigrate.)

[9] **Anti-Soviet N.Y. bombings.** A woman employee of Sol Hurok enterprises, an organization which booked Soviet cultural artists for U.S. tours, was killed Jan. 26 and 13 other persons, including Hurok, were injured in an explosion in the group's offices in New York. The blast and fire, police believed, were caused by an incendiary device. The explosion followed by several minutes a similar detonation at Columbia Artists, another talent-booking organization located a few blocks away. The Associated Press and the National Broadcasting Company received anonymous telephone calls shortly after the explosions from a person who declared that the fires had been set to protest the "deaths and imprisonment of Soviet Jews" for which "Soviet culture is responsible." The caller ended his message with the slogan of the militant Jewish Defense League (JDL)—"Never again." A federal grand jury in New York June 19 indicted three members of the JDL (Stuart Cohen, Sheldon Davis and Sheldon Seigel) in connection with the bombings. (In a related action, Acting Attorney General Richard G. Kleindienst announced May 24 that four members of the JDL had been arrested the previous day while assembling bombs to be used in blowing up the residence of the Soviet mission to the United Nations at Glen Cove, N.Y. The four—Mark I. Binsky, David Levine, Robert E. Fine and Ezra S. Gindi—were held without bail on federal and state charges of conspiracy and possessing a bomb.)

[10] **New rules for emigration.** Premier Aleksei N. Kosygin Aug. 3 handed down a decree providing for a new system of exit fees for emigrants. The measure was designed to apply equally to all Soviet citizens, but was expected to fall heaviest on Jews, who made up a large proportion of the educated community and of those seeking to leave the country. The regulations, which reportedly went into effect Aug. 14, required the payment of anywhere from $4,400 to $37,000, depending on the educational level of the applicant. The fees ostensibly were to reimburse the state for free education given the emigrants. The Soviet Union was reported Aug. 23 to be advising American Jews on how to insure that their relatives could emigrate—reportedly by transfering through an American bank the amount of the relatives' exit fees. The emigration tax evoked widespread criticism inside the Soviet Union and abroad. The head of the JDL, Rabbi Meir Kahane, warned Aug. 21 that his organization would kidnap Soviet diplomats and hold them for ransom unless the fees were abandoned within one month. Soviet Deputy Interior Minister Boris T. Shumilin Dec. 29 announced that the government planned to waive the fees for emigrants who were pensioners and to reduce the fees for emigrants who had worked after graduation.

[11]   Within the Soviet Union, an estimated 30 Soviet Jews were arrested Sept. 19 after staging a protest outside the Supreme Soviet building against ratification of the fees by the Supreme Soviet. At least 14 were released Sept. 23 after spending three days in a Moscow prison. Seven others were reported to have been secretly tried and given prison sentences of 15 days. Two others were believed to have been taken to mental hospitals *(see* [2]). In the United States, bipartisan amendments were added to House and Senate bills Oct. 4 denying the Soviet Union most-favored-nation trade benefits or participation in U.S. credit or investment programs while it imposed "more than a nominal tax . . . on any citizen as a consequence" of emigration. Both bills to which the amendments were added were in committee and not expected to reach the full House and Senate until spring of 1973.

See also AFGHANISTAN; ARAB REPUBLIC OF EGYPT; ATOMIC ENERGY [9, 11]; BAHAMAS; BANGLA DESH [1, 10]; BOLIVIA; CHEMICAL & BIOLOGICAL WARFARE; CHESS; CHINA, COMMUNIST; CONSERVATION; CUBA; CZECHOSLOVAKIA; DISARMAMENT; DRUG USE & ADDICTION [12]; ENVIRONMENT; ESPIONAGE; EUROPEAN SECURITY; FOREIGN POLICY; GERMAN CONSULTATIONS; GERMANY, WEST [2, 5-8, 10]; GREECE [5-6]; HIJACKING [7, 17]; HOCKEY; INDOCHINA WAR [15, 20-22]; IRAN; JAPAN [9]; MALTA; MIDDLE EAST [1, 32, 35-36]; NORTH ATLANTIC TREATY ORGANIZATION; OLYMPICS [6, 11]; PAKISTAN [1, 4]; PENTAGON PAPERS; PERU; POLAND; RUMANIA; SINO-SOVIET RELATIONS; SINO-U.S. RELATIONS [2, 7]; SOUTH AFRICA [4]; SOVIET-U.S. RELATIONS; SPACE [4, 7, 17, 20-22]; SPAIN; TRACK & FIELD; UNITED NATIONS

UNITED ARAB KINGDOM—*See* MIDDLE EAST [17]
UNITED AUTOMOBILE WORKERS OF AMERICA (UAW)—*See* LABOR
UNITED FARM WORKERS ORGANIZING COMMITTEE (UFWOC)—*See* LABOR
UNITED MINE WORKERS (UMW)—*See* MINES

UNITED NATIONS (U.N.)—**132 members.** At the beginning of 1972, the 132 members of the U.N. were:

Afghanistan	Chad	Ghana	Lesotho
Albania	Chile	Greece	Liberia
Algeria	China	Guatemala	Libya
Argentina	Colombia	Guinea	Luxembourg
Australia	Congo Republic	Guyana	Madagascar
Austria	Costa Rica	Haiti	Malawi
Bahrain	Cuba	Honduras	Malaysia
Barbados	Cyprus	Hungary	Maldive Islands
Belgium	Czechoslovakia	Iceland	Mali
Bhutan		India	Malta
Bolivia	Dahomey	Indonesia	Mauritania
Botswana	Denmark	Iran	Mauritius
Brazil	Dominican	Iraq	Mexico
Britain	Republic	Ireland	Mongolia
Bulgaria	Ecuador	Israel	Morocco
Burma	Egypt	Italy	Nepal
Burundi	El Salvador	Ivory Coast	Netherlands
Byelorussia	Equatorial	Jamaica	New Zealand
Cambodia	Guinea	Japan	Nicaragua
Cameroon	Ethiopia	Jordan	Niger
Canada	Fiji		Nigeria
Central African	Finland	Kenya	Norway
Republic	France	Kuwait	Oman
Ceylon	Gabon	Laos	Pakistan
	Gambia	Lebanon	Panama

Paraguay	Sierra Leone	Syria	Union of Arab
Peru	Singapore	Tanzania	Emirates
Philippines	Somalia	Thailand	United States
Poland	South Africa	Togo	Upper Volta
Portugal	Southern Yemen	Trinidad and	Uruguay
Qatar	Soviet Union	Tobago	Venezuela
Rumania	Spain	Tunisia	Yemen
Rwanda	Sudan	Turkey	Yugoslavia
Saudi Arabia	Swaziland	Uganda	Zaire
Senegal	Sweden	Ukraine	Zambia

Councils. Below is the membership of the U.N. Security Council, Economic and Social Council and Trusteeship Council as of Jan. 1. (Terms expire Dec. 31 of the year indicated.) *Security Council:* five permanent members—U.S., Britain, France, U.S.S.R. and China; 10 non-permanent members—Argentina (1972), Belgium (1972), Guinea (1973), India (1973), Italy (1972), Japan (1972), Panama (1973), Somalia (1972), Sudan (1973) and Yugoslavia (1973). *Economic and Social Council:* 27 non-permanent members—Bolivia (1974), Brazil (1972), Britain (1974), Burundi (1974), Ceylon (1972), Chile (1974), China (1974), Finland (1974), France (1972), Ghana (1972), Greece (1972), Haiti (1973), Hungary (1973), Italy (1972), Japan (1974), Kenya (1972), Lebanon (1973), Madagascar (1973), Malaysia (1973), New Zealand (1973), Niger (1973), Peru (1972), Poland (1974), Tunisia (1972), U.S.S.R. (1974), U.S. (1973) and Zaire (1973). *Trusteeship Council:* four permanent members—Britain, China, France and the U.S.S.R.; trust administering states—Australia and the U.S.

World Court. Membership of the International Court of Justice at The Hague (nine-year terms expire Feb. 5 of the year indicated): Cesar Bengzon, Philippines (1976); Federico de Castro, Spain (1979); Hardy Cross Dillard, U.S. (1979); Sir Gerald Fitzmaurice, Britain (1973); Isaac Forster, Senegal (1973); Andres Gros, France (1973); Louis Ignacio-Pinto, Dahomey (1979); Eduardo Jimenez de Arechaga, Uruguay (1979); Manfred Lachs, Poland (1976); Platon D. Morozov, U.S.S.R. (1979); Luis Padilla Nervo, Mexico (1973); Charles D. Onyeama, Nigeria (1976); Sture Petran, Sweden (1976). President: Muhammas Zafrullah Khan, Pakistan (1973). Vice President: Fouad Ammoun, Lebanon (1976).

Waldheim backs correspondents' ouster. Secretary General Kurt Waldheim Jan. 6 declined to reinstate the two Nationalist Chinese correspondents (Chen-chi Lin and Teh-cheh Tang) whose accreditation was withdrawn Dec. 17, 1971 in response to pressure from the People's Republic of China (Communist China). Goverdhan Lal Obhrai of India, the head of the U.N. press division, resigned June 21, effective Sept. 1, in a dispute with Waldheim over the expulsion of the two Nationalist correspondents. Obhrai maintained the explusion of Taiwan's diplomats "was not intended, and should never be permitted to mean, the expulsion of Chiang Kai-shek's journalists." In other China developments, the U.N. World Health Organization (WHO) general assembly voted May 10 to expel Nationalist China and admit the People's Republic of China. U.N. Development Program (UNDP) Administrator Rudolph A. Peterson announced March 17 that the U.N. would end its technical assistance to Taiwan within three months and recall the last of 26 experts working there. The action was taken in accordance with the U.N. General Assembly's 1971 vote to expel Taiwan as the representative of China and in response to "the expressed desire of the People's Republic of China that [the UNDP] terminate assistance to the 'province' of Taiwan." According to a report July 30, the U.N. had agreed, at the insistence of the People's Republic, to avoid any mention of Taiwan in its publications and documents. The decision meant that, as far as the U.N.'s widely quoted statistical reports were concerned, Nationalist China had ceased to exist as an entity.

Waldheim issues economy measures. Secretary General Waldheim Jan. 12 issued a memorandum outlining an economy campaign aimed at saving $6 million for the financially troubled U.N. The report indicated that the chief economies would be in salary expenditures, which accounted for 75% of the $213 million 1972 U.N. budget. Although there were no plans for discharging present staff members, posts becoming vacant might not be refilled automatically. Other proposed measures included a reduction in overtime, except in times of emergency, and tighter control over requests for additional or temporary staff during peak periods such as the 13-week General Assembly session each fall. A 15% reduction in documentation, which cost the U.N. $29 million in 1970, was also being sought, as well as decreases in rent and maintenance costs. The U.N.'s financial condition was aggravated by persistent rumors during 1972 that the U.S. would seek to reduce its assessed share of the organization's budget from 31.5% to 25%. The U.S. House of Representatives voted May 18 to reduce the U.S.'s 1973 contribution to the U.N. by 25%, while the Senate voted the full U.N. funding for 1973 but specified that the U.S. share of U.N. payments must be reduced to 25% of the U.N. budget beginning in 1974. U.S. Ambassador to the U.N. George Bush Oct. 4 said that a U.S. reduction would not be made unilaterally and would not take effect until 1974. He repeated U.S. contentions that a reduction in its assessment would make the U.N. less dependent on one power and stressed that reduction efforts were "not a response or retaliation for any U.N. issue that we don't like." The U.S. won its reduction Dec. 13 when the General Assembly voted 81-27 (22 abstentions) to reduce the U.S. share of the budget to 25%. In a related action, China said Oct. 9 that it was willing to raise its U.N. budget assessment from 4% to 7% in the following five years, but listed a number of budget items it would not pay for. (The items included certain expenses for maintaining a U.N. presence in Korea, U.N. offices dealing with refugees from Tibet and Mainland China, and the U.N. bond issue that paid for peacekeeping in the Middle East and the Congo. China also said it would not be responsible for the unpaid balance of Nationalist China's assessment before Taiwan's delegates were expelled.)

China veto bars Bangla Desh. China cast its first veto in the Security Council Aug. 25 to bar Bangla Desh from membership in the U.N. (Bangla Desh had formally applied for membership Aug. 8.) Eleven of the council's members, including the U.S., voted in favor of membership, and three abstained. The Chinese veto followed a bitter attack on the Soviet Union and

India by Ambassador Huang Hua. In voting against admission, China charged that Bangla Desh had violated two U.N. resolutions—one calling for the return of all prisoners taken in the December 1971 Indo-Pakistani war, and another demanding the removal of all foreign troops from Bangla Desh. About 90,000 Pakistani prisoners reportedly remained in Indian hands, but India claimed all of its troops were out of Bangla Desh. China maintained that Indian troops were still there, and called for a report by the secretary general on the matter. Before the final vote, China introduced a resolution that consideration of the Bangla Desh application be delayed until all prisoners of war were repatriated and all foreign soldiers taken out of Bangla Desh. Three nations voted for the measure, three voted against and nine abstained. However, despite Chinese opposition, the General Assembly Sept. 23 approved a measure providing for debate on admission of Bangla Desh. The item favoring debate had such side support among delegations that neither China nor Pakistan called for a formal vote on the matter, but Huang did take the floor to attack the Soviet Union for its alleged role in the Indo-Pakistani war. The assembly Nov. 29 adopted a compromise urging U.N. membership for Bangla Desh and calling for the release of Pakistani prisoners captured there.

General Assembly opens. The 27th annual session of the U.N. General Assembly convened in New York Sept. 19 amid tight security measures *(See* MIDDLE EAST [25]) and heard its new President, Stanislaw Trepczynski of Poland, deliver an unexpectedly harsh attack on the Vietnam war. Trepczynski discussed a wide range of world issues, but made only passing reference to the current wave of terrorism. Trepczynski, Poland's deputy foreign minister, had been unanimously elected to the presidency earlier Sept. 19, replacing Adam Malik of Indonesia. A career Communist party official, he was virtually unknown in the diplomatic world. He was only the second Communist to serve as president of the assembly, following Rumanian Foreign Minister Corneliu Manescu in 1967. The Assembly session ended Dec. 19. Its accomplishments, including a weak resolution on terrorism (establishing a committee which would hear reports of terrorism and report its findings to the assembly in 1973), were said to be few and tenuous.

East Germany joins UNESCO. In a move which ended years of efforts to keep East Germany out of U.N. agencies, the U.N. Educational, Scientific and Cultural Organization (UNESCO) voted in general conference Nov. 21 to approve East Germany's application for membership. (UNESCO's executive board Nov. 20 unanimously had approved West Germany's application for membership.) East Germany's admission to UNESCO qualified it for permanent observer status in the U.N. Secretary General Waldheim Nov. 24 granted such status to East Germany. The status, held by West Germany since 1953, was regarded as a step toward full U.N. membership.

See also ABORTION; AUSTRALIA [11]; BANGLA DESH [8]; BURUNDI; CHEMICAL & BIOLOGICAL WARFARE; CHINA, COMMUNIST; CONSERVATION; CYPRUS; DISARMAMENT; DRUG USE & ADDICTION [12]; ENVIRONMENT; ESPIONAGE; FOREIGN POLICY; GABON; GERMAN CONSULTATIONS; HIJACKING [1, 15-17]; INTERNATIONAL MONETARY DEVELOPMENTS [5]; INDOCHINA WAR [23]; IRAN; KOREAN RELATIONS; MICRONESIA; MIDDLE EAST [3, 18, 28, 30]; POLITICS [8, 15]; RHODESIA; SOUTH AFRICA [7, 9-10]; SOVIET-U.S. RELATIONS [6, 12]; UGANDA [10, 12]

UNITED REPUBLIC OF CAMEROON—*See* CAMEROON
UNITED SERVICE ORGANIZATION (USO)—*See* MILITARY [3]
UNITED STEELWORKERS OF AMERICA—*See* MINES
UNIVERSAL PARTY—*See* ELECTIONS [37]
UPPER VOLTA—*See* AFRICA
URBAN PROBLEMS—*See* HOUSING; NIXON, RICHARD MILHOUS; POPULATION; STATE & LOCAL GOVERNMENTS
URBAN RENEWAL—*See* HOUSING; STATE & LOCAL GOVERNMENTS

URUGUAY—The newly elected government of Uruguay *(see* [2-3]) declared a month-long "state of internal war" during April to help authorities combat the leftist Tupamaro guerrillas *(see* [5]). The state of war was extended during May and June; part of the legislation was lifted in July with the publication of a new national security law, but the remainder was again extended during September and November *(See* [6]).

[2] **Bordaberry named president.** The longest and most controversial vote recount in Uruguay's history ended Feb. 15 when the Electoral Court proclaimed Juan Maria Bordaberry president-elect of Uruguay. Bordaberry resigned as agriculture minister Feb. 2 and assumed the presidency March 1. Jorge Sapelli, Bordaberry's running mate on the Colorado ticket, was sworn in as vice president at the same time. Also taking office March 1 was a new minority Cabinet composed mostly of members of the Colorado party. The National (Blanco) party reportedly had refused to participate in the government. The new Cabinet: foreign affairs—Jose A. Mora Otero; interior—Alejandro Rovira; national defense—Gen. Enrique O. Magnani; economy and finance—Francisco Forteza; public health—Pablo Purriel; cattle and agriculture—Benito Medero; industry and commerce—Jorge Echevarria Leunda; public works—Walter Pintos Risso; labor and social security—Julio Amorin Larranaga; education and culture—Julio Maria Sanguinetti; transport, communications and tourism—Carlos Raul Ribeiro; planning and budget director (with rank of minister without portfolio)—Ricardo Serbino. (*See also* [8-9, 11-12].)

[3] *Election background.* Blanco partisans had raised accusations of government poll-rigging immediately after the Nov. 28, 1971 election. The charges against the government grew after the discovery early in January of extensive double voting for Bordaberry. Because former President Jorge Pacheco Areco was constitutionally barred from succeeding himself, the voting envelopes given voters by the Pacheco-Bordaberry faction of the Colorado party were to contain two lists of candidates: one headed by Pacheco and accompanied by a constitutional amendment which, if passed, would make Pacheco eligible; and another headed by Bordaberry, which would be valid if the amendment failed. Knowing that the amendment would not pass, however, Colorados in Montevideo handed out many envelopes containing two Bordaberry lists. In the original vote count after the election, tellers did not notice that many of the envelopes contained illegal double votes for Bordaberry. The electoral court, in its recount, said it could do nothing about the double voting, since there was no way of knowing which ballots were illegal. The ballot controversy led to demonstrations by Blanco students in Montevideo. Police reportedly dispersed demonstrators with tear gas Jan. 25, and other students were beaten Jan. 29 as police scattered demonstrators with tear gas and fire hoses. The controversy came to a head Feb. 4 and 6 with the discovery in factories in the town of Pando of sacks allegedly containing thousands of Blanco voting lists.

[4] **State of siege regulations repealed.** A joint session of Congress voted 67-1 March 10 to lift most of the curbs on civil liberties imposed by Pacheco in June 1969. The repeal measure was introduced by the Blancos and supported by the leftist Broad Front. The lone dissenting vote was cast by Vice President Sapelli, the only member of the Colorado party to attend the session. Restrictions on union rights, freedom of the press and the right of public assembly were lifted, but a ban on news of guerrilla activities remained in effect, as did other state of siege regulations which were consigned to study by a 15-member inter-party commission. Shortly after the vote, Congress received a bill from President Bordaberry replacing the restrictions. The bill would empower the executive branch to declare parts of Uruguay military zones, mobilize citizens to the nation's defense and impose new controls on the press.

[5] **State of war declared.** Congress April 15 declared a month-long "state of internal war" to help authorities combat leftist Tupamaro guerrillas. The

government had requested the state of war powers after Tupamaros April 14 ambushed and killed four officials of the country's anti-guerrilla campaign (police subcommissioner Oscar Delega, patrolman Alberto Leites, navy Capt. Ernest Motto Benvenutto and former Interior Undersecretary Armando Acosta y Lara). The powers were granted after 20 hours of heated congressional debate. (Opponents of the measure claimed it was unconstitutional and noted that it had not been used since 1904. They were assured that the powers would be used only in the search for violent subversives.) The measure suspended individual liberties and placed the country under martial law. The government was empowered to censor the press, declare curfews, search houses, detain or arrest persons and confiscate material at any time without judicial approval. Persons arrested would be tried in military courts and would not have the right to defense counsel. Some 35,000 members of the police, army, navy and air force began an intensive search for Tupamaros April 15, searching homes and businesses, stopping automobiles and demanding identification documents. Alleged right-wing terrorists April 16 set off explosives at three district offices of the Communist party, at the homes of three leftist politicians and the editor of a leftist magazine and at Montevideo's Evangelical Methodist Church (which had been used in one of the April 14 ambushes). In accord with the powers granted it April 15, the government April 17 prohibited newspapers, television and radio, under threat of military prosecution, from: revealing any information about military or police operations not given to them by authorities; contributing in any way to dissemination of information about subversive activities or of documents or statements issued by or related to subversive organizations; and reporting or making criticism of police and military activities against subversive elements.

[6] *War period extended.* Congress voted May 15 to extend the state of internal war for another 45 days. (Bordaberry had requested an indefinite extension.) Congress approved the extension 68-56 after an often bitter 45-hour debate in which opposition deputies accused the armed forces of wielding too much power without sufficient direction and called for the resignation of Defense Minister Magnani. Congress voted again June 30 to extend the state of internal war for another 90 days. The extension was passed 96-12 after more than 15 hours of debate. However, the part of the legislation placing the country under martial law was lifted July 11 with the publication of a new national security law which placed subversive crimes under military jurisdiction, empowered army courts to hand down sentences of up to 30 years for subversion and provided for jail terms of up to two years for journalists committing "press crimes." The part of the legislation suspending individual liberties was again extended Sept. 28 to Nov. 30. The extension was approved by a 73-52 congressional vote. The government later requested an indefinite extension of the law, but Congress voted 62-59 Nov. 30 to extend the legislation only to Feb. 15, 1973.

[7] **Official hears "death squad" testimony.** Hector Gutierrez Ruiz, president of the Chamber of Deputies, was kidnaped by Tupamaros April 24 and released April 25 after hearing testimony from captured police photographer Nelson Bardesio on the existence in Uruguay of Brazilian-style political "death squads." Gutierrez said April 25 that he had watched his captors interrogate Bardesio, who confessed to membership in an unofficial police squad that killed suspected subversives. Gutierrez said he had talked to Bardesio several times and had the impression he was telling the truth. The Tupamaros had sent letters to congressmen the week before in which Bardesio gave details of some of the death squad murders in which he had participated and asserted that three of the officals killed by the Tupamaros April 14 *(see* [5]*)* belonged to similar execution bands. Bardesio also claimed that the squads were backed by the Interior Ministry and had ties with Brazilian and Argentine security forces.

[8] Blancos join government. The right-wing minority of the Blanco party, led by Martin Recoredo Echegoyen, decided May 12 to join the government, giving President Bordaberry a majority in both houses of Congress. The development followed the collapse of negotiations on a legislative accord between Bordaberry and liberal Blanco leader Sen. Wilson Ferreira Aldunate. The negotiations had collapsed after Bordaberry rejected Ferreira's proposals for a complete change of policy, with far-reaching reforms at home and a nationalist stance abroad, and for fighting the Tupamaros by attacking Uruguay's deep-seated political, economic and social problems. The talks were renewed, but collapsed again in early June when Bordaberry rejected offers by the Broad Front to join the legislative accord. Despite the collapse of the negotiations with the Blanco's liberal wing, however, three members of the party's conservative wing assumed Cabinet posts June 9. The new officials were: Luis Balpardia Blengio, who replaced Echevarria as minister of industry and commerce; Carlos Abdala, replacing Amorin as labor and social security minister; and Jose Manuel Urraburu, who succeeded Ribeiro as transport, communications and tourism minister. (Urraburu was dismissed Dec. 28, after giving television and radio time to a Blanco senator.)

[9] Army colonel assassinated. Col. Artigas Alvarez, chief of civil defense and brother of the commander in chief of the combined military and police forces, was shot to death by Tupamaros in Montevideo July 25. He was the highest-ranking officer killed by the Tupamaros to date. The assassination came amid reports that the Tupamaros were secretly negotiating with members of the armed forces, who were said to be as disillusioned with Uruguay's politicians as were the guerrillas. (The reports of contacts between the guerrillas and the army were thought to have influenced President Bordaberry to dismiss Defense Minister Magnani July 19 and to replace him with Augusto Legnani, Uruguay's representative to the United Nations.) Sen. Zelmar Michelini of the Broad Front Aug. 1 confirmed that there had been a July truce between the Tupamaros and the army, during which guerrilla leaders negotiated with liberal army officers. The truce had ended with the assassination of Alvarez. The Tupamaros reportedly had rejected the army's proposals, which allegedly entailed the surrender of all guerrillas in exchange for lenient treatment at the hands of military judges and a number of social reforms.

[10] School crisis. All secondary schools and Montevideo's Labor University were ordered closed Aug. 12 and 14 after a series of attacks by right-wing terrorists in which one leftist student (Nelson Santiago Rodriguez) was killed when right-wing terrorists fired on a student-teacher meeting at his high school. High school authorities closed their schools and the Labor University went on strike to guarantee maximum attendance at a wake for Rodriguez Aug. 12. A Montevideo paper reported Aug. 13 that persons arrested in connection with Rodriguez's death had been released by authorities and that the shot which killed the student had come from a police vehicle, whose number it printed. (The government Aug. 18 pressed charges against the newspaper.)

[11] Cabinet resigns. The Cabinet resigned in three stages during October. The first resignation came Oct. 20 when Defense Minister Legnani and army commander in chief Gen. Florencio Gravina resigned and were temporarily replaced by Agriculture Minister Medero and Gen. Cesar Augusto Martinez, respectively. The resignations came after senior army commanders refused to obey a court order to release four doctors arrested earlier on suspicion of being Tupamaros and reportedly kept in custody because three of them had testified that they were "tortured savagely" by the military. The resignations were also related to investigation by the military of alleged profiteering, particularly among government officials. Senior officers and President Bordaberry reportedly had agreed in mid-October that the military's findings and the responsibility for further investigation should be turned over to a parliamentary investigative body. However, a group of air force captains, reportedly working on information supplied by Tupamaros, had refused to obey and had been supported in their refusal by superior officers. The second stage of the Cabinet resignations was also related to the military investigation. Economy and Finance Minister Forteza, Education and Culture Minister Sanguinetti and Public Works Minister Pintos resigned Oct. 28 to protest the arrest of Jorge Batlle, leader of a faction of the Colorado party and a major target of the investigation, after a radio broadcast in which Batlle criticized the armed forces. (The army had demanded Batlle's arrest immediately after the broadcast, but Bordaberry had refused until Gen. Martinez resigned in protest. In order to prevent further deterioration of army-government relations, Bordaberry relented. Martinez resumed his post after Batlle's arrest.) The resignation of the three Cabinet members of the Batlle faction was threatening to Bordaberry because his alliance with the faction had given him a majority in Congress. (Batlle was released Nov. 20.) The remainder of the Cabinet resigned Oct. 30 to give Bordaberry more freedom to deal with Uruguay's deepening political and economic crisis.

[12] **New Cabinet sworn in.** President Bordaberry Nov. 1 swore in five new Cabinet ministers. The new ministers were: foreign affairs—Juan Carlos Blanco; economy and finance—Moises Cohen; interior—Walter Ravenna; public works—Lt. Col. Angel Servetti; and defense—Armando Malet. Five other ministers remained at their posts, and Industry and Commerce Minister Balparda was given temporary control of the Education and Culture Ministry. (Jose Maria Robaina was named education and culture minister Nov. 28.) The Cabinet retained the political balance of its predecessor and received assurances of support from the Batlle faction of the Colorado party. The most important of the new Cabinet appointees was said to be Defense Minister Malet, named to stem the rapid increase of military influence in national politics. Malet, an economy minister in two previous governments, said Nov. 1 that he would act only "within the constitution and the law."

[13] **Opposition leader reveals secret documents.** Sen. Ferreira, leader of the majority wing of the Blancos, Nov. 16 revealed secret Foreign and Defense Ministry documents which he said "betrayed national sovereignty in the River Plata." The documents included one dated Feb. 24, in which Rear Adm. Guillermo Fernandez, then commander of the navy, ordered navy units not to interfere with transfer, lightening or fishing operations of Argentine ships in Uruguayan waters in the River Plata. Ferreira assigned the responsibility for the order to Fernandez and to ex-President Pacheco and ex-Foreign Ministers Otero and Federico Garcia Capurro. The government Nov. 17 denied Ferreira's charge and placed any legal action that might be taken against the senator under military jurisdiction. According to a report Dec. 1, military courts were questioning former ministers and even former President Pacheco on how Ferreira obtained the documents. The military reportedly also was considering lifting Ferreira's parliamentary immunity in order to prosecute him for insulting the armed forces and revealing military secrets.

Labor Developments

[14] **CNT strikes.** Only four days after Congress restored most union rights *(see* [4]), 20,000 state and private employees affiliated with the National Labor Confederation (CNT) staged two-hour work stoppages March 14 to demand immediate 40% wage increases, full restoration of civil liberties and rejection of the national security bill *(see* [6]). The CNT staged another general strike in Montevideo March 22 to re-emphasize its demands for higher wages. President Bordaberry March 31 authorized a 20% wage increase for private sector workers and 20%-30% price increases for virtually all essential goods and services. The left-wing press blasted the wage increases April 7, citing official statistics to show that the increase had already been wiped out by Uruguay's severe inflation. In response to the wage increases, the CNT April 5 adopted a "fight plan" against Bordaberry's economic and social policies. As part of the

fight plan, the CNT staged a general strike in Montevideo April 13, a 48-hour general strike in the city April 18 (extended from a planned 14-hour strike after police April 17 killed seven communists as part of the "state of internal war"), a general strike in the city April 25, a general strike May 31-June 1, a partial strike July 17-19 and a general strike July 20. Uruguay was paralyzed Nov. 9 by a general strike called by the CNT to demand solutions to labor problems and to protest the government's repressive education bill *(see* [17]). Montevideo was paralyzed Dec. 14 by another general strike called by the CNT to protest the education bill and the government's policy of "mini-devaluations" of the peso. (The peso was devalued 10 times between Bordaberry's election and the end of 1972.)

[15]   **Wage hikes pledged.** President Bordaberry Sept. 15 promised across-the-board wage increases, to take effect Oct. 1. Bordaberry's decision was reportedly influenced by rumors that the military would refuse to break up strikes by force. (Military officers were said to feel that workers' demands for higher wages were justified and to fear that actions against the strikers would commit them to the government's hard-line economic and social policies.) The government announced Sept. 29 that the wage increases would amount to 20%, but would be accompanied by 10%-25% price increases for food and clothing.

[16]   **Other strike developments.** The army took control of the state-owned railroads March 24 after workers refused to collect tickets in a protest against the railroad administration, which had refused to grant them wage increases. Nearly all Montevideo unions held short strikes April 29 to observe the death of Communist laborer Hector Cervelli, who died from wounds suffered in the police attack April 17 which killed seven other Communists (*see*[14]). Doctors and medical students belonging to the Uruguayan Medical Union May 9 staged a 24-hour work stoppage for better facilities, higher salaries and travel expenses. Teachers at Montevideo's secondary and trade schools June 26 began a 72-hour strike to protest the shooting of a teacher and a student during a demonstration outside the Economy and Finance Ministry June 23. Doctors in clinics, sanatoria and mutual help associations struck Aug. 2-3 to demand the release of several physicians arrested for alleged subversive activities. Some 9,000 owners of small shops, snack bars and restaurants struck Aug. 9 to protest a ban on beef imposed by the government in July. International flights of the state airline Pluna were suspended Aug. 12 when the workers struck to demand back pay. All educational institutions in Montevideo were closed Aug. 23 by a strike protesting low budgetary allocations for education and expressing solidarity with the strike at the Labor University *(see* [10]), which continued to protest right-wing attacks. Nearly all elementary schools were closed Aug. 30-31 as teachers struck to protest government policies.

[17]   Bar and cafe owners in Montevideo struck Sept. 2-3 to demand price increases from the government. Railroad workers struck Sept. 3, and railroad and urban and long-distance transport workers struck Sept. 8 to demand wage increases. About 10,000 workers in health services, state clinics and private hospitals struck Sept. 19-20. An estimated 100,000 government employees refused to work Sept. 21. More than 15,000 doctors, nurses and workers in private clinics and sanatoria struck in Montevideo Oct. 17 to demand higher wages and benefits. Public employees struck Oct. 25 and 31 to demand wage raises. Workers in the wool and meat industries Oct. 25 held one-day strikes, and small businessmen called a 24-hour stoppage Oct. 26 to protest the scarcity of goods and to demand "just prices." More than 6,000 state primary teachers in Montevideo and the neighboring department of Canelones struck Oct. 25-26 and launched an indefinite strike Oct. 30 to protest a government bill designed to reorganize and depoliticize Uruguay's schools. Montevideo physicians Oct. 24 began a seven-day strike to demand release of the four doctors arrested as Tupamaros *(see* [11]). (Four thousand doctors across the nation had struck Oct. 18-21 for the same reason.) The Montevideo physicians Nov. 1-2 extended their strike, but returned to work Nov. 3. They struck again Nov. 22-23, demanding

higher fees in public health facilities and the release of the four arrested doctors. (Two of the doctors were released Nov. 30.) Telecommunications workers struck Dec. 8-9 in a demand for increased benefits. Government bank workers struck across the country Dec. 7, following a stoppage by private bank workers Dec. 6. Postal employees struck Dec. 6-7.

See also BOLIVIA; DRUG USE & ADDICTION [16]

VACCINATION—*See* CONSUMER AFFAIRS [12]; HEALTH
VALUE-ADDED TAX (VAT)—*See* EUROPEAN ECONOMIC COMMUNITY [6, 14]; GREAT BRITAIN [2]; SWEDEN; TAXES
VATICAN—*See* ROMAN CATHOLIC CHURCH
VENERA 8—*See* SPACE [7]
VENEREAL DISEASE—*See* HEALTH

VENEZUELA—Student unrest. All secondary schools in Caracas were closed Jan. 25 after clashes between students and police resulted in more than 20 injuries and 100 arrests. The causes of the riots were not clearly known, but the outbreak apparently was related to the calling of student elections at the Central University of Venezuela in Caracas. Further street disturbances erupted Feb. 9 as students from Caracas high schools, reportedly protesting the alleged fatal shooting of a fellow student by police Feb. 8, raised barricades and threw rocks at cars and shop windows. Students protesting official repression, arrests of students and the killing of three youths by metropolitan police themselves clashed with police April 13 for seven hours. The clash, which organizers of the student demonstration said resulted when authorities tried violently to break up a peaceful rally, resulted in 15 injuries and dozens of arrests. A student was killed, reportedly by police, in clashes April 14 at the Central University. The death set off a wave of disturbances April 18-25 in Caracas, Barcelona, Cumana, Barinas, Merida, Maracaibo and Porlamar. The protests resulted in the death of two persons, the injuring of dozens and the arrest of more than 500. They included rock-throwing, sacking, arson and sniping incidents by students and "non-student agitators." In response to the unrest, Education Minister Enrique Perez Olivares suspended classes at all intermediate schools in Caracas and the central coastal region April 20-May 2.

Further student unrest erupted during May and June. A 12-year-old boy was killed and dozens injured May 23-June 2 as students rioted in Caracas and other cities to protest the return to Venezuela of two former presidents—Romulo Betancourt and Gen. Marcos Perez Jimenez—both of whom were expected to run in the 1973 presidential elections *(see below)*. Student riots again erupted June 5-6 as students protested the death of a medical student in the May clashes. The student, Marvin Marin Sanchez, reportedly had been hit in the head by a tear gas cannister fired at close range by a Caracas policeman. The disclosure of Marin's death June 5 provoked violent student demonstrations in Caracas and forced the suspension of classes at the Central University. The unrest grew June 6 after Marin's burial, which was attended by thousands of students, as well as by university and government officials. Clashes between police and students also occurred June 6 in Maturin, Merida, Barinas, Coro, Valencia, Barquisimeto, Barcelona, San Juan de los Morros, Porlamar and Puerto la Cruz. Further violence was reported in Caracas June 16 when high school students invaded the University City to protest the fatal shooting of a student by metropolitan police. Clashes between police and university and high school students in Caracas and other cities were again reported in November and December. They generally grew out of student demonstrations in support of political prisoners, who were on a hunger strike to urge the government to proceed with their trials.

U.S. envoy recalled. It was reported March 2 that U.S. Ambassador Robert McClintock had been summoned to Washington. Although a State Department spokesman claimed the trip had been scheduled for several months, it came amid strong criticism of the ambassador among members of the ruling COPEI party. McClintock reportedly had been summoned by the Venezuelan Foreign Ministry to explain a remark Feb. 22 that Venezuelan ministers had "fabricated myths" about the U.S. McClintock allegedly claimed he had made the remark because Americans in Venezuela were disturbed about the burning of a U.S. flag at a COPEI rally two weeks before. President Rafael Caldera had subsequently told the ambassador that the person responsible for the incident did not belong to COPEI.

Cabinet changes. President Caldera April 14 swore in five new Cabinet officials and a new governor of the Federal District. Nectario Andrade Labarca replaced Lorenzo Fernandez as interior minister; Luis Enrique Oberto became finance minister; Miguel Rodriguez Viso became agriculture and livestock minister; Alberto Martini Urdaneta was named labor minister; Rodolfo Jose Cardenas assumed leadership of the new Youth, Science and Culture Ministry; and Guillermo Alvarez Bajares became governor of the Federal District.

Ex-presidents return. Two former presidents—Betancourt and Perez Jimenez—returned to Venezuela during late May amid rumors that both would seek the presidency in 1973 elections. Betancourt, who had ruled the country in 1958-63, arrived in Venezuela May 23 from Switzerland after an eight-year self-imposed exile. Betancourt July 20 told officials of his Democratic Action party (AD) that he would not run in any future elections. He gave no specific reason for his decision, but observers cited his age (64) and the violent protests which had greeted his return to Venezuela *(see above)*. Perez Jimenez, whose military regime ruled Venezuela in 1948-58, arrived in Venezuela May 24, but returned to his home in Spain June 1 after being forced to testify in a federal court on the 1954 murder of an army lieutenant. (Lt. Leon Droz Blanco had claimed, shortly before his death, that the dictator had ordered his execution.) A Caracas criminal court judge Sept. 5 ordered Perez Jimenez's arrest in connection with the murder and announced that he would seek the ex-dictator's extradition from Spain. Perez Jimenez's candidacy for the Venezuelan presidency, announced in May, had aroused strong opposition from the COPEI, UD and the Republican Democratic Union (URD). All three parties had proposed separate constitutional amendments to bar the ex-president's candidacy. Congress Nov. 10 passed a constitutional amendment barring from the offices of president, senator, congressman and supreme court justice anyone sentenced by a court to more than three years in prison for crimes committed during a term of office. (Perez Jimenez had been sentenced in 1968 to four years in prison for embezzling state funds during his presidency.) The amendment had to go to the 20 state assemblies for approval, but its passage there was assured by the presence of anti-Perez Jimenez majorities in the assemblies.

Six killed in kidnap case. Police killed two suspected terrorists June 2 and another four June 4 as they searched unsuccessfully for Carlos Dominguez

Chavez, a wealthy industrialist kidnaped June 2 by professed members of the left-wing Zero Point guerrilla organization. (The two armed men killed June 2 were shot outside Dominguez's home when a policeman recognized one of them as a guerrilla. The four others were killed when police opened fire on a house where they believed Dominguez was being held.) President Caldera called off the manhunt June 4 after an appeal from Dominguez to stay out of the case. The industrialist was released June 15 after his family paid a record $1.1 million ransom.

See also ARMAMENTS, INTERNATIONAL; DRUG USE & ADDICTION [20]; LATIN AMERICA; OIL & NATURAL GAS

VENUS—See SPACE [7]

VIET CONG—See INDOCHINA WAR   [5-6, 17, 20, 41-44, 46-47, 49-50, 53]; SINO-U.S. RELATIONS [5, 7]

VIETNAM, NORTH (PEOPLE'S REPUBLIC OF VIETNAM)—India widens ties.

Indian and North Vietnam Jan. 7 expanded diplomatic relations by upgrading their respective consulates in New Delhi and Hanoi to embassies. New Delhi said the purpose of the action was "to strengthen further friendly relations" between India and North Vietnam. The U.S. and South Vietnam rebuked the Indian action and challenged Indian membership on the three-nation International Control Commission (ICC), which had been established by the 1954 Geneva conference on Indochina to supervise the cease-fire and partition agreements. The commission, made up of India, Poland and Canada, had been largely dormant since fighting began again in Vietnam in 1959. The U.S. State Department said that India, by strengthening its relations with North Vietnam, was endangering its status as the neutral member of the commission. Saigon retaliated against India Jan. 8 by barring the newly appointed ICC chairman, Indian L. N. Ray, from entering South Vietnam. According to South Vietnam, the Indian action, without a corresponding action to raise the level of diplomatic relations with the South from the consulate-general level, showed a partiality which could destroy the ICC. In a further retaliation against India, South Vietnam Sept. 29 expelled the entire Indian delegation to the ICC. The Indian and Polish members of the ICC then announced that the commission would shift its headquarters from Saigon to Hanoi.

See also DRAFT & WAR PROTEST; ELECTIONS [32]; GERMANY, WEST [3]; HIJACKING [3, 7]; INDOCHINA WAR [1, 5-6, 8-10, 13-35, 39-46, 48-54]; KOREA, SOUTH; MILITARY [7-8]; PENTAGON PAPERS; SINO-U.S. RELATIONS [2, 7]; SOVIET-U.S. RELATIONS [6, 11]

VIETNAM, SOUTH (REPUBLIC OF VIETNAM)—Defense aides, minister ousted.

Five top aides of Defense Minister Lt. Gen. Nguyen Van Vy were ousted by President Nguyen Van Thieu March 22, following a scandal involving possible misuse of a soldiers' retirement fund. Vy offered to resign after learning that his aides had been dismissed. Thieu Aug. 6 signed a decree retiring Vy and barring him from traveling abroad until a government investigation of the case was completed. (Vy was replaced as defense minister by Premier Tran Thien Khiem, who also served as interior minister.) The August decree also dismissed seven colonels and three civilians from the Defense Ministry and refused them permission to leave South Vietnam. No specific charges were filed against the officials, pending investigation. Soldiers had complained that they had not benefitted from the Mutual Aid and Savings Fund for Soldiers, administered by the Defense Ministry, although some money had been distributed to orphans, widows and the severely disabled.

Rule by decree. President Thieu May 9 pleaded for emergency powers that would enable him to rule by decree for six months to cope with the crisis created by the Communists' offensive in the Vietnamese war (see INDOCHINA WAR [14-19]). The president did not formally ask the National Assembly to grant him the special powers, but implied that he was putting the deputies on notice that he was leaving it up to them to approve his request. The House of

Representatives, by an 81-49 vote, May 14 approved Thieu's plea; but the Senate June 2, by a 27-21 vote, rejected the request. The measure was slightly rewritten and again passed the House. It was finally approved by the Senate June 27 by a 26-0 vote. The final Senate vote was held after Saigon's 10 p.m. curfew *(see below)*, when no opposition senators were present. The 26 opponents of the bill had walked out in protest against the invocation of a rule permitting five members to start a session. Opposition members argued that the invocation of the rule required the approval of the Senate chairman. Until the rule had been invoked, debate on Thieu's request had been delayed by the absence of five of the 57 senators. The measure was finally passed in the Senate by less than a quorum. It was signed by Thieu later June 27. (The Senate Sept. 23 passed a non-binding resolution asserting that Thieu had no authority to rule by decree.)

Martial law declared. President Thieu declared martial law throughout South Vietnam May 11 in another move to cope with problems caused by the Communists' offensive. It was the first time since the 1968 Communist Tet offensive that martial law had been imposed. A Cabinet decree announced May 11, implementing the martial law declaration, contained a series of measures affecting military mobilization and further restricted civil rights. Draft deferments were curbed, the draft age was lowered to 17 from 19, an estimated 45,000 draftees excused from military service were to be recalled and some militiamen were ordered transferred to the regular army. (All of Vietnam's colleges and universities were closed May 17 to allow for the conscription of students. Thieu July 8 rescinded the order lowering the draft age.) On civil matters, the Cabinet decree banned strikes and political demonstrations, required central and local authorities to control the distribution of essential goods, restricted travel to foreign countries and instituted a 10 p.m.-5 a.m. curfew. In a later development, President Thieu July 15 signed into law a martial-law decree providing jail terms for strikers, curfew violators, employers who fired workers during the state of war and persons who circulated news of pictures "detrimental to the national security" *(see also, below).* The edict also permitted police to shoot to kill motorists, looters, arsonists or saboteurs who attempted to flee.

Press curbed. In what newsmen and diplomatic observers regarded as a move to stifle criticism of the Saigon regime, President Thieu Aug. 5 announced a decree restricting South Vietnam's newspapers. Under the decree, every daily newspaper was required to deposit about $47,000 with the government treasury within 30 days as a guarantee to cover possible fines and court charges resulting from violations of the already strict press rules. The decree also provided for government shutdown of any newspaper, pending a court decision, if its daily issue were confiscated a second time for publishing "articles detrimental to the national security and public order." Two Saigon dailies immediately ceased publication rather than pay the required deposit. About one third of Saigon's 43 newspapers stopped publishing for one day Aug. 22 to protest the press law. The deadline for paying the deposit was extended to Sept. 15, but 14 newspapers and 15 periodicals ceased publication that day when they failed to meet the deadline. None of the publications which closed were pro-government. Only two opposition papers in Saigon paid their deposits and continued publishing.

Torture of opponents reported. An American newspaper Aug. 12 reported widespread torture of political prisoners rounded up in South Vietnam as suspected Communist sympathizers since the start of the Communist offensive. The report, which was denied by the South Vietnamese Interior Ministry Aug. 14, was based on smuggled interviews and documents purportedly written by inmates and prison guards. According to the report, more than 10,000 persons had been imprisoned, with the arrests still continuing. Many of the prisoners were being taken to Con Son jail, reportedly transported there in planes of Air America, the airline operated for the U.S. Central Intelligence Agency (CIA).

Hamlet elections abolished. The government Aug. 22 issued a decree abolishing popular democratic elections in the country's 10,775 hamlets and superseding a 1966 law establishing the election of hamlet and village officers. The new statute ordered the 44 province chiefs—military men appointed by President Thieu—to reorganize local governments and appoint all hamlet officials. (Thieu had earlier issued instructions to the province chiefs that they could replace elected village and hamlet officials at their discretion.) The decree was coupled with the issuance to the province chiefs of "general guidelines for the explanation and implementation" of the decree. The guidelines told province chiefs "to screen the ranks of village and hamlet officials including hamlet chiefs" and to dismiss those found "unqualified, negative or who had bad behavior." The reason for the decree and instructions reportedly was the discovery during the Communist offensive that many of the hamlet chiefs were Communists and had provided assistance to enemy forces.

Death penalty extended. Under the special powers granted him in June *(see above),* President Thieu Sept. 4 signed a decree ordering the death penalty for persons convicted of hijacking, armed robbery, rape and forcing women into prostitution. Thieu also ordered five years' imprisonment for persons involved in organized gambling.

Thieu curbs political parties. President Thieu Dec. 27 signed a decree which South Vietnamese political leaders claimed would eliminate almost all of the country's 24 political parties except Thieu's own Democracy party, whose formation had been completed in November. Thieu signed the statute on the last day before the expiration of his special decree powers. The new regulations required that every party must, within three months, set up branches in at least a quarter of the villages of half of South Vietnam's 44 provinces and in every city. Each branch must enroll as members at least 5% of the registered voters in each area. A party would be required to win at least 20% of the vote in any national election or be "automatically dissolved."

See also DRUG USE & ADDICTION [2]; ELECTIONS [34]; GERMANY, WEST [3]; HIJACKING [7]; INDOCHINA WAR [1-3, 6, 13-38, 41-54]; MILITARY [3, 6-8]; PENTAGON PAPERS; SINO-U.S. RELATIONS [8]; SOVIET-U.S. RELATIONS [6]; VIETNAM, NORTH; WAR CRIMES

VIETNAM VETERANS AGAINST THE WAR (VVAW)—*See* CIVIL DISORDERS; ELECTIONS [25-26]
VIOLENCE—*See* TELEVISION & RADIO [1-2]
VIRGIN ISLANDS—*See* CONGRESS; POLLUTION [8]
VOLPE, JOHN A.—*See* NIXON, RICHARD MILHOUS
VOLUNTEER ARMY—*See* ELECTIONS [9]; MILITARY [1, 4-5]; SELECTIVE SERVICE SYSTEM

VOTING RIGHTS—Postcard registration plan tabled. The Senate March 15 set aside, by a 46-42 vote, a bill to expand the franchise by allowing voters to register for federal elections by postcard. The bill, which was considered to be killed in the current session, was backed by the Senate Democratic leadership and opposed by a coalition of Republicans and Southern Democrats. Of the 12 senators absent from the voting, eight supported the bill.

1-year residency rule upset. In a 6-1 decision March 21, the Supreme Court struck down as unconstitutional a Tennessee law that set a one-year residency requirement as a prerequisite for voting in state and local elections and a three-month county residency requirement. The court held that bona fide residence was a legitimate voter qualification, but that "30 days appears to be an ample period of time" for states to register new arrivals to vote. The majority decision said that residency requirements burdened the constitutional right of citizens to travel from state to state and that the laws could not be upheld unless they were "necessary to promote a compelling state interest." Chief Justice Warren Burger dissented from the decision, noting that the court had upheld a one-year registration requirement for voting in 1904 and concluding that the 1904 ruling "is as valid today as it was at the turn of the century." The court's decision came in a case brought by James F. Blumstein, a native New Yorker who moved to Nashville, Tenn. in June 1970 and who was not allowed to register to vote in the August and November 1970 elections in that state. (Common Cause, a Washington-based citizens' lobby, estimated March 21 that the decision would enfranchise as many as five million Americans who were not permitted to vote in 1968 because of residency laws. According to Common Cause, only Minnesota had a 30-day residency requirement. Five states had three-month laws, and the rest had residency requirements of six months or a year.)

Youth vote in N.Y. primary cut. The Supreme Court voted 5-4 May 30 to let stand a lower court ruling that would bar 500,000 or more 18-20-year-old New York residents (about 80% of the group) from voting in the state's primary election June 20. At issue was a New York election law designed to prevent members of one party from crossing party lines to vote in another party's primary for a particular candidate. Under that law, a voter could not vote in a primary election unless he was an enrolled member of that party during the previous general election. The new voters had to register before Oct. 2, 1971.

See also LUXEMBOURG

WALDHEIM, KURT—*See* BURUNDI; CYPRUS; DISARMAMENT; INDO-
CHINA WAR [23]; IRAN; SOUTH AFRICA [10]; UNITED NATIONS
WALLACE, GEORGE—*See* CRIME [7-9]; ELECTIONS [4, 6-8, 10, 15-17, 21]
WANKEL ENGINE—*See* AUTOMOBILES

WAR CRIMES—Further Hersch disclosures. Seymour Hersh, the free-lance
journalist who won a Pulitzer Prize for his account of the Mylai massacre,
published four articles, Jan. 18 and 25 and June 3-4, giving more details and
making more charges concerning the 1968 massacre by U.S. Army men of
South Vietnamese in the hamlet of Mylai. Hersh attributed the source of the
information in all four articles to the transcript of the Army's 1969-70 inquiry
into the massacre. In the first article Jan. 8, Hersh said that a secret
investigation conducted by the Army's Criminal Investigation Division at the
request of the Army inquiry board concluded that 347 civilians died at Mylai, a
total Hersh said was "twice as large as has been publicly acknowledged." (It
was widely believed that less than 200 civilians were slain at Mylai; the Army
had consistently refused to say how many civilians had been killed in the
hamlet.) The first article also accused the Army of covering up factual material
about another alleged incident in which, Hersch said, 90 civilians were slain on
the same day as the Mylai attack in a hamlet known as Mykhe 4 (two miles
northwest of Mylai).

Charges Army destroyed papers. In his second article Jan. 25, Hersh
said that members of the Army's American Division destroyed documents about
the Mylai incident to protect officers involved in the attack. (Soldiers of the
11th Infantry Brigade of the American were the ones who swept through
Mylai.) Hersh said that the Army investigation, under Lt. Gen. William R.
Peers, had finished its inquiry "without being able to discover how the Mylai 4
files had disappeared" from the American's records in South Vietnam.

Panel indicts American. In his third article June 3, Hersh made public the
basic findings of the report of the Peers investigation. The article was
accompanied by excerpts from one chapter of the Peers Report. The report
concluded that the entire command structure of the American Division was
guilty of misconduct in connection with the Mylai incident. The report's most
serious finding was that the division's commander, Maj. Gen. Samuel W.
Koster, had committed 27 acts of misconduct or omission in connection with
the initial field investigation of the massacre, and his chief deputy, Brig. Gen.

George H. Young Jr., had committed 16 such acts. The report said there was no direct evidence that the two knew, in full, the details at Mylai. However, it concluded that "they probably thought they were withholding information concerning a much less serious incident than the one which had actually occurred." The report also said that information on the massacre was, "both wittingly and unwittingly," suppressed "at every command level" of the American Division. At the close of its inquiry, the Peers panel made three specific recommendations to then-Army Chief of Staff William C. Westmoreland and Stanley Resor, then Secretary of the Army. The recommendations were: that the officers accused of wrongdoing be required to undergo investigations pursuant to possible courts martial; that combat troops be more carefully advised about the international rules of war; and that the U.S. consider revising the procedures for reporting war crimes through the chain of command in which an officer in that command structure "participated in or sanctioned a war crime."

Second massacre described. In his fourth article June 4, Hersh expanded on the alleged massacre at Mykhe 4. According to the Peers Report, the soldiers involved in the Mykhe 4 massacre March 16, 1968 were attached to the Bravo Company in Task Force Barker. (The Charlie Company in Task Force Barker had been responsible for the Mylai killings.) The report said that Bravo Company infantrymen stormed into the hamlet and began indiscriminately shooting at civilians. The report said that most of the soldiers who took part in the assault on Mykhe 4 "have either refused to testify about the event or disclaimed any recollection of their observations." The Peers panel added: "For this reason, it has not been possible to establish the facts with any degree of certainty." However, the panel said, "both testimony and circumstantial evidence strongly suggest that a large number of noncombatants were killed during the search of the hamlet." Only one member of the Bravo Company, then-Capt. and platoon leader Thomas K. Willingham, had been publicly charged or prosecuted in connection with the Mykhe 4 slayings. Willingham had been accused of the unpremeditated murder of 20 civilians and with suppressing information about the Mylai killings; but both charges had been dropped by the Army in June 1970 because, according to an official statement, "based on available evidence, no further action should be taken in the prosecution of these charges."

U.S. sued for report. Rep. Les Aspin (D, Wis.) April 3 filed a suit in federal district court in Washington to force the Pentagon to release the unpublished Peers Report. Aspin, a member of the House Armed Services Committee, asked the court to order that the report be made public under the Freedom of Information Act. Named as defendants in the suit were Defense Secretary Melvin Laird and Secretary of the Army Robert F. Froehlke.

Army's case nears end. The Army Sept. 2 completed its administrative measures against those involved in the Mylai case, ordering Sgt. Kenneth L. Hodges dismissed from the Army and formally reprimanding Col. Nelson A. Parson and Capt. Dennis H. Johnson. Parson, who had been chief of staff of the American Division, was stripped of his Legion of Merit Decoration and given a letter of censure. Johnson, a division intelligence officer, was given a letter of reprimand, virtually ending any chance for promotion. Johnson, who had served in Charlie Company, Sept. 2 filed a suit in federal district court in Georgia protesting the action against him. (Murder charges against him in connection with Mylai had been dropped by the Army.) The only loose ends remaining in the Army's prosecution of those connected with Mylai were disposition of Hodges' suit and a review of the murder conviction of Lt. William L. Calley Jr., the only soldier to be convicted of a criminal charge in the incident.

Pacification assailed. Kevin Buckley, a correspondent who reported on the war in Vietnam for four years, charged in an article published June 19 that U.S. soldiers had deliberately killed thousands of Vietnamese civilians under the guise of "pacification." Buckley said: "It can, I believe, be documented that thousands of Vietnamese civilians have been killed deliberately by U.S. forces." At one point in his report, Buckley described a 1968 operation codenamed "speedy express," a pacification effort in the Mekong Delta province of Kien Hoa. He said that Americans listed 10,899 "enemy" killed in the operation, but only 748 weapons captured. He concluded that "a staggering number of noncombatant civilians—perhaps as many as 5,000 according to one official— were killed by U.S. firepower to pacify Kien Hoa." Buckley said Vietnamese civilians repeatedly told him that those "enemy" fatalities were, in many instances, unarmed farmers working in rice fields. Buckley said the death toll during the Kien Hoa operation "made the Mylai massacre look trifling by comparison."

More slayings near Mylai alleged. An Oklahoma City newspaper Sept. 27 disclosed that the Army was investigating allegations that another of its infantry units (Company C, 2nd Battalion, 35th Infantry Division) committed war crimes during a search and destroy operation between May 18 and May 23, 1967 in the same area as the Mylai massacre. According to the newspaper, former members of the company were reported to have said that the number of executed civilians and prisoners ranged from 80 to "the hundreds." Army investigators were also said to be looking into charges that villages and crops were burned and dead bodies mutilated. The Army Sept. 27 confirmed the existence of an investigation into allegations against Capt. James W. Lanning, commander of Company C during May 1967, in connection with the alleged atrocities. According to the Army, the report of the internal Army investigation had been completed in August and forwarded to Lanning's commander at Fort Bragg, N.C.

See also AUSTRIA; ELECTIONS [34]; GERMANY, WEST [1]; INDOCHINA WAR [24]; MIDDLE EAST [18]; NETHERLANDS

WARNER, JOHN W.—*See* MILITARY [2]; SOVIET-U.S. RELATIONS [4]
WARSAW PACT—*See* EUROPEAN SECURITY
WATERGATE—*See* ELECTION [2]; POLITICS [1, 9-12]
WATER POLLUTION—*See* CANADA [3]; CONSUMER AFFAIRS [8]; NIXON, RICHARD MILHOUS; POLLUTION [1-3, 9-16]; PUBLIC LAND
WATER POLLUTION CONTROL ACT OF 1972—*See* POLLUTION [15-16]
WEATHER UNDERGROUND—*See* CIVIL DISORDERS
WEINBERGER, CASPAR—*See* NIXON, RICHARD MILHOUS

WELFARE—Food stamp cutback restored. Agriculture Secretary Earl L. Butz Jan. 16 announced that the Nixon Administration had reversed a planned cutback in the food stamp program. Under 1971 legislation calling for a uniform eligibility standard, the Agriculture Department had set $360 as the top monthly income limit for participants in the food stamp program. The change would have allowed an additional 1.7 million persons, mostly in Southern and Western states, into the program while eliminating from it, or reducing benefits to, some 2.1 million persons, mostly in the Northeastern states where the cost of living was higher. The change had drawn protest in 1971 from 28 senators and Jan. 7 from 15 governors and New York City Mayor John V. Lindsay. In his Jan. 16 announcement, Butz said that he had issued new regulations to insure that "the benefits to each household are as high or higher than they were under the old regulations." Butz made it clear that funding for the new program would come from $202 million in funds allocated for food assistance but impounded by the Nixon Administration. (The Administration had requested $2 billion for the food stamp program in fiscal 1972, but Congress had appropriated $2.2 billion.) The Agriculture Department announced June 7 that $400 million of the funds appropriated for the food stamp program would not be spent because of errors in projecting program growth, delays in implementing new rules and delays by states in bringing new counties under the plan. (In a related development, a three-judge federal panel in Washington ruled May 30 that a 1971 law denying food stamps to unrelated persons living in the same household, aimed at "hippie" communes, was unconstitutional. The court held that the "hasty last-minute Congressional action" penalized other recipients unintentionally and that the law violated Supreme Court decisions on privacy and freedom of association.)

Residence laws voided. The Supreme Court Jan. 24, unanimously and without a hearing, upheld lower-court decisions barring one-year welfare residency rules in New York and Connecticut. The court had ruled in 1969 that a welfare residency law was an unconstitutional restriction on free interstate travel and made "invidious distinctions" between poor persons who were long-term residents and those who were not. Such a law could be justified, the court said, only by "compelling governmental interest." The New York and Connecticut laws, passed after that decision, cited budgetary problems as meeting that criterion. However, federal panels in both cases said the 1969 ruling excluded fiscal problems as a justifying factor.

Non-uniform relief aid upheld. With the Nixon appointees to the Supreme Court forming the backbone of the majority opinions, the court May 30 issued two rulings upholding the public assistance program in Texas. In a 6-3 decision, the court ruled that neither the Constitution's equal protection guarantee nor federal welfare laws prohibited states from granting lower benefits to child welfare recipients than to the aged and disabled. The Texas program paid families with dependent children (87% of whom were black or Mexican-American) 75% of their estimated need, while paying aged and disabled recipients (62% and 53%, respectively, of whom were white) 95%-100% of their estimated need. The court also ruled 5-4 that Texas did not violate federal law by making sharper cutbacks in certain assistance programs than in others. The majority opinion rejected the assertion that cutbacks in public assistance to dependent children discriminated against non-whites. (Texas and 18 other states reduced welfare payments by the amount of outside income brought into a family. In other states, the family could keep some of the earned money in addition to its regular welfare payments.)

State work plans OKd. The Department of Health, Education and Welfare (HEW) announced June 6 that it had reapproved experimental welfare reform programs proposed by New York and California and originally approved in 1971. The New York plan included an Incentives for Independence program in sections of three counties that would penalize welfare families that refused work and counseling services and would provide part-time jobs at $1.50 an hour for welfare schoolchildren 15-18 years old. It also included a Public Service Work Opportunities Project to require employable individuals in about one-fourth of the state's caseload of families with dependent children to accept training or community service jobs. A federal court in Washington had delayed implementation of the program in March to give welfare rights groups a chance to comment. The California plan would require about 30,000 welfare recipients in 35 counties to work off their grants in part-time jobs or lose their benefits. Only the handicapped or mothers with children under six years old would be exempt from the work requirement. An earlier California proposal, that would reportedly have covered all the state's welfare recipients, had been dropped due to HEW opposition.

Benefits for strikers upheld. The Supreme Court Oct. 16 affirmed a district court order overturning a Maryland law that denied welfare payments to families of workers on strike. (Six other states had similar laws.) The lower court had held that Maryland could not withhold aid-to-dependent-children assistance to the families of those who were on strike or who had been dismissed for misconduct. The lower court's ruling had held that HEW regulations required all states that furnished aid to unemployed workers' families to furnish it to all such families. However, HEW announced Oct. 16 that it would amend the regulations to make it clear that states could deny assistance to families of workers who were on strike or had been dismissed.

HR 1 cleared. Congress Oct. 17 completed action on HR 1, an omnibus welfare reform-Social Security bill introduced in 1971 at the beginning of the 92nd Congress. President Nixon signed the bill Oct. 30, despite earlier reports that a veto was being considered. HR 1 originally was passed by the House in June 1971. The Senate (after 15 months of consideration by the Senate Finance Committee) had completed action on a differing version Oct. 6, necessitating a House-Senate conference to reconcile the two bills. The conference bill was approved Oct. 17 by a 305-1 House vote and by a 61-0 Senate vote. The final version omitted any minimum family income plan, which had been passed by the House and supported by the Administration. It also omitted a Senate provision for a $400 million test program of the family income plan. (The Administration had opposed the Senate proposal.) The conference bill also dropped: a series of restrictive welfare rule proposals, including a plan to trace deserting fathers of welfare families and a restoration of residency requirements; a Senate provision to pay bonuses to low-income workers; Senate provisions to extend Medicare to cover some drugs for nonhospital payments and glasses, dental and podiatric devices; proposals to reduce the age at which workers or widows could retire at reduced benefit levels; and a Senate prohibition against state reduction of various benefits to those receiving increased Social Security benefits.

The bill included a provision for a federal takeover by 1974 of welfare assistance to the blind, aged and disabled—with a minimum monthly payment of $130 to single persons and $195 to couples, supplemented by up to $20 in Social Security payments, $65 in earnings and any additional supplements paid by states with already higher benefits. The bill also provided for the following new benefits: Medicare coverage for 1.5 million persons receiving disability benefits for at least 24 months; Medicare payments for some chiropractic and kidney dialysis treatments; an increase from $1,680 to $2,100 in the amount an elderly person could earn without losing benefits; and an increase in benefits to widows to 100% of their husband's benefits (from 82.5%). Minimum monthly payments of $170 were approved for low-income beneficiaries who had worked at least 30 years, and lesser increases for those working at least 17 years; a change was made in the method of computing retirement payments, resulting in an increase for most recipients; and an increase in benefit rates (1% a year) was made for workers over 65 who chose to delay receiving payments. The bill also set up doctor "peer review" groups to hold down Medicare and Medicaid inefficiencies. The first year costs of the omnibus bill were expected to be $6.1 billion, financed by an increase in the Social Security tax rate from 5.5% to 5.8%, and an increase in the maximum wage base from $9,000 to $10,800 in 1973 and to $12,000 in 1974.

U.S. threatens welfare cuts. HEW announced Dec. 4 that it would withhold up to $689 million in 1973 welfare payments to states that had failed to institute adequate procedures to eliminate ineligible recipients and overpayments. The department said that it had moved in order to "restore public confidence" in the welfare program. In justifying the decision, the announcement cited a March survey which estimated that 6.8% of families in the Aid to Families with Dependent Children (AFDC) program were ineligible, as were 4.9% of all adult blind, disabled and aged beneficiaries. The survey had also found that some 13.8% of AFDC families were receiving overpayments, as were 9.7% in the other programs. (The survey found underpayments in the cases of 7.6% and 5.6% of recipients, respectively.) In the 21 states that had not investigated the percentage of cases necessary to determine ineligibility rates, funds would be reduced according to the national average, HEW said. A Dec. 13 HEW announcement said that HEW would delay the threatened payment cut from Jan. 1, 1973 to April 1, 1973 in order to give state officials time to adjust to the new policy.

See also ELECTIONS [8, 16-17, 33]; GREAT BRITAIN[6];NIXON,RICHARD MILHOUS; SOCIAL SECURITY; STATE & LOCAL GOVERNMENTS

WEST AFRICAN ECONOMIC COMMUNITY (CEAO)—*See* AFRICA
WESTERN SAMOA—*See* EUROPEAN ECONOMIC COMMUNITY [7]; INTERNATIONAL MONETARY DEVELOPMENTS [8]

WOMEN'S RIGHTS—HEW bias report. Health, Education and Welfare (HEW) Secretary Elliot L. Richardson Jan. 14 issued a report prepared by the department's Woman's Action Program. He pledged to enforce over 100 recommendations for reform of HEW's employment practices and its social programs affecting women, and he ordered top assistants to establish timetables for implementation. Upgrading and counseling services were to be provided for female HEW employees, while part-time jobs and day-care arrangements would be provided for HEW working mothers. The report also recommended legislation to bar sex discrimination in HEW-supported vocational education. (Men currently were given preference in some state-run programs.) It also recommended that the Social Security Administration consider paying benefits to disabled housewives unable to continue homemaking activities. Tax deductions were asked for Social Security contributions by employers of domestics, to discourage nonpayment. The report also urged family planning programs to emphasize development and use of male contraceptives, to share birth control responsibilities between the sexes.

Equal rights amendment clears Congress. The Senate March 22 approved, by an 84-8 vote, the Equal Rights Amendment to the Constitution, mandating that "equality of rights under the law shall not be denied or abridged by the United States or by any state on account of sex." The amendment, passed by the House of Representatives in October 1971, was sent to the states for ratification within seven years. In considering the amendment, the Senate March 21 had defeated by wide margins provisions offered by Sen. Sam J. Ervin (D, N.C.) to exempt women from the draft, bar them from assignment to combat units and preserve laws that "extend protections or exemptions to women." The amendment had been endorsed by President Nixon March 18, and promoted by feminist organizations for 49 years.

EEOC tightens sex rules. The Equal Employment Opportunity Commission (EEOC) decided March 27 to issue new, tighter regulations barring sex discrimination in employment practices and compensation. The rules, which did not have the force of law, were meant to single out the practices which the EEOC might contest in court under its newly enacted enforcement powers *(see* CIVIL RIGHTS [13]). Under the rules, no woman could be denied employment solely because she was pregnant. Employers would have to provide the same leave, seniority and insurance benefits for pregnancy and abortion as for other temporary disabilities. All fringe benefits were to be equal, with no special distinctions for heads of households and no benefits limited to families of male employees. The EEOC ruled that federal employment laws would prevail over conflicting state laws, including any laws setting different working conditions or compensation on a sexual basis.

Nixon cites government job gains. President Nixon reported April 28 that the number of women in federal policy-making jobs earning over $28,000 had risen from 36 in April 1971 to 105 in April 1972. Over 1,000 additional women held middle-management positions earning $17,000-$24,200 a year. Civil Service Commission Vice Chairman Jayne Baker Spain, who helped direct the Administration's recruitment effort among women, said April 28 that progress had been hindered by the science or mathematics training requirements for 60% of middle- and high-level federal jobs.

Work status unchanged. The Women's Bureau of the Labor Department reported Aug. 26 that, while the proportion of women in professional, managerial and other high-status jobs had increased slightly between 1968 and 1971, average salaries for women had declined as a percentage of men's salaries during the period between 1955 and 1970. Women, who constituted 38% of the work force, increased their share of professional-technical and managerial jobs by about 1.5% over the period, rising to 39% in the first category and 17% in the second. However, in 1970 the average woman earned only 59% as much as a man in the same job, down from 64% in 1955. The gap was narrowest in professional jobs—where women earned 67%—and greatest in sales jobs— where they were paid only 43% of male salaries.

See also AUSTRALIA [11]; CIVIL RIGHTS [15-16, 18]; CONSUMER AFFAIRS [5]; EDUCATION [8]; ELECTIONS [14, 17, 23-24]; FEDERAL BUREAU OF INVESTIGATION; MILITARY [5]; PAKISTAN [10]; PERU; POLITICS [13]

WORKMEN'S COMPENSATION—*See* LABOR
WORLD BANK—*See* GHANA; INTERNATIONAL BANK FOR RECONSTRUCTION & DEVELOPMENT; LATIN AMERICA
WORLD CHAMPIONSHIP TENNIS (WCT)—*See* TENNIS
WORLD CONFERENCE ON THE HUMAN ENVIRONMENT—*See* ENVIRONMENT
WORLD COUNCIL OF CHURCHES—*See* CHURCHES
WORLD COURT—*See* ARGENTINA [3]; SOUTH AFRICA [7]; TERRITORIAL WATERS; UNITED NATIONS
WORLD HEALTH ORGANIZATION (WHO)—*See* HEALTH; PESTICIDES; UNITED NATIONS
WORLD SERIES—*See* BASEBALL

YABLONSKI, JOSEPH A.—*See* MINES
YAHYA KHAN, AGHA MOHAMMAD—*See* BANGLA DESH

YEMEN—Border tensions. Yemen March 11 accused Southern Yemen of massing troops along its borders, shelling Yemeni territory and violating its airspace. Southern Yemen March 13 leveled similar charges against its neighbor. The Yemeni statement asserted that villages in the southwestern Beidah district had been shelled by Southern Yemeni troops and that several persons had been killed or wounded on a mined road. The Southern Yemeni statement said "hireling former sultans and fugitives" had been waging border raids against Southern Yemen and implanting mines, killing at least seven persons in 1971. The statement said that large concentrations of Yemeni troops had been deployed along the border at the instigation of the U.S. and Saudi Arabia, which sought to encourage war between the two countries.

It was reported March 20 that 40 exiled Southern Yemeni opposition leaders in Yemen, members of the Front for the Liberation of Occupied Southern Yemen, had been invited the previous week to the Southern Yemeni town of Sbehha to take part in reconciliation talks and were then killed in a series of mine explosions.

Fighting across the border resumed Sept. 26, with each side blaming the other for precipitating the clashes. Southern Yemen charged Sept. 29 that Yemeni troops had overrun four of its villages, killing 25 civilians and an army officer. Yemen charged that the fighting erupted with Southern Yemeni artillery and air strikes against the border village of Qataba, in which more than 100 persons were killed. Ground fighting raged near Qataba, and capture of the town by Southern Yemeni forces was announced Oct. 1. Yemen denied the capture of Qataba. Southern Yemeni Prime Minister Ali Nasser Mohammed Oct. 1 called for a truce and proposed a joint committee of both nations to investigate the incidents that led to the border flare-up. Yemen rejected the truce offer Oct. 2 and said its forces would keep fighting until they had recaptured Qataba. Both countries Sept. 30 called on the Arab League to help end the fighting. (The league had formed a committee—made up of representatives of Egypt, Syria, Kuwait, Lebanon and Algeria—earlier in September to mediate the Yemeni dispute.)

Yemeni troops, using naval and air forces, Oct. 6 seized the Southern Yemeni island of Kamaran in the Red Sea. Southern Yemen said a large number of islanders were killed in the attack, but Yemen denied taking the island by force. The Arab League conciliation committee Oct. 13 arranged a cease-fire, but there was a brief outbreak of fighting Oct. 14 as Southern Yemeni forces reportedly shelled Qataba and Baida and occupied the village of Sakieh at the entrance to the Red Sea. Both sides accused each other of another cease-fire breach Oct. 18. Southern Yemen claimed that Yemeni troops had occupied strategic heights along the eastern and western border, and Yemen said that Southern Yemen had carried out renewed air and ground attacks.

Merger accord signed. Yemen and Southern Yemen Oct. 28 signed an accord pledging to merge into one country. The two countries had been conferring in Cairo since Oct. 21 under the auspices of the Arab League. The accord provided for the withdrawal of troops from the frontier areas and from territories occupied after the outbreak of the September fighting. Special committees of both nations were to begin arranging for the combining of all institutions in the two Yemens and for the drafting of a constitution within a year. An agreement formalizing the merger accord was officially signed Nov. 28. The new unified state was to be known as the Yemen Republic, with the capital in Sana. Its system of government would be "republican, nationalist and democratic." It would be ruled by a single presidential body and a unified legislature, executive and judiciary.

See also SOUTHERN YEMEN

YEMEN REPUBLIC—*See* YEMEN
YIPPIES—*See* ELECTIONS [24]
YORTY, SAM—*See* ELECTIONS [2, 4-5, 7]

YOUTH—Age of majority lowered. The states of California March 3, Maine March 4 and Wisconsin March 21 enacted laws to lower the legal age of majority to 18 from 21 in California and Wisconsin and 20 in Maine. Illinois, Michigan, New Mexico, North Carolina, Washington and Vermont already granted full rights at 18.

See also ELECTIONS [14, 17, 21, 23]

YOUTH INTERNATIONAL PARTY (YIPPIES)—*See* ELECTIONS [24]

YUGOSLAVIA—New party bureau named. The Yugoslav Communist party voted Jan. 23 to reduce the size of the party's Executive Bureau from 15 to eight. The new members (listed with their republic and area of specialty): Kiro Glirogov, Macedonia, foreign trade; Jure Bilic, Croatia, party discipline; Krste Avramovic, Serbia, industrial management; Stane Dolanc, Slovenia, foreign policy and interparty relations; Budislav Soskic, Montenegro, press and propaganda; Todor Kurtovic, Bosnia-Herzegovina, economy; Stevan Doronjski, Vojvodina Province (Serbia), agriculture; and Fadilj Hodza, Kosovo Province (Serbia), nationalities. Avramovic, Kurtovic and Bilic were new appointments.

Tito plans party overhaul. President Tito Jan. 24 urged a major reorganization in the structure of the Communist party. He suggested that "large, cumbersome party cells of up to 1,000 members" be replaced by "smaller, more active units" to enable workers to lead "a more intensive party life."

Terrorists killed. Government security forces were reported July 28 to have killed about 30 members of Ustashi (a Croatian emigre group which had long urged Croatian independence and which had been linked with violent activities in recent years) who had crossed the Austrian border into Yugoslavia earlier in July. The Croatians were understood to have come from Australia, where as many as 250,000 persons of Yugoslav orgin were living. (Australia Aug. 14 denied that it harbored members of the Ustashi.) The terrorists had overpowered a truck driver after crossing the border and had forced him to take them to the region of Bugojno in Bosnia-Herzegovina. The driver apparently escaped and warned the police, who sent soldiers to the area where the Croatians were hiding. The government reported July 30 that 17 of the terrorists had been killed and two had escaped. A report July 26 said that 13 government soldiers, including a captain, had been killed in shooting and that the two terrorists who had initially escaped were dead. Croatian government forces July 28 "sucessfully liquidated" eight terrorists who had crossed into Croatia from Bosnia-Herzegovina. No government version of the events attempted to explain the mission of the terrorists.

Croat students sentenced. A court in Zagreb Oct. 5 sentenced four Zagreb University students to prison in connection with disturbances at the university in 1971. The trial of the four students—Drazen Budisa, president of the Zagreb Student Association; Ivan Zvonimir Cicak, student pro rector at the university; Goran Dodig, deputy pro rector; and Ante Paradzik, president of the Student Association of Croatia—had begun July 5. The charges against them were planning to take Croatia out of the Yugoslav federation and planning to set up a terrorist organization on an Adriatic island. Budisa received four years imprisonment; Cicak and Paradzik were given three years; and Dodig was given one year. However, the time they had spent awaiting trial was to be counted as part of the sentences. After their release, Budisa, Cicak and Paradzik were to be forbidden to attend public meetings or express their opinions in news media for four, three and two years, respectively.

Other Croats sentenced. Three Croat intellectuals Nov. 12 were given prison terms for "hostile propaganda" against the government. Franjo Tudjman received two years in prison. Ante Bruno Busic and Dragutin Scukanec, both former journalists for a newspaper published by Matica Hrvatska (a Croat publishing house), were sentenced to two and four years, respectively. Three former officials of Matica Hrvatska were sentenced Nov. 24 to prison terms for formenting nationalism in the Croat republic and for planning to turn the publishing house into an opposition political party. Dr. Marko Veselica, a Zagreb University professor, received seven years; Joze Ivicevic-Bakulic was given four years, and Zvonimir Komarica was sentenced to two years in jail. All were forbidden to publish articles or speak at public gatherings for four years after their sentences expired.

Serbian party leaders quit. Marko Nikezic, chairman of the Serbian Communist party's Central Committee, and Mrs. Latinka Perovic, secretary of the committee, resigned their posts Oct. 21 after an apparent policy dispute with President Tito. In a report on the resignations Oct. 26, a U.S. newspaper said that Tito was known to favor a strong Communist party, while Nikezic was known to have sought "democratization of decision-making." Nikezic was replaced Oct. 26 by Tihomir Vlaskalic, a professor of economics at Belgrade University. Mrs. Perovic was replaced at the same time by Nikola Petronic, a metal worker. The resignations of Nikezic and Perovic began a series of resignations considered to be a response to Tito's efforts to oppose the growth of nationalism. Slavko Miloslavlevski, a Macedonian party secretary, asked Oct. 27 to be relieved of his post. Aora Pavlovik resigned as party secretary of the Belgrade party organization Oct. 28. Stane Kavcic, prime minister of Slovenia, was relieved of his office Oct. 29 and dismissed from membership in the federal party Presidium. Koca Popovic, a major Serbian political figure, resigned from the federal presidency Nov. 2.

See also ATOMIC ENERGY [6]; CHESS; DRUG USE & ADDICTION [12, 18]; HEALTH; HIJACKING [13, 15]; MIDDLE EAST [18]; OLYMPIC TERRORISM; POLAND

ZAIRE—Program for Africanization of names. President Joseph Desire Mobutu Jan. 12 began a government program of Africanization by changing his name to Mobutu Sese. The program roused opposition from the Catholic church and countermoves by the government against the church. Joseph-Albert Cardinal Malula, archbishop of Kinshasa, Jan. 24 was asked, as a result of an Executive Bureau meeting of the country's ruling People's Revolutionary Movement (MPR), to vacate his residence, owned by the party, within 48 hours and to leave the country because of his resistance to the Africanization of names. Mobutu Feb. 13 threatened to nationalize all schools organizing prayers for the cardinal. (Cardinal Malula's return to Zaire was authorized May 15 after he had "given evidence of his repentance.") The Political Bureau of the MPR Feb. 15 decreed that all citizens were required to drop their baptismal names and adopt African names.

Cabinet change. President Mobutu Feb. 21 announced a Cabinet change in which five senior ministers left the government. The five, with their replacements listed in parentheses, were: Foreign Minister Losembe Batawangele (Ngunza Karli Bongo); National Economy Minister Mbeka Makosa (Ndongala Tadi Lewa); Urbanism and Land Affairs Minister Kashamvu Ka Lwango Birhwelima (Kabuita Nyamabu); Commerce Minister Lanza Gatanga (Namwisi Ma Makoyi); and Posts and Telegraphs Minister Mushiete Mahamwe Mpale (Nyoka Jusu-Moengo).

Brazzaville ties resumed. The resumption of diplomatic relations with the Republic of Congo (Brazzaville) was announced Aug. 19. Normal traffic between the two countries was to go on across the Congo River, and economic and cultural cooperation was to be encouraged.

See also AFRICA; ANGOLA; ATOMIC ENERGY [6]; BURUNDI; GABON; INTERNATIONAL MONETARY DEVELOPMENTS [9]

ZAMBIA—New 4-year plan. President Kenneth Kaunda launched Zambia's second four-year plan Jan. 12. The plan envisaged an annual growth rate of 6.8%, which Kaunda said was "far more realistic" than the 12% expected under the previous plan which was "solely attributed to an unprecedented rise in the value of copper exports." The new five-year budget of nearly $3 billion was to be spent largely on road-building, low-cost housing, establishment of special zones for "intensive development" in rural areas and achievement of "self-sufficiency in staple foodstuffs, particularly maize."

Opposition banned. President Kaunda announced Feb. 4 that he had banned the opposition United Progressive Party (UPP) under "the preservation of public security regulations" and signed warrants for the detention of 123 of its officials, including UPP Chairman Simon M. Kapwepwe. Kaunda said his action was taken on the basis of investigations into the party since its formation in August 1970. He said observation of the party reveals that "it is a party bent on violence and destruction." He accused the UPP of having "engaged in bombing houses and buildings,... beaten innocent people, stoned and threatened people's lives, particularly national leaders and any others who have openly disagreed with them." A few days earlier, Kaunda said, an attempt had been made to blow up Freedom House, the headquarters of the ruling United National Independence party (UNIP) in Lusaka. Kaunda also accused the UPP of working "against the economic reforms" and of "sabotaging development plans in order to create dissent." (According to a report Oct. 2, members of the UPP were forming a new party, to be known as the United People's Party.)

One-party state approved. The National Assembly, by a vote of 78-0, Dec. 8 approved a bill to make the UNIP the only legal political party in Zambia. Kaunda signed the bill Dec. 13. Shortly before the bill was passed, all 17 members of the opposition African National Congress walked out of the chamber in protest. Opposition members criticized the government for its suspension of parliamentary procedures to allow second and third readings of the bill to take place the same day. (The bill was a result of recommendations made by an investigative committee established by Kaunda in February to recommend constitutional means of making the UNIP the only political party in Zambia.)

See also ANGOLA; INTERNATIONAL MONETARY DEVELOPMENTS [8]; MALAWAI; UGANDA [9]

ZANZIBAR—Sheik Karume killed. Sheik Abeid Amani Karume, chairman of the governing Revolutionary Council, was assassinated April 7 by four men as he played cards with friends at the headquarters of the ruling Afro-Shirazi party. Thabit Kombo, the party's secretary general, and Ibrahim Sadala, another member of the council, were wounded. Karume's bodyguard shot and killed one of the gunmen, but the others escaped. One of the assassins killed himself April 9 in the Stone House area of Zanzibar town, and the other two were killed by security forces at Bumbwini, 16 miles away. The men were described as three black Africans and an Arab. There was no immediate explanation for the attack, but the Revolutionary Council said April 8 over Radio Zanzibar that it would continue Karume's Socialist policies. Julius K. Nyere, who headed the union (Tanzania) of Tanganyika and Zanzibar which had taken place in 1964, April 12 appointed Aboud Jumbe, a minister of state under Karume, to succeed the sheik.

ZERO POPULATION GROWTH (ZPG)—*See* POPULATION
ZIPPIES—*See* ELECTIONS [24]